THE KEYNESIAN REVOLUTION, THEN AND NOW

ECONOMISTS OF THE TWENTIETH CENTURY

General Editors: David Colander, *Christian A. Johnson Distinguished Professor of Economics, Middlebury College, Vermont, USA* and Mark Blaug, *Professor Emeritus, University of London, Professor Emeritus, University of Buckingham and Visiting Professor, University of Exeter*

This innovative series comprises specially invited collections of articles and papers by economists whose work has made an important contribution to economics in the late twentieth century.

The proliferation of new journals and the ever-increasing number of new articles make it difficult for even the most assiduous economist to keep track of all the important recent advances. By focusing on those economists whose work is generally recognized to be at the forefront of the discipline, the series will be an essential reference point for the different specialisms included. Wherever possible, the articles in these volumes have been reproduced as originally published using facsimile reproduction, inclusive of footnotes and pagination to facilitate ease of reference.

A list of published and future titles in this series is printed at the end of this volume.

The Keynesian Revolution, Then and Now

The Selected Essays of Robert Eisner Volume One

Robert Eisner

William R. Kenan Professor Emeritus of Economics, Northwestern University, USA

ECONOMISTS OF THE TWENTIETH CENTURY

Edward Elgar

Cheltenham, UK • Northampton, MA, USA

Published by
Edward Elgar Publishing Limited
Glensanda House
Montpellier Parade
Cheltenham
Glos GL50 1UA
UK

Edward Elgar Publishing, Inc.
6 Market Street
Northampton
Massachusetts 01060
USA

A catalogue record for this book is available from the British Library

Library of Congress Cataloguing in Publication Data
Eisner, Robert.
The Keynesian revolution, then and now / Robert Eisner.
(The selected essays of Robert Eisner ; v. 1)
(Economists of the 20th century)
Includes bibliographical references.
1. Keynesian economics. 2. Economics—History—20th century.
3. United States—Economic policy—1993– 4. Budget deficits—United States. I. Title. II. Series : Eisner, Robert. Essays. Selections ; v. 1.
III. Series : Economists of the twentieth century.
HB119.E36A25 1998 vol. 1
[HB99.7]
330.1 s—dc21
[330.15'6] 98–29679
CIP

Eisner, Robert.
[Essays. Selections]
The selected essays of Robert Eisner / Robert Eisner.
(Economists of the 20th century)
Includes bibliographical references.
Contents: v. 1. The Keynesian revolution, then and now — v. 2. Investment, national income, and economic policy.
ISBN 1–85898–846–2 (v. 1). — ISBN 1–85898–847–0 (v. 2)
1. Economics—United States. 2. United States—Economic policy.
3. Fiscal policy—United States. I. Title. II. Series: Economists of the twentieth century.
HB119.E36A25 1998
330.1—dc21 98–161765
CIP

ISBN 1 85898 846 2

Printed and bound in Great Britain by MPG Books Ltd, Bodmin, Cornwall

Contents

Acknowledgements

The author and publishers wish to thank the following who have kindly given permission for the use of copyright material.

American Economic Association for articles: 'The Permanent Income Hypothesis: Comment', *American Economic Review*, **48** (5), December 1958, 972–90; 'The Keynesian Revolution Reconsidered', *American Economic Review*, **65** (2), May 1975, 189–94; 'Underemployment Equilibrium Rates of Growth', *American Economic Review*, **42** (1), March 1952, 43–58; 'Depreciation Allowances, Replacement Requirements and Growth', *American Economic Review*, **42** (5), December 1952, 820–31; 'Fiscal and Monetary Policy Reconsidered', *American Economic Review*, **59** (5), December 1969, 897–905; 'A New View of the Federal Debt and Budget Deficits', with Paul J. Picper, *American Economic Review*, **74** (1), March 1984, 11–29; 'Which Budget Deficit? Some Issues of Measurement and Their Implications', *American Economic Review*, **74** (2), May 1984, 138–43; 'Budget Deficits: Rhetoric and Reality', *Journal of Economic Perspectives*, **3** (2), Spring 1989, 73–93.

Blackwell Publishers Ltd for article: 'On Growth Models and the Neo-Classical Resurgence', *Economic Journal*, **LXVIII**, December 1958, 707–21.

Cambridge University Press for excerpt: 'US National Saving and Budget Deficits' in *Macroeconomic Policy after the Conservative Era*, Gerald A. Epstein and Herbert M. Gintis (eds), 1995, 109–42, references.

Eastern Economic Association for article: 'The Revolution Restored: Keynesian Unemployment, Inflation and Budget Deficits', *Eastern Economic Journal*, **XII** (3), July–September 1986, 217–21.

Econometric Society for articles: 'Another Look at Liquidity Preference', *Econometrica*, **31** (3), July 1963, 531–8, and 'Reply', 550; 'Non-Linear Estimates of the Liquidity Trap', *Econometrica*, **39** (5), September 1971, 861–4; 'Guaranteed Growth of Income', *Econometrica*, **21** (1), January 1953, 169–71.

Elsevier Science Publishers b.v. for excerpt and article: 'Self-Correcting Real Deficits: A New Lesson in Functional Finance', with Sang-In Hwang in *The Political Economy of Government Debt*, Harrie A.A. Verbon and Frans A.A.M. van Winden (eds), North Holland, 1993, 255–94; 'Real Government Saving and the Future', *Journal of Economic Behavior and Organization*, **23**, 1994, 111–26.

Harvard Business School Publishing Corporation for article: 'Sense and Nonsense about Budget Deficits', *Harvard Business Review*, May/June 1993, 99–111.

Kluwer Academic Publishers b.v. for excerpt: 'National Saving and the Twin Deficits: Myth and Reality', with Paul J. Pieper in *The Economics of Saving*, James H. Gapinski (ed.), 1993, 109–33.

Louisiana State University Press for article: 'Social Security, Saving, and Macroeconomics', *Journal of Macroeconomics*, **5** (1), Winter 1983, 1–19.

Macmillan Press Ltd for excerpt: 'Deficits, Monetary Policy, and Real Economic Activity', with Paul J. Pieper in *The Economics of Public Debt*, Kenneth J. Arrow and Michael J. Boskin (eds), 1988, 3–40.

M.E. Sharpe Inc. for article and excerpt: 'Will the Real Federal Deficit Stand Up?', *Challenge*, **29** (2), May-June 1986, 13–21; 'Deficits and Unemployment: Dogmas Blocking Economic Policy' in *Reclaiming Prosperity: A Blueprint for Progressive Economic Reform*, Todd Schafer and Jeff Faux (eds), 1996, 27–38.

MIT Press Inc. for article: 'National Saving and Budget Deficits', *Review of Economics and Statistics*, **LXXVI**, February 1994, 181–6.

National Affairs, Inc. for article: 'The Balanced Budget Crusade', *Public Interest*, **122**, Winter 1996, 85–92.

New Prospect Inc. for article: 'Our NAIRU Limit: The Governing Myth of Economic Policy', *American Prospect*, Spring 1995, 58–63.

Ohio State University Press for article: Review of *Information and Coordination: Essays in Macroeconomic Theory* by Axel Leijonhufvud, *Journal of Money, Credit and Banking*, **14** (3), August 1982, 413–20.

Review of Economic Studies Ltd for article: 'The Invariant Multiplier', *Review of Economic Studies*, **XVII** (3), 1949–50, 198–202.

University of Chicago Press for article: 'What Went Wrong?', *Journal of Political Economy*, **79** (3), May/June 1971, 629–41.

Every effort has been made to trace all the copyright holders but if any have been inadvertently overlooked the publishers will be pleased to make the necessary arrangements at the first opportunity.

Introduction

Minds and outlook are shaped early. In my case there was the backdrop of the depression of the 1930s, which did not touch me personally, but made my generation aware of possible failures of a market economy. Then there was World War II, which did affect my life, but also showed the tremendous potential of a capitalist US economy where adequate aggregate demand brought forth all the output that could be produced by all who wanted to work.

A brief stint in the labour movement – organizing in North Carolina and Virginia – sharpened my perception of the lives and problems of those whose well-being depended on jobs and decent incomes. It brought me to Johns Hopkins University in the fall of 1948, determined to put the rigour of Economics at the service of my ideals. There, Fritz Machlup showed me the beauty and the power of economic theory, and Evsey Domar exposed me to the crucial insight of John Maynard Keynes. My first articles, written while I was in graduate school, clearly reflected their influence and guidance. The path I started on then I have pursued, despite necessary reaction to changing times and changing fads as well as productive new ideas in our developing science, with what I hope will be felt to be welcome consistency.

As the anti-communist crusade began to gather momentum in the United States, I perversely chose to prepare myself for the German language exam, administered by Machlup, by reading Karl Marx's *Theorien über den Merhwert*, not then available in English. This exposed me to the thesis that a private-profit economy could produce great growth but that this growth, as well as a 'reserve army' of unemployed, were essential to its survival. I found in Keynes and Domar the confirmation that growth is essential to high employment and capital accumulation or investment in our future, but that unemployment is not essential to our economic system. These tenets have motivated much of my research and are reflected in resulting publications.

In my first regular academic appointment, at the University of Illinois, in a project directed by Franco Modigliani examining the role of expectations in economic behaviour, I conducted an interview study of business executives' views of the determinants of investment. I concluded that asking businessmen what caused investment was like asking patients what caused cancer. The answers were rather to be found in actual empirical relations. This led me into a considerable body of econometric work on business investment. The association with Modigliani made me an early partisan of both his life cycle theory of consumption and Milton Friedman's permanent income hypothesis, reflected in a number of my articles on consumption, investment and fiscal policy.

My contacts with Friedman, beginning with an exchange over his 'A Monetary and Fiscal Framework for Economic Stability' when I was a beginning graduate student and extending over the years of our proximity in the Chicago area, never brought me into his orbit, but had a profound effect on my work. I was his not infrequent debating partner or, rather, antagonist. There was little that I could write in macroeconomics without assuring myself that I could answer his criticisms if confronted with them.

Some of the Modigliani–Friedman concerns about relevant measures of income, along with my interest in the distribution of the national pie, led me to work on measures of 'non-income income' – real capital gains, three-martini lunches and other executive perks, and non-market output of all kinds, in households, non-profit institutions and government. This extended to comprehensive measures of investment, human as well as non-human, in all sectors of the economy and my 'Total Incomes System of Accounts' or TISA.

Attention to broader measures of income and capital reinforced my scepticism as to the motivation for a variety of tax 'incentives' for saving and investment, boons that seemed to reward particularly the holders of property rather than the have-nots. Econometric analyses added doubts as to their effectiveness.

From corrected measures of national accounts it was a short step to corrected measures of budget deficits and their impact on the economy. In books, professional articles and popular pieces in newspapers and elsewhere, I have laboured for a decade and a half to challenge conventional wisdom on the impact of debt and deficits.

That challenge brought me back to the critical issues of employment and growth and to a number of papers sharply questioning not only the robustness of any 'natural' or non-accelerating-inflation rate of unemployment (NAIRU) but its very existence. Clearly, trying to increase aggregate demand beyond the point of really full employment would have to be inflationary. But that there was a 'natural rate' of unemployment that would make it impossible to achieve full employment without accelerating inflation, I found to be bad theory – a modern dogma with curious Marxian roots – supported by conventional but not by relevant econometric tests and estimates.

Interspersed with all of my work in macroeconomic theory, econometrics and policy, but on occasion stemming from it, were a number of papers relating to issues of the time – the economics of the Vietnam War and of conscription, both of which I was against – the economics of disarmament which I was for, the general folly of air travel accident insurance, a co-authored work with my long-time friend and Northwestern University colleague, Robert Strotz, a tribute to the magnificent life-long defence of academic freedom by my great teacher, Fritz Machlup, defence of the elderly and their Social Security system, and reflections on French economic policy provoked no doubt by Francophile inclinations developed in my youth.

References

Friedman, M. (1948), 'A monetary and fiscal framework for economic stability', *American Economic Review*, **38**, June, 245–64. Reprinted in *Essays in Positive Economics*, Chicago: University of Chicago Press, 1953.

Marx, K. (1919), *Theorien über den Merhwert*, K. Kautsky (ed.), J.H.W. Dietz.

PART I

THE KEYNESIAN REVOLUTION – CONSUMPTION, INTEREST RATES AND GROWTH

[1]

The Invariant Multiplier[1]

In this note the writer will demonstrate an invariant multiplier " which holds good continuously without time-lag at all moments of time."[2] In so doing he will employ an appropriately defined economic period and a Keynesian (*General Theory*) concept of savings equal by definition to investment.

THE ROBERTSON-TYPE MODEL WITH CONSUMPTION-LAG

Hansen,[3] Samuelson,[4] Machlup[5] and others in their work in the multiplier have accepted the Robertsonian concept of the economic period.[6] This may be considered as proceeding from consumption through income: consumption means immediate income in the case of services and disinvestment in inventory in the case of goods. The disinvestment brings about new production to replace inventory depletions and hence consumption of goods also creates income, although in this case, indirectly. The period is considered to end with the creation of income. In this way, consumption becomes a function of the income of the preceding period: $C_t = f\ (Y_{t-1})$. Assuming a stable consumption function of the type, $C = a + bY$, the equation, actually, is $C_t = a + bY_{t-1}$. The multiplier, of course, is $\frac{1}{1-b}$.

In an analysis of this sort, saving is the difference between consumption of the present period and income of the preceding period, while investment plus consumption of the present period equal income of the present period. Algebraically, $S_t = Y_{t-1} - C_t$, while $I_t = Y_t - C_t$. Savings and investment are thus not equal by definition but reach equality at equilibrium, which, once the system is disturbed by an injection of investment, is only attained after an infinite number of periods.

[1] The author wishes to express particular indebtedness to Professors Evsey D. Domar, Fritz Machlup and G. Heberton Evans, of The Johns Hopkins University, and to Professor Paul A. Samuelson, of the Massachusetts Institute of Technology. Indeed, the basic concept of this note stems largely from lectures of Professor Domar, based on his own unpublished material on the multiplier. Professor Machlup has helped the author clarify the differences between this presentation and the Hansen-Machlup-Samuelson version of the multiplier. Professors Domar, Machlup, Evans and Samuelson have all been kind enough to read drafts of this note and to suggest significant corrections and improvements, but none of them, of course, can be held responsible for what shortcomings may remain. Professor Samuelson may be credited specifically with suggestion of the term " invariant multiplier," which would appear to correspond to Keynes' " logical theory of the multiplier."

[2] John Maynard Keynes: *The General Theory of Employment Interest and Money* (New York), p. 122.

[3] See Alvin H. Hansen: *Fiscal Policy and Business Cycles* (New York, 1941), pp. 264–88, especially p. 272.

[4] Paul A. Samuelson: " Interactions between the multiplier analysis and the principle of acceleration," as reprinted in American Economic Association, *Readings in Business Cycle Theory* (Philadelphia, 1946), p. 265 (from *The Review of Economic Statistics*, Vol. XXI, No. 2, May, 1939, pp. 75–8).

[5] Fritz Machlup: *International Trade and the National Income Multiplier* (Philadelphia, 1943), especially p. 1 and tables, e.g. Table 1A, page 28, and Table 1B, p. 29.

[6] D. H. Robertson: *Banking Policy and the Price Level* (London, 1926), pp. 60–70.

Similarly, the multiplier itself can, in line with this reasoning, be shown to reach its full value only after an infinite number of periods.[1]

Keynes cautioned against confusion of the invariant or "logical" multiplier "and the consequences of an expansion in the capital-goods industries which take gradual effect subject to time-lag and only after an interval." He continued: "The relationship between these two things can be cleared up by pointing out, firstly, that an unforeseen, or imperfectly foreseen expansion in the capital-goods industries, does not have an instantaneous effect of equal amount on the aggregate of investment, but causes a gradual increase of the latter."[2] Professor Haberler charges Keynes with just such a confusion of a "relationship by definition" with "a causal or empirical relationship between investment and income."[3] However, this definitional relationship or "barren algebraic relation"[4] may merit further examination.

MODEL OF SIMULTANEOUS CONSUMPTION WITH PRODUCTION-LAG

The relationship between multipliers can be more completely clarified in terms of a period analysis based on periods different from the Robertsonian periods mentioned above. Lundberg and Metzler, in particular, have worked with multiplier sequences using economic periods which prove to be more useful for the purposes of this note. Lundberg explains: "Receipts during one period will be turned into income during the next period."[5] With Metzler: "Sales during each . . . period depend upon income produced within the same period. . . . Production plans at the beginning of the period are made on the basis of past sales experience and the current state of inventories. . . ."[6] Metzler and Goodwin have also discussed the differing concepts of the economic period, which are so basic to the issue of the multiplier.[7] However, none of these writers has concerned himself with resolving the apparent contradiction between Keynes' "logical theory of the multiplier which holds good continuously, without time-lag, at all moments of time" and the varying multipliers found by Professor Machlup and others using Robertsonian concepts.

To explain this apparent contradiction, the invariant multiplier is presented, below, in terms of a model in which it is assumed that any purchase results, immediately, not in the creation of income, but only in the depletion of inventory, i.e. in disinvestment. Hence current consumption is always current disinvestment (and there are no "services" entering directly into consumption). The period begins with

[1] Cf. Richard M. Goodwin: "The Multiplier," in Seymour E. Harris (ed.) *The New Economics* (New York, 1947), especially pp. 482–93; Goodwin: "Secular and Cyclical Aspects of the Multiplier and the Accelerator," in *Income, Employment and Public Policy* (New York, 1948), especially pp. 112–3; Hansen: *Monetary Theory and Fiscal Policy* (New York, 1949), pp. 219–25; Machlup: "Period Analysis and the Multiplier Theory," as reprinted in American Economic Association, op. cit., especially p. 220 (from *Quarterly Journal of Economics*, Vol. LIV, November, 1939, pp. 1–27). Machlup shows the difference between the "short-run" multiplier and the "long-run" or "full" multiplier in a numerical example: with b equal to two-thirds and a period duration of three months, the multiplier at the end of three months is one and two-thirds; at the end of one year it is two and forty-nine eighty-firsts; it approaches the full value of three only asymptotically. Machlup has also demonstrated algebraically that, with essentially Robertsonian concepts, the multiplier at the end of any period, t, equals $\frac{1}{1-b}(1-b^t)$.—*International. Trade and the National Income Multiplier*, 1 p. 50; cf. Goodwin in *The New Economics*, p. 493.

[2] Keynes, op. cit., pp. 122–3.

[3] Gottfried von Haberler: "Mr. Keynes' Theory of the 'Multiplier': A Methodological Criticism," in *Readings in Business Cycle Theory*, p. 195.

[4] Ibid., p. 202.

[5] II. Erik Lundberg: *Studies in the Theory of Economic Expansion* (London, 1937), p. 191. See all of chapter 9.

[6] Lloyd A. Metzler: "Factors Governing the Length of Inventory Cycles," in *The Review of Economic Statistics*, February, 1947 (Vol. 29, No. 1), p. 2.

[7] Metzler: "Three Lags in the Circular Flow of Income," in *Income, Employment and Public Policy*, pp. 11–32.

production ; payment to the factors of production, or income, follows. Then comes consumption out of this income, which from the sellers' point of view, means disinvestment. Finally, orders are placed for the next period's production. Thus, consumption, in this model, is a function of the *present* period's income : $C_t = f(Y_t)$. And, with a stable, linear consumption function, $C_t = a + bY_t$, the multiplier is again $\frac{1}{1 - b}$.

All magnitudes in the model, which follows, refer to *changes* in amount per period from the amount in period 0, except in the case of " Inventory " (V), in which magnitudes refer to the change in stock from the amount existing at the end of the preceding period.

OPERATION OF MODEL WITH PRODUCTION-LAG

In this model, production of capital goods is increased by \$100 in period 1. Increased income of \$100 is therefore paid out in this period. Out of the new income, \$80 is consumed. This depletes inventory stocks of consumers' goods to the amount of \$80. Aggregate investment then equals \$100 (increased production of capital goods) minus \$80 (disinvestment of inventories of consumers' goods). The multiplier, or the change in income divided by the change in aggregate investment, at the end of period 1, thus equals 100 divided by 20, which equals five.

Changes Associated with an Autonomous Increase in Investment in the form of a \$100 Increase in Output of Capital Goods.

Marginal Propensity to Consume equals .8.

1 Period	2 Production of Capital Goods	3 Production of Consumers' Goods	4 Income (2 + 3)	5 Consumption	6 Inventory[1] (3 − 5)	7 Cumulative Inventory Disinvestment (Sum of 6)	8 Aggregate Investment (2 + 6)	9 Multiplier (4 ÷ 8)
t	Q	R	Y	C	V	ΣV	I	K
0	—	—	—	—	—	—	—	—
1	100	—	100	80	−80	−80	20	$\frac{100}{20} = 5$
2	100	80	180	144	−64	−144	36	$\frac{180}{36} = 5$
3	100	144	244	195.2	−51.2	−195.2	48.8	$\frac{244}{48.8} = 5$
4	100	195.2	295.2	236.16	−40.96	−236.16	59.04	$\frac{295.2}{59.04} = 5$
n (infinity)	100	400	500	400	0	−400	100	$\frac{500}{100} = 5$

[1] Change from *preceding* period rather than from level in period 0.

In period 2, the \$100 increase (over period 0) in the production of capital goods is, of course, maintained. But production of consumers' goods now rises by \$80 to meet orders of firms attempting to replace inventory depletions of period 1. Increased income paid out in period 2 hence amounts to \$180. Of this increase, 80 per cent, or \$144, is spent on consumption. Thus, although \$80 more of consumers' goods are added to inventory as a result of increased production of consumers' goods, the increase of \$144 in sales results in a *net* change in inventory of — \$64 in period 2. Since inventory has already dropped \$80 in period 1, the cumulative inventory disinvestment reaches

$144. The increase in aggregate investment in period 2 amounts to $36—the $100 increase in production of capital goods minus the $64 representing the period's disinvestment in inventory of consumers' goods. The multiplier at the end of period 2 is $180 divided by $36, which equals five.

As this sequence analysis is continued it is readily noted that the multiplier "holds good continuously." It equals five in every period. What does change is the amount of aggregate investment, or the multiplicand. Equilibrium is reached, after an infinite number of periods, when consumption equals the production of consumers' goods, thus making $-V$, the inventory disinvestment, equal zero, and aggregate investment equal 100. The model does, of course, make the assumption that firms attempt to keep inventories at some given level and determine their orders of production for the following period solely by this criterion, uninfluenced by expectations of further changes in income or sales. Thus, at the end of each period, firms *increase* their orders for production in the following period, over their orders for production in the period just ended, by the amount of *decrease* of inventory in that period. However, if the reader experiments with models in which expectations of changes in sales lead firms to behave otherwise, he will find that the multiplier, as here defined, does, in any event, remain constant. The only thing that will change is the number of periods which must elapse before V equals zero and hence Q equals I, thus attaining equilibrium. If firms alter their orders for inventory in accordance with expectations of the cumulative inventory adjustment that would take place by the end of the process, if only period-by-period adjustments were made, the process itself will be "telescoped" and the multiplicand will more rapidly assume the full value of the autonomous increase in production of capital goods. A great variety of results will follow if entrepreneurs behave otherwise in their orders. But in every model the value of the *multiplier*, $\frac{1}{1-b}$, remains constant, regardless of when or whether equilibrium is reached. The *multiplicand*, however, will vary, and will equal the autonomous investment only at equilibrium.[1]

ADVANTAGES OF THE INVARIANT MULTIPLIER

Presentation of an invariant multiplier in models such as those of this note, where consumption is a function of income of the same period, but production of consumers' goods (and hence, in part, income) is a function of the consumption (and inventory disinvestment) of the preceding period, facilitates analysis of the all-important components of aggregate investment in the sense in which this concept is usually applied by economists working with gross national product and national income data. Analysts and planners of national income changes may find it convenient to retain a relatively

[1] The following simple algebraic model should demonstrate mathematically that, within the limits of the assumptions, the multiplier will remain constant through all periods, and that the general argument will hold true regardless of the specific numerical values of the marginal propensity to consume and the multiplier :

It may be noted that the multiplier at the end of any period is simply the change in income divided by the change in investment. The actual change in income per unit of autonomous increase in investment, however, would be, for any period t, the value of $1 + b + b^2 + \ldots + b^{t-2} + b^{t-1}$. As Machlup and Goodwin have shown (footnote [1], page 199), this expression may be simplified to $\frac{1}{1-b}(1 - b^t)$. Thus, with an *invariant multiplier*, the *varying multiplicand* for any period, t, is found to be $1 - b^t$, per unit of autonomous increase in investment. Because of this varying multiplicand, the multiplier $\left(\frac{1}{1-b}\right)$ is therefore a "pseudo-multiplier" in the sense that this term is used by Samuelson in his essay in *Income, Employment and Public Policy* (Chapter VI, "The Simple Mathematics of Income Determination," pp. 133–55, especially pp. 142, 148 and 149).

constant short-term multiplier along with a " propensity " to consume tied closely to psychological rather than definitional variables ; the changing data such as inventory accumulation, foreign trade balances, and public and private " investment " expenditures may more readily be subsumed in a changing *multiplicand*.[1]

Changes per Unit of Autonomous Increase in Investment in the form of Increased Output of Capital Goods. Marginal Propensity to Consume Equals b.

1 Period	2 Produc Capital Goods	3 tion of Con-sumers' Goods	4 Income (2 + 3)	5 Consump-tion	6 Inven-tory[1] (3 − 5)	7 Cumulative Inventory Disinvest-ment (Sum of 6)	8 Aggre-gate Invest-ment (2 + 6)	9 Multiplier (4 ÷ 8)
t	Q	R	Y	C	V	ΣV	I	K
0	—	—	—	—	—	—	—	—
1	1	—	1	b	$-b$	$-b$	$1-b$	$\frac{1}{1-b}$
2	1	b	$1+b$	$b+b^2$	$-b^2$	$-b-b^2$	$1-b^2$	$\frac{1+b}{1-b^2} = \frac{1}{1-b}$
3	1	$b+b^2$	$1+b+b^2$	$b+b^2+b^3$	$-b^3$	$-b-b^2-b^3$	$1-b^3$	$\frac{1+b+b^2}{1-b^3} = \frac{1}{1-b}$
n (infinity)	1	$\frac{b}{1-b}$	$\frac{1}{1-b}$	$\frac{b}{1-b}$	0	$\frac{-b}{1-b}$	1	$\frac{1}{1-b}$

Washington, D.C. R. EISNER.

[1] As Professor Paul Samuelson has pointed out to the writer, the Robertson-type model with a consumption-lag ($C^t = a + bY^{t-1}$) may also be employed to demonstrate an invariant multiplier. In this case the multiplicand would be " Robertsonian saving," or the difference between the income of any period t, and the consumption of period $t - 1$ ($S^{t-1} = Y^t - C^{t-1}$). In order to discern conveniently the effect of inventory changes on this multiplicand it would be necessary to assume that consumption, disinvestment in inventory, production of new consumers' goods to make up for inventory depletions, and payment of income to the producers of these consumers' goods take place in sequence in the same period. Except for discomfort that such an assumption may cause and the reluctance that economists may feel to use " saving " as the multiplicand in an " investment multiplier," the Robertson-type model may certainly be employed to demonstrate the invariant multiplier.

[2]

The Permanent Income Hypothesis: Comment

In a critical review article,[1] H. S. Houthakker reports that an important testable implication of Friedman's theory of the consumption function[2] is contradicted by statistical data. Houthakker views his results as particularly significant because he believes the test he performed to have been suggested by Friedman.

In this paper I shall argue: (1) the test actually suggested by Friedman is an appropriate one. (2) Houthakker has not performed the test correctly. (3) When the test is performed correctly, utilizing the same data as Houthakker's, the results are entirely consistent with Friedman's permanent-income hypothesis. (4) A more powerful test, implicit in the underlying Friedman hypothesis, may be applied to these same data. (5) This more powerful test gives results strikingly consistent with the predictions of the Friedman model.

I. *Friedman's Theory and Proposed Test*

Friedman argues essentially that both income and consumption should be viewed as consisting of permanent and transitory components and that while the permanent components of income and consumption are positively related to each other, there is no correlation between transitory components or between either transitory component and the permanent component of the other variable. This means that total or "measured" consumption will vary systematically with total or "measured" income only to the extent that the variation in measured income represents a variation in permanent income. Where individuals receive a temporary increment in income one would expect an increase in their consumption only in response to the portion of that increase which, because of the addition to their wealth represented by the

[1] H. S. Houthakker, "The Permanent Income Hypothesis," *Am. Econ. Rev.*, June 1958, *48*, 396-404.

[2] Milton Friedman, *A Theory of the Consumption Function,* Nat. Bur. Econ. Research Gen. Ser. 63, Princeton 1957.

increment in income over any finite period of time, would be viewed as an increase in permanent income. The remainder of the temporary increase in income may be thought of as the transitory component of income and would have no effect on consumption.

Since Friedman argues that individuals are likely to consume a constant proportion of their permanent income, the elasticity of permanent consumption with respect to permanent income will be unity. It can then be shown to follow that when we compute regressions from cross-section data, if the mean transitory components of consumption and income are both zero the value of the elasticity of total consumption with respect to total income at the point of mean income will be an exact measure of P_y, the proportion of total variance of income that is due to its permanent component. And if linear regressions are calculated from the logarithms of consumption and income the estimated elasticity will of course be constant and will always measure P_y, regardless of the values of the mean transitory components. But, Friedman points out, "the permanent component of income is itself a resultant of a host of factors many of which are specifiable and observable, such as location, age, occupation and the like" (pp. 215-16). It follows that if we compute regressions within groups more or less homogeneous with respect to one or more of the factors affecting permanent income, regression coefficients (both those fitted to the arithmetical and the logarithmic data) will tend to be less than the regression coefficients computed from the data as a whole. Friedman thus proposes (p. 216, emphasis added) the following specific test:

> Suppose a regression were computed for a broad group of consumer units, say a sample of all units in the United States, and the corresponding elasticity estimated. Suppose this broad group were broken down into subgroups, say by the communities in which they reside, and separate regressions computed for each community. An *appropriately weighted* average of the corresponding elasticities should then be smaller than the elasticity for the group as a whole, and smaller by an amount calculable from the income data for the separate communities. The classification by communities eliminates one source of variability in permanent components, and so should reduce the variance of permanent components and hence the elasticity.

II. *Houthakker's Findings and the Nature of His Error*

It is this test that Houthakker has undertaken to perform. Utilizing some of the wealth of data provided by the budget survey carried out by the United States Bureau of Labor Statistics in 1950 and published jointly with the Wharton School of Finance and Commerce, Houthakker chose as his classifications: city class, occupation, and age of the head of the household. For each of 363 cells corresponding to the groups and subgroups so created, Houthakker calculated arithmetical linear regressions (marginal propensities to consume) and double-log regressions (elasticities of consumption with respect to income). He then compared the coefficients of each minor subgroup with those of the major group from which the subgroups had been formed. Each subgroup coefficient less than its corresponding major group coefficient

Houthakker classifies as "favorable" to the Friedman hypothesis. Where a coefficient of a subgroup is more than that of a major group, Houthakker classifies the result as "unfavorable." He then shows that "for almost every comparison the number of unfavorable cases exceeds that of the favorable cases." Comparing the coefficients of smallest cells with the coefficients computed for all households as a whole, Houthakker finds (p. 403):

> Perhaps the most devastating evidence . . .: of the marginal propensities to consume in the 215 smallest subcells less than one-third [67] agree with Friedman's theory, and only 40 per cent [86] of the corresponding elasticities agree. Even if the coefficients for the minor cells had a fifty-fifty chance of being smaller than the coefficients for all households, the observed results would have a probability of less than one per cent. A fortiori we are compelled to reject the hypothesis that the coefficients in the minor subcells are on the whole smaller than those for all households.

Houthakker then concludes (pp. 403-4) that this:

> . . . clearly reflects adversely on the permanent-income hypothesis of which it is the most direct test available so far. The fact that Friedman had confidently suggested it only adds to its significance. Nor can there be any doubt that if the concept of permanent income has any meaning at all, its numerical value must be more uniform in the minor than in the major subcells, so that the conditions for the test are indeed satisfied.

If Houthakker was right, Friedman's hypothesis, and indeed any hypothesis that consumption is related more to permanent than to transitory income (not merely the "extreme" Friedman view that consumption is related only to permanent income) would be badly damaged. But Houthakker is not right.

Houthakker has in fact "proved" too much. By his measure, the marginal propensities to consume and elasticities of consumption are actually *more* where apparently the variance of the permanent component of income is relatively less and the variance of the transitory component is relatively more. This would suggest that consumers vary their expenditures more with a transitory than with a permanent change in income. Such a result might follow from the fact that the data on consumption do not eliminate expenditures for the purchase of consumer durables, an elimination which both Friedman and Houthakker would perfer. While I believe that Houthakker is unwarranted in rejecting the possibility that this characteristic of the data is sufficient to explain the "negative" results, since I am no more prepared than Houthakker to offer data on this point I shall not press it.[3] But then what does account for Houthakker's literally negative results?

[3] While I share the view of Friedman, Houthakker and others that inclusion of only the rental or service value of consumer durables in "consumption" would permit estimation of a more stable "consumption" function, I must warn against misinterpretation of the implications of the parameters of such a function. For example, it would *not* follow then that a very low value (even zero, as suggested by Friedman) for the marginal propensity to consume out of transitory income implies that a temporary cut in personal income taxes on consumers would not be an effective antirecessionary measure. For if consumers were consequently to increase their purchases of durable goods, this increased "investment," explainable by the acceleration principle operating on an increased demand for the services

Before answering this directly, we should point to another curiosity in the Houthakker data which will help lead us to the source of the error. Recall Houthakker's finding that, taking all of the smallest subcells, the coefficients were actually significantly *un*favorable (not merely not significantly favorable) to the Friedman hypothesis. But when the major cell was "occupation" and the minor cell was "age and occupation" the "score" (on both the linear and the double-log coefficients) was 16 favorable and only 12 unfavorable. A chi-square test reveals that the ratio of "favorable" to "unfavorable" linear coefficients in this classification differs significantly from the corresponding ratio (of 67 to 148) involving the smallest subcells, which Houthakker, it will be recalled, found "most devastating." (With one degree of freedom, the adjusted chi-square of 6.325 on the comparison of linear coefficients in the two classifications is significant at the .02 probability level.) Indeed similarly significant (although not as sharp) discrepancies are found in other classifications where "occupation" is the major cell. Apparently some systematic factor which Houthakker has ignored is affecting his results.

To understand this factor we must digress briefly to elaborate on the theoretical basis for the test proposed by Friedman. He states that where the variance of the permanent component of income is reduced the regression coefficients should be less. But this is clearly on the assumption, which Houthakker forgets, that the variance of the transitory component of income is not reduced relatively as much as or more than the reduction in the variance of the permanent component. Now if permanent income is correlated with occupation, as of course it is, the variance of permanent income around the mean of permanent income of each occupation will, *on the average,* be less than the variance of permanent income around the mean of permanent income for all households. But it does not follow that the variance of permanent income within every occupation (or even within most occupations) will be less than the over-all variance of permanent income unless the *variance* of permanent income is unrelated to occupation. One of the basic empirical characteristics of income data is that the variance of income is highly related to occupation. Indeed it is probably this fact that has given rise to much of the more recent neo-Keynesian theory of the consumption function. In par-

---

of durables stemming from the (small) permanent component of the temporary increase in disposable income, and/or by the dependence of investment on the supply of funds in an imperfect capital market (one needs a down-payment for purchases of durable goods), might well increase expenditures more than one would expect even from the old incorrect estimates of marginal propensities to consume.

One should in this connection warn against the apparent misconception of Houthakker's that all of windfall gains or temporary increases in income constitute transitory income in the Friedman model. Thus, contrary to Houthakker's assertion (p. 398), a Friedman-type consumer "who has a lucky day at the races" might very correctly "buy his friends a drink." For a man who wins $100 at the races should, with the three-year horizon that Friedman postulates and a modest rate of interest, reckon that his permanent income is up by about $35. It would be only the remaining $65 that would constitute transitory income and have no effect on consumption. However, this consideration of the nature of the income components does suggest a problem as to the consistency of Friedman's definitions with his assumption of zero correlation of permanent and transitory components—a problem I shall not pursue further in this paper.

ticular, the variance of income in the "self-employed" occupation is notoriously vastly greater than in other occupations. And it is also clear that a very large part of the variance of total income in the self-employed category must be due to variance of transitory income. A self-employed person may have a high income one year and a low income or even a negative income the next.

What this means is that the variance of permanent income within the self-employed category may be much *more* than the variance of permanent income in all households, while the *ratio* of the variance of permanent income to the variance of transitory income within the self-employed category may be *less* than this ratio for all households. And what is more, and this is of crucial importance, so much of the variance of the transitory component of income may be concentrated in the "self-employed" category that the ratio of variance of permanent to variance of transitory components in all other occupations may be greater than this ratio for the self-employed category *and greater as well than the same ratio for all households as a whole.* But if this is so it would be entirely consistent with the Friedman theory to find that the "marginal propensity to consume" in the self-employed category is less than the marginal propensity to consume in each of the other categories and in all households combined, as Houthakker's work in fact reveals (see his Table I, p. 401). And it would also be consistent with Friedman's theory to find that the marginal propensities to consume in occupations other than that of the self-employed are generally *higher* than the marginal propensity to consume for all households, as Houthakker discovered.

Now the essential characteristics of the data with which Houthakker worked are in fact entirely consistent with the preceding analysis. Estimates of the variance (and standard deviation) of total income for all households and by occupation of head of household, as calculated from the mean incomes and frequencies within income intervals, made available in published B.L.S.—Wharton School budget data[4] are as follows:

	Variance	*Standard Deviation*
All households	6,805,262	2,609
Self-employed	21,934,339	4,683
Salaried professionals, officials, etc.	9,461,273	3,076
Clerical and sales workers	4,670,435	2,161
Skilled wage earners	2,279,554	1,510
Semiskilled wage earners	2,029,745	1,425
Unskilled wage earners	2,108,613	1,452
Not gainfully employed	4,871,268	2,207

In two of the occupations (the self-employed particularly) the variance of total income is greater than the variance of total income for all households. It is quite clear that the significant relation between income and occupation is not strong enough to outbalance the significant relation between occupation and the variance of income. But what about the ratios of permanent to transitory variances?

We can begin to answer this question on the basis of some casual em-

[4] The source of all of our basic data is *Study of Consumer Expenditures, Income and Savings,* Vol. I., *Family Accounts—1950,* Philadelphia, University of Pennsylvania, 1956.

piricism, observing that the variance of transitory income is likely to be proportionately very high both in the self-employed group, as already suggested, and in the changing, heterogeneous "not gainfully employed" group, which would include both unemployed and retired people.[5] But if transitory variance is proportionately greater relative to permanent income variance in these two categories then, since so much of the variance of total income is concentrated in the self-employed group, the ratio of transitory to permanent variance may well be less in all of the other occupations.

Fortunately, a related Friedman hypothesis enables us to be more precise in this analysis. According to Friedman the elasticity of consumption with respect to income, or $\frac{d\log C}{d\log Y}$, measures the ratio of the variance of permanent income to the variance of total income. Suppose that we take the double-log regression coefficients reported by Houthakker as our estimates of this ratio for both the self-employed group and all households as a whole. These estimates would then be, respectively, .523 and .696. But now suppose, to begin to anticipate the more powerful test that we have made, we assume that there is no significant difference in the mean transitory component for each occupation. Then all of the between-occupation difference in income would be due to differences in permanent income. This is an extreme assumption because in fact cyclical and other systematic factors may actually cause some differences in the mean transitory component of different occupations (for example the self-employed group probably had a greater mean transitory component in the inflation-war year of 1950 to which our data pertain). On this assumption and ignoring the estimate of the elasticity of consumption for the not-gainfully-employed group, we still find that analysis of variance (subdivision of sums of squares) reveals that the ratio of permanent income variance to total income variance for all of the other occupations, *appropriately weighted,* would average .697, slightly higher than this ratio for all households combined.

Whatever the method of estimating the proportion of transitory to permanent variance, it should be clear that where a very large proportion of the total sums of squares of deviations about the mean is concentrated in one (or two) groups and where the variance of this group (or these groups) consists disproportionately of variance of transitory income, the variance of most, if not all, of the other groups must consist disproportionately of permanent income. In such a situation, to the significance of which Friedman unfortunately did not explicitly call attention, it becomes particularly important that the marginal propensities and elasticities utilized in the Friedman test, be, as Friedman *did* state, appropriately weighted.[6] It is because of Houthak-

[5] The households headed by a retired person may contribute to low regression coefficients, which is really the essential statistical point, for reasons other than high relative variances of transitory income. For example, one would expect to find wide disparities in the ratios of nonhuman to human wealth in this group.

[6] Concentration of "sums-of-squares" is in fact great not only in the self-employed group (25.9 billion of a total within-occupation sum of squares of 71.0 billion) but in large cities. Thus, of a total sum-of-squares of deviations of income around the nine city class means, amounting to 80.9 billion, no less than 27.0 billion are generated in "Large Cities of the

ker's failure to weight his coefficients (for him each coefficient in effect has equal weight as he merely counts the number of coefficients "favorable" and "unfavorable") that he gets his negative results. But under these circumstances such results have no bearing on the Friedman hypothesis.

III. *A Correct Application of the Friedman Test*

Once we recognize this marked relation between the proportion of variance which is transitory and the contribution of the group to the total variance, the correct application of the Friedman test becomes clear. What we wish is a regression coefficient based on the within-group variance and covariance or the average of the within-group regression coefficients, *where each within-group coefficient is weighted by the sums of squares of the deviations of income around the group mean.* We can best make this clear in symbols:

Let C_{ig} equal the consumption of the ith household in the gth group

Y_{ig} equal the income of the ith household in the gth group;

n_g equal the number of households in the gth group;

G equal the number of groups;

$\bar{C}_g$ equal the mean consumption of households in group g;

$\bar{Y}_g$ equal the mean income of households in group g;

$\bar{C}$ equal the mean consumption of all households;

$\bar{Y}$ equal the mean income of all households;

$n = \sum_{g=1}^{G} n_g$ be the total number of households in the sample;

b_{CY} equal the regression coefficient of consumption on income for all households combined;

$b_{CY}^{i.G}$ equal the weighted average of within-group regression coefficients appropriate for the Friedman test.

Then, of course,

$$b_{CY} = \frac{\sum_{g=1}^{G}\sum_{i=1}^{n_g}(C_{ig} - \bar{C})(Y_{ig} - \bar{Y})}{\sum_{g=1}^{G}\sum_{i=1}^{n_g}(Y_{ig} - \bar{Y})^2},$$

North," where the within-group linear regression coefficient is distinctly lower than in most other city classes. Further, the between-group sum of squares of income deviations is in fact frequently relatively low; it is only 1.5 billion between-city-classes, for example, out of a grand total of 82.4 billion (although the corresponding ratio is markedly higher when occupation is the variable of classification). Thus, the amount that within-group variance (and regression coefficients) could be expected to be lower than over-all variance (and regression coefficients), because of the elimination of between-group variation, is small—perhaps smaller than Friedman anticipated in proposing his test—relative to the differences among within-group variances themselves. It is these peculiarities of the population which make the failure to "weight"—in many circumstances an innocent enough omission—so serious in this test.

but

$$b_{CY}^{i \cdot G} = \frac{\sum_{g=1}^{G} \sum_{i=1}^{n_g} (C_{ig} - \overline{C}_g)(Y_{ig} - \overline{Y}_g)}{\sum_{g=1}^{G} \sum_{i=1}^{n_g} (Y_{ig} - \overline{Y}_g)^2}.$$

So that the weighting may be seen more explicitly, we may also let $b_{CY}^{i \cdot g}$ designate the regression coefficient for consumption on income within the group g. Then,

$$b_{CY}^{i \cdot G} = \frac{\sum_{g=1}^{G} \left[b_{CY}^{i \cdot g} \sum_{i=1}^{n_g} (Y_{ig} - \overline{Y}_g)^2 \right]}{\sum_{g=1}^{G} \sum_{i=1}^{n_g} (Y_{ig} - \overline{Y}_g)^2}.$$

To summarize in words, what we need for the Friedman test is the regression of consumption on income for all households calculated on the basis of the total within-group variance and covariance, or the sum of the variances and covariances around the group means weighted in each case by the number of households in the group. In terms of within-group regression coefficients, what we need is the average of within-group regression coefficients weighted by the within-group sums of squares of deviations of income about the group mean.[7]

Then the test of the Friedman hypothesis is whether this within-group *weighted* regression coefficient is less than the over-all regression coefficient for all households combined. Since we have concentrated our discussion thus far on the classification by occupation let us first present the comparison of the over-all coefficients with the weighted averages of coefficients for occupations:

	Linear (MPC)	*Double-log* (Elasticity)
Weighted average of within-group occupation coefficients	.654	.702
Over-all coefficients	.679	.727

These differences are statistically significant at the .001 probability level. The Friedman hypothesis passes the test, a test that it "failed" decisively (by a ratio of 6 to 1) with Houthakker's unweighted (or equal-weight) comparisons.

In Table 1 we present comparisons of over-all coefficients (col. 4 and 7) and appropriately weighted within-group coefficients (col. 3 and 6) for many of the classifications employed by Houthakker. The table reveals results remarkably favorable to Friedman's hypothesis. Quite contrary to Houthakker's irrelevant comparisons, in every single one of 23 sets of correct comparisons, the appropriately weighted within-group marginal propensity to consume and the appropriately weighted within-group "elasticity of con-

[7] This is developed more fully in the appendix.

TABLE 1.—WITHIN-GROUP, OVER-ALL, AND BETWEEN-GROUP REGRESSION COEFFICIENTS OF CONSUMPTION ON INCOME*

Variable of Classification	Population	Linear Coefficients (Marginal Propensities)			Double-log Coefficients (Elasticities)		
		Within Group ($b^{i.g}_{CY}$)	Over-all (b_{CY})	Between-Group (b^{g}_{CY})	Within Group ($\beta^{i.g}_{CY}$)	Over-all (β_{CY})	Between-Group (β^{g}_{CY})
(1)	(2)	(3)	(4)	(5)	(6)	(7)	(8)
Age[d]	Total	.661	.681	.975[a]	.675	.709	.900[a]
Occupation[d]	Total	.654	.679	.806[a]	.702	.727	.798[a]
City class[e]	Total	.686	.691	.935	.715	.720	.995[c]
Age by city class[d]	Total	.656	.681	.949[a]	.668	.709	.900[a]
Occupation by city class[d]	Total	.650	.679	.808[a]	.696	.727	.806[a]
Age	Large cities, North	.639	.653	.864[c]	.679	.704	.849[c]
	Suburbs, North	.721	.736	1.046[a]	.729	.751	.899[a]
	Small cities, North	.668	.694	1.067[a]	.532	.589	.966[a]
	Large cities, South	.678	.692	1.067[c]	.776	.793	.946[c]
	Suburbs, South	.628	.652	.881[c]	.664	.699	.892[c]
	Small cities, South	.812	.822	.941	.788	.797	.855
	Large cities, West	.668	.703	1.002[a]	.652	.705	.885[a]
	Suburbs, West	.604	.645	.861[b]	.435	.524	.835[a]
	Small cities, West	.546	.587	1.018[a]	.626	.690	.951[a]
Occupation	Large cities, North	.624	.642	.749	.696	.704	.733
	Suburbs, North	.709	.718	.772	.736	.750	.807
	Small cities, North	.664	.681	.763	.690	.699	.718
	Large cities, South	.679	.719	.904[b]	.756	.792	.896[b]
	Suburbs, South	.606	.649	.836[b]	.696	.742	.876[c]
	Small cities, South	.780	.824	.956[c]	.714	.785	.982[a]
	Large cities, West	.680	.710	.841[a]	.678	.709	.782[c]
	Suburbs, West	.598	.644	.810[c]	.568	.624	.740[c]
	Small cities, West	.568	.597	.701	.652	.699	.800[c]

[a] Differences significant at .001 level.
[b] Differences significant at .01 level.
[c] Differences significant at .05 level.
[d] 567 observations.
[e] 81 observations.
[f] 63 observations in each city class.
* The basic data utilized were the arithmetic means of consumption and income and the number of households in the cell, for cells classified by income (9 groups), age (7 groups), occupation (7 groups), and city class (9 groups). There were 12,489 households in all. The numbers of households in the various city-class categories, in the order in which these are listed in the table, were, 3,853, 1,242, 629, 1,923, 503, 443, 2,192, 638, and 1,066. However, no more than 3 variables of classification were employed at one time and although each observation was weighted by the number of households in the cell, the maximum number of observations (cells) underlying any weighted regression was therefore 7×9×9, or 567. The "F" test was used to ascertain the statistical significance of differences (regardless of sign) among the within-group, over-all, and between-group regression coefficients, with the residual within-group variance (degrees of freedom equal to the total number of cells minus the number of groups minus one) as the lesser mean square. Differences significant at the .05 level or better are identified by superscripts in columns 5 and 8. Standard errors of the regression coefficients

sumption with respect to income" are *less* than the respective over-all coefficients. In addition, in further accord with Friedman's suggested test, as we stratify for more variables related to income we further reduce the within-group coefficients. Thus, for example, the within-age-and-city-class "marginal propensity to consume" of .656 is less than the within-age propensity of .661 and the within-city-class propensity of .686. Similarly, the within-occupation-and-city-class propensity of .650 is less than the within-occupation propensity of .654 (as well as, again, the within-city-class propensity of .686).

IV. *A More Powerful Test*

Transitory components of income, Y_{ig}^t, may be considered as themselves the sum of two components, the mean transitory component of the group, say $\overline{Y}_g^t$, and the deviation of the individual household's transitory income from the mean transitory component of the group, that is, $Y_{ig}^t - \overline{Y}_g^t$. The cross-section variance of the transitory component of income for a sample of n households may therefore be written:

$$S_t^2 = \frac{\sum_{g=1}^{G}\sum_{i=1}^{n_g}[(Y_{ig}^t - \overline{Y}_g^t) + (\overline{Y}_g^t - \overline{Y}^t)]^2}{n-1}$$

or

$$S_t^2 = \frac{\sum_{g=1}^{G}\sum_{i=1}^{n_g}(Y_i^t - \overline{Y}_g^t)^2 + \sum_{g=1}^{G} n_g(\overline{Y}_g^t - \overline{Y}^t)^2}{\sum_{g=1}^{G}(n_g - 1) + G - 1}.$$

have also been estimated. These, as well as further details as to the underlying calculations are available upon request to the author.

Each of our coefficients is derived from all observations of the groups indicated. For this reason they differ somewhat from those of Houthakker, who eliminated a number of cells "in order to avoid meaningless results based on very small numbers of households" (p. 402). In particular, Houthakker excluded all households where the age of the head was over 65 or under 25, thus restricting himself to 4 of the 7 age groups in which the data were classified, and also eliminated all remaining subcells in which fewer than 5 income groups were represented. Such eliminations were unnecessary in the case of our weighted measures. Each set of our coefficients ($b_{CY}^{i.g}$, b_{CY}, and $b_{\overline{C}\overline{Y}}^{g}$; and $\beta_{CY}^{i.g}$, β_{CY}, and $\beta_{\overline{C}\overline{Y}}^{g}$) for any group or groups is of course based on data for the same set of households.

Coefficients derived from weighted means of consumption and income of cells defined by income and other classificatory variables depend somewhat upon the identity of the other classificatory variables employed. Minor discrepancies apparent in our table among over-all regression coefficients for identical populations reflect inequalities of the amounts and proportions of *within-income group* variance and covariance (of course unavailable from the tabulated frequency distributions both Houthakker and I have utilized), when income groups are subdivided by age, occupation, city class, age and city class, or occupation and city class. Problems of lack of uniqueness of the resultant coefficients, occasioned by the form of the available published tabulations, are apparently trivial in numerical magnitude and are, in any event, largely irrelevant to the comparisons of within-group, over-all, and between-group coefficients with which we are concerned. It should of course be clear throughout that "between-group" refers to groups other than income and that all of the "within-group" coefficients are actually "between-income-group" coefficients.

Then, if the transitory component of income is uncorrelated with the variable of classification, the larger the values of n_g, the more the mean transitory component for any group, $\overline{Y}_g^t$, will approximate the over-all mean transitory component, $\overline{Y}^t$. Let us now introduce the "between-group regression coefficient," based upon the group means of consumption and income weighted by the number of households in each group. Denoting this coefficient by $b_{\overline{C}\overline{Y}}^g$, we have:

$$b_{\overline{C}\overline{Y}}^{g} = \frac{\sum_{g=1}^{G} n_g(\overline{C}_g^p - \overline{C}^p)(\overline{Y}_g^p - \overline{Y}^p) + \sum_{g=1}^{G} n_g(\overline{C}_g^t - \overline{C}^t)(\overline{Y}_g^t - \overline{Y}^t)}{\sum_{g=1}^{G} n_g(\overline{Y}_g^p - \overline{Y}^p)^2 + \sum_{g=1}^{G} n_g(\overline{Y}_g^t - \overline{Y}^t)^2}.$$

According to Friedman, the second term of the numerator, which corresponds to the covariance of the transitory components of consumption and income, should approximate zero. However, if the transitory component of income is unrelated to the variable of classification (g), the value of the second term of the denominator will also be nonzero only because of sampling fluctuations, and the ratio of its value to that of the first term of the denominator will approach zero as the values of n_g increase. For, it will be noted that, if the variable of classification *is* related to *permanent* income the values of $(\overline{Y}_g^p - \overline{Y}^p)$ will *not* approach zero, while, if the variable of classification is uncorrelated with the *transitory* component of income, the value of $(\overline{Y}_g^t - \overline{Y}^t)$ *will* approach zero.

From this it follows that, if we pick our variables of classification properly, as we increase the number of households in each group the second terms of the numerator and denominator above will tend to vanish and the between-group regression coefficient will approach the value of the coefficient of regression of the permanent component of consumption on the permanent component of income.[8] The same result will follow for the elasticity of consumption with respect to income, that is, the coefficient of regression of the logarithm of consumption on the logarithm of income. Thus, we should expect the elasticity of consumption with respect to income estimated from the group means of the logarithms of consumption and income to be close to unity if the Friedman hypothesis is correct. More accurately, we should expect this elasticity to be significantly closer to unity than the elasticity calculated from the data with regard to individual households, which we have referred to as the "over-all" coefficient. How close to unity the calculated between-group elasticity will be will depend upon the extent to which the variable of classification, while correlated with permanent income, is in fact uncorrelated with the transitory component of income.

While much of the transitory component of income is unique to the individual—layoffs, illness, windfall gains and losses—and individual differences

[8] Expressed another way, for appropriate choices of the variable of classification, g, $b_{\overline{C}\overline{Y}}^g$ will be an asymptotically unbiased estimate of Friedman's k $\left(\text{or } \frac{C_p}{Y_p}\right)$.

will tend to wash out in any large-group averaging, which is the basis of our hypothesis, some of it does, of course, vary systematically. Thus, for example, year-to-year changes in relative prices and in averages or indices of prices may have different effects upon the transitory income of different groups. In 1950, in particular, it may be expected that the rise in prices and money incomes and other consequences of the beginning of the Korean war would influence unequally the transitory incomes of different occupations, city classes, and age groups. One might expect the self-employed group, and possibly wage earners, to have sharply positive transitory components. Similarly, retired people and older age groups might suffer declines in real income which would in part represent declines in transitory components.[9] Cities containing plants operating on military contracts might evidence greater increases in transitory income than other cities, and so forth.

In spite of all these qualifications, it would seem clear that if our hypothesis is correct (and ultimately if Friedman's hypothesis as to the roles of permanent and transitory income is correct) we should expect our between-group regression coefficients to be substantially higher than the over-all coefficients and, a fortiori, consistent with the original Friedman test proposal, to be higher than the within-group coefficients. And, particularly, we should expect the between-group elasticities of consumption with respect to income to be substantially closer to unity than the over-all elasticities (and again, a fortiori, than the within-group elasticities). Thus while the Friedman test involves only the prediction that within-group coefficients will be less than the over-all coefficients, our test demands that the between-group linear regression coefficient approximate the ratio of permanent consumption to permanent income, k, and that the between-group log-linear coefficient (elasticity of consumption with respect to income) approximate unity for appropriately selected variables of classification. And we should be able to anticipate at least relatively the amount of departure from unity as a result of the nature of the variable of classification and its relation or lack of relation to the transitory component of income (presuming, of course, that the variable of classification is related to the permanent component of income).

The results of our test are striking (see Table 1, col. 5 and 8). The between-group city-class cross-section marginal propensity to consume based upon the means of income and consumption in the 9 different city classes was .935, far above the corresponding .691 figure for the over-all marginal propensity to consume, as well as, of course, the within-city-class weighted MPC of .686. The between-city-class elasticity is .995, about as close to unity as anyone could wish,[10] and far above both the over-all elasticity of .720 and the weighted within-city-class elasticity of .715. The between-occupation marginal propensity to consume based upon means of consumption and income of each occupational group is .806, which is again substantially above the over-all figure of .679, as well as the weighted within-occupation coefficient of .654.

[9] Some members of older age groups whose retirement had been postponed or who had been called out of retirement as a result of the war-induced increase in the demand for labor might, of course, have substantial, largely transitory *increases* in income.

[10] Standard error of .038.

The between-occupation elasticity is .798, again substantially above both the over-all elasticity of .727 and the weighted within-occupation elasticity of .702.

The between-group coefficients, while bound mathematically to conform (in the opposite direction) to the relation of the within-group to over-all coefficients, are thus particularly revealing. That the elasticities are in many instances close to unity is in accord with Friedman's view of the relation between consumption and the permanent component of income and our suggestion that for appropriate variables of classification the variance in the transitory component of income "washes out" between groups. It may be noted, however, that the elasticities between-occupations are conspicuously less than unity. But is this not precisely what we might have expected in view of the likelihood that the transitory component of income would in fact be much less *unrelated* to occupation than to other variables of classification? Particularly, in the year of 1950, to which our data pertain, the transition from recession to war-induced inflation would appear likely to have involved transitory components of income that were markedly related to the occupation of the head of the household.

Our between-group coefficients suggest strongly that with appropriate variables of classification unrelated to the transitory component of income, with other relevant variables accounted for, and with consumption defined so as to include only the service or depreciation (not the purchase price) of durable goods, the elasticity of consumption with respect to income may indeed be close to unity. What is more, it may be noted, the "marginal propensity to consume" derived from such intergroup data would appear strangely close to unity, as well. Is all of the Keynesian concern about saving without base? Lest we leap to unwarranted conclusions we should remind ourselves that the relevant (and Keynesian) marginal propensity relates consumption to *national* income. We deal only with disposable personal income. These statistics may, however, be a useful reminder that most of saving is to be accounted for and explained in terms of undistributed corporate profits and "capital gains," rather than personal income. But all this is another story.

V. *Conclusion*

Both the test proposed by Friedman, involving appropriately weighted within-group regression coefficients, and our test, involving between-group regression coefficients, give results which are consistent with the Friedman hypothesis that consumption is unrelated to nonpermanent components of income. This should not be taken to mean that Friedman's theory of the consumption function is sufficient for all purposes of prediction and analysis. Our results are consistent as well with the hypothesis that consumption is positively related to temporary components of income, but not as positively related as it is to the permanent component. It should also be recognized that the averaging process involved in working with group means may have "washed out" many relevant variables, other than the transitory component of income, which should play a significant role in the development of a stable consumption function. It would be in order, too, to utilize data such as we have employed to choose between elements of the Friedman model and the frequently similar but sometimes critically different elements of the Modigliani-Brumberg model of consumption.

But with all of these challenging issues still to be resolved, it should be clear that contrary to Houthakker's report, Friedman's permanent income hypothesis does not fail one of the important appropriate tests Friedman proposed. And further, it comes through with flying colors on the more powerful test of between-group coefficients presented in this paper.

Appendix

The basis for both the Friedman test and our own may be indicated rigorously as follows. Utilizing symbols introduced in the text and, to simplify the exposition, letting:

$$c_{ig} = C_{ig} - \overline{C}, \qquad y_{ig} = Y_{ig} - \overline{Y},$$
$$c_{i.g} = C_{ig} - \overline{C}_g, \qquad y_{i.g} = Y_{ig} - \overline{Y}_g,$$
$$c_g = C_g - \overline{C}, \text{ and } y_g = \overline{Y}_g - \overline{Y},$$

we have, for the sums of squares of deviations of income from its mean,

$$(1) \quad \sum_{g=1}^{G}\sum_{i=1}^{n_g} y_{ig}^2 = \sum_{g=1}^{G}\sum_{i=1}^{n_g} (\overset{p}{y}_{ig} + \overset{t}{y}_{ig})^2 = \sum_{g=1}^{G}\sum_{i=1}^{n_g} (\overset{p}{y}_{i.g} + \overset{p}{y}_g + \overset{t}{y}_{i.g} + \overset{t}{y}_g)^2.$$

Similarly, we have for the sums of products of deviations of consumption and income from their means,

$$(2) \quad \begin{aligned} \sum_{g=1}^{G}\sum_{i=1}^{n_g} c_{ig}y_{ig} &= \sum_{g=1}^{G}\sum_{i=1}^{n_g} (c_{i.g} + c_g)(y_{i.g} + y_g) \\ &= \sum_{g=1}^{G}\sum_{i=1}^{n_g} c_{i.g}y_{i.g} + \sum_{g=1}^{G} n_g c_g y_g. \end{aligned}$$

Then in terms of total or measured consumption and income the "overall" least squares regression coefficient is:

$$(3) \quad b_{CY} = \frac{\sum_{g=1}^{G}\sum_{i=1}^{n_g} c_{i.g}y_{i.g} + \sum_{g=1}^{G} n_g c_g y_g}{\sum_{g=1}^{G}\sum_{i=1}^{n_g} y_{i.g}^2 + \sum_{g=1}^{G} n_g y_g^2}.$$

The within-group coefficient appropriate to the Friedman test, based only on within-group variances and covariances, is:

$$(4) \quad b_{CY}^{i.G} = \frac{\sum_{g=1}^{G}\sum_{i=1}^{n_g} c_{i.g}y_{i.g}}{\sum_{g=1}^{G}\sum_{i=1}^{n_g} v_{i.g}^2}.$$

The between-group coefficient which we have proposed is:

$$b^{g}_{CY} = \frac{\sum_{g=1}^{G} n_g c_g y_g}{\sum_{g=1}^{G} n_g y_g^2}. \tag{5}$$

It may be noted first that since

$$\sum_{i=1}^{n_g} c_{i.g} y_{i.g} = (n_g - 1) S_{c_{i.g} y_{i.g}}; \tag{4.1}$$

where $S_{c_{i.g} y_{i.g}}$ is of course the covariance of C and Y within the group g, and

$$\sum_{i=1}^{n_g} y_{i.g}^2 = (n_g - 1) S^2_{y_{i.g}}, \tag{4.2}$$

where $S^2_{y_{i.g}}$ is the variance of Y within the group g, we may give (4) the alternative formulation which makes clear the appropriately weighted average of regression coefficients that we require. Substituting (4.1) and (4.2) in (4), we secure:

$$b^{i.G}_{CY} = \frac{\sum_{g=1}^{G} (n_g - 1) S_{c_{i.g} y_{i.g}}}{\sum_{g=1}^{G} (n_g - 1) S^2_{y_{i.g}}} = \frac{\sum_{g=1}^{G} \left[b^{i.g}_{CY} \left(\sum_{i=1}^{n_g} y_{i.g}^2 \right) \right]}{\sum_{g=1}^{G} \sum_{i=1}^{n_g} y_{i.g}^2}. \tag{4.3}$$

Now by Friedman's assumption that permanent and transitory components of income are uncorrelated in the population from which our sample is drawn, or that:

$$r_{Y^p Y^t} = 0, \tag{6}$$

we can, from (1) write the mathematical expectation of the variance of income in a sample of n households, recalling that

$$n = \sum_{g=1}^{G} n_g,$$

as:

$$E\left[\frac{1}{n-1} \sum_{g=1}^{G} \sum_{i=1}^{n_g} y_{ig}^2\right] = E\left[\frac{1}{n-1}\left(\sum_{g=1}^{G} \sum_{i=1}^{n_g} (\overset{p}{y}_{i.g} + \overset{p}{y}_g)^2 + \sum_{g=1}^{G} \sum_{i=1}^{n_g} (\overset{t}{y}_{i.g} + \overset{t}{y}_g)^2 \right)\right]$$

$$
(7) \qquad = E\left[\frac{1}{n-1}\left(\sum_{g=1}^{G}\sum_{i=1}^{n_g}(\overset{p}{y}_{i.g})^2 + \sum_{g=1}^{G} n_g(\overset{p}{y}_g)^2 + \sum_{g=1}^{G}\sum_{i=1}^{n_g}(\overset{t}{y}_{i.g})^2 + \sum_{g=1}^{G} n_g(\overset{t}{y}_g)^2\right)\right].
$$

Similarly, we can write the mathematical expectation of the covariance of consumption and income as:

$$
\begin{aligned}
&E\left[\frac{1}{n-1}\sum_{g=1}^{G}\sum_{i=1}^{n_g} c_{ig}y_{ig}\right] \\
&= E\left[\frac{1}{n-1}\left(\sum_{g=1}^{G}\sum_{i=1}^{n_g}(\overset{p}{c}_{i.g} + \overset{t}{c}_{i.g})(\overset{p}{y}_{i.g} + \overset{t}{y}_{i.g}) + \sum_{g=1}^{G} n_g(\overset{p}{c}_g + \overset{t}{c}_g)(\overset{p}{y}_g + \overset{t}{y}_g)\right)\right] \qquad (8) \\
&= E\left[\frac{1}{n-1}\left(\sum_{g=1}^{G}\sum_{i=1}^{n_g}(\overset{p}{c}_{i.g}\overset{p}{y}_{i.g} + \overset{t}{c}_{i.g}\overset{p}{y}_{i.g} + \overset{p}{c}_{i.g}\overset{t}{y}_{i.g} + \overset{t}{c}_{i.g}\overset{t}{y}_{i.g}) + \sum_{g=1}^{G} n_g(\overset{p}{c}_g\overset{p}{y}_g + \overset{t}{c}_g\overset{p}{y}_g + \overset{p}{c}_g\overset{t}{y}_g + \overset{t}{c}_g\overset{t}{y}_g)\right)\right].
\end{aligned}
$$

Then, on Friedman's hypothesis that only the permanent components of consumption and income are systematically related, or that, for the population,

$$
(9) \qquad r_{C^tY^t} = r_{C^pY^t} = r_{C^tY^p} = 0,
$$

we can reduce (8) to

$$
\begin{aligned}
&E\left[\frac{1}{n-1}\left(\sum_{g=1}^{G}\sum_{i=1}^{n_g} c_{ig}y_{ig}\right)\right] \qquad (10) \\
&= E\left[\frac{1}{n-1}\left(\sum_{g=1}^{G}\sum_{i=1}^{n_g}\overset{p}{c}_{i.g}\overset{p}{y}_{i.g} + \sum_{g=1}^{G} n_g\overset{p}{c}_g\overset{p}{y}_g\right)\right].
\end{aligned}
$$

Thus, if Friedman's assumptions are correct, by rearranging terms and dividing (10) by (7) we can derive a consistent[11] estimate of the over-all least-squares coefficient of regression of total consumption on total income, as:

[11] We cannot be sure that our estimates are unbiased because the mathematical expectation of a ratio is not generally equal to the ratio of the mathematical expectations of the numerator and denominator taken separately.

$$(11)\quad \operatorname*{plim}_{n\to\infty} b_{CY} = \lim_{n\to\infty}\left\{\frac{\sum_{g=1}^{G}\sum_{i=1}^{n_g} \overset{p}{c}_{i.g}\overset{p}{y}_{i.g} + \sum_{g=1}^{G} n_g \overset{p}{c}_g \overset{p}{y}_g}{\sum_{g=1}^{G}\sum_{i=1}^{n_g}\left[(\overset{p}{y}_{i.g})^2 + (\overset{t}{y}_{i.g})^2\right] + \sum_{g=1}^{G} n_g\left[(\overset{p}{y}_g)^2 + (\overset{t}{y}_g)^2\right]}\right\}.$$

The corresponding consistent estimate of the within-group regression coefficient is indicated by:

$$(12)\quad \operatorname*{plim}_{n\to\infty} \overset{i.G}{b}_{CY} = \lim_{n\to\infty}\left\{\frac{\sum_{g=1}^{G}\sum_{i=1}^{n_g} \overset{p}{c}_{i.g}\overset{p}{y}_{i.g}}{\sum_{g=1}^{G}\sum_{i=1}^{n_g}\left[(\overset{p}{y}_{i.g})^2 + (\overset{t}{y}_{i.g})^2\right]}\right\},$$

and for the corresponding estimate of the between-group coefficient,

$$(13)\quad \operatorname*{plim}_{n\to\infty} \overset{g}{b}_{\bar{C}\bar{Y}} = \lim_{n\to\infty}\left\{\frac{\sum_{g=1}^{G} n_g \overset{p}{c}_g \overset{p}{y}_g}{\sum_{g=1}^{G} n_g\left[(\overset{p}{y}_g)^2 + (\overset{t}{y}_g)^2\right]}\right\}.$$

Now, if the covariance of c^p and y^p is not related to the variable of classification, g,

$$(14)\quad k = b_{C^pY^p} = \lim_{n\to\infty}\left\{\frac{\sum_{g=1}^{G}\sum_{i=1}^{n_g} \overset{p}{c}_{i.g}\overset{p}{y}_{i.g}}{\sum_{g=1}^{G}\sum_{i=1}^{n_g} (\overset{p}{y}_{i.g})^2}\right\} = \lim_{n\to\infty}\left\{\frac{\sum_{g=1}^{G} n_g \overset{p}{c}_g \overset{p}{y}_g}{\sum_{g=1}^{G} n_g (\overset{p}{y}_g)^2}\right\}.$$

Friedman's argument, then, is that the ratio of permanent to total income variance within groups is likely to be less than this ratio over-all, or that,

$$(15)\quad \lim_{n\to\infty}\left\{\frac{\sum_{g=1}^{G}\sum_{i=1}^{n_g} (\overset{p}{y}_{i.g})^2}{\sum_{g=1}^{G}\sum_{i=1}^{n_g}\left[(\overset{p}{y}_{i.g})^2 + (\overset{t}{y}_{i.g})^2\right]}\right\} < \lim_{n\to\infty}\left\{\frac{\sum_{g=1}^{G}\sum_{i=1}^{n_g} (\overset{p}{y}_{i.g})^2 + \sum_{g=1}^{G} n_g (\overset{p}{y}_g)^2}{\sum_{g=1}^{G}\sum_{i=1}^{n_g}\left[(\overset{p}{y}_{i.g})^2 + (\overset{t}{y}_{i.g})^2\right] + \sum_{g=1}^{G} n_g\left[(\overset{p}{y}_g)^2 + (\overset{t}{y}_g)^2\right]}\right\}.$$

But for Friedman's argument [inequality (15)] to hold it is necessary that the ratio of permanent to total income variance *within* groups also be less than this ratio *between* groups, or

$$(16)\quad \lim_{n\to\infty}\left\{\frac{\sum_{g=1}^{G}\sum_{i=1}^{n_g}(\overset{p}{y}_{i.g})^2}{\sum_{g=1}^{G}\sum_{i=1}^{n_g}[(\overset{p}{y}_{i.g})^2+(\overset{t}{y}_{i.g})^2]}\right\} < \lim_{n\to\infty}\left\{\frac{\sum_{g=1}^{G} n_g(\overset{p}{y}_g)^2}{\sum_{g=1}^{G} n_g[(\overset{p}{y}_g)^2+(\overset{t}{y}_g)^2]}\right\},$$

which is the basis for our own test.

This last condition will in fact be met if the variable of classification, g, is related to permanent income but unrelated (or at least relatively less related) to transitory income. A sufficient, but of course not necessary, condition for this last is that:

$$(17)\quad \lim_{n_g\to\infty} \overline{Y}_g^t = 0 \qquad g = 1, \cdots, G$$

whence it will follow that:

$$(18)\quad \lim_{n\to\infty} \overline{Y}^t = 0$$

and

$$(19)\quad \lim_{n\to\infty} \frac{1}{n}\sum_{g=1}^{G} n_g(\overset{t}{y}_g)^2 = 0.$$

Then if the Friedman hypotheses as to the relationships among the covariances of the permanent and transitory components of income and consumption [(6) and (9)] are correct, and the variables of classification are such that equation (14) and inequality (16) are also satisfied, we may multiply (14) by (16) to obtain

$$(20)\quad \lim_{n\to\infty}\left\{\frac{\sum_{g=1}^{G}\sum_{i=1}^{n_g}\overset{p}{c}_{i.g}\overset{p}{y}_{i.g}}{\sum_{g=1}^{G}\sum_{i=1}^{n_g}[(\overset{p}{y}_{i.g})^2+(\overset{t}{y}_{i.g})^2]}\right\} < \lim_{n\to\infty}\left\{\frac{\sum_{g=1}^{G} n_g\overset{p}{c}_g\overset{p}{y}_g}{\sum_{g=1}^{G} n_g[(\overset{p}{y}_g)^2+(\overset{t}{y}_g)^2]}\right\},$$

whence, substituting from (12) and (13),

$$(21)\quad \operatorname*{plim}_{n\to\infty} \overset{i.G}{b}_{CY} < \operatorname*{plim}_{n\to\infty} \overset{g}{b}_{\overline{C}\overline{Y}}$$

and, since numerators and denominators of (20) are all nonnegative, inspection of (11) reveals that:

$$(22)\quad \operatorname*{plim}_{n\to\infty} \overset{i.G}{b}_{CY} < \operatorname*{plim}_{n\to\infty} b_{CY} < \operatorname*{plim}_{n\to\infty} \overset{g}{b}_{\overline{C}\overline{Y}}.$$

It may also be seen readily that in the limiting case where

$$\lim_{n\to\infty} \frac{1}{n} \sum_{g=1}^{G} n_g (\overset{t}{y}_g)^2 = 0, \tag{19}$$

that is, where the mathematical expectation of the mean transitory component of income is the same in all groups (including hence the case where $E(\bar{Y}_g^t) \equiv 0$),

$$\operatorname*{plim}_{n\to\infty} \overset{g}{b}_{\bar{C}\bar{Y}} = \lim_{n\to\infty} \frac{\sum_{g=1}^{G} n_g \overset{p}{c}_g \overset{p}{y}_g}{\sum_{g=1}^{G} n_g (\overset{p}{y}_g)^2} = k. \tag{23}$$

An analogous exposition in terms of the logarithms of consumption and income can be used to demonstrate that if the Friedman hypotheses are correct, with appropriate variables of classification, *g*,

$$\operatorname*{plim}_{n\to\infty} \overset{i.G}{\beta}_{CY} < \operatorname*{plim}_{n\to\infty} \beta_{CY} < \operatorname*{plim}_{n\to\infty} \overset{g}{\beta}_{\bar{C}\bar{Y}} = 1, \tag{24}$$

where β refers to the least-squares estimate of the log-linear coefficient in a stochastic relation of the form

$$\ln C = \alpha + \beta \ln Y + u. \tag{25}$$

ROBERT EISNER*

* The author is associate professor of economics at Northwestern University. He is indebted to R. H. Strotz for helpful comments and discussions of an earlier draft, and to the Northwestern University Computing Center and to D. L. Harris, Donald Meyer and T. N. Srinivasan for assistance in carrying out the calculations.

[3]

Econometrica, Vol. 31, No. 3 (July, 1963)

ANOTHER LOOK AT LIQUIDITY PREFERENCE

BY ROBERT EISNER

IN A RECENT PAPER in this journal [1], Bronfenbrenner and Mayer concerned themselves with "five fundamental questions of liquidity theory" (p. 811) relating to the observability of a "liquidity function," its interest elasticity, its stability, the causes of its shifts over time, and whether it does "appear to impose an observable floor to interest rates." While admitting some problem of identification of the relations observed among data on money and interest rates, they concluded that they apparently had estimated demand functions, because "their coefficients seem to point in this direction" (p. 820). And they report (p. 818) that "the interest elasticity . . ., the nub of liquidity theory, is estimated at between 0.3 and 0.5 for idle balances . . . . There is no evidence for the proposition that any of these elasticities goes to zero for high rates of interest or for the proposition that some 'floor' or 'bottom stop' exists for interest rates at which the elasticity goes to infinity."

Restudying these issues, utilizing additional data for the same 1919–56 period[1] along with the original series which Bronfenbrenner and Mayer have generously made available to me, I shall argue that:

1. At least for the early part of the period, shifts in the demand function have been such that it has not been properly identified and estimated.
2. Measurement of appropriate elasticities and slopes does in fact give strong support to the Keynesian proposition "that some 'floor' or 'bottom stop' exists for interest rates."

My differences with Bronfenbrenner and Mayer will relate to:

1. Their confounding issues of elasticity with those of slope.
2. Their use of a short-term rather than a long-term rate of interest.
3. Particular arbitrary qualities in their definition of "idle balances."
4. Their failure to follow through the implications for identification of changing supply functions as between different periods of time.
5. Questions as to the nature of the error term or direction of the relation that should be estimated.

I shall first indicate the essential argument in regard to each of these points and then set forth the empirical data, as I have reworked and expanded them, that show the relevance of the arguments.

[1] For the gathering of which I am indebted chiefly to Mrs. Patricia Wishart. I have also been assisted at the Northwestern University Computing Center by Mrs. Betty Benson and have benefitted from further computational assistance by Jack Barnes. A grant from the National Science Foundation has quite generally facilitated the work.

CONCEPTUAL ISSUES

1. *Elasticity, slope, and the liquidity trap.* It can be seen readily that any constant elasticity of demand, such as is given by the relation

$$\ln M_d = a + b \ln i \qquad (b \text{ assumed less than zero}) \tag{1}$$

is consistent with the liquidity trap, for in arithmetic form this would appear as

$$M_d = \frac{A}{i^{-b}}, \tag{2}$$

and clearly as i goes to zero, M_d goes to infinity. It may indeed be noted that by estimating the logartihmic form indicated above, Bronfenbrenner and Mayer were assuming a constant elasticity and thus implying a nonnegative lower bound to the rate of interest which would satisfy their relations. Evidence that the elasticity goes to infinity or even gets larger at lower interest rates is quite unnecessary for the proposition that the money demanded goes to infinity as the interest rate is lowered. Findings that the elasticity does not get smaller in absolute amount as the interest rate gets smaller would be sufficient—but not necessary—evidence for the liquidity trap.

In view of this implication of a "floor or bottom stop" from any constant interest elasticity, information bearing on the liquidity trap might better be got from estimates of arithmetic (as opposed to logarithmic) slopes. For the Keynesian theory would require the slope of the demand curve to be closer to horizontal for low interest rates or high amounts of idle balances.[2] (Bronfenbrenner and Mayer show some awareness of the significance of the slope (p. 833) but it does not enter into their main argument.)

2. *Short-term versus long-term interest rates.* While undoubtedly many arguments can be made from an empirical standpoint that better measures of some "pure" rate of interest can be gotten with short-term rates than with yields to maturity on long-term bonds, it must be recognized that the Keynesian theory about the demand for money tending to become "absolute" at low rates of interest, applies to long-term rates. For that theory states that because of the "speculative motive" with regard to capital gains and losses which are peculiar to long-term securities, the rate of interest on long-terms cannot get indefinitely low without the market becoming dominated by those who prefer to hold cash in expectation of a fall in prices of long-terms. The peculiarly Keynesian issue is that of getting down the

[2] It should be recognized that the search in time series data for a *perfectly* horizontal demand curve for money is foredoomed to failure. Keynes himself wrote, "... whilst this limiting case might become practically important in future, I know of no example of it hitherto. Indeed, owing to the unwillingness of most monetary authorities to deal boldly in debts of long term, there has not been much opportunity for a test" ([2, p. 207]). We might stress that even an occasional actual descent all the way into the liquidity trap, such as Keynes argued had not occurred prior to his writing, would not result in an estimate of a horizontal demand curve from a time series including observations both within the trap and outside of it.

long-term rate (which is most relevant to investment). It is hardly meeting this issue to relate the quantity of money to the short-term rate. If one is interested in an estimate of the efficacy of monetary policy in influencing economic activity, one should measure elasticities and slopes in regard to long-term rates, and one should indeed expect the interest elasticity to be higher and the slope of the money demand curve closer to horizontal for long-term than for short-term rates of interest.[3]

3. *The definition of idle balances.* Building on a formulation ascribed to Tobin, Bronfenbrenner and Mayer in effect define idle balances as

$$L_t = M_t - Y_t\,(M/Y)_{\min}\,, \tag{3}$$

where L represents idle balances, M represents the quantity of money (demand deposits plus currency), and Y represents private GNP, all in billions of dollars, and $(M/Y)_{\min}$ represents the minimum ratio of the quantity of money to private GNP in the period under consideration, which was achieved in 1926. The effect of this definition was to consider idle balances as zero in 1926, creating obvious embarrassment in any logarithmic analysis. Bronfenbrenner and Mayer attempted to get around this consequence of their definition by calling idle balances 0.1 billion in 1926, so that the logarithm of idle balances for that year was −1, but making no adjustment in the idle balances of other years. Since all other logarithms of idle balances ranged between 0.1761 and 1.8507, it may be seen that this 1926 value was quite extreme. As Bronfenbrenner and Mayer acknowledge by eliminating 1926 and 1927 from a number of regressions, with substantial alteration of the results, this extreme value had much effect.

A general transformation of the Bronfenbrenner-Mayer idle balances which would have merit in terms of both its economic and statistical properties is one that would allow a constant minimum component of idle balances, even in years of maximum velocity. Then we should write idle balances as

$$L_t = M_t - Y_t\,(M/Y)_{\min} + L_o\,, \tag{4}$$

where L_o are the minimum idle balances that exist even in years of maximum velocity.

4. *The supply function and identification.* As Bronfenbrenner and Mayer point out, the identification problem can be met if it can be assumed that the demand function remained fixed throughout the relevant period while the supply function shifted. Observations of actual quantities of money and interest rates would then trace out the demand function. However, there is historical insight which suggests a different hypothesis. This is that until roughly 1934 (perhaps a year or two earlier or later but this is not a bad selection for the Keynesian divide), monetary policy (at least in the United States, to which the data under consideration relate)

[3] It may be noted further that any constant elasticity of the demand for money with respect to the short-term rate of interest, as assumed by Bronfenbrenner and Mayer in the form of the function they estimate, implying a lower bound of zero for the short-term rate, is consistent with a positive lower bound for the long-term rate.

consisted of meeting the "demands of trade," which implied maintaining a relatively fixed supply function in which the actual quantity of money made available increased with increased demand. This increased demand would be indicated by, among other things, increases in the rate of interest. Thus the supply curve in this early period was more or less fixed, with the quantity of money supplied increasing with the rate of interest.

However, with the advent of Keynesian notions of "easy money" (aided by Treasury views of the desirability of keeping down the rate of interest on the large federal debt), the supply curve was made to move in such a way that, although its movements were quite imperfectly timed, they matched or more than matched movements in demand (recognizing that the demand function is defined to include income and wealth, as well as the interest rate, among its arguments). All this would suggest that in the early period, up to 1934, the observed relation between money and interest rates would be of relatively indeterminate sign or positive, reflecting in considerable part the shape of the supply curve. But after 1934, the observed relation would more closely approximate that associated with the demand function: the quantity of money would be higher, the lower the rate of interest.

5. *Assumptions as to error terms and the direction of the relation.* Implicit in the estimation of the demand for money by Bronfenbrenner and Mayer is the assumption that the rate of interest can be taken as an exogenous variable or "known number" to which responds, according to a structural relation but with an error term, the quantity of money. But this hardly accords with the economic theory to which it relates. Is not our idea rather that the quantity of money varies exogenously (perhaps on the basis of monetary policy) and that the rate of interest then responds in accordance with the structural relation defined by the demand curve, but with an error term (which may be based on frictions, rigidities, speculative factors, or the like)? It is surely true, as expositors of monetary theory must confirm, that the quantity of money is taken as the known number, and it is the rate of interest which, with a disturbance, reacts. The effect of this kind of misspecification of the error is to cause underestimates of the elasticity of money with respect to the rate of interest or, perhaps more appropriately, to lead one to infer greater than true elasticities of the rate of interest with respect to the quantity of money.

THE DATA

Short-term versus long-term interest elasticities. The first two equations ((5) and (6)) in Table I indicate that the elasticity of idle balances as defined by Bronfenbrenner and Mayer, designated L, is decidedly greater with respect to the Aaa corporate bond rate, which I take as a measure of the long-term interest rate, i_L, than it is with regard to the commercial paper rate or short-term rate i_s. The first set of coefficients (5) correspond to those presented by Bronfenbrenner and Mayer (p. 817; theirs differ slightly from mine because of minor computational errors in their calculations of logarithms). It is to be noted that the elasticity of idle balances with respect to the commercial paper rate is —.545. The corresponding elasticity with respect to the Aaa corporate bond rate[4] is -2.026. These results are consistent with the analytical considerations indicated above which suggested that high elasticities of demand for idle balances would, in line with Keynesian theory, be expected on long-term rather than short-term interest rates.

In view of my criticism of the Bronfenbrenner-Mayer definition of idle balances, I have also conducted the analysis for L^*, where, in terms of the Bronfenbrenner-Mayer idle balances, L, we can write $L^* = L + 1.0$, both variables defined in billions of dollars. It turns out that this redefinition does, as we anticipated, have a substantial effect, because in the Bronfenbrenner-Mayer analysis the extreme value of -1 for the logarithm of L was associated with a year (and a general period) of relatively high interest rates. Corresponding regressions of L^* show considerably lower interest elasticities, in absolute terms, $-.278$ instead of $-.545$ for i_s, and $-.891$ instead of -2.026 for i_L, as may be noted in the third and fourth sets of results presented in Table I. We may also note that the unbiased estimates of the coefficient of determination are higher for the regressions involving L^*, and I should argue again that on both economic and statistical grounds L^* is a better definition of idle balances[5] than L.

Finally, in regard to Table I, we may note that the elasticity of i_L with respect to i_s is a low .278. Clearly, long and short rates moved together, but the record of these years indicates as clearly that movements of the short rate were associated with much smaller movements of the long rate, roughly one-quarter as great. One may quickly concede that the montary authority can change the short-term interest rate. But this does not have very much effect on the long-term rate.

1919 to 1934 versus 1935 to 1956. Comparisons between these two sets of years are illuminating with respect to two problems, that of identification and the question of the appearance of a liquidity trap as idle balances become high and interest rates low. In regard to the second of these, we should observe first that the mean of Aaa bond rates for the years 1919–34 was 4.89 per cent while for the years 1935–56 the mean was 2.93 per cent. And idle balances (the Bronfenbrenner-Mayer definition, L) averaged \$5 billion in the 1919–34 period and \$41 billion in the years from 1935 to 1956. Keynesian theory suggests that the slope of the demand for money (or idle balances) on an *arithmetic* scale should be flatter in the later period. Table II indicates that this is so for the short-run interest rate

[4] Similar results were obtained throughout our analysis when the long-term government bond rate was used instead of the Aaa corporate bond rate. In the interest of simplicity the presentation is limited to results of regressions involving the commercial paper and Aaa corporate bond rates as representative of short-term and long-term interest rates, respectively. The Aaa corporate bond rates were annual averages taken from *Moody's Industrial Manual*, 1958, p. A19.

[5] L^* is of course arbitrary in its assignment of the value of 1.0 to L_0 in equation (4) above. A more general treatment might entail estimating maximum velocity and the amount of idle balances along with the other parameters in which we are interested. However, I have not endeavored in this paper to depart from the (Tobin-) Bronfenbrenner-Mayer formulation.

TABLE I

SHORT-TERM VERSUS LONG-TERM ELASTICITIES

Form of Regression	Dependent Variable	Regression Coefficients and their Standard Errors					$\hat{R}^2$	n
		Constant Term	Commercial Paper Rate (i_s)	Aaa Corp. Bond Rate (i_L)	Wealth (W)	Prev. Idle Bal. (L_{-1})		
(5) log	Bronf.-Mayer Idle Bal., L	−4.542 (2.642)	−.545 (.209)		1.803 (.947)	.535 (.135)	.786	37
(6) log	Bronf.-Mayer Idle Bal., L	.651 (3.017)		−2.026 (.891)	.359 (.971)	.517 (.153)	.777	37
(7) log	Bronf.-Mayer Idle Bal. + 1.0, L^*	−1.741 (1.408)	−.278 (.111)		.742 (.516)	.738 (.094)	.920	37
(8) log	Bronf.-Mayer Idle Bal. +1.0, L^*	.617 (1.522)		−.891 (.552)	.072 (.496)	.746 (.124)	.912	37
(9) log	Aaa Corp Bond Rate, i_L	.485 (.014)	.278 (.032)				.661	38

TABLE II

DIFFERENCES BETWEEN 1919–34 AND 1935–56, ARITHMETIC REGRESSIONS

Form of Regression	Dependent Variable	Regression Coefficients and their Standard Errors					$\hat{R}^2$	n
		Constant Term	i_s	i_L	W	L_{-1}		
(10) arithmetic	L, 1919–34	−1.61 (9.49)	−.324 (.669)		.0057 (.0096)	.938 (.246)	.782	15
(11) arithmetic	L, 1935–56	−10.00 (18.00)	−8.43 (4.14)		.0298 (.0267)	.894 (.081)	.862	22
(12) arithmetic	L, 1919–34	−31.27 (14.76)		3.054 (1.663)	.0233 (.0102)	1.156 (.151)	.830	15
(13) arithmetic	L, 1935–56	65.60 (21.57)		−15.82 (7.09)	−.0067 (.0122)	.685 (.128)	.867	22

with which Bronfenbrenner and Mayer concerned themselves, accepting their supposition that these are demand relations. The values of $\partial L/\partial i_s$ are −.324 and −8.43 for the earlier and later periods, respectively.

It must be confessed, however, that the money-interest slope of the measured regression for the earlier period (abstracting from the other variables) is so nearly vertical as to renew the doubts Bronfenbrenner and Mayer endeavored to exorcise with regard to whether the observed magnitudes relate to the demand curve, the supply curve, or both. These doubts are increased sharply by examination of the corresponding partial derivatives of idle money with regard to the Aaa corporate bond rate. For, as we may also note in Table II, while $\partial L/\partial i_L$ is -15.82 for the later period, appropriately larger in absolute amount than the corresponding derivative with regard to the short-term rate, for the earlier period, $\partial L/\partial i_L$ is positive, 3.054. I suggest again my explanation above, that monetary policy through this period can best be characterized as meeting the demands of trade, which implied keeping a relatively constant supply function, in terms of the variables we have been observing. Thus, in the face of shifts in demand in this period we have, to a considerable extent, traced out the supply function, rather than the demand function, as Bronfenbrenner and Mayer presumed.

Inverting the relation: interest rates as a function of idle balances. Table III indicates the results of regressions run on the basis of considerations as to the nature of the underlying function and error terms as discussed above. Using L^* as the measure of idle balances and experimenting with its lagged as well as current values in view of the presumed direction of the relation, we observe, over the entire 1919–56 period, a total short-term interest rate elasticity with respect to idle balances of about —0.69. The long-term interest rate elasticity, on the other hand, was only about —0.2. The estimates imply that a 50 per cent increase in the quantity of money, other things remaining constant so that the increase would be an increase in "idle money," would generate only a 10 per cent fall in the corporate bond rate, on the average from 3.72 per cent to 3.35 per cent. Hardly a contradiction of the Keynesian notion that monetary policy might be limited in its scope of operation!

Finally, Table IV may be noted briefly, first for its evidence of a low elasticity of long-term interest rates with repect to idle balances in the later years, similar to that observed above for the entire period. And, second, we see what may be again interpreted as evidence of an unresolved identification problem in the particularly

TABLE III

INTEREST RATES AS A FUNCTION OF IDLE BALANCES, 1919–56

Form of Regression	Dependent Variable	Regression Coefficients and their Standard Errors					$\hat{R}^2$	n
		Constant Term	W	W_{-1}	L^*	L^*_{-1}		
(14) log	i_s	-4.946 (1.885)	2.083 (.674)		$-.575$ (.228)	$-.117$ (.228)	.638	37
(15) log	i_L	1.131 (.440)		$-.120$ (.158)		$-.194$ (.020)	.835	37
(16) log	i_L	1.149 (.418)	$-.122$ (.149)		$-.082$ (.051)	$-.117$ (.050)	.844	37

TABLE IV

LONG-TERM INTEREST RATES AS A FUNCTION OF IDLE BALANCES, LOGARITHMIC AND ARITHMETIC REGRESSIONS, 1919–34 AND 1935–56, COMPARED

Form of Regression	Dependent Variable	Regression Coefficients and their Standard Errors				$\hat{R}^2$	n
		Constant Term	W	L^*	L^*_{-1}		
(17) log	i_L, 1919–34	2.424 (.426)	−.608* (.152)		−.018 (.030)	.554	15
(18) log	i_L, 1935–56	−.372 (.272)	.394* (.099)		−.200 (.027)	.719	22
(19) log	i_L, 1919–34	2.706 (.464)	−.702 (.164)	.020 (.037)	−.050 (.040)	.578	15
(20) log	i_L, 1935–56	−.071 (.249)	.301 (.088)	−.146 (.065)	−.073 (.063)	.768	22
(21) arith	i_L, 1919–34	8.910 (.754)	−.0054 (.0011)	.077 (.042)	−.120 (.048)	.687	15
(22) arith	i_L, 1935–56	3.086 (.293)	.00056 (.00034)	−.0137 (.0061)	−.0017 (.0061)	.651	22

* Lagged value of wealth, W_{-1}, used instead of W.

low absolute values of elasticities, and at least a suggestion of a positive relation for unlagged L^*, in the pre-Keynesian years of high interest rates and low idle balances.

I do not presume to make too much of all of this analysis. There are, I believe, serious conceptual difficulties, not all of which I have discussed, in the kind of study Bronfenbrenner and Mayer attempted. It appears in the light of this reexamination, however, that neither the Bronfenbrenner-Mayer view of the shape of the demand for money nor, in particular, their negative judgment with regard to the existence of the Keynesian "liquidity trap" are supported by further analysis of their own and other appropriate data within the general framework they employed.

Northwestern University

REFERENCES

[1] BRONFENBRENNER, M., AND T. MAYER: "Liquidity Functions in the American Economy," *Econometrica*, Vol. 28 (1960), pp. 810–834.

[2] KEYNES, J. M.: *The General Theory of Employment, Interest and Money*, New York: Harcourt, Brace and Company, 1936.

Econometrica, Vol. 31, No. 3 (July, 1963)

REPLY

BY ROBERT EISNER

THE TENET of "the trap" would appear to be a critical issue of "faith." But the genesis of the "faith" was the notion that salvation for persistent employment was not to be found in automatic adjustment of the rate of interest and that even a managed adjustment of the rate of interest was limited in its potential. As must be clear from this exchange, the relevant rate of interest was the long-term rate, and the problem was peculiarly that the long-term rate could not fall sufficiently low.

In the always treacherous application of quantitative data to theoretical issues, one must be clear as to the theory to be confronted. As I sought to recall (footnotes 2 and 3), citing *The General Theory*, Meltzer's "demand for money become[s] infinite or the slope of a demand function for money become[s] flat" are *not* the theory, and not part of the faith. And the fact that short-term interest rates can be pushed close to zero, entirely consistent with any constant short-term interest elasticity of demand for money (which is surely more than a "debater's point" since it was short-term interest elasticities which Bronfenbrenner and Mayer estimated), offers no evidence as to whether any monetary policy in the past or the forseeable future could have reduced the long-term rate below an economically significant non-zero "bottom stop." For this purpose, whatever the semantic history, evidence of a flattening of the slopes of the curve relating money to the *long*-term interest rate at lower rates would seem a more subtle test than comparisons of elasticities, which might still remain constant down to a bottom stop we have never quite reached. That Meltzer's own work, to which he alludes, bears critically on this point is not clear, but there is not the space to discuss that. As for the liquidity trap, we have never been caught in it—more is the pity! The quest for corpses, as well as the heralding of their absence, would seem out of place.[1]

Northwestern University

[1] While eschewing the further substantive discussion that would prevent compliance with an editorial injunction of brevity, it may be in order to correct one misinterpretation of my position. I cannot accept the statement by Bronfenbrenner and Mayer (page 542) that "for our later period . . . we agree that monetary supply functions . . . approximated horizontal lines . . ." Quite the contrary, my argument (top of page 534) implies that the relevant supply of money for *idle* balances in the later period was a *vertical* line which shifted over time (generally to the right). As for the earlier period, it must also be recognized that since the dependent variable ("*idle*" balances) is already adjusted for income, and since wealth is included in the relation, a relatively fixed vertical line (or one tilted slightly in a clockwise direction) is exactly the supply curve to be expected for idle balances if the total supply of money, as Bronfenbrenner and Mayer state, was essentially "shifting with cycles and growth".

[4]

FACTORS AFFECTING THE LEVEL OF INTEREST RATES*

PART II

SOME YEARS AGO I was engaged in the probably dubious task of interviewing executives of generally very large manufacturing corporations in an effort to discover the determinants of business investment. Fortunately, I was theory-oriented and had some good notions of what I was looking for and the stubbornness to persist until I found what I was after.

One of the key questions was the role of the supply of money capital, whether measured by price or availability, in determining the rate of investment. What do you think I learned, every time I spoke to a comptroller, treasurer or financial vice president? That money was very important. Everything depended on the terms on which money could be raised and, of course, on the ability of the officer to whom I was speaking to obtain the money on favorable terms. To epitomize it all, in one substantial company in the Midwest a financial vice president said, "Of course money is important. If I can't get the money at reasonable terms we can't invest." As this remark was completed, the company's executive vice president entered. I politely briefed him on what I had just asked: "Do shortages of money or the difficulty of securing favorable terms influence your rate of capital expenditures or prevent you from undertaking or carrying through on investment?" Without waiting to hear what his financial vice president had answered, the executive vice president quickly replied, "Not at all! We make capital expenditures if they appear profitable or if we need the plant or equipment. It's his job to get the money," indicating the hapless financial vice president.

---

*This presentation was prepared while the speaker was a fellow at the Center for Advanced Study in the Behavioral Sciences, Stanford, Calif. He is appreciative of comments of John G. Gurley, Patric A. Hendershott, Axel Leijonhufvud, Abba P. Lerner, Robert H. Strotz, and William Vickrey, none of whom, of course, may be held accountable for the current contents.

ROBERT EISNER

The moral of my story, aside from what you may think it implies about the determinants of investment, is that everyone likes to think he is important. Particularly, people who deal in money—in the creation of money and in monetary policy—including those who invest a good bit of time teaching, writing, theorizing and doing research about money, like to think it is important. But that does not make it so. And more particularly, people concerned with money may well think it important in ways that it is not, and ignore some of the more important ramifications of their doings with money, which go beyond them.

Money Only Small Element

The first thing to acquire is humility, the humility which comes from recognition that no matter what particular definition of money we use, "money" is only a small element or set of elements in the vast spectrum of assets (and debts) which serve or may serve the various pecuniary functions. If an individual, or the economy, is short of one instrument of money or near money, it will turn to another.

As a general proposition this notion that pecuniary assets are substitutes for each other is hardly startling. I should like to carry it to something of an analytical extreme, and perhaps we shall find that extremism in the pursuit of knowledge has some virtue. After noting the limits of what we can expect any monetary authority, qua monetary authority, to be able to do in the way of affecting interest rates, we may be able to sense more clearly what is affecting the rates we observe in the market place.

I start with one extreme, the Keynesian liquidity trap. What we have in mind here is the right-hand end of the well-known liquidity preference curve, which indicates that no matter how great the (real) quantity of money, there is some positive lower bound below which the long term rate of interest cannot be made to fall. This relates, of course, to the idea, built on a combination of historical experience and perhaps even the analytical insight that financial transaction costs at the least necessitate some non-zero price to borrowing, that future rates of interest may be higher than current rates. The lower the current rate, the greater the number of actual and potential lenders who feel that future rates will be higher and, more directly significant, the greater the demand for money rather than the bonds expected by these bears to go down in price.

That there need be no analytical difficulty in the notion of "absolute" liquidity preference because of a violation of budget constraints—Patinkin has postulated one[1]—may be seen by recognizing that, in principle, if the monetary authority were to continue to try to buy bonds beyond the point at which all existing bonds had been sold by the private sector of the economy, rational speculators would then issue new bonds or promises to repay and sell them to the monetary authority.

[1] [5], pp. 216, 225.

LEVEL OF INTEREST RATES

For, expecting the rate of interest to rise, they could later make their gain by buying back their bonds from the monetary authority. (It would of course not matter if the monetary authority stubbornly refused to sell at the new lower prices; the lenders could make the same gain by buying just enough other bonds at the new lower prices to receive an interest return equal to the interest they were paying the monetary authority.)

Where Is Liquidity Trap?

The issue of where the lower bound to the rate of interest might be located and how actions of the monetary authority itself may affect it has been neglected by latter-day Keynesians. This may be related to a curious confusion in some econometric work, where historical data are used in an effort to find—or even determine the existence of—the liquidity trap.[2] As Keynes himself argued, we have never been in the trap; the monetary authority has never acted sufficiently "boldly" to get us there.[3]

Corollary to the view that the monetary authority may be limited in its control over the rate of interest—and in the limiting case, may lose "effective control over" it—is the view that the more the monetary authority seeks to effect changes in the rate of interest the less it will be able to do so. "The market" will hardly expect a current counter-cyclical easy money policy to persist if the monetary authority has shown by its actions that it will engage regularly in a counter-cyclical monetary policy. Unless the market has concluded that cycles are a thing of the past, it will reason that easy money today will be followed by tight money at some future date and vice versa. Hence, any attempt to lower long-term interest rates now will be at least somewhat thwarted by the very rational conviction, on the part of all those who understand monetary policy, that the gears will be reversed so that rates will be higher in the future. A counter-cyclical monetary policy thus militates against reduction of the long-term rate of interest to the lowest rate possible

---

[2] See, for example, Bronfenbrenner and Mayer, [1].

[3] "There is the possibility, . . . after the rate of interest has fallen to a certain level, liquidity-preference may become virtually absolute in the sense that almost everyone prefers cash to holding a debt which yields so low a rate of interest. In this event the monetary authority would have lost effective control over the rate of interest. But whilst this limiting case might become practically important in future, I know of no example of it hitherto. Indeed, owing to the unwillingness of most monetary authorities to deal boldly in debts of long term, there has not been much opportunity for a test." (Keynes, [4], p. 207.) Cf. Milton Friedman, who states, "Keynes and most other economists of the time believed that the Great Contraction in the U.S. occurred despite aggressive expansionary policies by the monetary authorities—they did their best but their best was not good enough." ([2], p. 3.) A correct rendition of Keynes and, I believe, of reality would be, "They did *not* do their best, but their best would not have been good enough."

ROBERT EISNER

and, *pari passu,* militates against reduction of the "required rate of return on capital" which Tobin and Brainard [6] aptly characterize as "the basic criterion of the effectiveness of a monetary action" (p. 387).[4]

It is old hat that monetary policy may prove relatively impotent in combating a substantial depression. It is clearly not so widely recognized that use of monetary policy as a first resort against minor fluctuations of economic activity can be self-defeating and can militate against keeping the long-term rate of interest as low as possible. Indeed, the prevailing view seems to be that monetary policy should be used frequently for counter-cyclical purposes, with fiscal policy, presumably for institutional, political reasons, reserved for the combat of major fluctuations in demand. Yet to the extent that we thus keep interest rates over time on the average higher than they need to be, we risk a welfare loss, provocatively discussed by Friedman in an unpublished paper on "The Optimum Quantity of Money," as we permit a price for a good—money—to rise substantially above its marginal cost of production, which is essentially zero.[5]

What may strike us as truly novel—I hope I can convince you not bizarre—is the view I should like to develop that the traditional asymmetry associated with Keynesian monetary theory is wrong. I suppose I am a bit suspicious of asymmetries in economics. Perhaps this is merely an aesthetic prejudice, but somehow I find the frequent invocation of asymmetrics troublesome in suggesting that the economy is forever being determined by special cases. Maybe so, but this would make the world infinite in its complexity and hopeless to untangle. So, out of faith in our professional capacities, would it not be more appealing to look for consistency and symmetry? By way of consistency, therefore, I am ready to argue, as should now be apparent, that the influence of monetary policy on both the rate of interest and the aggregative level of economic activity is quite generally limited. By way of symmetry, I would suggest that monetary policy is especially limited not only by the liquidity trap in depression, where the elasticity of demand for money is viewed as approaching infinity. It is quite similarly especially limited in analogous efforts to combat inflation by making the quantity of money very low. For again one finds oneself approaching an infinite elasticity of demand for money—another kind of liquidity trap or, better, a "liquidity leak."

---

[4] Again citing Keynes, "Thus a monetary policy which strikes public opinion as being experimental in character or easily liable to change may fail in its objective of greatly reducing the long-term rate of interest . . ." [4, p. 203]. Short-term rates may indeed be moved considerably by action of the monetary authority but, for a complex of reasons which I shall not develop here, I do not see in short-term rates a major determinant of investment or of the general level of economic activity.

[5] We lay aside Friedman's suggestion of a steadily falling quantity of money and steadily falling price level as the instruments for reducing the marginal yield of money and the nominal rate of interest to zero.

LEVEL OF INTEREST RATES

The geometry of all this, in terms of conventional liquidity preference figures, is disarmingly simple. All we have to do, as shown in Figure 1, is draw a liquidity preference curve which not only flattens out to the right (on the money axis) but which at the left intersects the vertical (interest rate) axis. What this, of course, implies is that not only is there some rate of interest below which the monetary authority cannot get us by increasing the quantity of money. There is also some rate above which the monetary authority cannot get us by decreasing the quantity of money.

Figure 1

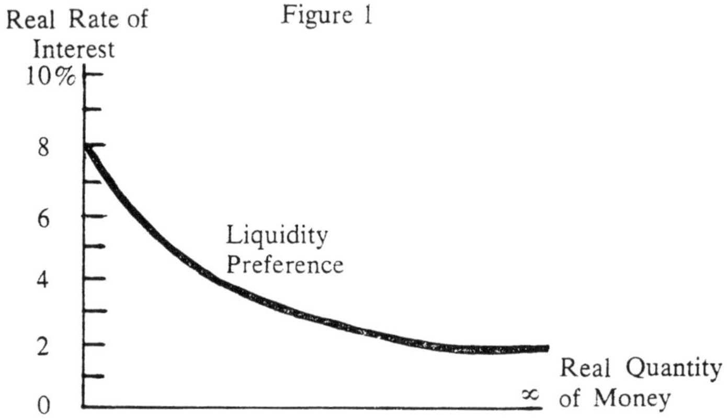

With the liquidity trap, we may recall, there were certain underlying real factors relating to transactions costs and, perhaps, borrowers' and lenders' risks which, along with historical considerations, set an expectation of a floor to the long-term rate of interest. The expected minimum rate then becomes such a floor, since at this rate demand for money on the part of those expecting rates to go up becomes completely dominant or "absolute." But now, analogously, there are certain real considerations which will limit what, in equilibrium, will be paid for whatever the monetary authority is offering in the way of "money." As we argued earlier in this paper, "money," whether coin, currency, demand deposits or time deposits, is only a small subset of the elements in the total spectrum of pecuniary assets, actual and, certainly, potential. True, this "money" is particularly convenient. One may well pay a premium to have it. It has its substitutes, however, and there is a limit to the premium which will be paid.[6]

[6] The liquidity trap is defined at a nominal rate of interest which is identically the real rate of interest in the Keynesian case of downward inflexibility of prices, since the liquidity trap situation is hardly one in which to look for upward movement of prices. The liquidity leak, however, is better defined at a real rate, since here there would appear to be no good reason to rule out the relevant, upward flexibility of prices. The nominal rate of interest at which the leak becomes absolute would then depend upon the expected rate of increase of prices.

ROBERT EISNER

We may ask ourselves, in quest of explication, what would happen if the monetary authority began to cut down on the supply of nickels. Suppose the supply were cut virtually to zero. Would much of a premium be paid in dimes or pennies by those desperately anxious to have nickels to make change conveniently, or to use chewing gum machines? Suppose the monetary authority were to cut the supply of all coins to virtually zero? Would much of a premium be paid for coins? Or would there be a general switch to substitutes, which would include transportation tokens sold by the dollar, checks for payment or change of less than a dollar, and perhaps extensive use of ledger books and IOU slips? There might even be fewer items selling for 98 cents. This is not to say that the all but complete shortage of coins—even a complete shortage—would not inflict some cost on economic activity and have some effect. And the effect would be differential—little on the real estate agent and not much more on the new car salesman, significant for the corner grocer and perhaps quite substantial for the corner newspaper dealer.

Suppose the monetary authority went further and endeavored, by selling securities in the open market, to reduce to close to zero the total amount of "money," including coin, currency and demand deposits. Money would become very scarce. Because of the reserve requirements for time deposits, they too would be drastically curtailed as banks lost reserves and depositors "withdrew" their deposits to buy securities. Rates of interest would rise—6.5%, 7%, 7.5%, 8%—but how high? Would they rise indefinitely, or would there be some point, admittedly more distant than in the case of nickels, all coin, or all coin and currency, where those who normally use "money" would say, in effect, "At that price, who needs it?"

Economy Would Adjust to Money Substitute

At such a point, General Motors might pay United States Steel and United States Rubber with its IOUs, instead of those of some bank. And U.S. Steel could pay its suppliers of coal and iron ore with the GM IOUs or its own. What would back these up if necessary? Actually, something much more tangible than "full faith and credit": the plant, equipment, inventories and product of the issuing companies. It is true that there would be some inconvenience in all of this but, perhaps sooner than one might expect, the economy would get used to "trade money," or whatever one might call it. It might not even prove so infinitely varied. Economies of scale would show themselves and good trade money would probably drive bad trade money out of circulation. If the antitrust division of the Department of Justice did not intervene we might quickly find a concentration in the issue of trade money, perhaps by Sears, A & P and large air lines as well as GM, which would make present day banking look perfectly competitive by comparison. Credit card companies would have a booming business.

For our purposes the question would be what premium would have to be paid to delay payment by one year. To get $100 of equipment, inventories or services now, how much would General Motors or Sears have to offer in the way of claims on its product one year from now? Would it really be much more than, say, \$108? If it would not, could the liquidity preference function for "money," that peculiar instrument issued or controlled by the monetary authority, intersect the vertical axis much above 8%? We suggest not. As the quantity of money is reduced so that we approach that point of intersection, we may add, the elasticity of demand for money with respect to the rate of interest, in this case of the liquidity leak as in the liquidity trap, would approach infinity.[7]

Once we have established some upper bound beyond which it is not reasonable to expect individuals or businesses to go in paying for that special financial instrument usually known as "money," we should again look to become dominant all the expectational, "speculative" factors which were dominant at the other extreme of the liquidity preference function. Perhaps in a moment of temporary stress the monetary authority can push the short-term rate above, say, 8%. If a large number of people reason that General Motors and Sears and the like will not long continue to pay more than 8% when they have the alternative of issuing their own debt instruments, there will be a dominant demand for

---

[7] The assumption of an intersection with the vertical axis is, of course, the assumption that

$$\frac{dQ}{dP} < \varepsilon, \quad \varepsilon < 0, \text{ as } Q \to 0,$$

whence

$$\frac{dQ}{dP} \cdot \frac{P}{Q} \to -\infty \quad \text{as } Q \to 0.$$

By running a sufficient budget surplus and insisting that taxes must be paid in "money," not trade money, the Treasury can presumably drive the rate on "money" above what we have defined as the rate of the absolute liquidity leak. Individuals and businesses could be forced to pay more than this, on pain of imprisonment, to meet their tax obligations. But then surely "money" would be used only to pay taxes and would have ceased to be the medium of exchange relevant to economic activity. Money might be borrowed for taxes but not to invest. And, as noted below, we would be dealing with certain implications of fiscal policy, not monetary policy.

Similarly, it might be made a criminal offense to issue or use the kind of trade money which I suggest, and the literal-minded among us may insist that this is already largely true. One has to have a charter to create bank money, and General Motors would not get one. But, I would argue, there would be and are an infinite number of ways of economizing on "money," of which conventional trade credit is already recognized as one of the most widespread. My argument is essentially that the ready availability of money substitutes in a developed economy such as our own sets clear and relatively narrow limits on the real power of the monetary authority. One can, of course, change the structure of our system and insist that one *has* to use "money," and spell out myriad rules to stop the "leak." None would deny, as I suggest below, that various forms of compulsion can stop the economy from doing many things, including, ultimately, functioning at all, but surely this takes us far beyond the realm of what is usefully thought of as monetary policy.

any bonds paying more than 8%. Investors expecting the rate of interest to fall below a current rate of more than 8% of course anticipate a capital gain on any bonds they can obtain. Their "speculative motive" would dictate the holding of bonds just as their brothers in the liquidity trap would speculate on cash. The speculative motive might thus, as in Figure 2, make the liquidity preference curve flatten out as it approached the vertical axis; with whatever slope it intersected, however, as noted, the elasticity would be infinite at the point of intersection.

Issue: Exchange of Money for Nonmonetary Assets

One might suggest that the trouble with this analysis is that we are claiming to reduce the quantity of money but actually we are letting money leak back in through the back door or, should we say, the front door of Sears or General Motors. If we are talking about reducing the supply of money we should really reduce the supply of all money, not just "money." We should perhaps think in terms of prohibiting the issue or use of the trade money we have been postulating. Is this not the nub of the matter? The monetary authority deals in "money." There is no doubt that the authority, some authority, can have very great effects upon the economy. The Department of Defense could conceivably bring economic activity to a virtual halt by threatening destruction to all who would produce and, if necessary, carrying out the threat. Monetary analysis, however, relates to the instruments which a monetary authority, properly speaking, can control. By a monetary authority we should make clear—clearer than I believe it is always made—that we mean an authority with the power to exchange its obligations for others and to control the power of certain specialized institutions to do likewise, where their instruments of superior liquidity are *defined* as money. This must involve an exchange of obligations, not the giving away of obligations (or money) for nothing. The latter involves fiscal policy, and a different set of considerations, just as authority in the form of the Department of

Figure 2

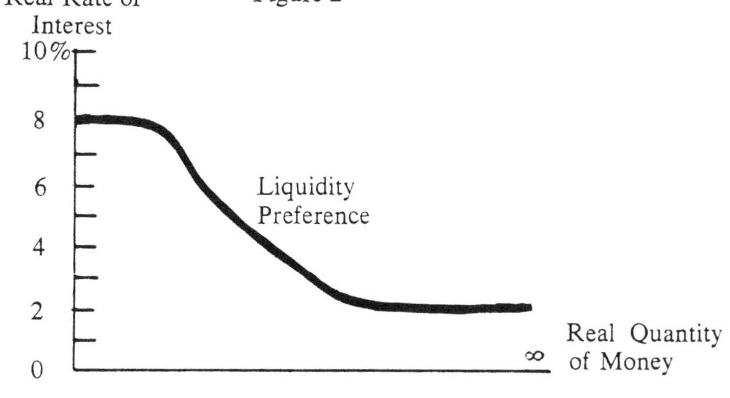

LEVEL OF INTEREST RATES

Defense, as suggested above, involves a different set of considerations. The issues which confront us under the rubric of monetary policy, at least in the United States, involve not the creation of net additions to the assets of the private sector of the economy, but merely the exchange of money for nonmonetary assets.[8]

What does this extreme vision of an economy in which the monetary authority cuts the quantity of "money" to the ultimate have to do with the United States of 1967 and 1968? I would argue, "A good deal." Monetary authorities were nowhere bold enough to get us into the liquidity trap during the great depression and monetary authorities can hardly be expected to be bold enough to get us to the liquidity leak in a time of pressing inflation. I am not prepared to argue that monetary authorities have always or even most of the time done the right thing. Vitiating some of the complaints that monetary authorities have not done enough to combat inflation (if much at all) is the probability that they could not have done much more. If I may be permitted just a bit of asymmetry after all, I might suggest that while the effectiveness of the monetary authority in combating serious deflation is largely one of impotence, the difficulty in combating inflation is that long before the final manifestation of impotence in the liquidity leak, a great deal of damage can be done by monetary attempts to combat inflation.

Tight Money Has Selective Effect

The fact is that different units in the economy have different capacities to obtain money, to economize in its use and to create or obtain money substitutes. If 1967 showed anything it was that tight money, at least as measured by high nominal rates of interest, has a very selective effect on the economy. Residential housing construction, as we all know, felt the pinch badly, and took a severe beating. Business capital expenditures, particularly those of the largest firms which account for most of them, showed no discernible impact of monetary stringency, and indeed reached new record highs (however its precipitate rate of growth slackened). Had money been made more difficult to borrow, the pinch on residential housing construction and some other sectors of the economy would have been even tighter. Yet paradoxically, some of the rest of the economy might have boomed all the more, as resources flowed from the victims of tight money to those with readier access to money or its myriad substitutes.

It may well be argued that, during part of 1967, bank reserves and the money supply were rising so rapidly that by no stretch of the imagi-

---

[8] In this sense, I might suggest, much of what passes for monetary analysis involving real asset effects is irrelevant. The world of monetary policy is the implicit world of Keynes's *General Theory* in which all money held by the private sector is balanced by private debt; there can be no "Pigou effect."

ROBERT EISNER

nation could the Fed be viewed as playing a restraining hand. (One retort might be that you do not know the stretch of my imagination.) I may concede that monetary policy was, like fiscal policy, victim of the same political machinations relating to a lack of candor in anticipating and admitting the inflationary impact of the partly surreptitious continued escalation of war expenditures. I would insist, however, that the inflation has been fiscally induced by the escalating war expenditures and the failure, for political reasons, to impose a tax increase early in the escalatory process; the increasing quantity of money at most kept uneven pace with rising rates of output, demand and expectations which it did not induce. One may well argue, in view of what happened to both nominal rates of interest and residential construction, that the money supply did not really keep pace.

I should pause to meet at least one potential cry of outrage, that we should be talking about not the nominal rate of interest but the "real" rate of interest. The real rate of interest, it might then be claimed, did not really rise. Rather, inflation amounted to at least as much as, possibly more than, the increased nominal interest rates, so that the real rate actually declined. Hence the monetary authority *was* acting in an inflationary fashion.[9] I do not believe it, and I can at least offer some casual empirical evidence to sustain my disbelief.

Lack Reliable Data on Expectations

For one thing there is frequently in economics a confusion between past trends and expectations as to the future. It is true that we usually do not have much in the way of reliable data on expectations, so that in our empirical work we frequently use past variables as proxies (pretty poor ones) for expectations of the future. But it remains expectations of the future which are relevant. He who acts on the future on the basis of simple extrapolations of past rates of change is not the one on whom I would bet my money, whether in the stock market or anywhere else. The "real" rate of interest relevant to economic activity would be the nominal rate adjusted for the *expected* rate of change in prices. Who is very sure that a 3% increase over the past year makes likely a 3% increase over the next year, and the year after that, and many years still further in the future?

By way of that casual empiricism, I note that, from January 1965 to December 1967, Moody's Aaa corporate bond rates rose from 4.43% to 6.19%. The rate of price inflation may well depend on the measure

---

[9] Attention should be called to the striking analysis of my colleague, Patric Hendershott [3], who finds that it is quite generally the endogenous elements of the money supply, stimulated by economic activity itself, which have given the mistaken impression of pro-cyclical action by the monetary authority. The exogenous contributions of the Fed have actually been counter-cyclical.

LEVEL OF INTEREST RATES

we use, but on the chance that prices for fixed investment goods may be those most relevant to corporate borrowing, we may note that their index rose over this same period from 107.0 to 114.6, which comes to about 2.5% per year rate of increase. At first glance, we might say that we have more than accounted for the increase in the nominal bond rate of some 1.76% points. But have we? First we might note that price increases in investment goods had not begun in this period of rising interest rates. For the three-year period from 1962 to 1965, the investment goods price index rose from 104.1 to 107.7, roughly 1.2% per year. Hence, the rate of increase of the rise in prices was only in the order of about 1.3%, from 1.2% to 2.5%. Since corporate bond rates had been fairly stable before, we apparently had an increase of some 1.76% in nominal interest rates accompanied by an increase in the rate of increase of prices of only 1.2%. More to the point, is it likely that such an increase in the rate of rise of prices generated an expectation of a corresponding rise in prices over all the long years for which corporate bonds might be borrowed? If the long-run elasticity of expectations for *rates of increases* of prices is substantially less than unity, and I can hardly believe in the present situation that it has not been substantially less than unity (I suspect it is close to zero), then the real rate of interest has indeed risen substantially since 1965 and, probably, in every month in 1967 since April. If you are still doubtful, look at residential housing. Clearly somewhere expected price increases were not sufficient to outweigh the rise in nominal rates of interest (although, again, in some cases they certainly were).

Limits to What Monetary Authority Can Do

Where does all this leave us with regard to factors affecting interest rates? Essentially, it argues that interest rates are largely determined by some fairly pervasive forces in the economy, relating to productivity and thrift and risk, the shape of production functions and parameters of intertemporal utility functions. Expected future price movements will play a part, but this part can readily be exaggerated, particularly by a confusion between past and current rates of change of prices and these future expectations which alone are relevant. The monetary authority assuredly does play a substantial role, since money substitutes are not without additional cost. In the short run, no doubt, the monetary authority can raise interest rates significantly—or allow them to rise. This is not without effect on the economy, although much more at the non-aggregative level, involving transfer of resources from those with poorer access to credit to those with better access. Curbed by liquidity traps and liquidity leaks and, generally, by the expectational links of past, current and future, there are decided limits to what the monetary authority can do to counteract real forces in the economy. When depression destroys investment demand, interest rates will fall. When an expanding war calls for resources at a faster rate than a growing economy will freely grant them, interest rates rise. Purely monetary measures to cope

ROBERT EISNER

with such developments are limited in effectiveness and sometimes so selective in their impact as to offend seriously our sense of equity and, in some instances, the efficient working of the economy.

Money Close to Free Good

So I come around, by what may seem a somewhat devious route, to a conclusion familiar to most of you from the work of my distinguished colleague, Milton Friedman. Money, bless it, is really as close to a free good as we are ever likely to run into. With modern banking systems its marginal cost of production is virtually zero. There is every reason to keep its price as close as possible to its marginal cost. Both contrived scarcity and repeated swings in monetary policy will prevent attainment of that low price.

I cannot fathom the applicability, whatever their elegance, of models which suggest that the way to achieve this virtually zero cost of money (and nominal rate of interest) is to bring about somehow a steadily declining money supply and corresponding declining price level. Among other things, for better or for worse, prices (and not just wages) are fairly rigid in a downward direction in the economy we know, and not so fully flexible upwards either, for that matter. I find myself drawn to the suggestion that the best policy to follow is one which will make the money supply increase at some substantial steady rate and let interest rates then adjust to real forces but hopefully, thus, keep them as low as possible. This may strike many of you as an humble objective—but perhaps, after all this, it is on a note of humility that I should close.

REFERENCES

[1] M. Bronfenbrenner and T. Mayer: "Liquidity Functions in the American Economy," *Econometrica,* Vol. 28 (1960), pp. 810-834.

[2] M. Friedman, "The Role of Monetary Policy," *American Economic Review,* Vol. 58 (1958), pp. 1-17.

[3] P. A. Hendershott, *The Neutralized Money Stock: An Unbiased Measure of Federal Reserve Actions,* Irwin, 1968.

[4] J. M. Keynes, *The General Theory of Employment, Interest and Money,* New York: Harcourt, Brace and Company, 1936.

[5] D. Patinkin, *Money, Interest and Prices,* second edition, Evanston: Harper and Row, 1965.

[6] J. Tobin and W. C. Brainard, "Financial Intermediaries and the Effectiveness of Monetary Controls," *American Economic Review,* Vol. 53 (1963), pp. 383-400.

[5]

Econometrica, Vol. 39, No. 5 (September, 1971)

NON-LINEAR ESTIMATES OF THE LIQUIDITY TRAP

BY ROBERT EISNER[1]

1. INTRODUCTION

HOWARD W. PIFER [3] has recently presented estimates of parameters of a non-linear formulation of the Keynesian liquidity trap. Making the quantity of money, M, depend upon national income, NI, assets, A, and the difference between the rate of interest, r, and a liquidity floor, r_{min}, Pifer estimated r_{min} between 2.0 per cent and 2.2 per cent. He then, however, reported these estimates "not significantly different from zero as measured by the likelihood ratio test" (p. 329). Next, following a suggestion of Eisner [2] that the rate of interest be viewed as a function of the quantity of money, Pifer inverted his relation and reported now that no lower bound to the interest rate could be observed. He concluded that "results obtained using a non-linear, maximum likelihood method provide no significant evidence to support the existence of the liquidity trap" (p. 332).

Re-estimation with Pifer's data and application of appropriate statistical tests contradict Pifer's conclusions. First, where the quantity of money is taken as the dependent variable, his estimates of a positive floor to the rate of interest are found to be statistically significant. Second, Pifer's procedure for estimating the inverse function, where the quantity of money is taken as exogenous, is incorrect. Using maximum likelihood estimators described by Box and Cox [1], we confirm estimates of an interest rate floor in the neighborhood of two per cent, and find these too significantly above zero.

2. THE DEMAND FOR MONEY WITH INTEREST RATE EXOGENOUS

Re-estimates of Pifer's equations (3.1) to (3.4), as indicated in Table I, place the floor of the liquidity trap at from 2.03 to 2.18 per cent. (Some slight discrepancies with Pifer's reported

TABLE I

PIFER'S EQUATIONS[a] WITH MONEY DEPENDENT: TEST STATISTICS FOR HYPOTHESIS THAT $r_{min} > 0$

Equation and variables included in addition to $r - r_{min}$	$\hat{r}_{min}$	$\Sigma \hat{e}^2$ (for $\hat{r}_{min}$)	$n - k$	Σe^2 (for $r_{min} = 0$)	F^* $\left(\frac{\Sigma e^2 - \Sigma \hat{e}^2}{\Sigma \hat{e}^2/n - k}\right)$	L^* $\left(n \ln \frac{\Sigma e^2}{\Sigma \hat{e}^2}\right)$	Significance levels: $P(F > F^*)$ Less than	Significance levels: $P(\chi^2 > L^*)$ Less than
(3.1) None	2.18	30.84	55	33.15	4.11	4.18	.05	.05
(3.2) A	2.03	.3195	54	.3830	10.73	10.51	.005	.005
(3.3) A, NI	2.12	.2239	53	.2811	13.52	13.19	.001	.0005
(3.4) A, NI, M_{t-1}	2.16	.0943	52	.1144	11.09	11.20	.005	.001

[a] While Pifer wrote his equations in multiplicative form, he and I have actually in all cases estimated their logarithmic transformations. Thus statistics presented are, for example, for

$$\ln M_t = \ln \alpha + \beta_1 \ln (r_t - r_{min}) + \beta_2 \ln A_t + \beta_3 \ln NI_t + \beta_4 \ln M_{t-1} + \ln u_t, \tag{3.4*}$$

and similarly for the other equations in this table and the tables below. We have followed Pifer in labelling the estimated variance of $\ln u_t$ as σ_u^2. We denote the sum of the squared residuals as Σe^2 for $r_{min} = 0$ and as $\Sigma \hat{e}^2$ for the maximum likelihood estimate, $\hat{r}_{min}$, the residual variance degrees of freedom for n (= 58) observations as $n - k$, the sample F ratio (with one numerator degree of freedom) as F^*, and the logarithmic transformation of the likelihood ratio (a chi-square variable with one degree of freedom) as L^*.

[1] The author is indebted to the National Science Foundation for financial support, to Howard Pifer for the data, originally gathered by Allan Meltzer, to Keith McLaren and Bernard Reddy for various calculations, to Robert W. Clower, Meyer Dwass, Walter D. Fisher, and Michael Lovell for helpful reactions and comments and, most importantly, to Edgar L. Feige and Kenneth J. White and to Robert Welch.

results, which ranged from 2.04 to 2.20, are apparently explainable by the greater accuracy of our regression program, as indicated in slightly lower estimates of the variance of residuals.) Approximate tests of the significance of the positive estimates of r_{min} may be found in the F-statistic for the ratio of the increase in the sum of squared residuals, resulting from constraining r_{min} to be zero, to the estimated variance of residuals with the maximum likelihood, non-linear estimation of r_{min}, or in the likelihood ratios. Contrary to Pifer's report, it is clear that in all cases, with either test, r_{min} is significantly positive at at least the .05 probability level and, wherever assets, income, or the lagged quantity of money are introduced into the regressions, r_{min} is significant at better than the .005 probability level.

3. THE INTEREST RATE FUNCTION WITH MONEY EXOGENOUS

Pifer endeavors in his equations (4.1) and (4.2) to follow the Eisner suggestion that estimation of the liquidity preference function may better embody the assumption that interest rates move in response to exogenous shifts in the money supply. Pifer finds, however, that in regressions involving logarithmic transformations of (4.1) and (4.2), the variance of residuals keeps decreasing as lower and lower values of r_{min}, including 0 and -1.0 per cent in his Table II, are assumed. Asserting that "the variance of residuals . . . [is] the statistic that we must minimize in order to obtain the maximum likelihood estimate," Pifer suggests that "(i) a low-level liquidity trap does not exist, and that (ii) a logarithmic function with its assumption of constant elasticity may not be the best formulation of the demand equation" (p. 330).

The source of difficulty should become evident in Table II, which presents relevant statistics for a number of trial values of r_{min} in (4.2*), the logarithmic transformation (also used by Pifer)

TABLE II

σ_u^2 AND OTHER STATISTICS AS FUNCTIONS OF r_{min}, PIFER EQUATION (4.2*) $\ln(r_t - r_{min}) = \ln\alpha + \lambda_1 \ln M_t + \lambda_2 \ln A_t + \ln u_t$

r_{min}	$\hat{\lambda}_1$	$\sigma_{\hat{\lambda}_1}$	$\hat{R}^2$	σ_u^2	Variance of $\ln(r_t - r_{min})$
2.34999	−5.958	.942	.4758	1.6056	3.0630
2.34	−4.551	.380	.7734	.2616	1.1546
2.0	−2.679	.170	.8538	.0525	.3589
0.0	−1.016	.072	.8164	.0095	.0517
−1.0	− .786	.057	.8073	.0060	.0310
−10.0	− .262	.020	.7831	.00075	.0035
−1000.0	− .0035	.0003	.7692	$15(10)^{-8}$	$64(10)^{-8}$

of his (4.2). The variance of the residuals, as Pifer suggested, is apparently a monotonic, positive function of r_{min}; as r_{min} is lowered from 2.34999 per cent, just below 2.35 per cent, the minimum value of r_t in the series, σ_u^2 declines from 1.6056 to virtually zero. But the variance of the residuals keeps declining because the variance of the dependent variable which we are trying to explain keeps declining as r_{min} is lowered, as is made abundantly evident in the final column of Table II.

An appropriate maximum likelihood estimator where a parameter enters non-linearly in the dependent variable is described by Box and Cox [1, see especially pp. 214–216]. In the current instance the logarithm, except for a constant, of the likelihood function to be maximized with respect to r_{min} and the linear parameters, Λ, is:

$$L(\Lambda, r_{min}) = -\tfrac{1}{2}n \log \sigma_u^2(\Lambda, r_{min}) - \Sigma \log (r_t - r_{min}),$$

and what Pifer has done is to omit the second term, which accounts for the transformation from r to $\log(r - r_{min})$. Searching the least squares estimates, σ_u^2, for given values of r_{min} at intervals of

.01, we locate maximum likelihood estimates of $\hat{r}_{min} = 1.66$ per cent and 1.95 per cent, respectively, as shown in Table III, for Equation (4.1), where the interest rate is a function only of money, and (4.2), where the interest rate is a function of money and assets. In additional Equations (4.3) and (4.4), where money and income, and money, assets, and income are taken as independent variables, $\hat{r}_{min} = 2.06$ per cent and 2.02 per cent. Further, the likelihood ratio test leads to rejection of the hypothesis that $r_{min} = 0$, at the .01 probability level or better in all cases except that of the poorly fitting (and certainly misspecified) relation (4.1) involving only money. Far from contradicting evidence of the liquidity trap noted in equations with money dependent, correct estimates of the inverse relation are amply confirming.[2]

TABLE III

CORRECTED ESTIMATES OF EQUATIONS WITH INTEREST RATES DEPENDENT[a] AND LIKELIHOOD RATIO TEST OF $r_{min} > 0$

Equation	$\hat{r}_{min}$	$\hat{\lambda}_0$	$\hat{\lambda}_1$ (M)	$\hat{\lambda}_2$ (A)	$\hat{\lambda}_3$ (NI)	$\hat{R}^2$	L^*	Significance level $P(\chi^2 > L^*)$ is less than
(4.1)	1.66	1.526	−.288	—	—	.349	1.64	.20
		(.174)	(.050)	—	—			
(4.2)	1.95	−5.854	−2.559	2.492	—	.850	10.32	.005
		(.557)	(.164)	(.184)	—			
(4.3)	2.06	−2.284	−3.068	—	2.861	.786	7.71	.01
		(.395)	(.255)	—	(.271)			
(4.4)	2.02	−5.484	−3.021	1.909	1.021	.869	12.51	.0005
		(.625)	(.192)	(.350)	(.315)			

[a] The equations are in the form

$$\ln(r_t - r_{min}) = \lambda_0 + \lambda_1 \ln M_t + \lambda_2 \ln A_t + \lambda_3 \ln NI_t + \ln u_t,$$

with variables deleted as indicated.

4. CONCLUSION

This paper, like Pifer's, has ignored what well may be serious questions as to the consistency of estimators of single equations plucked from an implicitly simultaneous system. It has also ignored effects on consistency and/or efficiency stemming from serial correlation of disturbances.[3] It hardly claims to have offered definitive estimates of liquidity preference functions.

[2] It may be observed, in all of the equations presented in Table III, that the signs of the coefficients of $\ln M$ are negative but approximately equal in absolute value to the positive coefficients of $\ln A$ or $\ln NI$ or to the sum of these coefficients. This suggests that interest rates are dependent upon the ratios of money to assets or national income, with the small but significantly negative sum of the coefficients of money, assets, and income (−.091, standard error of .037) implying, however, some secular decline in interest rates with equiproportionate increases in these variables over time. It further suggests that increases in the quantity of money markedly less rapid than those of national income, as in each of the years beginning with the 1965 escalation of the war in Vietnam, would be expected to cause interest rates to rise, as of course they did. (This is not to assert that growing expectations of continued price inflation did not also contribute to rising interest rates.)

[3] We have, however, supplemented the analysis in this paper by assuming that the disturbances in the equations presented in Table I are generated by the first order auto-regressive relation, $\ln u_t = \rho \ln u_{t-1} + \varepsilon_t$, and attempting maximum likelihood estimates of ρ and r_{min}. For (3.4*) and (3.3*) they were, respectively: $\hat{\rho} = .36$, $\hat{r}_{min} = 1.98$ per cent, and $\hat{\rho} = .97$, $\hat{r}_{min} = 2.20$ per cent. For (3.2*), involving only assets as an additional independent variable, the estimates were $\hat{\rho} = .94$, $\hat{r}_{min} = 1.26$ per cent. For (3.1*), with no other independent variables, $\hat{\rho}$ was apparently just above its prescribed upper bound of unity. The estimate of r_{min} for $\rho = 1.0$, in this case, was 2.02 per cent.

But it is clear that Pifer's findings cannot properly be considered to have sprung the liquidity trap. Perhaps those of us so inclined can still argue that money doesn't always matter very much.

Northwestern University

Manuscript received May, 1970; revision received July, 1970.

REFERENCES

[1] Box, G. E. P., and D. R. Cox: "An Analysis of Transformations," *Journal of the Royal Statistical Society*, Series B, 26 (1964), 211–243.
[2] Eisner, Robert: "Another Look at Liquidity Preference," *Econometrica*, 31 (1963), 531–538.
[3] Pifer, Howard W.: "A Non-Linear, Maximum Likelihood Estimate of the Liquidity Trap," *Econometrica*, 37 (1969), 324–332.

[6]

The Keynesian Revolution Reconsidered

By ROBERT EISNER*

It all seemed so simple once. A new generation of economists, nurtured "in the new ideas," had less difficulty "in escaping from the old ones." We understood the determinants of underemployment and knew what to do about it. But now the previously rearguard actions of separate groups of neoclassicists and monetarists have been seen by some as a full-fledged challenge to basic Keynesian theory. And at the policy level, professional as well as public bewilderment grows through months of increasing inflation *and* unemployment.

Whence emanated the "underemployment equilibrium" fondly exposited to a captive generation of students and all others who would listen? We all did see the truth of Keynes's denial of the second of the two "classical . . . postulates," that "the utility of the wage . . . is equal to the marginal disutility of . . . employment." But why? Was it rigid wages because of irrational or institutional constraints? Was it rigid wages due to perfectly rational choice in view of imperfect information, search costs, and inelasticity of expectations with regard to future wage offers? Or after all, is wage rigidity, whatever the reason, an explanation of "equilibrium" in the general level of prices and unnecessary to an explanation of underemployment?

It is this last that we can properly attribute to Keynes, not merely the "Keynesians," to evoke Axel Leijonhufvud's distinction—and I mean by Keynes, *The General Theory*, not necessarily the *Treatise* to which Leijonhufvud would also have us refer. To Keynes, wages were not perfectly flexible downward; we need not be detained as to the reason, whether Keynes's own explanation or the current, sophisticated views in terms of information and search costs. And it is also true that Keynes viewed the monetary authority as deficient in its efforts and methods to keep the quantity of money sufficient to minimize long-term rates of interest. But it is important to see, both in terms of theory and policy, that wage frictions and monetary restrictions, while both sufficient conditions, were not necessary for Keynesian unemployment. This relates rather to an aggregate of individual preferences which do not bring about current consumption of total product and the lack of an *intertemporal* price structure which can insure the production now of capital goods for the future in an amount equal to the gap between consumption and the total production that would be effected by full employment.

It has been customary to compartmentalize the deficiencies in effective demand. On the one hand, consumption, for a variety of reasons relating to individual preferences, would be both bounded and fairly inelastic over plausible ranges of rates of intertemporal substitution. Investment, or the demand for current production of capital goods, is constrained by two blades of a scissors: production possibilities of functions which underlie expected rates of return and the long-run rates of interest which may be viewed as a cost or rental price of capital or rate of capitalization of expected future returns. Looked at either way, the possible rate of

* William R. Kenan Professor of Economics, Northwestern University, and research associate of the National Bureau of Economic Research. I am indebted for helpful comments to R. A. Gordon, Harry G. Johnson, and Robert M. Solow.

investment in a free economy is also bounded, and this I would insist is Keynes and not merely "Keynesian," as Leijonhufvud argues.

Implications of rational choice and some evidence (Eisner, 1963, 1971) substantiate the possibility of a positive liquidity trap. Past history, including a history of rate variability, risk, risk aversion and information and transaction costs, indicates that at any point of time the public may be ready at some positive rate of interest to turn all of its bonds or other income-earning assets into cash and indeed, contrary to Don Patinkin (p. 349), issue more promises to future payments—bonds—than are currently in existence in return for additional cash. The liquidity blade of the scissors, however, need not be set at a positive rate of return. It suffices for the theory of underemployment that the blade be nonnegative; and we can hardly suggest a willingness to lend or invest at negative rates of return as long as there is any nonwasting, noncostly asset such as money.

It is the other blade of the scissors that has been questioned, originally explicitly by Frank Knight, with antecedents going back at least to Eugen v. Böhm-Bawerk, later by "Keynesians" such as Robert Solow and James Tobin, by Dale Jorgenson implicitly in his self-named "neoclassical investment function," and most recently by Leijonhufvud. One can appeal to considerable if disputable econometric evidence that investment demand is relatively inelastic, over plausible ranges, to available rates of intertemporal substitution, where these should depend upon both nominal interest, or expected earnings rates, and expected rates of price change. One can resort to casual empiricism or *gedank*-experiments which might suggest that, at any available technology, *profitable* investment opportunities are finite, or recall that a capital addition must, to be profitable, not only add to gross product but must add more than its original cost. Or one may merely look to the total structure of Keynesian theory and recognize that, were there no problem of matching *attainable* rates of interest to *acceptable* rates of return, Keynesian underemployment would vanish in reasonably functioning markets. Saving in excess of the investment demand at full employment would simply enough bring about a fall in the rate of interest sufficient to raise investment demand, if not reduce saving, to the appropriate equilibrium.

Clearly, rigid or downwardly inflexible wages are a sufficient condition for persistent unemployment in the face of a decline in aggregate demand. But while wages may in fact not be perfectly flexible, Keynes's argument was that, even if they were, full employment would not be assured. Given unemployment, with a nominal quantity of money held constant or which does not decline in full proportion with wages and prices, real cash balances would rise, thus lowering the rate of interest and raising the real value of outstanding bonds. The lower rate of interest would increase investment demand, but because of the shape of the liquidity preference function and ultimately, if it ever came to that, the liquidity trap, and the limited interest elasticity of investment demand, this "Keynes effect" would prove insufficient. The higher real value of bonds could raise consumption by those who are net holders of bonds. But unless there were an outside debtor such as a government, for whose real obligations the public (out of money illusion) would have no concern, or which would have a different horizon or set of time preferences, the increased real value of bonds for net creditors would be offset by a corresponding increase in the real obligations of net debtors. As for cash itself, this would have to be or correspond to a net asset of the public, perhaps as "outside" or government money, and the government would have to follow a "monetary" policy which in effect, by holding the money supply constant or not letting it fall in proportion to prices, transfers real purchasing power to holders of cash.

The policy implications involved in all of this seemed clear for a long time to most economists. For one thing, keep interest rates as low as possible and have the central bank operate directly on the rates relevant to investment by buying *long*-term bonds. This would be a step in the right direction, but given the limits to how low the rate of interest could be pushed and given the limits to investment demand, further action in the way of fiscal policy to raise consumption might prove necessary, along with direct government participation to "socialize" investment.

An important implication of the theory and policy, sometimes implicit and sometimes explicit, was that "stabilization" meant maintenance of full employment. The appropriate policy was not to lop off booms but to fill in recessions. While Keynes was explicit on this last, a full consideration of the system, both as originally formulated and as we should see it more clearly now, reveals basic weaknesses and contradictions in conventional countercyclical policy.

With regard to monetary policy and the interest rate, countercyclical policy is inconsistent with full employment policy. For full employment, we want no monetary bar to maximum investment. This means that we want no shortage of liquidity, *current or expected*, to drive long-term interest rates above a minimum which might, with appropriate consumption and investment functions, be the natural rate. But every time the monetary authority curbs the money supply to fight an inflation or cut off a boom it raises interest rates. In so doing it makes all the less credible any policy of low long-term rates and vitiates its efforts to lower rates in the next recession.

While the self-cancelling effect of monetary shifts should have been implicit in original Keynesian formulations, difficulties in affecting consumption by countercyclical tax measures have become apparent with later formulations of the consumption function, particularly by Franco Modigliani and Richard Brumberg and by Milton Friedman (1957), and the ineffectiveness of the 1968 surcharges in combating inflation. If current consumption depends not merely on current income but on wealth and expected future income as well, a temporary increase in tax rates may have only a minor effect in curbing aggregate demand. And with regard to the investment function, we have come to see that the paths of the acceleration principle and, perhaps a fortiori, substitution effects involve fairly long, well-distributed lags and expectations of the profitability of investment which, however mercurial on occasion, are not always easily swayed by transitory considerations.

The common thread to difficulties that even a fully competitive system may have in returning to full employment, or in ever attaining it, stems from the often uncertain and often inconsistent ties between the present and the future. Thus interest rates may not fall far enough now because of expectations by many that they will be higher in the future. Workers will not accept lower wages now because they expect that if they wait or look longer they may find a better paying job in the future. Abandoning the fiction of tâtonnement and recontracting, sellers of goods and services may hold out in the expectation that if they wait their reservation prices will be met. (Of course, in a world of imperfect competition, a fall in demand may raise or lower prices or leave them the same, depending upon changes in elasticities of demand and the nature of marginal cost curves.) And there is no guarantee that expectations of future wants and future prices will determine consumption plans for the present and the future which will mesh with current and future investment.

Through all the recapitulations and revisions of theory, we should keep prominent the recognition that money is not omnipotent. Its supply and demand equations are undoubtedly more important than those for peanuts, but not in principle different. If the supply of peanuts is reduced, even to zero, there would be repercussions in other equations as the demand for substitutes is felt. Similarly, the supply of money, by any particular definition, can be reduced with a demand for (and creation of) money substitutes then increased. Since, as Robert Clower and others have reminded us, money may usefully be viewed as a factor of production, reducing its supply may well reduce real output precisely in association with rising costs, a matter to which we shall return.

And then tied to our recognition of long-run consumption functions, related to far more than current income, and investment functions which are inelastic, unstable, yet hard to affect, is the critical fact of lack of perfect information and futures markets which would meet that lack. The only pervasive futures markets that exist are in money but even these are almost always in nominal terms. Except on cost-plus government contracts (the significance of which, as John Kenneth Galbraith has eloquently reminded us, should not be overlooked) producers can rarely guarantee their profits by sales of futures to match spot purchases of capital, labor, and materials. The lack of such futures markets at every stage may lead sellers, producers, and buyers to hold back, in risk aversion and uncertainty, leaving demand and output deficient in comparison with what they might be if all markets, for present and future goods and services, could be cleared currently.

This suggests, by way of policy, fiscal measures to change intertemporal price expectations. Instead of varying taxes on income, which have a wealth effect almost certain to be in the same direction for both current and future consumption, government should vary tax rates on goods and services. In some periods tax rates may become negative, that is, turn into subsidies, in order to encourage expenditures. In other periods, tax rates would be raised in order to discourage expenditures. Changes would be pointedly temporary to encourage intertemporal substitution. Thus when demand is deficient, tax rates on goods and services can be reduced temporarily with an explicit warning that they are likely to be raised in the future when demand may prove too high. The difference between a 10 percent subsidy and a 10 percent tax, for example, may well entail a sufficient shift in intertemporal price expectations to have a substantial effect on current demand.

And instead of permanent equipment tax credits, investment allowances, or accelerated tax depreciation, government might much better institute high but variable tax and subsidy combinations on investment expenditures generally, including nonprofit institutions and state and local governmental units as well. Thus, in periods when investment expenditures are to be encouraged, subsidies might run not to 7 percent but to 14 or 28 percent of any expenditures above, say, depreciation charges or an average of the last three years' investment expenditures. Where investment expenditures are to be discouraged, the subsidy can be converted to a tax. Again, knowledge that taxes and subsidies are temporary would generate a low, possibly negative, elasticity of effective price expectations and major intertemporal substitution of investment expenditures.

Tax policy may also be used to affect directly the demand for labor services. Where employment is slack, payroll taxes can be cut or suspended, or even converted into subsidies to encourage employers to hire workers. Where inflationary bidding up of wages has taken place, payroll taxes can be raised, perhaps particularly on *increases* in payrolls beyond what they were previously. And all of this focuses directly on the root cause of Keynesian departures from (hopefully not inflationary) full employment equilibria: a lack of an appropriate set of intertemporal prices or price expectations.

By further way of policy, certain old prescriptions for full employment still offer a sound foundation. As Evsey Domar long ago suggested, a governmental "guarantee" of a steady growth of income, in part presumably through a steady growth in "autonomous" government expenditures, tends to generate the investment and consumption demand which brings the economy to full employment. Along with this should go a fairly steady growth of the money supply, consistent with both Friedman (1968) and Keynes.

But beyond that, recognition of public concern with inflation, if nothing else, dictates the formulation of policies to improve the inflation-unemployment tradeoff. There are many obvious things that could be said about firm government action to promote competition. Too often ignored are the mass and maze of government institutions, actions, and policies which contribute to inflation. These include tariffs, import quotas, price supports, resale price maintenance, petroleum prorationing, regulatory authorities that keep rates up, purchasing and hiring policies that raise prices not only for what government buys, but for all buyers in direct or indirect competition with government.

To the objection that elimination of barriers to competition may have a once-over effect of lowering prices but no long-run influence on the rate of inflation, one should raise the "ratchet effect." Inflation may stem as much from nonfalling as from rising prices. In any functioning economy, demands and supplies are perennially changing. Some prices must hence be expected to rise while others fall. If tariffs, regulators, or monopolists "protect" us from price declines, the average movement of all prices can only be upward.

On the positive side, government can move to improve markets in general, and notoriously imperfect labor markets in particular, by utilization of modern information-processing techniques to match jobs to workers, not only locally but anywhere in the nation. Planning, encouragement, training and retraining, and subsidization should be used to bring to full employment both the transiently unemployed and the stubborn hard core. Indeed, beyond usually defined full employment, much can be done to expand the voluntary labor force by facilitating the freeing of slaves of domestic labor and seeing to it that there is optimal investment in the human capital of all of our population, including women, minorities, and the historically disadvantaged.

While we have suggested sobering considerations regarding the efficacy of both monetary and fiscal policy for combating cyclical fluctuations, there are a number of things that can be done, both to bring about greater stability and achieve "prosperity without inflation and without war," to repeat some words which might well be taken as more than rhetoric. For one thing, cut massive military expenditures, which have peculiar inflationary properties. In addition to adding to the income-expenditure stream without offering corresponding supplies of goods to private markets, the nature and aura of military purchases and the symbiotic relation of public buyers and private suppliers offer a strong suggestion of inflationary potential. But government taxes which relate directly to final products or factors clearly raise prices. One could stimulate demand *and* combat inflation by cutting excise taxes and payroll taxes and by subsidizing certain production, such as mass transit services, which may be particularly desirable in terms of positive externalities (or the ability to substitute for other production with negative externalities). Further, we could abandon the curious combination of high interest rates and business taxes, which in the long run must in at least considerable part be passed on to consumers, and special tax subsidies, such as equipment tax credits and accelerated depreciation, which compensate or more than compensate for some these charges which are imposed on all. And finally, while I have not introduced distributional considerations, I might venture a considered judgment that the package of policies to which I have pointed would on balance cater well to egalitarian tastes.

If economists can free themselves from old *political* ideas and advocate boldly what makes economic sense, the Keynesian revolution, appropriately refined and revised, may yet carry the day. For "soon or late, it is ideas, not vested interests, which are dangerous for good or evil."

REFERENCES

R. W. Clower, "Is There an Optimal Money Supply?," *J. of Fin.*, May 1970, *25*, 425–33.

E. D. Domar, "Capital Expansion, Rate of Growth, and Employment," *Econometrica*, Apr. 1946, *14*, 137–47.

R. Eisner, "Another Look at Liquidity Preference," *Econometrica*, July 1963, *31*, 531–38.

———, "On Non-linear Estimates of the Liquidity Trap," *Econometrica*, Sept. 1971, *39*, 861–64.

M. Friedman, *A Theory of the Consumption Function*, Princeton 1957.

———, "The Role of Monetary Policy," *Amer. Econ. Rev.*, Mar. 1968, *58*, 1–17.

J. K. Galbraith, *The New Industrial State*, 2d ed., Boston 1971.

J. M. Keynes, *The General Theory of Employment, Interest and Money*, New York 1936.

D. W. Jorgenson, "Capital Theory and Investment Behavior," *Amer. Econ. Rev. Proc.*, May 1963, *53*, 247–59.

A. S. B. Leijonhufvud, *On Keynesian Economics and the Economics of Keynes*, New York 1968.

F. Modigliani and R. Brumberg, "Utility Analysis and the Consumption Function: An Interpretation of Cross-Section Data," in K. K. Kurihara, ed., *Post-Keynesian Economics*, New Brunswick 1954, 388–436.

D. Patinkin, *Money, Interest and Prices*, 2d ed., New York 1965.

R. M. Solow, "A Contribution to the Theory of Economic Growth," *Quart. J. of Econ.*, Feb. 1956, *70*, 65–94.

J. Tobin, "A Dynamic Aggregative Model," *J. Polit. Econ.*, Apr. 1955, *63*, 103–15.

BOOK REVIEWS

Information and Coordination: Essays in Macroeconomic Theory

By Axel Leijonhufvud. New York: Oxford University Press, 1981. x + 388 pp. $19.95 (cloth); $11.95 (paper)

Two Review Essays

Over the last half century we have moved from a period in which John Maynard Keynes was a symbol of subversion to much of both the business establishment and the economic profession, through an era where Richard Nixon asserted "I am now a Keynesian" and Milton Friedman said "We are all Keynesians now,"[1] to Leijonhufvud's conclusion that unless his "Z-theory" can be sustained, "all of Keynesian economics will have to be judged a big mistake" (p. 187).

Leijonhufvud's own work played no small part in the ferment and shifts in views. Appreciated if not hailed at one point or another by economists as disparate as Milton Friedman, Joan Robinson, and James Tobin, Leijonhufvud contributed substantially to raising important new issues, and to laying to rest some old ones, perhaps as yet unresolved. His new collection of twelve articles and essays (two previously unpublished) dating from 1967 to 1976, offers a good opportunity to review where we were and where we are.

As Leijonhufvud and Keynes saw the issue, correctly, a fundamental question for macroeconomic theory, as well as policy, is whether the system is self-regulating. Is there a homeostatic mechanism which will keep the economy at full employment or quickly counteract any disturbances which bring a departure from such an equilibrium? The answers, Leijonhufvud perceives, again correctly, can depend on those to two other questions: (1) is there an attainable or economically relevant price vector at which all markets, including the labor market will clear? and (2) if there is such a vector, can we be confident that the system will find it or, given any departure from that vector, will return to it?

Leijonhufvud's answer to the first question is an unequivocal yes. He rejects the "revolutionary orthodoxy" with its "elasticity pessimism" as a caricature of Keynes invented by "Keynesians." The consumption function multiplier is not high, the interest elasticity of investment demand is not low, and liquidity preference is no permanent obstacle. On this last, Leijonhufvud would reject the Master

[1]As quoted by Samuelson [10, 1976, p. 205 or 1980, p. 194].

0022-2879/82/0882-0413$00.50/0
JOURNAL OF MONEY, CREDIT AND BANKING, vol. 14, no. 3, (August 1982)

as well as his misguided followers. The system is not overdetermined. There is a full employment price vector.

Leijonhufvud rejects the American Keynesians who accepted the ''neoclassical synthesis,'' conceding the Walrasian solution but resting their case for unemployment on wage rigidity. Leijonhufvud argues, and here I agree, that Keynes did not base his case against the self-adjusting properties of the system on wage rigidity. Keynes indeed devoted considerable attention to the effects of wage changes and concluded that while wages were in fact not fully flexible, more flexibility would cause more rather than less instability.

The problem, Leijonhufvud insists, is not that a full employment equilibrium solution does not exist. It is not that rigid wages (or any other ''spanner in the works'') blocks the path to the solution. It is rather, simply enough, that there is no Deus ex machina in the form of Walrasian auctioneer with his infinite series of instantaneous ''tâtonnenents'' to keep the system at its solution price vector. As a consequence, in the well-known formulations of Clower and Leijonhufvud, transactions take place at *dis*equilibrium prices. Some suppliers (of output or labor) then do not realize full employment equilibrium receipts. As a consequence they in turn reduce their expenditures below what they would have spent at full employment. The disequilibrium is self-aggravating rather than self-correcting.

The central point is that, lacking the auctioneer, there is a formidable and at times insurmountable problem in the dissemination of costly information and the coordination and reconciliation of inconsistent perceptions. This relates most acutely to differing views about the future among the consumers who save, the entrepreneurs who invest, and the lenders or bankers who affect interest rates with their own anticipations of future returns. In a ''Wicksellian context,'' Leijonhufvud sees the key price out of equilibrium as the rate of interest. Other prices and wages would not necessarily be wrong if the interest rate were at its full employment solution value. There is thus no point to price or wage adjustments since the issue is not one of their relative prices. The system responds then to excess supply not by immediately and speedily lowering particular prices, which in fact may not be ''wrong,'' but by reducing output. The Marshallian price-to-output sequence is reversed.

Is there no hope for adjustment? If entrepreneurial expectations have resulted in lower investment demand than is consistent with consumers' desires to provide for the future and if those in financial markets do not change their perceptions of the future so as to bring down rates of interest sufficiently to generate enough investment, will the inconsistent plans and expectations be reconciled? Leijonhufvud suggests that in a ''corridor'' not too far from equilibrium the problems of information and coordination are likely to be readily solved. Outside of that corridor—read the Great Depression or substantial inflation—the homeostatic devices are likely to fail. In the first case, however, Leijonhufvud would look hopefully to corrective monetary policy.[2] Interest rates above equilibrium would imply bond prices below the supply prices of the real assets that they would finance. The monetary authority, by lowering interest rates, can presumably raise these bond prices (indefinitely?) or, correspondingly, raise the present value and hence the demand price for any real asset promising a stream of future returns.

[2]In the case of inflation ''outside the corridor,'' Leijonhufvud interestingly concludes, ''monetary policy action should be expected to be less effective than normally—and particularly if operated against the current of a contrary fiscal policy'' (p. 267). I have, on a number of occasions, made a similar argument [2, 3].

There is much in all of this that macroeconomists, Keynesian or neoclassical or monetarist, can ignore only at great peril. Surely, the Walrasian auctioneer and all markets clearing at general equilibrium prices, however useful as analytical tools, are inadequate guides—or hardly any guides at all—for major issues in macroeconomics. Surely, costly information, imperfect coordination, differing views about the future, and transactions at other than "equilibrium" prices are more the rule than the exception. But is that all of the Keynesian contribution? In his sometimes unseemly impatience with the priests, has Leijonhufvud been too free or irreverent with the truths they claimed to have found?

"The difficulty lies," wrote Keynes, "not in the new ideas, but in escaping from the old ones, which ramify, for those brought up as most of us have been, into every corner of our minds" [5, p. viii]. For all his attention to Keynes, Leijonhufvud appears somehow more comfortable with Wicksell on saving and investment and interest rates, with D. H. Robertson on loanable funds and, most importantly, with the axioms and assumptions that make for full employment, however relevant the difficulties in attaining it.

Thus Leijonhufvud, like the early objectors to the Keynesian revolution, has great difficulty with the saving-investment identity. He sees it as ignoring the role of the rate of interest in the saving-investment relation, quite failing to recognize that the introduction of that highly useful accounting definition does not contradict the role of the rate of interest (along with income) in the saving-investment *demand* relation.[3] Neither Keynes nor any but his most vulgar and misinformed expositor would ignore the interrelation between the rate of interest and investment demand and their interacting roles in an equilibrium solution.

I learned as a graduate student (from both Fritz Machlup and Evsey Domar) that, whatever one's tastes for one concept or the other as better keeping track of key elements of financial behavior, loanable funds and liquidity preference are in a one-to-one correspondence.[4] Whatever parametric assumptions are desired for the one could be handled in the other. Leijonhufvud's rather strident rejection of Keynes's liquidity preference seems more related to his rejection of "absolute" demand for liquidity in relation to any long-run rate of interest. As should be well known, Keynes never did claim that absolute liquidity preference or the liquidity trap described any existing or historical state of the economy, but it did represent an analytically important limiting case, as we shall note below.

Leijonhufvud denounces repeatedly both the notion that investment demand is fairly inelastic with respect to the rate of interest and the idea that Keynes ever thought it so. I differ here with Leijonhufvud on both counts and our differences are fundamental to our view of the economy and the economy that Keynes was trying to explain. As to what the economy is really like, there was and is a very considerable body of direct empirical evidence indicating that the elasticity of investment demand with respect to the rate of interest (or more generally its rental or user cost or

[3]Leijonhufvud's lack of fluency in national income accounting (perhaps not uncommon among nonempirical theorists) is evidenced by his argument that real GNP would include "the real service output" of both government price controllers and the corporate managers hired to resist them (p. 257). Such activities of added corporate managers might affect costs and prices but would not, in fact, be final output or enter into real GNP.

[4]Cf. Hicks [4, pp. 153–62] and Patinkin [8, pp. 375–78]. Leijonhufvud, I may note, was a graduate student at Northwestern and I was a (minor) member of his dissertation committee. But he somehow never took a course with me and I am tempted to paraphrase a line Machlup once used about a student of his (not me): nothing in this book did Leijonhufvud learn from me. But I hope that is not entirely true.

rate of return), while not zero, is not enormous. But even aside from the direct empirical evidence, the world would be vastly different from what we observe, if investment demand were highly elastic. For if it were, it would be difficult indeed to know why investment demand could not readily accommodate itself, regardless of expected returns, to the flow of saving forthcoming at full employment. We would need a "spanner" in the form of failures of information and coordination that go beyond the point of "rationality." With a highly interest-elastic investment demand schedule, it should surely be possible for some "reasonable" fall in the rate of interest to counteract any demand shocks that lower the marginal efficiency of investment curve.

It is important to distinguish between the short run in which adjustment costs may make the investment demand curve less elastic and the longer run (how long?) in which this source of inelasticity disappears. But even in the infinitely long run, the investment demand curve may still intersect the horizontal axis. Investment demand even at a zero rate of interest may be, and I would assert is, finite. Additional capital may always add to output (or potential output) but may not promise a positive net return. And, it may be noted that at the point where the investment demand curve crosses the horizontal axis, that is, at a rate of interest of zero, the interest elasticity of investment demand is zero.

Confusion on this matter not infrequently stems from the failure to distinguish between gross and net returns of capital. Going back at least to Böhm-Bawerk, we are accustomed to the productivity of more roundabout methods and the positive partial derivative of capital in production functions. But all possible more roundabout methods do not add to production more than their increased cost. And we cannot assume that, with a given production function, all additions of machinery will prove worth their cost of production, even if their necessarily finite stream of expected returns is discounted at a zero rate of interest.

It is not proper to assume that real assets have perpetual streams of nonnegative net returns or that the integral of the gross returns over time is necessarily higher than the original cost. And hence adjustments in the rate of interest *may* not necessarily be sufficient always to raise investment demand to the full employment rate of saving or, in a Leijonhufvudian formulation, bring the expectations of lenders and bond holders, as manifested in bond prices, into conformity with the expectations of investors in real assets under conditions of full employment.

As to what Keynes really said or meant, for those such as Leijonhufvud and I who still care, my reading is that Keynes certainly did view his "marginal efficiency of capital" schedule or investment demand as insufficiently elastic to guarantee the homeostatic property or self-regulating return to full employment which was indeed the central issue of the *General Theory*. Keynes was at pains to argue for lower rates of interest to bring about greater investment and this argument is to be found in the *General Theory*. But, by way of buttressing the point that Keynes did see an insufficiently elastic investment demand schedule as central to the economy's failure to home in on full employment, note the following:[5]

> It seems likely that the fluctuations in the market estimation of the marginal efficiency of different types of capital. . . will be too great to be offset by any practicable changes in the rate of interest. (p. 164)

[5] All from Keynes [5].

> With a given labour force there is a definite limit to the quantity of labour embodied in roundabout processes which can be used to advantage. (p. 214)

> Thus even if the rate of interest is zero, there is a strict limit to the proportion of prospective consumers' demand which it is profitable to begin providing for in advance. (p. 217)

> When there is change in the prospective yield of capital or in the rate of interest, the schedule of the marginal efficiency of capital will be such that the change in new investment will not be in great disproportion to the change in the former; i.e., moderate changes in the prospective yield of capital or in the rate of interest will not be associated with very great changes in the rate of investment. (p. 250)

Given Leijonhufvud's rejection of an inelastic investment demand function and his rejection of a long-run elastic liquidity preference function, he has already repudiated the notion that parameters may be such that a full employment equilibrium solution does not exist. If investment demand is sufficiently interest elastic and the reservation of liquidity or credit sufficiently inelastic, there is a rate of interest consistent with preferences of lenders, savers, and entrepreneurial investors under conditions of full employment. There is hence no need for the Pigou effect, which Leijonhufvud referred to as nailing the coffin on the corpse and ending ''virtually the rear-guard action of those Keynesians who have tried to maintain a place for Keynes on this lofty plane of abstraction'' (p. 50).

With Leijonhufvud, there *is* a full employment equilibrium with a ''normal'' rate of interest for which, no matter what the real forces or entrepreneurial expectations affecting the marginal efficiency of investment schedule, investment demand equals full employment saving. In a full information macroeconomic (FIM) model everyone has learned and accepted that rate of interest. Liquidity preference relates not to the normal rate of interest but to the difference between the existing limited information rate and the normal rate. Since incomplete information without rescue from rational expectations prevents immediate adjustment of the actual rate of interest to changes in real forces which have changed the normal rate, and permits monetary changes to create departures of the actual rate from a stable normal rate, real changes have output and price effects and monetary changes have output and interest effects. But since that (sometimes changing) normal or full employment solution interest rate exists, unemployment is only a disequilibrium, if sometimes persistent, phenomenon. A correct monetary policy though, except with extreme departures from the equilibrium solution, Leijonhufvud concludes, should restore the rate of interest to its normal full employment value.

If the initial discrepancy between the rate of interest and the solution rate and consequent shortfall of investment demand generate accelerator effects which cause a further decline in the MEC schedule, the rate of interest may fall to a solution rate but the further depressed MEC schedule may be ''too low to restore full employment. This transition from one type of disequilibrium to another puts the system into a state where discretionary fiscal spending is the preferred policy'' (p. 199). Otherwise, one presumes, monetary policy should be sufficient and, indeed, one may wonder why a market endowed with rational expectations and financial experts and economists as good as those at the call of the Federal Reserve or the Bank of England should not even more quickly bring the real quantity of money and hence interest rates back to their appropriate level.

Despite all his attention to the disequilibria in which interest rates and hence output and employment have departed from their equilibrium values, Leijonhufvud remains dominated by his—and the classical and the Walrasian—notion of an existing full employment solution. This keeps him or repeatedly pulls him back into the old ideas of the Euclidean, full employment world where parallel lines never cross [5, p. 16] and an increased propensity to save must raise investment, productivity, and growth. It is perhaps what leads him to what I can best describe as a petulant, heavily semantic attack on Lange's formulations of Say's Law and Walras's Law and a contemptuous rejection of the paradox of thrift as an unworthy survivor of crude macroeconomic textbooks.[6] Of course, if we can accept the full employment solution as relevant, excess demand for money and excess supply of goods must surely be eliminated by lower commodity prices. A greater propensity to save must *both* lower the rate of interest and increase investment. Above-equilibrium interest rates thus look for explanation in a "search theory of the unemployment of financial capital" (p. 198). With a permanent income theory of consumption, shortfalls of consumer expenditures with current unemployment despite expected "normal" full employment are explainable in terms of the illiquidity of human capital, which Leijonhufvud offers as "an essentially 'monetary' view of Great Depressions" (p. 78).

I would not denigrate Leijonhufvud's emphasis on issues of information and coordination in a market system. And this emphasis is in the *General Theory*, most fundamentally in the difficulty of reconciling differing views (and preferences) about the future on the part of households who save, entrepreneurs who invest, and lenders (including private banks and the monetary authority), who finance the transition from now to later. But I may paraphrase Robertson, in likening Keynes's theory of liquidity preference to the "grin without the cat" [9], to suggest that Leijonhufvud, in his return to (or failure to escape from) the old full employment norm, has disembodied the perplexed frown of misinformation. If that full employment equilibrium is always there, waiting to be found, why do information and coordination problems persist and recur? The answer may be that conditions keep changing so that searches for the new equilibrium must begin repeatedly before the old one is "discovered." In the long run, in a stationary world, there would be no problem; we need hardly be reminded of Keynes's obvious retort as to what happens to us all in the long run. But that may not be the whole story.

Let me therefore essay to restore the Keynesian model with which Leijonhufvud, monetarists, neo-Walrasians, neoclassical synthesizers, and, more recently, rational expectationalists in varying degrees have made so free, or have ignored. We start from the premise that both in theoretical purity and in the "real world," we cannot at any point in time be sure of the *existence* of a full employment equilibrium solution. The consumption function *may* be so low and the associated propensity to save so high, the production function and the (flexibly) associated entrepreneurial expectations of the return on capital so unpromising, and the curb set by the preference for liquidity, even if only at a zero rate of interest, so binding, that there is no price vector at which all markets will clear. Leijonhufvud's normal real rate of interest may be negative and hence, even without the Keynesian speculative-motive liquidity trap, and without general price inflation, cannot possibly be attained.

[6]Cf. Lange's systematic treatment of the "optimal propensity to consume" in his original review article on *The General Theory* [6].

Despite oft-reputed assertions to the contrary, as Patinkin pointed out originally [8], the Pigou effect does not offer a *sure* way out, either at theoretical or policy levels. At the theoretical level, the corrective wealth effects to departures from full employment, resulting in a lower general level of prices, flow not from the existence of money but from public perception of net government liabilities to the private sector. These in fact are trivial in the form of money and in principle need not exist in that form at all. The nonmonetary or interest-bearing government debt is what chiefly constitutes directly, or as a backing for money, the private wealth to which the Pigou effect might be relevant. The whole effect is hence eliminated in a completely privately oriented market system where the government, as conservatives might have it, always balances its budget and provides no "outside" money.

Even with a government debt, it is important, as Barro [1] has reminded us (if carrying his argument to a doubtful extreme), that current government debt, after taking into account possible future public responsibility for interest and principal, be viewed as a net asset of the private sector. (Here I personally would express some reserve to the Barro argument, as differences in discount rates and perceptions of risk and uncertainty as well as the paths of expected utility of current and future generations do not guarantee public evaluation of net debt as zero.)

Beyond all this, as again Patinkin pointed out originally, the wealth effect will raise consumption but, even aside from problems of dynamics, expectations, and frictions, there can be no guarantee, from a pure theory of consumer choice, that it will raise consumption sufficiently to fill the gap between full employment output and attainable investment demand. We have here Patinkin's distinction between "the Pigou effect" and "the Pigou theorem" [7, 1951, pp. 266–68, 271].

To these doubts in even the purest theory, we can add the observations that the wealth effect on consumption, as most have acknowledged, is likely in practice to be small. How then can we be sure at any point in time that a full employment solution exists? We can certainly have no confidence that it is always attainable without significant government intervention.

The issues of information and coordination are major. But they persist and take on added and crucial dimensions in considerable part because we can never be sure that the solution is to be found. This is not to say, and Keynes did not say, that there is never a solution. Consumption and investment demand may be sufficient at some point in time, particularly with strong exogenous (possibly governmental) contribution, for that solution vector with an attainable "normal" rate of interest to exist. But we cannot accept this as an axiom; we cannot be sure.

In a world of *this* kind of uncertainty both the old economics and its recent reincarnations are seriously misleading. It is *not* rational to assume that we are in a world of no involuntary unemployment. With the possibility of involuntary unemployment we have to recognize that wages and prices are not fully flexible, not as a requirement for the existence of unemployment but as a requirement for a determinate price level. And with that recognition it is no longer rational to operate from a model of the world in which money is neutral, government policy can only affect employment by the short-lived consequences of deceit, and, sad or happy as it may appear, depending upon our place in the world, all is for the best in an essentially self-regulating system.

The issues of information and coordination of expectations are critical to the workings of the economy and to our understanding of it. Leijonhufvud's work, as this collection of essays reminds us, has been a significant contribution, but the full truth, in Keynes and in the world we know, lies deeper.

LITERATURE CITED

1. Barro, Robert J. "Are Government Bonds Net Wealth?" *Journal of Political Economy*, 82 (Nov./Dec. 1974), 1095–117.
2. Eisner, Robert. "Factors Affecting the Level of Interest Rates." In *Conference on Savings and Residential Financing, 1968 Proceedings*, pp. 28–40. Chicago: United States Savings and Loan League, 1968.
3. ______. "Fiscal and Monetary Policy Reconsidered." *American Economic Review*, 59 (December 1969), 897–905.
4. Hicks, John R. *Value and Capital*. Second edition. Oxford: Clarendon, 1946.
5. Keynes, John M. *The General Theory of Employment, Interest and Money*. New York: Harcourt Brace, 1936.
6. Lange, Oscar. "The Rate of Interest and the Optimal Propensity to Consume." *Economica*, 5 (February 1938), 12–32. Reprinted in American Economic Association, *Readings in Business Cycle Theory*, pp. 169–92. Philadelphia: Blakiston, 1944.
7. Patinkin, Don. "Price Flexibility and Employment." *American Economic Review*, 38 (September 1949), 543–64. Reprinted with revisions in American Economic Association, *Readings in Monetary Theory*, edited by F. P. Lutz and L. W. Mint, pp. 252–83. Homewood, Ill.: Irwin, 1951.
8. ______. *Money, Interest and Prices*. Second edition. New York: Harper and Row, 1965.
9. Robertson, Dennis H. "Mr. Keynes and the Rate of Interest." *Essays in Monetary Theory*, 1940. Reprinted in American Economic Association *Readings in the Theory of Income Distribution*. Homewood, Ill.: Irwin, 1951.
10. Samuelson, Paul A. *Economics*. Tenth and Eleventh editions. New York: McGraw-Hill, 1976, 1980.

ROBERT EISNER*

William R. Kenan Professor of Economics
Northwestern University

[8]

*Social Security, Saving, and Macroeconomics**

Arguing within the framework of a life-cycle hypothesis of consumption of the individual household, Martin Feldstein has claimed that a pay-as-you-go, unfunded social-security system implies a private-sector perception of wealth which both depresses private saving and raises aggregate consumption. But the effects in a macroeconomic context are not the same. With less than full employment, perceived increments to private wealth in social security or any other government obligations should increase current and planned future consumption and saving, raising employment and output. With full employment, as long as monetary policy is appropriately accommodating, such increments to wealth should raise prices but leave all real variables, including capital accumulation, unaffected. Increases in social-security wealth would merely substitute for real private wealth in the form of explicit government bonds. Econometric estimates from corrected U.S. data on social security, public debt, income, and employment are consistent with these hypotheses.

1. Introduction

To many it has become an article of faith that business investment and saving are too low and that this is the fault of government. Contributing to that faith, Martin Feldstein claimed in 1974 that social security had reduced both total private saving and the private capital stock by 38 percent! This provoked a substantial professional debate.[1] Most recently, Dean R. Leimer and Selig D.

*I am grateful to Robert J. Gordon, Christophe Chamley, Gerald S. Goldstein, Fumio Hyashi, Truman Bewley, Arlie G. Sterling, W. Kip Viscusi, and an anonymous referee for helpful comments, and to James E. Glassman for enlightening research which stimulated my own efforts. Steven Bender has been of invaluable assistance in the empirical analysis, which has used data presented by Dean R. Leimer and Selig D. Lesnoy (1980, 1982) as well as series on public debt made available by Stephen Taylor of the Flow of Funds Division of the Federal Reserve Board.

[1]Feldstein claimed support for his dramatic conclusions in the work of Munnell (1974a and 1974b). His findings were challenged by Drazen (1978) as well as by Barro (1978), who argued that private bequests would negate governmental intergenerational transfers. He argued his case further in a number of subsequent articles (1976a, 1976b, 1976c, 1977a, 1977b, 1977c, 1978, 1979a, 1979b, 1979c, 1980, 1982 and, with Pellechio, 1979).

Journal of Macroeconomics, Winter 1983, Vol. 5, No. 1, pp. 1–19

Robert Eisner

Lesnoy (1980, 1982) found that Feldstein's own original empirical argument stemmed from a computer programming error.[2]

I propose to demonstrate that Feldstein's theoretical model, as well as his data, was wrong. He, and others, have been guilty of the basic fallacy of composition. The rate of consumption and saving by the individual household has been improperly applied to the analysis of aggregate consumption and saving. At the neglected macroeconomic level, microeconomic effects wash out or are reversed. And newly developed data, including explicit government debt as well as improved measures of social-security wealth, yield estimates consistent with the predictions of appropriate macroeconomic theory.

At the level of the individual household, social security will imply a net addition to perceived wealth if the present value of expected benefits exceeds the present value of associated taxes. If it does, it will add to current and planned consumption, thus reducing saving defined as the difference between private income and consumption.

For the economy as a whole, however, net social-security wealth will have effects upon income, employment, prices, and the real value of government debt. Where unemployment exists because of inadequate effective demand, additions to wealth in the form of social security may be expected, abstracting from distributional effects and supply considerations, to increase aggregate employment, income, output, consumption, *and* saving.

Under conditions of full employment, the perception of increased net social-security wealth creates excess effective demand and raises the price level. The real value of private assets in the form of government debt other than social-security obligations is

[2]Feldstein (1980) claimed that estimates from corrected and updated data "imply that social security depresses saving by about fifty percent of its current value." The assumptions underlying this claim were also challanged by Leimer and Lesnoy (1981, 1982). Negative empirical results were reported earlier by Sterling (1979), by Kotlikoff (1979), by Kopits and Gotur (1979), and by Glassman (1979). Barro and MacDonald (1979) stated, "Overall economic theory provides neither an a priori argument for a strong depressing effect of social security on saving nor decisively rules out an important influence. The crucial issues are empirical," p. 276. After their own analysis of international cross sections and time series they concluded: "Our general assessment of present empirical knowledge is that, either in terms of individual components of evidence or in terms of the overall picture, there is no support for the proposition that social security depresses private saving. The effect of social security on saving and capital formation remains an open empirical issue."

reduced. Unless monetary policy is perverse, the social-security debt of the government then merely substitutes in real terms for other government debt, with no change in the private perception of total wealth and hence with no change in total consumption or saving.

Again reasoning at the level of the individual household, Feldstein and others do anticipate a positive social-security effect on saving from any inducement to early retirement. In a growing economy, the greater saving of the working young will outweigh the dissaving of older retirees. But with earlier retirement the lifetime income of households is reduced, and aggregate income and output and, very likely, aggregate consumption and saving are reduced as well.

2. Microeconomic Foundations and Issues

The Life-Cycle Hypothesis and Social Security

According to the life-cycle hypothesis, as presented originally by Modigliani and Brumberg (1954) and developed and applied by Modigliani (for example, 1966 and 1970) and by Ando and Modigliani (1963) in a number of subsequent articles, individuals act to maximize the utility of consumption in the current year and in all of the expected future years of their lives. Given well-behaved utility functions, this leads them to allocate their initial wealth and current and expected incomes so as to more or less even out consumption over their earning spans and their years of retirement. We hence have a confirmation of the "hump saving" of Harrod (1948) in which positive saving takes place during years of work and the wealth so accumulated is spent or dissaved during subsequent years of retirement. Planned consumption of the current and all future years is a positive function of initial wealth and of current and expected incomes of all future years.

If there are no bequests, so that each individual starts his life with zero wealth and ends it with zero wealth, net saving for each individual over his lifetime is zero. Net saving for the economy arises, estate motives aside, from growth either in population or real income per capita, or both. If each generation earns more than the preceding one, those in the working generation will always be saving more than those in the older, preceding generation are dissaving out of the wealth that they have accumulated from their lower incomes. Similarly, even if income per capita is not growing, if the population is growing, the younger generation will always be larger

Robert Eisner

and saving more in the aggregate than the smaller older generation is dissaving.

Social security in the United States is essentially on a pay-as-you-go basis. Thus, no significant trust fund is built up and current beneficiaries are paid out of receipts from current taxpayers. In a real sense, the consumption of current beneficiaries is produced by the labor services of those currently working, since no additional capital has been provided to produce these services. Each wage earner has his disposable income reduced by the amount of his tax contributions to social security (and by the employer's contributions which he might otherwise receive in wage income, as well). He reduces his consumption according to his marginal propensity to consume out of disposable income. If consumption depended only upon current income, that reduction would be counterbalanced by equally increased consumption of current beneficiaries.[3]

Were the government to initiate social security on a fully contributory basis, taking taxes from each working person and in return giving him at a certain age benefits equal to the return that he could have earned if he had set aside these taxes in personal saving, there would be no effect on consumption. As long as the government rate of return is equal to the rate of return in (presumably perfect) private capital markets, there is no reason in the life-cycle model for the introduction of social security to change the consumption of individual workers. What will increase consumption (and decrease saving according to Feldstein) is the awarding of current or prospective retirement benefits to some individuals without a corresponding increase in their tax liabilities. Social security will introduce a positive wealth effect on consumption if, for all current households, the present value of current and expected benefits is greater than the present value of current and expected taxes.[4]

This, however, is precisely what happens in an essentially unfunded, pay-as-you-go social-security system such as ours, when there

[3]At least to a first approximation. Differing marginal propensities to consume relating to age may have a second-order effect under the life-cycle hypothesis.

[4]Feldstein and I discount Barro's argument that expected increased taxation for future generations would induce compensatory intergenerational transfers that would lower current consumption. The underlying hypothesis that greater social-security wealth would increase consumption is weakened, however, by the factors of liquidity constraints and bequests. Evidence of major household capital accumulation taking place through bequests rather than life-cycle saving [Kotlikoff and Summers (1982)] goes along with evidence of less-than-life-cycle predicted consumption by the old [Blinder (1983)]. Liquidity constraints may be such that taxes for social security, even if balanced by greater prospective future benefits, actually reduce consumption by the young.

is growth in the population of contributors and/or working income per contributor. For then taxes of current working contributors are sufficient to pay benefits to the smaller previous generation of current retirees in proportion to smaller current working wages but are less than the benefits to be expected by current workers who will be paid out of the higher incomes in the more numerous future generation.

Private Saving and Government Saving

In the aggregate, the introduction of social-security taxes and a concomitant commitment to offer retirement benefits such that the present values of benefits and taxes are equal will have no effect upon consumption and hence upon saving if there are no other changes in taxes or government expenditures. What this implies is that the introduction of the social-security system will cause a government budget surplus (or a lesser deficit); government "saving" will replace private saving. In a stationary economy, the surplus would accumulate year by year until the completion of a complete life cycle. Thereafter the surplus would be back to zero (or to the amount of the original deficit) but the government debt would have been reduced (or the government would have acquired private assets) by the amount of the accumulated surpluses over the interval.

None of this then will affect consumption, saving, or wealth. Without social security, individuals choosing to save for their retirement would have reduced their consumption by the same amount, using the difference between their income and consumption to buy private assets or government bonds. With social security, they will not buy the government bonds or private assets. To the extent that the reduction is merely in the purchase of government bonds, individuals will hold an implicit debt of the government in the form of social-security obligations rather than an explicit debt in the form of government bonds.[5] To the extent that individuals buy less in

[5]The distinction between private and government saving then becomes one essentially of semantics and accounting. Assume two individuals with the same income and the same consumption. If one has deductions taken from his pay to buy government bonds, he is deemed to have saved. The other, who has deductions for social-security taxes which also give him a claim on government in prospective retirement benefits, has not, as personal income is defined net of all contributions for social security. An individual who buys government bonds contributes to private saving. One who pays social-security taxes into a trust fund which buys government bonds on his behalf does not. The retiree consuming from the proceeds of sales of his government bonds is then considered to be dissaving. The retiree consuming out of his social-security benefits is not dissaving because realization of this government debt is counted in disposable personal income.

the way of private assets, business including financial intermediaries will hold more, or the government will buy more of such assets, presumably in the form of loans to private borrowers in a nonsocialist economy.

Thus, where government may be a creditor or debtor to the private sector, even if only by issuing money, the introduction of social security in such a way that the net worth of the private sector is not changed will have no effect upon consumption, saving, or wealth. This will be true, at least, in a pure economy of perfect capital markets where individuals are always free to borrow or lend, consume or save, and work or retire according to their choices.

All of this, by the way, has nothing to do with whether the economy is stationary or growing, in either of the senses we have indicated above. Since no individual's consumption would be changed by the introduction of social security, whatever rate of net saving had been brought about by growth of the economy without social security would be maintained with it. This result would hold in an economy with the possibility of bequests or other forms of private intergenerational transfers. The introduction of social security on the terms we have thus far defined has involved no intergenerational transfer and has changed no one's consumption. There is hence no need for any change in private intergenerational transfers.

The aspect of social security which can change consumption is its noncontributory component. If individuals receive or expect to receive benefits whose present value is greater than the present value of associated increases in taxes, they are presumed to consume more, as is illustrated in Figure 1. Here

T_1 = social security tax;
$A = (1 + g)T_1$ = social-security benefits expected in period 2;
A_O = fully contributory social-security benefits ($g = r$);
A_G = "give-away" social-security benefits ($g > r$);
g = rate of growth of income and benefits per generation;
r = real rate of interest;
$\hat{C}_i$ = consumption in period i without social security (or with fully contributory social security); $i = 1, 2$;
$\hat{C}_i^S$ = consumption in period i with pay-as-you-go, "give away" social security; $i = 1, 2$.

This wealth effect, by the way, is of course not unique to social-security benefits. It may exist in all government transfer payments, such as veterans' bonuses and pensions, welfare benefits,

Figure 1

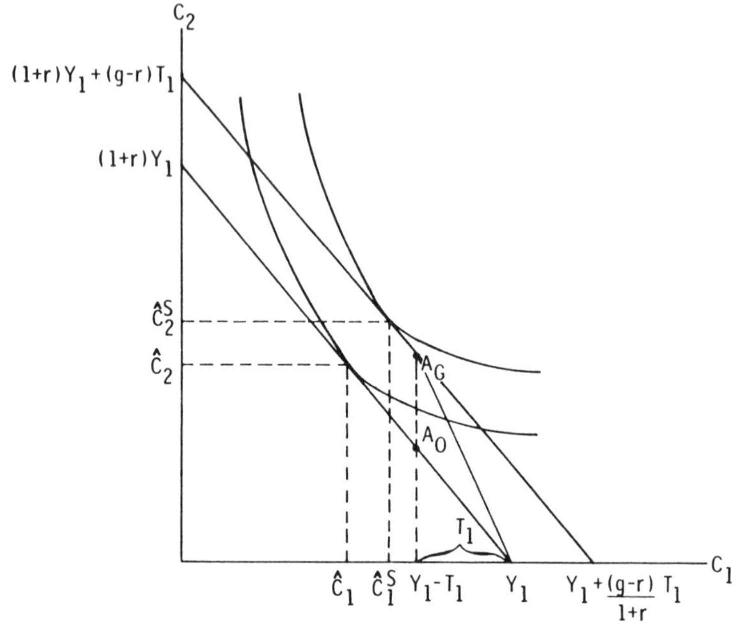

and subsidies to farmers, which raise the *net* debt of the government to the public. It is the "give-away" component—the awarding of benefits for which equally present-valued tax liabilities are not imposed—that causes social security to contribute to individual consumption, not the fact that government, rather than the private sector, is providing for retirement, or that anything is unique about social security as opposed to "private security."[6]

[6]There may also be some reduction in saving if the introduction of social security offers a more perfect market for retirement annuities than would be available privately. Individuals may feel that they have to save more with private insurance if they consider private insurance less reliable or less able to cope with uncertainties regarding price levels and length of life. Conversely, however, private insurance may discourage saving because it is too costly. The introduction of cheaper social insurance may then lead to a choice of more saving. Social security may have another, long-run effect, of lower birth rates which is, as far as I know, ignored in most analysis. For social security may reduce the incentive in individual households to produce children for old age support. Fewer children would then probably mean lower consumption by households with young adults, and hence more conventionally measured saving, but less accumulation of human capital.

Robert Eisner

3. Macroeconomic Relations

Unemployment and the Paradox of Thrift

When an individual household increases consumption while other variables including its income remain unchanged, it saves less. But for the economy as a whole the ceteris paribus assumption is surely unwarranted. What does social security imply at the macroeconomic level for employment, income and output, the rate of interest, and the real value of public holdings of explicit government debt?

Can gross national product and national income properly be held invariant with respect to social security? Feldstein cites Keynes as believing that social security would depress the rate of saving (1979a, p. 3). What he fails to distinguish is that what Keynes had in mind, along with "earlier Keynesians like Seymour Harris" also cited, was the ratio of saving to income but not necessarily the rate of saving. One of the earliest presentations of the Keynesian model, by Oscar Lange (1938), addressed itself specifically to the question of the "optimal propensity to consume," pointing out that up to some point more consumption, by increasing income, would increase saving and investment more than it would decrease it. This possibility has been of course emphasized to a generation of students of economic principles as the so-called "paradox of thrift." Social security may encourage individuals to save less and consume more, without reducing aggregate saving. Given the variability of income and output, social security may actually increase consumption *and* aggregate saving and capital formation.

Feldstein could not properly infer anything from his model as to what he calls "The Impact on Aggregate Saving" (1974, p. 919).[7]

[7]Feldstein here equated effects on consumption with equal and opposite effects on personal saving and also appeared to assume that effects on personal saving are carried over to aggregate saving. He argued that with an estimated marginal propensity to consume out of disposable income of 0.65, since in 1971 "social security taxes and contributions reduced disposable income by $51 billion in 1971 prices [, t]he corresponding reduction in personal saving is, therefore, $18 billion." Then, on the basis of his estimated marginal propensity to consume out of gross social-security wealth of 0.021 he added, "The social security wealth . . . for 1971 was $2,029 billion, implying a reduction in saving of $43 billion. . . . The total fall in personal saving was therefore $61 billion in 1971 prices," p. 920.

But a reduction in "personal saving" caused by introducing social-security taxes, which reduces personal income, does not raise consumption. Taking Feldstein's estimated parameters, we should argue that the $51 billion in social-security taxes and contributions reduced consumption by $33 billion. Then, still accepting his

To do so one would have to introduce a complete model which would indicate the effect of any estimated changes in consumption upon income. Saving is of course the difference between income and consumption. Only on the crude assumption that income is unchanged, can one say that changes in consumption involve equal and opposite changes in saving.

Let us introduce a simple macroeconomic model in which output is a function of effective demand up to the point of full employment. Where aggregate demand exceeds full-employment output, prices rise until a real-balance effect, directly and/or through higher rates of interest, reduces real demand to full-employment output. We can reduce this system to its barest essentials in the following equations:

$$C/P = C(Y/P, K, GD/P, M_x/P, i);$$

$$0 < C_1 < 1, \quad C_2, C_3, C_4 > 0, \quad C_5 \lesseqgtr 0; \tag{1}$$

$$I/P = I(C(t)/P(t), i); \quad I_1 > 0, \quad I_2 < 0, \; - C_5; \tag{2}$$

$$M/P = L(Y/P, K, GD/P, i); \quad L_1, L_2, L_3 > 0, \quad L_4 < 0; \tag{3}$$

$$Y/P \equiv C/P + I/P; \tag{4}$$

$$Y/P \lesseqgtr (Y/P)_f \tag{5}$$

where

C = nominal consumption;
Y = nominal income or output;

---

estimated parameters, social-security wealth increased consumption by \$43 billion. The net effect upon consumption was thus plus \$10 billion, quite different from Feldstein's "fall in personal saving" of \$61 billion. And what in fact happened to aggregate saving is still to be determined. If the increased consumption of \$10 billion resulted in higher income and output, aggregate saving would be reduced by less than \$10 billion and perhaps even increased.

With income unchanged, the decrease of \$61 billion in personal saving is of course offset by a \$51 billion increase in government saving (increased budget surplus or decreased deficit) from the social-security taxes, so that aggregate saving is reduced by \$10 billion rather than Feldstein's \$61 billion. And again, if income is raised, both private and government saving will be increased, reducing or reversing the \$10 billion drop in aggregate saving.

K = real capital;
GD = government debt to the private sector;
M_x = outside money; M = total quantity of money, inside and outside;
P = the price level;
i = the rate of interest;
I = nominal investment;
$C(t)$, $P(t)$ = the expected paths of nominal consumption and prices;
$(Y/P)_f$ = full-employment output;

and numeral subscripts indicate partial derivatives with respect to arguments of the behavioral functions.

Thus, real consumption is a function of real output, of wealth in the form of real capital, of outside money and government debt to the private sector, and of the rate of interest (1). Real investment is a function of the rate of interest and of the expected path of real consumption (2). The rate of interest is determined by the condition that the real supply of money equal the demand for money, which is a function of real output, of the stock of nonmonetary wealth, and of the rate of interest (3). Finally, real output equals real consumption plus real investment (4) but is bounded by the supply constraint of full employment (5).

We have made the customary assumptions regarding partial derivatives. The only crucial one for our argument is C_3, the partial derivative of real consumption with respect to wealth in the form of real government debt to the private sector. If the Barro argument (1974) that government debt is not perceived as a net asset were correct, that would be true both of explicit government debt and implicit debt in the form of social security and this entire discussion would be without foundation.

Let us now assume that the system is altered by the introduction of net social-security wealth. We may then write (1) as

$$C/P = C(Y/P, K, GD/P + SSWN/P, M_x/P, i) \qquad (1')$$

where $SSWN$ = net social-security wealth.

Thus, consumption demand would be higher if households perceive greater wealth in the form of holdings of either explicit government debt or implicit government debt in the form of the present value of the excess of social-security commitments over social-security taxes. Now, if the introduction of net social-security wealth increases the total government debt to the private sector, explicit and implicit, consumption demand will rise. If real output is less than full-employment output, investment may also rise, accommodated of course by a marginal propensity to consume less than one. Just how investment will change will depend upon interest elasticities and the reaction of the money supply. Since, in accordance with the life-cycle hypothesis, increased wealth will generate higher planned consumption not only currently but over the entire life cycle, rational firms will strive to invest more in anticipation of greater future consumption.

The Full-Employment Case

The case of less than full employment, while perhaps frequently relevant, may seem to some to avoid the central issue. What would be the effect of the introduction of net social-security wealth in a full-employment economy, which is presumed by some to represent "the long run"? Here the answer, at least for the equilibrium or steady-state case, can be remarkably simple. According to Equation (1′), at the existing price level the demand for real consumption would increase. The anticipation that real consumption would increase would generate increased investment demand according to (2). But since real output cannot increase, the price level, P, will rise. If the money supply, M, is not increased, the new equilibrium will entail a higher rate of interest (associated with a lower ratio of money to total government debt), less investment, and more consumption.

But this result, it should be clear, stems only from the assumption that the money supply is not accommodative. If the initial real value of the explicit government debt, GD/P, is sufficiently high, at least higher than the addition of real (indexed) social-security wealth, there would appear to be no reason why the price level, the money supply and all nominal variables cannot be increased by some proportion, δ, such that the sum of explicit and implicit government debt, $GD/\delta P + \delta SSWN/\delta P$ will equal the original explicit debt, GD/P. Since, with the usual assumption of no money illusion, all real functions are homogeneous of degree zero in nominal variables and the price level, if the initial system can be in full-employment equilibrium, there is no reason why there cannot be a corresponding new equilibrium with prices, the money supply (including outside money), and total government debt all proportionately higher, but the interest rate, real consumption, real investment, real output, and the stock of real capital all unchanged.[8]

Finally, what of the retirement effect? Suppose that either the perception of added wealth or the peculiarities of eligibility for social-security benefits induce earlier retirement. This would cause individuals to save more during their working years in order to consume over a longer period of retirement. In the usual case of growing populations and/or growing per capita earnings, it would generate lower per capita consumption.

But if individuals are retiring earlier a smaller proportion of the population will be working. Full-employment output will therefore be less and under conditions of full employment that, of course, means that output will be less. Thus, by reducing aggregate output, earlier retirement may leave us with less saving as well as less consumption. Whether saving in fact will be less will depend upon whether the reduction in consumption by the working population is less than the loss in output due to earlier retirement.

4. Empirical Estimates

It is possible to use the original Feldstein data, as corrected by Leimer and Lesnoy (1980), as a base for time series to look for empirical support for some of these relations. While retaining the skepticism of Leimer and Lesnoy and others that any measurable perceptions of social-security wealth have in fact had much effect upon consumption and saving, we can estimate the essentials of (1′), taking account of both unemployment and what happens to the explicit government debt. To do so, I have used Feldstein's per capita series in 1972 dollars, as provided and corrected by Leimer and Lesnoy, for consumption (C), disposable income (YD), net retained earnings (RE), and household wealth (HW, real plus financial assets less liabilities), and series on population and the personal-consumption-expenditure price deflator.

I have added the percent of the labor force unemployed and a measure of domestically held public debt. This last was calculated (from data provided by Stephen Taylor of the Flow of Funds Division of the Board of Governors of the Federal Reserve System) by subtracting the portion of the debt held by foreigners from total

[8]The reader should not confuse this comparative-static argument with questions of rates of actual or expected inflation, which are not part of the social-security issue which has been raised.

federal debt held by the public. The latter series corresponds to the data published until recently in tables under the title "Net Public and Private Debt" in the *Economic Report of the President*, which I used with minor adjustment for years prior to 1946. Conversions from par to market value were accomplished by application of government bond price indices [to be found in Eisner (1980), p. 324].

I began by reproducing and verifying the original Feldstein estimates of

$$C = b_0 + b_1 YD + b_2 YD_{-1} + b_3 RE + b_4 HW + b_5 SSWN + u, \quad (6)$$

and the Leimer–Lesnoy reestimates based upon their corrected series. In column 2 of Table 1, we show initially the estimates for the Leimer–Lesnoy data using the Feldstein perceptions of net social-security wealth. We see here little or no role either for social-security wealth or other household wealth.

To test our hypotheses, we have undertaken two modifications in the empirical relationship. First, we have constructed the variable *DPD*, for the market value of domestically owned public debt, again in per capita, 1972 dollars. We then broke the household-wealth variable, *HW*, into *DPD* and the remainder, adjusted household wealth, *ADJHW*. Second, we constructed a variable to measure the level of unemployment, *LU*, defined as $(U - 2.9)/2.9$, where *U* is the level of unemployment in percent and 2.9 is the lowest percent of unemployment in the years included in our sample. The range of *LU* thus extends from the low of zero in 1953 to 5.55 in 1938 when unemployment was 19 percent, to a high of 7.59 in 1933, before social security was established, when unemployment was measured at 24.9 percent. We define a new variable, *LU*SSWN*, the product of *LU* and *SSWN*, to capture the role of unemployment in the effect of social-security wealth on real consumption.

The results, as shown in column 3 of Table 1, are at least highly suggestive. Both components of household wealth, the domestically held public debt and the remainder, now have substantial and highly significant positive coefficients. The coefficient of net social-security wealth is again negative but the new variable, *LU*SSWN*, indicating the effect of social-security wealth with unemployed resources, is a significantly positive 0.008, with a *t*-statistic of 3.73.

The estimates of coefficients of *SSWN* and *LU*SSWN* sug-

Robert Eisner

TABLE 1. *Consumption and Net Social-Security Wealth, Domestically Held Public Debt and Unemployment; Regression Coefficients and t-Statistics*

Variable or Statistic	*Feldstein Equation 1930 to 1977*	*With Public Debt and Unemployment (excluding 1941–46)*	*Post-war with Public Debt 1947 to 1977*
Constant	51	−101	−303
	(1.11)	(−1.82)	(3.29)
YD	0.766	0.734	0.730
	(12.09)	(14.16)	(8.40)
YD_{-1}	0.100	0.046	0.081
	(1.70)	(0.89)	(0.88)
RE	0.070	−1.33	−0.030
	(0.66)	(1.11)	(−0.17)
HW	0.012		
	(1.61)		
ADJHW		0.038	0.036
		(4.32)	(2.46)
DPD		0.078	0.124
		(4.26)	(4.00)
SSWN	−0.015	−0.021	0.028
	(−1.36)	(−2.23)	(1.25)
*LU*SSWN*		0.008	
		(3.73)	
R^2	0.998	0.999	0.998
D-W	1.06	1.62	1.50
n	42	42	31
[b]*DPD.SSWN*		0.0938	−0.4374

gest that the parameter for social-security wealth in 1938, when unemployment was at 19 percent, was +0.023. In 1933, with unemployment at 24.9 percent, that parameter would be +0.042, even higher than the estimated 0.037 obtained from the Feldstein equation and the Feldstein data, computing error and all. Alas, there was no social security in 1933.

Our estimates of the coefficients of *SSWN* and *LU*SSWN*

imply that 10.1 percent unemployment was the dividing line. For rates of unemployment above 10.1 percent, social-security wealth had a positive direct effect on consumption.[9] For unemployment below 10.1 percent, social-security wealth had a negative effect on consumption.

There is still one final section to our empirical report. By Feldstein's measures, as corrected and replicated by Leimer and Lesnoy [(1980), Table A3 or (1982), Table A5, pp. 625–6.], net social-security wealth stood at 1,045 billion 1972 dollars in 1977 (on the assumption of a real rate of discount of 3 percent and an expected growth of real per capita income of 2 percent per annum). This amounted to an increase in net social-security wealth from 1946 to 1977 of 794 billion 1972 dollars. But over the same period real capital *losses* of the private sector on net U.S. Government and Monetary Authority obligations came to 844 billion 1972 dollars [Eisner (1980), Table 5.56]. Indeed, the simple correlation coefficient of domestic public debt and net social-security wealth per capita over the years 1947–77 was −0.938.

In column 4 of Table 1, we present estimates for the post-war period—when there were no long periods of substantial unemployment—without the unemployment variable. We now find a very large and significantly positive coefficient of 0.124 for *DPD*, suggesting that the real decline in the domestically held public debt was associated with lower per capita consumption. We also find some evidence, although much less substantial, of a positive *partial* effect of rising social-security wealth on consumption, as indicated in the coefficient of 0.028 of *SSWN*.

A simple regression of the domestically held public debt on net social-security wealth in the post-war period yields a coefficient of −0.4374, as also shown in column 4 of Table 1. Taking all other variables as unaffected, but noting this relation between domestically held public debt and social-security wealth, we may write the total derivative of consumption with respect to social-security wealth as

$$\frac{dC}{dSSWN} = \frac{\partial C}{\partial SSWN} + \frac{\partial C}{\partial DPD} \cdot \frac{d\,DPD}{d\,SSWN} \quad . \tag{7}$$

[9]It should be acknowledged, however, that the indicated relation may also be explained by the cyclical tendency of the consumption–income ratio to rise in depressions, quite apart from social security. See Barro (1978).

Robert Eisner

Substituting into (7) the relevant estimated parameters of column 4 yields $dC/dSSWN = 0.028 - 0.4374\ (0.124) = -0.026$.

I would not want to claim that all or much of recent inflation has been caused by social security, but what do these results imply? During the post-war period, when unemployment was in relatively modest ranges, inflation and, ultimately, higher interest rates were associated with substantial declines in the real per capita value of the explicit public debt. Any positive effect on consumption of increased government obligations in the form of social security would then have been more than offset by the negative effect on consumption of decreased government obligations in the form of explicit public debt.

5. Conclusion

I would not take the empirical results as more than suggestive. As Leimer and Lesnoy (1980, 1981, and 1982) have made abundantly clear, there are difficulties with any particular assumed perception of social-security wealth. It may well be that the public acts as if net social-security wealth is zero, or even negative. Further, there are sizeable differences among our own estimates of the parameter of domestically held public debt, which appear implausibly high, and that of the remainder of household wealth, although some of this may relate to measurement errors in the original household-wealth series. Disposable income, it may be added, is also not the proper variable, as it includes earnings from capital which enter into household wealth. Estimates of unemployment effects may be sensitive to the definition of our unemployment variable and we may be picking up essentially the well-known negative relation between unemployment and the ratio of saving to income. One may well wonder further about estimates, by Feldstein or me, of single equations without regard to endogeneity of variables in a complete model.

We can observe, nevertheless, that the empirical results are broadly supportive of the theoretical implications of social-security wealth in a *macro*-economic model consistent with the life-cycle hypothesis for consumption behavior:

1. Perceived net social-security wealth would add to real consumption in periods of substantial unemployment. Increases in consumption at such times can be expected to have positive effects on income which induce positive effects on saving and investment.

2. In periods of relatively full employment, any positive effects of perceived social-security wealth on nominal consumption would be dissipated in associated higher prices and lower real values of the explicit public debt. Thus perceived increases in social-security wealth would not, in periods of relatively full employment, raise real consumption. Indeed, if the data are to be believed—perhaps because of lower anticipated lifetime income associated with earlier retirement—increased social-security wealth actually reduces real consumption.

Received: August, 1981
Final version received: April, 1982

References

Ando, Albert K. and Franco Modigliani. "The 'Life Cycle' Hypothesis of Saving: Aggregate Implications and Tests." *The American Economic Review* 53 (March 1963): 55–84.

Barro, Robert J. "Are Government Bonds Net Wealth?" *Journal of Political Economy* 82 (Nov./Dec. 1974): 1095–1117.

———. *The Impact of Social Security on Private Savings: Evidence from the U.S. Time Series*. Washington, D.C.: American Enterprise Institute, 1978.

Barro, Robert J. and Glenn M. MacDonald. "Social Security and Consumer Spending in an International Cross Section." *Journal of Public Economics* 11 (June 1979): 275–89.

Blinder, Alan. "Social Security, Bequests, and the Life Cycle Theory of Savings: Cross-Sectional Tests." In *The Determinants of National Savings and Wealth*. R. Heming and F. Modigliani eds. International Economic Association, 1983. (Also National Bureau of Economic Research, Working Paper No. 619, 1981.)

Drazen, Allan. "Government Debt, Human Capital, and Bequests in a Life-Cycle Model." *Journal of Political Economy* 86 (June 1978): 505–16.

Eisner, Robert. "Capital Gains and Income: Real Changes in the Value of Capital in the United States, 1946–1977." In *The Measurement of Capital, Studies in Income and Wealth*. Dan Usher, ed. Chicago: University of Chicago Press for National Bureau of Economic Research, Vol. 45, National Bureau of Economic Research, 1980.

Feldstein, Martin. "Social Security, Induced Retirement, and Aggregate Accumulation." *Journal of Political Economy* 82 (September–October 1974): 905–25.

———. "Perceived Wealth in Bonds and Social Security: A Comment." *Journal of Political Economy* 84 (April 1976a): 331–36.

———. "Social Security and Saving: The Extended Life Cycle Theory." *The American Economic Review* 66 (May 1976b): 77–86.

———. "Social Security and the Distribution of Wealth." *Journal of the American Statistical Association* 71 (December 1976c): 800–807.

———. "Social Insurance." *Public Policy* 25 (Winter 1977a): 81–115.

———. "Social Security and Private Savings: International Evidence in an Extended Life-Cycle Model." In *The Economics of Public Services*. Martin Feldstein and R.P. Inman, eds. London: Macmillan Press, 1977b.

———. "The Social Security Fund and National Capital Accumulation." In *Funding Pensions: The Issues and Implications, for Financial Markets*. Federal Reserve Bank of Boston, (1977c).

———. "A Reply to Barro." In *The Impact of Social Security on Private Saving, Evidence from U.S. Time Series*. Robert J. Barro. Washington, D.C.: American Enterprise Institute, 1978.

———. "The Effect of Social Security on Private Saving: The Time Series Evidence." National Bureau of Economic Research, Working Paper No. 314, 1979a.

———. "The Effect of Social Security on Saving." National Bureau of Economic Research, Working Paper No. 334, 1979b.

———. "International Differences in Social Security and Saving." National Bureau of Economic Research, Working Paper No. 355, 1979c.

———. "Social Security, Induced Retirement, and Aggregate Capital Accumulation: A Correction and Updating." National Bureau of Economic Research, Working Paper No. 579, 1980.

———. "Social Security and Private Saving: Reply." *Journal of Political Economy* 90 (June 1982): 630–42.

Feldstein, Martin and Anthony Pellechio. "Social Security and Household Wealth Accumulation." *The Review of Economics and Statistics* 61 (August 1979): 361–68.

Friedman, Milton. *A Theory of the Consumption Function*. Princeton University Press for NBER, 1957.

Glassman, James E. *The Impact of Social Security on Private Saving*. Unpublished doctoral dissertation. Northwestern University, 1979.

Harrod, Roy E. *Towards a Dynamic Economics*. London: Macmillan and Company, 1948.

Kopits, George and Padma Gotur. "The Influence of Social Security on Household Savings: A Cross-Country Investigation." Unpublished. International Monetary Fund: 1979.

Kotlikoff, Laurence J. "Testing the Theory of Social Security and Life Cycle Accumulation." *The American Economic Review* 69 (June 1979): 396–410.

Kotlikoff, Laurence J. and Lawrence H. Summers. "The Role of Intergenerational Transfers in Aggregate Capital Accumulation." *Journal of Political Economy* 89 (August 1981): 706–32.

Lange, Oscar. "The Rate of Interest and the Optimal Propensity to Consume." *Economica* 5 (February 1938): 12–43. (Reprinted in *Readings in Business Cycle Theory*. American Economic Association. Blakiston, 1944.)

Leimer, Dean R. and Selig D. Lesnoy. "Social Security and Private Saving: A Reexamination of the Time Series Evidence Using Alternative Social Security Wealth Variables." Presented at the American Economic Association annual meetings in Denver, September 1980. (Manuscript dated August 21, 1980, Social Security Administration, Washington, D.C. Also ORS Paper No. 19, Nov. 1980.)

———. "Social Security and Private Saving: New Time Series Evidence with Alternative Specifications." Social Security Administration. Washington, D.C., ORS Working Paper No. 22, Sept. 1981.

———. "Social Security and Private Saving: New Time-Series Evidence." *Journal of Political Economy* 90 (June 1982): 606–29.

Modigliani, Franco. "The Life Cycle Hypothesis of Saving, the Demand for Wealth and the Supply of Capital." *Social Research* 33(2), 1966.

———. "The Life Cycle Hypothesis of Saving and Intercountry Differences in the Savings Ratio." In *Induction, Growth and Trade, Essays in Honor of Roy Harrod.* W.A. Eltis, M.F.G. Scott, J.N. Wolfe, eds. Oxford: Clarendon Press, 1970.

Modigliani, Franco and Richard Brumberg. "Utility and the Consumption Function: An Interpretation of Cross-Section Data. In *Post-Keynesian Economics.* K. Kurihara, ed. New Brunswick: 1954.

Munnell, Alicia H. "The Impact of Social Security on Personal Savings." *National Tax Journal* 27(4) (December 1974a).

———. *The Effect of Social Security on Personal Saving*. Cambridge, Mass.: Ballinger, 1974b.

Sterling, Arlie G. *Social Security and Inflation in a Life Cycle Model: Implications for the Savings Rate.* Unpublished manuscript. Northwestern University, 1979.

Eastern Economic Journal, Vol. XII, No. 3, July-September 1986

THE REVOLUTION RESTORED: KEYNESIAN UNEMPLOYMENT, INFLATION AND BUDGET DEFICITS

ROBERT EISNER*

Just about half a decade ago Martin Feldstein chaired a session in which he introduced me as "the outstanding Keynesian, indeed, probably the only surviving Keynesian." It was not clear that the description was intended to be flattering, particulary to the somewhat business-oriented group I was addressing. But the description was hardly accurate even then. I suppose, though, that those of us who held the faith were all in some sense "outstanding," in contrast to the roars from sometimes clashing supply-siders, monetarists, and market-clearing rational expectationalists.

That Keynesians no longer stand out so much may be attributed in considerable part to the force of the great recession of 1981-82. The pressure of 10.7 percent unemployment can bring some rethinking among all but the most stubborn. But in the spirit that "soon or late, it is ideas ... which are dangerous for good or evil," let me suggest some which may explain the recession in Keynesian influence and grounds for its resurgence. These ideas center about the wealth effects of government obligations to the private sector in the face of changing levels of prices.

I. Prices and Underemployment in a Keynesian Model Without Inflation

That significant lessons of the Keynesian model can be and have been drawn with the assumption of fixed prices—or more exactly, in Keynes' phrase, with a given wage unit—has apparently misled many over the years. For the most essential Keynesian conclusion is that, *with or without* fixed prices or wages, a modern competitive economy may not endogenously maintain full employment or correct departures from full employment within any reasonable period of time, if at all.

The problem, of course, is the possibility of inadequate effective demand. This is readily demonstrated with a fixed price level (or wage unit) in terms of saving and investment demand curves which intersect at less than the full employment level of output or, when defined for full employment, intersect at unattainable rates of interest. These rates are unattainable either in the sense that they are below the levels at which the supply of money would, if ever pushed that far, spill into a liquidity trap or, ultimately, are negative.

*Northwestern University, Evanston, Illinois.

But all of this is not to assert that the price level or wage unit is in fact fixed. Indeed much of *The General Theory* involved consideration of what would happen were wages and prices flexible. The usefulness of the simplifying assumption of a fixed price level resides precisely in Keynes' demonstration that abandonment of the assumption does not invalidate his fundamental conclusion.

In a Walrasian model we assume that excess supply of any good or factor of production will generate a decline in its price. But the remedial effects of lower wages on employment must be found in a substitution of labor for other factors of production or in an increase in aggregate demand.

The substitution of labor for other factors of production depends upon essentially fortuitous changes in relative prices or expected relative prices, difficult to reconcile with assumptions of perfect competition and generally flexible prices. Increases in aggregate demand relate to lower interest rates or a real balance effect which increases public perceptions of its real wealth.

Lower interest rates can help but the question is how much? Can the help be expected to be sufficient to end any departure from full employment? Declines in the rate of interest would be bounded ultimately by zero or by the height of the liquidity trap, even if, as Keynes points out, we have never allowed ourselves or pushed ourselves into the trap. The interest effect will then be insufficient unless the interest elasticity of aggregate demand and, particularly, investment demand, is sufficiently great. As I have insisted elsewhere, 1) Keynes argued that this critical interest elasticity of investment demand did not seem to be sufficiently large, 2) credible econometric estimates, of course including my own, confirm that it is not very great and, 3) not the least, the whole Keynesian explanation of underemployment would lose its foundation if that elasticity were great. Any slack in effective demand would readily be eliminated by automatic declines in the rate of interest.

What then can be the role of flexible wages and prices? The excess supply of labor, generating a decline in money wages, must be assumed under competitive conditions to generate a fall in the general level of prices. This may be seen, in turn, as generating a fall in the demand for money in nominal terms or, in Keynes' formulation, an increase in the real supply of money. In either event, interest rates decline. But if the potential fall in interest rates is limited and if the interest elasticity of investment demand is correspondingly insufficient, this path to the return to full employment is blocked.

We are left then with the propositions that lower price levels generated by an excess supply of labor may eliminate the excess supply if they have a sufficiently positive effect upon perceptions by the public of their real wealth, the so-called Pigou effect after the arguments of Haberler and Pigou, well discussed by Patinkin [5]. As is perhaps not sufficiently widely recognized, this argument loses its foundation in a truly private, competitive economy where there is no government debt, interest-bearing or non-interest-bearing. For here there is no "outside" asset fixed in money terms that will increase in real value as the price level fails.

There are of course further difficulties. As Patinkin pointed out, they may relate to the dynamic problem of how *declines* in prices, as opposed to a lower level of prices, can be achieved in the face of bankruptcies en route and/or elastic price expectations which will induce delays in purchases. But finally, the saving function may be such that, as wealth increases, the desire to save or accumulate more may eventually dominate the decreasing marginal utility of consumption. In the short run, given the limited speed at which prices can be expected to fall, the wealth effect may prove inadequate in generating the additional demand necessary to restore full employment. But even in the long run, at least the theoretical possibility remains that the wealth effect will be insufficient. In the words of Patinkin, the "Pigou effect," that a lower level of prices, ceteris paribus, will generate greater effective demand and lower unemployment may be true but the "Pigou theorem," that this must imply a return to full employment, may not be true. Hence, in the non-inflationary Keynesian model, price movements may not serve the role of guaranteeing full employment.

If we accept the view that Keynesian unemployment does not require imperfectly flexible wages and prices, what is their role? It is, simply enough, to give definition to the price level. By this view, the intense search for "microfoundations of macroeconomics" and, in particular, the excellent work on implicit and explicit contracts, serve the function not of explaining why there is unemployment but, rather, why wages and prices, as Keynes suggested, have some stability and do not fall to zero when effective demand is less than the output associated with full employment or, as some would define it, the "natural" rate of employment.

II. Unemployment and Inflation

On the one hand, the contras insisted that Keynesian theory was fatally flawed in failing to account properly for the role of prices in preventing involuntary unemployment. On the other, particularly in the 1970s, they argued that the Keynesian model was inapplicable to a world of inflation. Playing on earlier adoption by some Keynesians of simplistic Phillips curves, they maintained that the coincidence of unemployment and inflation dictated rejection of the Keynesian model. It is instructive to note the explanation offered by Robert Lucas, for prime example, of the economic evidence that led him to question and reject the Keynesian model to which he had initially sought to contribute, and to build his own substitute paradigm. It was that the Keynesian theory led to the policy conclusion that government budget deficits and easy money would bring about the curbing and reduction of unemployment, and that conclusion was contradicted by the facts. Keynesians had conceded that the fiscal and monetary stimulus might cause some inflation, but this would be accompanied, it was argued by lesser unemployment. Lucas observed, with Thomas Sargent, that the lesson of the 1970s was that "massive government budget deficits and the high rates of monetary expansion" were accompanied not by decreasing unemployment but by *growing* unemployment *and* growing inflation[1] .

If significant fiscal and monetary stimulus bring on accelerating inflation while leaving unemployment high, the Keynesian view of the world would indeed seem out of kilter. But is that accurate recent history? Was it really true, as one witty graduate student is reported to have said after release of official unemployment figures during the depth of the 1981-82 recession, "The natural unemployment rate has just reached 10.8 percent"? Or is there something else to the story? Is it possible that fiscal policy can prove very potent, as Keynesians have insisted, but that it was not really expansionary in the 1970s and on into the beginning of this decade. Perhaps the causes of what appear to be accelerating inflation are to be found in a succession of supply shocks in petroleum and world agricultural markets. And the unemployment then stemmed very considerably from fiscal and monetary policies which, in response to inflation were, avowedly or implicitly, contractionary.

What then of the charge by Lucas and others that large budget deficits which, according to Keynesian theory, should have reduced unemployment, were in fact associated with increasing unemployment? The answer is that budget deficits that reduce unemployment would have to be *real* budget deficits. And real budget deficits, in the tradition of Haberler and Pigou in their arguments that a declining price level would reduce unemployment by raising the real value of private claims on the government, would have to increase the *real* value of net debt.

[1]See, for example, [3], p. 2, and [4], p. 295.

In this sense, then, the deficits that Lucas—and Keynesians—saw in the 1970s, were not real deficits. As I have now pointed out in a number of places[2], the combination of rising interest rates which lowered the market value of debt held by the public, and inflation lowering the real value all the more, converted the nominal budget deficits into real surpluses. From 1977 through 1980, for example, cumulative reported federal budget deficits came to $152 billion. Adjusting for price and interest effects on the real value of federal net debt, we find not cumulative deficits, but cumulative surpluses of $72 billion over this period. When we turn to the more relevant high employment budget, we find that it has been reported in deficit for every single year from 1970 to 1984. But again including the inflation tax stemming from rising prices and interest rates, the *adjusted* high employment budget was very substantially in surplus for the years 1977 through 1981. And by a finer measure of fiscal thrust, taking into account the generally rising share of federal expenditures which were transfer payments and payments of nominal interest rather than purchase of goods and services, fiscal tightness was probably all the greater.

Inflation could thus hardly be ascribed to excess demand associated with increasing fiscal ease and stimulus if there was no such movement to fiscal ease. Rather, a substantial explanation of sluggishness in the economy, climaxed by the severe 1981-82 recession, might be found in a relatively tight fiscal policy as well as in the widely blamed (or credited) role of monetary policy. Since Keynesian theory—and the "Keynesian-neoclassical synthesis"—would have predicted that the combination of really tight fiscal and monetary policy would depress aggregate demand and hence increase unemployment, there is nothing in this economic history which can properly motivate rejection of the Keynesian model.

This also leads to a new view of the seemingly shifting and unstable Phillips curves originally thought to show a negative relation between inflation and unemployment. The acceleration of inflation over a number of years should not have been attributed to movement up the vertical Phillips curve at the "natural rate of unemployment." For if demand was insufficient, employment was below its "natural" rate and the causes of the acceleration of inflation were to be found elsewhere. The relevance of the new "equilibrium" macroeconomics is also called into question. If increasing unemployment is found again to be associated with inadequate aggregate demand because of real, if unrecognized, budget surpluses, there seems less point in the equilibrium explanations. It becomes all the harder to believe that unemployment grew because workers increasingly decided that the real wages being offered were inadequate.

And similarly, we need not explain reductions in unemployment in terms of workers, not recognizing that prices are rising as rapidly as wages, being fooled into thinking that the real wage is higher and hence accepting work or jobs that they would otherwise reject. The explanation of the sharp economic recovery and reduction of unemployment from 1983 through 1985 is to be found very clearly, within the Keynesian model, in terms of a vast shift in fiscal as well as monetary posture. Not only did massive tax cuts and increases in military expenditures move the budget to huge nominal deficit, the declining inflation—both from exogenous oil price movements and the recession itself—and falling interest rates sharply reduced and even reversed the corrections for price and interest effects on the real value of outstanding debt. The high employment budget shifted from an adjusted surplus equal to 1.45 percent of GNP in 1981 to an adjusted *deficit* of 2.01 percent of GNP in 1982, the largest such shift to deficit on record. In this, along with easing of monetary policy, we find a clear explanation of the major, if still insufficient, reduction in involuntary unemployment.

[2] [1] and [2], for example.

III. Conclusion

There is perhaps a moral to all of this. Good theoretical models should always be subject to fleshing out with facts. And facts can be troublesome. There is some folly in viewing the economy as one in which all prices are perfectly flexible, when it is clear that most of them are not. It is useful to try to explain why they are not and what makes them move.

But it is also important when some facts seem to contradict an otherwise useful theory, to make sure the facts are relevant and right. In the case of conventional measures of fiscal policy and, as deregulation would appear to make increasingly clear, very likely with monetary variables as well, the facts have not been what they seemed.

As the full impact of all of this becomes apparent, *The General Theory*, after half a century, will prove more alive than ever.

References

1. Eisner, Robert. *How Real Is the Federal Deficit?*. New York: The Free Press, A Division of Macmillan, 1986.

2. Eisner, Robert and Paul J. Pieper, "A New View of the Federal Debt and Budget Deficits." *The American Economic Review*, March 1984: 11-29.

3. Lucas, Robert E., Jr. *Studies in Business Cycle Theory*. Cambridge, Mass.: MIT Press, 1981.

4. Lucas, Robert E., Jr. and Thomas J. Sargent. "After Keynesian Economics," in *After the Phillips Curve: Persistence of High Inflation and High Unemployment*. Federal Reserve Bank of Boston Conference Series 19, 1978. Reprinted in *Rational Expectations and Economic Practice*, edited by Robert E. Lucas Jr. and Thomas J. Sargent. Minneapolis: University of Minnesota Press 1981: pp. 295-319.

5. Patinkin, Don, "Price Flexibility and Full Employment." *The American Economic Review*, September 1948, pp. 543-64. Reprinted in Williams, Harold R. and John D. Huffnagle, Eds. *Macroeconomic Theory: Selected Readings:* New York: Appleton-Century-Crofts, 1969, pp. 380-404.

[10]

UNDEREMPLOYMENT EQUILIBRIUM RATES OF GROWTH

By ROBERT EISNER*

I.—*Introduction: Aggregative Theory Tackles the Problem of Growth*

There is evidence that the Keynesian revolution is moving into a new phase. After over a decade of discussion, the aggregative concepts of the determination of the levels of income and employment have become well-intrenched in the core of economic theory. "Saving and investment curves" and the approach which they symbolize have become the common property of the professional economic theorist and the college sophomore. But at this point an advance guard has plunged on. Harrod, Domar, Hicks and others have left behind the stationary equilibria of saving, investment and employment to lead us into a turbulent new world of growing economies.[1]

In this new world a first casualty of the older Keynesian system is the wage unit. Measurement is now undertaken in terms of real output. Next, a new dimension is added to the aggregate supply function; productive capacity increases over time—that is, the zero elasticity portion of the curve of aggregate supply moves to the right as the economy grows. With these and other changes which will become apparent in the course of this article, it is possible to make secure certain gains of the first phase of the revolution and to afford new insights into the long-run determinants of employment. In furtherance of this latter objective, we shall offer new sets of schedules or curves of aggregate *growth* which may in some measure expose and clarify fundamental relationships of growing economies in the manner that our older schedules of aggregate *flows* of investment and saving revealed essential relationships of econ-

* The author is assistant professor of economics at the University of Illinois. He is indebted to Professors Evsey D. Domar and Fritz Machlup of The Johns Hopkins University for discussion of some of the concepts of this article when it was still in a formative stage. He has profited as well from helpful criticisms of a later draft by William M. Capron of the RAND Corporation and Professor C. Addison Hickman of the University of Illinois.

[1] Pertinent works by R. F. Harrod include: "An Essay in Dynamic Theory," *Econ. Jour.*, Vol. XLIX (Mar., 1939), and *Towards a Dynamic Economics* (London, 1948). Evsey D. Domar's works on growth include: "Capital Expansion, Rate of Growth, and Employment," *Econometrica*, Vol. 14, no. 2 (Apr., 1946), pp. 137–47; "Expansion and Employment," *Am. Econ. Rev.*, Vol. XXXVII, No. 1 (Mar., 1947), pp. 34–55; and "The Problem of Capital Accumulation," *Am. Econ. Rev.*, Vol. XXXVIII, no. 5 (Sept., 1948), pp. 777–94. J. R. Hicks has made Harrod's concepts an important foundation of his *A Contribution to the Theory of the Trade Cycle* (Oxford, 1950). These names, of course, while they represent early or prominent arrivals, far from exhaust the growing group of explorers in this field.

omies in stationary equilibrium. Development of these new curves of growth will, however, involve us in consideration (and perhaps some reconsideration) of the traditional functions of saving and investment upon which certain of the new curves will be found to depend.

We shall take as a starting point, and as a framework for much of this analysis, the intriguing algebraic models of Professor Domar on the relationship between rates of growth and levels of employment. Professor Domar has devoted much of his work to an examination of the rate of growth necessary for the maintenance of full employment. I shall, after presenting the Domar tools, essay to apply those tools and some others to a further demonstration of the underemployment implications of rates of growth less than the full-employment rate.

II.—*Domar and the Full Employment Equilibrium Rate of Growth*

Domar defines σ as the ratio of the change in productive capacity which takes place in an economy in any period to the change in capital stock (investment) which occurs during the same period.[2] He uses the symbol α for the proportion of income saved (invested). Thus, denoting investment by I, income by Y, and productive capacity by P,

$$\sigma I = \Delta P, \tag{1}$$

$$I = \alpha Y, \tag{2}$$

and

$$\Delta P = \alpha\sigma Y. \tag{3}$$

Now if the maintenance of equilibrium requires either that excess capacity remain at zero (full employment: $Y = P$) or that the amount of excess capacity does not change ($Y = P -$constant), the equilibrium growth in income must equal the growth in productive capacity. Operating under the assumption, for purposes of simplification, that equilibrium involves full employment ($Y = P$), Domar finds that to maintain equilibrium, income (Y) must grow by the amount $\alpha\sigma Y$ in every period. Quoting Domar directly:

> $\alpha\sigma$ is the equilibrium rate of growth. So long as it remains constant, the maintenance of full employment requires investment to grow at a constant compound-interest rate.[3]

[2] "Expansion and Employment," *op. cit.*, p. 40. The wording of this definition, it should be noted, is such that σ may well be a function of other variables than investment. In particular, increases in population which involved increases in the supply of labor would raise the value of σ.

[3] "Capital Expansion, Rate of Growth, and Employment," *op. cit.* p. 141. *Cf.* "The Problem of Capital Accumulation," *op. cit.*, p. 781. The constancy of $\alpha\sigma$ will depend, of course, on the constancy of α, the proportion of income saved, and of σ, the productivity of investment, or on mutually counterbalancing changes in these variables. We shall abandon Domar's assumption that α is constant, in the course of our analysis. We shall, however, retain the assumption of a

If α remains constant as income changes, it must represent both the average and marginal propensities to save. For since

$$I = \alpha Y \tag{2}$$

differentiation reveals that

$$\frac{dI}{dY} = \alpha. \tag{2a}$$

However, according to the multiplier theorem, the change in income equals the change in investment divided by the marginal propensity to save. Thus,

$$\Delta Y = \frac{\Delta I}{\alpha} \tag{4}$$

and, dividing by (2) above,

$$\frac{\Delta Y}{\alpha Y} = \frac{\Delta I}{\alpha I} \tag{5}$$

or

$$\frac{\Delta Y}{Y} = \frac{\Delta I}{I} \cdot \tag{6}$$

In words, the proportionate rate of growth of income equals the proportionate rate of growth of investment. In order to maintain an equilibrium rate of growth of income the economy must also, if α is constant, maintain the same rate of growth of investment. Under the assumption of Domar's model that equilibrium involves full employment, therefore, $\alpha\sigma$ is the equilibrium rate of growth of investment.

III.—*Underemployment Rates of Growth*

We must at this point modify Domar's formulation by declaring explicitly that $\alpha\sigma$ can be considered the equilibrium rate of growth only as long as full employment is considered a condition of equilibrium. In this connection, it must be pointed out that a wide range of economists have denied that full employment is an equilibrium condition. Marx argued that capitalism could not exist without a "reserve army of the unemployed." Keynes is perhaps most famed for his theory of under-

constant value of σ. It may be noted that among elements contributing to stability in the value of σ would be a constant rate of growth of the supply of labor. The maintenance of a constant value of σ in the face of irregular variations in the supply of labor would require counterbalancing changes in other determinants of σ such as technology and the marginal productivity of capital.

employment equilibrium. And most contemporary economists, one would suspect, feel that relatively "full" employment can be approximated in a private capitalistic economy only in exceedingly unstable periods of boom which would not be thought of as conditions of "equilibrium."

Developing further the underemployment element of the Domar system, we may state that if equilibrium involves a constant proportion of idle capacity, equilibrium demands that

$$Y = \theta P, \tag{7}$$

where θ is the "coefficient of utilization" or the per cent of productive capacity which is utilized.

Then, if we start from a position of equilibrium such that

$$Y_0 = \theta P_0, \tag{7a}$$

maintenance of equilibrium requires that

$$\Delta Y = \theta \Delta P \tag{8}$$

or

$$\Delta P = \frac{\Delta Y}{\theta} \cdot \tag{8a}$$

But

$$\Delta P = \alpha\sigma Y. \tag{3}$$

Hence, substituting (3) in (8a), and rearranging terms,

$$\frac{\Delta Y}{Y} = \alpha\sigma\theta. \tag{9}$$

The equilibrium rate of growth, if equilibrium involves less than full employment, is thus $\alpha\sigma\theta$, where θ is the proportion of productive capacity utilized at equilibrium.

It is interesting to present these relationships in terms of Harrod's system of "dynamic economics" which considers expressly a concept of underemployment equilibrium in economies with rising levels of output. Harrod's G_w or "warranted rate of growth" is "that over-all rate of advance which, if executed, will leave entrepreneurs in a state of mind in which they are prepared to carry on a similar advance."[4] Further, Harrod adds, G_w "in Keynesian fashion contemplates the possibility of growing 'involuntary' unemployment." Now, in Harrod's system a condition of equilibrium obtains when the actual rate of growth (G) equals G_w. Since to maintain full employment, on Domar's terms, the rate of growth must equal $\alpha\sigma$, a requirement for full-employment equilibrium

[4] *Towards a Dynamic Economics*, p. 82.

for Harrod must be that $G=G_w=\alpha\sigma$. If a certain proportion of unemployment (slack resources) is the condition for putting "entrepreneurs in a state of mind in which they are prepared to carry on a similar advance," then G_w must equal $\alpha\sigma\theta$, where θ is again the utilized proportion of productive capacity, *i.e.*,

$$G = G_w = \alpha\sigma\theta. \tag{10}$$

This extension and application of Domar's concepts to Harrod's system reveals, then, that where the equilibrium level of employment is a constant proportion of full employment, the equilibrium or "warranted" rate of growth decreases as this ratio of the equilibrium level of employment to the level of full employment decreases. *The maintenance of full employment equilibrium demands a higher rate of growth than the maintenance of underemployment equilibrium.*

While Domar's mathematical demonstration of the outcome of any constant rate of growth, r, should be convincing to those who prefer such rigorous reasoning,[5] arithmetic exploration may make the matter clearer to the general reader. Assume, therefore, that $\alpha=0.1$, $\sigma=0.4$, and $r=0.03$. Then, $\theta=0.75$; equilibrium will be approached with only 75 per cent of productive capacity utilized. Roughly speaking (assuming that the proportion of existent human resources utilized is equal to the proportion of capital resources utilized),[6] we may say that 25 per cent

[5] See, particularly, "Capital Expansion, Rate of Growth, and Employment," *op. cit.*, pp. 140–44. The essence of this may be reproduced as follows:
"Since

$$I = I_0 e^{rt}, \tag{11}$$

capital [K], being the sum of all net investment, equals

$$K = K_0 + I_0 \int_0^t e^{rt} dt = K_0 + \frac{I_0}{r}(e^{rt} - 1). \tag{12}$$

As t becomes large, K will approach the expression $(I_0/r)e^{rt}$, so that capital will also grow at a rate approaching r. As $Y=(1/\alpha)I_0e^{rt}$, the ratio of income to capital is

$$\frac{Y}{K} = \frac{\frac{1}{\alpha} I_0 e^{rt}}{K_0 + \frac{I_0}{r}(e^{rt} - 1)} \tag{13}$$

and

$$\lim_{t\to\infty} \frac{Y}{K} = \frac{r}{\alpha}.\text{"} \tag{14}$$

Then, substituting $K=P/\sigma$ into (14), above, we obtain

$$\lim_{t\to\infty} \frac{Y}{P} = \frac{r}{\alpha\sigma} = \theta. \tag{15}$$

[6] The relative magnitudes of unemployment of capital and of labor resulting from redundant capacity is, of course, actually a function of price, wage and interest flexibilities, capital and labor mobilities and various other institutional factors. However, it seems reasonable to assume a fairly high correlation between the utilization of capital and labor.

of the labor force will be unemployed. The reader may demonstrate for himself, with self-constructed period analysis based on the assumed parameters, that this will be so whether the economy starts from a position of full employment, 25 per cent unemployment, or more than 25 per cent unemployment. However, it is important to keep in mind that the actual rate of growth, r, is assumed to be constant.

When we allow r to vary and, further, to become largely a function of the proportion of productive capacity which is utilized, we move from Domar's system to Harrod's system, from Domar's r to Harrod's actual rate of growth, G. We then get results frequently much different from the convergence to a given coefficient of utilization suggested by Domar.

Domar, in effect, has shown the relationship between what Harrod might designate as the maintenance of various possible "warranted" or equilibrium rates of growth, the productivity of investment and the employment ratio (the ratio of actual to "full" employment). He has not considered the effects of departures of the actual rate of growth from the equilibrium rate of growth. Domar's system thus enables us to present underemployment (or full employment) equilibrium. Harrod emphasizes this equilibrium's essential instability—an instability which leads to the underemployment *dis*equilibria which form a major element of the system of Hicks.

IV.—*Underemployment "Equilibrium" or Disequilibrium*

Many economists objected strenuously to Keynes' concept of underemployment equilibrium. Would-be objectors to the theoretical concept of underemployment equilibrium rates of growth considered in this article may, however, find little tangible to attack. For our "equilibrium" is a formal mathematical condition defined merely as stability over time of the variables which enter our system. In most of this analysis we do not consider the requirements which such stability must impose upon variables outside of our system such as wages, interest rates, price levels and expectations. Thus, when we indicate that a certain *constant* rate of growth of income, *if maintained*, must involve a certain constant proportion of unemployment, we are reasoning in a quite formal manner and do not consider what factors would have to be operative for such a constant rate of growth actually to be maintained. In this respect we are, after all, conforming to the usual theoretical exercises with saving and investment schedules, in which we assert that *if* a certain investment schedule is operative, a certain equilibrium level of income must follow. We abstract here from the underlying determinants of the actual and "equilibrium" rates of growth of income as we abstract, temporarily, in the saving and investment schedule analysis, from the problem of the underlying determinants of the saving and investment schedules.

As Harrod points out, however, the "equilibrium" of growing economies is essentially unstable. If the actual rate of growth exceeds the "warranted" or equilibrium rate of growth, a shortage of capital goods (raw materials, finished products, machinery, etc.) develops; new orders and increases in output to make up this shortage accelerate the growth of income. Conversely, if the actual rate of growth falls short of the warranted rate, a relative surplus of goods must manifest itself; entrepreneurs, in an effort to work off this surplus, cut orders and output. The rate of growth, already too low, declines and, indeed, becomes negative.

Readers familiar with Harrod's model may ask now what an equilibrium condition involving underemployment signifies for C_r, the *equilibrium* value of C (which is the ratio of aggregate *ex post* investment to changes in income, $I/\Delta Y$). Before answering this question it is well to point out that C_r does not actually have any particular subjective meaning to the individual entrepreneur. Rather it is merely the *self-consistent* value of C. Thus, C_r is that value of C for a given period which will lead entrepreneurs to undertake actions which will, in the aggregate, give rise to the same value of C in the ensuing period. Other things, including s, the proportion of income saved, remaining equal, this constant value (C_r) of C will then involve a constant value (G_w) for G, the rate of growth of income. A value of C in excess of C_r means, however, that entrepreneurs on balance find more investment has taken place (more inventories have accumulated, more machinery has been constructed, etc.) than the actual growth in aggregate demand (income) warrants. Hence orders and output are reduced.

Our concept of underemployment equilibrium includes, in effect, a greater value for C_r than would be the case if the equilibrium condition involved full employment. When we suggest that a rate of growth involving underemployment *can* be self-perpetuating, we are suggesting as well, therefore, that the accumulation of capital at a rate which, because of its relation to the rate of growth, involves the creation of a constant proportion of excess capacity, will lead entrepreneurs to actions which, in the aggregate, continue this rate of growth.

Understanding of these relationships may be enhanced by the reflection that this increase in the value of C_r and decrease in the value of G_w from the values which could be compatible with full employment are *not* what present the system with underemployment. A high, full-employment value for G_w would, as Harrod points out, merely make more difficult the maintenance of full employment by setting a requirement for G (which would have to equal or exceed G_w) which would be more difficult to fulfill. The consequence, in Harrod's model, would be chronic periods of underemployment *dis*equilibrium. During these periods, because the actual rate of growth, G, would be less than the warranted or equilibrium rate of growth, G_w, and consequently, C would have to exceed C_r, unwanted or excess capital would accumulate and cause the levels of production and income to drop precipitously. It would then only be in periods of mass unemployment, with an abundance of slack resources, that it would be possible for the economy to grow at such a rate that G would be in excess of G_w, with C consequently less than C_r, and the downward pressures could be briefly dispelled.

The lowering of G_w and the raising of C_r from their full employment values, in this system, reduce the danger of chronic underemployment *dis*equilibrium and substitute the possibility of an (unstable) equilibrium growth, involving underemployment. The admitted instability of this equilibrium invites consideration of restraining mechanisms which must be added to our model to prevent its "exploding" to infinite heights or impossible depths at the first departure from the line of stable growth. Restraining mechanisms, such as capacity "ceilings" in booms and real limits to the rate of disinvestment in periods of decline, prove quite useful in developing "Hicksian" models of the business cycle within the framework of growing economies. The present writer has worked extensively with those models and the failure to consider them in this paper implies no unfavorable judgment as to their significance.

V.—*Growth Curves: A Diagrammatic Presentation of Underemployment Equilibrium*

The Keynesian revolution may, perhaps, make secure its conquest of the new world of growth by recourse to diagrammatic presentation of the sort that was so significant in its earlier triumphs. For in a fashion strikingly analogous to creation of the familiar "saving-investment" curves of current textbooks it is possible to devise curves connecting rates of growth and the relative level of employment.

In the following pages we shall demonstrate growth curves appropriate for various saving functions. The relationship between saving and growth and employment thus revealed will suggest interesting hypotheses as to the hitherto frequently baffling nature of the aggregate saving function.

Figure 1 illustrates this relationship when all of Domar's simplifying assumptions, including the assumption that saving is a constant proportion of income, are accepted. On the horizontal axis, instead of income or employment, as in the traditional Keynesian analysis, we plot (in percentage figures) Y/P, the ratio of output to productive capacity. "Full employment" is indicated by output equal to productive capacity, or the abscissa, Y/P, equal to 100%. We shall boldly refer to the value Y/P as the "employment ratio," thereby assuming that the proportion of labor which is unemployed is always equal to the proportions of other resources which are idle.[7] On the vertical axis we plot, instead of saving and investment, percentage rate of growth of productive capacity (which is a function of real saving and the productivity of investment) and percentage rate of growth of income (which is a function of the rate of growth of investment; in Figure 1 the percentage rates of growth of income and investment are equal because investment has been assumed to be a fixed proportion of income, that is, $I=\alpha Y$). We may refer to the percentage rate of growth of productive capacity per unit of time as $(dP/dt)/P$ or as $(dP/P)/dt$. Similarly, we may refer to the percentage rates of growth of income and investment, per unit of time as, respectively, $(dY/Y)/dt$ and $(dI/I)/dt$. But inasmuch as the time dimension, implicitly thought of as a year, will in any event be the same for the various magnitudes, and since time symbols are conventionally omitted in referring to "stationary" variables such as income and investment, we shall omit the "*dt*" from our rate of growth symbols. The percentage rates of growth of productive capacity, income and investment per unit of time are thus denoted in Figure 1, and in the rest of this paper, as respectively dP/P, dY/Y, and dI/I.

Now, since σ is defined as the change in productive capacity accompanying each unit of investment,[8]

$$\frac{dP}{P} = \frac{I\sigma}{P} \tag{16}$$

where I is the volume of investment.

However,

$$S = I = \alpha Y. \tag{2b}$$

Hence,

$$\frac{dP}{P} = \alpha\sigma \frac{Y}{P} \cdot \tag{17}$$

In common sense terms, the growth of productive capacity depends (at least in part) upon investment, which equals saving. But saving, in turn, is a positive function of income. Thus with any given level of productive capacity, the rate of growth of productive capacity will vary directly with income, that is, with the proportion of productive capacity which is utilized.

[7] See footnote 6.

[8] In order for σ to have enough stability to be meaningful it must be associated with a unit of intended or desired investment which entrepreneurs find useful in the productive process. It cannot refer to the unwanted inventories or other excess investment which help confirm the Keynesian saving-investment identity. Thus, though not necessarily rejecting this identity, we must restrict the application of this analysis to "equilibrium" conditions, in which investment will be so constituted as to have a meaningful and reasonably consistent relation to productivity.

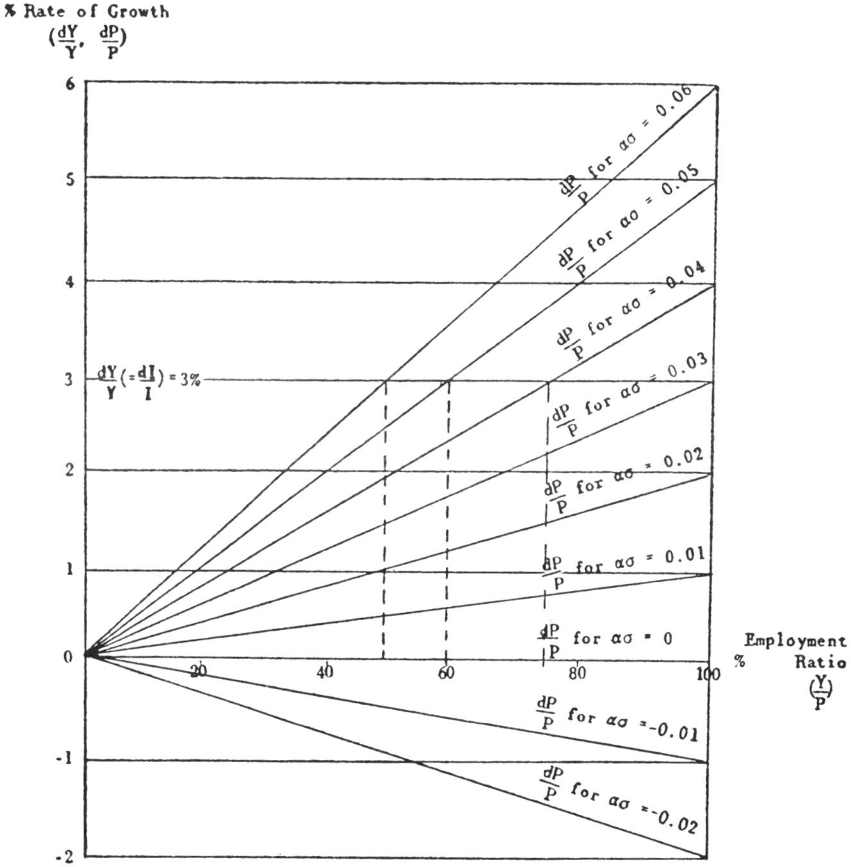

FIGURE 1. INVESTMENT A CONSTANT PROPORTION OF INCOME;

$$I = \alpha Y$$

$$\frac{dP}{P} = \alpha\sigma \frac{Y}{P}.$$

It is therefore possible to construct a family of dP/P curves (rate of growth of productive capacity curves) which slope upward from left to right. The magnitude of slope of these curves depends upon the values of α and σ. In Figure 1, curves are shown for each of the values of $\alpha\sigma$ from -0.02 to 0.06. Then, on the same graph we may let a horizontal line indicate the rate of growth of income (dY/Y). The equilibrium ratio of income to productive capacity (or "employment ratio") is now indicated by the intersection of the growth of income curve with the appropriate growth of productive capacity curve. For example, if $\alpha = 0.2$ and $\sigma = 0.2$, the appropriate dP/P curve is the one designated "$\alpha\sigma = 0.04$." Then, if income were to grow at a three per cent rate (annually—an assumption which would approximate historical data and which consequently will be applied for illustrative purposes also in Figures 2, 3, and 5), the equilibrium Y/P ratio would be 75%, the abcissa of the intersection of the curves, $dY/Y=3\%$ and $dP/P=\alpha\sigma(Y/P)$, where $\alpha\sigma=0.04$.

In the traditional "saving-investment" analysis, either raising the investment curve or lowering the saving curve would raise the equilibrium level of employment. In our diagram, either raising the "growth of income curve" or lowering the "growth of productive capacity curve" will raise the equilibrium *ratio* of employment. To extend the analogy further, in our diagram, lowering α, the average propensity to save, will lower the dP/P curve (rotating it clockwise, with the origin as a fulcrum) and thus raise the employment ratio. And increasing dI/I, the rate of growth of investment, will raise the dY/Y curve, via the multiplier effect, thus raising the employment ratio.

In Figure 2 we drop the assumption that investment is a constant proportion of income but we retain a constant *marginal* propensity to save. As a further modification, we replace the traditional saving function,

$$S = \alpha Y - b \tag{18}$$

by a function in which our second parameter makes saving depend, in part, upon productive capacity, *i.e.*,

$$S = \alpha Y - \beta P. \tag{19}$$

This new function, we may suggest, may solve some of the persistent difficulties encountered in attempts to derive a long-run saving function from time series data.[9] It also points to a negative partial correlation

[9] It may be noted that if we accept the traditional saving function,

$$S = \alpha Y - b, \tag{18}$$

then

$$\frac{S}{P} = \frac{\alpha Y - b}{P}. \tag{18a}$$

Since

$$\frac{dP}{P} = \frac{I\sigma}{P} \quad \text{and} \quad I = S,$$

$$\frac{dP}{P} = \alpha\sigma\frac{Y}{P} - \frac{b\sigma}{P}. \tag{20}$$

Thus in a growing economy, with P rising, at any given employment ratio (Y/P) the value of dP/P will be increasing. However, this is merely a corollary of the fact that in a growing economy, with Y rising while b remains constant, saving would be a rising proportion of income, approaching the proportion α. The saving function actually used in Figure 2, on the other hand, is based on the hypothesis that there is no long-run change in the proportion of income saved.

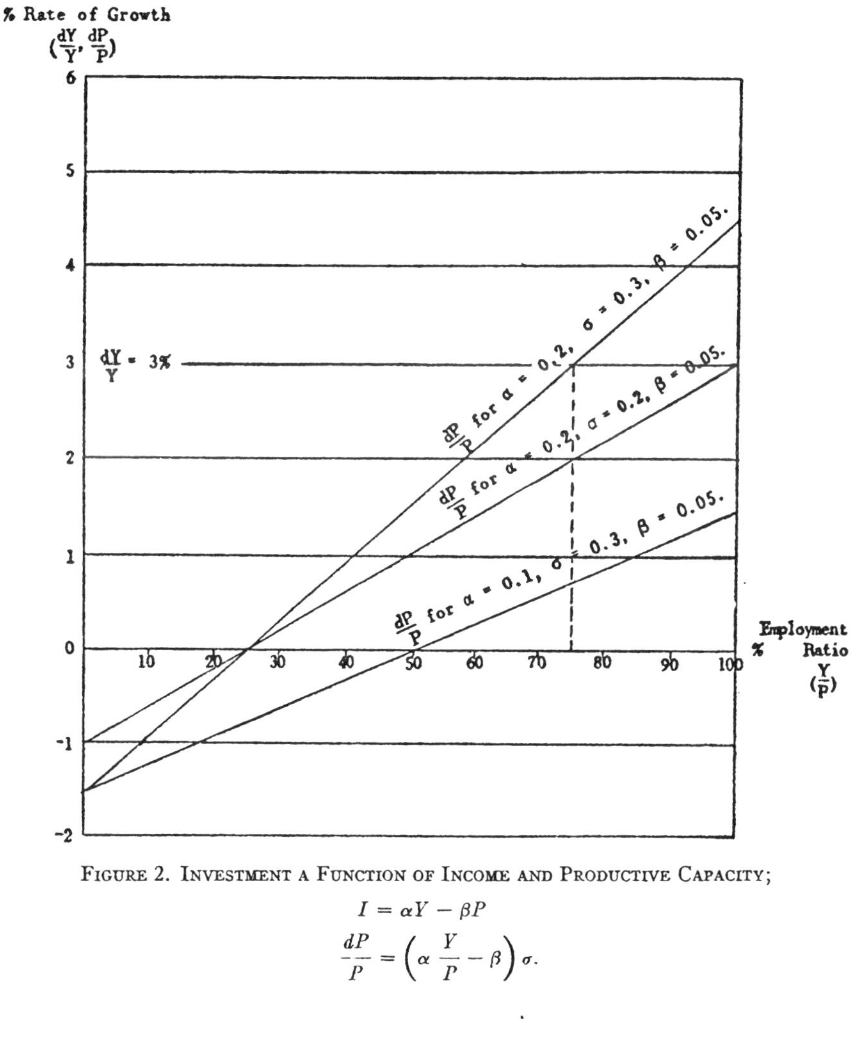

FIGURE 2. INVESTMENT A FUNCTION OF INCOME AND PRODUCTIVE CAPACITY;

$$I = \alpha Y - \beta P$$

$$\frac{dP}{P} = \left(\alpha \frac{Y}{P} - \beta\right)\sigma.$$

between productive capacity and investment, which would appear to conform to both statistical data (low levels of investment during periods of unemployment), and economic theory.[10]

The "growth of productive capacity (dP/P) curves" of Figure 2 may be derived quickly. Since $S = I$,

$$I = \alpha Y - \beta P. \qquad (19a)$$

[10] Since investment is frequently designed to increase productive capacity, as productive capacity increases, with income remaining constant, the demand for investment goods and the amount of investment may be expected to drop.

But

$$\frac{dP}{P} = \frac{I\sigma}{P} \tag{16}$$

and hence

$$\frac{dP}{P} = \left(\alpha \frac{Y}{P} - \beta\right)\sigma. \tag{21}$$

Thus, as in Figure 1, the dP/P curves are positively sloped straight lines. For any given values of α, β and σ, the rate of growth of productive capacity varies directly with the employment ratio. However, in Figure 2 extremely high rates of unemployment (low employment ratios) are associated with absolute declines in productive capacity. And in Figure 2, the dP/P curves, in order to attain a moderate positive value at a high (but not 100%) employment ratio, must be more sharply sloped than the dP/P curves of Figure 1, which begin from the origin.

This last characteristic of our curves assumes considerable interest when translated into ordinary language. So expressed, it states: our saving and productivity of investment functions may be such that the maintenance of full employment demands a high rate of growth; a stationary economy can exist, with dP/P curves such as those illustrated, but only with large proportions of unemployment.

Figure 3 introduces a savings function which adds realism and also sharpens the suggestive relationships which we have just been considering. Now saving (investment) is made a function of both income and the employment ratio (Y/P). This may be explained, at least in part, by the dis-saving necessary to care for the unemployed. As income increases, there is a rise in the volume of saving as well as in the living standards of those who are earning. However, where productive capacity (P) grows faster than income (Y), thus reducing the value of Y/P, unemployment rises and a greater proportion of income is used in providing for consumption of the unemployed. We may also point out that this function, suggesting relatively high levels of investment in periods of full employment, squares well with statistical data on cyclical fluctuations of income and investment.

The specific function exhibited in Figure 3 (though not statistically derived) expresses in a reasonably simple fashion the general relationships just cited. Thus:

$$S = I = \alpha Y\left(\frac{Y}{P}\right) - \beta P \tag{22}$$

$$\frac{I}{P} = \alpha\left(\frac{Y}{P}\right)^2 - \beta \tag{22a}$$

$$\frac{dP}{P} = \left[\alpha\left(\frac{Y}{P}\right)^2 - \beta\right]\sigma. \tag{23}$$

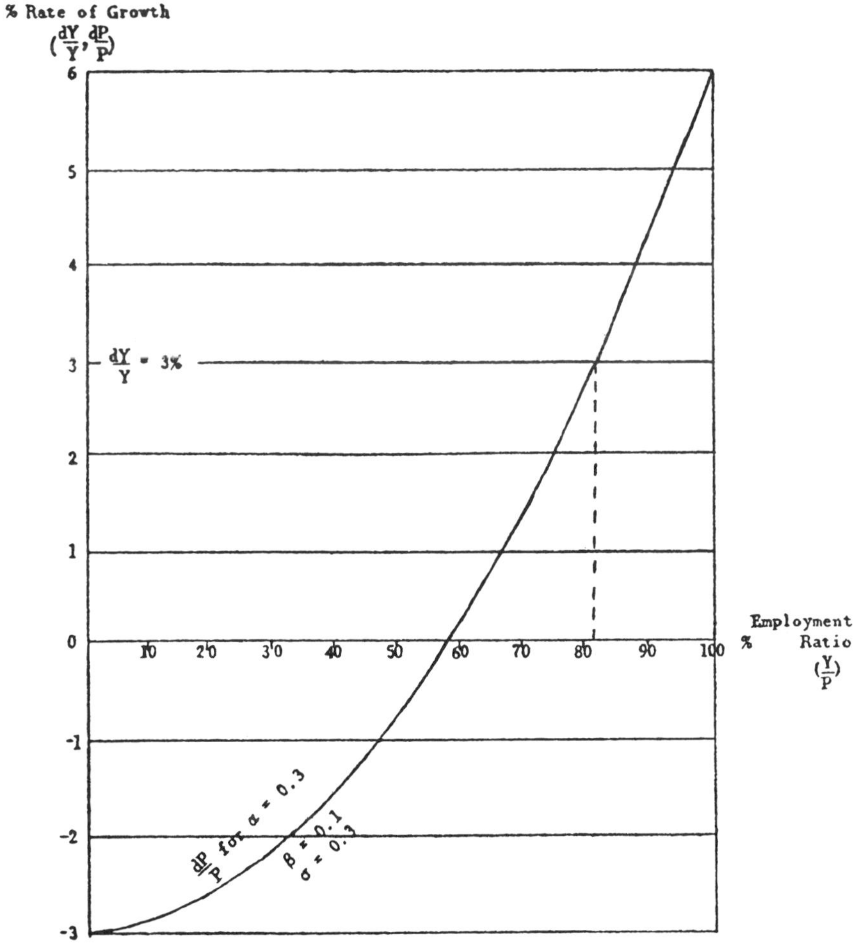

FIGURE 3. INVESTMENT A FUNCTION OF INCOME, PRODUCTIVE CAPACITY AND THE EMPLOYMENT RATIO;

$$I = \alpha Y\left(\frac{Y}{p}\right) - \beta P$$

$$\frac{dP}{P} = \left[\alpha\left(\frac{Y}{P}\right)^2 - \beta\right]\sigma.$$

Examination of Figure 3 reveals that as full employment is approached, the employment ratio becomes less and less responsive to increases in the rate of growth of income. Put another way, it appears possible that the investment and productivity functions are such that it is impossible to secure full-employment equilibrium without rates of growth which, on the basis of past performance, our economy cannot be expected to maintain.

The attainment and maintenance of full-employment equilibrium in growing economies is then the problem of raising the rate of growth of income and/or reducing the rate of growth of productive capacity at

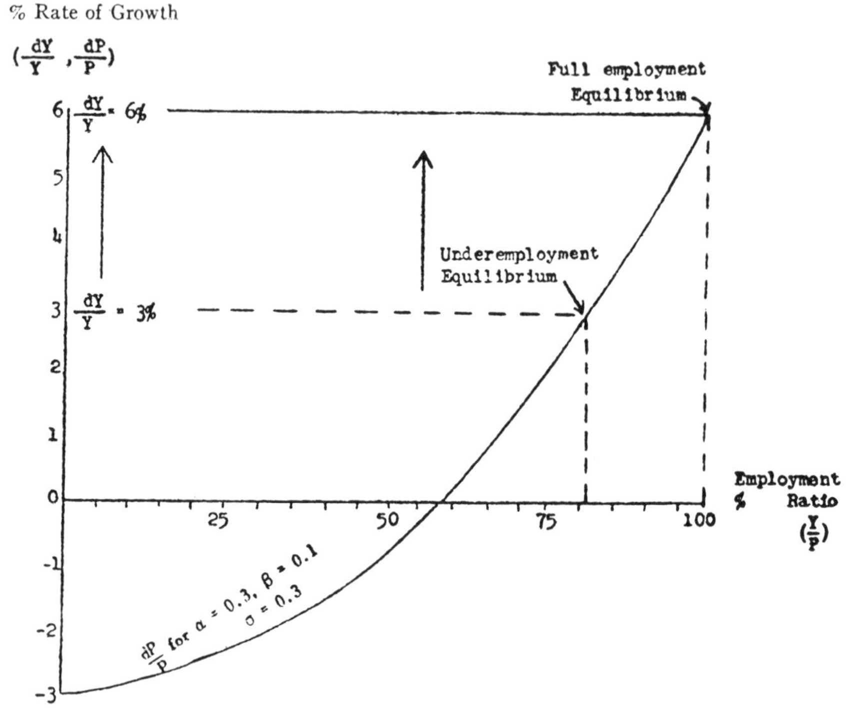

FIGURE 4. ATTAINING FULL EMPLOYMENT BY RAISING RATE OF GROWTH OF INCOME CURVE;

$$\frac{dP}{P} = \left[\alpha\left(\frac{Y}{P}\right)^2 - \beta\right]\sigma.$$

levels of full employment. These complementary approaches are exhibited diagrammatically in Figure 4 and in Figure 5. In Figure 4, raising the income growth curve from 3% to 6% brings a movement of the equilibrium employment ratio, as indicated by the intersection of the curves for growth of productive capacity and of income, from just over 80% to 100%, or full employment. In Figure 5, a similar movement to full employment is accomplished by lowering the value of α from 0.3 to 0.2, thus moving to the right and lowering the growth of productive capacity curve sufficiently to make it intersect the income growth curve at a 100% employment ratio.

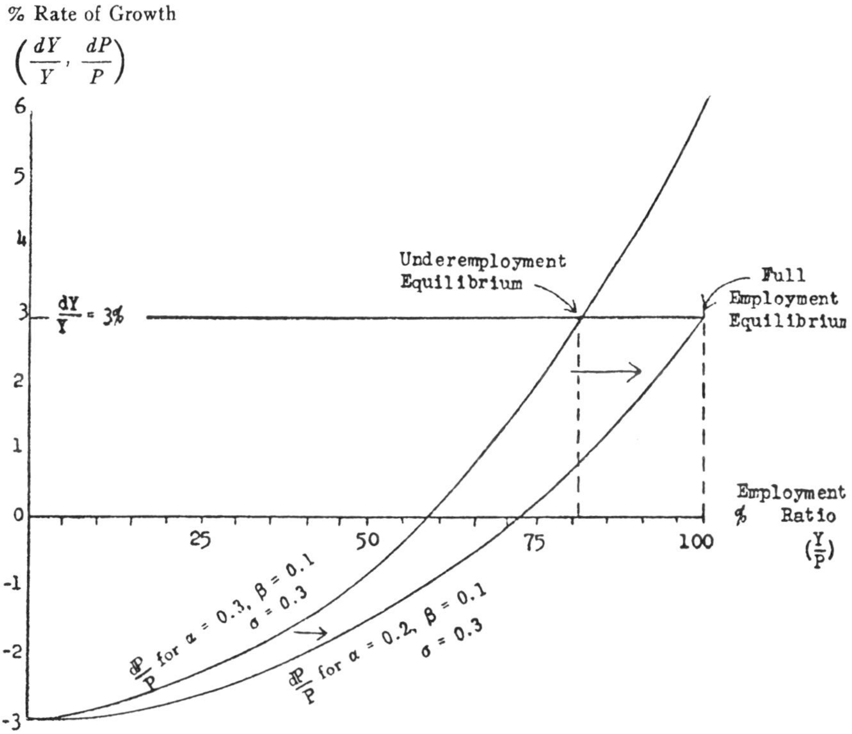

FIGURE 5. ATTAINING FULL EMPLOYMENT BY REDUCING SAVING, THUS LOWERING RATE OF GROWTH OF PRODUCTIVE CAPACITY CURVE;

$$\frac{dP}{P} = \left[\alpha\left(\frac{Y}{P}\right)^2 - \beta\right]\sigma.$$

The diagrams presented in this section, as well as the general concepts of this article which they portray, have weaknesses similar to those of the aggregative, "Keynesian" diagrams and concepts of stationary economies. Specifically, these diagrams and concepts abstract from the micro-economic functions and relations from which, ultimately, they must derive their content. In addition, it should be pointed out that these diagrams and concepts, in their present development, have not been applied to the essential process of transition from one equilibrium to another. However, they may be of some value both in assisting the forward march of the advance guard of "revolutionizing" economic theorists and in helping to consolidate for the rest of the profession some of the newly won ground. In substance, they may facilitate analysis of the modern capitalistic economic system without abstracting out the element of growth which has seemed to so many—private profit enthusiasts as well as the system's critics—to be of its essence.

[11]

DEPRECIATION ALLOWANCES, REPLACEMENT REQUIREMENTS AND GROWTH

By ROBERT EISNER*

I. *Setting of the Problem*

Recent years have witnessed an increasing attention to the size of depreciation allowances. It has been realized that the magnitude of depreciation charges is a major determinant in the distribution of income. Fundamentally, the larger are depreciation allowances the larger the proportion of the national product which will be absorbed by business enterprises before any "distribution" of income takes place. For one thing, the higher are depreciation charges, other things remaining unchanged, the lower must be "profits"; hence the lower will be profits taxes. And a corporation whose official profit figures are low may also be better able to resist trade unions, stockholders and others who might covet the corporate gain.

A not uncommon defense against charges by labor and consumer groups that corporate profits have been unconscionably high has been the argument that depreciation allowances are too low and hence profits are overstated. This argument, in perhaps unsophisticated fashion, declares that the cost of replacing expiring equipment in today's inflated market is actually much greater than current depreciation charges, which are related to original cost of assets.

There are various levels at which those who are so inclined may care to meet this argument. For one thing, they may raise the effect of technological advance and increases in productive efficiency. It may be quite possible, in spite of inflated prices, to replace old assets with new ones whose dollar cost per unit of productive capacity or output is less than that of the cheaper but less efficient assets being replaced. Secondly, some question may be posed as to the basic relevance of replacement requirements to the consideration of depreciation allowances. Many accountants will insist that depreciation accounting is merely a device for allocating original cost and is entirely unrelated to replacement requirements.

It is not my purpose to do more than call attention to the challenge as to the relevance of replacement requirements to depreciation allow-

* The author is assistant professor of economics at Northwestern University. He expresses indebtedness to Edward Budd, William M. Capron, Everett E. Hagen, C. Addison Hickman, Leonid Hurwicz, Robert K. Mautz and Owen H. Sauerlender, for advice and assistance in various phases of the preparation of this article.

ances. A more complete treatment would have to consider depreciation allowances as an aspect of basic social, political, and moral problems of the rights of ownership. Since, however, replacement requirements and depreciation allowances have been connected directly in professional and popular discussions, it seems appropriate, regardless of the correctness of that connection, to apply certain tools of formal analysis to their joint consideration.

II. *Assumptions*

Let us lay the groundwork for our formal analysis by setting forth the following symbols. Our subsequent assumptions will enable us to evade the aggregation problem and relate our variables to either the economy as a whole or the individual firm.

I = gross investment
R = replacement requirements
D = depreciation charges
$E = (D/R) - 1$, the ratio by which depreciation charges exceed or fall short of replacement requirements
a = length of life of assets (in years)
b = period of amortization (in years)
t = the year to which a magnitude refers; thus
I_t = gross investment in the year t,
R_t = replacement requirements in the year t
$E_t = (D_t/R_t) - 1$, etc.
r = the rate of growth of gross investment

$$\left(r_t = \frac{I_t}{I_{t-1}} - 1\right). \tag{1}$$

Then let us add the following simplifying assumptions.

(1) All capital assets have the same length of life, a years.
(2) All capital assets have periods of amortization of the same length, b years.
(3) Gross investment grows at a constant rate, r.
(4) All depreciation charges are made by the "straight-line" method, that is, by allocating an equal amount of the original cost of each asset to each year of its amortization period.
(5) Depreciation charges are begun for each asset at the beginning of the calendar year following the year of its acquisition.[1]
(6) There is no change in the general level of prices.
(7) All capital assets are of the "one-horse-shay" variety, giving the

[1] Firms generally charge at least part of a year's depreciation to an asset in the year in which it is purchased. However, recognition of this fine point would merely complicate our mathematical expression without altering significantly our conclusions. We assume, in effect, that one full year's depreciation charge is made for each asset exactly one year after its installation and that subsequent charges on each asset are made at exactly annual intervals.

same level of service until their moment of extinction, at which point serviceability drops abruptly to zero.

The first three assumptions above should cause no difficulty. For our assumptions of identical time spans for all assets and identical rates of growth for all time periods the reader may substitute in his mind concepts of mean length of life, mean period of amortization and mean rate of growth. The fourth assumption, of straight-line depreciation, is both simplifying and reasonably realistic, since probably close to 90 per cent of all corporate capital assets are depreciated by the straight-line method.

We shall employ initially assumption (6), barring general price increases, to delineate the implications of real growth. We shall relax this assumption in the course of our analysis.

The one-horse-shay assumption (7) is the troublesome one, on which critics might well focus their attention. Its complete abandonment would complicate tremendously and perhaps vitiate much of the simplified analysis in this article. Fortunately, there seem to be weighty justifications for its use.

First, there does seem to be some agreement, particularly among accountants, that productive efficiency (not to be confused with value) of most capital goods drops more sharply when assets are old than when they are new. "One-horse-shay" assets are merely the limiting case of assets whose serviceability declines over time at an increasing rate. We may clarify this by a brief algebraic and geometric digression.

Let P=productive capacity and let g=age of asset.

Then, in our "general" case, which we shall refer to as Case A, we may state that

$$P = f(g) \qquad (2)$$

such that

$$\frac{dP}{dg} < 0 \qquad (2.1)$$

and

$$\frac{d^2P}{dg^2} < 0. \qquad (2.2)$$

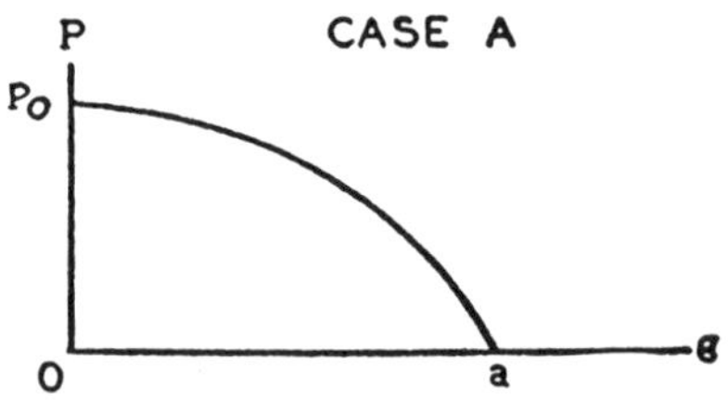

In the "one-horse-shay" situation which we shall dub Case A-1,

$$P = f_1(g) \qquad (3)$$

such that

$$P = \begin{cases} P_0 & \text{for } 0 \leqq g < a \\ 0 & \text{for } g \geqq a. \end{cases} \qquad (3.1)$$

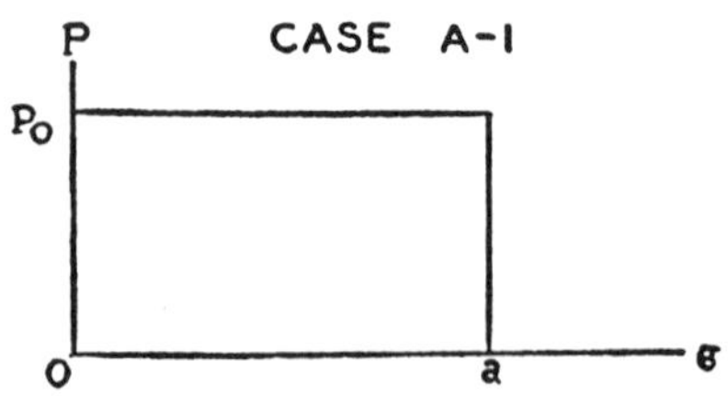

Our conviction that the common situation in the real world is certainly within the general category indicated by Case A and is probably close to that of Case A-1 is strengthened by the reflection that depreciation charges do not include charges for maintenance costs. It is thus quite legitimate in the function above to define P as the productive capacity of an asset which has been kept in good operating condition by appropriate repair and maintenance expenditures.

We may grant the existence of Case B, in which $(dP/dg)<0$ but $(d^2p/dg^2)>0$, but we shall ignore it in most of our subsequent analysis.[2]

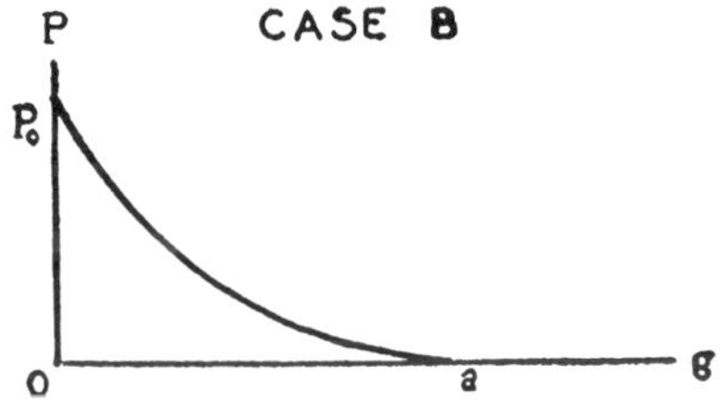

III. *Replacement Requirements*

With the aid of the definitions and assumptions presented above we may now approach the problem of replacement requirements in straightforward fashion. From our definitions and assumption (3), that r is constant, we can write,

$$I_{t-a} = I_t(1 + r)^{-a}. \tag{4}$$

Now, on the basis of assumptions (1), (6), and (7), according to which there is no general change in prices and all assets remain fully productive for a years and then die a sudden death, replacement requirements are equal to the value of the assets installed a years earlier, whence

$$R_t = I_t(1 + r)^{-a}. \tag{5}$$

It is well to be fully aware of the implications of equation (5). In a stationary economy, since $r=0$, replacement needs of any year are equal to gross investment of the current year. However, in a constantly

[2] For this dismissal of Case B we may offer the following justification:

1. Case B situations are likely to include a large proportion of the assets which are handled by methods other than straight-line depreciation. Though replacement requirements for Case B assets will be higher in growing firms than is indicated in our Case A-1 analysis, depreciation allowances may also be higher than is indicated by our assumption of straight-line depreciation.

2. To the extent that firms with Case B assets maintain straight-line depreciation they may be expected to write off their assets over a shorter period than the entire time of the assets' useful lives. This, as will be seen below, will increase depreciation allowances in growing firms and thus counterbalance the increased replacement requirements which we have ignored by our Case A-1 assumption.

This positive effect of growth on the ratio of depreciation allowances and replacement requirements requires only the general Case A assumption. However, the specific quantitative relationships which we shall advance below do depend on our Case A-1 ("one-horse-shay") assumption.

growing economy, replacement requirements in real terms are *less* than gross investment. The ratio of replacement requirements to gross investment varies inversely with the length of life of capital and the rate of growth.

IV. *The Basic Algebraic Relationship*

So far, our results, while perhaps not previously presented in this formal mathematical manner, are not new to economists. Indeed, George Terborgh emphasized that replacement requirements could account for an increasing proportion of gross investment in an economy with a declining rate of growth.[3] However, Terborgh, who was concerned in this emphasis with refuting Professor Hansen's doctrine of secular stagnation, did not concern himself with the rather inverse problem of "excessive"[4] depreciation allowances in their context of resultant lower statements of net income, investment and profits.

We shall examine now, with the explicit assumptions we have indicated, the specific relationship between replacement requirements, depreciation allowances and the rate of growth, under the system of straight-line depreciation. We shall shortly distinguish two situations: (1) the period of depreciation of each asset is identical with the life of the asset; (2) the period of depreciation is shorter than the life of the asset. Situation 1, to which we shall refer as "unaccelerated amortization," may be taken as a limiting possibility in growing economies or growing firms, indicating a minimum disparity between depreciation allowances and replacement requirements. Situation 2, to which we shall refer as "accelerated amortization," indicates that this disparity may be, actually, of very substantial magnitude.

In both situations 1 and 2, if an asset is fully depreciated in b years, the proportion of the asset charged to depreciation in any one year is $1/b$. Therefore, the total depreciation charge in any year, t, is equal to $1/b$ multiplied by the value of assets installed in the years $t-b$ through $t-1$.[5] Thus, recalling (4),

$$D_t = \frac{I_t}{b} \sum_{n=1}^{b} (1 + r)^{-n}. \qquad (6)$$

[3] *The Bogey of Economic Maturity* (Chicago, 1945), pp. 99–119.

[4] The term "excessive" is employed here merely to indicate the arithmetic relation to current replacement requirements. No implications are intended as to desirable policy from the point of view of financial reserve, investment decisions or other such matters.

[5] Depreciation charges would be larger and our conclusions would actually be strengthened somewhat if our assumption (5) were relaxed to recognize the fact that depreciation charges are generally made before an asset is one year old. For this would mean that the bulk of depreciation of each asset would be completed somewhat sooner and the charges made in any one year then would relate on the average to assets which were installed later. In a growing economy these later assets are, of course, of greater value than the assets installed at an earlier period.

Then, applying the usual rules for the sum of such a series, we find

$$D_t = I_t\left[\frac{1 - (1 + r)^{-b}}{br}\right]. \tag{7}$$

Dividing (7) by (5) and recalling that we have defined $E_t = (D_t/R_t) - 1$, we obtain

$$E_t = \frac{(1 + r)^a - (1 + r)^{a-b}}{br} - 1, \tag{8}$$

where E_t indicates the ratio by which depreciation charges exceed replacement requirements in the year t.

Situation 1: *Unaccelerated Amortization*

In the situation which we categorize as "unaccelerated amortization," the period of depreciation for each asset is identical with the period of its useful life or, in terms of our symbols, $a = b$. Substituting in (8) we secure,

$$E_t = \frac{(1 + r)^a - 1}{ar} - 1. \tag{8.1}$$

Similarly, we may rewrite (7),

$$D_t = I_t\left[\frac{1 - (1 + r)^{-a}}{ar}\right]. \tag{7.1}$$

Our major findings can now be deduced quite readily. First, substituting, we see that when

$$r = 0, \quad D_t = I_t, \quad R_t = I_t,$$

and

$$E_t = \frac{I_t - I_t}{I_t} = 0.$$

But, differentiating (8.1) with respect to r, it can be proved that

$$\frac{\partial E_t}{\partial r} > 0 \text{ when } a > 1 \text{ and } r > -1 \text{ but not equal to zero,} \tag{8.2}$$

and

$$\frac{\partial E_t}{\partial a} \gtreqless 0 \quad \text{as} \quad r \gtreqless 0. \tag{8.3}$$

Then, so long as $r > -1$ (which includes all meaningful values of r),

$$E_t \gtreqless 0 \quad \text{as} \quad r \gtreqless 0. \tag{8.4}$$

Literary presentation of our equations may appropriately accentuate their impact.

1. On the aggregative level, replacement requirements equal depreciation allowances only in the very special case of a stationary economy. On the level of the individual firm, similarly, replacement requirements equal depreciation allowances only in the firm whose net investment is zero.[6]

2. Replacement requirements are more than depreciation allowances only in declining economies or shrinking firms.

3. Depreciation allowances exceed replacement requirements in growing economies and in growing firms. Since growth is clearly a dominant characteristic of both the American economy and its firms, this finding would seem to be of decisive significance.

4. The amount of the "excess" of depreciation allowances over replacement requirements varies directly with the rate of growth. Where the rate of growth is positive, the greater is the rate of growth the greater is the ratio by which depreciation allowances exceed replacement requirements. Where the rate of growth is negative, the smaller is the rate of growth (the faster gross investment is declining), the greater is the ratio by which depreciation allowances fall short of replacement requirements.

5. In growing economies or in growing firms the "excess" of depreciation allowances is greater as the life of assets is longer. In declining economies or in shrinking firms the proportion by which depreciation charges are less than replacement requirements is greater as the length of life of assets is greater.

Illustrative values of E_t for various values of r and a may help convey the significance of the relationships expressed in the equations above. Thus we may note that in an economy which grows steadily at a 3% rate and which applies straight-line depreciation methods throughout the life of its assets, the excess of depreciation allowances over replacement requirements for assets which last five years is 6.2%. For assets which last 10 years, this excess is 14.6%; for 15-year assets the excess is 24.0% and for 20-year assets the excess is 34.4%, etc. These excesses would be more for a more rapidly growing economy and less in a less rapidly growing economy.

[6] Where $r=0$, $D_t=I_t$; hence net investment $=I_t-D_t=0$.

Situation 2: Accelerated Amortization

The effect of changing the period of amortization may be determined by going back to equation (8) and securing the partial derivative of E_t with respect to b. Accordingly,

$$\frac{\partial E_t}{\partial b} = \frac{(1+r)^{a-b}}{b^2 r}\left[1 + b \log_e (1+r) - (1+r)^b\right]. \tag{8.5}$$

It may then be demonstrated that

$$\frac{\partial E_t}{\partial b} < 0 \quad \text{when} \quad r > 0, \tag{8.6}$$

and

$$\frac{\partial E_t}{\partial b} > 0 \quad \text{when} \quad r < 0. \tag{8.7}$$

In words, where the rate of growth is positive, the shorter is the period of amortization, the greater is the ratio by which depreciation allowances will exceed replacement requirements. Accelerated amortization means increased depreciation charges (and, consequently, lower "profits" and profits taxes). Conversely, in a declining economy or firm, shortening the period of amortization increases the amount by which depreciation allowances fall short of replacement requirements.

The magnitude of the effect of acceleration of amortization is substantial. In an economy growing at a constant three per cent per annum rate with assets lasting ten years, *excess* depreciation (E_t) is raised from 14.6% to 23.1% of replacement requirements if amortization is accelerated from ten years to five years.[7] With twenty-year assets, acceleration of amortization to a five-year period would increase *excess* depreciation from 34.4% to 65.4% of replacement requirements. With thirty-year assets, *excess* depreciation, already at 58.6% of replacement requirements with unaccelerated amortization, is raised to 122.3% if amortization is speeded to a five-year period.[8]

V. *The Effect of Price Changes*

So far we have operated with the assumption that there is no change

[7] Five years has been the depreciation period which federal authorities have allowed to be used for tax purposes in much of the accelerated amortization during the second World War and again in the last two years.

[8] It may be noted that where the amortization period is *longer* than the useful life of assets, depreciation allowances may be less than replacement requirements, even in growing economies. In such cases an increased rate of growth would accentuate the deficiency of depreciation allowances vis-à-vis replacement requirements.

A fuller treatment of the subject of accelerated amortization, including consideration of relevant statistical data, may be found in the author's "Accelerated Amortization, Net Profits and Growth," in the November 1952 issue of the *Quarterly Journal of Economics.*

in the general level of prices. Our analysis should indicate that those who would unhesitatingly adduce price increases as proof that current depreciation allowances are insufficient to meet replacement requirements have ignored the effect of growth. Specifically, they have failed to consider that in our growing economy depreciation allowances would substantially exceed replacement requirements if there had been no price increases. Correct statement of the issue would present the problem of whether price increases have been sufficient to eliminate the excess of depreciation allowances which would exist with an unchanging price level. Let us apply our formal system to this problem.

Therefore, let us now assume that the general price level or, for our purposes, the price level of investment goods, changes at the constant rate i. Then, let us use r' to denote the constant rate of change of the monetary value of gross investment. Thus,

$$1 + r' = (1 + r)(1 + i). \tag{9}$$

Also using the prime symbol (′) to designate our other variables under conditions of changing prices, we find that depreciation charges may be expressed as

$$D_t' = I_t'\left[\frac{1 - (1 + r')^{-b}}{br'}\right], \tag{7.2}$$

while replacement requirements become,

$$R_t' = I_t'\left(\frac{1 + i}{1 + r'}\right)^a. \tag{5.1}$$

Then, dividing (7.2) by (5.1), and simplifying,

$$E_t' = \frac{(1 + r')^a - (1 + r')^{a-b}}{br'(1 + i)^a} - 1. \tag{8.8}$$

We may pause to deduce the unaccelerated amortization case which, although of some general economic interest, is mathematically merely a special case of the relationship expressed above. Thus under our new assumptions of price changes we may describe situation 1 (where $a=b$) by substituting a for b in (8.8). Then,

$$E_t' = \frac{(1 + r')^a}{ar'(1 + i)^a} - 1. \tag{8.9}$$

Equations (8.8) and (8.9) confirm clearly the common sense notion that price increases raise the cost of replacement requirements in relation to depreciation allowances. Put algebraically, it is apparent that, with the usual qualification that $r > -1$ but not equal to zero,

$$\frac{\partial E_t'}{\partial i} < 0. \tag{10}$$

However, it can also be made quite clear that the fact of an increase in prices is no proof that replacement requirements are not more than covered by depreciation allowances. It is indeed possible to state the function which indicates precisely how much prices would have to increase to warrant the charge that replacement requirements cannot be met by depreciation allowances. The price increase $\bar{\imath}$, which would just eliminate the excess of depreciation allowances may be calculated by setting $E_t' = 0$. It can then be shown that

$$= \left[\frac{(1 + r')^a - (1 + r')^{a-b}}{br'}\right]^{1/a} - 1. \tag{11}$$

It is a simple exercise to calculate the rate of increase of prices which would be necessary to wipe out the excess of depreciation allowances for any particular combination of our variables. For example, if $r' = 8\%$, $a = 20$ and $b = a$, substitution in (11) reveals that $\bar{\imath} = 0.042$. Unless prices increased at more than a 4.2% per annum rate depreciation allowances would continue to exceed replacement requirements.

Accelerated amortization would increase substantially the rate of increase of prices necessary to cancel the excess of depreciation allowances. To illustrate numerically, again, if $r = 8\%$, $a = 20$ and $b = 5$, then $\bar{\imath} = 1.051$. Thus, unless prices increased at more than a 5.1% per annum rate, depreciation allowances would exceed replacement requirements.

It is important to bear in mind that the rate of change of gross investment in monetary terms is itself a function of the rate of change of prices. Recall that

$$1 + r' = (1 + r)(1 + i). \tag{9}$$

Therefore, an increase in the rate of change of prices, i, which would raise replacement requirements, would also raise r' and hence raise depreciation allowances. However, the increase of depreciation allowances resulting from an increase in the rate of change of prices would be less than the increase in replacement requirements. We may note, in connection with the magnitudes which we have used for illustrative purposes, that the rate of increase of prices necessary to wipe out the excess of depreciation allowances is somewhat more than half of the rate of increase of gross investment in monetary terms. Another manner of expressing this relationship would be to state that the rate of increase of prices must be somewhat more than the rate of increase in the real volume of gross investment in order for price increases to wipe out the excess of depreciation allowances over replacement requirements.[9]

VI. *Summary and Conclusions*

We may summarize our major findings as follows:

A. Abstracting from price changes

(1) Depreciation allowances exceed replacement requirements in growing economies or growing firms.

(2) The excess of depreciation allowances over replacement requirements varies positively with (a) the rate of growth of gross investment and (b) the length of life of assets.

[9] Those who prefer geometric presentations may find in the following diagram a convenient synthesis of the relationships which we have been considering.

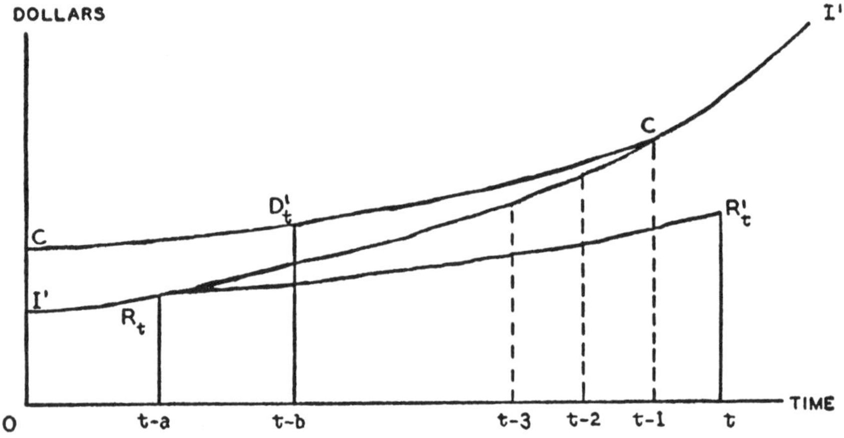

$I' = I_0'(1+r')^j \qquad (j=0, \cdots, t)$

indicates the annual rate of gross investment in monetary terms.

$C = \int_{t-k}^{t-1} \frac{I'}{k}$ = depreciation charges in the year t expressed as a function of the length of the depreciation period, k.

D_t' = the height of C at $t-b$ (the value of C when $k=b$).

R_t = the height of I' at $t-a$.

R_t' = the height at t of a curve which grows at a $(1+i)$ rate from I_{t-a}' (or R_t).

It should be apparent that increasing the value of r' will tilt I' further upward and in turn raise C, thus increasing D_t'. If $b=a$, D_t' exceeds R_t by the distance between C and I' at $t-a$. On the other hand, if $a<b$ (for example, if $a<3$), R_t may exceed D_t'. One may observe generally that as long as I' rises over time, the slope of C is also positive, and decreasing the value of b must increase D_t'. Similarly, decreasing the value of a must increase R_t and, by thus raising the price increase curve which leads from R_t to R_t', must also increase R_t'. Finally, if price increases account for a sufficiently large proportion of the growth in investment, the curve leading from R_t to R_t' will be so close to the I' curve that R_t' will equal or exceed D_t'.

(3) The excess of depreciation allowances over replacement requirements varies negatively with the length of the period of amortization; accelerated amortization increases depreciation allowances.

B. When price changes are considered

(1) Increases in prices may not be sufficient to wipe out the excess of depreciation allowances over replacement requirements caused by growth in the real volume of investment.

(2) The extent of price increases necessary to cancel the effects of growth in the real volume of investment is a function of the rate of growth of investment (in monetary terms, which is a product of the real growth and the change in prices), the length of life of assets, and the period of amortization. Illustrative examples reveal that only when prices increase somewhat faster than real investment do replacement requirements approach the magnitude of depreciation allowances.

We may conclude that the phenomenon of growth places on shaky ground those who would argue that depreciation allowances are insufficient to meet replacement requirements. To the extent that replacement requirements may offer a criterion for the size of depreciation allowances a contrary hypothesis would appear appropriate. Perhaps depreciation allowances are too high and net profits, as well as net income and net investment, are understated by conventional accounting practices! And perhaps our traditional analyses of the distribution of "income" overlook, consequently, a substantial component of the social product which accrues to business enterprises in the form of generous depreciation allowances. Finally, our analysis may have suggested that in this entire area—as perhaps in others—economists must avoid explaining our developing world with models which ignore the phenomenon of growth.

[12]

GUARANTEED GROWTH OF INCOME

By Robert Eisner[1]

Professor Domar, several years ago, raised the interesting question of whether a governmental guarantee that income would grow at the full-employment equilibrium rate of growth will actually call forth sufficient private investment to generate the increase in income necessary to maintain full employment [**1**]. This note will call attention to certain pitfalls for unwary explorers of Domar's challenging work.

In the Domar model, σ equals the increase in productive capacity of the economy, s equals that increase for an individual firm associated with a unit of investment, while α equals the average and marginal propensity to save. Then, assuming that investment which does not depend on growth in income (via the acceleration principle) is completely absent and eschewing consideration of "the numerous practical questions that the income guarantee would raise," Domar argues, "If an economy starts from an equilibrium position, an expected rise in income of $Y\alpha\sigma$ will require an investment equal to $Y\alpha\sigma/s$" [**1**, see p. 145]. "If σ equals s," Domar continues, ". . . a mere guarantee of a rise in income (if taken seriously by the investors) will actually generate enough investment and income to make the guarantee good without necessarily resorting to a government deficit." But, ". . . if σ is appreciably below s, investment will probably fall short of savings and equilibrium will be destroyed" [**1**, see p. 146].

Now, by the magnitude of investment which "an expected rise in income of $Y\alpha\sigma$ will require," Domar must mean the aggregate of the investment undertaken by each individual entrepreneur under the assumptions: (1) that each entrepreneur *knows* (is 100% certain) that he will experience an increase in the demand for his products which is exactly proportionate to the guaranteed increase in national income and (2) that each entrepreneur will operate under the conviction (held with 100% certainty) that each unit (or dollar) of investment which he undertakes will raise his productive capacity by the amount s.

With these two assumptions, we may state that entrepreneurs will seek to expand productive capacity by the amount $Y\alpha\sigma$ but that their initial effort in this direction will involve aggregate investment of $Y\alpha\sigma/s$. Then, of course, if σ is less than s, the amount of investment forthcoming must be less than $Y\alpha$ and, in accordance with multiplier theory, income must fall.

However, if it were appropriate to view the problem on the basis of these assumptions—and Domar must indeed so envisage the problem

[1] The author is indebted to Professors Evsey D. Domar, Fritz Machlup, and C. Addison Hickman for discussions and criticisms of the content of this note.

Reprinted from
Econometrica, Journal of the Econometric Society, Vol. 21, No. 1, January, 1953
The University of Chicago, Chicago 37, Illinois, U.S.A.
Printed in U.S.A.

in order to conclude that "an expected rise in income of $Y\alpha\sigma$ will require an investment equal to $Y\alpha\sigma/s$"—it would still be susceptible of easy solution. Domar need then only have the government "guarantee" an income rise of $Y\alpha s$. The investment generated should now equal $Y\alpha$, which would be sufficient to increase productive capacity by $Y\alpha\sigma$ and to maintain the equilibrium level of income.[2]

But such manipulations offer no clue as to real world possibilities. For Domar, like R. F. Harrod,[3] has been guilty of what F. Hayek might call "methodological collectivism."[4] From another camp, the criticism might be offered that here again an economist has confused the generalized concept of "production" and the "specifically defined *bourgeois* or capitalistic mode of production."[5] Domar ignores that what is pertinent to the individual investor is not how much *national* income or *aggregate* demand will rise but rather how much the demand for the product of the firm in which he contemplates investment will rise. The individual investor, even if possessed of complete confidence in the government's ability to fulfill its guarantee as to *national* income, must be less than 100% certain that demand for the product of his firm will increase at the "guaranteed" rate.[6]

This uncertainty may be regarded as a cost which retards investment. A business man who is 100% certain that demand for his product will rise 5% will invest more, according to generally accepted economic theory, than one who views his future demand as having equal probabilities of falling 5%, rising 5%, or rising 15%. Yet clearly it is the latter businessman who must be the capitalist prototype. It is only the manager of a plant in a planned or socialized society that can know, because governmental orders or the five-year plan calls for such an increase, that demand for his product will increase by 5%.

[2] Domar seems unaware, perhaps because of his use of infinitesimal calculus rather than discrete period analysis, of the need for "leading" a steady increase of income rather than merely maintaining a given level of income. Without offering a precise mathematical solution here we may suggest that with the assumptions implicit in Domar's models, the government may have to "guarantee" an increase in income greater than $Y\alpha s$ so that the investment generated is more than $Y\alpha$ and a constant, multiplier-induced rate of increase of income is maintained.

[3] See [3] and [4]. Note particularly the definition of Harrod's, "warranted rate of growth," [4] p. 82.

[4] See [7] pp. 41–46. I employ the term, in this note, to denote improper use of aggregates as explanations or determinants of individual actions. It should be clear that there remains a large area where the use of aggregates is highly beneficial, if not essential. Certain of the relationships between aggregate growth and the level of employment are explored at some length in [2].

[5] Author's translation of a criticism of Ricardo by Marx, see [5] p. 279.

[6] This point has been made effectively in [6]; see especially pp. 868–871.

We may observe then, that because of the uncertainty of each entrepreneur as to his share of the national income increase of $Y\alpha\sigma$, the aggregate of investment is likely to be less than $Y\alpha\sigma/s$. Hence, even if σ equals s, the amount of investment generated will be less than $Y\alpha$ and income will have to fall from its equilibrium rate.

The problem thus becomes considerably less tractable. Earlier it was suggested that if insufficient investment were forthcoming because σ were less than s, one had only to raise the rate of growth of national income from $\alpha\sigma$ to αs. But now we see that the amount of investment generated, or forthcoming, while doubtlessly profoundly influenced by the course of *national* income, is in the last analysis determined by the expectations of individual entrepreneurs as to the change in demand for their own products as well as their own (and competitors') productivity.

We must conclude, therefore, that a mere guarantee of the growth of national income, without further governmental intervention, will not insure a stable growth of income. It may bring a stable growth for a brief time but then, as individual economic relationships and expectations change, the ratio of income increase to investment generated may change; the growth will then lose its stability and, perhaps, cease. Thought provoking and enlightening as is Domar's generally aggregative treatment, it must be observed that a purely aggregative approach cannot cope with major theoretical obstacles to the success of a guarantee of a stable growth of income.

Northwestern University

REFERENCES

[1] Domar, Evsey D., "Capital Expansion, Rate of Growth, and Employment," Econometrica, Vol. 14, April, 1946, pp. 137–47.

[2] Eisner, Robert, "Underemployment Equilibrium Rates of Growth," *American Economic Review*, Vol. 42, March, 1952, pp. 43–58.

[3] Harrod, R. F., "An Essay in Dynamic Theory," *Economic Journal*, Vol. 49, March, 1939, pp. 14–33.

[4] ———, *Towards a Dynamic Economics*, London: Macmillian, 1948, 168 pp.

[5] Marx, Karl, *Theorien über den Merhwert*, Vol. 2, Part 2, Edited by Karl Kautsky, Stuttgart: J. H. W. Dietz, 1919, 384 pp.

[6] Shelling, T. C., "Capital Growth and Equilibrium," *American Economic Review*, Vol. 37, December, 1947, pp. 864–876.

[7] von Hayek, F. A., "Scientism and the Study of Society: Part II," *Economica*, Vol. 10, February, 1943, pp. 34–63.

[13]

ON GROWTH MODELS AND THE NEO-CLASSICAL RESURGENCE [1]

I. The Attack on the Growth Models

The relatively prosperous decade of the fifties has been replete with retreats from the economics of the thirties. It is good that economists are ready to meet the social issues of their own day; the problem of under-employment in a developed capitalist economy has hardly the urgency of yesteryear. But ills rooted deep in the structural relations of an economic system have a way of recurring, unless those structural relations are adequately and permanently changed. There is hence purpose in clarifying and preserving from distortion in later lights some of the now older diagnoses.[2]

In recent journals several respected economists have joined the attack on growth-cyclical models of the Harrod–Domar–Hicks variety. I submit that these models are such, in their inspiration and assumptions, that the attacks can be successful only with the inclusion of an apparently unintended target—Keynes. I propose to make clear the Keynesian content of the growth models and to redress somewhat the current balance by defending and building upon the Keynesian heritage.

The banners of the attackers are strikingly similar. James Tobin rebels against the concept of " straight and narrow paths from which the slightest deviation spells disaster." [3] Kenneth Boulding ridicules the " H–D–H " or " Hiccup " dynamic with its " dismal," " gloomy," " masochistic " prophecies.[4] Robert Solow rejects " the characteristic and powerful conclusion of the Harrod–Domar line of thought . . . that even for the long run the economic system is at best balanced on a knife-edge of equilibrium growth." [5] All three see the basic problem raised by the Harrod–Domar–Hicks growth model enthusiasts as the unique result of (arbitrary and unwarranted) assumptions of fixed proportions of the factors of production. More completely, in the words of Tobin, " Contemporary theoretical models of the business cycle and of economic growth typically possess two related

[1] The writer is indebted to Norman F. Byers, Alfred H. Conrad, F. H. Hahn, Harry G. Johnson, Alvin L. Marty, Tibor Scitovsky, Robert Solow, James Tobin and Fred M. Westfield for helpful reactions and suggestions. He wishes to acknowledge, in particular, the valuable and detailed comments of Robert H. Strotz. The paper was prepared in part during the tenure of a Social Science Research Council Faculty Research Fellowship.

[2] This paragraph was written, with perhaps pardonable truculence, in the pre-recession summer of 1957.

[3] " A Dynamic Aggregative Model," *Journal of Political Economy*, Vol. LXIII (April 1955), 103–15.

[4] " In Defense of Statics," *Quarterly Journal of Economics*, Vol. LXIX (November 1955), especially pp. 492–5.

[5] " A Contribution to the Theory of Economic Growth," *Quarterly Journal of Economics*, Vol. LXX (February 1956), 65–94.

characteristics: (1) they assume production functions that allow for no substitution between factors and (2) the variables are all real magnitudes; monetary and price phenomena have no significance " (p. 103).[1] Generally, the attackers argue that with consideration of variable-factor proportions and flexible prices, *unlike* in the Harrod–Domar–Hicks models, not one but a variety of warranted rates of growth become possible and the economy will be free to adjust to whatever rate is appropriate for full employment.

II. What Harrod, Domar and Hicks Really Said

It can be shown quickly that the growth models *did* encompass variable factor proportions and reasonable operation of the money–price mechanism. First, in Harrod's formulation, G_w, the warranted or self-sustaining rate of growth, depends upon s, the proportion of income saved (or that proportion remaining after saving is utilised in " autonomous " investment and export balances), C_r, the " required " or equilibrium, current capital–output ratio which leaves entrepreneurs satisfied, and d^* (for " deepening "),[2] the proportion of output absorbed in lengthening the production process or increasing the capital–output ratio. Algebraically,

$$G_w = \frac{s - d^*}{C_r} \quad \ldots\ldots\ldots \quad (1)$$

or

$$G_w C_r + d^* = s \quad \ldots\ldots\ldots \quad (1.1)$$

In this latter form the above equation expressed directly the condition of equality between the proportion of output for which there is investment demand ($G_w C_r + d$) and the proportion of output saved (s).[3] If the actual

[1] In " Complementarity and Long-range Projections," *Econometrica*, October 1956, pp. 429–50, which came to the writer's attention when this paper was in penultimate draft, P. J. Verdoorn also relates the Harrod–Domar models to an assumption of complete lack of substitutability of factors. The implication of Verdoorn's work is that this complementarity assumption may prove not unreasonable for purposes of prediction or as a description of the medium-long-run adjustment powers of the economy. But Verdoorn's thesis is also consistent with the argument we shall develop, that there *is* substitutability but that *economic* constraints limit crucially the range of admissible factor ratios.

[2] Harrod used the symbol d to denote deepening; we have changed this to d^* in order to avoid confusion with the differential and derivative symbol, d.

[3] If we write capital as

$$K = Y \cdot \frac{K}{Y} \quad \ldots\ldots\ldots \quad (1.2)$$

investment can be written

$$I = \frac{dK}{dt} = \frac{K}{Y}\frac{dY}{dt} + Y\frac{d(K/Y)}{dt} \quad \ldots\ldots\ldots \quad (1.3)$$

and the ratio of investment to income is

$$\frac{I}{Y} = \frac{d \log Y}{dt} \cdot \frac{K}{Y} + \frac{d(K/Y)}{dt} \quad \ldots\ldots\ldots \quad (1.4)$$

For the equilibrium condition described by the warranted rate of growth it is presumed that K/Y, rate of growth is less than the warranted rate, investment demand must then be less than saving, and the rate of growth of output and (eventually) the rate of output must turn down. But if G_n, the "*natural*" rate of growth or maximum rate of growth of which the economy is capable under conditions of full employment, is less than G_w, then the *actual* rate at full employment would have to be less than G_w. It follows that investment demand would have to be less than saving at full employment. Thus full employment could at best represent a momentary position of disequilibrium. A critical aspect of the problem, then, can be formulated as how to prevent G_w from exceeding G_n. One way to do this is to have deepening—a positive value of d^*. Harrod states explicitly, "*d* may have a positive value because of the nature of the inventions occurring. It may also have a positive value because the rate of interest is falling. Our aim should be to get such a progressive reduction in the rate of interest that

$$G_w C_r = s - d = G_n C_r."$$

Harrods adds, "If *d* is positive, C_r will increase through time, and may eventually become so great as to enable us to dispense with *d*." [1]

Now, increasing capital intensity stemming from lower interest rates implies changing factor proportions and indeed, with linear, homogenous production functions (as assumed by Solow and Tobin), changes in the capital–output ratio must mean changes in factor proportions. Thus Harrod is saying that factor proportions *may* change so much—the economy *may* get so capital intensive—that the rate of growth necessary to absorb saving (the "warranted" rate, G_w) will be reduced to an acceptable level. But, Harrod continues, "The question we now have to ask is whether there will be any natural tendency for the rate of interest to come down sufficiently. *This is the crux of the matter* [emphasis added, R. E.], the crux, perhaps, of that modern economic situation to which we shall revert, when the post-war shortages cease." I submit that there can be no doubt that in Harrod's model factor proportions are quite variable and the money–price mechanism is free to operate as it will; there is no uneconomic, arbitrary, technological

the actual, current capital–output ratio, is the ratio currently *demanded*, and therefore equals C_r. Then if $\frac{d(K/Y)}{dt}$, or "deepening," is taken as the time rate at which entrepreneurs *demand* (*desire*) that the capital–output ratio change, $\frac{I}{Y}$ is the ratio of investment *demand* to output. The warranted rate of growth is that value of $\frac{d \log Y}{dt}$ (Harrod's *G*) for which

$$\frac{d \log Y}{dt} \cdot \frac{K}{Y} + \frac{d(K/Y)}{dt} = \frac{I}{Y} = s = \frac{S}{Y}, \quad \ldots \ldots \quad (1.5)$$

or that value which makes investment demand equal saving.

[1] *Towards a Dynamic Economics* (London, 1948), p. 96. This corresponds precisely, as should become clear below, to Solow's positive value for the rate of change of the capital–labour ratio ($r > 0$), leading eventually to an equilibrium ratio, r^* (*loc. cit.*, p. 70).

constraint.[1] However, as more capital is used, other things remaining equal, the return on capital must fall. The difficulty is that this fall may conflict with the Keynesian floor to the rate of interest or, more generally, with the rate of return on capital which entrepreneurs will find acceptable.

Domar, similarly, is clear in pointing out that the crucial issue is not whether capital–output ratios are fixed but rather whether they are free to adjust in such a manner as to eliminate " The Problem of Capital Accumulation." [2] Raising the question of the American economy's ability to continue indefinitely absorbing new capital at its rapid post-war rate, Domar writes:—

> " Implicit in this worry is the belief that the possibilities of the so-called deepening of capital (in the sense of an increasing ratio of capital to output) are limited. Therefore the amount of capital that the economy can absorb, at a given income level and over a given period of time, is limited as well. . . . We have thus assumed, at least for the purpose of this discussion, that there exists a fairly stable ratio between annual output (or national income) and the capital stock needed for its production, this ratio to be indicated by the letter *s*. While, strictly speaking, we shall treat *s* as a given constant, it need not be so. It is certainly not the same among various firms and industries. The national average (if such exists) can be made a function of time, interest rate, or of something else. *But it must have some stability, because if s can be anything, our argument falls through and we are back at the Knight–Simons Position* " [that " investment opportunities are practically unlimited "].[3]

Finally, Hicks would have cyclical fluctuations about a growth trend develop with any of a wide variety of capital–output ratios (as well as saving ratios and lags).[4] Hicks argues that any values of the accelerator above the " Upper Point " will generate a " strong " cycle when equilibrium is disturbed, values merely above the " Middle Point " will lead the system into strong cycles, and even values merely above the " Lower Point " will contribute to some (damped) cyclical fluctuations. And Hicks devotes much space in his " inspection of the ceiling " and his analysis of " the monetary factor " to a consideration of whether the forces that transform the accelerator or the desired capital–output ratios are likely to eliminate the troublesome instability and departures from full employment which the H–D–H models all suggest. Hicks' answer, of course, is not encouraging. But again, the difficulty is due to incapacities of adjustment of the monetary framework and of the economic system generally and not an arbitrary assumption of (technologically determined) corners in the production isoquants.

[1] Cf. Harrod's amplification of this point in his " Comment " on Harold Pilvin's " Full Capacity *vs.* Full Employment Growth," *The Quarterly Journal of Economics*, Vol. LXVII (November 1953), pp. 553–9.

[2] *American Economic Review*, Vol. XXXVIII (December 1948), pp. 777–94.

[3] *Ibid.*, pp. 777–9, emphasis added.

[4] J. R. Hicks, *A Contribution to the Theory of the Trade Cycle* (Oxford, 1950).

III. "A Dynamic Aggregative Model" with Some Keynesian Parameters

The issues may be fairly joined by constructing a model which draws heavily upon the elegant presentations of two of the critics, Solow and Tobin, and utilises such a model to consider conditions or assumptions sufficient to give the peculiar or particular Harrod–Domar–Hicks results. We shall consider first the factor-proportion question, assuming initially that private saving equals the change in physical capital and is some constant ratio of output. Later we shall enlarge the area of debate by introducing a more general saving function, complete with a "Pigou effect" and a new "dynamic Pigou theorem."

The Production Function, Factor Proportions and the Rate of Profit

Let us assume, with Solow and Tobin, that net output is a linear, homogeneous function of capital and labour:

$$Y = F(K,L) \qquad \ldots\ldots\ldots \qquad (2)$$

and that output consists of only one good, which may be consumed or retained as capital (invested). Writing $r = K/L$ for the capital–labour ratio, we may, on the basis of the homogeneity assumption, factor out L and rewrite the production function:

$$Y = L \cdot F(r,1) \qquad \ldots\ldots\ldots \qquad (3)$$

We may further assume diminishing marginal returns to each factor of production, throughout the economically relevant range of factor proportions, so that, in particular,

$$\frac{d^2F}{dr^2} < 0 \qquad \ldots\ldots\ldots \qquad (4)$$

But since in equilibrium the rate of profit, i, is presumed to equal the net marginal product of capital, we may write

$$i = F_K \equiv F_r \qquad \ldots\ldots\ldots \qquad (5)$$

and, consequently, substituting in (4),

$$\frac{di}{dr} < 0 \qquad \ldots\ldots\ldots \qquad (6)$$

In words, i must be a monotonic, decreasing function of r; an increase in the capital–labour ratio must mean a decrease in the rate of profit.

Taking Harrod's system as representative for our purposes, we may express his symbols as

$$C_r = \frac{K}{Y} = r\frac{L}{Y} = \frac{r}{F(r,1)} \qquad \ldots\ldots \qquad (7)$$

and

$$d^* = \frac{d(K/Y)}{dt} = \frac{dC_r}{dr}\cdot\frac{dr}{dt} \qquad \ldots\ldots \qquad (8)$$

where r is the capital–labour ratio corresponding to the equilibrium capital–output ratio, C_r, and

$$\frac{dC_r}{dr} = \frac{F(r,1) - rF_r}{[F(r,1)]^2} \quad . \quad . \quad . \quad . \quad . \quad . \quad . \quad (9)$$

Hence, substituting in (1) and simplifying terms, and denoting $F(r,1)$ by F,

$$G_w = \left(\frac{d \log \Upsilon}{dt}\right)_w = \frac{s}{r} \cdot F - \frac{d \log r}{dt} + \frac{d \log F}{dt} \quad . \quad (10)^1$$

But since $F(r,1)$ is total output per unit of labour and rF_r is the return to capital per unit of labour, for all economically relevant values of r (where the share of capital is less than unity) we obtain from (9) the condition that

$$\frac{dC_r}{dr} > 0 \quad . \quad . \quad . \quad . \quad . \quad . \quad . \quad (11)$$

or that Harrod's C_r, the capital–output ratio, varies in the same direction as the capital–labour ratio. From (8) and (11),

$$d^* \gtreqless 0 \text{ as } \frac{dr}{dt} \gtreqless 0 \quad . \quad . \quad . \quad . \quad . \quad . \quad . \quad (12)$$

or deepening depends upon an increase in the capital–labour ratio: moreover,

$$\frac{dd^*}{d\left(\frac{dr}{dt}\right)} > 0 \quad . \quad . \quad . \quad . \quad . \quad . \quad . \quad (13)$$

.e., deepening is a monotonically increasing function of the rate of change of the capital–labour ratio. Now, dismissing negative values of C_r, as

[1] Noting that

$$\frac{d \log F}{dt} = \frac{d \log \Upsilon/L}{dt} = \frac{d \log \Upsilon}{dt} - \frac{d \log L}{dt} \quad . \quad . \quad . \quad . \quad . \quad . \quad (10.1)$$

we may write the actual rate of growth of output

$$\frac{d \log \Upsilon}{dt} = \frac{d \log K}{dt} - \left(\frac{d \log K}{dt} - \frac{d \log L}{dt}\right) + \frac{d \log F}{dt} \quad . \quad . \quad . \quad . \quad . \quad (10.2)$$

Since saving is presumed to be realised (whether consistent with entrepreneurial equilibrium or not),

$$\frac{s}{r} \cdot F = \frac{sL \cdot F}{K} = \frac{1}{K} \cdot \frac{dK}{dt} = \frac{d \log K}{dt} \quad . \quad . \quad . \quad . \quad . \quad . \quad (10.3)$$

so that, substituting in (10.2),

$$\frac{d \log \Upsilon}{dt} = \frac{s}{r} \cdot F - \left(\frac{d \log K}{dt} - \frac{d \log L}{dt}\right) + \frac{d \log F}{dt} \quad . \quad . \quad . \quad . \quad (10.4)$$

But then, where

$$\frac{d \log K}{dt} - \frac{d \log L}{dt} = \frac{d \log r}{dt} \quad . \quad . \quad . \quad . \quad . \quad . \quad . \quad . \quad (10.5)$$

(10.4) becomes identical with (10): the actual rate of growth of output equals the warranted rate when the capital–labour ratio is actually changing at the rate $\frac{d \log r}{dt}$ consistent with entrepreneurial equilibrium.

economically irrelevant, and negative values of $s - d^*$ as unlikely and uninteresting in the present context, we see from (1) that

$$\frac{\partial G_w}{\partial C_r} < 0 \quad . \quad . \quad . \quad . \quad . \quad . \quad . \quad (14)$$

and

$$\frac{\partial G_w}{\partial d^*} < 0 \quad . \quad . \quad . \quad . \quad . \quad . \quad . \quad (15)$$

Then, combining (14) and (11),

$$\frac{\partial G_w}{\partial r} = \frac{\partial G_w}{\partial C_r} \cdot \frac{dC_r}{dr} < 0 \quad . \quad . \quad . \quad . \quad . \quad . \quad (16)$$

and combining (15) and (13),

$$\frac{\partial G_w}{\partial\left(\frac{dr}{dt}\right)} = \frac{\partial G_w}{\partial d} \cdot \frac{dd^*}{d\left(\frac{dr}{dt}\right)} < 0 \quad . \quad . \quad . \quad . \quad . \quad (17)$$ [1]

In words again, Harrod's warranted rate of growth may be reduced by an increase in the capital–labour ratio (16) as well as by an increase in the rate of change of the capital–labour ratio (17).

But now we shall introduce some reasonable parameters into our production function. Critics of the growth models deal with functions which implicitly or explicitly (like the Cobb–Douglas illustration Solow employs) imply the assumption that the marginal net product of capital is always positive, regardless of how high the capital–labour ratio rises; barring demand problems it must always pay to invest. This, indeed, is one of the "crucial" assumptions [2] on which the growth model *critiques* rest. It embodies again

[1] These results may also be obtained directly in terms of r. Again denoting $\frac{Y}{L} = F(r,l)$ by F, we may write

$$C_r = \frac{K}{L} \cdot \frac{L}{Y} = \frac{r}{F} \quad . \quad . \quad . \quad . \quad . \quad . \quad . \quad . \quad . \quad (16.1)$$

Then, substituting in (1),

$$G_w = (s - d^*)\frac{F}{r} \quad . \quad . \quad . \quad . \quad . \quad . \quad . \quad . \quad . \quad (16.2)$$

The partial derivative of G_w with respect to r, assuming s and d^* constant, is then

$$\frac{\partial G_w}{\partial r} = -(s - d^*)\frac{(F - rF_r)}{r^2} \quad . \quad . \quad . \quad . \quad . \quad . \quad . \quad (16.3)$$

As explained above in regard to (11), we may take $F - rF_r$, the relative share of labour, as positive. Hence, where

$$s - d^* = \text{constant} > 0, \frac{\partial G_w}{\partial r} < 0 \quad . \quad . \quad . \quad . \quad . \quad (16.4)$$

And the partial derivative of G_w with respect to d^*, with s and r assumed unchanged, is

$$\frac{\partial G_w}{\partial d^*} = -\frac{F}{r} < 0 \quad . \quad . \quad . \quad . \quad . \quad . \quad . \quad . \quad . \quad (17.1)$$

[2] Solow warns that: "A 'crucial' assumption is one on which the conclusions do depend sensitively, and it is important that crucial assumptions be reasonably realistic. When the results of a theory seem to flow specifically from a special crucial assumption, then if the assumption is dubious, the results are suspect" (*loc. cit.*, p. 65). But he charges this to the Harrod–Domar model.

the optimistic notion of unlimited investment opportunities; it should not be surprising that it yields optimistic conclusions. Let us, however, in curiously more classical vein,[1] recognise that in any given period, or with a given production function, there is a limit to the extent to which greater round-aboutness of production will pay for itself. All we are arguing is that with a given quantity of labour there is some finite amount of capital at which the diminishing *net* marginal return to capital will reach zero. With more than that amount of capital the marginal net product of capital will be negative; additional capital will not realise, and hence should not be expected to realise, sufficient returns during its life-time to pay for itself. We thus add the further description of our production function,

$$F_K \gtreqless 0 \text{ as } K \lesseqgtr K_0,\ L = L_0 \quad . \quad . \quad . \quad . \quad (18)$$

or utilising the homogeneity assumption and defining $r_0 = \frac{K_0}{L_0}$,

$$i = F_K \equiv F_r \gtreqless 0 \text{ as } r \lesseqgtr r_0 \quad . \quad . \quad . \quad . \quad . \quad (19)$$

Now the existence of r_0, a limit to the profitable extensibility of the capital–labour ratio, will prove sufficient to admit the possibility of the "H–D–H" difficulties,[2] but, if we wish to get more Keynesian, we can add a liquidity trap at say i_1, where $i_1 > 0$ and is the rate of return equal to the floor to the rate of interest. To i_1 will correspond some capital–labor ratio, say r_1, where $r_1 < r_0$ and

$$i = F_K \equiv F_r \gtreqless i_1 \text{ as } r \lesseqgtr r_1 \quad . \quad . \quad . \quad . \quad (20)$$

Hence there is an upper limit to the value of r, which may be denoted by r_0 or r_1, depending upon whether we wish to assume that the rate of (net) profit can fall to zero or only to some value above zero. Since from (16) it can be seen that G_w is a monotonically decreasing function of r, for any given values of s and d^* $\left(e.g., d^* = 0 = \frac{dr}{dt}\right)$, there is then a lower limit to G_w. If this lower limit is still higher than the actual or maintainable rate of growth the economy is in for the H–D–H maladies.

But what if there is deepening, that is, d^* and $\frac{dr}{dt}$ are positive? Here we

[1] Consistently, for example, with the formulation by John M. Cassels, "On the Law of Variable Proportions," reprinted from *Explorations in Economics* in *Readings in the Theory of Income Distribution*, pp. 103–18.

[2] The simplifying assumption of linear homogeneity of the production function enables us to meet the Solow–Tobin type *critiques* on their own ground, but it is a stronger assumption than we require. The Harrod–Domar–Hicks problem may be exhibited by any production function in which, with the given (presumably exogenous) growth of labour supply and the rate of capital accumulation consistent with the saving function, the marginal net product of capital is declining, and has no non-negative lower bound.

are referring not to a *higher* but to an *increasing* capital–labour ratio. As we noted in (17), the greater the rate of increase of the capital–labour ratio, other things equal, the less the warranted rate of growth. Thus we may concede that if the warranted rate of growth is too high there is always some rate of change of factor proportions which will be sufficient to make the warranted rate of growth any necessary lower figure. We are not, however, out of the woods. For, in accordance with (6), an increasing value of r must mean a decreasing rate of profit. But since $i \geqq 0$ or $i \geqq i_1$, eventually (with $\frac{dr}{dt} > \epsilon;\ \epsilon > 0$),

$$\text{as } r \underset{\rightarrow}{=} r_0 \text{ or as } r \underset{\rightarrow}{=} r_1,\ \frac{di}{dt} \underset{\rightarrow}{=} 0 \quad . \quad . \quad . \quad . \quad . \qquad (21)$$

Then, writing

$$\frac{dr}{dt} = \frac{dr}{dF_r} \cdot \frac{dF_r}{dt} \quad . \quad . \quad . \quad . \quad . \quad . \quad . \qquad (22)$$

we can see that since, as stated in (5), in equilibrium, the rate of profit equals the marginal product of capital or $i = F_r$, as

$$\frac{di}{dt}\left(= \frac{dF_r}{dt}\right) \underset{\rightarrow}{=} 0,\ \frac{dr}{dt} \underset{\rightarrow}{=} 0 \quad \text{unless } \frac{dr}{dF_r} \underset{\rightarrow}{=} -\infty \quad . \quad . \qquad (23)$$

and, substituting $di = dF_r$ in (22) and (22) in (8), we derive,

$$d^* = \frac{dC_r}{dr} \cdot \frac{dr}{di} \cdot \frac{di}{dt} \quad . \quad . \quad . \quad . \quad . \quad . \quad . \qquad (24)$$

To paraphrase our equations once more, where the capital–labour ratio is increasing $\left(\frac{dr}{dt} > 0\right)$, deepening is taking place ($d^* > 0$), and then, as Harrod (among others) points out, the warranted rate of growth is reduced and thereby relief is found. But deepening ($d^* > 0$) requires a falling marginal net product of capital, and hence a falling rate of profit $\left(\frac{dF_r}{dt} = \frac{di}{dt} < 0\right)$. There is a limit to how far the rate of profit can fall, and hence, unless the marginal net product of capital falls asymptotically to this limit (so that $\frac{dr}{dF_r} \rightarrow -\infty$, the unlimited investment opportunities argument again), there is a limit to how long any given rate of deepening (any given positive value of d^*) can be maintained. Thus we should observe that the rate of deepening is curbed not only by price and money rigidities and direct institutional constraints on the rate of fall of the equilibrium rate of return on investment $\left(\frac{di}{dt}\right)$; whatever the freedom from constraints, as long as there is a lower limit to i (even if only at $i = 0$), i cannot fall fast for long without hitting bottom.

The Saving Function, Asset Preferences and "Pigou Effects"

We shall now abandon the assumption that saving equals the change in physical capital and is a constant proportion of output. We shall instead introduce the saving function,

$$\frac{dW}{dt} \equiv S = S\left(Y, i, K, \frac{M}{P}\right) \quad . \quad . \quad . \quad . \quad (25)$$

where W stands for wealth or total accumulated savings and is defined as

$$W \equiv K + \frac{M}{P} \quad . \quad . \quad . \quad . \quad . \quad . \quad . \quad (26)$$

the total of physical capital and the real value of cash balances, so that saving is defined as

$$\frac{dW}{dt} \equiv S \equiv \frac{dK}{dt} + \frac{M}{P}\left(\frac{d\log M}{dt} - \frac{d\log P}{dt}\right) \quad . \quad . \quad (26.1)^1$$

We may therefore, substituting in (10), rewrite the formulation of the warranted rate of growth as

$$G_w = \left(\frac{d\log Y}{dt}\right)_w = \frac{1}{K} \cdot S\left[L \cdot F, i, K, \frac{M}{P}\right] - \frac{M/P}{K}\left(\frac{d\log M}{dt} - \frac{d\log P}{dt}\right) - \frac{d\log r}{dt} + \frac{d\log F}{dt} \quad . \quad (27)$$

We shall assume that saving is positive (at least initially) and linear, homogeneous in income and wealth. Thus with a constant rate of profit and a constant ratio of wealth to income the saving–income ratio will likewise remain constant.[2] To the extent that the converse is true and, in particular, that the desire to save is dissipated with increasing income and wealth, our whole problem would, of course, at least ultimately, disappear. But that converse assumption has not to my knowledge been argued to be

[1] Saving is thus identically equal not to investment but to the sum of investment and the change in the Government's real, net obligation to the private sector of the economy. The definition is analogous to that used in national-income accounts, where saving is made equal to the sum of investment and the government deficit. It should be realised that, consistent with this definition, private saving equals income (after taxes) plus government transfer payments and capital gains, including the increase in the real value of cash balances, minus consumption. This formulation, in view of our concern with price flexibility, would seem superior to that usually offered (and accepted by Tobin), where saving is identified only with the change in capital stock. That formulation is, of course, identical with ours if the real value of cash balances is assumed to be fixed. But in a model including variable prices and ruling out money illusion, it seems preferable to identify the behavioural saving function as that describing the aggregate of individual additions to net worth, whatever the form in which these additions are embodied. We join Tobin in adopting the simplifying assumption that there are no bonds and that the only stores of value are physical capital and government-issued money.

[2] This would appear consistent with the statistical and theoretical work by Kuznets, Modigliani, Duesenberry, Friedman and others. Tobin's assumption that saving is zero for some positive income (*loc. cit.*, p. 104) is not appropriate for the long-run saving function which is relevant.

currently relevant, and will not be entertained. Our saving function may be further described by the following partial derivatives:

$$S_Y > 0 \quad \ldots \quad (25.1)$$

$$S_i \gtreqless 0 \quad \text{but} \cong 0 \quad \ldots \quad (25.2)$$

$$S_K < 0 \quad \ldots \quad (25.3)$$

and

$$S_{M/P} < 0 \quad \ldots \quad (25.4)$$

With the possible exception of (25.2), in which it is assumed that the interest elasticity of saving is not sufficient to make any difference, these would not appear, in the present context at least, to be controversial. And in this context (25.2) need be disturbing only to those who stand on the original neo-classical position that the rate of interest can be expected to vary sufficiently to ensure the equality of investment demand and saving under conditions of full employment.

The form in which savings are held will be described by an asset preference function,

$$\frac{M}{P} = M(K, i, Y) \quad \ldots \quad (28)$$

the satisfaction of which defines a condition of portfolio balance. This function has the general specifications,

$$M_K > 0 \quad \ldots \quad (28.1)$$

$$M_i < 0 \quad \ldots \quad (28.2)$$

and

$$M_Y > 0 \quad \ldots \quad (28.3)$$

But we shall also endow it with the Keynesian characteristic that the demand for liquidity becomes absolute as the rate of return on investment approaches some lower limit. Thus we add,

$$M_i \underset{\rightarrow}{=} -\infty \text{ as } i \underset{\rightarrow}{=} i_1 \text{, or merely, as } i \underset{\rightarrow}{=} 0 \quad \ldots \quad (28.4)$$

since money is presumed to be a non-depreciating store of wealth, and hence

$$i \geqq i_1 \text{ or } i \geqq 0 \quad \ldots \quad (28.5)$$

Our system is now complete, and the issue can be specified as follows. Is an actual rate of growth of output equal to the solution for the warranted rate in (27) necessarily consistent (or attainable) with the full-employment conditions,

$$\begin{cases} L = L_s, \text{ the labor supply,} & (29) \\ \dfrac{d \log L}{dt} = \dfrac{d \log L_s}{dt} \quad \ldots & (29.1) \end{cases}$$

and the profit maximisation or " economic " relationship

$$F_r = i \geqq i_1 \text{ or } \geqq 0 \quad \ldots \quad (30)$$

along with the related constraints upon r and $\frac{dr}{dt}$ expressed in (19), (20) and (23)? Or we may pose the issue in perhaps more familiar guise: can we be sure of equality between the rate of change in the capital–labour ratio determined by saving and changes in labour supply and the rate of change in this ratio acceptable to entrepreneurs under the constraints of the production function and market-determined asset preferences, *i.e.*, can

$$\frac{S}{K} - \frac{M/P}{K}\left(\frac{d\log M}{dt} - \frac{d\log P}{dt}\right) - \frac{d\log L_s}{dt} = \frac{d\log r}{dt}\,? \quad . \quad (31)$$

Within the framework of an analogous set of relationships,[1] it has been argued (by Tobin), " In this model, unlike those of Harrod, Hicks and others, failure of the labor supply to grow at the rate necessary for balanced growth [constant capital–labor ratio] does not mean that growth at a slower rate is impossible." [2] The rate of profit must fall, it is conceded, as the capital–labour ratio grows, and " Portfolio balance requires, therefore, that a given increment of capital be accompanied by a greater price decline than in the case of balanced growth. But there is some rate of price decline that will preserve portfolio balance, even in the extreme case of completely inelastic labor supply."

This argument, however, is clearly invalid if the " given increment of capital " would bring the marginal net product of capital below i_1 (or below zero), thus violating condition (30). Portfolio balance can then be preserved only if the price decline reduces the increment of capital (saving) sufficiently so that $F_r \geq i_1$ (or 0).

But can the static " Pigou effect " rescue us? Must there always be *some level* of prices (above zero) for which real cash balances will be so large that the supply of saving will be reduced to whatever amount is consistent with the exogenous growth of the labour force and an *economic* capital–labour ratio? For this to be true it must be made clear that our assumption that $S_{M/P} < 0$ is not sufficient.[3] As indicated by Patinkin,[4] the reduced rate

[1] In which, however, functional saving is defined as the change in capital stock (cf., footnote 1, p. 716, above) and is dependent only upon income, thus excluding the Pigou effect, but is assumed (" crucially ") to be zero for some positive income producible under conditions of full employment (cf., footnote 2, p. 716, above).

[2] Tobin, *loc. cit.*, p. 107. The word " possible " in the text seems clearly to have been a misprint, and I have taken the liberty of changing it to " impossible " in my quotation.

[3] It is interesting to note that the Pigou effect, which we are here admitting, implies a curious type of money illusion to which illusion-hostile neo-classicists might wish to take exception. For an increase in the real value of cash balances makes society no wealthier in " real " terms, that is in goods. The illusion of greater wealth is accepted by private individuals in so far as they consider the balance sheet of only the private sector of the economy, and do not reckon that society is in some sense the debtor as well as the creditor of each dollar of government obligation.

[4] Don Patinkin, " Price Flexibility and Full Employment," as reprinted in American Economic Association, *Readings in Monetary Theory*, especially pp. 267–9, and *Money, Interest, and Prices* (Evanston, Illinois, 1956) p. 236.

of saving resulting from increased cash balances may involve an asymptotic relation in which the total possible effect is finite:

$$\frac{\partial^2 S}{\partial (M/P)^2} > 0 \text{ so that } S_{M/P} \rightarrow 0 \text{ as } M/P \rightarrow \infty \quad . \quad (25.5)$$

The economic plausibility of this argument is suggested by the observation that the acquisitive motive, as well as the desire to better oneself, to pass more on when one leaves this world than one had when one entered, are fundamental parts of the capitalist ethic. Who really finds that he is rich enough and ceases trying to get richer? But if society, no matter how great its wealth, will always strive to accumulate more, we can have no assurance that, even aside from expectational and other dynamic considerations,[1] the saving ratio can be made sufficiently low.[2]

But there is still a way out for the growth model critics. Under the restrictive conditions we have assumed, there must be a consistent solution for the warranted rate of growth as defined in (27)—if we do not require price stability. For with a constant nominal quantity of money, M, we can, from (25) and (26.1), write the increment of capital

$$\frac{dK}{dt} = S\left(Y, i, K, \frac{M}{P}\right) + \frac{M}{P} \cdot \frac{d \log P}{dt} \quad . \quad . \quad . \quad (32)$$

With falling prices $\frac{M}{P} \cdot \frac{d \log P}{dt}$ is, of course, negative and (at least mathematically) there is nothing to prevent this negative value from being indefinitely great, reducing $\frac{dK}{dt}$ to any necessary level, regardless of the supply of saving.

" Equilibrium " can thus be maintained by a perpetual fall in prices, in which the community " saves " by increasing the real value of cash balances. Paraphrasing somewhat Patinkin, we have a " dynamic Pigou theorem," [3] which suggests that there is some *rate of fall* of prices sufficient to satisfy the excess of the full employment desire to save over whatever investment demand may be forthcoming. The reader may estimate for himself the probability of finding expectations functions, let alone institutional flexibilities, which would make such a solution economically plausible.

[1] Of course, few to-day, in any event, would argue that the Pigou effect could be expected to maintain generally full employment in a dynamic system with the substantial fluctuations in demand which have characterised Western economies.

[2] It has been argued that underlying the portfolio balance equation is the desire of individuals (and the community) to split increments of wealth as between physical and monetary assets in order to minimise risk (Tobin, pp. 106–7). This would suggest that increments of wealth in the form of cash balances would increase the demand for physical capital, although its expected return were not thereby improved. But it can also be argued that as wealth increases, in line with the saving motives discussed above, its marginal utility approaches a positive asymptote and the hedging incentive would disappear as marginal utility became constant.

[3] Cf., Patinkin's *static* " Pigou theorem " in " Price Flexibility and Full Employment," p. 271.

Our system has been endowed explicitly with the neo-classical complements of variable factor proportions, flexible prices, cash-balance effects and a *fixed* linear, homogeneous production function (thus ruling out the employment of capital-using innovations like a *Deus ex machina* to set the plot straight). By way of summary, we shall describe the operation of this system when confronted with a rate of growth in the labour supply (ultimately Harrod's " natural rate of growth ") less than the " proper " full-employment rate warranted by the supply of saving. And by way of simplification of exposition we shall consider the case (suggested by Tobin) where the supply of labour is " completely inelastic . . . with respect to the real wage and with respect to time."

Since the rate of saving is (by hypothesis) positive, the ratio of capital to labour must increase continuously and the rate of profit must fall continuously. As the rate of profit falls the community becomes disposed to take larger and larger proportions of increments of wealth in the form of money. With a fixed stock of money, successive increments of wealth will then require successive declines in the level of prices. But as the rate of profit approaches the value of i at which M_i approaches minus infinity we find the community approaching a situation where no further increase in the stock of capital and decline in the rate of profit is consistent with portfolio balance, regardless of the decline in the price level (or alternately, increase in the quantity of money). The rate of profit cannot (in equilibrium) fall below the point of infinite elasticity of the demand for money because the community stops accepting further increases in capital (which is what lowers the value of i) as i reaches that lower limit. But this means that positive saving can take place only in the form of the increased cash balances stemming from falling prices. And it is only thus that the relatively too large (positive) warranted rate of growth is reducible to equality with the natural rate.

There is no assurance that such a solution, of perpetually falling prices, would prove dynamically stable when we admit the role of expectations. For price declines generating expectations of further price declines would increase the relative attractiveness of money as compared to physical capital, and might leave no point of equilibrium as long as there were physical capital of which individuals might dispose. I shall not attempt to explore further the difficulties along these lines, but, in any event, it is on this solution of perpetually *falling* prices—a " dynamic Pigou theorem "—that a rejection of the *possibility* of the growth model problems would have to rest.

IV. Conclusion

The implications of recent models of economic growth and fluctuation of the Harrod–Domar–Hicks variety have been challenged as the consequence of arbitrary assumptions of rigid technological relationships and/or rigid price relationships. This challenge is unfounded.

For the Harrod–Domar–Hicks models require no more in the way of a production function than most of us would be willing to grant as reasonable. Specifically, they do require a schedule of *net* marginal productivity of capital declining in such a way that there is a limit to the capital–labour (or capital–output) ratio which is economically feasible. This limit may be reached at the point where the marginal efficiency of investment equals the rate of interest set by the Keynesian liquidity trap. It may even be reached only at the point where the marginal net product of capital is zero (and the marginal efficiency of investment also zero if expectations are founded on reality). But limit there must be.

And if there must be an *upper* limit to the capital–output ratio, there must, for any saving ratio, be a *lower* limit to the rate of growth of output (or labour) which will be consistent with the saving forthcoming. This minimum " required " rate of growth can then be reduced only to the extent the saving ratio can be reduced. If the saving ratio will not adjust automatically, via interest-rate changes or " Pigou effects," to whatever value is consistent with whatever rate of growth of output obtains, then there remains some minimum " warranted," " equilibrium " or " full-employment " rate of growth. This rate of growth is thus determined jointly by the upper limit to the automatic, free adjustment of the capital–output ratio and the lower limit to the automatic free adjustment of the saving ratio. If we do not obtain this rate of growth we are in some kind of trouble—an underemployment trouble which the models merely seek to explain, not create.

We are not always in this kind of trouble. We may not always face a problem of capital–output ratios and saving ratios determined by free economic forces being inconsistent with underlying determinants of economic growth such as population and the development of additional natural resources. The problem may become remote for substantial periods of time because of various social or governmental pressures (intended or unintended) upon these ratios. But whether or not the problem is at any moment of time crying for solution, it does exist. And in view of the historical record of cyclical instability, uneven growth and recurring periods of unemployment in the (private-profit-motivated) capitalistic economies we have known, the problem seems important. It is perhaps a mark of the technological backwardness of economic theory that the " H–D–H dynamic " arrived so late. It will certainly (in the view of this observer) be a mistake to hasten to discard it.

ROBERT EISNER

Northwestern University.
Evanston.

PART II

FISCAL AND MONETARY POLICY AND BUDGET DEFICITS

[14]

Fiscal and Monetary Policy Reconsidered

By ROBERT EISNER*

Does the 1968–69 period of continued inflation in the U.S. economy in the face of higher tax rates and a huge swing from budget deficit to surplus prove that fiscal policy is impotent? One-third of a century after Keynes' *General Theory* are we to return to the policy prescriptions of a crude—or sophisticated—quantity theory of money? Is salvation yet to be found in a restrictive monetary policy which has sharply reduced the rate of growth of the money supply to some 3 percent per annum, seen bank prime rates rise to 8-1/2 percent, rates on top corporate bonds to over 8 percent, and average mortgage yields to 7-3/4 percent?[1] All this coincides with relatively full employment—a seasonally adjusted unemployment rate of 3.6 percent in June 1969—and, after over a year of the 10 percent income tax surcharge and perhaps nine months of tight money, accelerating price inflation now approaching an annual rate of 6 or 7 percent.

We shall argue in this paper that contemporary economic theory implies severe limitations in the effectiveness of both tax policy and monetary policy in curbing an inflation brought about by high government expenditures, such as are typically related to war. In so doing, we shall review the balanced budget theorem in light of the permanent income hypothesis. We shall also review monetary theory in terms of interaction of wealth and liquidity factors in current demand.

I. *Weakness of Compensatory Tax Policy*

The balanced budget theorem indicated that, with appropriate *ceteris paribus* assumptions, an increase in government expenditures for goods and services matched by a corresponding increase in tax revenues will under certain circumstances imply an increase in the new equilibrium level of national income equal to the increase in government expenditures (and taxes). A ready implication of the theorem is that an increase in government expenditures at full employment would have to be matched by a somewhat greater than equivalent increase in tax revenues, or a tightening of monetary policy, if inflation is to be avoided. Conversely, of course, to maintain full employment in the face of a fall in government demand for goods and services, there must be a greater than equivalent reduction in tax revenues and/or an easing of monetary policy. Applying a very simple example of the balanced budget relation to the problem of maintaining aggregate demand constant, since the multiplier effect of an increase in government expenditures for goods and services is $1/1-b$ while that of an increase in taxes is $-b/1-b$, the increase in taxes necessary to counterbalance a one dollar increase in government expenditures must be $1/b$, where b is, of course, the marginal propensity to consume.

Inflationary ills of the last several years in the U.S. economy are, consistent with the analysis above, frequently traced to the major escalation of Vietnam war expendi-

* Professor of economics, Northwestern University, and research associate, National Bureau of Economic Research. The author is most grateful for comments by the Editor, Frank Brechling, Otto Eckstein, Walter D. Fisher, Milton Friedman, Sherman J. Maisel, and Charles L. Schultze on an earlier draft of this paper. They are, of course, all absolved of responsibility for any of the current version with which they are in disagreement.

[1] The Federal Reserve Bank of New York reported in August 1969, "... While there are suggestions of slowing in some sectors of the economy, there is little evidence that financial restraint has as yet sufficiently dampened the excessive pace of economic activity." [11, p. 155]

tures beginning in 1965, unmatched by a reasonably prompt tax rise. Over the years from 1965 to 1968, indeed, Federal expenditures for national defense rose from $50.1 billion to $60.6 billion to $72.4 billion to $78.9 billion, or from 8.6 percent of 1965 Gross National Product (*GNP*) to 9.2 percent of an already inflated 1968 *GNP*. The surcharge of 1968 is estimated to have amounted to somewhat more than $6 billion in personal income taxes[2] and probably came to another $4 billion in increased corporate income taxes plus a few billion more in the accompanying extension of certain excise rates. Operating on the apparent assumption that much of the increase in defense expenditures had already been absorbed in the real and inflationary growth of the economy, some observers ascribed the failure of the tax increases of 1968 to curb further inflation to a premature move by the Federal Reserve System to easy money, which counteracted what would otherwise have proved an effective, if belated, anti-inflationary fiscal policy. It is the thesis of this paper that the tax surcharge should never, on basic theoretical grounds, have been considered an effective anti-inflationary device and that, given a sufficiently excessive rate of government spending, there is little that any meaningful monetary policy can do to stop inflation.

The basic economic error of those who saw in the 10 percent income tax surcharge an adequate measure against inflation may be charged to failure to take into account the implications of the permanent income hypothesis, both for consumption and, in correlative fashion, for business investment. Dealing in terms of equilibrium or permanent income, an increase in tax withdrawals of some ten or eleven billion dollars per year may be expected to have a very substantial depressant effect on aggregate demand, in the order of perhaps $8 billion on consumption alone. But the tax increase legislated in the surcharge did not represent a corresponding reduction in *permanent* after-tax income. It did clearly represent a reduction, in itself, in *current* or measured after-tax income for roughly a twelve month period. Before we can make any meaningful predictions of the effect of this on consumption, we must note its relation to permanent income, or more precisely, to a fully specified consumption function.

To do so, let us invoke a simplified version of the Modigliani-Brumberg formulation [7] and write consumption of any period as

$$C = C(Y, Y^e, W), \tag{1}$$

where Y is current income, Y^e some appropriately weighted and discounted average of expected future incomes, and W is initial wealth. For the average individual, with a number of years of income-earning and probably a somewhat larger number of years of life in prospect and, frequently, some substantial body of wealth already accumulated, current income is the least important argument of this function. The notion that current income has much at all to do with current consumption is probably rooted in two confusions, one theoretical and the other empirical. The theoretical confusion involves the tendency to carry over reduced forms of a system of equilibrium relations to cyclical and dynamic problems where they do not apply. Thus, if we were to compare two states, for an individual household or for an economy, in which expected income and assets were in a fixed and equilibrium relation to current income, we should properly expect consumption in these two states to differ by a very high proportion of the differences in current income. But there is no good reason to think that the two states of comparison, as an economy before and after surtax, should involve such an equilibrium relation among the relevant variables. And the complementary error in empirical analysis is to infer that because in some sets of data there is a fairly high "marginal propensity to consume" out of current income, there is any stable relation between consumption and current income that is not crucially dependent upon the relation involving current income and the other, omitted variables in the consumption function. This may be seen readily by examining the marginal propen-

[2] [10, p. 463].

sity to consume out of current income, derived from (1), which may be written:

$$\frac{dC}{dY} = \frac{\partial C}{\partial Y} + \left(\frac{\partial C}{\partial Y^e}\cdot\frac{dY^e}{dY}\right) + \left(\frac{\partial C}{\partial W}\cdot\frac{dW}{dY}\right). \tag{1.1}$$

The main point to be gleaned from (1.1) and the most casual empiricism is that the *partial* derivative of consumption with respect to current income, $\partial C/\partial Y$, even for income measured over a period as long as a year, is likely to be very small. Indeed, in the simplest Modigliani-Brumberg case, for a not atypical household with, say, 25 years of anticipated future existence, aside from discounting factors, it would be .04. Bringing in a positive rate of time discount would certainly increase this *mpc* above .04, but it may still be seen as likely to be very low. If a household's assets and expected income are unaffected, we can expect little in the way of change in consumption from a temporary reduction in income brought on by an increase in tax rates.

Yet, it is precisely this issue that has been largely ignored in discussions of likely effectiveness of the 1968–69 surcharge as a counterbalance to escalated Vietnam war expenditures. For the latter were very substantially a direct contribution to the domestic demand for goods and services. The tax increase would offset this demand via its indirect effect on consumption and investment demand. But its initial effect on consumption, we may note in (1.1), is likely to be very small. First, the contribution of the last term may reasonably be expected to be zero, on the ground that assets held by households should be no more after the imposition of the tax than before. In fact, if anything, the role of the last term turned out to be perverse, as the concurrent declines in interest rates entailed higher prices for outstanding bonds and equities. The influence of the second term may reasonably have been expected to be small, insofar as it applies to the direct or initial effect of taxes, if only because the tax increase was widely advertised as temporary, scheduled to end in little more than one year. Indeed, even apart from the legal status of the tax as temporary, individuals would hardly be expected quickly to adjust their long-run future income expectations in response to a tax change of this sort. The change in consumption due to a change in expected future income should not therefore have been foreseen as large. We are thus left with the small direct effect of the change in current after-tax income as the major component of what initial anti-inflationary impact on consumption might reasonably have been expected from the tax surcharge. Is it really any wonder that consumption continued to rise after the imposition of the surtax in 1968, while personal saving, the difference between current or measured after-tax income and consumption, dropped precipitously, from almost 7.5 percent of disposable income in 1967 and the first half of 1968, to 6.6 percent in the final half of 1968, and 6.1 percent in the first quarter of 1969?[3]

As all students of multiplier theory know, however, each initial "injection" of purchasing power generates further demand as secondary income recipients excercise their propensities to consume. While perceptive income recipients might reckon the induced changes in income which they experience as no more permanent than the original tax change itself, it is probably more likely that they will fail to distinguish tax-induced changes in income from changes unrelated to taxes. The propensity to consume which

[3] [10, p. 467]. It should be recognized that the Modigliani and Friedman models relate directly to the consumption of services and not to consumer expenditures, which include investment in consumer durables. A small change in the demand for consumer services might conceivably generate an accelerator effect entailing more substantial investment (or disinvestment) in the consumer goods which would provide these services. There may well be some magnification of the role of income tax changes along these lines. It may appear doubtful, however, that a small short-run change in the demand for consumer services would generate any great investment in the durable goods which would provide services for a long time. The arguments in favor of a permanent income theory for business investment [2] may reasonably apply also to consumer investment.

we may wish to apply, while still not an *mpc* out of permanent income, or one reflecting equilibrium relations of current income to wealth and expected future incomes, may hence perhaps be higher than that out of the initial tax-created change in after-tax income.

Modifying one of the formulations of William Salant [9] in his treatment of the balanced budget theorem, we note that the relative change in income resulting from the increase in a tax proportionate to income may be written

$$(2) \qquad \frac{Y_2 - Y_1}{Y_1} = - \frac{b_i(t_2 - t_1)}{1 - b_s(1 - t_2)},$$

where b_i is the marginal propensity to consume out of the initial, tax-generated change in disposable income, b_s is the marginal propensity to consume out of the secondary or subsequent rounds of changes in disposable income, t_1 and t_2 are the tax rates and Y_1 and Y_2 the income equilibria, before and after the tax rate changes, respectively. While somewhat inappropriately applying this equilibrium relation to the issue at hand, we may still recognize b_i as very small. If then, for example,[4] $b_i = .1$, $b_s = .5$, $t_1 = .18$ and $t_2 = .198$, the relative depressant effect of the surcharge on income would be

$$(2.1) \qquad \frac{Y_2 - Y_1}{Y_1} = \frac{.1(.198 - .18)}{1 - .5(1 - .198)} \cong .003$$

or three-tenths of one percent—less than \$3 billion, even at our current inflated rate of *GNP*.

If the predictable restraining effect of the surcharge on consumption should have been small, it should have been smaller still on business investment. Some conventional wisdom might have argued that the surcharge on corporate income should have made business investment less profitable and hence reduce it. I have on a number of previous occasions argued against this view.[5] The major aggregative effect of profits on investment must relate to the expected profitability or marginal efficiency of investment. This surely involves expectations of a long-run future or "permanent" income or output and demand.[6] The momentary ripple in corporate profits after taxes should and did have little effect on business investment demand. And since the impact of the surcharge on consumption was negligible, as we have noted, little or no acceleration effect of the surcharge on investment was to be found either. To some extent, as business endeavors to smooth production, inventory investment might even have been expected to compensate for slight short-run fluctuations in consumption.[7]

Was there hence nothing that fiscal policy could have done to curb inflation? This does not follow, but the political constraints accepted by otherwise sophisticated advocates of fiscal policy in the economics profession led them to ignore or even oppose the possible fiscal measures which would have brought a speedy end to inflation. By doing so, they curiously left the field on the one hand to conservative opponents of government social programs and, on the other, to the current "I-told-you-so" band of monetary enthusiasts. For there were those insisting, as the surcharge was being debated, that they would support an increased tax rate only if it were accompanied by reduced government expenditures. To some others mesmerized by simplistic application of the lessons of Economics/1—before the permanent income theory took hold—this insistence seemed to contain the elements of heresy and blackmail. If the surcharge were set at an appropriate level, why have a reduction of government expenditures *in addition*? Would this not be "overkill?" Indeed, fears of "overkill" apparently swept enough of the fiscal-minded economic community in the waning months of the Johnson Administration for the Federal Reserve Board to be

[4] Basing figures other than b_i very roughly on equations (A.1) to (A.5) and on (A.34) in Fromm and Taubman [6, pp. 126–27 and p. 133].

[5] In [1], for example.

[6] See [2].

[7] The corporate tax surcharge may actually also stimulate business capital expenditures! Current investment entails current start-up costs and additional depreciation charges which are balanced against the expectation of added future income. Higher current tax rates which are not expected to persist would encourage current investment and charges against current highly taxed income in the expectation of future income subject to lower rates of taxation.

induced to ease monetary restraints shortly after the enactment of the surcharge in 1968.

Of course, as it turned out, the ceiling on Federal expenditures proved decidedly porous. It was inapplicable, to begin with, to the original source of inflationary pressure, expenditures for Vietnam. What with other "loopholes," Federal expenditures for goods and services continued to creep up all through 1968 and into 1969. (And state and local government expenditures increased at a faster rate.) Inflation therefore continued, partly as the lagged response to, and projection of, pressures and movements begun earlier, partly because government expenditures continued to increase, and in considerable part because the tax increase did little, and should have been expected to do little, to reduce private demand.

There was of course one fiscal measure which might have been expected to do the trick: a real and substantial reduction in the war and other defense spending which had contributed to the inflation in the first place.[8] There were a considerable number of economists who advocated this, and who went a step further, arguing that rejection of the surcharge would help force the hand of the Administration in the direction of reversing the prevailing escalation of the war. This was, of course, a political judgment, but not an implausible one to many of us then, and certainly not now in retrospect, in view of the pressures which were at the time leading President Johnson to proclaim a change in policy and his own withdrawal from the forthcoming presidential race. It may also be well to note that war and defense demand are likely to be more inflationary, dollar for dollar, than other components of aggregate demand. The nature of procurement practices and the psychological aura of necessity that accompanies military purchasing have undoubtedly led to acquisition of military goods at particularly inflated prices. Major military expenditures then have the effect of raising prices throughout the economy in the competitive bid for factors and materials fueled by firms with little pressure to keep down costs.

But the path of ending the war and/or drastically cutting military expenditures was not the one followed. Prices continued to rise, apparently at an accelerating rate! And with the failure of an improperly conceived fiscal policy has come a growing disenchantment with fiscal policy in general and new strength for the notion that it is money which really matters. We are now told that, if only the quantity of money can be kept from growing immoderately, inflationary forces will, with due lags, subside. This would occur, it is implied, regardless of fiscal policy, that is, regardless of the rate of Federal expenditures and, for that matter, taxation. Having noted the ineffectiveness of the tax surcharge in checking inflation, we have now to demonstrate that tight money, or a tight rein on the money supply in the face of substantial continued inflationary pressure from government expenditures, will be similarly ineffective.

II. *Inadequacy of Monetary Policy*

Let us elucidate the theoretical relations by constructing a simple model in which aggregate demand is the sum of government and private demand, and private demand is in turn a function of current after-tax income, expected future after-tax income, the rate of interest and privately held assets, including the real stock of money. The nominal stock of money may be taken, for simplicity, to be entirely Treasury currency; that is, an obligation of the government to the private sector of the economy, and a parameter to be fixed by the monetary authority. The demand for money will be taken as a function of the rate of interest, output, and assets. Income, assets and demand and its components are real. These

[8] It is curious that so many arguing for reductions in Federal spending have until very recently treated military expenditures as sacrosanct and concentrated their fire on nonmilitary or domestic programs. Yet in 1968, for example, those wishing to cut nonmilitary Federal expenditures for goods and services—and it is spending for goods and services which has a direct, full effect on aggregate demand—had only $21.1 billion at which to whittle away, while National Defense expenditures were $78.9 billion, almost four times as much. We may hence stress, on the basis of plain arithmetic, questions of priorities aside, that meaningful cuts in the direct Federal contribution to inflationary demand would have to involve cuts in war and defense spending.

relations and the conventional partial derivatives may be conveniently written as follows:

(3) Private Commodity Demand
$C \quad = C(Y, Y^e, i, A, M)$
where $0 < C_Y, C_{Y^e}, C_A, C_M < 1, \quad -\infty > C_i > 0$

(4) Real Money Demand
$M^D = M^D(X, i, A)$
where $M_X > 0, \; M_i < 0, \; M_A > 0$

(5) Output Equilibrium
$X \quad = C + G$

(6) Money Market Equilibrium
$M \quad = M^D$

(7) Money—Price Identity
$M \quad = Q/P$

C = the sum of consumption and investment demand
Y = current income after taxes
Y^e = an appropriately weighted average of expected future income after taxes
i = the rate of interest or rate of time discount
A = the net real value of nonmonetary assets held by the private sector
M = real cash balances held by the private sector
M^D = real cash balances demanded by the private sector
X = output = income = Y + taxes
G = government demand for goods and services
Q = the nominal quantity of money
P = the commodity price index[9]

The model presented in equations (3)–(7) would appear to embody the essential considerations and parametric assumptions of fiscal and monetary enthusiasts alike. Yet, given this model, the limitations of monetary policy and the speciousness of the developing notion that *only* money matters may be made readily apparent.

In our model, the nominal quantity of money, Q, and the real rate of government demand for goods and services, G, are given. Let us then first ascertain whether an increase in government demand, measured by a corresponding increase in government expenditures for goods and services can be offset by maintenance of a constant stock of money. To further simplify the exposition, we will assume initially that the increase in government expenditures is unmatched by an increase in tax revenues, although more generally we might merely assume initially that the increase in government expenditures is less than fully matched by an increase in tax revenues. Such deficit-financed government expenditures must imply an increase in the quantity of money, Q, an increase in interest-bearing Treasury obligations, or both. Let us assume that the deficit financing is covered by direct borrowing from the public so that the quantity of money remains constant while private holdings of interest-bearing Treasury obligations increase. If we further assume full employment, there can be no increase in output, X, which means that the new equilibrium must involve a lower level of private commodity demand, C. But with tax revenues unchanged, an unchanged full employment level of output implies that current real income after taxes, Y, must also be unchanged. There is no a priori reason to assume any change in expected income, Y^e. Hence, this means that the reduction in private commodity demand must be associated with changes in the rate of interest, i, the real value of nonmonetary assets, A, or real cash balances, M.

Now, as long as the government budget deficit persists, unless prices or interest rates rise, A must rise as a consequence of the increase in interest-bearing Treasury obligations held by the private sector.[10] As indicated in (3), this in itself would raise commodity demand. It follows that the reduced commodity demand required by the new equilibrium would have to be associated with an increase in the rate of interest, i, which would also serve to lower A, and/or a reduction in M brought about by an increase in the level of prices. This last would further

[9] It will be noted below that in this system of five equations which is not explicitly closed, C, i, M, M^D, and P are endogenous. Y, Y^e, X, G, and Q are exogenous, either fixed or determined by relations not set forth above. A is partly exogenous and partly dependent on other variables in the system.

[10] The argument advanced in some quarters that Treasury borrowing may only prove a substitute for business or other private borrowing is irrelevant in that we are concerned here with the ***net*** value of nonmonetary assets held by the private sector. We join Patinkin [8], for example, and others in ruling out distribution effects of assets and liabilities so that if Paul is given an I.O.U. by Peter, thus increasing Paul's net assets but decreasing Peter's by an equal amount, we assume no resultant change in private commodity demand.

serve to reduce or even reverse the increase in A.

If the reduction in private commodity demand is associated with an increase in prices which reduces M and, possibly A as well, our point has already been demonstrated. The increase in government expenditures, with the nominal quantity of money kept constant, has forced a new equilibrium level of prices higher than the old. But the result would be the same even if no increase in prices is generated directly in the commodity demand equation. For the increase in the rate of interest, which may be looked at from the securities side as resulting from the increase in supply of Treasury interest-bearing obligations, or from the real side as implicit in the bidding of resources away from private investment to production for government, must have its consequences, in any event, in the money market. If the increase in the rate of interest is sufficient to prevent the value of nonmonetary assets from rising, it is immediately clear from (4) that the real demand for money must be less. This means that, to satisfy (6), in accordance with the constraint shown in (7), the real supply of money, M, must be reduced by an increase in prices, P. If the value of nonmonetary assets has risen because the net increase in Treasury obligations corresponding to the budget deficit outweighs losses in capital values due to higher interest rates, it would still seem clear that the real demand for money must fall. To claim otherwise would be to argue that the higher rate of interest necessary to induce investors to move from money to bonds had somehow left them content to hold more money than initially. Recognizing the interdependence of markets, it would be to argue that the increase in interest rates necessary to reduce commodity demand despite the increase in the net value of assets would not be sufficient to reduce the real demand for money, implying a shift from commodities to money as interest rates and bond holdings rise. Indeed, as will be seen below, this would be to to argue that a deficit-financed increase in government expenditures can be deflationary while the same increase in government expenditures would be inflationary if fully supported by increased taxes.

The general argument which we have just developed follows through on the assumption that the increase in government demand is fully financed by taxes. If the increased taxes are taken to be temporary, it is clear that since, according to (3), $C_Y<1$, an increase in tax withdrawals equivalent to the increase in government expenditures does not reduce private commodity demand by as much as government demand has increased. To preserve output equilibrium (5), therefore, with no increase in Treasury interest-bearing obligations which would raise A, there must be an increase in the rate of interest, i, or a decrease in real cash balances, M. With the nominal quantity of money, Q, kept constant, real cash balances can be reduced only by an increase in the price level. And if we were to argue that the necessary reduction in private commodity demand could be accomplished entirely by an increase in the rate of interest, along with a concomitant reduction in the value of assets, we would still be faced with repercussions in the money market. Real money demand would now be reduced by both interest and asset effects, as indicated in (4), and to preserve the equilibrium condition (6), real cash balances would have to be reduced, in accordance with (7), by an increase in the price level.[11]

III. *Conclusion*

It should thus be clear that an increase in government demand for goods and services will prove inflationary with an equivalent increase in current tax revenues and the prevention of growth in the money supply.[12]

[11] It may be added that even if the tax increase is expected to be permanent we may have inflationary pressure in the instance above. For unless the sum of the first two derivatives in (1.1), that is, the marginal propensity to consume out of current and expected future income, is equal to or greater than unity, hardly generally likely in view of the role of assets, an increase in government expenditures matched by a permanent increase in tax revenues will require a downward shift in investment demand, or a higher price level, to restore equilibrium.

[12] How inflationary—that is, magnitudes as opposed to mere directions of effects— is not indicated by the

It is of course conceivable that a greater than equivalent increase in tax revenues and an actual reduction of the money supply might be sufficient to offset the increase in government demand. But as I have argued elsewhere [3], monetary measures are likely ultimately to be as limited in their impact in combating inflation as they have long been recognized to be limited in combating a deep depression. There may well be a "liquidity leak" of money substitutes, in the face of an attempt to stifle inflation by traditional monetary controls, akin to the liquidity trap facing those who would use monetary policy to combat a depression.[13] Yet we must note that conventional counter-cyclical fiscal policy will also prove severely limited precisely to the extent that it is recognized as counter-cyclical. For the permanent income theory should have forewarned us that the usual attempts to manipulate demand by varying taxes on income, as with the tax surcharge, would require fluctuations in tax rates far beyond those usually considered. These, in turn, given our difficulty in knowing precisely the magnitude as well as the timing of consequences of tax rate alterations, might well lead to less rather than more stability.[14]

All this should not leave matters entirely hopeless, at least in terms of fiscal policy. For one thing, as we have stressed, variation in government expenditures for goods and services remains a direct and highly potent factor, for good or for evil. Public works or, more generally, government investment and consumption, reemerge in their early role as prime weapons in the arsenal against depression and take on analogous importance in any struggle against inflation. If the government begins to contribute to inflation by rapidly escalating expenditures for a war such as in Vietnam, the indicated fiscal measures would include: 1) cut government expenditures for nonmilitary goods and services (to the extent this is feasible), as conservatives are generally quick to advocate; 2) cut other military expenditures—if we are to spend more in fighting a current war, reduce investment in strategic weapons for some future war; 3) recognizing the true, unavoidable cost to the economy of a Vietnam-type escalation, nip it in the bud, and the inflation along with it.

Further, however, there are other fiscal measures which, at the cost of varying degrees of distortion in the economy, might alter private demand sufficiently. On consumption, for example, there might be a set of very substantial sales taxes and/or subsidies which would be known to vary over time. Thus, there might be a very high excise tax attached to certain consumer goods and services, particularly those more easily postponable or for other reasons with a high elasticity of demand, with clear and widely publicized information that such rates would be changed as economic conditions change. One might introduce a 50 percent additional tax for buying a new automobile now with the suggestion that such tax would be removed a year from now and even that it

formal analysis of this paper. Conceivably, if the absolute values of C_i and C_M or, better, the elasticities of commodity demand with respect to the rate of interest and real cash balances, are very large, there need be little change in the rate of interest or in the price level in order to reduce commodity demand in (3) by the amount of increased government expenditures. Then further, if the absolute value of M_i, or the interest elasticity of the real demand for money, is very low, the small change in the rate of interest emanating from (3) would require little in the way of increases in the price level to reduce the supply of money and restore equilibrium in the money market. If commodity demand were perfectly interest-elastic—a kind of "investment trap"—no change in prices would be involved but commodity demand itself would be indeterminate over the range of perfect elasticity. Similarly if we have zero elasticity of the demand for money, depending on asset effects, there might be no price movement necessary to restore equilibrium. In the obviously realistic intermediate cases, relative potency of fiscal and monetary policies may then be seen to hinge on relative values of the interest and asset elasticities of the demands for commodities and the demand for money. Monetary enthusiasts must, implicitly or explicitly, see the commodity demand elasticities as high and the money demand elasticities, at least that with respect to the interest rate, as low.

[13] In addition, we should be aware that higher costs of money, like sales and excise taxes and, in the long run, business income taxes as well, tend to raise prices by raising costs of production.

[14] See the fine discussion of this matter by Milton Friedman [5].

might be replaced with a 20 percent subsidy. Indeed, promised future subsidies might be used generously as a desirable alternative to current excise taxes which would combat inflation by actually raising current prices to the ultimate consumer. Better still, there might be substantial delayed tax or interest benefits made available on nonnegotiable Treasury saving bonds.

Similar measures directed at inter-temporal substitution may also be applied to investment. Thus, a system of investment tax credits and investment allowances or subsidies with particularly high marginal impact, for example, in the order of 25 percent on investment above 80 percent of a past average rather than 7 percent on all investment, and also known to be variable over time, should have some very substantial effect on this component of private demand. A business firm might well delay purchase of equipment or construction during an inflationary situation in which it would have to pay an added tax of 25 percent on the investment while anticipating that the same investment a year or two from now would have no tax or perhaps a subsidy of 25 percent.

It would seem important for those attempting to manage the economy to learn some of these lessons, at least implicit in recent economic theory, before, for want of correct analysis and prescriptions, the "dismal science" falls into dismal repute, and our fates are turned back to know-nothings, within or without the profession.

References

1. R. Eisner, "Capital Expenditures, Profits and the Acceleration Principle," in *Models of Income Determination*, Nat. Bur. Econ. Res., Stud. In Income and Wealth, Vol. 28, Princeton 1964.
2. ———, "A Permanent Income Theory for Investment: Some Empirical Explorations," *Amer. Econ. Rev.*, June 1967, *57*, 363–90.
3. ———, "Factors Affecting the Level of Interest Rates: Part II" (orginally "The Liquidity Trap and the Liquidity Leak") in *Conference on Savings and Residential Financing, 1968 Proceedings of United States Savings and Loan League*, Chicago 1968, pp. 28–40.
4. M. Friedman, *A Theory of the Consumption Function*. Princeton 1957.
5. ———, "The Effects of a Full Employment Policy on Economic Stability: A Formal Analysis," in *Essays in Positive Economics*. Chicago 1953.
6. G. Fromm and P. Taubman, *Policy Simulations With An Econometric Model*. Washington 1968.
7. F. Modigliani and R. E. Brumberg, "Utility Analysis and the Consumption Function," in K. K. Kurihara, ed., *Post-Keynesian Economics*, New Brunswick 1954. Reprinted in H. R. Williams and J. D. Huffnagle, *Macroeconomic Theory: Selected Readings*. New York 1969.
8. D. Patinkin, *Money, Interest, and Prices*, 2nd ed., New York 1965.
9. William A. Salant, "Taxes, Income Determination, and the Balanced Budget Theorem," *Rev. Econ. Statist.*, May 1957, *39*, 152–61, reprinted in R. A. Gordon and L. R. Klein, eds., *Readings in Business Cycles*, Homewood 1965.
10. *Federal Reserve Bulletin*, "Consumption and Saving Patterns Since Mid-1968." Washington, June 1969.
11. *Monthly Review*, Federal Reserve Bank of New York, August 1969.

[15]

What Went Wrong?

Robert Eisner

Northwestern University and National Bureau of Economic Research

Failure to stop war-induced inflation is traced to: (1) higher tax rates inducing higher government expenditures; (2) limitations of countercyclical tax changes predictable from the permanent-income hypothesis; (3) perverse effects of certain tax changes on investment demand; (4) tax increases, especially but not exclusively of the excise variety, which raise prices by reducing supply; (5) a liquidity leak, analogous to the liquidity trap, which sharply limits the impact of tight money; (6) inelastic interest-rate expectations which limit real long-term movements, while permanent changes in long rates rule out intertemporal substitution effects; (7) the cost element in higher interest charges, which raises supply prices; (8) possibly decreasing elasticity of lower demand in an imperfectly competitive world; and (9) lags which may be variable as well as long.

1. Introduction

We all know those standard items of instruction in modern economics: to fight a recession, spend more, tax less, and increase the money supply; to stop inflation, reduce government spending, raise the rate of taxation, and tighten money! In the light of recent developments—in the economy and in economic theory—are these rules adequate?

Good Keynesians have long argued that monetary actions might be limited in their aggregative effectiveness. They warned that the proximity of the liquidity trap in depression[1] would cause expansionary mone-

An earlier version of this paper was presented to the Midwest Economic Association meetings, April 1970, in Detroit. The author is indebted for helpful comments to Thomas F. Cargill, who discussed the paper at those meetings, to Harry G. Johnson, and to Keith R. McLaren.

[1] Contrary to the presumption of some who have looked for data to confirm or deny the existence of a liquidity trap, Keynes did not argue that the historical record will exhibit one. He wrote, rather (1936, p. 207): "There is the possibility . . . that, after the rate of interest has fallen to a certain level, liquidity-preference may become virtually absolute in the sense that almost everyone prefers cash to holding a debt

tary policy to resemble pushing on a string, but the conventional wisdom continued to attribute potency to money as a weapon against inflation.

As to fiscal advice, we have been bedeviled by popular hang-ups on debt burdens; spending more and taxing less would increase the federal debt, but we were ready within the profession (for example, Domar 1944 and Lerner 1948) to explain away all the false analogies and false burdens, however little the political leaders whom we advised dared reveal Truth to the uninitiated. Some troublesome arguments developed, particularly those suggesting that a larger federal debt would imply lower private saving and hence the burden on the future of a lower stock of capital (Modigliani 1961), but these were generally dismissed as second-order complications. Friedman (1948, 1953, and elsewhere) warned persistently of the limitations of human prescience, but his warnings were generally well noted and absorbed into the body of our science without widely affecting its course.

On the left, there were those, frequently on the fringe of the profession, who insisted that the basic misconception was that of government as an exogenous force that could be expected to stabilize or in any way rectify the system of which it was an integral part. But this line of objection was generally dismissed as politically motivated or unnecessarily defeatist.

And so the new economists did establish a new frontier. Having conquered the classroom from graduate level down even to some enlightened high schools and having largely swept the textbook field, they were finally able to take over at the highest levels of government. They told how to get the country moving again and were heard. Unemployment dropped as government spending (in considerable part, military spending) increased. And after some at first abortive efforts, a major tax-reduction bill was enacted. By the end of 1964, one could point with pride to our real growth rates, and unemployment was close to the announced 4 percent target.

Then came the massive escalation of the war in Vietnam. Perhaps out of miscalculation, perhaps out of political considerations which dictated a refusal to acknowledge the extent of the escalation or the costs likely to be involved, President Johnson at first rejected the economic advice that higher tax rates were necessary to curb inflation from sharply increased government expenditures for goods and services in an economy at or near full employment. (For some of the background of this, see Okun

---

which yields so low a rate of interest. In this event the monetary authority would have lost effective control over the rate of interest. But whilst this limiting case might become practically important in future, I know of no example of it hitherto. Indeed, owing to the unwillingness of most monetary authorities to deal boldly in debts of long term, there has not been much opportunity for a test."

[1970, chap. 3] and, for a somewhat more acerbic view, Eisner [1968*b*, esp. p. 15].) Eventually, the administration asked for tax increases, but the path to their enactment proved choppy and delayed. Military expenditures in particular and government expenditures in general continued to rise, and with them grew the rate of inflation. The 10 percent income tax surcharge was finally imposed by the middle of 1968 and, a year later, extended in full through the end of 1969. And despite a number of errant twists and sharp reversals of field, monetary policy moved through 1968 into what, by many meaningful measures, has been considered the tightest phase in our national history. (Keynesians may note record interest rates, while quantity theorists see a money supply which, in the face of ever increasing demand, was sharply limited for well over a year and showed no growth at all for at least six months.) Thus, we now have the denouement of the tragedy of the economists! By the end of the decade, despite the arguments of many that the surcharge would do the trick and despite the arguments of many (not necessarily identical with the first "many") that tight money would do the trick, the rate of inflation was, by at least some measures, greater than ever.

In the early thirties, an increasingly disbelieving and distrusting public was assured that "prosperity was around the corner." At the end of the sixties, economists in considerable number had joined administration spokesmen, or acted as them, in urging that the end of inflation was around the corner, although historical recollections may have made them a bit cautious in using that particular phrase. In more sophisticated terminology, explanations were couched in terms of "lags," with some acknowledgment that the lags were turning out to be somewhat longer than anticipated. As a generation before, the public was not entirely believing, and the stock of economists, among others, plummeted.

What is the problem? What (if anything) did go wrong?

2. Fiscal Pitfalls

A primary question involves the applicability of the usual *ceteris paribus* assumption in predicting the impact of changes in tax rates. In particular, is it reasonable to claim that the rate of government expenditures remains the same when tax rates are increased?

This issue may have been better perceived by politicians than by the political economists of the administration during the 1968 struggle on passage of the income tax surcharge. Noneconomist senators and congressmen then insisted upon stipulations of curtailment of government spending as a condition to the enactment of higher tax rates. A number of economists saw this as "overkill." Having fixed upon a set of increased tax rates to slow the economy, there seemed little logic in being forced to choose between no tax increase or a tax increase *and* an accompanying limitation on government expenditures.

But were the noneconomists perhaps in a broader view wiser? If a large budget deficit arises, as it did in fiscal 1968, and reaches the limits of toleration, might an increase in tax rates merely permit high or higher government expenditures without exceeding the tolerable limit on the deficit? Such an increase in tax rates, accompanied by correspondingly larger government expenditures for goods and services, would be inflationary.[2]

But even assuming that government expenditures are unaffected, what may we really expect, in the light of "the permanent-income theory," from a temporary change in income tax rates such as those of the surcharge enacted in 1968? The substantial positive magnitude usually attributed to the marginal propensity to consume out of current income is dependent upon the usual long-run relation between current income and expected income or wealth. A change in individual income tax rates designated as countercyclical—all the more so, one slated to expire in a year—should have little effect on expected income and hence little effect on current consumption. Indeed, what should have been clear here from economic theory (as suggested in Eisner 1969) was quickly confirmed after the fact by the sharp drop in personal saving in the latter half of 1968 and only a gradual and small reduction in the rate of growth of consumption.[3]

Changes in corporate (or other business) income tax rates may prove not merely ineffective but actually perverse. To the extent that they influence stock prices, as they should, they will affect aggregate demand in the right direction via the wealth arguments in the consumption function. The direction of effect on business investment may be another matter, however. Where business is influenced by imperfect capital markets, the reduction in funds currently available as a consequence of an increase in profits taxes may bring about some delay in investment. But, except where liquidity is a critical problem, one should expect business to be guided primarily by the expected profitability of investment. Aside from technological change, this should relate essentially to expected de-

[2] Something close to an explicit avowal of the connection between tax rates and government expenditures is to be found in Nixon's *Economic Report of the President* (1970): "The tax bill passed in December [1969] reduced revenues for the next fiscal year by close to $3 billion, compared to my original proposals, requiring the Administration to reduce spending plans further in order to retain a surplus" (p. 7).

[3] Personal saving as a proportion of personal income fell from 7.2 to 5.6 percent from the second to the third quarter of 1968. The average saving ratio for the six quarters before imposition of the surcharge was 7.3 percent; the average ratio for the six quarters after was 6.0 percent. Consumption grew at an annual rate of 10.5 percent from the latter half of 1967 to the first half of 1968 and continued on at an 8.5 percent rate from the first to the second half of 1968 and at 7.2 and 6.0 percent rates in the successive six-month periods of 1969.

mand for products, relative prices which would influence the desired capital-labor and capital-output ratios, and capital replacement requirements.

Given a wealth-maximization model, even a permanent change in the rate of business taxation has no unique direction of effect on business investment. By applying formulations of Jorgenson (1963), Hall and Jorgenson (1967), and Coen (1968), it can be shown that an increase in the rate of business income taxation would *raise* the rate of business investment to the extent that capital-goods prices are expected to rise and there is a high present value to each dollar of depreciation applied for tax purposes. It seems quite possible, with recent inflation and the major liberalization of tax depreciation over the last two decades, that these conditions were being met.

Further, *countercyclical* changes in business income taxes may have a perverse effect on investment. Investment is undertaken currently in expectation of after-tax profits in the future. A higher rate of business taxation that is expected to be temporary offers firms an inducement to incur tax-deductible costs now in expectation of profits later when tax rates will be lower. Capital expenditures, bringing with them short-term charges against income in the form of planning, development, start-up, interest, and depreciation costs, with expected returns over the long term, might thus have been stimulated by the corporate-profits tax surcharge of 1968. And business investment did in fact boom, reaching heights throughout 1968 and 1969.[4]

A careless assumption seems to be widespread that all increases in tax rates are deflationary in the sense of slowing price rises. In fact, efforts to restrain inflation should be directed to reducing effective demand. As was argued eloquently by Hotson (1967), changes in tax rates which raise the aggregate supply curve may reduce real demand, but precisely as a consequence of stimulating the price rise they were designed to discourage. Yet, part of the tax law of 1968 enacting the personal income and corporate income tax surcharges involved an extension of various excise taxes which were due to expire. These excise taxes were extended again in the tax law of 1969. At the beginning of 1970, there were even suggestions that the Nixon administration might ask for new excise or value-added taxes as a means of balancing the budget and hence combating inflation. And as was pointed out by Hansen (in press), income taxes, too, along with other fiscal measures which reduce real income, may raise the supply curve of labor (that is, reduce labor supply) as workers endeavor to maintain real incomes by demanding higher money wages.

[4] Nonresidential total fixed investment, at $81.6 billion in 1966 and $83.7 billion in 1967, rose to $88.8 billion in 1968 and $99.3 billion in 1969, an 11.8 percent increase the year *after* the imposition of the surcharge, which was retroactive to April 1968 for corporations.

The fault in the logic should be clear. A balanced budget will be less inflationary than one in deficit if it is balanced by lowering government expenditures for goods and services. Inflation may be checked by balancing a budget by means of those increases in tax rates which lower the money aggregate demand for goods and services. Balancing the budget by increases in tax rates which raise the money aggregate supply curve, however, will reduce real effective demand, that is, the real value of aggregate demand at the point of intersection with the aggregate supply curve, but will do this at the expense of higher prices. A reduction in real effective demand may well ultimately have an impact on prices via induced changes in demand such as may stem from application of the investment accelerator. But this is another story and indeed one not entirely different from that which one might expect from a continuing inflation without imposition of higher excise, value-added, or sales taxes. For, given a cessation of refueling from governmental inflationary action, the surge of rising prices may in any event be expected to spend itself against the ceiling imposed by limitations of real growth and, consequently, real demand (see Hicks 1950, pp. 124–35).

3. Monetary Paradoxes

The old Keynesian arguments as to the limitations of monetary policy in combating a depression are well known. The interest elasticity of consumer demand is low and not even of certain sign. The interest elasticity of investment demand, while more clearly of the right sign (negative), is also small. But there is a floor below which the rate of interest may not be driven, and a positive floor at that. Monetary policy (presumably dealing with "inside" money which does not change the net asset position of the private sector of the economy) may be viewed as operating through its effects upon the rate of interest. It can then have only a limited and very likely inadequate influence in raising aggregate demand sufficiently to end any serious recession or depression.

Flexible prices, with the nominal quantity of money at least not decreasing as rapidly as the price level, may serve as a substitute for or reinforcement of an explicitly countercyclical monetary policy. They have the possible disadvantage, however, of generating perverse expectational effects. *Lower* prices may invoke a "positive monetary effect" (Lange 1952, p. 7), but *falling* prices may well stimulate a shift from goods to money. The existence of outside money—positive, net monetary assets of the private sector of the economy—permits a cash balance effect or "Pigou effect," but this is generally recognized to be seriously limited in its practical or empirical impact, if not in concept.

Skepticism of the role of monetary policy as a counterrecessionary tool has not generally been as widely felt with regard to its anti-inflationary potency. But economists may well look with suspicion at claimed asymmetries—and with at least as much suspicion at this one as at others. Closer examination reveals limitations in the effectiveness of tight money in combating inflation which are analogous to those of easy money in ending a recession.

I have elsewhere suggested the existence of a "liquidity leak" at the upper end of the liquidity preference curve to match the "liquidity trap" at the lower end (Eisner 1968*a*, illustrated on p. 33, fig. 1). In both cases, where the curve depicting the demand for money approaches a horizontal slope at some positive rate of interest and where it intersects the vertical axis at some (also positive) finite rate of interest, the interest elasticity of the demand for money approaches or equals minus infinity. If we are dealing with a world of changing prices, our vertical axis must be explicitly denominated in *real* rates of interest, that is, the nominal rate of interest minus the expected rate of price inflation. We may then imagine our money markets ensconced in a sea of money substitutes. As the cost of money is raised by a central bank which further and further curtails the money supply, more and more money substitutes leak into the system. The money substitutes may have certain technical deficiencies and hence be more costly to produce or use. But clearly, as the cost of Treasury or bank money becomes in some sense prohibitive, Sears Roebuck, General Motors, and other large companies will resort increasingly to their own substitutes, whether credit cards, trade credit, unsecured commercial paper, certificates of deposit, or myriad other existing instruments and new ones yet unheard of. What we define as money, essentially those obligations of commercial banks called demand deposits, are after all but one very small part of a wide spectrum of assets (liabilities) which can be used for the various functions which we associate with money.[5] The obligation of any large and well-known company could serve almost as well as the obligation of a bank. If we were forced to, we could use obligations of smaller companies, known only in smaller areas. To try to constrict the economy by operating on the very narrow part of the spectrum currently defined as money is, to apply a metaphor recently used by Friedman in objecting to price controls, like attempting to constrict the volume of a large balloon by pressing in some particular spot; the balloon will bulge elsewhere.[6] It is a long, long path from the curtailment, even the total elimination, of bank money to barter.

[5] See Tobin (1968, p. 859), who refers to "some narrow category of financial assets, arbitrarily designated as 'money.' "

[6] This is not to deny that tight money may not cause some extreme dislocations in certain sectors of the economy, witness financial markets in general and housing in particular.

What is more, the same expectational problems which relate to the lower-end liquidity trap come into the upper-end liquidity leak. The higher are interest rates, and hence the lower are bond prices, the more investors and borrowers there will be with expectations that bond prices will be higher in the future. Particularly if tight money is recognized as a temporary, countercyclical phenomenon, at some floor to long-term bond prices and, hence, ceiling to long-term interest rates, the prospective capital gains to holders or buyers of bonds and prospective losses to issuers would be overwhelming and decisive.

But if real interest rates could somehow be made very high because tight money and high interest rates were expected to persist, their effect on aggregate demand would be minimized. For surely the interest elasticity of investment demand will be much lower if differences in interest rates are looked upon as permanent rather than temporary. A firm contemplating capital expenditures with expected returns over, say, a twenty-year period may postpone the investment for a year if interest rates are viewed as temporarily high (although it may be more likely that the long-term financing rather than the investment itself will be delayed). It would be much less likely to do so if the advantage of delay is eliminated by the expectation of continued high interest costs.[7]

A further problem in the use of countercyclical monetary policy relates to perverse price effects. We currently observe high money rates of interest emerging as major elements in the high costs of capital-intensive industries. As capital costs rise—and this is particularly apparent in regulated and generally capital-intensive utilities—costs of service and prices of products rise. Indeed, these higher prices contribute to further increases in costs as wage earners endeavor to compensate for a higher cost of living. The expectation of such wage increases leading to further increases in prices implies a continued high rate of expected inflation and hence contributes in turn to maintaining high money rates of interest. Similar forces can be found at work in the housing markets

[7] The expectation problem raises more profound difficulties at least implicit in the *General Theory* but largely ignored in current discussions. Keynes argued the desirability of driving down the long-term rate of interest. Recent discussions of monetary theorists have come back to the notion of eliminating the costs to the economy of artificially costly (or unnecessarily inefficient) money (see, for example, Clower 1969, Friedman 1969, and Tobin 1968). In this context, countercyclical variation of the money supply may be expected to bring about secularly higher long-term rates of interest. Increasing numbers of investors may prove wary, for example, of bonds whose prices are temporarily high because of antirecessionary measures expected soon to be replaced by a policy designed to drive bond prices down, as the phase of the cycle changes. What is more, since interest rates might normally be expected to be lower in recessions and higher in booms even without countercyclical intervention by the monetary authority, such intervention would serve to increase the variance of interest rates over the cycle. Thus, if investors are on balance risk averters, the greatest variability of bond prices introduced by countercyclical monetary activity would force payment of higher yields to compensate for the greater risk so introduced.

and indeed wherever the high cost of money intended to stop inflation is of consequence.[8] This "inflationary" aspect of tight money is a monetary analog to the cost-increasing fiscal measures discussed earlier.[9]

4. Imperfections, Expectations, and Lags

Limitations of monetary and fiscal policy are compounded by the realities of the market. One could specify a set of conditions, including downwardly rigid wage rates, whereby wages and prices would be constant up to the point of absolutely full employment, but aggregate money demand in excess of the aggregate supply price of full employment at existing wages and prices would merely result in equal proportionate increases in wages and prices. If wages and prices were then fully flexible downward to their initial level, a subsequent decrease in money aggregate demand could reduce wages and prices to this point. Beyond that, further reduction in aggregate demand would only reduce employment and output.

This picture is clearly a caricature of the economy we know, but what other clear representation justifies the faith that the battery of increases in tax rates and costs of money will have substantial and reasonably prompt restraining effects on price increases rather than on employment and output? Might there, for example, be perverse tendencies in the relation between output and prices in some industries or sectors of the economy? Business respondents argue frequently that lower output implies higher average costs and the necessity of raising prices to maintain even minimal profits.[10] This may make little sense in a perfectly competitive market, but in the world of imperfect competition and oligopoly are we so sure? May decreasing demand be associated with decreasing elasticity of the demand curves perceived by the firm? This may indeed be true in industry demand curves. The relatively small numbers of oligopolists sharing the markets in many industries may well, experiencing less and less elastic demand curves, take rising average unit costs, accentuated by higher tax and interest costs, as a meaningful clue or trigger for general price increases. May not unions reason similarly, in

[8] In housing we may note upward pressure on rents as the elasticity of demand for current housing services is low and the supply of new housing is curtailed.

[9] Higher interest rates have the further not insignificant effect of raising income to the private sector from government debt. Federal interest payments rose from $13.7 billion to $15.8 billion from fiscal 1968 to fiscal 1969 and were projected to rise to $17.8 billion in fiscal 1970, the increases due almost entirely to increased rates of interest on new Treasury issues replacing maturing obligations.

[10] Some Chicago area suburban realtors early in 1970 announced that, because of decreased sales and falling profits due to tight money, they were raising their commissions from 6 to 7 percent! Wall Street brokers have reasoned similarly in striving to increase commission charges in the face of falling transactions.

such circumstances, with regard to the derived demand for the labor of their members? May it not be in the general interest of employers and unions in oligopolistic industries to raise wages and prices if reduced demand implies a lower price elasticity of demand for the products of the industry? And indeed, one can hardly dismiss the possibility that certain reductions in aggregate demand may manifest themselves first in withdrawal from the market of purchasers with relatively higher price elasticities of demand.[11]

The Phillips curve suggests that the rates of increase of wages and consequently of prices are inverse functions of the rate of unemployment. This strand of thought may perhaps be traced back to the Marxian view that it was the reserve army of the unemployed that kept wages from rising. But despite recent rigorous exploration of possible underpinnings for the Phillips curve, it remains shiftable and uncertain and particularly influenced by the rate of expected inflation. Indeed, it has been argued (Phelps 1968, pp. 702–3; Lucas and Rapping 1969, esp. pp. 738–39) that the long-run Phillips curve appropriate for a condition of fully anticipated wage and price inflation is vertical, signifying no relation between the rate of unemployment and a fully anticipated price inflation (without money "illusion").

A common defense against the failure thus far to make a significant dent in inflation is to attribute the difficulty not to equilibrium theory but to lags in adjustment. It may be quickly conceded that lags may be long. Estimates of investment functions (Eisner 1960; Hall and Jorgenson 1967, 1969; Jorgenson and Stephenson 1967; Eisner and Nadiri 1968 and 1970; Bischoff 1969) suggest median lags of several years from changes in determinants to actual expenditures, with no good reason for assuming that lags are the same for all determinants. Current theory of the consumption function suggests, as indicated above, that substantial changes in consumption must await changes in wealth and in expected future income.

Forecasters, in and out of government, have repeatedly revised their estimates of the timing of results of anti-inflationary action. By now, enough previous forecasts of a slowing of inflation have been belied by events to breed caution in at least some administration predictions. With the GNP price deflator having risen by 2.7 percent from 1965 to 1966, by 3.2 percent from 1966 to 1967, by 4.0 percent from 1967 to 1968, and by 4.7 percent from 1968 to 1969, the Council of Economic Advisers in early 1970 must still caution, "The sharp rise of wholesale prices at the end of 1969, however, holds out the possibility that the rise of over-

[11] More traditional theorists may find this a more convenient explanation of the downward stickiness of prices. If not, they may wish to entertain the radical restructuring implicit in Galbraith's arguments for producers' (or sellers') rather than consumers' "sovereignty" (1958, 1967. and, most recently, 1970).

all prices (as measured by the GNP deflator) in early 1970 may differ little from that in late 1969."[12] After two years of supposedly anti-inflationary fiscal policy, and after well over a year of clearly anti-inflationary monetary policy, we are still looking uncertainly for evidence of even a turning point in the rate of price inflation, let alone a reduction below rates existing when anti-inflationary actions were begun. One may begin to wonder whether, if the underlying equilibrium theory can still be considered sound in itself, the length of the lags makes it relatively irrelevant in terms of effective policy.

The changing views of lags held by unsuccessful prophets may, in fact, have some foundation in the real instability of lag structures of response by the behavioral units of the economy. For, while certain elements of the lag structure are determined by relatively unchanging technological parameters, lags may vary with their economic determinants and are undoubtedly due in considerable part to the varying times accountable to dissemination of information and the adaptation of expectations on which decisions are made. Outbreak of war and an increase in government orders may change expectations overnight and set in motion almost immediate changes in prices (as in 1950, when the Korean war began) and sharp upturns in production. In some instances where autonomous changes are immediately seen as "permanent," the economy may respond extremely rapidly. In other instances where longer-run expectations of the future are slower to be affected, long lags will relate to the lengths of time necessary for relevant expectations to change. What this means is that shifts of current exogenous variables may not only have repercussions spread out over a considerable future but that it may also be very difficult to know the lag pattern when economic consequences must stem from the actions of independent forces in the economy.

5. Conclusion

All this may leave us with the sober realization that sharp and major changes in the rate of government expenditure for goods and services are likely to have effects which may not readily be counteracted, if at all, by the instruments of control ordinarily used. A $30 billion per year

[12] *Economic Report of the President* (1970, p. 58). The GNP deflator has now (May 1970) been reported to have risen at a 6.2 percent annual rate in the first quarter of 1970, the highest rate of increase since 1951, during the Korean war. The Consumer Price Index rose at an annual rate of 7.2 percent in April 1970. (The rates of increase of various price indices have of course fluctuated from month to month, but updating the figures to those available as this paper is going to press would have no appreciable effect on the argument. The September–October 1970 increase in the CPI, for example, was from 136.6 to 137.4, virtually identical in magnitude to the 133.2–144.0 rise from March to April.)

increase in defense expenditures *plus* the withdrawal from the civilian labor force of a million or more men cannot be absorbed without corresponding cost in a full employment economy. An offsetting reduction in the real demand for goods and services cannot readily be engineered if one restricts oneself to operating on the private sector of the economy with relatively indirect aggregative tools whose effectiveness at best is restricted to the relatively long term.

Offsetting action might be found in the reduction of government expenditures for goods and services elsewhere. Fairly drastic action to change intertemporal price ratios by combinations of current taxes and promised future subsidies may induce some postponement of demand for investment and consumption of particular goods and services with relatively high elasticity of demand with respect to intertemporal price ratios. Even here, however, limited mobility or transferability of resources and spillover effects may lead to somewhat less than the desired results.

Political considerations aside, the economist has only one sure answer. To avoid the inflation or other unhappy shocks to the economy from involvement in foreign wars, don't get involved!

References

Bischoff, C. W. "Hypothesis Testing and the Demand for Capital Goods." *Rev. Econ. and Statis.* 51 (August 1969): 354–68.

Clower, R. W. "Is There an Optimal Money Supply?" Paper presented to joint meetings of the American Finance Association and the Econometric Society, New York, December 1969.

Coen, R. M. "Effects of Tax Policy on Investment in Manufacturing." *A.E.R.* 58 (May 1968): 200–211.

Domar, E. D. "The 'Burden of the Debt' and the National Income." *A.E.R.* 34 (December 1944): 798–827. Reprinted in E. D. Domar, *Essays in the Theory of Economic Growth.* New York: Oxford Univ. Press, 1957.

Economic Report of the President, February 1970. Washington: Government Printing Office, 1970.

Eisner, R. "A Distributed Lag Investment Function." *Econometrica* 28 (January 1960): 1–29.

———. "Factors Affecting the Level of Interest Rates: Part II." In *Conference on Savings and Residential Financing, 1968 Proceedings.* Chicago: U.S. Savings and Loan League 1968. (*a*)

———. "War and Taxes: The Role of the Economist in Politics." *Bull. Atomic Sci.* 24 (June 1968): 13–18. (*b*)

———. "Fiscal and Monetary Policy Reconsidered." *A.E.R.* 59 (December 1969): 897–905.

Eisner, R., and Nadiri, M. I. "Investment Behavior and the Neo-Classical Theory." *Rev. Econ. and Statis.* 50 (August 1968): 369–82.

———. "Neo-Classical Theory of Investment Behavior: A Comment." Ibid. 52 (May 1970): 216–22.

Friedman, M. "A Monetary and Fiscal Famework for Economic Stability." *A.E.R.* 38 (June 1948): 245–64. Reprinted in *Essays in Positive Economics*. Chicago: Univ. Chicago Press, 1953.

———. "The Effects of a Full Employment Policy on Economic Stability: A Formal Analysis." In M. Friedman, *Essays in Positive Economics*. Chicago: Univ. Chicago Press, 1953.

———. *The Optimum Quantity of Money and Other Essays*. Chicago: Aldine, 1969.

Galbraith, J. K. *The Affluent Society*. Boston: Houghton Mifflin, 1958.

———. *The New Industrial State*. Boston: Houghton Mifflin, 1967.

———. "Economics as a System of Belief." *A.E.R.* 60 (May 1970): 469–78.

Hall, R. E., and Jorgenson, D. W. "Tax Policy and Investment Behavior." *A.E.R.* 57 (June 1967): 391–414.

———. "Tax Policy and Investment Behavior: Reply and Further Results." Ibid. 59 (June 1969): 388–401.

Hansen, Bent. "The Anti-inflationary Effects of Fiscal Policy: A Comment." *A.E.R.* (in press).

Hicks, J. R. *A Contribution to the Theory of the Trade Cycle*. Oxford: Clarendon, 1950.

Hotson, John H. "Neo-Orthodox Keynesianism and the 45° Heresy." *Nebraska J. Econ. and Bus.* 6 (Autumn 1967): 34–49.

Jorgenson, D. W. "Capital Theory and Investment Behavior." *A.E.R.* 53 (May 1963): 247–59.

Jorgenson, D. W., and Stephenson, J. A. "The Time Structure of Investment Behavior in United States Manufacturing, 1947–60." *Rev. Econ. and Statis.* 49 (February 1967): 16–27.

Keynes, J. M. *The General Theory of Employment, Interest and Money*. New York: Harcourt Brace, 1936.

Lange, O. *Price Flexibility and Employment*. Bloomington, Ind.: Principia, 1952.

Lerner, A. P. "The Burden of the National Debt." In *Income, Employment and Public Policy*. New York: Norton, 1948.

Lucas, R. E., and Rapping, L. A. "Real Wages, Employment, and Inflation." *J.P.E.* 77 (September/October 1969): 721–54.

Modigliani, F. "Long-Run Implications of Alternative Fiscal Policies and the Burden of the National Debt." *Econ. J.* 71 (December 1961): 730–55.

Okun, A. M. *The Political Economy of Prosperity*. Washington: Brookings Inst., 1970.

Phelps, E. S. "Money-Wage Dynamics and Labor-Market Equilibrium." *J.P.E.* 76 (July/August 1968): 678–711.

Tobin, J. "Notes on Optimal Monetary Growth." *J.P.E.* 76 (July/August 1968): 833–59.

[16]

A New View of the Federal Debt and Budget Deficits

By ROBERT EISNER AND PAUL J. PIEPER*

Much again has recently been made of the purportedly large government debt and deficits. To some, the sheer magnitude of the federal debt, passing $1.3 trillion in 1983, suggests the danger of some kind of national bankruptcy. To others, the large and growing budget deficits, which have now reached 6 percent of Gross National Product, are a harbinger of a new acceleration of inflation. Fiscal policy, it is further argued, has been incessantly stimulative, as is indicated by the movement to deficit of even the high-employment budget in the last two decades.

A number of recent papers have pointed to the need for adjustment of conventional measures of government debt and, in particular, the deficit.[1] As is of course well known, in its failure to distinguish between current and capital expenditures, the federal budget is widely at variance with prevailing accounting practice for private business. Application of government accounting methods to the private sector would move many major American corporations toward deficit. Conversely, conventional private accounting methods would generally move government accounts toward surplus.

But of further and critical importance, in government accounts as in private accounts, inflation plays vast tricks. If we are to avoid the cardinal economic sin of money illusion, we must look at real market values of debt and real deficits that correspond to changes in the real value of debt. In the first substantive section of this paper, therefore, we develop and present measures of the real value of federal government net debt, offering as a byproduct associated measures of net worth.[2] The net revaluations calculated in developing a time-series of real net federal debt are applied to develop a series of "adjusted" budget surpluses and deficits.

The second substantive section of the paper entails an application of these measures to develop adjusted figures for the recently revised official high-employment budget surplus and deficit.[3] The official and adjusted series for the high-employment budget are then related to changes in real Gross National Product and the rate of unemployment. It is found that lagged series of the official high-employment budget surplus and, even more clearly, our adjusted measures taking into account the impact of inflation and changing interest rates on the real value of the debt, show clear and sharp negative relations with the real path of the economy. With increasing inflation, a balanced official high-employment budget proved less and less consistent with the maintenance of high employment or adequate economic growth. Recent declines in real *GNP* and increases in unemployment are remarkably closely associated with a substantial move to surplus in the adjusted high-employment budgets.

*William R. Kenan Professor of Economics, Northwestern University, Evanston, IL 60201, and Assistant Professor of Economics, University of Illinois, Chicago, IL 60680, respectively. We are indebted to Elizabeth Fogler of the Flow of Funds Division of the Federal Reserve Board, and to John J. Seater, W. Michael Cox, and Eric Hirschhorn for guidance through published and unpublished data. We are particularly indebted to Laurence Kotlikoff for suggesting that earlier work of Eisner (1980) be updated for use by the Council of Economic Advisers. We are further indebted to the Council for financial support and to the National Science Foundation (grant SES-7717555) for support of the initial research. We are grateful to Otto Eckstein, H.S. Houthakker, and Allen Sinai for comments on an earlier draft of part of this paper, and to Moses Abramovitz, Michael Boskin, E. Cary Brown, Paul Evans, Benjamin Friedman, Robert J. Gordon, Bert G. Hickman, Frank de Leeuw, Frederic Mishkin, Dale T. Mortensen, and George Neumann for comments on later versions, and to anonymous referees. We alone are responsible for its contents.

[1]See, for example, Michael Boskin (1982), Michael Cox and Eric Hirschhorn (1983), *Economic Report of the President* (1982), Brian Horrigan and Aris Protopapadakis (1982), Rudolph Penner (1982), Richard Ruggles and Nancy Ruggles (1982), and John Seater (1981).

[2]Measures including state and local government are presented in Appendix A.

[3]See Frank de Leeuw and Thomas Holloway (1982).

TABLE 1—MARKET TO PAR INDICES (100 = PAR), SELECTED YEARS[a]

	U.S. Government Securities				Bonds		Mortgages	
	Total	Bills	Notes	Notes; Bonds	State; Local	Corporate	State; Local	Federal
1946	102.71	99.95	100.47	103.58	100.30	98.14	103.90	104.10
1959	94.07	98.80	98.00	91.73	96.00	83.77	94.50	95.60
1969	92.04	97.69	94.99	89.23	88.20	72.12	92.30	93.40
1976	101.15	98.68	103.42	102.72	101.80	97.03	96.70	97.80
1977	98.31	98.10	99.64	98.43	102.30	93.13	97.60	98.40
1978	95.30	97.15	95.80	94.38	97.40	86.43	94.50	95.90
1979	94.44	96.64	95.47	93.38	95.40	80.40	89.80	91.20
1980	92.86	96.00	94.34	91.29	86.10	74.04	86.80	88.50

[a]Complete tables corresponding to this table and to Tables 3, 4 and 5, with data for all of the years from 1946 to 1980, are available from the authors on request.

I. Actual Budget Deficits and Debt

A. *The Debt: From Par to Market and Gross to Net*

Government debt figures usually reflect the par value of government obligations. If the debt were overwhelmingly in very short-term securities, or if interest rates did not change much over the life of securities, the difference between par and market values would be small. Particularly in recent years, neither of these conditions was met. Interest rates soared and market values of outstanding fixed securities collapsed.

As a first step, therefore, we have built upon work of John Seater (1981) and Michael Cox and Eric Hirschhorn (1983) to construct market-to-par indices for major financial components of government balance sheets. We find that, with par equal to 100, the market index for the composite of all U.S. government securities had fallen by the end of 1980 to 92.86, as shown in Table 1. (The index for state and local government bonds fell further, to 86.10.)

A second step is to recognize that the gross public debt is a correct measure of neither the total liabilities (interest-bearing and non-interest-bearing) of the federal government (including its associated credit agencies and the Federal Reserve) nor of the net debt, that is, the difference between total liabilities and total financial assets. We find, as indicated in Table 2, that total liabilities associated with the U.S. government came at the end of 1980 to $1,220 billion at par. The par value of financial assets amounted to $592 billion. Par value of *net* government debt was thus only $628 billion.

But the *market* value of total U.S. government liabilities was $1,154 billion, $66 billion less than its par value. The market value of U.S. government financial assets was $707 billion, or $115 billion more than par, reflecting a market value of gold $141 billion greater than the statutory figure based on the $42 per ounce at which it is held in Treasury accounts. Thus, the market value of U.S. government net debt in 1980 was $448 billion, a considerable cry from the original "gross public debt" figure of $930 billion.[4]

[4]In addition to explicit debt or accounting liabilities, the federal government and its agencies of course have substantial other contractual obligations. As of the end of the 1982 fiscal year, the Treasury listed "liabilities" accountable to the public of $1,085.5 billion, "undelivered orders" (mainly of the Departments of Defense and Housing and Urban Development) of $474.7 billion and, dwarfing both, "contingency" obligations which summed to $6,981.5 billion.

These last comprised $346.7 billion in loan and credit guarantees and $2,079.6 billion in insurance commitments, largely for the Federal Deposit Insurance Corporation and the Federal Savings and Loan Investment Corporation. They also included amounts for "annuity programs," which totalled $4,473.8 billion. Of these, $835.9 billion were for retirement pay, chiefly for the armed forces and the civil service. The other major items were the actuarial values of net obligations for the three Social Security Trust Funds, coming to $577.9 billion for hospital insurance, $2,297.6 billion for old age and survivors insurance, and $656.3 billion in net *assets* for disability insurance. Adding together all of the figures

TABLE 2—THE BUDGET DEFICIT, GROSS PUBLIC DEBT, AND MARKET VALUE OF NET DEBT, 1980 (Billions of Dollars)

A. Reconcilation of Gross Public Debt and Market Value of Net Debt	
Gross Public Debt	$ 930.2
+ Other Liabilities of Federal Government	120.1
+ Liabilities of Credit Agencies	188.2
+ Liabilities of Federal Reserve	173.8
− Debt held by Federal Government	− 192.46
Total U.S. Government Liabilities at Par	$1,220.0
+ Par-to-Market Conversion	− 65.7
Total U.S. Government Liabilities at Market	$1,154.3
Federal Government Financial Assets	$ 225.3
+ Credit Agency Assets	192.54
+ Federal Reserve Assets[a]	173.8
Total U.S. Government Financial Assets at Par[a]	$ 591.7
+ Par-to-Market Conversion	115.0
On Gold	141.1
On Other Assets	− 26.1
Total U.S. Government Financial Assets at Market	$ 706.7
U.S. Government Net Debt	$ 447.5
B. Reconcilation of Budget Deficit and Changes in Gross Public Debt	
Budget Deficit on National Income Account	$61.2
+ Insurance Credits to Households	+ 8.8
+ Change in U.S. Financial Assets	+ 26.0
+ Change in Treasury Debt Held by U.S. Government	+ 7.4
− Change in other U.S. Liabilities	− 11.0
− Mineral Rights Sales	− 6.5
− Statistical Discrepancy (Flow of Funds)	− 0.8
Change in Gross Public Debt	$ 85.1

[a]Includes small amount of tangible Federal Reserve assets.

(which the Treasury does not do), we come to a total of $8,541.7 billion, far in excess of direct liabilities and our net debt figures.

Such vast government programs and obligations may well have a substantial impact on the economy. They are clearly, however, in varying ways different in character and implications from the formal, current debt. A considerable amount of recent work has endeavored to detect effects on consumption and saving of the major item of implicit Social Security debt. But even measures of the magnitude of that debt vary widely with plausible assumptions as to future government policy and as to public perceptions and expectations, as has been well shown by Dean Leimer and Selig Lesnoy (1982). Eisner (1983) has also noted the apparently varied impact of "net Social Security wealth" in a macroeconomic model, along with a substantially greater and clearer role for direct government debt. As pointed out by the U.S. Treasury, "Clearly, there is a vast difference between items... where the liability is certain and relatively precise... and... where the possible future liability is highly speculative and may never arise.... The [latter] amounts, if they can be projected at all, are stated... without regard to probability of occurrence and without deduction for existing and contingent assets which would be available... ." (1982, p. 2).

It is clear that construction of relevant measures of government commitments that go beyond net current liabilities would take us far afield. It would also be subject to huge uncertainty regarding the anticipated tax receipts which may eventually be generated to meet the commitments. One not entirely implausible assumption, particularly after recent changes in the Social Security Law, may be that we can expect taxes to be raised so that the net actuarial value of government obligations and the taxes to pay for them will be zero, and certainly not a growing ratio of national income.

In any event, the federal liabilities calculated in this paper, as in the Treasury tabulations, do not include the present value of government personnel retirement provisions, the projected Social Security commitments under current law, or other "contingent" obligations, nor do assets include an estimate of the present value of associated future taxes. Liabilities do include, however, the value of assets held in federal employee and railroad retirement funds, so that their net contribution to the debt comes to zero.

Like any business, the federal government also has some tangible assets. These include reproducible assets in the form of residential structures, nonresidential structures, equipment and inventories, which by BEA estimates at the end of 1980 had a net replace-

TABLE 3—FEDERAL GOVERNMENT NET DEBT AND NET WORTH, BILLIONS OF DOLLARS

	1946	1950	1960	1970	1980
Assets					
Tangible	170.1	112.2	207.3	301.0	727.0
Reproducible Assets	162.6	102.6	188.9	264.6	607.6
Residential Structures	2.6	2.2	3.2	5.7	20.6
Nonresidential Structures	33.1	39.1	60.8	100.2	251.6
Equipment	75.4	34.4	65.6	95.3	202.4
Inventories	51.6	26.9	59.2	63.4	132.9
Land	7.5	9.5	18.4	36.4	119.5
Financial	74.2	93.9	117.8	218.0	706.7
Currency, Demand + Time Deposits	8.8	9.7	12.8	18.0	33.9
Gold	20.7	22.8	17.8	12.0	152.3
U.S. Government Securities	24.3	21.3	28.5	63.6	123.4
Treasury Issues	24.3	21.3	28.5	63.4	114.2
Agency Issues	0.0	0.0	0.0	0.2	9.2
Mortgages	2.1	2.8	10.9	31.5	126.2
Other Loans	8.1	16.0	25.0	64.8	199.7
Taxes Receivable	8.2	16.5	12.7	5.7	9.3
Miscellaneous Assets	2.0	4.7	10.0	22.2	62.0
Total Assets	244.3	206.0	325.1	519.0	1,433.7
Liabilities					
Treasury Currency + SDR Certificates	2.4	2.4	2.7	6.0	13.6
Demand Deposits + Currency	30.4	28.2	30.6	52.0	121.5
Bank Reserves + Vault Cash	18.2	19.9	20.4	31.2	47.3
Credit Market Instruments	234.3	219.5	240.2	324.9	834.6
Savings Bonds	44.4	50.0	46.5	53.1	68.4
Other Treasury Issues	188.8	168.1	185.9	232.4	617.8
Agency Issues	1.2	1.8	7.8	39.3	148.4
Insurance, Retirement Reserves	8.0	12.7	20.5	34.9	85.5
Miscellaneous Liabilities	6.8	7.4	10.9	21.8	51.9
Total Liabilities	300.1	290.0	325.2	407.7	1,154.3
Net Debt[a]	225.9	196.2	207.4	252.7	447.5
Net Worth	−55.9	−84.0	−0.1	48.3	279.4

[a]Total liabilities minus financial assets.

ment cost, which we will take as market value, of $608 billion.[5] We estimate land owned by the federal government at $119 billion. Total tangible assets at the end of 1980 were thus $727 billion.

We add $707 billion of financial assets to reach a total assets figure at the end of 1980 of $1,434 billion. We subtract liabilities of $1,154 billion. The result, shown in Table 3, is a positive net worth of $279 billion.

The contrasting results for the series of gross Treasury debt and total liabilities on the one hand, and net debt and net worth on the other, are striking. Gross Treasury debt of $259 billion in 1946 had risen only to $321 billion by 1965, but then increased at an accelerating rate to the $930 billion by the end of 1980 (and now of course well over $1 trillion). Net debt as late as 1966 was, at $223 billion, still below the 1946 high point of $226 billion. Net debt climbed thereafter to a total of $448 billion by the end of 1980.[6]

[5]Of the $251 billion of federal nonresidential structures in 1980, "conservation and development" (including dams and power plants) amounted to $101 billion; military was $82 billion; industrial was $23 billion; highways and streets were $14 billion; hospitals were $8 billion; other buildings and structures were $23 billion. Of the $202 billion of federal equipment, $167 billion was military and $35 billion was nonmilitary. Residential structures were valued at $21 billion and inventories at $133 billion.

The propriety of taking the BEA replacement costs as estimates of market value is open to question, but to go beyond this would entail an effort, with still questionable results, considerably greater than we have been able to undertake at this time.

[6]Looking at what would for a private business be the bottom line, the net worth figures tell a different story, although a story that would hardly be unfamiliar to any successful large corporation. For all the while that gross Treasury debt, or even the difference between total

TABLE 4—THE REAL VALUE OF FEDERAL DEBT

	Billions of 1972 Dollars					1972 Dollars	
	Gross Public Debt	Net Debt	Budget Surplus (Deficit−)	Net Revaluation of Net Debt	Change in Net Debt	Net Debt per Capita	Change in Net Debt per Capita
1946	539.2	470.1	8.0	−83.6	−	3,384	−
1950	459.1	350.8	17.2	−31.8	44.0	2,326	−338
1960	421.4	299.1	4.4	8.7	5.8	1,679	6
1970	415.3	269.9	−15.3	1.7	15.4	1,338	60
1975	445.9	278.9	−55.2	−2.2	57.3	1,320	259
1976	481.3	318.2	−40.2	−4.2	39.3	1,482	162
1977	498.6	320.5	−33.2	−37.9	2.3	1,482	−0
1978	503.4	296.7	−19.5	−51.1	−23.8	1,364	−118
1979	496.6	244.8	−9.1	−71.4	−51.9	1,120	−244
1980	495.9	238.6	−34.5	−42.9	−6.2	1,078	−42

B. *Deficits and Real Changes in Net Debt*

While the federal government reported budget deficits totalling $336 billion from 1947 to 1980, the market value of net federal debt grew by only $222 billion from the end of 1946 to the end of 1980 (Table 3). And over that period, the real market value of that debt (in 1972 dollars) declined by $231 billion (Table 4). Even the usual measure of Treasury debt known as the gross public debt was no larger in 1980 in real terms than in 1946. In fact, it declined in 1972 dollars from $539 billion to $496 billion. This reduction in real gross debt reflects large negative net revaluations. Higher interest rates lowering the market value of debt, higher prices of gold increasing the value of that government asset and, particularly, general inflation, combined further to cut the real market value of the *net* debt virtually in half since the end of World War II.

This suggests that our conventional measure of the budget deficit is particularly misleading in periods of significant inflation, and high and fluctuating nominal interest rates. Federal government net interest payments of $53.1 billion in 1980 were only modestly less than the $61.4 billion deficit (on National Income Accounts). With interest rates on Treasury securities rising from about 11.5 percent to over 14 percent, net interest payments in 1981 came to $71.9 billion, well exceeding a $60.0 billion reported deficit.[7] (For 1982, however, while net interest payments rose to $85.0 billion, the deficit on national income account soared to $149.5 billion.)[8] But measures of real interest, taking into account changes in the real market value of the federal debt, would have been small fractions of nominal payments, or actually negative. Substitution of real for nominal interest costs in budget expenditures would indicate that the budget was close to balanced in 1980, a result consistent with the changes in the real value of the debt (Table 5).[9]

liabilities and total financial assets which we have been calling net debt, was growing, so was net worth. By our measures, net worth was a negative $56 billion at the end of 1946, as shown in Table 3. It became even more negative, finally reaching a lower bound of minus $92 billion at the end of 1949. But, by the end of 1956, the federal government was at least briefly in the black, with a net worth of $8 billion. Net worth was then trivially negative, hovering around zero, for the years 1960–62, before it again began to rise. It dipped in the 1974–75 recession and its wake, but came up very sharply in the next five years, when gross Treasury debt was soaring dramatically. We measure federal net worth at the end of 1980 at $279 billion. Our federal government, like many individuals and business that borrowed heavily in an inflationary period, came out pretty well with its investments in tangible assets—and in gold.

[7,8] *Economic Indicators*, May 1983, p. 34.

[9] Of course, the population has been growing over the last 35 years. Our ultimate measure of the trend in debt then may well be the real net debt per capita. This figure declined (in 1972 dollars) from $3,384 at the end of 1946 to $1,078 at the end of 1980, as also shown in Table 4.

(over)

TABLE 5—RECONCILIATION OF FEDERAL BUDGET SURPLUS (DEFICIT) AND CHANGE IN REAL NET DEBT

(1)	Surplus (Deficit −) on National Income Accounts (2)	Interest Rate Effects (Par-to-Market Adjustment) (3)	Price Effects (Nominal to real adjustment) (4)	Adjusted Surplus (Deficit −) (5)	Off-Budget Items[a] (6)	Net Revaluation on Gold (7)	Decrease (Increase −) in Real Net Debt in Current Dollars (8)
1976	−53.1	−12.5	21.2	−44.5	−4.2	−3.3	−52.0
1977	−46.4	16.9	29.3	−.2	−9.0	6.0	−3.3
1978	−29.2	18.6	43.3	32.7	−8.7	11.8	35.7
1979	−14.8	1.7	44.1	31.0	−9.8	63.6	84.9
1980	−61.2	12.6	55.9	7.3	−2.1	6.0	11.2

Note: Column 5 is total of cols. (2), (3), and (4); Column (8) is total of cols. (5), (6), and (7).

[a]This is the sum of insurance credits to households, federal mineral sales, credit agency surplus, net revaluations on foreign exchange and miscellaneous assets, and the Flow of Funds statistical discrepancy.

A proper measure of the government's current surplus is the reduction in real value of government net debt or, consistent with the Haig-Hicks definition of income, the amount of additional expenditures that can be made while keeping net debt intact. If there were no net revaluations of existing financial assets and liabilities, this definition would correspond to conventional measures of the deficit. Net revaluations have in fact generally been considerable, however, as we have just noted, and all the more so in periods of significant inflation and high and fluctuating nominal interest rates.

As with the debt, therefore, we make two adjustments to the deficit, a par-to-market adjustment and a nominal-to-real adjustment. The first of these is the change in net debt due to changing market rates of interest, which we term the interest effect. With generally rising interest rates, this effect has been on balance positive in the postwar era, thus reducing the adjusted deficit.

The second and usually larger adjustment, incorporating what we denote as the price effect, is the change in the real value of the net debt due to changes in the price level. It has of course become of major importance with the higher inflation of the 1970's.

By reducing our measure of the deficit by the amount of decrease in the real value of existing net government debt, we are in effect including the so-called "inflation tax" in budget revenues. Since inflation (and expected inflation) forces borrowers to offer higher nominal interest rates to compensate for the inflation tax on holders of securities, the price-effect adjustment may alternatively be viewed as a conversion of interest expenditures from nominal to real.

In Table 5 we add the interest and price effects to present an adjusted measure of the federal budget surplus or deficit. The conventional and adjusted budgets prove quite different. The officially reported deficit of $61.2 billion in 1980, for example, is converted to a $7.4 billion surplus when price and interest effects are considered. And the adjustments have not been constant in amount; in earlier years, when inflation was lower, they were decidedly smaller.[10]

II. The High-Employment Budget

A. *The Official High-Employment Budget Surplus and Relevant Adjusted Measures*

The high-employment budget, currently calculated for an unemployment level of 5.1

Real debt per capita was thus at the end of 1980 less than one-third of what it was at the end of 1946.

[10]The adjusted surplus differs from the real change of government net debt, expressed in current dollars, by the amounts of the off-budget items and net revaluations of gold. We have excluded net revaluations on gold from the adjusted surplus on the principle that an increase in the value of government gold holdings, unlike an increase in the value of government holdings of private debt, does not decrease private net worth. It may indeed be argued, rather, that an increase in the value of gold will be perceived by the private sector as increased backing for government debt and thus as increased private wealth. Similar considerations apply to the off-budget items.

percent, is generally understood to provide a first-order measure of the thrust of federal fiscal policy on aggregate demand. Increases in the high-employment budget surplus or decreases in the deficit are viewed as contractionary. The tendency of the high-employment budget to be in deficit in recent years, in contrast to those before 1966, has perhaps contributed to the view that, despite generally increasing inflation, the federal budget has been, perversely, expansionary. The depth and severity of the recession of 1981–82 have then been attributed to the great potency of a tight and tough monetary policy which has overbalanced an easy fiscal policy.

These views, at least of fiscal policy, are fundamentally flawed. In particular, in a period of significant and rising inflation, the traditional high-employment budget, as usually measured, is no longer an unbiased measure of fiscal thrust. It in fact measures nominal rather than real impacts on income, and confuses nominal flows with changes in real stocks.

For the high-employment budget to measure correctly the thrust of federal fiscal policy, it must measure correctly its contribution to aggregate demand. We abstract here from not unimportant questions relating to the balanced budget multiplier, and to the mix among both expenditures and receipts. We abstract as well from the question of monetization of the debt or possible interaction of fiscal and monetary policy. These issues aside, a relevant high-employment deficit must add to correctly measured private income and wealth.

It is clear, for example, that a "deficit" which involves expenditures by the Treasury to purchase existing securities held by the public would not be a relevant deficit. Neither, indeed, would a deficit used to finance purchase of existing assets which merely involves a change in private portfolios—the substitution of government bonds for the assets sold to the Treasury. Similarly, a surplus brought on by the sale of public lands to the private sector does not change private wealth holdings—except possibly to raise them if the sales are at prices below market value. And a deficit that does not increase the net debt of the government does not increase the net income or net worth of the private sector, and hence does not per se have an expansionary effect on aggregate demand.[11]

Perception of the gap in the relation between measured deficits and changes in net debt of the government, or net worth of the private sector, points to the major effect of inflation on a relevant high-employment budget. For inflation and changing rates of inflation quite break whatever links have existed between budget deficits and real income or changes in net worth of the private sector.

A measure of the real actual surplus or deficit may be viewed as essentially the sum of three components: 1) the nominal surplus or deficit as currently measured; 2) an adjustment for changes in market value of government financial assets and liabilities due to changing market rates of interest; and 3) changes in the real value of net debt due to changing general price levels incident to inflation. An identical or analogous set of adjustments is appropriate for the high-employment budget surplus or deficit.

It should be understood that the inflation adjustments deal with rates of change in the price level and rates of change in the rate of change in the price level. Price level effects are included in the definition and measure of the high-employment budget currently. Frank de Leeuw and Thomas Holloway (1982) present in some detail the sophisticated measures utilized in tabulating automatic effects of inflation and higher price levels on the high-employment budget surplus or deficit as defined by the Bureau of Economic Analysis. Higher price levels and inflation cause more than proportionate increases in corporate taxes, and in personal taxes as long as the

[11]We do view increases in net debt as, *ceteris paribus*, increasing private perceptions of financial wealth and hence private demand for goods. With Ricardo himself we hence reject the Ricardo "equivalence theorem," by which the private sector would perceive increases in the present value of future tax liabilities equal to any current increases in government debt. And whether increased real government budget deficits would result in "crowding out," with no net increase in total output, as argued by William Fellner (1982), we would suggest would depend upon how close the economy is in fact to full employment. With ample unutilized resources, it is hard to see why fiscal stimulus must prove abortive.

TABLE 6—HIGH-EMPLOYMENT BUDGET SURPLUS (DEFICIT) AS PERCENT OF *GNP*, OFFICIAL AND ADJUSTED

	High-Employment Surplus (Deficit –)		
	Official	Adjusted for Price Effects	Adjusted for Price and Interest Effects
1955	1.30	2.81	3.71
1956	1.87	3.83	4.63
1957	1.37	2.47	1.26
1958	0	.93	2.21
1959	1.11	2.09	2.90
1960	2.39	2.84	.98
1961	1.35	1.99	2.44
1962	.53	1.29	.91
1963	1.24	1.79	2.26
1964	.17	.78	.73
1965	.13	.98	1.42
1966	–.74	.34	.09
1967	–1.89	–.89	–.38
1968	–1.26	.06	.20
1969	.52	1.95	2.68
1970	–.46	.77	–.64
1971	–1.05	.12	–.21
1972	–1.02	.02	.42
1973	–.72	.89	1.13
1974	–.02	2.16	1.97
1975	–1.88	–.37	–.55
1976	–1.01	.22	–.52
1977	–1.13	.39	1.27
1978	–.70	1.30	2.16
1979	–.09	1.74	1.81
1980	–.81	1.31	1.63
1981	.15	1.92	1.97

rate structure is progressive and not indexed. While many expenditure programs (Social Security most conspicuously) are also inflated by higher prices, and interest payments, as observed, are increased by the higher nominal rates associated with higher inflation, the effect of inflation on balance is to increase the high-employment budget surplus or decrease the deficit.

But these effects of inflation on the high-employment budget surplus as defined are quite another matter than the effect of inflation on the real high-employment budget. For the greater the rate of inflation, the greater is the decline in the real value of net private holdings of government debt or, put another way, with real interest costs substituted for nominal interest payments, the greater is the real high-employment budget surplus (or the less the deficit).[12]

We have hence undertaken to calculate a high-employment budget that, by correcting for these inflation effects, comes closer to measuring the real surplus or deficit and consequent thrust of fiscal policy on aggre-

[12]The high-employment budget, while aimed at eliminating the cyclical effects on the actual budget, is of course not exogenous to what is going on in the economic system. To consider it a measure of fiscal thrust is not to view it as entirely at the discretion of the fiscal authorities. And just as an easy monetary policy lowering Treasury interest payments, or inflation as a consequence of external supply shocks, will move the official high-employment budget to surplus, so will *tight* money and inflation move our price- and interest-adjusted high-employment budget further to surplus, with no independent government action.

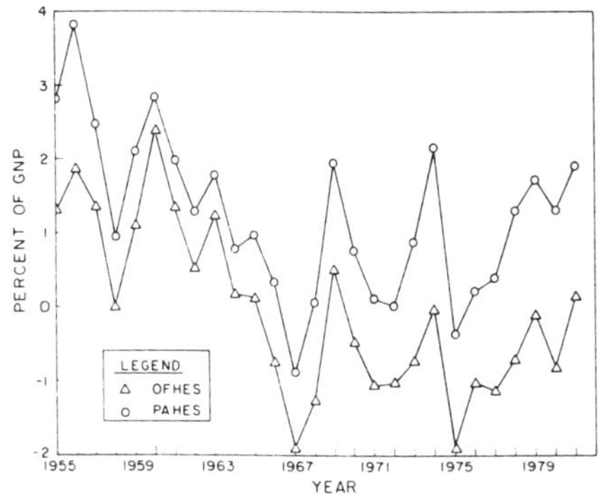

FIGURE 1. OFFICIAL AND PRICE-ADJUSTED HIGH-EMPLOYMENT SURPLUS

gate demand. Applying our calculations of net revaluations on actual net federal debt, we have adjusted the high-employment budget surplus series presented by de Leeuw and Holloway for the years 1955 through 1981. The results shown in Table 6, and partially in Figure 1, are dramatic. Inflation and rates of interest were low and relatively steady in the early years of the period prior to escalation of our military involvement in Vietnam. Corrections to the high-employment budget surplus are hence small in those early years. In the years from our heavy Vietnam involvement on, however, when the high-employment budget as well as the actual budget moved substantially to deficit, the effect of our corrections is dramatic. The entire perceived trend in the direction of fiscal ease or expansion is eliminated or reversed. The adjusted high-employment budget surplus, as a percent of *GNP*, for every year from 1977 through 1981 was, except for the tax-surcharge year of 1969 and the oil-price-shock year of 1974, higher than the surplus of any single year going back to 1965. With similar exceptions, the surplus adjusted only for price (and not interest) effects was higher in every year from 1978 to 1981 than that of any single year back to 1963.

This suggests a need for some significant rewriting of recent economic history. Inflation can hardly be ascribed to excess demand associated with increasing fiscal ease and stimulus if, at least by the high-employment budget measure, appropriately defined, there was no such movement to fiscal ease.[13] Some explanation of sluggishness in the economy in the last several years, climaxed by the current recession, may then be found in a relatively tight fiscal policy, as measured by the adjusted high-employment budget surplus, as well as in the widely perceived role of monetary policy.

B. *Empirical Relations*

Movements in real economic activity in the United States have in fact been negatively related to the high-employment budget surplus. This is confirmed dramatically in relations between percent changes in real *GNP* and unemployment on the one hand, and lagged values of the high-employment budget surplus as a percentage of *GNP* on the other.

Recognizing 1967 as something of a watershed inaugurating accelerating inflation and subsequently slower rates of growth and higher unemployment, we have divided our observations into two groups: 1956–66 and 1967–81 (or 1982). Looking first at the official high-employment budget surplus (*OFHES*), we note in equations (1) and (4) of Table 7 that it was clearly negatively

[13]That federal government expenditures as a share of *GNP* rose, from 17.0 percent in 1955 to 23.4 percent in 1981 (while receipts rose from 18.2 to 21.4 percent), is also not evidence of an expansionary fiscal policy. Some part of the expenditure increase involves the increase in nominal interest payments which would be viewed as akin to a purchase of government liabilities of real debt. Federal expenditures net of net interest paid increased only from 15.9 to 21.0 percent of *GNP*. More generally, the balanced budget multiplier will apply to government expenditures for goods and services, not to the transfer payments financed by taxes. The share of goods and services of *GNP* purchased by the federal government declined sharply from 11.1 percent in 1955 to 7.8 percent in 1981. Only when state and local expenditures are included is the picture altered. Total government expenditures for goods and services rose from 18.8 percent of *GNP* in 1955 to 20.3 percent in 1981. In the latter year, federal grants in aid to state and local governments came to 3.0 percent of *GNP*. (Percents calculated from dollar figures in *Economic Report of the President*, February 1982, pp. 233 and 320; *Economic Indicators*, May 1983, pp. 1 and 34; and, for 1955 net interest, *National Income and Product Accounts, 1929–74*, p. 96.)

TABLE 7—HIGH-EMPLOYMENT BUDGETS AND CHANGES IN REAL *GNP* AND UNEMPLOYMENT

Equations	Measure of *HES*	Dependent Variable (Y)	Regression Coefficients[a] 1956–66 b_{01}	b_{11}	1967–81 b_{02}	b_{12}	$\hat{R}^2$	*D-W*
(1)	*OF*	%Δ*GNP*	5.678 (.930)	−1.837 (.733)	.519 (.750)	−2.896 (.730)	.451	1.61
(2)	*PA*	%Δ*GNP*	7.189 (1.089)	−1.730 (.499)	4.432 (.496)	−2.318 (.439)	.595	2.02
(3)	*PIA*	%Δ*GNP*	4.838 (1.240)	−.505 (.508)	−1.055 (.625)	−1.561 (.470)	.291	2.12
(4)	*OF*	%Δ*UN*	−.881 (.437)	.792 (3.44)	1.281 (.352)	1.258 (.343)	.399	2.25
(5)	*PA*	%Δ*UN*	−1.182 (5.93)	.569 (.272)	−.384 (.270)	.955 (.250)	.403	2.31
(6)	*PIA*	%Δ*UN*	−.116 (.319)	−.182 (.259)	.333 (.632)	.493 (.240)	.085	2.01
			1956–66		1967–82			
(2′)	*PA*	%Δ*GNP*	7.189 (1.068)	−1.730 (.490)	4.450 (.504)	−2.524 (.438)	.638	2.01
(5′)	*PA*	%Δ*UN*	−1.182 (.594)	.569 (2.272)	−.389 (.268)	1.018 (.233)	.462	2.31

Notes: *HES* = high-employment budget surplus; *OF* = official; *PA* = price adjusted; *PIA* = price and interest adjusted; %Δ*GNP* = percent change in real Gross National Product; %Δ*UN* = percentage point change in unemployment.

$$Y_t = b_{01} + b_{11} HES_{t-1} \qquad t = 1955\text{–}66$$

$$Y_t = b_{02} + b_{12} HES_{t-1} \qquad t = 1967\text{–}81,\ 1982$$

[a]Standard errors are shown in parentheses.

related to subsequent growth in real *GNP* and positively related to subsequent changes in employment in both periods, apparently more sharply so (although the differences are not statistically significant) in the later period. Also note that in the earlier period, a balanced official high-employment budget would "predict" a 5.7 percent growth in real *GNP* and an annual decline of 0.9 percentage points in unemployment. In the later period, however, a balanced official high-employment budget would predict only a 0.5 percent growth in real *GNP*, along with a 1.3 percentage point annual increase in unemployment. Each percentage point increase in the official high-employment budget surplus (measured as a percent of *GNP*) is associated with a reduction of 2.9 percentage points in the rate of growth of real *GNP* and an increase of almost 1.3 percentage points in unemployment.

Why is a balanced official high-employment budget now associated with a stagnant economy and increasing unemployment? A clue to the answer is found in the relations involving the price- or inflation-adjusted high-employment budget, shown in equations (2) and (5) of Table 7 and remarkably sharply in Figures 2 and 3. We note first, from the values of b_{02} in equations (2) and (5), that a balanced, *price-adjusted* high-employment budget in the later periods predicts a 4.4 percent growth in real *GNP* and a 0.4 percent decline in unemployment. But, recall from Table 6 that in 1981, when the official high-employment surplus was 0.15 percent of *GNP*, the high-employment surplus adjusted for price effects was 1.92 percent of *GNP*—a difference of 1.77 percentage points. Our relations suggest that if the official high-employment budget had been in deficit by that much, real growth would

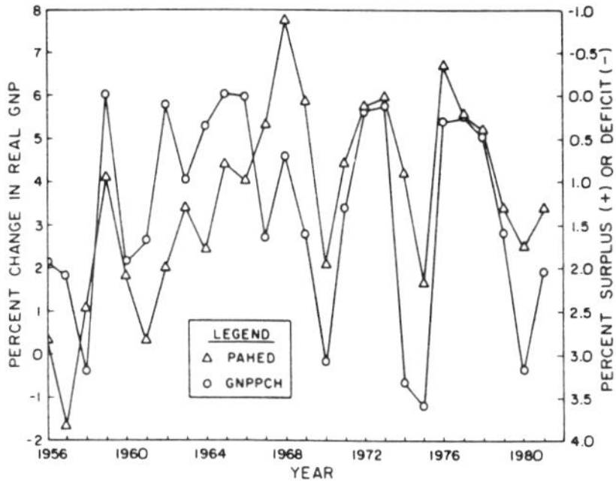

FIGURE 2. LAGGED PRICE-ADJUSTED H-E DEFICIT AND CHANGE IN *GNP*

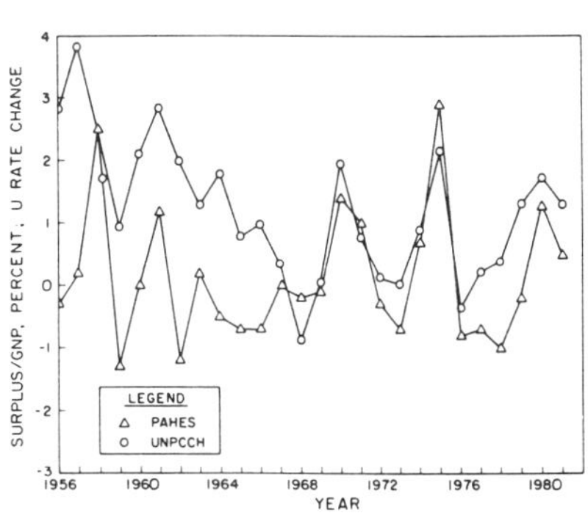

FIGURE 3. LAGGED PRICE-ADJUSTED H-E SURPLUS AND CHANGE IN UNEMPLOYMENT

have risen to 5.6 percent and unemployment would have declined by 0.9 percentage points.[14]

What is more, the coefficients of determination in the relations involving the price-adjusted surplus, particularly the value of .595 in the *GNP* change equation, suggest that the inflation effect does at least as well, and possibly better, in capturing the impact of fiscal thrust than the components of the official high-employment budget surplus. This would indeed be consistent with the hypothesis that in the official unemployment budget relation we have an errors-in-variable problem. The true relation then involves the price-adjusted high-employment budget. In the earlier period, when inflation was small, the relations were fairly similar. In the later period with high inflation, the differences in the relations cannot safely be ignored.

Our relations involving one-year lagged, adjusted high-employment budget surpluses became poorer, however, when the corrections relating to par-to-market adjustments of the value of the debt were incorporated. As shown in equations (3) and (6), estimated parameters retained the hypothesized signs in all cases, except the earlier period for the unemployment equation, but absolute values of the estimates, levels of significance, and coefficients of determination were less. These results may stem in part from the high variability of interest rates and consequent par-to-market corrections which may cause private creditors to view interest effects to a considerable extent as transitory. A par-to-

---

[14]

$$b_{11} + b_{12}(-1.77) = .519 - 2.896(-1.77)$$
$$= 5.644 \text{ in } (1),$$
$$b_{11} + b_{12}(-1.77) = 1.281 + 1.258(-1.77)$$
$$= -0.946 \text{ in } (4).$$

These are, of course, disequilibrium relations. We do not suggest on the basis of (2) that a balanced price-adjusted high-employment budget would generate a permanent growth in real *GNP* of 4.432 percent or, on the basis of (5), permanent rates of decline in unemployment of 0.384 percentage points per year. Indeed, one might infer that it would prove impossible to maintain a balanced, adjusted high-employment budget indefinitely. For as unemployment reached truly full-employment levels, further stimuli to demand would increase the rate of inflation until the price-adjusted high-employment budget were sufficiently in surplus to be consistent with no further changes in the rate of unemployment. By way of illustration, without taking the specific numbers too seriously, equation (5) suggests that the rate of unemployment would be constant with a price-adjusted high-employment surplus equal to 0.402 percent of *GNP*. This would imply a 3.5 percent per annum growth in real *GNP*.

Similarly, equation (4) indicates that zero change in unemployment would require an official high-employment deficit equal to 1.018 percent of *GNP*. This would also imply real per annum growth in *GNP* of some 3.5 percent.

TABLE 8—HIGH-EMPLOYMENT BUDGETS AND CHANGES IN REAL *GNP* AND UNEMPLOYMENT

Equations	Measure of *HES*	Dependent Variable (Y)	Regression Coefficients[a] 1957–66 b_{01}	b_{11}	b_{21}	1967–81 b_{02}	b_{12}	b_{22}	$\hat{R}^2$	*D-W*
(7)	*OF*	%Δ*GNP*	5.634	−1.798	.104	.522	−2.896	.003	.399	1.63
			(1.296)	(.799)	(.865)	(.976)	(.777)	(.726)		
(8)	*PA*	%Δ*GNP*	7.794	−1.504	−.488	4.301	−2.349	.236	.565	2.04
			(1.403)	(.608)	(.621)	(.590)	(4.87)	(4.95)		
(9)	*PIA*	%Δ*GNP*	7.903	−.281	−1.554	4.474	−1.494	−.648	.603	1.97
			(1.265)	(4.27)	(.395)	(.531)	(.359)	(.366)		
(10)	*OF*	%Δ*UN*	−.897	.808	.040	1.497	1.265	.278	.361	2.33
			(.600)	(.370)	(.401)	(.452)	(.360)	(.336)		
(11)	*PA*	%Δ*UN*	−1.710	.498	.353	−.455	.938	.126	.403	2.40
			(.735)	(.320)	(.327)	(.311)	(2.36)	(.260)		
(12)	*PIA*	%Δ*UN*	−1.289	−.244	.790	−.340	.457	.347	.484	2.15
			(.648)	(.219)	(.202)	(.272)	(.184)	(.187)		
			1957–66			1967–82				
(9′)	*PIA*	%Δ*GNP*	7.903	−.281	−1.554	4.513	−1.623	−.764	.633	2.05
			(1.240)	(.418)	(.387)	(.548)	(.348)	(.361)		
(12′)	*PIA*	%Δ*UN*	−1.289	−.244	.790	−.355	.504	.347	.521	2.20
			(.656)	(.221)	(.205)	(.273)	(1.95)	(.181)		

Notes: See Table 7.

$$Y_t = b_{01} + b_{11}HES_{t-1} + b_{21}HES_{t-2} \qquad t = 1957 \text{ to } 1966$$

$$Y_t = b_{02} + b_{12}HES_{t-1} + b_{22}HES_{t-2} \qquad t = 1967 \text{ to } 1981, 1982$$

[a]See Table 7, fn. a.

market correction based on market values of securities on December 31 may not be promptly reflected in aggregate demand of the subsequent year.

We have therefore estimated relations in which changes in *GNP* and employment are functions of both one- and two-year lags of the high-employment budget surplus. The results, presented in Table 8, are again dramatic.

The effects of the official and price-adjusted high-employment surplus are essentially felt with only a one-year lag, as indicated in equations (7), (8), (10), and (11). In the *PIA* (price- and interest-adjusted) equations, adjusted coefficients of determination ($\hat{R}^2$) are uniformly lower with the extra lagged variables in the *OFHES* and *PAHES* equations, while they are markedly higher in *PIAHES* equations. Indeed, the two-year distributed lag equations for the *PIAHES* (the fully adjusted high-employment budget surplus) show, at least trivially, the best fit of all, with adjusted coefficients of determination of .603 and .484 for the percent change in *GNP* and the percentage point change in unemployment, respectively.[15]

[15]The distributed-lag, price- and interest-adjusted equations (9) and (12) suggest that a balanced, adjusted budget would, after two years, generate per annum rates of growth of real *GNP* of 4.5 percent and annual declines of unemployment of 0.34 percentage points. A steady state in unemployment would require an adjusted budget in surplus by 0.423 percent of *GNP*. This would in turn imply a rate of growth of real *GNP* of 3.57 percent.

As this paper was completed, preliminary estimates of changes in real *GNP* and unemployment for 1982 became available. We used them in estimating equations (2′) and (5′), respectively, in Table 7, and (9′) and (12′) in Table 8. They improved the fit and confirmed the relations estimated for the years through 1981. The originally estimated equations indeed went a considerable way in predicting the deepening recession in 1982. Real *GNP* in 1982 was down 1.7 percent after a 1.9 percent rise in 1981. Equation (1), based on the official high-employment budget surplus, would have predicted *GNP* growth in 1982 of 0.08 percent. Equation (2), based on the price-adjusted surplus would have come a bit closer in catching the slowdown, forecasting a de-

III. Summary and Conclusions

We have noted first that official measures of the federal debt and budget deficits are misleading by any of several reasonable standards. Gross public debt figures ignore financial asset accumulation as well as the real assets which have contributed to a growing government net worth. Budget flows have failed to distinguish between current and capital accounts, and measures of surplus and deficit have been inconsistent with changes in the real value of net debt.

Adjustment for the changing relations between the par and market value of government financial assets and liabilities and further adjustments for the effects of inflation on the real value of net debt reveal a very great secular *decline* since the end of World War II in the explicit net claims (excluding Social Security and other future retirement benefits) of the private sector on the federal government. This suggests that by relevant economic measures, consistent with changes in the real value of the debt, the federal budget may properly be viewed as more frequently in surplus than in deficit.

Similar adjustments applied to the official high-employment budget surplus or deficit alter sharply the conventional picture of recent fiscal policy, particularly in periods of substantial inflation. An appropriately adjusted high-employment budget turns out to have been not in deficit in recent years, as usually supposed, but in considerable surplus. The view that fiscal policy has generally been too easy and overstimulatory is contradicted. Even with the new tax cuts, as late as 1981 the adjusted high-employment budget was very substantially in surplus and a relatively contractionary force in the economy.

Empirical confirmation of this view may be found in simple, lagged relations between changes in real *GNP* and changes in unemployment on the one hand, and the official and adjusted measures of the high-employment budget surplus or deficit on the other. The official high-employment budget surplus and, even more clearly, the inflation-adjusted and fully adjusted high-employment budget surpluses were substantially and significantly negatively related to real growth and positively related to changes in unemployment.[16] A return to recovery rates of growth of *GNP* and reduction in unemployment, at the rates of inflation and interest rates through 1981, would call for balanced, inflation-adjusted high-employment budgets, or much larger deficits in the official high-employment budget.[17]

This suggests two important correctives to widespread views of fiscal and monetary policy. First, the 1981–82 recession cannot be properly interpreted as the triumph of all-powerful monetary constraints over relatively ineffective fiscal ease. Without denying the significant effects of a tight money policy in depressing the economy, it is necessary to point out that the verdict is not in on what might have happened if tight money had been pitted against real fiscal stimulus.

Second, the absence of real fiscal stimulus —and indeed the presence of some measure of fiscal tightness—makes clear the extent of the overkill of monetary restraint which contributed to the highest unemployment levels in almost two generations. Those who acqui-

cline of 0.02 percent. Equation (9) forecast *GNP* growth of 0.47 percent.

The one-year lag equations predicted about half of the increase in unemployment which occurred from 1981 to 1982. Might we attribute the remaining half to monetary policy and the gathering force of cyclical decline?

[16] Our estimates are of course essentially of reduced-form relations. We should hope that the results are sufficiently suggestive to induce application of our adjustments in full macroeconometric models. This might permit clarification of the extent to which price and interest movements are affecting consumption and investment directly via their effects on net debt or via associated real interest rates which may in turn be related to monetary policy. It might also illuminate the extent to which federal surpluses and deficits have been offset at the state and local level.

[17] Presently anticipated official high-employment deficits in the future are another matter. As indicated in Appendix B and Table A2, current Congressional Budget Office projections of actual deficits and rates of interest, inflation, and unemployment suggest adjusted high-employment budget deficits of 1.60, 1.99, and 2.55 percent of *GNP* in 1986, 1987, and 1988, respectively, implying an extremely expansionary but unsustainable fiscal policy.

esced in tight money as "the only game in town" to slow a presumably overheated inflationary economy were wrong on two counts. The absence of increasing fiscal thrust reinforces the inference that the inflation came on the side of supply shocks rather than excess demand. And the strong-willed rejection of accommodative monetary policy, rather than balancing budget excesses, offered a near-lethal combination of monetary and fiscal contraction.

Appendix

A. *Total Government: Federal, State, and Local*

Total liabilities of state and local governments grew from $16 billion at the end of 1946 to $296 billion at the end of 1980, as shown in Table A1. For that same period, however, their financial assets grew from $12 billion to $205 billion. Net debt was close to zero in 1946, and had increased only moderately to a peak of $120 billion at the end of 1976 before turning down.

When we take into account tangible assets —highways, water and sewer systems, public buildings, land, and the like—we find that net worth of state and local governments, always positive, grew enormously. From 1946, when it stood at $82 billion, it rose to $1,605 billion by the end of 1980.

We may look at the sum of the balance sheets for federal, state, and local governments to find the total government picture. There we note that while liabilities grew by over a trillion dollars, from $316 billion in 1946 to $1,450 billion by the end of 1980, financial assets grew over that same period from $87 billion to $912 billion. Thus net debt grew only from $230 billion to $538 billion.

Total government tangible assets, however, grew by over $2 trillion, from $255 billion at the end of 1946 to $2,423 billion at the end of 1980. Thus, the value of total assets of government grew by almost $3 trillion, from $342 billion at the end of 1946 to $3,335 billion at the end of 1980. The net worth of total government also grew by nearly $2 trillion, from $26 billion at the end of 1946 to $1,884 billion at the end of 1980.

B. *Projected Future High-Employment Budgets and their Effects*

With massive tax cuts and increases in military spending dwarfing reductions in nonmilitary government outlays, fiscal policy took a sharp turn towards stimulus in 1982. This was measured in the official high-employment budget, which moved from a surplus equal to 0.15 percent of *GNP* in 1981 to a deficit of 1.08 percent of *GNP* in 1982. Congressional Budget Office calculations consistent with projected budget deficits from 1983 to 1988 indicate that the official high-employment deficit will grow further, to 1.75 percent of *GNP* in 1983, reaching 4.14 percent in 1988.

Utilizing Congressional Budget Office projections of movements in the *GNP* implicit price deflator and Treasury bill rates, along with Wharton Annual Model projections of interest rates on U.S. government notes and bonds, and a future series for federal debt developed from forecasts of actual deficits, we have also been able to calculate the high-employment budget adjustments for price and interest effects. To do so, we constructed market-to-par indices for future years by extrapolating relations between these indices and the relevant interest rates over the earlier period, relations which fit quite well, and then applied these and the projected price changes to projections of financial assets and liabilities assumed to have the same distribution as in 1981.

The results shown in Table A2 for the years 1982–88 indicate a pattern quite different from the corresponding data in Table 6 for earlier years. Where our adjustments for price and interest effects in the recent period of high inflation and rising interest rates showed adjusted budgets moving more sharply to restraint, the impact of the adjustments now is in the direction of relatively greater stimulus. While the official high-employment budget moved from 0.15 percent in surplus in 1981 to 1.08 percent in deficit in 1982, as noted above, the adjusted high-employment budget, with declining rates of inflation and falling interest rates, moved much more. The high-employment budget adjusted only for price effects went from 1.92 percent in surplus to a virtual balance, of

TABLE A1—ASSETS, LIABILITIES, AND NET WORTH, BILLIONS OF DOLLARS, FEDERAL, STATE AND LOCAL, AND TOTAL GOVERNMENT

	Assets					
Year (1)	Tangible (2)	Financial (3)	Total (4)	Total Liabilities (5)	Net Debt (6)	Net Worth (7)
Federal						
1946	170.1	74.2	244.3	300.1	225.9	−55.9
1950	112.2	93.9	206.0	290.0	196.2	−84.0
1960	207.3	117.7	325.0	325.2	207.5	−.2
1970	301.0	218.0	519.0	470.7	252.7	48.3
1975	433.6	359.3	793.0	720.0	360.7	72.9
1976	462.9	397.0	859.9	829.0	432.0	31.0
1977	509.7	428.5	938.2	890.6	462.1	47.6
1978	571.8	504.9	1,076.7	970.1	465.2	106.6
1979	647.4	632.6	1,280.1	1,049.3	416.6	230.8
1980	727.0	706.7	1,433.7	1,154.3	447.5	279.4
State and Local						
1946	85.2	12.5	97.7	16.2	3.7	81.5
1950	114.4	17.6	132.0	26.6	9.0	105.4
1960	237.2	32.8	270.0	74.2	41.5	195.8
1970	548.5	70.6	619.1	149.8	79.2	469.3
1975	977.8	121.6	1,099.4	223.4	102.3	875.5
1976	1,049.9	134.1	1,184.0	253.9	119.8	930.1
1977	1,159.7	155.7	1,315.8	273.5	117.7	1,042.3
1978	1,317.8	173.0	1,490.8	283.9	110.9	1,206.9
1979	1,504.0	189.7	1,693.7	297.7	108.0	1,396.0
1980	1,695.9	205.1	1,901.0	296.0	90.9	1,605.0
Total Government						
1946	255.3	86.7	342.0	316.3	229.6	25.7
1950	226.6	111.5	338.1	316.6	205.2	21.5
1960	444.4	150.6	595.0	399.5	248.9	195.5
1970	849.5	288.6	1,138.1	620.5	331.9	517.6
1975	1,411.4	480.9	1,892.3	943.9	463.0	948.4
1976	1,512.8	531.1	2,043.9	1,082.9	551.8	961.0
1977	1,669.4	584.2	2,253.6	1,164.1	579.8	1,089.5
1978	1,889.6	678.0	2,567.6	1,254.1	576.1	1,313.5
1979	2,151.4	822.4	2,973.8	1,347.0	524.6	1,626.8
1980	2,422.9	911.9	3,334.8	1,450.3	538.4	1,884.5

Note: Column (6) is col. (5) − col. (3); Column (7) is col. (4) − col. (5).

TABLE A2—PROJECTED HIGH-EMPLOYMENT BUDGET SURPLUS OR DEFICIT AS PERCENT OF *GNP*, OFFICIAL AND ADJUSTED

	High-Employment Budget Surplus (Deficit −)		
Year	Official[a]	Adjusted for Price Effects	Adjusted for Price and Interest Effects
1981	0.15	1.92	1.97
1982	−1.08	.01	−1.77
1983	−1.75	−.48	−1.46
1984	−2.49	−1.08	−.47
1985	−2.87	−1.37	−1.13
1986	−3.25	−1.80	−1.60
1987	−3.74	−2.26	−1.99
1988	−4.14	−2.59	−2.55

[a]Years from 1982 to 1988 calculated from Congressional Budget Office figures furnished by Frank Russek; the projected deficit for 1988 was the average of the first three quarters with the third quarter weighted twice.

0.01 percent in surplus. And the fully adjusted high-employment budget, including price and interest effects, moved almost 4 percentage points, from 1.97 percent in surplus to 1.77 percent in deficit!

It may be instructive to note what our equations with the various high-employment budgets predict for 1983, and beyond. Equations (2′), (5′), (9′), and (12′), shown in Tables 7 and 8, and new equations for the official high-employment budget estimated on data through 1982, all indicate an upturn in 1983. The official high-employment budget equation predicts the smallest increase in real *GNP*, 3.7 percent, and unemployment essentially unchanged (up about 0.1 percentage points). The price-adjusted high-employment budget, recognizing the lesser effects of inflation on the real value of the debt, indicates a growth of 4.4 percent in real *GNP* and decline of 0.4 percentage points in unemployment. Finally, the price- and interest-adjusted high-employment budget equations point to a growth in real *GNP* of some 5.9 percent and a decline in unemployment of 0.45 percentage points.

As this is written (June 1983), the Bureau of Economic Analysis has released its second-quarter "flash" estimate of real *GNP* growing at a 6.6 percent annual rate, which Martin Feldstein, Chairman of the Council of Economic Advisers, and other administration officials indicate may presage a (presumably) fourth-quarter over fourth-quarter increase of 5.5 percent.[18] The adjusted budget equations point more closely to that mark than does the equation with the official high-employment budget, but as year-over-year projections, the estimates of the adjusted equations appear somewhat high. By the time this paper is in print, the reader should have the opportunity to check the various forecasts against the actual data for 1983.

Looking further into the future, with forecasts of lower inflation and declining or steady interest rates, our adjustments do relatively little to temper projections by the Congressional Budget Office of a high-employment budget very substantially in deficit. We cannot consistently apply our projections of adjusted deficits to forecast the path of the economy because this path may diverge from the Congressional Budget Office projections on the basis of which both the official high-employment budget and our adjustments are calculated. Without taking into account the feedback which would alter the underlying Congressional Budget Office projections, our equation (12′), for example, would point to rates of growth of real output ranging from the 5.88 percent in 1983 to 8.37 percent in 1988, and an unemployment rate which would be down to 2.2 percent by 1988; applications of the official high-employment budget would indicate a 1988 unemployment rate of minus 0.8 percent!

All this has obviously ignored supply constraints. The aggregate demand which would call for these paths of output and employment must in fact be expected to generate considerably higher rates of inflation than those in the Congressional Budget Office forecasts. These in turn would affect interest rates and our price and interest adjustments to the high-employment budget. Consequently, the fully adjusted high-employment budget may in fact turn out to be less in deficit than assumed in our productions. Indeed, as increases in inflation increasingly erode the value of debt created by increases in deficits, the projected adjusted deficits may well prove unattainable.

C. *Sources and Methods*[19]

The major basic sources of data are the Bureau of Economic Analysis (BEA) of the Department of Commerce and the Flow of Funds Accounts of the Federal Reserve Board.

Data on reproducible tangible assets of government (including government enterprises) are the revised series, at current (replacement) cost, on the BEA capital stock

[18] As reported in *The Wall Street Journal*, June 22, 1983, p. 3.

[19] A more detailed and precise description of sources and methods, including construction of the various indices developed, is available from the authors on request.

data tape.[20] Land estimates for 1952 through 1968 originated with Grace Milgram in Raymond W. Goldsmith (1973). These were extrapolated backward and forward on the basis of total private land estimates taken from the Flow of Funds.[21]

The Flow of Funds data on financial assets and liabilities were at face value or par. Federal government data were totals for U.S. government, federally sponsored credit agencies, and the Monetary Authority. Assets held in federal employee and railroad retirement funds appeared both as assets and equal offsetting liabilities. The state and local government data excluded employee retirement funds. No attempt was made to estimate and include retirement liabilities or associated future receipts at either the federal or state and local levels.

Conversion of values from par to market for financial assets and liabilities was accomplished as follows:

Currency, demand and time deposits, other loans, taxes receivable, and miscellaneous assets and liabilities. These items were taken at face value as indicated in the Flow of Funds accounts.

Gold. Prior to 1968, gold was taken at the official price of $35 per ounce. From 1968 through 1980, market values for the last trading day of the month were taken from the *Report of the Director of the Mint*, 1968, 1969,...1980, "Daily market prices of industrial gold in the United States, quoted by Engelhard Minerals and Chemical Corporation, Murray Hill, New Jersey."

U.S. government securities. Indices were taken or derived from published and unpublished data prepared by Cox and Hirschhorn. We applied the index for total U.S. government debt to Treasury issues, the index for U.S. Treasury notes to savings bonds and a weighted average of indices for Treasury bonds and notes to federal credit agency issues.

[20]BEA Capital Stock Tape (1980). Data for 1980 were obtained by telephone from Jerry Silverstein.

[21]Flow of Funds Accounts, Division of Research and Statistics, Board of Governors of the Federal Reserve System, Flow of Funds data tape (September 1981).

State and local obligations. For short-term obligations, that is, those of less than one year, we used the Cox and Hirschhorn index for U.S. Treasury bills. For other state and local bonds, we constructed an index by assuming that bonds have maturities of ten years, biannual interest payments, and coupon rates equal to the Standard and Poor's annual yields on long-term state and local bonds in the years they were issued. The volumes of new bond issues were taken from *Business Statistics* and from the *Federal Reserve Bulletin*. Market values were then calculated as the sum of interest and principal commitments, discounted by the Standard and Poor's end-of-year yield on state and local bonds, of the bonds issued over the ten most recent years.

Mortgages. We used a similar method in constructing a market-to-par index for mortgages, in this case assuming a 15-year life and discounting by the Federal Home-Loan Bank Board new home mortgage yield.

Corporate and foreign bonds (held by state and local governments). We used the New York Stock Exchange bond index for all listed U.S. companies, as found in the New York Stock Exchange *Fact Book*.

For net revaluations, we generally followed the formulation and procedures described in Eisner (1980). Thus,

$$\text{(A1)} \quad NR_t = \left(K_t - \frac{P_{t,end}}{P_{t-1,end}} K_{t-1} - \frac{P_{t,end}}{P_t} IN_t \right) \frac{P_t}{P_{t,end}},$$

where NR_t = net revaluations of the year t, K_t = net value of stock at the end of the year t, P_t = the *GNP* implicit price deflator for the year t, $P_{t,end} = (P_{t,IV} + P_{t+1,I})/2$, with $P_{t,IV}$ and $P_{t+1,I}$ denoting *GNP* implicit price deflators for the fourth quarter of the year t and the first quarter of the year $t+1$, respectively, and IN_t = net investment or net flows in the year t.

For all financial assets other than gold and corporate equities, net investment in year t is the difference in the par value of stocks between years t and $t-1$.

Net investment in corporate equities is the net flow in the Flow of Funds accounts. Net investment in gold is equal to the change in the physical stock of gold, multiplied by the average market price.

For conversions of budget surplus or deficit to 1972 dollars, we used the *GNP* implicit price deflator. For gross public debt and net debt, we used our estimate of the end-of-year deflator, the mean of the fourth-quarter deflator and the deflator for the first quarter of the subsequent year.

The official high-employment budget surplus data were taken from de Leeuw and Holloway.

Interest rate effects equal the total change in par-to-market revaluations:

$$(A2)\quad IRE_t = \sum_{i=1}^{4} [(1 - MP_{i,t})K_{i,t} - (1 - MP_{i,t-1})K_{i,t-1}],$$

where $K_{i,t}$ is the par value of the ith financial instrument in year t, expressed as a positive quantity if it is a liability and a negative quantity if it is an asset, and $MP_{i,t}$, $i = 1$ to 4, are the market-to-par indices for the four financial instruments—savings bonds, mortgages, net holdings of agency issues, and other Treasury issues.

Price effects, expressed in current prices, relate to changes, due to inflation, in the real value of existing net debt exclusive of gold. They are calculated as the net revaluations described in (A1) above, but net of the interest rate effects defined in (A2), where K_t is the market value, exclusive of gold, of federal net debt at the end of year t, and IN_t is the market value of the change in net debt, exclusive of gold, in the year t.

REFERENCES

Boskin, Michael J., "Federal Government Deficits: Some Myths and Realities," *American Economic Review Proceedings*, May 1982, *72*, 296–303.

Cox, Michael and Hirschhorn, Eric, "The Market Value of U.S. Government Debt: Monthly, 1942–1980," *Journal of Monetary Economics*, March 1983, *11*, 261–72.

de Leeuw, Frank and Holloway, Thomas M., "The High-Employment Budget: Revised Estimates and Automatic Inflation Effects," *Survey of Current Business*, April 1982, *62*, 21–33.

Eisner, Robert, "Capital Gains and Income: Real Changes in the Value of Capital in the United States, 1946–1977," in Dan Usher, ed., *The Measurement of Capital*, Chicago: University of Chicago Press, 1980, 175–346.

______, "Social Security, Saving and Investment," *Journal of Macroeconomics*, Winter 1983, *5*, 1–19.

Fellner, William, "The High-Employment Budget and Potential Output: A Critique," *Survey of Current Business*, November 1982, *62*, 26–33.

Goldsmith, Raymond W., *Institutional Investors and Corporate Stock — A Background Study*, New York: National Bureau of Economic Research, 1973.

Horrigan, Brian R. and Protopapadakis, Aris A., "Federal Deficits: A Faulty Gauge of Government's Impact on Financial Markets," *Business Review*, Federal Reserve Bank of Philadelphia, March/April 1982, 3–16.

Leimer, Dean R. and Lesnoy, Selig D., "Social Security and Private Saving: New Time-Series Evidence," *Journal of Political Economy*, June 1982, *90*, 606–29.

Penner, Rudolph G., "How Much is Owed by the Federal Government?," *Carnegie-Rochester Conference Series on Public Policy: Monetary Regimes and Protectionism*, Spring 1982, *16*, 233–56.

Ruggles, Richard and Ruggles, Nancy D., "Integrated Economic Accounts for the United States, 1947–1980," *Survey of Current Business*, May 1982, *62*, 1–53.

Seater, John J., "The Market Value of Outstanding Government Debt, 1919–1975," *Journal of Monetary Economics*, July 1981, *8*, 85–101.

Congressional Budget Office, *The Outlook for Economic Recovery*, Washington: USGPO, February 1983.

U.S. Council of Economic Advisers, *Economic Indicators*, May 1983, Washington: USGPO, 1983.

______, *Economic Report of the President*, Washington: USGPO, February 1982.

Federal Reserve Bulletin, selected issues, 1979–82.

New York Stock Exchange, *Fact Book*, 1951...1980.

The Wall Street Journal, June 22, 1983.

U.S. Department of Commerce, Bureau of Economic Analysis, *The National Income and Product Accounts of the United States, 1929–74, Statistical Tables*, Washington: USGPO, 1976.

______, *Business Statistics*, Washington: USGPO, 1979.

______, BEA Control Stock Tape, BEA-N1W-80-002, Washington, 1980.

U.S. Department of the Treasury, Bureau of Government Financial Operations, *Statement of Liabilities and Other Financial Commitments of the United States Government as of September 30, 1982*.

______, Bureau of the Mint, *Report of the Director of the Mint*, 1968...1980.

Wharton Econometric Forecasting Associates, *Wharton Long-Term Forecast, April 1983*, Philadelphia: 1983.

[17]

Which Budget Deficit? Some Issues of Measurement and Their Implications

By ROBERT EISNER*

A budget deficit is like sin. To most of the public it is morally wrong, very difficult to avoid, not always easy to identify, and susceptible to considerable bias in measurement.

To the body politic, and perhaps also to many economists, the apparent underlying reality is that every dollar of deficit—of a person, business or government—adds a dollar to debt. And debt is bad!

In commentary on that last, I like to recall pleasurably the late Sumner Slichter, a respected conservative economist of at least a generation ago. Churlishly responding to a pressing questioner on a TV program, he suggested increasing debt could be very good; he would generally counsel young people to go into significant debt to buy homes.

More- and less-sophisticated economists have long come to recognize a number of measures of federal budget deficits and their varied implications. Deficits are not always bad, or at least at certain times their alternatives are worse. And we must distinguish among cyclical deficits, structural deficits and high employment deficits, to name a few. But matters are more complicated than many of us have thought to note. We do not usually measure government budget deficits in economically relevant fashion. When we do, we can get results at variance from much conventional wisdom. Just consider the following sketchy set of issues.

1) Should we have included in the fiscal 1983 budget deficit of $195.4 billion some $17 billion of outlays of off-budget federal entities largely to finance direct loan programs? In fact, we did not.

2) As of the end of the 1982 fiscal year, the Treasury listed "contingency" obligations which totalled $6,982 billion, largely for retirement pay and Social Security. Should we try to estimate the year's increase in present value of obligations, net against them the increase in present value of anticipated associated receipts and add that remainder to the deficit? We do not.

3) In general, when the federal government incurs a liability in order to acquire an asset, whether borrowing to make a loan or to acquire real capital, should we net the additional asset from the additional liability in calculating our deficit? Federal investment-type outlays have been estimated by the Office of Management and Budget at $182 billion fiscal 1983. Should the federal government, like private business and state and local governments, have separate capital and current budgets? It does not.

4) We all know that inflation plays huge tricks on conventional accounting. Paul Pieper and I (1984) have estimated that adjusting for changes in the real market value of federal financial assets and liabilities would change the high-employment budget surplus by large *and varying* amounts, ranging between 2.86 percent and −0.18 percent of *GNP* in the years 1969 to 1982. Adjustments would be broadly similar for actual budget deficits. Should we make inflation adjustments? We do not.

5) The $195.4 billion deficit for fiscal 1983 cited above, we are told, is a historical record for the United States. We have never had a budget deficit that large. And it is anticipated by the Congressional Budget Office that if no corrective action is taken (even assuming that defense spending will grow at a rate of "only" 5 percent after inflation, lower than administration requests) the deficit will rise to about $250 billion in fiscal 1988 and $280 billion in 1989. But so what? What do these mind-boggling numbers mean? Gross National Product in calendar 1983 will be over $3,300 billion

*William R. Kenan Professor of Economics, Northwestern University, Evanston, IL 60201. I am indebted to Paul Pieper for his contribution to joint work on which this paper leans heavily.

and, by 1989, according to one set of forecasts, it will be in excess of $5,400 billion. Should we perhaps recognize that in an economy in which everything is growing—output, income, liabilities and assets—a quite substantial deficit may leave ratios of financial assets and liabilities in our government and national balance sheets unchanged? We generally do not.

6) With all the questions relative to knowing what budget deficits are or have been, problems are vastly compounded in forecasting deficits in budgets yet to be realized. As is well known, huge portions of federal receipts and expenditures are endogenous, determined not merely by decisions as to rates of expenditures and taxes, but by economic and demographic developments, and, indeed, interactions between the budget and the economy. We can perhaps forecast how many people will be in each category eligible for Social Security, but we do not know how many will choose to draw benefits rather than continue working. What assumptions should we make about employment, unemployment, real growth, inflation, corporate profits, and so many other lesser variables which will so critically affect future budget deficits? Should we have a single forecast of these variables, agreed upon by Congress and the administration, so that differences in deficit estimates and predictions can be separated from differences in underlying assumptions? We do not.

7) Finally, how do differences among the measures of budget deficits, past and prospective, relate to their possible impact on the economy? Have we considered which are relevant for the various issues of so much concern—inflation, employment, investment, consumption, distribution of income, role of government, incentives, efficiency and the allocation of resources?

Having sketched out a set of questions, I shall be so bold as to offer some comments, including even a few numbers on which to reflect.

I. Off-Budget Items and Credit Extension

Off-budget items relate almost entirely to credit extension, generally by the Federal Financing Bank to federal lending agencies. It has been argued that direct off-budget loans advanced under federal auspices, $14 billion in 1982, plus a portion of guaranteed loans (the total of which was $21 billion in 1982, and estimated at over $50 billion in 1983) represent unrecognized contributions to the true budget deficit.

Clearly, federal loans or loan guarantees which result in private expenditures which would not otherwise be undertaken must be recognized, aside from possible substitution effects, as augmenting aggregate demand. I should caution, however, against viewing them as, except possibly in small part, elements of a budget deficit in most, economically relevant senses. For Treasury borrowing to finance loans to the public, directly or indirectly, except as a second-order effect, adds neither to the net debt of the federal government nor the net financial assets of the public. (To the extent that the federal government borrows at the market rate of interest but lends at a below-market rate, it is, however, acquiring loan assets whose market value is less than the market value of its liabilities.) Hence (except for the parenthetical qualification), these off-budget federal borrowings do not have the essential wealth effects on consumption usually attributable to true budget deficits.

By another criterion as well, that of net claims on credit markets, federal borrowing to finance loans to the public would also qualify very partially, if at all, as components of a relevant budget deficit. For while, on the one hand, the Treasury borrowing draws on the public supply of credit, the Treasury or agency lending offers an essentially equivalent offset by meeting some of the public demand for credit.

II. Contingency Expenditures

Constructing a budget of "contingency expenditures" and associated receipts may well be a useful exercise. The relevant numbers, as we have suggested, are enormous, as may be the associated deficits (or surpluses). I should object, however, to incorporating measures of year-to-year increase in net contingent liabilities in current budget deficits.

Proclamations (usually intended to be alarmist) of huge net contingent liabilities and accruals to these net liabilities which might be considered annual deficits are in fact highly conjectural. What expenditures or outlays will finally be will depend frequently upon legislation of the future. Similarly, associated receipts will depend upon future legislation as well as highly uncertain economic and demographic developments. And how to balance projected expenditures and receipts depends further on uncertain and changing rates of discount.

An interesting and major case in point is the whole matter of Social Security, on which many have become exercised. We have been told that huge increases in net Social Security debt were having a major impact on aggregate consumption and saving. But after the initial sensationalist articles and arguments, a number of works (including my 1983 article) raised fundamental doubt as to the existence of any clear, measurable impact. And finally, in a few strokes of legislation, the balance between contingent expenditures and contingent liabilities was changed drastically. Who could even say accurately that the public over the last several decades has perceived annual increases in net Social Security wealth? And who can argue persuasively that they are perceiving such increases now?

III. Capital Budgets

Failure to separate current and capital expenditures in the formal federal budget and the associated failure to account systematically for capital assets contributes to confusion in economic analysis and consequent formulation of policy. It does make a difference whether a budget "deficit" finances transfer payments, current services, accumulation of stocks, or long-term investment. For example, the argument, to which I give little weight, that public perception of assets in the form of government debt is offset by anticipated associated tax liabilities, is negated to the extent that real income-producing government assets lie behind the debt. Federal capital accounts might of course well relate, further, not only to investment in physical assets owned by government, but to investment in the human capital and the private and public resources of the nation.

Objection to separating out capital expenditures from the current federal budget seems to stem considerably from concern that any resultant lowering of measured budget deficits would reduce resistance to excessive government spending. Aside from the ideological and unsubstantiated nature of the premise, however, there is no reason why, as I shall illustrate below, separate current and capital accounts cannot be combined to reach a bottom line showing precisely the unified budget deficit to which so much attention is now given. The separate subtotals, though, would give us a better clue as to the extent government was leaving a burden for future generations or building the houses—and other assets—that Sumner Slichter recommended for the young.

IV. Inflation Adjustments

The failure to account separately for capital expenditures quite breaks the publicly perceived connection between a budget deficit and spending beyond our means or squandering the public treasure. Recurring budget deficits have in fact been accompanied by *in*creasing federal net worth, as noted in my article with Pieper. What has also until recently been remarkably underplayed, if not ignored, is that in periods of inflation, our conventionally measured budget deficits are accompanied by *de*creasing values of real federal net debt. The "underlying reality...that every dollar of deficit...adds a dollar to debt" is simply not true in a real sense if price levels are not constant. And if interest rates fluctuate, the statement is not true even with reference to the market value of nominal debt. Adjustments of the official budget deficit to make it correspond to changes in net financial liabilities entail interest rate effects on market value of federal financial assets and liabilities and price or inflation effects on the real values of the corrected market values.

In general, we may write the adjusted or corrected deficit as

$$D_C = D - \dot{P}_A A + \dot{P}_B B - \dot{P}(B + M - A)$$

where D = the "official deficit," A = federal

financial assets (excluding gold), B = federal interest-bearing liabilities held by the public, $\dot{P}_A$ and $\dot{P}_B$ = the relative (weighted average) rates of price change of A and B, respectively, $\dot{P}$ = the inflation rate, M = non-interest-bearing federal liabilities held by the public, essentially "high-powered money" or the monetary base, and $B + M - A$ = the "net debt."

As noted in my article with Pieper, the corrected deficit is vastly reduced and frequently converted to surplus in years of rapid inflation and rising interest rates (hence falling bond prices). The real federal net debt as defined above hence fell enormously since World War II, declining in per capita 1972 dollars from $3,694 at the end of 1946 to $1,445 by the end of 1980, despite a heavy preponderance of officially measured budget deficits in the intervening years.

What is more, turning to the high-employment deficit as a first-order measure of fiscal thrust, while the official measure of generally increasing deficit through the 1970's and up to 1981 suggested a stimulatory fiscal policy, the corrected measure showed quite the opposite. The severe recession of 1981 and 1982 was associated with high previous surpluses in the interest- and price-corrected high-employment budget—2.2, 1.8, 1.6, and 2.0 percent of *GNP* in the years 1978 to 1981. Interestingly, the recovery of 1983 is well accounted for by the sharp 1982 move to a deficit equal to 1.8 percent of *GNP* in the corrected high-employment budget; this was the product of a growing official deficit, slowing inflation and lower interest rates.

Recent work of Alex Cukierman and Jorgen Mortensen (1983) suggests that inflation corrections call for similar drastic revisions in perceptions of fiscal policies in Western Europe. In particular, the United Kingdom and Italy, with high official budget deficits, turn out to have had very low budget deficits, or even surpluses, after correction for inflation, perhaps accounting for their high unemployment rates. By contrast, the corrected budgets in West Germany, with relatively low rates of inflation and little or no net government debt, were sufficiently in deficit to have been stimulatory, possibly accounting for the low unemployment and rapid growth in Germany.

V. Equilibrium Growth

Whatever our measure of the deficit in dollars, pounds, lira, or marks, to what is it relevant in a large, changing, and generally growing economy? Recent work has suggested some apparent—if dubious—paradoxes involving deficits and rates of growth of interest-bearing securities and "money." We may get some needed perspective by exploring briefly one, simple overall relation. Netting out the acquisition of financial assets, essentially the off-budget items discussed above, we may write the official deficit as $D = \dot{B} + \dot{M} - \dot{A}$. Then, denoting $\gamma = (B + M - A)/Y$ = the ratio of net debt to *GNP*, and $g = \dot{Y}/Y$ = the rate of growth of *GNP*, it is readily apparent that $D/Y = \gamma g$ is the "equilibrium" condition for a stable ratio of net debt to *GNP*.

With the current value of γ in the United States approximately 0.3 and the growth of *GNP* in nominal terms about 10 percent, one notes that the "equilibrium" value of D/Y, far from zero, is some 0.03. Thus, at current or immediately anticipated rates of growth, we can accommodate an official deficit of 3 percent of *GNP* without increasing the relative debt burden. In fact, the deficit for fiscal 1983 ran closer to 6 percent of *GNP*, but it may be argued that this was largely a cyclical deficit and the structural or reasonably high-employment deficit would be considerably less.

Ignoring interest rate effects, we may write for our inflation-corrected, "equilibrium" budget deficit ratio, $D_C/Y = \gamma(g - \dot{P})$ or, more precisely, $D_C/Y = \gamma n$, where $n = (1 + g)/(1 + \dot{P}) - 1$. With $\gamma = 0.3$ and a real rate of growth, $n = 0.03$, an inflation-corrected budget deficit which would keep the ratio of net debt to output constant at its current value of 0.3 would then be in the order of 0.9 percent of *GNP*. This is in the neighborhood of the current price-adjusted high-employment deficit. Congressional Budget Office projections of an official high-employment deficit approaching 4 percent of *GNP* by 1988 would imply, on the basis of the concomitantly assumed 5 percent rate of inflation, however, a price-adjusted deficit ratio of some 2.5 percent. Such an *adjusted* deficit might well prove unsustainable. Relations estimated by Pieper and me suggest that resultant inflation and increases in debt would widen the gap between official and adjusted deficits until the latter were back at a more modest, equilibrium level.

VI. Conclusion—A Variety of Deficits

A few definitions and associated dollar figures for 1982 can help bring all this together. In Table 1, we note a variety of budgets or accounts to be considered. From them one can concoct a very large variety of deficits, only a subset of which are listed in Table 2. Some will be of greater relevance for certain purposes and some for others.

The current budget deficit, D1, would be most consistent with the more usual private business and state and local government measures, but the current adjusted deficit, D4, would be more economically relevant. In terms of macroeconomic policies for high-employment and stable price paths, my preference would go to D6, the national income account adjusted deficit, which would essentially indicate the change in net debt of the federal government to the public. As remarked above, in the years leading up to 1981, inflation and rising interest rates had both contributed to reducing national income adjusted deficits sharply or even converting some to surplus, but there was a marked shift in the correction in 1982.

We might also keep a close eye on D7, which would include price or inflation adjustments but not the (partially related) sharply fluctuating interest effects on the market value of debt. For a bottom line on the long-run trend in government activities, we might regard D8 and D12, the changes in net worth and "total net worth," the latter including contingent assets and liabilities. We should indeed, for many purposes go much further and recognize the intangible wealth to which government ostensibly contributes by expenditures for research and development, education and health.

What about D3, the official national income account budget deficit (or its unified budget twin)? We may as well continue to calculate it. We need the basic data in orderly form and we should have the series for continuity. But it may not merit prime focus. If we are concerned with economic analysis and consequences, we should not be shy about looking further.

TABLE 1—A VARIETY OF BUDGETS

Account (1)	Credits (2)	Debits (3)	Deficit[a] (4)
A. Current	617	744[b]	127
B. Capital	43[c]	63[d]	20
C. National Income	617	764	147
D. Net Revaluations of Financial Capital	−10	11	21
D*. Price Component	−28	−61	(34)
D**. Interest Component	18	72	55
E. Net Revaluations of Tangible Capital	9	–	(9)
F. Off-Budget (ΔV)	18	17	(1)
G. Contingent[e] (ΔV)	−390	−256	134

Note: Calendar 1982 unless otherwise indicated; ΔV is change in value of balances, and parentheses indicate surplus.

[a]Col. 4 is col. 3 minus col. 2.

[b]Includes capital consumption allowances and $701 billion in current outlays.

[c]Capital consumption allowances.

[d]Capital expenditures.

[e]Fiscal 1982.

TABLE 2—A VARIETY OF DEFICITS

Deficit Components[a] (Designation)	Deficit[b] (1)	(2)
D1 = *A* (Current)	126.7	4.1
D2 = *B* (Capital)	20.4	0.7
D3 = *A* + *B* = *C* (National Income)	147.1	4.8
D4 = *A* + *D* (Current Adjusted)	147.8	4.8
D5 = *A* + *D** (Current Prices-Adjusted)	93.1	3.0
D6 = *C* + *D* (*NI* Adjusted)	168.1	5.5
D7 = *C* + *D** (*NI* Prices-Adjusted)	113.4	3.7
D8 = *A* + *D* + *E* (Net Worth)	139.1	4.5
D9 = *C* + *F* (*NI* plus Off-Budget)	146.1	4.8
D10 = *C* + *F* + *G* (Total)	280.1	9.1
D11 = *C* + *D* + *F* + *G* (Total Adjusted)	301.1	9.8
D12 = *A* + *D* + *E* + *F* + *G* (Total Net Worth)	272.1	8.9

Note: Calendar 1982, except for D10, D11, and D12, which includes the G component for fiscal 1982; *NI* = National Income.

[a]As designated in Table 1.

[b]Col. 1 is billions of dollars; col. 2 is percent of *GNP*.

REFERENCES

Cukierman, Alex and Mortensen, Jorgen, "Monetary Assets and Inflation Induced Distortions of the National Accounts–Conceptual Issues and Correction of Sectoral Income Flows in 5 EEC Countries," *Economic Papers* No. 15, June 1983, Commission of the European Communities, Directorate-General for Economic and Financial Affairs, Internal Paper.

Eisner, Robert, "Social Security, Saving, and Macroeconomics," *Journal of Macroeconomics*, Winter 1983, *5*, 1–19.

______ **and Pieper, Paul J.,** "A New View of the Federal Debt and Budget Deficits," *American Economic Review*, March 1984, *74*, 11–29.

ROBERT EISNER

Will the Real Federal Deficit Stand Up?

Deficits do matter. But to know their economic impact, we must use the high-employment deficit and adjust it for the effects of changing inflation and interest rates.

In some circles, the federal budget deficit has become the hottest political issue since Vietnam. Democrats and Republicans echo each others' proclamations of disaster and largely restrict their differences to proposed remedies and the casting of blame. Scoring political points has replaced almost all efforts at sober economic analysis.

Deficits do matter, but to know how and how much, you have to measure them right. And deficits can be good as well as bad.

By official measure, the federal budget has been in deficit in all but eight of the fifty-five years from 1931 through 1985. In fact, in the twenty-five years since 1960 only one, 1969, had no deficit. The last sixteen years have presented an unbroken picture of deficits.

World War II saw what were then huge deficits, totaling $170 billion for the years 1942 through 1945. The total gross federal debt over that period rose by $203 billion.

From 1946 through 1984, budget deficits, net of surpluses, totaled $988 billion; including off-budget outlays, they totaled $1,112 billion. Over that period, the gross federal public debt increased by $1,317 billion. This is a history that, at least in general terms, is well etched into the public consciousness. It has been the stuff of many sober pronouncements and warnings and has frequently agitated political debate. A number of additional items of information, however, compli-

ROBERT EISNER is William R. Kenan Professor of Economics, Northwestern University. This article is adapted for *Challenge* from a much longer paper presented at the Symposium and is drawn from the author's new book, *How Real Is the Federal Deficit?* (New York: The Free Press, A Division of Macmillan, Inc., May 1986).

May-June 1986/Challenge

cate the picture and also put it in better perspective.

First, when numbers are changing rapidly over time, particularly with economic growth and inflation, it is important to put the figures in some kind of relative terms. The gross federal debt held by the public, for example, grew from $235 billion at the end of the 1945 fiscal year to $1,313 billion by the end of the 1984 fiscal year. But our national income and gross national product grew relatively more over these years. The gross federal debt held by the public was 108.4 percent of GNP at the end of fiscal 1945. Despite the very large dollar growth in that debt over the following years, it had fallen, as a percentage of GNP, to 27.8 percent by the end of the 1980 fiscal year. And with all the subsequent red ink and increase in the debt, at the end of the 1984 fiscal year the debt as a ratio of GNP had risen to only 36.7 percent, still well below the 108.4 percent figure of 1945 (and the 119.8 percent figure of 1946).

There are some analogous observations to make with regard to our annual budget deficits. They surged during the years of World War II, but then were generally modest until they rose toward the end of the Vietnam War and surged again after 1981. Over all these years federal outlays and receipts have been fluctuating—albeit growing—and GNP has increased enormously. How can we get an appropriate view of the *relative* size of the deficit?

One way to get a broader perspective is to note what has happened to the deficit as a percentage of budget outlays. We see in Table 1 that, while the proportion of federal outlays that are deficit-financed stood at a substantial 21.8 percent in fiscal 1984, this was far from a record. During the Depression fiscal year of 1932 (from July 1, 1931, through June 30, 1932), although the deficit was "only" $2.7 billion, 58.7 percent of federal outlays were deficit-financed. And during the war years that proportion soared, rising to 70 percent in 1943. In the presumably fiscally responsible administration of Dwight Eisenhower, in fiscal 1959, the ratio rose to 13.96 percent. During the peak-deficit, Vietnam fiscal year of 1968, the ratio was slightly higher, some 14.13 percent.

The size of the deficit relative to the economy as a whole may be reasonably captured by the ratio of the deficit to GNP. That ratio was also relatively high in Depression and war years, but fairly small over the rest of the period until 1982.

Deficits and the economy

But how can we measure the effects of deficits on the economy? Do they cause inflation or recession? Do they reduce unemployment or crowd out investment? Do they stifle economic growth or stimulate it? Do they increase our foreign debt and wreck our balance of trade, or do they contribute to world prosperity?

A simple, naive approach would be to relate the federal deficit to some of the broad aggregates in which we are interested. We might check the correlations among deficits and GNP, business investment, or the rates of unemployment or inflation. The difficulty, a common one in economics, is especially serious here: we cannot distinguish between cause and effect.

The problem is that the economy affects the deficit, perhaps as much as or more than the deficit can be expected to affect the economy. When economic conditions are good, incomes, profits, and employment are high. Treasury receipts, tied as they are to individual and business income taxes and payroll taxes on employment, are hence high. Further, government expenditures for unemployment benefits and welfare payments will be less when the economy is prosperous.

The combination of higher tax receipts and lower expenditures means a lower deficit. But it is clearly the high GNP, income, profits, and employment that have caused the low deficit, and not the reverse. Since high rates of saving and investment generally accompany high GNP, incomes, and profits, they too would be associated with smaller deficits. The inference that the smaller deficits brought on the higher saving and investment would be similarly unwarranted.

The inverse relation between deficits and inflation is somewhat more complex. At first blush it might appear that inflation would have a neutral effect on the deficit. While higher prices would mean larger nominal incomes and hence greater tax payments to the Treasury, the government would also have to pay more for what it buys. If federal salaries and Social Security benefits are indexed to the cost of living, we might conclude that expenditures and receipts would both be increased by inflation and the deficit therefore not changed.

There are, however, a number of complications. First, income taxes historically have risen more, proportionately, than increases in income brought on by inflation. This has happened because of the notorious "bracket creep"—inflation has pushed more of income into taxable brackets and into higher brackets with higher tax rates.

Table 1 **Federal Receipts and Outlays, and Surplus or Deficit as Percentage of Outlays and GNP, Fiscal Years 1929–84**

Fiscal year	Receipts	Outlays†		Surplus or deficit (−)		
(1)	(2)	(3)	(4)	(5)	(6)	(7)
	Billions of dollars	Billions of dollars	Percentage of GNP	Billions of dollars	Percentage of outlays	Percentage of GNP
1929	3.9	3.1	3.03	0.7	23.47	0.71
1932	1.9	4.7	6.96	− 2.7	−58.70	− 4.09
1943	23.6	78.5	44.37	− 54.9	−69.89	−31.01
1945	45.2	92.7	42.71	− 47.5	−51.22	−21.88
1946	39.3	55.2	27.32	− 15.9	−28.73	− 7.85
1959	79.2	92.1	19.41	− 12.9	−13.96	− 2.71
1960	92.5	92.2	18.52	0.3	0.29	0.05
1965	116.8	118.2	17.92	− 1.6	− 1.35	− 0.24
1966	130.8	134.5	18.57	− 3.8	− 2.82	− 0.52
1967	148.8	157.5	20.26	− 8.7	− 5.53	− 1.12
1968	153.0	178.1	21.42	− 25.2	−14.13	− 3.03
1969	186.9	183.6	20.16	3.2	1.76	0.36
1970	192.8	195.6	20.19	− 2.8	1.45	− 0.29
1971	187.1	210.2	20.38	− 23.0	−10.96	− 2.23
1972	207.3	230.7	20.44	− 23.4	−10.13	− 2.07
1973	230.8	245.7	19.62	− 14.9	− 6.06	− 1.19
1974	263.2	269.4	19.53	− 6.1	− 2.26	− 0.44
1975	279.1	332.3	22.45	− 53.2	−16.01	− 3.59
1976	298.1	371.8	22.67	− 73.7	−19.82	− 4.49
1976*	81.2	96.0	22.21	− 14.7	−15.31	− 3.40
1977	355.6	409.2	21.97	− 53.6	−13.10	− 2.88
1978	399.7	458.7	21.93	− 59.0	−12.86	− 2.82
1979	463.3	503.5	21.36	− 40.2	− 7.98	− 1.71
1980	517.1	590.9	22.94	− 73.8	−12.49	− 2.87
1981	599.3	678.2	23.50	− 78.9	−11.63	− 2.73
1982	617.8	745.7	24.48	−127.9	−17.15	− 4.20
1983	600.6	808.3	25.09	−207.8	−25.71	− 6.45
1984	666.5	851.8	23.79	−185.3	−21.75	− 5.17

Source: *Economic Report of the President, February 1985*, Table B-72, p. 318, U.S. Department of the Treasury, Office of Management and Budget, Bureau of Economic Analysis, and author's own calculations.

Note: Fiscal years until 1976 ran from July 1 of the preceding calendar year to June 30. From 1977 on, the fiscal years began on October 1.

* Transition quarter, July 1 to September 30, 1976.

† Including off-budget outlays.

While indexing of exemptions and tax brackets to the price level has now essentially ended that contribution of inflation to a more-than-proportional enhancing of individual income-tax payments, the effect of inflation in bringing more-than-proportional increases in business tax payments remains. This stems from the failure of original-cost depreciation deductions to rise with inflation, as well as from swollen inventory profits of firms that use FIFO ("first-in, first-out") accounting. This occurs because revenues reflect current higher prices, while accounting costs of materials and fixed capital are based on the lower prices of bygone days.

Inflation also brings about more-than-proportionate increases on the expenditure side. These stem from the higher interest rates and hence greater Treasury interest payments as inflation expectations take hold.

In the past, bracket-creep effects of higher prices were such that inflation tended on balance to reduce deficits. But such an association of higher inflation and lower deficits does *not* imply the inverse relation—that deficits reduce inflation.

Actual budget deficits are therefore not a good measure of fiscal policy. The administration and the Congress might be following a tight fiscal policy, keeping discretionary expenditures down and tax rates up, and yet a recession would create a substantial deficit. Indeed the tight fiscal policy, by depressing aggregate demand, might bring on such a recession.

The high-employment budget

To ascertain what deficits do to the economy, we need a measure that is uncontaminated by what the economy does to deficits. Economists have been able to develop one that removes some of the contamination—brought on by cyclical fluctuations in income and employment. It has been variously called the full-employment, high-employment, standardized-employment, cyclically adjusted, and structural budget.

Whatever its name, the important thing about this budget is that it presents estimates of what expenditures and receipts, and hence the deficit, *would be* if the economy were at a level of activity independent of cyclical variations in employment, output, and income. Since the cyclical variations in output and income are closely associated with those of employment and unemployment, the budget has usually been defined for a constant rate of unemployment.

Beginning in 1955, the Bureau of Economic Analysis of the Department of Commerce constructed a series of high-employment budget surpluses and deficits. "High" employment was initially taken to mean 4 percent unemployment, but that figure was subsequently raised, apparently on the assumption that structural or demographic change in the economy was increasing the amount of unemployment—unfortunately often called the "natural" rate of unemployment—which should be accepted as consistent with high employment. It was argued, particularly, that the population contained increasing proportions of youths and urban blacks, with high rates of even noncyclical unemployment, and these increasing proportions were forcing up the national average of unemployment which was attainable.

Table 2

Actual and High-Employment Federal Budget Surpluses and Deficits on National Income Account, 1955–84

Year	Actual	High-employment	Actual	High-employment
	Billions of dollars		Percentage of GNP	
(1)	(2)	(3)	(4)	(5)
1955	4.4	5.2	1.10	1.30
1956	6.1	7.9	1.44	1.87
1957	2.3	6.1	0.51	1.37
1958	−10.3	0.0	−2.28	0.00
1959	−1.1	5.4	−0.23	1.11
1960	3.0	12.1	0.60	2.39
1961	−3.9	7.1	−0.74	1.35
1962	−4.2	3.0	−0.75	0.53
1963	0.3	7.4	0.04	1.24
1964	−3.3	1.1	−0.51	0.17
1965	0.5	0.9	0.08	0.13
1966	−1.8	−5.6	−0.24	−0.74
1967	−13.2	−15.1	−1.65	−1.89
1968	−6.0	−11.0	−0.69	−1.26
1969	8.4	4.9	0.89	0.52
1970	−12.4	−4.6	−1.25	−0.46
1971	−22.0	−11.3	−2.04	−1.05
1972	−16.8	−12.1	−1.42	−1.02
1973	−5.5	−9.5	−0.42	−0.72
1974	−11.5	−0.3	−0.80	−0.02
1975	−69.3	−29.1	−4.47	−1.88
1976	−53.1	−17.4	−3.09	−1.01
1977	−45.9	−20.4	−2.39	−1.06
1978	−29.5	−15.9	−1.36	−0.73
1979	−16.1	−2.0	−0.67	−0.08
1980	−61.2	−17.1	−2.33	−0.65
1981	−64.3	−3.2	−2.17	−0.11
1982	−148.2	−32.6	−4.83	−1.06
1983	−178.6	−57.0	−5.40	−1.72
1984	−175.8	−91.8	−4.80	−2.51

Sources: Frank de Leeuw and Thomas M. Holloway, "The High Employment Budget: Revised Estimates and Automatic Inflation Effects," *Survey of Current Business*, 62 (April 1982), pp. 21–33, subsequent issues of the *Survey of Current Business*, and author's adjustments to maintain a 5.1 percent base for "high employment" in 1983 and 1984. These last estimates have been revised downward somewhat from those published in *How Real Is the Federal Deficit?*

The comparison of actual and high-employment budgets is intriguing. From 1955 to 1965, as shown in Table 2, the actual budget was in deficit five times and in surplus six. The high-employment budget was never in deficit. When the actual budget was in surplus, the high-employment budget was more so. All this reflected the fact that actual unemployment was more than the high-employment rate over this period. Hence, actual tax revenues were less while government expenditures were more.

From 1966 to 1969, with the boom aggregate demand produced by the Vietnam War, actual unemployment was less than the 4 percent rate associated with high employment. (That is an interesting commentary on our view of "high employment" even then. Quite ignoring the Humphrey-Hawkins Full Employment and Balanced Growth Act, we now cheerfully project unemployment in the 6 and 7 percent range.) The low unemployment of those years caused the three actual deficits to be *less* than the deficit associated with high employment and the 1969 surplus to be greater.

The 1970s ushered in the era of unrelenting federal deficits. For none of the last sixteen years has the budget been balanced, let alone in surplus. Those who saw deficits as evidence of unbridled government spending contributing to inflation seemed to have some support for their views. Inflation rose through most of the decade of the seventies, peaking in 1981. But then, as deficits soared to unprecedented heights in 1982, inflation rates dropped precipitously.

The deficits were widely interpreted, nevertheless, as evidence of expansionist fiscal policy. Richard Nixon had said in 1972, "We are all Keynesians now." If the Keynesian analysis, which had presumably come to dominate policymaking, were correct, should not unemployment have been low and the economy sizzling? In fact, unemployment was inching up and the economy was sluggish. What was wrong?

One try at an answer was that it was the actual budget that was showing the repeated and generally growing deficits. As we have observed, these deficits may have been essentially the product of poor economic conditions, rather than their cause. We may point, for example, to the then-record deficit of $69 billion in 1975. Clearly that was largely the result of the sharp 1974–75 recession. Unemployment, after all, averaged 8.5 percent in 1975. If we had looked at the high-employment budget might we have had a different picture?

But now comes the shocker. The high-employment budget deficit was less than the actual deficit throughout the 1970s and into the 1980s, but it too was never quite balanced, coming close only in 1974. Indeed, in 1975 the high-employment deficits seemed generally to be getting larger, not smaller.

It might be said that with growth in the economy and inflation everything was getting larger. The deficit figures would be more comparable over time if they were adjusted for this growth. A simple way to do this is to present the deficit figures as percentages of GNP. As we can also see in Table 2, however, this does not change the basic picture. Actual deficits as a percentage of GNP set post–World War II records. Even high-employment budgets showed an unmistakable trend to deficit.

At least until the Vietnam War, the high-employment budget was never in deficit and was usually substantially in surplus. By 1966, however, the high-employment budget moved to deficit, and stayed in deficit, with the solitary exception of the tax-surcharge year of 1969. It would thus appear that the original charge that fiscal policy had been overly expansive is supported—or at least not contradicted—by the history of the high-employment budget deficit.

Table 3 **High-Employment Surplus as Percentage of GNP, 1955–84**

Year	Official	Adjusted for price effects	Adjusted for interest effects	Adjusted for price and interest effects	Percent change in GNP
	Percentage of GNP				
(1)	(2)	(3)	(4)	(5)	(6)
1955	1.30	2.81	2.26	3.77	6.72
1956	1.87	3.83	2.79	4.74	2.14
1957	1.37	2.46	0.11	1.20	1.82
1958	0.00	0.93	1.32	2.24	−0.42
1959	1.11	2.09	1.96	2.94	5.99
1960	2.39	2.83	0.45	0.89	2.15
1961	1.35	1.99	1.81	2.45	2.63
1962	0.53	1.25	0.12	0.87	5.78
1963	1.24	1.79	1.70	2.25	4.02
1964	0.17	0.78	0.12	0.72	5.27
1965	0.13	0.98	0.58	1.43	6.04
1966	−0.74	0.33	−0.97	0.11	5.97
1967	−1.89	−0.89	−1.33	−0.34	2.70
1968	−1.26	0.06	−1.14	0.18	4.62
1969	0.52	1.94	1.32	2.74	2.79
1970	−0.46	0.77	−1.87	−0.64	−0.18
1971	−1.05	0.11	−1.41	−0.25	3.39
1972	−1.02	0.02	−0.66	0.39	5.66
1973	−0.72	0.89	−0.46	1.14	5.77
1974	−0.02	2.15	−0.16	2.01	−0.64
1975	−1.88	−0.38	−2.04	−0.54	−1.18
1976	−1.01	0.22	−1.75	−0.52	5.41
1977	−1.06	0.46	−0.23	1.30	5.51
1978	−0.73	1.26	0.15	2.15	5.03
1979	−0.08	1.72	0.11	1.91	2.84
1980	−0.65	1.45	−0.13	1.97	−0.30
1981	−0.11	1.57	−0.23	1.45	2.52
1982	−1.06	0.02	−3.10	−2.01	−2.13
1983	−1.72	−1.66	−0.44	−0.62	3.70
1984	−2.51	−1.36	−3.07	−1.92	6.78

Sources: Frank de Leeuw and Thomas M. Holloway, "The High Employment Budget: Revised Estimates and Automatic Inflation Effects," *Survey of Current Business*, 62 (April 1982), pp. 21–33, subsequent issues of the *Survey of Current Business*, *Economic Report of the President, February 1985*, author's adjustments to maintain a 5.1 percent base for "high employment" in 1983 and 1984, and author's calculations explained in *How Real Is the Federal Deficit?* with deficit figures for 1983 and 1984 revised downward from those published there.
Note: Surplus or deficit (-) on national-income-accounts basis.

Deficits adjusted for inflation

We come now to our critical departure. We must adjust deficits for inflation. The real surplus or deficit may be viewed as essentially the sum of three components: (1) the nominal surplus or deficit as currently measured; (2) an adjustment for changes in the market value of government financial assets and liabilities due to changes in interest rates; and (3) an adjustment for changes in real value due to changing general price levels incident to inflation. An identical or analogous set of adjustments is appropriate for the high-employment budget surplus or deficit.

We can then calculate the adjusted high-employment budgets, which, by correcting for these inflation effects, come closer to measuring real surpluses or deficits and the consequent thrust of fiscal policy on aggregate demand. Applying our calculations of net revaluations on actual net federal debt, we originally adjusted the official high-employment budget surplus series for the years 1955 through 1981. Maintaining

Figure 1 **Official and Price-Adjusted High-Employment Budget Surplus**

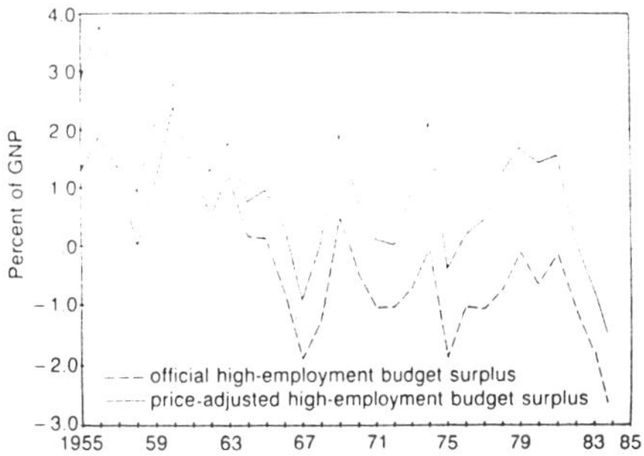

the 5.1 percent unemployment benchmark for high employment in effect in the official series since 1975, we have now extended our calculations to 1984.

The results, shown in Table 3, are dramatic. Inflation and rates of interest were low and relatively steady in the early 1960s prior to escalation of our military involvement in Vietnam. Corrections to the official high-employment budget surplus are hence generally small in those early years.

But in later, more inflationary years, when the official high-employment budget as well as the actual budget moved substantially into deficit, the corrections are striking. In the 1970s, the entire perceived trend in the direction of fiscal ease or expansion is eliminated or reversed. The high-employment budget surplus, fully adjusted for price and interest effects, was higher as a percent of GNP for every year from 1977 through 1981 than the surplus of all but two of the years from 1966 through 1976. The only exceptions were the tax-surcharge year of 1969 and the oil-price-shock year of 1974.

With similar exceptions, the surplus adjusted only for price (and not interest) effects was higher in every year from 1978 to 1981 than in any other year back to 1963. And since we have accepted Bureau of Economic Analysis increases in the "high-employment" bench mark from 4.0 percent to 5.1 percent unemployment over the period of its "official" series, we may well understate the move to fiscal tightness. The high-employment surpluses would have been even greater in later years if calculated at 4.0 percent unemployment.

New light on economic history

So some significant rewriting of recent economic history is in order. Inflation could hardly be ascribed to excess demand associated with increasing fiscal ease and stimulus if, at least by the appropriately corrected high-employment budget measure, there was no such movement to fiscal ease. Some explanation of sluggishness in the economy, climaxed by the severe 1981–82 recession, might then be found in a relatively tight fiscal policy, as measured by the adjusted high-employment budget surplus, as well as in the widely blamed (or credited) role of monetary policy.

The record of deficits beginning in 1982 is another matter. We shall come to that later. For now we want to show the relation of budget deficits to the economy. And we will find that prevailing views reflect the distortions of improper measures, the most important of which, again, are those tricks played by the effects of inflation.

A few charts can begin to set the record straight and tell a dramatic new story. First, Figure 1 shows the widening gap between official and price-adjusted high-employment budget surpluses or deficits as inflation began to heat up in the late 1960s. The two measures moved up and down in broadly similar fashion. But by the mid-1970s the inflation-adjusted budgets were some 1.5 to 2 percentage points more in surplus or less in deficit than the unadjusted, official high-employment budgets.

What about the relation between budget deficits and the economy? A single picture may be worth a thousand words, or as many statistics. Figure 2 juxtaposes the percentage change in real GNP and the previous year's price-adjusted high-employment deficit as a percentage of real GNP.

The two curves, it must be conceded, show a remarkable fit. The greater the deficit, the greater the next year's increase in GNP. The less the deficit, the less the increase or the greater the decline in the next year's GNP.

Changes in real GNP, as is well known, are closely but inversely related to changes in unemployment.

Production requires labor, and the more people working the greater the output. When unemployment goes up, real GNP growth slackens or actually becomes negative. When unemployment goes down, GNP goes up. And the faster unemployment goes down, the faster GNP rises.

In view of the relation between the deficit and GNP, we should thus expect a similar close, but inverse, relation between the deficit and changes in unemployment. Figure 3 confirms this. Converting the inverse relation with the deficit into a direct one, it plots the percentage-point change in unemployment and the *previous* year's ratio of the price-adjusted high-employment *surplus* (the negative of the deficit).

The close fit of the two curves is again outstanding. Higher surpluses—or lower deficits—are associated with greater increases or smaller decreases in unemployment.

This relation indicating the stimulative effect of budget deficits has held up under a substantial amount of more vigorous statistical analysis, reported in my new book, *How Real Is the Federal Deficit?* That analysis indicates that monetary policy, as measured by changes in the monetary base, also affects rates of growth of gross national product and unemployment. The independent effect of budget deficits remains substantial, however, probably greater (when the deficit is adjusted for inflation) than effects of changes in the monetary base.

Figure 2 **Lagged Price-Adjusted High-Employment Deficit and Change in GNP**

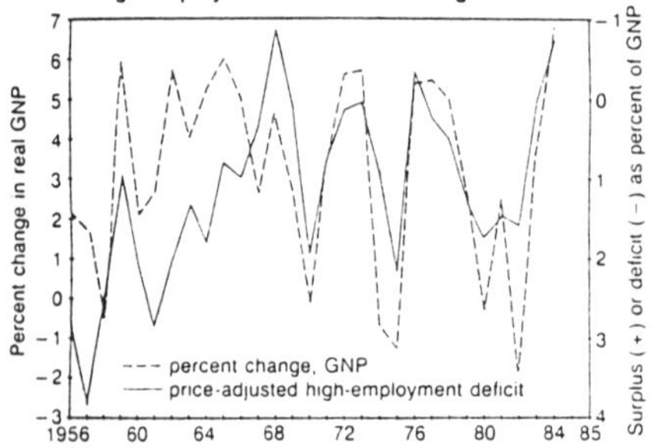

Budget deficits are found to be positively associated not only with increases in consumption but also with increases in investment. Deficits in the past have generally "crowded in" investment, not crowded it out. There is evidence as well, however, that budget deficits have contributed to the increase in our trade deficit, particularly in their association with substantial increases in imports. It should be added that these increases in our imports have in turn stimulated growth in output in our OECD partners. And it may be added,

Figure 3 **Lagged Price-Adjusted High-Employment Surplus and Change in Unemployment**

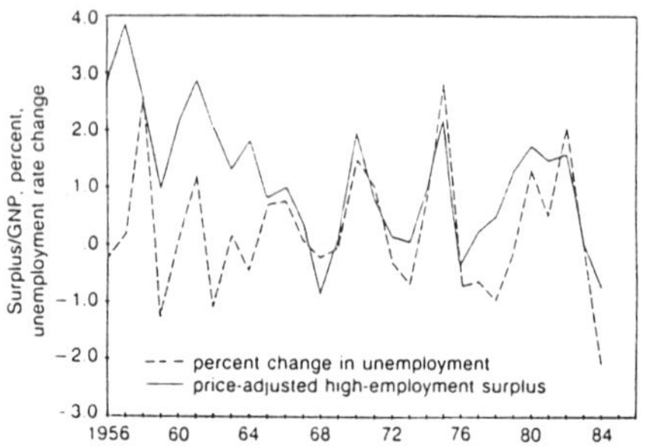

finally, that, after adjustment for inflation, it turns out that Japan had the greatest deficits in recent years along with the fastest growth. And the very slow-growing United Kingdom had substantial budget surpluses after inflation adjustment.

The impact of the deficit

Where does all this leave us? The officially reported federal debt has been growing at astronomical rates. Since President Reagan took office in 1981 the gross public debt has more than doubled, from $930 billion to $1.9 trillion. The increase has reflected huge and repeated annual deficits, reaching $212 billion in fiscal 1985.

But this has not been all bad! Indeed, given the economic collapse of 1981–82, smaller deficits would have made the deep recession worse. Unemployment would have risen above the official 10.7 percent figure, which was already the highest since the Great Depression of the 1930s. Total production and business profits would have been less. Without the huge deficits, we would not have had the brisk recovery of 1983 and 1984. And the 1984 election results—for good or for ill—might well have been quite different.

Up to about 1966, when inflation was relatively

minor, budget deficits were really budget deficits. In the period from 1966 on, however, when inflation became substantial, the officially balanced budget turned into one of surplus after inflation corrections were made. A balanced, inflation-adjusted, high-employment budget would have been substantially expansionary, producing high rates of growth of GNP and declines in unemployment. As late as 1981, however, we had a roughly balanced *official* high-employment budget, while the budget adjusted for inflation was substantially in surplus.

The Carter administration, which, along with most outside critics, ignored indications of sluggishness in the economy, interpreted the combination of apparent deficits and inflation as indicating excess demand. It initiated moves to combat inflation by encouraging a tight-money policy and, in its final years, striving to reduce budget deficits. This policy continued through the first year of the Reagan administration, as domestic spending was further restrained and more taxes rose than declined.

But in fact, fiscal policy was not stimulative. The high inflation and rising interest rates meant that budgets seemingly in deficit were actually in substantial surplus. Our statistical relations indicate strongly that these inflation-adjusted surpluses contributed significantly to the 1981-83 recession.

This suggests two important correctives to widespread views of fiscal and monetary policy. First, the 1981-83 recession cannot properly be interpreted as a triumph of all-powerful monetary constraints over relatively ineffective fiscal ease. Tight monetary policy *and* tight fiscal policy were its proximate causes.

Thus, those who acquiesced in tight money as the only way to slow a presumedly overheated, inflationary economy were wrong on two counts. First, the inflation had come from supply shocks—with critical energy prices up some 500 percent in a decade—rather than excess demand, an inference reinforced by the absence of real increases in fiscal thrust. And second, strong-willed rejection of accommodative monetary policy, rather than balancing budget excesses, offered a near-lethal combination of monetary and fiscal contraction.

But fiscal policy moved in a sharply different direction in 1982. A combination of major tax cuts and increases in military expenditures with a fall in inflation and interest rates converted the adjusted high-employment budget from a very high surplus to a very high deficit. Indeed, the change of 3.46 percentage points, from a surplus of 1.45 percent of GNP in 1981 to a deficit of 2.01 percent in 1982, was one of the greatest such swings to expansion on record. Our estimate of relations between budget deficits and changes in GNP and unemployment predicted a major swing to economic recovery and lower unemployment in 1983 and on into 1984, and that is of course precisely what occurred.

Prior to both the fiscal 1986 Congressional Budget Resolution and the Gramm-Rudman program to "balance the budget" by 1991, Congressional Budget Office estimates indicated very large and increasing deficits in the years ahead. August 1985 projections of the official high-employment ("standardized-employment") budget, reduced to a 5.1 percent unemployment rate, showed a deficit of $185 billion by 1990. This corresponds to an actual projected deficit in the national income accounts of $258 billion for that year.

Adjustment for price effects, however, brings the high-employment deficit down substantially, to $29 billion in 1986, but shows it rising to $79 billion by 1990. The price- and interest-adjusted deficit in 1990 is projected at $76 billion. We thus had projections of substantial high-employment deficits over the rest of this decade. The adjustments for anticipated inflation reduced those projected deficits, but still left them high. The projected adjusted deficits, therefore, while initially less than their 1982-84 peaks, were substantial, and turning higher.

Indeed, make no mistake about it. From a historical perspective, these deficits are enormous. From 1986 to 1990 they would average 2.15 percent of GNP, while up to 1982 the largest inflation-adjusted deficit we had ever had, in any year since the high-employment series began in 1955, was 0.64 percent. From 1955 to 1981, the adjusted high-employment budget was, on average, in *surplus* by 1.35 percent of GNP.

Deficits this large, according to my analysis—and probably those of any major econometric model—imply considerable excess demand. Unchecked, they would be pushing the economy toward rates of growth of GNP and declines of unemployment—the latter to negative figures!—that are clearly unattainable.

Initially, however, it should be recognized that the large deficits would be expected to contribute to a reduction of our 7 percent overall unemployment rate. Once unemployment is driven as low as possible with aggregative measures, further fiscal stimulus would generate inflation. The Federal Reserve would then be expected to tighten the money supply, and interest rates, both nominal and real, would rise.

The curious consequence is that associated declining real market values of the public holdings of government debt would mean that the *real* federal deficit would be reduced. It would have been reduced, however, by an inflation tax rather than explicit tax increases or reductions in government expenditures.

The deficit reductions envisaged in the Congressional Budget Resolution for fiscal 1986 were in fact substantial. With adjustment for inflation, the high-employment budget, calculated at an unemployment rate of 5.1 percent, would be brought into balance in 1986 and would be in some surplus in subsequent years. While none of this can be predicted with great accuracy or confidence, it would appear that such a path for the high-employment budget, and the associated relatively moderate actual budget deficits that it implies, would be consistent with relatively low unemployment and reasonably noninflationary economic growth.

The Gramm-Rudman program, on the other hand, envisages very drastic deficit reduction from 1987 on. By bringing the actual budget to balance by 1991, it would create a surplus in the official high-employment budget and, most important, very substantial surpluses in the high-employment budget adjusted to include the inflation tax. Gramm-Rudman would, in a real sense, give us high-employment budget surpluses, when adjusted for inflation, comparable to those that have usually been associated in the past with a sluggish economy or sharp recessions.

A new look at deficits

Once we get over the notion that deficits are automatically sinful, and once we learn to measure them right, a lot of the easy answers have to be rejected. It is not true that deficits must always be reduced. The current mix of fiscal and monetary policy, with high real interest rates and a huge trade imbalance accountable to an expensive dollar, is far from ideal. Our budget priorities may be all wrong. But it is hard to sustain the knee-jerk reaction that wiping out all the overall official deficit will solve our problems.

The public has feared that budget deficits add to their own debt burden and that of future generations. What we really bequeath to the future, however, is our physical and human capital. A "deficit" that finances the construction and maintenance of our roads, bridges, harbors, and airports is an investment in the future. So are expenditures to preserve and enhance our natural resources or to educate our people and keep them healthy. Federal budgets that are balanced by running down our country's capital or mindlessly selling public assets to private exploiters are real national deficits.

As for that bottom line on what to do about the current federal deficit—it depends. If we were to carry out the projections of the fiscal 1986 Joint Congressional Budget Resolution, and we are seriously committed to a high-employment economy, we would probably have gone far enough in overall budget cutting. The increase in debt for the last five years has been such that even our slower rate of inflation generates a substantial inflation tax. The inflation tax rate is less, but the public debt on which it is paid is more.

Inflation-adjusted budget deficits, on the basis of the budget resolution projections, did not promise to be unduly large. For those who prize economic growth and low unemployment, the risk of insufficient fiscal stimulus must be weighted heavily. One cannot properly counsel budget-balancing in an economy with unemployment still at 7 percent and real economic growth well below its potential. A budget balanced by current federal rules of accounting is an invitation to the worst economic downturn in half a century.

The budget mix is another matter. We may wish to spend more on investment in our public infrastructure and human capital and less on subsidies and support to those with the most political clout. We may also wish to devote more to our nation's welfare and less to warfare. And we may wish to finance our expenditures with a more equitable tax system.

With a sound and balanced fiscal policy, we should look all the more to a monetary policy that permits the economy to move at full speed. No artificial shortage of money should be allowed to drag down private investment or so distort the value of the dollar as to cripple the significant sectors of the American economy that do and should compete in world markets.

A competitive, market-oriented economy is capable of stunning successes. But there remains a major role for government policy to ensure the aggregate demand necessary for full employment and maximum growth. With correct measures, the macroeconomic theory of the past half century can continue to show the way.

[19]

Deficits, Monetary Policy, and Real Economic Activity

Robert Eisner
NORTHWESTERN UNIVERSITY

and Paul J. Pieper
UNIVERSITY OF ILLINOIS

1 INTRODUCTION

The coincidence in the 1970s of apparently large, structural federal deficits, substantial and growing unemployment and inflation rising to double-digit levels brought widespread questioning of the hitherto dominant Keynesian paradigm. Indeed, Robert Lucas (Lucas and Sargent, 1978; Lucas, 1981) indicated this coincidence as a motivation for his own rejection of that paradigm and search for new macroeconomic theory. In short, he explained, the Keynesian model suggested that expansive fiscal and monetary policies might cause some inflation but would reduce unemployment. But to the contrary, he indicated, these policies begot accelerating inflation *and high unemployment.*

In earlier work (Eisner and Pieper, 1984), we have argued that conventional measures of federal deficits – both actual and structural or high employment – along with associated views of fiscal policy, were fundamentally flawed. We showed that they were particularly biased measures of fiscal thrust in periods of significant inflation. Conventional measures ignored changes in the market value of outstanding government debt due to changing interest rates and further changes in their real value due to changes in the general level of prices or inflation. Making appropriate adjustments for changes in the real value of debt forces revision of conventional measures of fiscal policy. Particularly from 1977 to 1981, what appeared to be substantial deficits, both actual and due to high employment, became substantial surpluses.

We reported further that high employment deficits adjusted to correspond to changes in the real value of net debt were positively associated with subsequent increases in real GNP and reductions in unemployment. In other work (Eisner and Pieper, 1985) we noted that the United States high employment budget deficits adjusted for inflation were positively associated with subsequent real growth in Canada, France, West Germany, Italy, Japan and the United Kingdom.

The relations we estimated were all single equation, reduced forms and doubts may reasonably be expressed as to whether our results will prove robust against underlying structural changes. Dealing only with the reduced forms, however, the question immediately arises as to whether deficits may have been associated with changes in the money supply, which had been omitted in the relations we estimated. Perhaps it was excluded monetary variables that accounted for the relations we observed.

In this chapter we will seek to answer that question. We will further estimate separately the role of the interest effect on the market value of the debt and deficit. In addition, we will extend our previous analysis with annual data to estimation of distributed lag relations involving quarterly time series. Finally, we will go beyond effects on the aggregate of gross national product to examine movements of the various components of GNP. This will enable us to cast some light on the extent to which deficits 'crowd out' or 'crowd in' investment. We will also find, in the impact of deficits on net exports, an explanation of the previously observed relation between United States deficits and GDP growth among our major trading partners.

2 THE ROLE OF MONEY AND DEFICITS: ANNUAL DATA

We have introduced two different measures of monetary policy into our relations, the monetary base and non-borrowed reserves, both expressed as the change in end-of-period real stocks as a percentage of GNP.[1] We use the high employment deficit, calculated for an unemployment level of 5.1 per cent, as a first order measure of the thrust of fiscal policy on aggregate demand. However, our preferred fiscal measure differs in two important respects from other studies. First, since it is clearly real wealth which is relevant to real economic activity, we have adjusted the high employment deficit for changes in the real market value of government debt due to both inflation and changes in interest rates. The latter affect the market value of federal debt while inflation further affects its real value.

Secondly, we relate changes in real economic activity to the level of the high employment deficit, expressed as a percentage of GNP, rather than its rate of change. Consumption is a function of wealth, and not just current income, in both the life-cycle and permanent income theories. A federal budget deficit increases desired consumption by raising current wealth in the form of the federal debt to the private sector.[2] To the extent that it is expected to continue it also raises expected future income. Thus the change in consumption should be a function of the change in government net debt, or the level of the deficit. The higher the deficit, the greater the increase in wealth and the greater the increase in consumption.

A greater federal debt may also stimulate investment, both directly and indirectly. A direct effect may stem from portfolio considerations. Firms finding themselves with greater wealth in the form of government securities may strive to restore balance by acquiring real assets. A perhaps more powerful indirect effect may stem from perceptions of increased current and planned future consumption which would generate demand for more capital to supply an increased output of consumer goods.

In our earlier work, since time series for high employment budgets have been constructed back to 1955, we were able to regress changes in gross national product and unemployment on lagged high employment budget surpluses for observations beginning with 1956. A consistent series for the monetary base is available from the Federal Reserve only for years beginning with 1959. Our regressions were therefore able to use observations from 1960 through 1984. We had previously estimated separate sets of constants and regression coefficients for observations in the less inflationary, pre-1967 period and for the ones beginning with 1967. With so few pre-1967 observations now available, we have specified separate parameters only for the constant terms but calculated common regression slopes.

In Table 1.1[3] we present regressions of changes in GNP on the lagged high employment surplus and the lagged real change in either the monetary base or non-borrowed reserves, all expressed as percentages of GNP. The results for the high employment surplus variables are consistent with our previous work with a somewhat different set of observations. First, a balanced official high employment budget would appear to produce a very substantial growth in GNP in the earlier less inflationary period but virtually no growth in the later more inflationary period. The difference is much less, as shown by the constant terms, in the price adjusted surplus regression. Secondly, the high employment surplus is significantly negatively related to subsequent growth in GNP

6

Table 1.1 High-employment budget, monetary aggregates and GNP

$$\Delta GNP_t = b_{01}X_1 + b_{02}X_2 + b_1 HES_{t-1} + b_2 \Delta M_{t-1}$$
$$X_1 = 1,\ X_2 = 0:\ t = 1961\text{–}6$$
$$X_1 = 0,\ X_2 = 1:\ t = 1967\text{–}84$$

(1)	(2)	(3)	(4)	(5)	(6)	(7)	(8)	(9)
	Regression coefficients[a]							
Equation	Constants		High employment surplus		Change in monetary base	Change in non-borrowed reserves	$\hat{R}^2$	D–W
	1961–6	1967–84	Official	Price-adjusted				
	(b_{01})	(b_{02})	(b_1)	(b_1)	(b_2)	(b_2)		
(1.1)	7.450 (0.879)	0.772 (0.602)	−2.577 (0.530)				0.547	1.68
(1.2)	8.662 (0.856)	4.328 (0.422)		−2.306 (0.370)			0.662	1.88
(1.3)	3.228 (0.722)	2.023 (0.409)			12.888 (2.282)		0.618	1.99
(1.4)	4.525 (1.034)	3.099 (0.588)				10.574 (7.311)	0.125	1.59
(1.5)	5.159 (0.977)	1.123 (0.499)	−1.426 (0.546)		8.790 (2.556)		0.701	1.58

(1.6)	6.417 (1.257)	3.353 (0.576)		−1.461 (0.501)	6.628 (2.907)		0.719	1.70
(1.7)	7.041 (0.882)	0.999 (0.594)	−2.501 (0.512)			8.331 (5.082)	0.581	1.86
(1.8)	8.423 (0.941)	4.343 (0.429)		−2.237 (0.390)		3.162 (4.781)	0.653	1.88

Notes:
[a] Ordinary least squares; standard errors are shown in parentheses.
ΔGNP = per cent change in GNP
HES = high employment surplus as per cent of GNP
ΔM = real change in monetary base as per cent of GNP, or real change in non-borrowed reserves as per cent of GNP.

and again the relation is sharper, in terms of standard errors and coefficients of determination, for the price adjusted surplus.

As hypothesised, however, the real change in monetary base also proves a good predictor of subsequent increases in GNP. In the 1967–84 period, a constant real monetary base was associated on average with a 2.0 per cent increase in real GNP (and 3.2 per cent growth in the years 1961–7). Each tenth of a percentage point increase in the ratio of the real change in monetary base to gross national product (corresponding on average to a 2.13 per cent increase in the rate of growth of the monetary base) was then associated with a 1.3 percentage point greater growth in GNP. The coefficient of determination in the monetary base relation was 0.618, higher than the 0.547 value of $\dot{R}^2$ for the official high employment surplus equation, but less than the 0.662 for the price adjusted surplus equation. The real change in non-borrowed reserves performs poorly, with little explanatory power and a coefficient not significantly different from zero.

Regressing the real change in GNP on both the high employment surplus and change in monetary base reveals that both were significant. The absolute values of both sets of coefficients, however, were less than when they were the sole regressors. In the best fitting equation, involving the price adjusted high employment surplus and the change in monetary base, the role of the monetary base variable is minimised, with a coefficient of 6.628, as compared with 12.888 when it is the sole regressor and 8.790 when it is coupled with the official high employment surplus. The coefficient of the price adjusted high employment surplus variable is a robust −1.461, almost three times its standard error of 0.501. The coefficient of the price adjusted high employment surplus increases to −2.237 when the monetary base is replaced by non-borrowed reserves, while the coefficient of non-borrowed reserves continues to be not significant.

We have noted in earlier work that the price and interest adjusted high employment surplus required two years of lags to show most of its effect on GNP. We attributed this to the possibility that agents would view short-term changes in the market value of securities as in considerable part transistory. We have thus regressed real changes in GNP on lagged values of the high employment surplus and two year lagged values of the interest effect. Results are shown in Table 1.2.

As hypothesised, the lagged interest effects are significantly negatively related to changes on GNP. The high employment surplus, both unadjusted and price adjusted, is highly significant in all four regressions. Introduction of separate interest effects generally reduces the significance

Table 1.2 High employment budget, delayed interest effect, monetary aggregates and GNP

$$\Delta GNP_t = b_{01}X_1 + b_{02}X_2 + b_1 HES_{t-1} + b_2 IE_{t-2} + b_3 \Delta MB_{t-1} + b_4 \Delta NR_{t-1}$$

$$X_1 = 1,\ X_2 = 0 \text{ for } t = 1961\text{–}6$$

$$X_1 = 0,\ X_2 = 1 \text{ for } t = 1967\text{–}84$$

(1)	*(2)*	*(3)*	*(4)*	*(5)*	*(6)*	*(7)*	*(8)*	*(9)*	*(10)*
		Regression coefficients[a]							
Equation	*Measure of HES*	*Constants*		HES_{t-1}	IE_{t-2}	ΔMB_{t-1}	ΔNR_{t-1}	$\hat{R}^2$	*D–W*
		1961–6 (b_{01})	*1967–84* (b_{02})	(b_1)	(b_2)	(b_3)	(b_4)		
(2.1)	OF	5.226 (0.872)	1.323 (0.453)	−1.330 (0.488)	−0.901 (0.364)	6.875 (2.408)		0.762	1.67
(2.2)	PA	6.300 (1.136)	3.357 (0.520)	−1.323 (0.456)	−0.846 (0.359)	5.166 (2.697)		0.771	1.70
(2.3)	OF	6.550 (0.763)	1.310 (0.513)	−2.065 (0.457)	−1.167 (0.389)		6.930 (4.319)	0.701	1.86
(2.4)	PA	7.722 (0.867)	4.093 (0.388)	−1.860 (0.370)	−0.997 (0.377)		2.880 (4.196)	0.733	1.80

Notes:
[a] Ordinary least squares; standard errors in parentheses.
GNP = per cent change in GNP
HES = high employment surplus as per cent of GNP
OF = official
PA = price adjusted
IE = interest effect as per cent of GNP
MB = real change in monetary base as per cent of GNP
NR = real change in non-borrowed reserves as per cent of GNP

of the monetary variables. The coefficient of the lagged monetary base is no longer significant in the equation with the price adjusted surplus (although it is significant, at the 0.05 probability level, in Cochrane–Orcutt autoregressive relations, now shown here), while non-borrowed reserves are not significant in both equations. The price adjusted high employment surplus variable performs slightly better than the official high employment surplus, in terms of goodness of fit, with either monetary variable (but not consistently so in the Cochrane–Orcutt estimates).

Further confirmation of the robustness of the fiscal variables may be seen in Table 1.3, which shows the results of annual regressions with the change in unemployment as the dependent variable. Holding the monetary base constant, an increase in the official high employment deficit of one per cent of GNP is associated with a reduction of 0.69 percentage points in the unemployment rate, while a similar increase in the price adjusted deficit is associated with a 0.63 percentage points decline in unemployment. As in the GNP regressions, the coefficients of both surplus variables and the lagged interest effects are highly significant, with *t*-statistics in most instances greater than three. The monetary base is significant only in the official surplus equation, while the coefficient of non-borrowed reserves is positive. Again, a balanced official budget (and constant real monetary base) appears expansionary in the earlier period, but contractionary, bringing significantly greater unemployment, in the more inflationary later years.[4]

3 RESULTS WITH QUARTERLY TIME SERIES

In analyses of quarterly time series we first worked with four quarter lags of official and price adjusted high employment budget surpluses and four quarter lags, as well, of three sets of monetary variables. Regressing the change in GNP on the budget variables alone produced a sum of the coefficients of the price adjusted surplus with a lower standard error while the difference in constant terms as between earlier and later periods was greater in the official surplus equations. These results again suggest an inflation error in the official surplus variables, partly corrected by separate constant terms for more inflationary and less inflationary periods. Two sets of monetary variables – the monetary base and total reserves – also showed sums of regression coefficients which were significant at least the 0.05 probability level, with the

Table 1.3 High-employment budget, delayed interest effect, monetary aggregates and unemployment

$$\Delta \text{UN} = b_{01}X_1 + b_{02}X_2 + b_1\text{HES}_{t-1} + b_2\text{IE}_{t-2} + b_3\Delta\text{MB}_{t-1} + b_4\Delta\text{NR}_{t-1}$$

$$X_1 = 1,\ X_2 = 0 \text{ for } t = 1961\text{–}6$$

$$X_1 = 0,\ X_2 = 1 \text{ for } t = 1967\text{–}84$$

(1)	*(2)*	*(3)*	*(4) (5)*	*(6)*	*(7)*	*(8)*	*(9)*	*(10)*	
		Regression coefficients[a]							
Equation	*Measure of HES*	*Constants*		HES_{t-1}	IE_{t-2}	ΔMB_{t-1}	ΔNR_{t-1}	$\hat{R}^2$	*D–W*
		1961–6 (b_{01})	*1967–84* (b_{02})	(b_1)	(b_2)	(b_3)	(b_4)		
(3.1)	OF	−0.611 (0.387)	0.936 (0.201)	0.692 (0.217)	0.506 (0.161)	−2.208 (1.068)		0.746	1.93
(3.2)	PA	−1.052 (0.523)	−0.073 (0.239)	0.634 (0.210)	0.482 (0.165)	−1.539 (1.242)		0.736	1.72
(3.3)	OF	−1.171 (0.332)	1.010 (0.223)	0.944 (0.199)	0.621 (0.169)		0.788 (1.881)	0.691	1.83
(3.4)	PA	−1.738 (0.363)	−0.273 (0.162)	0.868 (0.155)	0.536 (0.158)		2.690 (1.757)	0.746	1.57

Notes:

[a] Ordinary least squares; standard errors are shown in parentheses.

UN = percentage point change in unemployment rate

HES = high employment surplus as per cent of GNP

OF = official

PA = price adjusted

IE = interest effect as per cent of GNP

MB = real change in monetary base as per cent of GNP

NR = real change in non-borrowed reserves as per cent of GNP monetary base variables most clearly significant. The differences were not great but the coefficient of determination was higher in the budget equations and highest when the price adjusted surplus was used as the regressor.

When fiscal and monetary variables are both used as regressors, t-statistics are generally reduced. However, the price adjusted surplus variables remain significant in all regressions, while the official surplus variables are no longer significant at the 0.05 level in the monetary base equation and the only significant set of coefficients for the monetary variables is found in the equation including the official surplus and non-borrowed reserves.

The four-quarter lag regressions reported in Table 1.4 include price adjusted budget variables but exclude interest effects, that is, the par-to-market adjustment which captures capital gains and losses in the market value of outstanding federal debt. To estimate their role we again turn to longer lags and introduce, in this case as separate variables, interest effects lagged five to eight quarters. The sums of coefficients of the interest effect variables, as shown in Table 1.5, prove highly significant in all equations and are close in magnitude to the sums for the budget surplus variables. (Interest effects are defined as positive to the extent that they reduce the market value of net debt and thus contribute to a surplus. We should hence expect similar signs of coefficients of the budget surplus and the separate interest effects.) The monetary variables remain significant only in the regression including the official surplus and non-borrowed reserves. To the extent monetary variables do affect the rate of growth of output their role would appear to be largely captured in their wealth effect on the market value of government debt.

The results of quarterly regressions involving the change in unemployment are shown in Table 1.6. The sums of coefficients of the fiscal variables are consistently significant with a value in the neighbourhood of unity, or somewhat greater than the estimates from annual time series. None of the sets of monetary variables is significant in any of the six regressions.

Table 1.7 presents regressions, for both GNP and unemployment, involving eight quarterly lags of the price and interest adjusted high employment surplus and the change in monetary base. Once more, the adjusted budget variable fares considerably better when each is a sole regressor. When both sets of variables are introduced into the regressions, estimated parameters of the high employment surplus variables prove robust and highly significant. The monetary base variables lose all significance and actually reverse sign.

Table 1.4 High-employment budget, monetary aggregates and GNP, quarterly data, four-quarter lags

$$\Delta GNP_t = b_{01}X_1 + b_{02}X_2 + \sum_{i=1}^{4} b_{1i}HES_{t-1} + \sum_{i=1}^{4} b_{2i}\Delta M_{t-i}$$

(*1*) Equation	(*2*) Measure of HES and money	(*3*) Regression coefficients[a] Constants 1960.2–1966.4 (b_{01})	(*4*) Constants 1967.1–1984.4 (b_{02})	(*5*) HES (Σb_{1i})	(*6*) ΔM (Σb_{2i})	(*7*) $\hat{R}^2$	(*8*) $\hat{\rho}$
(4.1)	OF	6.459 (1.122)	1.411 (0.826)	−2.101 (0.695)		0.260	0.272
(4.2)	PA	8.153 (1.197)	4.235 (0.614)	−2.199 (0.528)		0.279	0.223
(4.3)	MB	3.047 (1.003)	1.940 (0.594)		13.788 (3.622)	0.248	0.211
(4.4)	NR	4.617 (1.109)	3.156 (0.665)		11.857 (6.769)	0.207	0.344
(4.5)	TR	4.654 (1.029)	3.267 (0.626)		21.950 (9.979)	0.212	0.292
(4.6)	OF, MB	4.798 (1.424)	1.113 (0.768)	−1.399 (0.813)	8.486 (4.472)	0.283	0.208
(4.7)	PA, MB	6.646 (2.036)	3.538 (0.974)	−1.630 (0.810)	4.998 (5.532)	0.272	0.200
(4.8)	OF, NR	6.267 (1.068)	1.306 (0.786)	−2.190 (0.669)	13.309 (6.326)	0.303	0.238
(4.9)	PA, NR	7.811 (1.218)	4.331 (0.606)	−2.107 (0.533)	8.286 (6.318)	0.316	0.224
(4.10)	OF, TR	6.222 (1.134)	1.458 (0.869)	−1.925 (0.712)	12.780 (9.789)	0.282	0.242
(4.11)	PA, TR	7.936 (1.400)	4.211 (0.617)	−2.055 (0.634)	5.485 (10.714)	0.279	0.225

Notes:
[a] Least squares with Cochrane–Orcutt first order autoregressive corrections; standard errors are shown in parentheses.

X_1 = 1, $X_2 = 0$, for $t = 1960.2$ to 1966.4; $X_1 = 0$, $X_2 = 1$, for $t = 1967.1$ to 1984.4

HES = high employment surplus as per cent of GNP

OF = official, PA = price adjusted

ΔM = real change in monetary aggregates as per cent of GNP

MB = monetary base; NR = non-borrowed reserves; TR = total reserves.

14

Table 1.5 High employment budget, monetary aggregates, interest effects and GNP, quarterly data

$$\Delta GNP_t = b_{01}X_1 + b_{02}X_2 + \sum_{i=1}^{4} b_{1i}HES_{t-i} + \sum_{i=1}^{4} b_{2i}\Delta M_{t-i} + \sum_{i=5}^{8} b_{3i}IE_{t-i},$$

(1) Equation	*(2)* Measure of HES and M	*(3)* Regression coefficients[a]: Constants, 1960.2–1966.4 (b_{01})	*(4)* Constants, 1967.1–1984.4 (b_{02})	*(5)* HES (Σb_{1i})	*(6)* ΔM (Σb_{2i})	*(7)* IE (Σb_{3i})	*(8)* $\hat{R}^2$	*(9)* $\hat{\rho}$
(5.1)	OF, MB	5.169 (1.301)	1.343 (0.708)	−1.462 (0.749)	5.155 (4.260)	−1.443 (0.565)	0.340	0.152
(5.2)	PA, MB	6.791 (1.876)	3.751 (0.898)	−1.574 (0.751)	2.169 (5.223)	−1.411 (0.571)	0.324	0.149
(5.3)	OF, NR	5.904 (0.959)	1.615 (0.714)	−1.848 (0.624)	11.873 (5.906)	−1.520 (0.535)	0.361	0.164
(5.4)	PA, NR	7.157 (1.151)	4.139 (0.558)	−1.750 (0.520)	7.000 (6.036)	−1.376 (0.547)	0.365	0.170
(5.5)	OF, TR	6.115 (1.016)	1.458 (0.786)	−1.834 (0.657)	4.584 (9.248)	−1.705 (0.574)	0.346	0.177
(5.6)	PA, TR	7.622 (1.301)	4.049 (0.569)	−1.891 (0.602)	−1.793 (10.232)	−1.581 (0.582)	0.335	0.177

Notes:
[a] Least squares with Cochrane–Orcutt first order autoregressive corrections; standard errors are shown in parentheses.
X_1 = 1, $X_2 = 0$, for $t = 1960.2$ to 1966.4; $X_1 = 0$, $X_2 = 1$, for $t = 1967.1$ to 1984.4
HES = high employment surplus as per cent of GNP
OF = official, PA = price adjusted
ΔM = real change in monetary aggregates as per cent of GNP
MB = monetary base; NR = non-borrowed reserves; TR = total reserves.

Table 1.6 High-employment budget, monetary aggregates, interest effects and unemployment, quarterly data

$$\Delta \mathrm{UN}_t = b_{01}X_1 + b_{02}X_2 + \sum_{i=1}^{4} b_{1i}\mathrm{HES}_{t-i} + \sum_{i=1}^{4} b_{2i}\Delta M_{t-i} + \sum_{i=5}^{8} b_{3i}\mathrm{IE}_{t-i}$$

(1) Equation	*(2)* Measure of HES and M	*(3)* Regression coefficients[a] Constants 1960.2–1966.4 (b_{01})	*(4)* Constants 1967.1–1984.4 (b_{02})	*(5)* HES (Σb_{1i})	*(6)* ΔM (Σb_{2i})	*(7)* IE (Σb_{3i})	*(8)* $\hat{R}^2$	*(9)* $\hat{\rho}$
(6.1)	OF, MB	−0.494 (0.613)	1.214 (0.347)	0.931 (0.330)	−3.115 (1.909)		0.501	0.499
(6.2)	PA, MB	−1.575 (0.869)	−0.308 (0.434)	1.012 (0.339)	−1.144 (2.335)		0.500	0.509
(6.3)	PA, MB	−1.520 (0.799)	−0.341 (0.394)	0.961 (0.315)	−0.523 (2.177)	0.526 (0.218)	0.532	0.456
(6.4)	OF, NR	−0.911 (0.530)	1.107 (0.378)	1.131 (0.296)	−1.370 (2.335)		0.508	0.555
(6.5)	PA, NR	−1.814 (0.579)	−0.442 (0.305)	1.106 (0.241)	0.622 (2.327)		0.526	0.536
(6.6)	PA, NR	−1.524 (0.517)	−0.378 (0.263)	0.961 (0.224)	0.253 (2.199)	0.557 (0.212)	0.560	0.469

Notes:
[a] Least squares with Cochrane–Orcutt first order autoregressive corrections; standard errors are shown in parenthesis.
X_1 = 1, X_2 = 0, for t = 1960.2 to 1966.4; X_1 = 0, X_2 = 1, for t = 1967.1 to 1984.4.
HES = high employment surplus as per cent of GNP
OF = official, PA = price adjusted
ΔM = real change in monetary aggregates as per cent of GNP
MB = monetary base; NR = non-borrowed reserves; TR = total reserves
UN = percentage point change in unemployment

17

Table 1.7 High employment budget, monetary base, GNP and unemployment, quarterly data, eight-quarter lags

$$\Delta Z_t = b_{01}X_1 + b_{02}X_1 + \sum_{i=1}^{8} b_{1i}\text{HES}_{t-i} + \sum_{i=1}^{8} b_{2i}\Delta\text{MB}_{t-i}$$

(1) *Equation*	*(2)* *Dependent variable* (ΔZ_t)	*(3)* *Regression coefficients*[a] *Constants* *1961.2–1966.4* (b_{01})	*(4)* *1967.1–1984.4* (b_{02})	*(5)* *HES* (Σb_{1i})	*(6)* ΔMB (Σb_{2i})	*(7)* $\hat{R}^2$	*(8)* $\hat{\rho}$
(7.1)	ΔGNP	9.113 (1.231)	4.674 (0.630)	−2.544 (0.546)		0.316	0.217
(7.2)	ΔGNP	3.295 (1.189)	2.034 (0.631)		12.377 (4.759)	0.223	0.200
(7.3)	ΔGNP	9.498 (2.472)	4.758 (1.155)	−2.601 (0.909)	−1.207 (6.939)	0.291	0.216
(7.4)	ΔUN	−2.335 (0.577)	−0.601 (0.303)	1.146 (0.243)		0.531	0.515
(7.5)	ΔUN	0.381 (0.621)	0.657 (0.331)		−6.411 (2.330)	0.442	0.525
(7.6)	ΔUN	−2.491 (1.104)	−0.633 (0.534)	1.186 (0.391)	0.177 (3.146)	0.494	0.521

Notes:

[a] Least squares with Cochrane–Orcutt first order autoregressive correction: standard errors are shown in parentheses.

$X_1 = 1, X_2 = 0$ for $t = 1961.2–1966.4$
$X_1 = 0, X_2 = 1$ for $t = 1967.1–1984.4$
HES = price and interest adjusted high employment surplus as per cent of GNP
MB = real change in monetary base as per cent of GNP
GNP = per cent change in GNP, at annual rates
UN = percentage point change in unemployment

We conclude, on the basis of these single equation estimates, that monetary policy, as evidenced by changes in either the monetary base or in total or non-borrowed reserves, does not explain – or explain away – the association of budget deficits with increases in gross national product and decreases in unemployment. Quite to the contrary, the high employment budget deficit, adjusted for changes in the real value of the debt due to inflation and changing interest rates, accounts for a substantial portion – in the eight-quarter regressions virtually all – of the effects otherwise attributable to the role of money. The monetary variables do not prove robust.[5] The adjusted surplus variables do.

4 COMPONENTS OF GNP

Government deficits may be viewed as constituting public dissaving, absorbing private saving and hence, if private saving is given, reducing private investment. Of course, if output is not fixed it is unreasonable to assume that private saving is given. As the issue was posed half a century ago, a stimulus to non-investment spending may bring about more or less private investment, depending on the relative reactions of the demand for money and of investment to interest rates and output (Lange, 1938). These in turn will relate to how close the economy is to full employment and hence how much output can in fact increase. Indeed, even at full employment it would appear that a deficit induced increase in aggregate demand need not reduce investment if the money supply is increased in proportion to the increase in interest bearing government debt. The only result then would be a higher price level, with no change in the real debt, real quantity of money, interest rates or investment (see Eisner, 1986, pp. 182–4).

In an open economy, government deficits may also affect the balance of payments via interest and output effects. To the extent they increase output they will increase imports. To the extent they raise interest rates they will attract foreign capital, raise exchange rates and add to the impetus to an 'unfavourable' balance of trade and a reduction in net exports. The inflow of foreign capital and goods would, however, both help accommodate an increase in investment.

The evidence that adjusted structural deficits have been positively related to the growth of GNP makes clear that it cannot be assumed that a deficit-induced stimulus to consumption must result in less private investment. The issue is an empirical one, and we are able to offer some striking results of further examination of our annual time series.

The effects on GNP of the budget deficit, and other variables such as changes in the monetary base, are the sum of their effects, direct or indirect, on the various components of GNP. We have hence regressed changes in these components, each expressed as percentages of GNP so that estimated parameters are comparable, on the price adjusted high employment surplus and changes in the monetary base. As shown in Table 1.8, equation (8.1), the surplus is, as expected, negatively related to consumption. Each percentage point of price adjusted high employment deficit as a ratio of GNP was associated over the years 1961 to 1984 with an increase in personal consumption expenditures equal to 0.646 per cent of GNP. But as also shown in Table 1.8, each percentage point of deficit was also associated with an even larger increase in gross private domestic investment, amounting to 1.371 per cent of GNP (8.2). While of course neither of these point estimates should be taken too seriously, it is worth noting that the signs of the coefficients are clearly statistically significant. Results shown in Table 1.9 indicate further that the deficit was similarly positively associated with the durable and the non-durable and services components components of consumption, and with the fixed and inventory components of investment. The adjusted high employment deficits were thus correlated positively with increases in *both* consumption and investment. Deficits were 'crowding in' investment, not crowding it out.

As predicted, however, deficits did have a distinct negative effect on net exports. Each percentage point of adjusted high employment deficit as a ratio of GNP was associated with a reduction of net exports of 0.392 per cent of GNP, as shown in Table 1.8, equation (8.4). And this was more than fully accounted for by an increase of imports equalling 0.436 per cent of GNP, as shown in Table 1.9, equation (9.8).

There are important consequences, domestic and foreign, of this negative effect of our budget deficits on net exports. On the domestic side, we have a 'leakage' of income and demand outside of our economy. We see in equation (8.6) in Table 1.8 that each percentage point of price adjusted high employment deficit is associated with an increase in 'domestic demand' equal to 2.125 per cent of GNP. With a reduction in net exports equal to 0.392 per cent of output, however, the estimated impact of one percentage point of deficit on GNP is only 1.571 per cent.[6] We find then that the deficit leads Americans to spend more and that stimulates more production, but some of it involves Japenese Toyotas and Sonys, French wine and English sweaters. The increase in imports thus permits a greater increase in domestic consumption and investment than the increase in domestic output.

22

Table 1.8 High-employment budget, changes in monetary base and changes in components of GNP

$$\Delta COM_t = b_{01}X_1 + b_{02}X_2 + b_1 PAHES_{t-1} + b_2 \Delta MB_{t-1}$$

$$X_1 = 1, X_2 = 0 \text{ for } t = 1961\text{–}6$$

$$X_1 = 0, X_2 = 1 \text{ for } t = 1967\text{–}84$$

(1) Equation	*(2)* Component	*(3)*	*(4)*	*(5)*	*(6)*	*(7)*	*(8)*
		Regression coefficients[a]					
		Constants		*Surplus* $PAHES_{t-1}$	*Monetary base* ΔMB_{t-1}	$\hat{R}^2$	$\hat{\rho}$
	(*COM*)	*1961–6* (b_{01})	*1967–84* (b_{02})	(b_1)	(b_2)		
(8.1)	Consumption	3.400 (0.676)	2.344 (0.305)	−0.646 (0.266)	2.427 (1.582)	0.580	0.095
(8.2)	Investment	2.569 (1.189)	1.133 (0.551)	−1.371 (0.422)	3.727 (2.425)	0.562	0.283
(8.3)	Government	1.178 (0.560)	0.478 (0.272)	−0.106 (0.174)	−0.629 (0.978)	0.352	0.476
(8.4)	Net exports	−1.682 (1.450)	−0.829 (1.202)	0.392 (0.137)	1.600 (0.813)	0.503	0.850
(8.5)	GNP	6.195 (1.301)	3.381 (0.591)	−1.571 (0.485)	7.266 (2.827)	0.733	0.173
(8.6)	Domestic demand	7.338 (1.527)	3.929 (0.689)	−2.125 (0.570)	5.380 (3.314)	0.700	0.161

Notes:

[a] Least squares with Cochrane–Orcutt, first order autoregressive corrections; standard errors are shown in parentheses.

ΔCOM = change in component as per cent of GNP
PAHES = price adjusted high employment surplus as per cent of GNP
ΔMB = change in monetary base as per cent of GNP

Table 1.9 High employment budget, monetary base, and fine components of GNP

$$\Delta \text{COM}_t = b_{01}X_1 + b_{02}X_2 + b_1\text{PAHES}_{t-1} + b_2\Delta\text{MB}_{t-1}$$

$$X_1 = 1,\ X_2 = 0 \text{ for } t = 1961\text{–}6$$

$$X_1 = 0,\ X_2 = 1 \text{ for } t = 1967\text{–}84$$

(1) *Equation*	*(2)* *Component*	*(3)*	*(4)*	*(5)*	*(6)*	*(7)*	*(8)*
		Regression coefficients[a]					
		Constants		*Surplus*	*Monetary base*	$\hat{R}^2$	$\hat{\rho}$
	(COM)	*1961–6* (b_{01})	*1967–84* (b_{02})	$PAHES_{t-1}$ (b_1)	ΔMB_{t-1} (b_2)		
(9.1)	Consumer durables	1.034 (0.364)	0.603 (0.165)	−0.382 (0.140)	1.082 (0.802)	0.548	0.197
(9.2)	Nondurables and services	2.349 (0.400)	1.732 (0.180)	−0.258 (0.154)	1.438 (0.936)	0.510	0.085
(9.3)	Fixed investment	1.597 (0.696)	0.827 (0.333)	−0.800 (0.214)	2.780 (1.261)	0.664	0.448
(9.4)	Change in inventories	0.777 (0.593)	0.229 (0.265)	−0.444 (0.240)	0.848 (1.411)	0.340	−0.128
(9.5)	Federal	0.591 (0.530)	0.173 (0.256)	−0.091 (0.167)	−0.863 (0.936)	0.281	0.466
(9.6)	State and local	0.540 (0.252)	0.307 (0.128)	−0.011 (0.062)	0.187 (0.361)	0.515	0.611

(9.7)	Exports	0.004 (0.513)	0.277 (0.240)	0.007 (0.186)	1.742 (0.972)	0.204	0.400
(9.8)	Imports	0.942 (0.381)	0.734 (0.176)	−0.436 (0.149)	0.280 (0.856)	0.428	0.081

Notes:
[a] Least squares with Cochrane–Orcutt first order autoregressive corrections; standard errors are shown in parentheses.
ΔCOM = change in component as per cent of GNP
PAHES = price adjusted high employment surplus as per cent of GNP
ΔMB = change in monetary base as per cent of GNP

But if this 'leakage' reduces the favourable impact of budget deficits on our own output, it correspondingly contributes to the demand for foreign product. With US gross national product in the neighbourhood of \$4,000 billion, each percentage point of deficit contributes a net increase in demand for foreign goods and services of \$17.5 billion (0.436 per cent of \$4,000 billion). We should then anticipate a role for the US budget deficit in the economies of other nations. The lesser increase in domestic output will have a counterpart in greater growth of output elsewhere.

This is of course precisely what we discovered in relating price adjusted high employment deficits in the United States to changes in gross domestic product in six major OECD countries. The US budget deficit contributed significantly to those nations' economic growth. The effects of deficits on the net exports component of US GNP point out the multiplicand in a substantial foreign trade multiplier.

We have again been able to improve the fit of our relations by introducing the interest effect lagged two years. Table 1.10 shows significant negative coefficients for the contribution of the interest effect to an adjusted high employment surplus in the equations for consumption (10.1) and investment (10.2) as well as for GNP (10.5) and domestic demand (10.6). The price adjusted high employment surplus remains highly significant in all of these equations as well as in the equation for net exports. The total effect of the adjusted high employment surplus, including the two-year lagged interest effect is uniformly increased.

Our regressions of components of GNP offer a few other interesting results. For those concerned that budget deficits fuel increases in government expenditures the message is apparently, 'Not to worry!' Each percentage point of adjusted high employment deficit, again as a ratio of GNP, was associated, as shown in (8.3) of Table 1.8, with increases in government expenditures of only 0.106 per cent of GNP, with the increase in federal expenditures alone accounting for 0.091 per cent of output, as shown in equation (9.5) of Table 1.9. And finally, the monetary base variable, while significant in the total GNP regressions (8.5 and 10.5) and uniformly showing the 'right' (generally positive) sign for the GNP components, was significantly different from zero at the 0.05 probability level only in the case of fixed investment (9.3), and even then only when the interest effect variable was excluded – which is also what a good Keynesian might have predicted[7].

Table 1.10 High employment budget, changes in monetary base and changes in components of GNP

$$\Delta COM_t = b_{01}X_1 + b_{02}X_2 + b_1 PAHES_{t-1} + b_2 IE_{t-2} + b_3 \Delta MB_{t-1}$$

$$X_1 = 1, X_2 = 0 \text{ for } t = 1961\text{–}6$$

$$X_1 = 0, X_2 = 1 \text{ for } t = 1967\text{–}84$$

(1) Equation	(2) Component	(3)	(4)	(5)	(6)	(7)	(8)	(9)
		Regression coefficients[a]						
		Constants		Surplus $PAHES_{t-1}$	Interest effect IE_{t-2}	Monetary base ΔMB_{t-1}	$\hat{R}^2$	$\hat{\rho}$
	(COM)	1961–6 (b_{01})	1968–84 (b_{02})	(b_1)	(b_2)	(b_3)		
(10.1)	Consumption	3.280 (0.630)	2.326 (0.285)	−0.575 (0.243)	−0.383 (0.184)	1.898 (1.477)	0.642	0.153
(10.2)	Investment	2.250 (1.075)	1.037 (0.495)	−1.132 (0.436)	−0.671 (0.351)	2.698 (2.448)	0.617	0.096
(10.3)	Government	1.032 (0.586)	0.466 (0.296)	−0.069 (0.162)	−0.167 (0.118)	−0.885 (0.945)	0.381	0.558
(10.4)	Net exports	−1.472 (1.136)	−0.694 (0.864)	0.379 (0.128)	0.193 (0.100)	1.929 (0.758)	0.574	0.834
(10.5)	GNP	6.033 (1.152)	3.390 (0.522)	−1.467 (0.432)	−0.836 (0.336)	5.852 (2.551)	0.792	0.178
(10.6)	Domestic demand	7.145 (1.255)	3.945 (0.568)	−1.973 (0.479)	−1.151 (0.392)	3.349 (2.844)	0.793	0.127

Notes:
[a] Least squares with Cochrane–Orcutt, first order autoregressive corrections; standard errors are shown in parentheses. ΔCOM = change in component as per cent of GNP. PAHES = price adjusted high employment surplus as per cent of GNP. ΔMB = change in monetary base as per cent of GNP

5 CONCLUSIONS

1. Money does not explain away a strong relation between the inflation adjusted high employment surplus and changes in gross national product and unemployment. In regressions involving both fiscal and monetary variables, the fiscal variables prove generally robust. The relations are stronger and the monetary variables, while usually maintaining some role, generally lose significant when the high employment surplus is adjusted for price and interest effects. Thus failure to measure deficits correctly has not only contributed to a false view of fiscal impotence, but has possibly lead to an overestimate of the importance of money.

2. The adjusted high employment budget deficit is positively related to increases in both consumption and investment. Far from crowding out investment, deficits apparently crowd it in.

3. A damping effect of deficits is to be noted, however, in the negative relation between the adjusted high employment surplus and net exports. Aggregate demand of Americans is stimulated considerably more than the aggregate demand for American output. Thus, US budget deficits add a foreign trade multiplier stimulus to the growth in output in US major trading partners.

4. In the light of all the above, overly enthusiastic monetarists, those who would infer policy ineffectiveness from rational expectations, and those who would reject the Keynesian revolution of a half century ago – or its 'neoclassical synthesis' – might all take pause.

APPENDIX 1

Table 1.A1 Lag structure: official and price-adjusted high-employment surplus, real change in non-borrowed reserves and interest effect, and per cent change in GNP

(1)	*(2)*	*(3)*	*(4)*	*(5)*	*(6)*	*(7)*
Lag	*Equation (5.3) Official surplus*			*Equation (5.4) Price-adjusted surplus*		
	HES	*ΔNR*	*IE*	*HES*	*ΔNR*	*IE*
1	−0.799 (0.599)	0.863 (2.023)	—	−0.862 (0.488)	−0.883 (2.099)	—
2	0.450 (0.680)	5.855 (2.098)	—	0.371 (0.497)	5.407 (2.136)	—
3	−1.880 (0.644)	4.384 (2.227)	—	−1.333 (0.486)	2.711 (2.326)	—
4	0.381 (0.582)	0.772 (2.147)	—	0.075 (0.456)	−0.235 (2.140)	—
5	—	—	−0.504 (0.183)	—	—	−0.495 (0.185)
6	—	—	−0.574 (0.204)	—	—	−0.530 (0.207)
7	—	—	−0.199 (0.207)	—	—	−0.147 (0.210)
8	—	—	−0.242 (0.181)	—	—	−0.204 (0.183)
Sum	−1.848 (0.624)	11.873 (5.906)	−1.520 (0.535)	−1.745 (0.520)	7.000 (6.036)	−1.376 (0.547)

Notes:
HES = high employment surplus as per cent of GNP
ΔNR = real change in non-borrowed revenues as per cent of GNP
IE = interest effect on federal debt as per cent of GNP

Table 1.A2 Eight-quarter lag structure: price and interest adjusted high employment surplus and real change in monetary base, GNP and unemployment equations

(1) Lag	*(2)*	*(3)*	*(4)*	*(5)*	*(6)*	*(7)*	*(8)*	*(9)*
	ΔGNP Equations				ΔUN Equations			
	(7.1) $PIAHES$	*(7.2)* ΔMB	*(7.3)* $PIAHES$	ΔMB	*(7.4)* $PIAHES$	*(7.5)* ΔMB	*(7.6)* $PIAHES$	ΔMB
1	−0.366	6.324	−0.306	3.290	0.084	−1.406	0.073	−0.503
	(0.165)	(2.099)	(0.183)	(2.304)	(0.052)	(0.666)	(0.058)	(0.733)
2	−0.394	3.699	−0.330	−0.577	0.191	−1.645	0.182	0.129
	(0.176)	(2.130)	(0.215)	(2.624)	(0.063)	(0.766)	(0.078)	(0.962)
3	−0.565	2.000	−0.563	−2.195	0.141	−1.004	0.155	0.744
	(0.173)	(2.186)	(0.223)	(2.571)	(0.061)	(0.759)	(0.084)	(0.949)
4	−0.177	0.046	−0.273	−3.086	0.175	−1.333	0.202	0.427
	(0.173)	(2.282)	(0.220)	(2.651)	(0.060)	(0.784)	(0.084)	(0.962)
5	−0.349	2.028	−0.456	0.354	0.223	−0.851	0.252	0.128
	(0.173)	(2.269)	(0.219)	(2.537)	(0.060)	(0.776)	(0.083)	(0.894)
6	−0.415	1.516	−0.423	1.916	0.124	−0.324	0.129	−0.439
	(0.174)	(2.215)	(0.219)	(2.263)	(0.061)	(0.738)	(0.082)	(0.962)
7	−0.068	−1.759	−0.028	0.283	0.139	−0.078	0.127	−0.353
	(0.174)	(2.053)	(0.214)	(2.160)	(0.061)	(0.737)	(0.078)	(0.766)
8	−0.210	−1.476	−0.223	−1.193	0.069	0.231	0.065	0.044
	(0.166)	(2.017)	(0.189)	(2.029)	(0.052)	(0.643)	(0.060)	(0.642)

Sum	−2.544 (0.546)	12.377 (4.759)	−2.601 (0.909)	−1.207 (6.939)	1.146 (0.243)	−6.411 (2.330)	1.186 (0.391)	0.177 (3.146)
$\hat{R}^2$	0.316	0.223	0.291		0.531	0.442	0.494	

Notes:
PIAHES = price and interest adjusted high employment surplus as per cent of GNP
ΔMB = real change in monetary base as per cent of GNP
ΔGNP = per cent change in real GNP
ΔUN = percentage point change in unemployment rate

Table 1.A3 High employment surplus, changes in real monetary base and real non-borrowed reserves, as percentage of GNP, 1960–84

Year	*High-employment surplus*			*Change in real monetary base*	*Change in real non-borrowed reserves*
	Official	*Adjusted for price effects*	*Adjusted for price and interest effects*		
1960	2.39	2.83	0.89	−0.09	0.18
1961	1.35	1.99	2.45	0.08	0.03
1962	0.53	1.28	0.87	0.08	−0.02
1963	1.24	1.79	2.25	0.27	0.00
1964	0.17	0.78	0.72	0.25	0.05
1965	0.13	0.98	1.43	0.22	0.00
1966	−0.74	0.33	0.11	0.02	−0.09
1967	−1.89	−0.89	−0.34	0.20	0.15
1968	−1.26	0.06	0.18	0.15	−0.05
1969	0.52	1.94	2.74	−0.04	−0.11
1970	−0.46	0.77	−0.64	0.08	0.08
1971	−1.05	0.11	−0.25	0.13	0.05
1972	−1.02	0.02	0.39	0.44	0.06
1973	−0.72	0.89	1.14	−0.08	−0.10
1974	−0.02	2.15	2.01	−0.13	−0.04
1975	−1.88	−0.38	−0.54	−0.02	−0.06
1976	−1.01	0.22	−0.52	0.15	−0.04
1977	−1.06	0.46	1.30	0.13	−0.06
1978	−0.73	1.26	2.15	0.01	−0.06
1979	−0.08	1.72	1.91	0.00	−0.07
1980	−0.65	1.45	1.97	−0.10	−0.04
1981	−0.11	1.57	1.45	−0.15	−0.01
1982	−1.06	0.02	−2.01	0.16	0.03
1983	−1.66	−0.60	0.68	0.28	0.01
1984	−2.51	−1.36	−1.92	0.42	0.02

APPENDIX 2: SOURCES AND METHODS

1 Net Debt

Net debt is defined as total financial assets less financial liabilities. Federal government net debt includes totals for the government of the

United States, federally sponsored credit agencies, and the monetary authority. Current assets in federal employee and retirement funds are treated as offset by current liabilities. No consideration was made for future retirement obligations or associated future receipts.

The Flow of Funds section of the Federal Reserve Board is the data source for the par value of the net debt. US government securities, agency issues and savings bonds are converted to market values by indices taken directly or derived from Cox (1985). A market-to-par index for mortgage holdings was developed by discounting mortgage flows by the end of period yield on new home mortgages. A precise description of the procedure can be found in Eisner (1986).

2. Price Effects – Nominal-to-Real Conversion

Price effects are calculated as the change in the real market value of existing net debt, excluding gold, measured in average prices of the period. They may be described as:

$$PE_t = [(A-1)DM_{t-1} + (B-1)(DM_t - DM_{t-1})1/B$$

where

PE = price effects,
P = GNP implicit price deflator in period t,
P^e = end of period price deflator,
DM = end of period market value of net debt excluding gold
$A = p_t^e / P_t$, and
$B = P_t^e / P_{t-1}^e$.

The end of year price deflator is calculated as the arithmetic average of the deflators in the fourth and first quarters. The deflator for personal consumption expenditures, which is available monthly, is used to calculate the end of quarter GNP price deflator. The formulation used is:

$$P_t^e = P_t(P_t^{c,e}/P_t^c)[(P_{t+1}P_t^c)/(P_tP_{t+1}^c)]^{.5}$$

where

P = GNP implicit price deflator
P^c = implicit price deflator for personal consumption expenditures

$P^{c,e}$ = end of quarter implicit price deflator for personal consumption expenditures. This is calculated as the average of the deflators for the last month of the quarter and the first month of the next quarter.

The last term, the ratio of growth in the GNP deflator to the PCE deflator, is intended to control for differences between the two indexes in trend rates of growth.

3 Interest Effects

Interest effects equal the total change in par-to-market revaluations:

$$IE_t = \sum_{i=1}^{5} [(1 - \mathrm{MP}_{i,t})\mathrm{K}_{i,t} - (1 - MP_{i,t-1})K_{i,t-1}],$$

where

$K_{i,t}$ = par value of the i-th financial instrument at the end of year t, expressed as a positive quantity if it is a liability and a negative quantity if it is an asset

$MP_{i,t}$ = market-to-par index for the i-th financial instrument at the end of the year t.

The five financial instruments are savings bonds, mortgages, agency issues, Treasury issues held by the Federal Reserve and US government and Treasury issues held by the public. Market-to-par indexes for all instruments except mortgages are taken or derived from Cox (1985). A market-to-par index for mortgages was developed by discounting mortgage flows by the end of period yield on new home mortgages. A precise description of the methodology used can be found in Eisner (1986). Quarterly interest effects are calculated in the same manner except that end of quarter per values and market-to-par indexes are used, and the total change in par-to-market revaluations is multiplied by four to convert from quarterly to annual rates of change.

4 High-Employment Budgets

The high employment surplus is defined for a 4.0 per cent level of unemployment in 1955, gradually increasing to 5.1 per cent in 1975 and remaining constant thereafter, as indicated below.

Year	*High employment unemployment rate*
1955–8	4.0
1959	4.1
1960–2	4.2
1963–4	4.3
1965	4.4
1966	4.5
1967	4.4
1968	4.5
1969	4.6
1970	4.7
1971	4.8
1972–3	4.9
1974	5.0
1975–84	5.1

Data from 1955 to the third quarter of 1983, are taken from de Leeuw and Holloway (1982) and the *Survey of Current Business* (*SCB*) November 1983. The US Department of Commerce now uses a 6 per cent unemployment rate in estimating the high employment surplus, which is presented periodically in the *SCB*. The series based on a 5.1 per cent rate is extrapolated through 1984 on the basis of the following equation:

$$\mathrm{HES}(5.1)_{t,j} = \mathrm{HES}(6)_{t,j} + \mathrm{HEGNP}_t[\mathrm{HES}(5.1)_{83.3} - \mathrm{HES}(6)_{83.3}]/\mathrm{HEGNP}_{83.3}$$

$$t = 83.3 \text{ to } 84.4.$$

where

HES(5.1) = high employment surplus estimated for 5.1 per cent unemployment
HES(6) = high employment surplus estimated for 6 per cent unemployment
HEGNP = nominal high employment GNP for 6 per cent unemployment and the numerical subscripts refer to year and quarter.

5 Monetary Base

The data source for the monetary base, non-borrowed reserves and total reserves is the Federal Reserve Board's 'Reserves of Depository Institutions'. All monetary aggregates are seasonally adjusted and adjusted for changes in reserve requirements. The monetary variables used in the regressions are defined as the change in end of period real stocks divided by real GNP. Thus, for annual data

$$MCH_t = 100\left[\left(\frac{M_t^e}{P_t^e} - \frac{M_{t-1}^e}{P_{t-1}^e}\right)/GNP72_{t-1}\right],$$

where

MCH = change in real money stock (either the monetary base, non-borrowed reserves or total reserves) as a percentage of real GNP
M^e = nominal money stock at the end of period, taken to be the last week of the period
P^e = end of period GNP implicit price deflator
$GNP72$ = gross national product in US 1972 dollars.

The quarterly monetary variable is defined in the same manner except the change in real stocks is multiplied by 400.

6 Gross National Product

Data for GNP and its components are from the *National Income and Product Accounts*, 1929–76, the July 1982 *Survey of Current Business* and the 1985 *Economic Report of the President*. The dependent variable in the annual GNP regressions is the percentage change in real GNP (1972 US dollars). The dependent variable in the quarterly GNP regressions is the quarterly growth in real GNP, expressed as an annual rate. This is defined as

$$\mathrm{GNP}CH_t = \left[\left(\frac{\mathrm{GNP72}_t}{\mathrm{GNP72}_{t-1}}\right)^4 - 1.\right] * 100.$$

7 Unemployment

The unemployment variable is the percentage point change in the unemployment rate, defined as

$$UNCH_t = 100\left[\frac{UN_t}{UN_t + CIV_t} - \frac{UN_{t-1}}{UN_{t-1} + CIV_{t-1}}\right],$$

where

$UNCH_t$ = percentage point change in the unemployment rate
UN_t = total unemployment
CIV_t = total civilian employment.

The quarterly change in the unemployment rate is multiplied by four to express as annual rate. Annual data are from the 1985 *Economic Report of the President*. Quarterly data are calculated by averaging the monthly totals from *Business Statistics 1982* and the 1985 *Economic Report of the President*.

Notes

The authors are vastly indebted for the assistance of Sang In Hwang.

1. The monetary base and unborrowed reserves, both essentially policy instruments of the Federal Reserve, seemed more appropriate than broader monetary aggregates subject to direct endogenous fluctuations with movements in the economy. Experiments with M1 and M2, however, indicate that their use as monetary variables would not alter the conclusions of our analysis of annual data.
2. Antecedents of this formulation may be found in Haberler (1941), Pigou (1943) and Patinkin (1948). Clearly, we reject the argument by Barro (1974) that government debt and deficits do not affect aggregate demand, the so-called 'Ricardian equivalence effect.'
3. Sources and methods and some basic data for these and subsequent tables are given in the Appendices.
4. The dual constant terms in effect proxy for differences in inflation corrections in the two periods. They contribute what may be viewed as a greater spurious component to the coefficient of determination (R^2) in the regressions including the official high employment surplus.
5. This is true for the monetary base and reserve variables but M1 and M2, unlike in the annual data, perform somewhat better as regressors with quarterly time series. We conjecture that this is due to their more endogenous character in short-term fluctuations. As output rises, increased transaction demand generates an increased supply of M1, and higher interest rates, at least in recent years, generate an increased demand and supply of M2.

6. The sums of the estimated parameters for components do not equal precisely the estimated parameters for the aggregates, of which these are part, because of our use of the Cochrane–Orcutt estimator, with different autoregressive corrections.
7. There are similar substantial improvements in fit when the two-year lagged interest effect is introduced into Table 1.9 equations for the 'fine components' of GNP. The coefficients of the price adjusted surplus ($PAHES_{t-1}$) remain generally robustly negative while coefficients of the monetary base variable are again reduced substantially.

References

Barro, Robert J. (1974) 'Are Government Bonds Net Wealth?', *Journal of Political Economy*, vol. 82, November/December, pp. 1095–117.

Cox, W. Michael (1985) *The Behaviour of Treasury Securities: Monthly, 1942–84*, Federal Reserve Bank of Dallas, February.

Eisner, Robert (1986) *How Real is the Federal Deficit* (New York: The Free Press).

Eisner, Robert and Pieper, Paul J. (1984) 'A New View of the Federal Debt and Budget Deficits', *The American Economic Review*, vol. 74, March, pp. 11–29.

Eisner, Robert and Pieper, Paul J. (1985) 'Measurement and Effects of Government Debt and Deficits', in *Studies in Banking and Finance*, vol. 2, (Amsterdam, North Holland), pp. 115–44.

Haberler, Gottfried (1941) *Prosperity and Depression*, 3rd ed (Geneva: League of Nations).

Lange, Oscar (1938) 'The Rate of Interest and The Optimal Propensity to Consume', *Economica*, vol. V, February, pp. 12–32. Reprinted in *Readings in Business Cycle Theory*, American Economic Association, (1944).

de Leeuw, Frank and Holloway, Thomas M. (1982) 'The High-Employment Budget: Revised Estimates and Automatic Inflation Effects', *Survey of Current Business*, April, pp. 21–33.

Lucas, Robert E., Jr. (1981) *Studies in Business Cycle Theory* (Cambridge, Mass.: MIT Press).

Lucas, Robert E. and Sargent, Thomas J. (1978) 'After Keynesian Economics', in *After the Phillips Curve: Persistence of High Inflation and High Unemployment*, Federal Reserve Bank of Boston Conference, series no. 19, reprinted in Lucas, Robert E. Jr. and Sargent, Thomas J. (eds), *Rational Expectations and Economic Practice* (Minneapolis: University of Minnesota Press, 1981), pp. 295–319.

Patinkin, Don (1948) 'Price Flexibility and Full Employment', *The American Economic Review*, vol. 38, September, pp. 543–64.

Pigou, Arthur C. (1943) 'The Classical Stationary State', *Economic Journal*, vol. 53, December pp. 343–51.

DISCUSSION

This paper is a continuation of other work done by Eisner and Pieper. The basic premise is that conventional measures of fiscal deficits and debt (both actual and high employment) are fundamentally flawed. Eisner and Pieper correct for changes in the market value of government debt due to changes in interest rates and changes in the real value due to inflation. In earlier work, the authors show that these adjusted deficit figures are strongly related to economic activity. This paper studies the effects of the adjusted figures and selected monetary aggregates on changes in overall economic activity and on components of GNP.

Principal conclusions are that (1) the introduction of monetary aggregates does not mitigate the explanatory power of fiscal variables, (2) adjusted deficits are positively related to consumption and investment; that is, deficits 'crowd in' investment, (3) adjusted deficits are negatively related to net exports, (4) the evidence is strongly supportive of standard Keynesian propositions. Followers of other doctrines 'might all take pause'.

The regressions use annual data for 1960–84, with series on the high employment surplus, non-borrowed reserves, and the monetary base. The basic format is a linear regression of the change in economic activity on once lagged high employment surplus and the change in a monetary figure.

Professor John Taylor agreed that the adjusted deficits are, in principle, better measures than conventionally reported deficits. His main reservation was that the concept of an adjusted deficit may be abused in countries where deficits are financed largely by money creation.

Taylor interpreted the basic regression format as an aggregate demand equation, and noted that the paper could be interpreted as a rejuvenation of the Ando–Modigliani/Friedman–Meiselman debate on the relative strength of monetary and fiscal policy. He finds this 'contest' to be unsatisfactory, for several reasons. First, he objects to the use of narrow monetary figures that do not include deposits. He suggested M1 or M2 as alternatives.[1] Moreover, there is no demonstration that other lags do not matter. A vector autoregression would be more reasonable as a reduced form, and a structural model would be even more interesting.

The 'crowding in' result occurs, Taylor believes, because price adjustment is ignored. Deficits crowd out net exports because a fiscal stimulus raises both output and interest rates. Both effects reduce net exports. Finally, Taylor does not 'take pause' at the results, because the major issues, as he sees them, relate to price adjustment and aggregate supply, whereas the authors have focused on aggregate demand.

Professor Eisner responded that M1 and M2 were thought to be too endogenous to be useful. He agreed that structural modelling is an important next step. He is not a fan of vector autoregressions, but does not think that his models unduly restrict parameter values. To him, the fundamental issue is whether aggregate demand is important. He interprets the results as showing that aggregate demand has proved relevant for economic fluctuations.

Professor Pieper pointed out that the regressions used net debt: total financial assets minus financial liabilities.

Professor Marc Robinson suggested it may be useful to separate the components of net debt in the study. Moreover, the changing constant term (before and after 1967) suggests some structural changes.

Professor Bert Hickman objected to the treatment of prices as exogenous. The division of nominal income changes into price and output changes is critical. *Professor Michael Boskin* suggested it may be difficult to study the effect of fiscal policy on net exports without correcting for the change from fixed and floating exchange rates.

Dr Vito Tanzi noted that the authors adjusted the public debt for inflation, but not the private debt. He had difficulty accepting the idea that individuals are as rational as the model required them to be. Finally, he questioned whether there was double counting in the deficit adjustment since high inflation brings about high interest rates.

Professor Eisner responded that the market value adjustments induced by interest rates and real value adjustments induced by inflation were conceptually different. At a constant inflation and interest rate, the real value erodes. If interest rates then changed, with inflation constant, this would induce a further change in the market value of the debt.

Professor Kleiman suggested that the debt position *vis-à-vis* the rest of the world should be considered. *Professor Joseph Stiglitz* suggested that the unanticipated deficits should matter. *Professor Kenneth Arrow* pointed out that investment has exogenous components, so that it also should be included in the regressions.

Note

1. A note on this point has been added to the revised version of the paper with one or two other minor alterations.

Journal of Economic Perspectives—Volume 3, Number 2—Spring 1989—Pages 73–93

Budget Deficits: Rhetoric and Reality

Robert Eisner

Whatever the real or imagined ills of the economy, the news media, most politicians and a fair proportion of the economics profession are quick to point to the culprit: "the budget deficit." No matter that few appear to know or care precisely what deficit they are talking about or how it is measured. No matter that few bother to explain in terms of a relevant model just how government deficits may be expected to impact the economy. No matter that few offer any empirical data to sustain their judgments.

So budget deficits cause inflation. Budget deficits raise interest rates. Budget deficits bring on the trade deficits. Budget deficits crowd out investment. Budget deficits are an irresponsible mortgage on the future. And budget deficits caused the October 1987 stock market crash and now threaten further financial cataclysms! Is there truth in any of these assertions? Or does it all depend?

Budget deficits do matter and their effects, contrary to Barro's "Ricardian equivalence theorem," can be substantial. As most economists have recognized for at least half a century, budget deficits can, however, be too small as well as too large. To know which, you have to measure them right. And you have to analyze their role in the world in which we live. Pure Walrasian and rational-expectation market-clearing models may prove more useful for academic advancement than for promotion of economic health.

I need not repeat many of the objections to the equivalence theorem raised by Bernheim and Gramlich and addressed by Barro in this symposium. However, there is

■ *Robert Eisner is William R. Kenan Professor of Economics, Northwestern University, Evanston, Illinois.*

one overriding objection that cannot be overstressed. We simply do not live in a Walrasian, market-clearing world, and all our economic agents—as opposed apparently to some economists—know it. Aside then from all the issues of uncertainty as to who might pay any future taxes occasioned by a current deficit, real world economic agents have no reason to assume that there will be any additional tax burden at all. With the existence of what, in the older vernacular, we used to call simply "less-than-full-employment"—the so-called "natural" (God-given?) rate of unemployment belongs perhaps with those who accept the doctrine of creationism—increases in current consumption need not involve any borrowing from the future or from any future generation of taxpayers. The consumption is supplied from otherwise unutilized resources.[1] With the consumption then will come more, not less investment. The economy will move to a higher growth path. Extra taxes in the future, if there are to be any, may then readily be paid out of higher future incomes.

I believe there are serious problems with our fiscal policy. These relate to fundamental national priorities and the provision of public goods, now and for the future. But the current size of the federal deficit is not "our number one economic problem," if indeed it is a problem at all.

[1]One should properly be startled by Bernheim's assumptions of market clearing and an economy that "gravitates towards a full employment equilibrium" on which his arguments for the "neoclassical paradigm" depend, after his suggestion that "Keynesians are to be applauded for recognizing the importance of unemployed resources." He then adds, "Without a complete (or "fully satisfactory") theory of unemployment, Keynesian analysis is an exercise in blind faith." Would that all economic analysis were held to such a standard!

Where indeed is that full employment equilibrium of Bernheim's "long run"? Even the current "low" official unemployment rate of 5.4 percent is a full two percentage points above what it was some 20 years ago. Have we become accustomed to rationalizing our failures? There can hardly be many who doubted the existence of unemployed resources in December 1982 when the rate of unemployment was 10.7 percent. There should not have been many in the subsequent years when too many of our colleagues informed us that that natural rate was 6.5 percent or even more. With unemployment now well below that, the appropriate reaction, I should think, is not that we must *now surely* be at the full (or "natural"?) employment equilibrium, but rather a certain humility at our past errors.

It should be added that despite Bernheim's insistence that the Keynesian view requires a significantly "myopic" or liquidity-constrained population, Keynes never argued that consumption depended only on current disposable income. At least this reasonably unreconstructed Keynesian has long accepted with enthusiasm the major thrust of the life cycle and permanent income theories of consumption. One hardly need be myopic to increase consumption in the face of increases in current disposable income, and to increase it all the more if the prospects of continuing deficits raise expected disposable income along with a public debt very rationally viewed as private wealth. The failure by consumers to foresee *added* future tax burdens as a consequence of current deficits should be credited not to myopia but simply a lack of the faith (or old-time religion or plain old dogma?) that seems to have captured a number of economists.

Bernheim sees the view that "Keynesian analysis concerns the short run while Neoclassical analysis concerns the long run" as "close to the truth" but "misleading." He sees a permanent deficit as determining "national saving in some 'full employment' equilibrium." However glib Bernheim finds the characterization, the long run is a succession of short runs. Long run equilibrium models for dynamic economies in perpetual states of short run disequilibria can prove analytically useless and disastrous as guides to policy. The reduction of budget deficits and current consumption, as we shall note below, is clearly associated with less current investment. That such short run sacrifice will lead to long run success is again better supported by acts of (Calvinist?) faith than empirical evidence.

On Measures of Deficits, Government Liabilities and Assets

One might think it obvious that in order to talk about budget deficits, one must first have an accurate measure of their size. But the measurement of budget deficits has generally been a highly ignored issue. Here are some of the most fundamental problems.

First, the national income accounts measure of budget deficits, furnished by the Bureau of Economic Analysis, is a handier economic tool than the official "unified" budget. This measure focuses on current income flows and avoids some of the nonsense of counting sale of real or financial assets as "receipts" (or as offsets to expenditures) and the purchase of financial assets as "outlays." Such sales and purchases are essentially portfolio changes, having no first-order effect on the net debt or net worth of government or the private sector. The unified budget and the NIA budget can differ by nontrivial amounts. In fiscal 1985 the deficit on a national income accounts basis was indeed $28 billion less than the unified budget deficit. The difference was only $7 billion in fiscal 1986 and $1 billion in 1987 but was $11.7 billion in 1988.

Second, while what goes on within the beltway is important, Washington is not the only seat of government in the United States. Along with the fiscal 1988 federal deficit of $141.5 billion on a national income accounts basis, there was a state and local government aggregate *surplus* of $54.4 billion. It would certainly seem in order to take this into account, if only because the federal deficit was swollen by grants-in-aid to state and local governments totalling $108.6 billion. Including the non-federal surpluses knocks the total government deficit for fiscal 1987 down to $87.1 billion, or about 1.8 percent of GNP.

Third, the federal accounts make no distinction, in the expenditures contributing to a "deficit," between current expenses and investment. Most of the large corporations in the United States would find themselves in deficit if they had to include capital expenditures rather than depreciation charges in their profit and loss statements.[2] The Office of Management and Budget classified $127 billion of projected "Federal, investment outlays" for fiscal 1988 as expenditures on physical assets and another $80 billion of non-physical investment, for education, training, research, and development (*Special Analyses*, p. D-3). If we were to substitute a reasonable estimate of capital consumption for these $207 billion of investment expenditures, we would reduce the measure of the federal deficit by another $70 billion or so. With similar adjustments for state and local budgets, particularly if we were to capitalize the vast expenditures for education and include in the national income account budget only the depreciation of human capital, the entire government budget deficit would disappear. And with it would have to go the oft-repeated charge that our budget

[2] For example, from 1970 to 1984, the liabilities of General Motors grew 546 percent, from $4.3 billion to $27.9 billion, and those of IBM 530 percent, from $2.6 billion to $16.3 billion. Both companies have of course been eminently profitable and neither reported "deficits." The gross federal debt over this period grew 361 percent, to the accompaniment of myriad warnings about the federal deficit.

deficits mean that we are reckless with our future. Our public policy may well be mortgaging the next generation, but it is not "the deficit" that is doing it.[3,4]

Indeed, there is only one way in which we can allow today to injure tomorrow. That is to act today so that tomorrow has less productive capital, and that includes capital of all kinds—business plant, equipment, and inventories *and* government, household and nonprofit institution tangible capital, and human and intangible capital in all sectors. The impact of budget deficits—and budget deficit reduction—on intertemporal distribution then comes back smack to their impact on net investment, on *all* net investment.

We may get some perspective by sober study of federal balance sheets on the one hand and estimates of the *nation's* capital stock on the other. First, as seen in Table 1, despite year after year of deficits by official, conventional measure, from 1945 to 1980 the net worth of the federal government *rose* from a negative $44 billion to a positive $382 billion. The values of its tangible assets of land, structures, equipment and inventories and of its financial assets of gold, securities, mortgages and loans had grown more than its liabilities. Indeed, even ignoring real assets, the federal "net debt,"[5] the excess of liabilities over financial assets, had grown only from $230 billion to $441 billion, far less relatively than the more than 400 percent increases in prices over this period. It is true, however, that net worth turned down again after 1980 as deficits soared—although accounting for the value of federal mineral rights under the land and offshore might still leave it positive (Boskin et al., 1985).

[3]Sales of public assets of land and mineral rights and other acts of "privatization," if accomplished at bargain basement prices, have the effect of adding to the burden of future taxpayers even as they reduce the current official deficit. By Federal accounting rules we could indeed reduce the deficit to zero by the simple expedient of selling off government assets on a lease-back arrangement. In the initial years the government rental payments could easily be kept enough below assets sales receipts to meet Gramm-Rudman balanced budget targets. Of course, the rental payments would mount each year as more and more assets are sold. And eventually the Government would run out of assets to sell!

[4]It has been suggested that a comprehensive budget should also include the vast amounts of "contingent expenditures" or commitments, of which prospective social security and Federal employee retirement benefits loom largest. We should then, in principle, take their present value and offset them by the present value of corresponding prospective tax receipts. Certainly, it would be important for economic analysts to keep these contingency obligations, which have varying amounts of immediacy, in mind. Including them in calculations of "the budget deficit," however, would appear to be fraught with mischief. Projected expenditures and tax receipts are subject to wide variation with demographic, economic and, not least, legislative changes. The Social Security amendments of 1982, for example, would have created a fiscal 1983 surplus of some $1.3 trillion (see Eisner, 1986, pp. 36–38), as a consequence of the reduction in the present value of prospective benefits and increase in the present value of prospective taxes.

It would hardly seem that economic agents should be expected to respond to the same extent, if at all, to such changes in uncertain prospects as they would to changes in their assets of explicit government debt. And empirical investigation generally confirms that (see Eisner, 1983, *inter alia*). Very few Americans, except perhaps some of those at the point of retirement, have the vaguest notion of their future Social Security benefits. It is probably most reasonable to assume that they act as if, in the aggregate, their net wealth in contingency obligations is zero, that is, that the government will periodically adjust taxes to benefits. On this assumption, which may be taken as one of "equal ignorance," contingency obligations contribute nothing, one way or the other, to the general budget deficit.

[5]The Federal government and its associated credit agencies are lenders as well as borrowers. To the extent Federal expenditures are financing loans to small business, farmers, students or others, government debt held by the public is matched by the public's debt to the government.

Table 1
Federal Government Consolidated Balance Sheet: Liabilities and Tangible and Financial Assets

	Year and Amount (Billions of Dollars)			
Item	*1945*	*1960*	*1980*	*1984*
Tangible assets	186.2	205.8	822.5	1,118.0
Reproducible assets	179.3	187.4	648.1	915.2
Land	6.8	18.4	174.4	202.8
Financial assets	102.8	124.7	720.9	887.4
Total assets	289.0	330.4	1,543.4	2,005.4
Total liabilities	332.6	331.8	1,161.6	2,063.3
Net debt (total liabilities minus financial assets)	229.8	207.1	440.7	1,175.9
Net worth	−43.7	−1.3	381.8	−57.9

Including Federal Reserve and credit agencies, based on market or replacement values.
Source: Eisner (1986), Table 3.3, p. 29.

After the dramatic increases in debt taken out to finance the fighting of World War II, the history of U.S. debt until the early 1980s was one of major reduction in its relevant, *relative* magnitude. The gross federal debt as a ratio of GNP, shown in Table 2, actually fell from 110 percent at the end of 1945 (and 114 percent at the end of 1946) to 26 percent in 1980, before rising to its current level of about 42 percent. And net federal debt per capita fell, in constant 1982 dollars, from $8639 at the end of 1945 to $2219 in 1980, before rising to something over $6000 currently.

The bottom line, though, should be the capital or wealth of the nation. Table 3 provides an estimate of $23.7 trillion (at the end of 1981) for total capital, of which government and government enterprise capital comprised $2.7 trillion or 9.4 percent. The largest portion of the total by far, some $14.6 trillion or 61.6 percent, is accountable, however, to households. And most of that is the intangible or human capital attributable chiefly to government-financed education.[6]

The Real Deficit and Growth, Employment and Inflation

The issues of substituting depreciation for federal investment expenditures, including state and local budgets in the total deficit calculation, and examining net national worth are major. But rather than trying now to manufacture all of the figures

[6]These capital estimates are all constructed on a cost basis, adjusted to current prices. The value of education reflects both market expenditures and the opportunity costs of students 14 years of age and older. A full description of sources and methods is to be found in Eisner (1989).

Table 2
Measures of the Federal Debt

	Gross Federal Debt Held by Public		*Net Debt per Capita*
Year	*Billions of Dollars*	*% of GNP*	*1982 Dollars*
1945	232.2	110.2	8,639
1946	241.9	113.9	7,227
1960	237.2	46.0	3,576
1970	284.9	28.1	2,815
1980	715.1	26.2[a]	2,219
1984	1,312.6	34.5	4,496
1986	1,746.1	40.9	5,963
1987	1,888.1	41.3	
1988	2,050.0	41.8	
Change, 1945–1980	+479.9	−84.0	−6,420
Change, 1980–1984	+597.5	+8.3	+2,277
Change, 1984–1986	+433.5	+6.4	+1,467
Change, 1986–1988	+303.9	+0.9	

Adapted and updated from Eisner (1986), Tables 2.3 and 2.5, pp. 18–19, 21.
[a]Percent of third quarter GNP for this and subsequent years. For years up to 1970, where fiscal years ended June 30, percents were of corresponding calendar year GNP.

relevant to those issues, I should like to focus at this point on a simpler but crucial measure: the otherwise unadjusted federal budget deficit, itself, corrected for inflation.

As Paul Pieper and I have indicated in a series of papers—starting with Eisner and Pieper (1984)—and as I have elaborated in *How Real Is the Federal Deficit?* (Eisner, 1986) and elsewhere—we must look at the *real* deficit. This means, for many critical purposes, a measure of the deficit that corresponds to real changes in the government's debt, and hence to changes in the public's perception of the value of its holdings of that debt.

The change in the real value of the net federal debt may be viewed as the sum of three components: the nominal deficit exclusive of offsetting changes in financial assets and liabilities; changes in the nominal market value of existing financial assets and liabilities due to changes in nominal interest rates; and changes in the real values due to changes in the general level of prices (inflation). When we add these "interest effects" and "price effects" to the federal budget surplus (or subtract them from the deficit) we get a measure of the *real deficit*. The real deficit corresponds to the change in the real value of the net government debt, which it should be noted is not at all the nominal deficit divided by a price deflator. That measure, the real value of the nominal change, appears to be an arithmetic construct devoid of economic content.

Table 3
Capital Stocks, 1981

Component of Capital	*Billions of Current Dollars*
Business	6,085.9
Tangible	5,528.9
Intangible (R & D)	557.0
Nonprofit	248.2
Government	2,220.4
Government enterprise	476.3
Household	14,626.0
Tangible	3,949.7
Intangible (human)	10,676.3
Total	23,746.4

Source: Eisner (1985), Table 13, p. 47.

The real deficit, until the last six years of the Reagan Administration, was very different from the nominal one that drew all the attention. As shown in Table 4, the $153 billion of nominal deficits during the four Carter years, from 1977 through 1980, were actually surpluses totaling $72 billion. Rising prices, reducing the real value of the dollar, was serving as an inflation tax on the holders of government obligations. Rising interest rates, in part associated with *rising* rates of inflation, further reduced the market value of outstanding debt. In effect, measures of the official, nominal deficit include in expenditures nominal rather than real interest payments. They fail to impute as offsetting receipts the component of nominal interest payments which goes only to compensate holders of Treasury debt for their capital losses, and the Treasury's gains.

The nominal *high-employment* deficits, which averaged 0.53 percent of GNP from 1977 through 1981, correspond to real high-employment surpluses averaging 1.76 percent. All this suggests the need for some substantial revision of economic history and perhaps of the economic theory inspired by a misreading of the facts. In the words of Robert Lucas and Thomas Sargent (1981, pp. 295–296), the lesson of the 1970s was that "massive government budget deficits and high rates of monetary expansion" were accompanied not by decreasing unemployment but by *growing* unemployment *and* growing inflation. It was indeed the failure of the Keynesian paradigm in this regard to which Lucas (1981, p. 2) points as the motivation for his own search for a new macroeconomic model.

But viewing the real budget surpluses we are led rather to conclude that it was aggregate demand, in the face of the inflationary supply shocks of soaring petroleum prices and rising raw material prices on world markets, that failed after all. These exogenous forces brought on an inflation tax that reduced the real value of private wealth in the form of government debt, aggravating a loss due to the lower market

Table 4

Nominal and Real Budget Surplus or Deficit on National Income Account, Billions of Dollars, and Nominal and Real High-Employment Budget as Percent of GNP

	Surplus or Deficit			
	Actual Billions of Dollars		*High-Employment As Percent of GNP*	
Year	*Nominal*	*Real*	*Nominal*	*Real*
1977	−45.9	−0.6	−1.06	1.30
1978	−29.5	32.9	−0.73	2.15
1979	−16.1	32.1	−0.08	1.91
1980	−61.2	7.6	−0.65	1.97
1981	−64.3	−18.3	−0.11	1.45
1982	−148.2	−177.2	−1.06	−2.01
1983	−178.6	−101.2	−1.72	0.62
1984	−175.8	−154.1	−2.51	−1.92
Totals				
1977–80	−152.7	72.0		
1981–84	−566.9	−450.8		
Means				
1977–81	−43.4	10.7	−0.53	1.76
1982–84	−167.4	−144.2	−1.76	−1.10

Derived from Eisner (1986), Table B.7, p. 192, and Table 8.3, p. 87.

values associated with rising interest rates. It was then relatively tight fiscal policy, combined with the new tight monetary policy initiated in 1979, both continued through the first half of 1982, which brought us to 10.7 percent unemployment by December of that year.

What is the appropriate underlying theory? Going back to Pigou, Haberler, Lange and Patinkin, increased real holdings of government obligations by the private sector—money or interest-bearing—create an excess demand for goods. This must drive up output or prices or both. In the somewhat more recent formulation of Modigliani's life cycle theory of consumption, they enter as an increase of wealth in the individual's budget constraint. As he or she tries to maximize lifetime utility or welfare, the increased wealth is allocated to present and future needs and thus serves to generate increases in current and planned future consumption.

In terms of portfolio allocation theory, increased holdings of government debt also generate a demand for real, income-earning assets.[7] This, along with rational

[7]If returns to government debt and to real assets were highly correlated, government debt would be a substitute for real assets. But so long as they are not perfect substitutes, an increase in real wealth resulting from an increase in government debt would result in some increase in the demand for real assets.

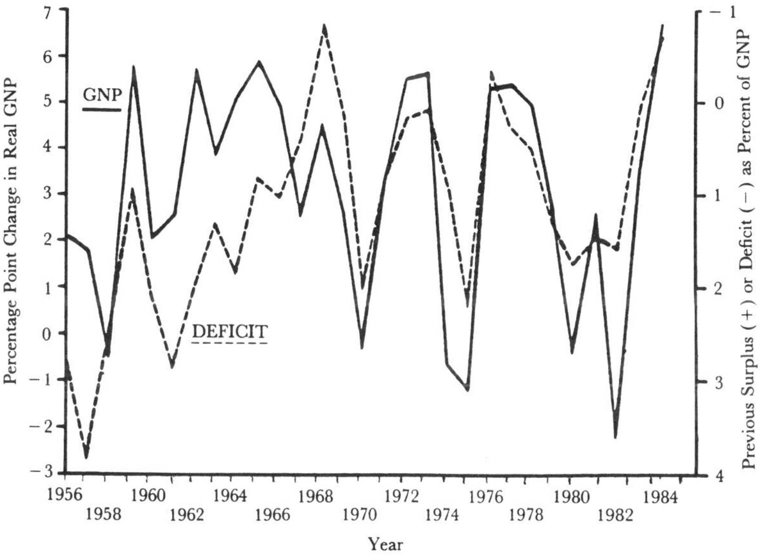

Fig. 1. Adjusted Deficit and Change in GNP

business behavior in the face of anticipations of increased future consumption, generates increased investment demand as well. And indeed there are other channels by which demand may be increased. In models of credit and equity rationing (for example, Stiglitz and Weiss, 1988; Greenwald and Stiglitz, 1988), deficits from either tax reductions or increases in government outlays create essentially riskless collateral and lead to more private expenditures, both by firms and individuals.

Whether this increased demand can be effected in real goods depends upon whether the economy is capable of increased production. And this comes back to the issue that provoked modern macroeconomics half a century ago, and which remains critical to any policy decisions today. That is the issue of unemployment and unused resources. If there is no involuntary unemployment and there are no idle resources, increased demand cannot generate more output; it can only bring higher prices. This is apparently the world of Milton Friedman (1968) and then Lucas, although they allow for various short run real effects as economic agents are slow or asymmetrical in their assimilation of information. But if you doubt that somehow our economy has generally been at its "natural rate" of employment, you may not be shocked to learn that real structural budget deficits have over the last several decades proved stimulatory to the economy.

And that is exactly the fact. As Figure 1 makes abundantly clear, the greater the real or inflation-adjusted high-employment federal deficit from 1955 to 1983, the greater was the next year's increase in GNP. The less the deficit, or the more the surplus, the less was the subsequent increase in GNP, or the more the GNP tended to

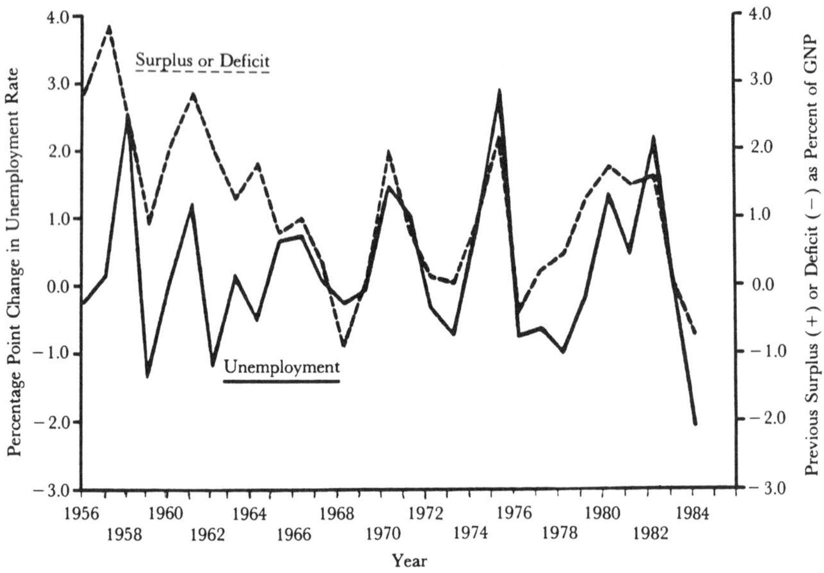

Fig. 2. Adjusted Surplus and Change in Unemployment

decline. And since more rapid increases in output are associated with declines in unemployment, and less rapid increases (or decreases) with increases in unemployment, a corresponding close fit is seen between the curves in Figure 2 for the adjusted budget surplus and subsequent changes in unemployment.

While the charts tell the story, all this is demonstrated more rigorously in the regression results of Table 5 where, for both the relatively noninflationary period from 1956 to 1966 and the more inflationary years from 1967 to 1984, the previous real high-employment budget surplus was significantly negatively related to changes in output and employment. Over the years 1966 to 1983, each percentage point that the inflation-adjusted or real high employment budget was in deficit was associated on the average, the following year, with 2.491 percentage points of growth in real GNP and 1.087 percentage points of decline in unemployment. The corresponding figures in the earlier years, when the economy was generally growing at rates closer to capacity and with less employment slack, were 1.731 percentage points for GNP growth and 0.566 percentage points for reduction in unemployment.[8,9,10]

But that is only part of the story. Budget deficits have not only been related positively to growth of GNP as a whole, but also to growth of its components of both

[8]This has not, it should be added, been a spurious consequence of coincidental monetary policy. Real changes in the monetary base have indeed also been associated positively with changes in real GNP (although actually not correlated with the structural budget deficits), but multiple regressions involving both the adjusted federal deficit and the real change in money supply (included in Table 6) leave the deficit parameters robust, and with pride of place.

Table 5

Real High-Employment Budgets and Changes in GNP and Unemployment

$Y_t = b_{01} + b_{11} PAHES_{t-1}$ for $t = 1956, \ldots, 1966$

$Y_t = b_{02} + b_{12} PAHES_{t-1}$ for $t = 1967, \ldots, 1984$

Y = dependent variable: *DGNP* or *DUN*

PAHES = price-adjusted high-employment budget surplus as percent of GNP

DGNP = percentage change in gross national product

DUN = percentage point change in unemployment

Dependent Variable (Y)	Regression Coefficients[a] 1956–66 b_{01}	1956–66 b_{12}	1967–84 b_{02}	1967–84 b_{12}	Significance Level of Difference in Regressions	$\hat{R}^2$	D-W
DGNP	7.187	−1.731	4.421	−2.491	0.0001	.622	2.10
	(1.125)	(0.516)	(0.447)	(0.416)			
DUN	−1.175	0.566	−0.455	1.087	0.002	.494	2.27
	(0.585)	(0.269)	(0.233)	(0.216)			

Source: Eisner (1986), Table 9.1, p. 97.

[a] Ordinary least squares; standard errors are shown in parentheses.

consumption and investment. We may note in Table 6 that each percentage point of real high-employment deficit was associated with growth of consumption the next year amounting to 0.642 percentage points of consumption. It was also associated with growth in gross private domestic investment equal to 1.383 percentage points of GNP. The evidence is thus that deficits have not crowded out investment. There has rather been "crowding in." And this should come as no surprise except to those devotees of "the new macroeconomics" who have embraced the old Euclidian world where employment and output are fixed (at those nefarious "natural" rates). We are in fact not only on the rising slope of the infamous Laffer curve but also on the rising slope of the curve for investment implicit in Lange's old (1938) article on the optimal

[9] The split in the time series may also be related to the general slowdown in growth in GNP, apparently associated with productivity. The earlier years were generally characterized by greater growth in GNP, less inflation and lower real budget deficits or greater surpluses. Within each period, as may be noted in the regression results, greater deficits were followed by greater increases in GNP.

[10] The size of the budget deficit is of course not the only parameter of fiscal policy that may be expected to affect aggregate demand, output and employment. Government expenditures for goods and services are themselves a component of GNP while interest and transfer payments will stimulate the economy only to the extent that they are spent. Thus, a given budget deficit will contribute less to aggregate demand if its interest and transfer payment components are greater. Some expenditures, as for roads and bridges, may prove complimentary with some private expenditures, as for cars and trucks, and substitutes for some others, such as railroad freight cars. And various taxes and tax subsidies are intended to discourage or encourage specific expenditures or consumption or investment in general. Our equations are clearly only reduced forms, and estimated parameters are affected by (probably changing) relations among unspecified variables and equations.

Table 6
Real High-Employment Budgets, Changes in Monetary Base, and Changes in Components of GNP

$$DCOM_t = b_{0l}X_l + b_{02}X_2 + b_l PAHES_{t-1} + b_2 DMB_{t-1}$$
$$X_1 = 1, \quad X_2 = 0 \quad \text{for } t = 1962, \ldots, 1966$$
$$X_1 = 0, \quad X_2 = 1 \quad \text{for } t = 1967, \ldots, 1984$$

$DCOM$ = change in component as percent of GNP
$PAHES$ = price-adjusted high-employment surplus as percent of GNP
DMB = real change in monetary base as percent of GNP

	Regression Coefficients[a]						
	Constants						
Component (*COM*)	*1962–66* (b_{01})	*1967–84* (b_{02})	$PAHES_{t-1}$ (b_1)	DMB_{t-1} (b_2)	$\hat{R}$	$D - W$	rho
Consumption	3.401	2.339	−0.642	2.393	.580	1.91	.092
	(0.675)	(0.303)	(0.263)	(1.592)			
Investment	2.613	1.135	−1.383	3.587	.570	1.99	.282
	(1.176)	(0.541)	(0.414)	(2.411)			
Government	1.195	0.483	−0.113	−0.660	.354	1.52	.473
	(0.558)	(0.270)	(0.172)	(0.981)			
Net Exports	−1.615	−0.766	0.399	1.625	.512	1.45	.836
	(1.273)	(1.012)	(0.137)	(0.811)			
GNP	6.208	3.371	−1.568	7.172	.735	2.03	.174
	(1.296)	(0.585)	(0.479)	(2.830)			
Domestic	7.405	3.934	−2.141	5.149	.767	1.93	.155
Demand	(1.506)	(0.675)	(0.560)	(3.295)			

Source: Eisner (1986), Table 9.8, p. 110.
[a] Least squares with Cochrane-Orcutt, first-order autoregressive corrections; standard errors are shown in parentheses.

propensity to consume.[11] Where more resources are available, and perverse monetary policy does not raise interest rates so as to preclude their use, more consumption may indeed be expected to be associated with more investment. The life cycle model, as we have noted, and Friedman's permanent income theory as well, both imply that

[11] Lange pointed out that increasing consumption may be expected to have two effects on investment. On the one hand, following the Keynesian analysis—although one would expect a similar result in a neoclassical framework—it would raise income, the transactions demand for money and interest rates. The rise in interest rates would indeed tend to reduce investment—the familiar crowding out. But as income rose there would, on the other hand, be demand for more capital to produce the associated increase in output, thus an increase in investment. The "optimal propensity to consume," which would maximize investment, would be reached when the marginal negative effects on investment of higher interest rates reached equality with the positive marginal effects of greater output. In the new classical and neoclassical worlds of natural or full employment, with changes in output generated only by changes in supply, there is only the negative interest effect. In the Keynesian (real) world where employment and output vary as a consequence of changes in aggregate demand, there is usually, unfortunately, plenty of room for increased production so that investment is likely to be crowded in, rather than crowded out, by increased consumption.

deficits will bring more consumption now and in the future. This should lead rational producers to try to produce more to meet current consumption demand but also to undertake more investment to provide the capital to produce more in the future.[12]

It is true that the deficits have also related negatively to net exports. The private wealth corresponding to increased public debt has meant more consumption of foreign goods as well as domestic goods and hence larger imports.[13] Although United States budget deficits have contributed to increases in current account deficits (along, of course, with net investment by foreigners in the United States) our corresponding capital account surplus is not all bad for the rest of the world, despite chronic complaints from international financial circles. In other work with Pieper (Eisner and Pieper, 1987), I have found that U.S. real budget deficits have been significantly and substantially related to subsequent increases in gross domestic product over the years 1971 to 1982 in the major OECD countries: Canada, France, Germany, Italy, Japan and the United Kingdom. Indeed, each percentage point of U.S. deficit (as a percent of GNP) was associated on the average with about 1.7 percentage points of foreign increase in GDP.

In fact, the now widely repeated argument that the United States has become "the world's largest debtor nation" proves on consideration to be somewhat confusing and confused. For one thing, net investment income as late as 1987 was a whopping positive $20.4 billion which, unless rates of return on U.S. investment abroad were far higher than foreigners' returns on investment in the U.S., suggests a *prima facie* contradiction of U.S. net debtor status. Part of the explanation may be that U.S. direct investment abroad is generally older than foreign investment in the U.S. and considerably reflects earlier, lower price levels. In that case, U.S. assets abroad would be undervalued and might even exceed the value of foreign assets in the United States.[14]

[12]Prudence in accepting anyone's regression results, including one's own, is always in order. I do not claim mine are unimpeachable. Fully specified structural equations in full models have their advantages. They also bring their problems, but I am working on them and encourage others to do so. I have less enthusiasm for vector autoregressions.

Bernheim's reserves regarding my reduced forms, however, seem strained. It does not seem overwhelmingly credible that my inflation-adjusted high employment surpluses were negatively related to subsequent real increases in aggregate demand for the fortuitous reasons he adduces. Bernheim's argument is essentially that exogenous policy-makers reduced those surpluses (increased deficits) in recessions in the mistaken notion that they would stimulate the economy. In fact, he suggests that they did not, but cyclical variations were such that just one year after they took these actions, real GNP and its components did recover for reasons that had nothing to do with fiscal policy.

My results for consumption are after all in line with those he cites approvingly. And since he does admit the existence of unemployed resources, he should not be surprised that deficit-induced increases in consumption are associated with increases in GNP (to which my regressions relate directly, not national income as indicated by Bernheim) and its components.

[13]The surplus on investment income disappeared in the first two quarters of 1988 but, as explained by the Bureau of Economic Analysis, this "reflected a decrease in receipts of income on U.S. direct investment abroad that was more than accounted for by a shift to capital (currency translation) losses associated with appreciation of the dollar" (DiLullo, 1988, p. 33).

[14]See Eisner and Pieper (1989).

But second, what is frequently forgotten is that the U.S. "net debtor" (or net creditor) position, since we have few obligations in foreign currencies, is appropriately measured in dollars. As the dollar falls (as it should be allowed to in accordance with market forces and a sensible monetary policy), the value of foreign currency rises and the dollar value of our foreign assets rises. That appreciation in the value in dollars of U.S. foreign investments is a significant corrective to the increase in indebtedness brought on by our current account deficit.

And third, the long run impact of even the unadjusted current account deficits we have been enduring is frequently exaggerated. Assume they continue at $150 billion per year for five more years—a highly unlikely event if the dollar is allowed to move freely. That would add $750 billion to our international "net debt." At even a substantial 4 percent real rate of interest, this would entail $30 billion of net payments to foreigners. With 7 percent growth, GNP would be approximately $6.7 trillion in five years, so that the net outpayment would come to less than half of one percent of what we are producing. I do not mean to advocate continued current account deficits adding to U.S. "debt" but, to keep matters in perspective, it should be recognized that half of one percent of GNP is not the stuff of disaster. Two-tenths of one percent of unemployment cost us about that amount of real income. The difference between 5.4 percent and the full employment target of 4 percent unemployment amounts to far more.

All this is pertinent to the widely expressed concern over the alleged inadequacy and decline of "national saving," on which Gramlich focusses much of his discussion. For it turns out that the fall is quite fully accounted for by increases in reported capital consumption allowances and, recently and most importantly, negative U.S. foreign investment.

The ratio of GNP to real capital consumption allowances (with adjustment) increased by 3.76 percentage points from 1951 to 1987, causing an equivalent reduction in net investment and net saving. The capital consumption increase apparently stems from shifts in investment from structures to equipment and from equipment such as railroad cars with expected lives of 30 years to trucks with expected lives of 10 years. If we believe investment is properly guided by the lure of profits, may we not expect some at least of the presumed increase in replacement requirements to be offset by increased capital productivity?[15]

Real *gross* private domestic investment as a percent of real GNP was 18.0 percent in 1979 and exactly the same figure, 18.0 percent, in 1987, despite a 3.8 percentage point move in the National Income Account federal budget, from a surplus of 0.4 percent of GNP to a deficit of 3.4 percent. Over the same period, however, net exports, which essentially account for net foreign investment, moved from +0.1

[15]Suppose we reject the inference that the shifts were productive, arguing that they were brought on by (the now abandoned) investment tax credit for equipment and the huge acceleration of tax depreciation culminating in the tax changes of 1981, and sustained by the high real interest rates of most of the current decade, which may be expected to discourage long-lived investment. The remedy would then appear to lie clearly not in a general lament over the resultant decline in net investment but in the sustained reversal of these policies that brought on the increase in capital consumption.

percent of GNP to −3.5 percent. The move to real structural budget deficit had something to do with this, by stimulating the economy and thereby increasing our imports. But in 1983, when the recession-swollen deficit was 5.2 percent of GNP, net exports were only −0.6 percent—and gross private domestic investment was down to 15.4 percent of GNP.

The large move to negative net exports and negative foreign investment from 1983 to 1987 is very largely accountable to the one-third previous rise, from 100.8 to 132.0, in a trade-weighted index of the real exchange rate for the dollar. The fall in the dollar since early 1985 has increased the value of U.S. assets abroad, thus offsetting the negative foreign investment. If the Federal Reserve were to permit the dollar to fall further, our measured foreign investment, and hence net saving, would increase with the stimulation to our exports. And we would have a further gain in the dollar value of our mainly foreign-currency denominated foreign assets and in the dollar earnings from those assets.

The evidence that budget deficits have caused a decline in correctly measured national saving, even as a percent of GNP, is thus doubtful indeed.[16] And in terms of a comprehensive measure of national saving, including public investment in infrastructure, education and research, misguided efforts to reduce the budget deficit are by far the greatest threat to investment in our future.

Deficits and Inflation

It is widely suggested that structural budget deficits contribute to inflation. This is presumably implied by the assumption that the economy is generally at its "natural" or "non-accelerating inflation rate of unemployment" (NAIRU), unless perverse policy temporarily drives it off that rate. I have mined the data of the last 30 years shamelessly in an effort to test that argument and I challenge others to do likewise. I find no support for the proposition that the federal budget deficit, by any measure, contributes to inflation. If anything, the opposite appears to be true.

As shown in Table 7, when annual observations from 1956 to 1985 are used to regress the rate of inflation on its own lagged value and lagged values of the inflation-adjusted structural deficit and rate of unemployment (with a shift variable

[16] My argument should be distinguished from that of Barro that private saving adjusts to public dissaving. In support of his argument, Barro points to recent Israeli experience where offsetting movements in public and private saving were associated with huge changes in the rate of inflation. With higher inflation there were greater deficits and greater private saving. With lesser inflation there were smaller deficits and less private saving.

But with greater inflation, seignorage or the inflation tax would be greater, and thus there would be no inflation-induced rise in the *real* budget deficit or *real* private saving. And with less inflation, and lesser nominal deficits and private saving, the inflation tax would be less. The offsetting movements of measured public and private saving might then merely reflect the fact that private agents are not guilty of money illusion and that both the real government deficit and real private saving, measured to include the inflation tax on monetary debt and assets, were relatively constant. The force of this comment would depend on the amount of seignorage left in an economy where high inflation has vastly diminished real holdings in local-currency denominated assets.

Table 7
Budget Deficits and Inflation

$$DGNPDEF_t = b_{0l}X_l + b_{02}X_2 + b_l DGNPDEF_{t-1} + b_2 U_t + b_3 PAHES_{t-1}$$
$$X_1 = 1, \quad X_2 = 0 \quad \text{for } t = 1956, \ldots, 1966$$
$$X_1 = 0, \quad X_2 = 1 \quad \text{for } t = 1967, \ldots, 1985$$

$DGNPDEF$ = percent change in GNP price deflator
$PAHES$ = price-adjusted high-employment surplus as percent of GNP
U = unemployment rate as percent of labor force

Variable or Statistic	*Regression Coefficients and Standard Errors*		*Means and Standard Deviations*
X_1 (1956 to 1966)	2.378	0.248	4.853[a]
	(1.004)	(0.670)	(2.646)
X_2 (1967 to 1985)	3.694	2.392	
	(1.060)	(1.042)	
$DGNPDEF_{t-1}$	0.877	0.597	4.849
	(0.185)	(0.168)	(2.618)
U_t	−0.469	—	5.983
	(0.177)		(1.663)
$PAHES_{t-1}$	0.193	0.350	1.004
	(0.292)	(0.318)	(1.228)
$\hat{R}^2$	.795	.747	
D–W	2.13	1.74	

[a] Dependent variable.

again for the relatively higher inflation of the two latter decades of the period), the surplus coefficient is close to zero, *and positive*. Taken literally (and ignoring the large standard error) it suggests that each percentage point of deficit as a ratio of GNP *subtracts* 0.2 percentage points from the rate of inflation the next year, and 1.6 percentage points in the long run. Omitting the unemployment variable to test the possibility that the effects of larger deficits on inflation have been picked up in lesser unemployment, which they would have brought about, offers no comfort. The coefficient of the price-adjusted high employment surplus variable is still positive and suggests that each percentage point of deficit subtracts 0.35 percentage points from the rate of inflation the next year, and 0.9 percentage points in the long run.

And lest one think this is all an artifact of my inflation adjustment to the deficit, I can report that relations involving the nominal or unadjusted high-employment deficit are similar, as are those with the actual deficit, nominal and real. Adding changes in the monetary base to the regressions does no good either. There should of course be much more to properly specified structural relations, including variables measuring supply shocks and variables reflecting changing expectations, but it may well be argued that the evidence that structural budget deficits have contributed to inflation has not been found.

The true story is apparently that major inflation of the 1970s and the beginning of the 1980s stemmed not from budget deficits or excess demand but from the major supply shocks of hugely escalating oil costs and rising prices of agricultural products in world markets. Increases in unemployment were associated with reductions in inflation, but at a cost which many of us might properly find exorbitant, less than half of one percent decrease in inflation in the current year for each one percentage point increase in unemployment, if we wish to take seriously the estimated parameter of -0.469 for U_t in Table 7.

A New View of the Past, and Balance for the Future

What has been going on and where do we go from here? First, budget deficits did not contribute to the inflation of the 1970s, which reached its peak in 1981. This stemmed from the supply shocks in petroleum and world markets for agricultural products, not a surge in demand. The inflation tax converted supposed deficits into substantial real surpluses until the latter half of 1982. It was large structural surpluses, along with tight money, that brought us the worst recession since the great depression of the 1930s and an unemployment rate of 10.7 percent by December 1982.

It was then the huge swing to real deficit in the latter half of 1982, along with the switch to easier money, and the continued deficits thereafter which sparked our substantial economic recovery. It may of course be noted, as was probably reflected in the earlier regression results, that the large deficits were accompanied by a sharp reduction in the rate of inflation as well as interest rates. The recovery has been long but sluggish in considerable measure because of large and growing trade deficits. While these may be laid partly at the door of the deficit-fueled growth of the economy, which raised imports, key responsibility must be attributed to still too restrictive monetary policy. This has kept real interest rates and the value of the dollar too high. With all of its fall over the past four years, the dollar remains at or above the levels of 1980. The major surge in productivity among our key international competitors since 1980 clearly called for a considerably lower value of the dollar.

What does that indicate now? To begin, with all of the nonsense in current calculations of the deficit, "balance" in the conventional sense makes no sense. At the 1988 inflation rate of 4 percent, for example, the inflation tax on the $2,100 billion of our current federal debt held by the public implies that nominal balance would be a real surplus of $84 billion. The federal government would be reducing the real value of its debt, and the assets of the public in the form of that debt, by $84 billion per year, with all that this would imply for consumption, portfolio adjustment, investment, output and employment.

A much better concept of balance, in a growing economy such as ours, with or without inflation, would be one in which the debt-income ratio were constant. The necessary and sufficient condition for this, of course, is that the debt grow at the same rate—no faster or slower—as income. I offer this not as an iron-clad imperative, regardless of circumstances, but rather as a rule of thumb which would, one may note, be equally appropriate for an individual or a corporation.

For the federal government, with GNP growing at about 7.5 percent per year, the debt could then grow at 7.5 percent per year. With the gross federal debt at $2100 billion, this comes to an increase in debt, and hence a nominal current deficit, of $157 billion. It may be noted that this "balanced deficit" is almost exactly the actual nominal deficit of $155 billion for fiscal year 1988 and is exceeded only trivially by the gloomier projections, without further reductions, for 1989. And if we take into account state and local government budgets, we find that for total government we are in substantial surplus. Despite all the furor, total government debt is currently a declining ratio of GNP.[17]

This rule of balance should not be engraved in stone—or in the Constitution. Even this measure should at times show a deficit, at times a surplus. It depends on the shape of the economy, on associated monetary policies and on relative needs for public and private investment. At least until the reductions legislated in late 1987 and early 1988, the nation's current federal deficits did appear large for the long run. They implied an increasing ratio of federal debt-to-GNP. Over the long run, it might have been argued then, the federal deficits should be brought down. But that judgment should depend on what is happening to state and local governments. And most fundamentally, it should depend on how much of the nation's resources are being devoted and should be devoted to private versus public investment.

If public investment in the education and health of America, in the nation's stock of basic scientific and technological knowledge and in its collective resources and infrastructure are to be increased, continued large nominal deficits may well be in order, and even large real deficits.

It is tempting to suggest, recalling Abba Lerner's old principle of "functional finance," that nominal deficits will never cause permanent real deficits that are too large. If an economy has unemployed resources, a large nominal deficit will increase aggregate demand, both real and nominal, until it reaches full (or "natural") employment. At that point (if not before), inflation will have risen, and will keep rising until the inflation tax, reducing the real value of existing government debt, is sufficient to bring the rate of increase in the real value of that debt—the real deficit—down to equality with the rate of growth in real GNP. Any still greater nominal deficit will then only raise the rate of inflation but not the rate of increase in the real value of government debt and hence not the real deficit. There is hence no further increase in real consumption, and no crowding out of investment, even at full employment. There will, however, be crowding out of investment if the monetary authority acts to reduce the inflation by tightening credit and raising interest rates.

If we are not facing a full-employment, excess-demand inflation, the case for nominal and real deficit reduction, despite what has apparently become dominant conventional wisdom among politicians, press and pundits and, I must confess, considerable numbers of economists, is shaky indeed. If deficits are to be reduced, a prime concern should be avoidance of a recession, and this, as Keynes argued a half

[17]The ratio of *deficit* to GNP, d, consistent with a constant debt-GNP ratio, b, is simply the product of that ratio and the rate of growth of GNP, g, thus expressed as $d = bg$. Hence, for b approximately equal to 0.42 and g at about 7.5 percent, we can maintain a deficit at 3.15 percent of GNP forever without raising the debt-GNP ratio.

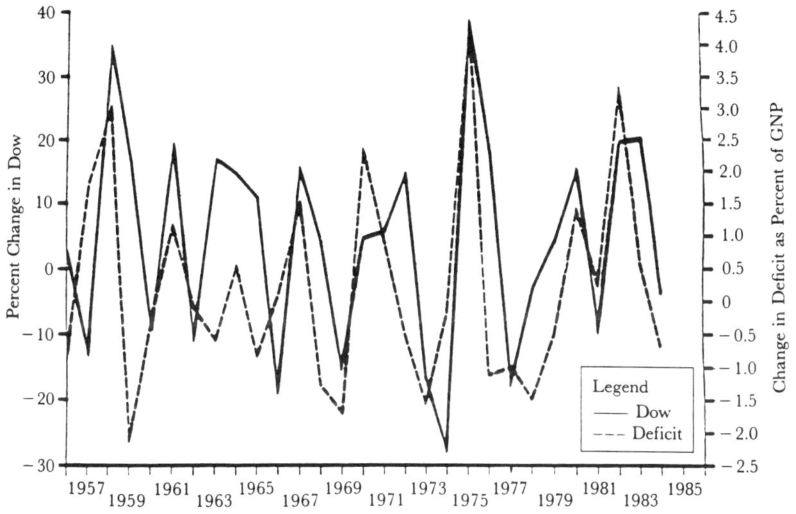

Fig. 3. Changes in Dow Industrials and Price-Adjusted Deficit

century ago, is not to be accomplished by lopping off a boom. Too many of us have allowed our targets of full employment to recede with the political winds and misguided concern for inflation. We may take comfort that, from the 10.7 percent official measure of December 1982, unemployment had declined (as of November 1988) to 5.4 percent. But whatever happened to that "full employment" target of 4 percent unemployment? The unemployment rate was 3.5 and 3.4 percent twenty years ago.

At this time, therefore, the prime aggregate policy instrument should be monetary policy, and it should be more stimulatory. Significant and sustained increases in the monetary base would lower interest rates and encourage a further decline in the dollar.[18] Both gross private domestic investment and exports would thus increase. Not

[18]The curious notion that a more rapid growth in the quantity of money can only in the long run raise nominal interest rates and leave the real rate unchanged, again attributable to Friedman (1968), rests largely on the equally curious notion that we are always at that fully market-clearing, "natural," full-employment rate of output. If we are (and all agents know we are), then increases in demand as a consequence of a greater quantity of money can only raise prices. By a further leap of imagination—or of assumption—increases in the quantity of money (or the monetary base) somehow entail equiproportionate increases in all obligations and claims denoted in money, including the very government debt created quite independently by budget deficits. Alternatively, money neutrality in the face of Federal Reserve open market operations can be rescued by unreserved acceptance of Barro-Ricardian equivalence; since government debt is not viewed as a private asset, substitution of money for that debt merely adds equivalent amounts to private wealth and proportionately increases nominal spending. For those not fully committed to the equivalence theorem, the proposition that increasing the money supply, in the manner in which this actually occurs in our economy, will have no real effects would appear to be as preposterous as the assumption that,since there is some rate of taxation so high that it will kill off all taxable income, we are, in fact, in the current United States economy, on the falling portion of the Laffer curve so that lower tax rates will actually raise tax revenues.

only would the U.S. trade deficit finally come down, but the nominal budget deficits themselves would be reduced. Lower interest rates would contribute directly; each percentage point drop would save the Treasury over $20 billion in annual interest payments within two or three years, as the debt is rolled over.[19] And the stimulus to the economy would further reduce the deficit as tax revenues rise and unemployment benefit payouts decline.

And what about the stock market? Those who have trumpeted budget deficits as the cause of share price declines would do well to think again. I have for some time now been gleefully passing out copies of charts such as Figure 3 and regressions from my 1986 book showing that increases in deficits were strongly correlated with *in*creases in the Dow. Of course, I can add that the October 1987 crash followed immediately on the news that "the deficit" had declined from $221 billion in fiscal 1986 to $148 billion in 1987. Further *reductions* in the deficit might bring new, dismal reverberations on Wall Street!

■ *I am grateful for valuable comments and suggestions by the editors, Timothy Taylor, Joseph E. Stiglitz and Carl Shapiro. I have benefitted as well from the financial support of a series of National Science Foundation grants, including the current SES-8707979.*

[19]The real deficit would of course rise temporarily as the *falling* interest rates would raise the market value of outstanding government debt. Once interest rates reached their lower value, both the nominal and real deficits would be less.

References

Boskin, Michael J., M. S. Robinson, T. O'Reilly, and P. Kumer, "New Estimates of the Value of Federal Mineral Rights and Land," *American Economic Review*, December 1985, *5*, 923–936.

Dilullo, Anthony J., "U.S. International Transactions, Second Quarter 1988," *Survey of Current Business*, Sept. 1988, *68*, 33–38.

Eisner, Robert, "Social Security, Saving and Investment," *Journal of Macroeconomics*, Winter 1983, *5*, 1–19.

Eisner, Robert, "The Total Incomes System of Accounts," *Survey of Current Business*, Jan. 1985, *65*, 20–25.

Eisner, Robert, *How Real Is the Federal Deficit?* New York: The Free Press, A Division of Macmillan, 1986.

Eisner, Robert, *The Total Incomes System of Accounts*, Chicago: University of Chicago Press, 1989.

Eisner, Robert and Paul J. Pieper, "A New View of the Federal Debt and Budget Deficits," *American Economic Review*, March 1984, *74*, 11–29.

Eisner, Robert and Paul J. Pieper, "Measurement and Effects of Government Debt and Deficits." In *Economic Policy and National Accounting in Inflationary Conditions*, *Studies in Banking and Finance*. Amsterdam: North Holland, 1987, pp. 116–144.

Eisner, Robert and Paul J. Pieper, "The World's Greatest Debtor Nation?," forthcoming, 1989.

Friedman, Milton, "The Role of Monetary Policy," *American Economic Review*, March 1968, *58*, 1–17.

Greenwald, Bruce C., and Stiglitz, Joseph E., "Financial Market Imperfections and Business Cycles," NBER Working Paper No. 2494, Cambridge MA, January 1988.

Lange, Oscar, "The Rate of Interest and the Optimal Propensity to Consume," *Economica*, February 1938, New Series *5*, 12–32. Reprinted in American Economic Association, *Readings in Business Cycle Theory*. Philadelphia: Blakiston, 1944, pp. 169–192.

Lerner, Abba, "Functional Finance and the Federal Debt," *Social Research*, 1943, *10*, 38–58.

Lucas, Robert E., Jr., *Studies in Business Cycle Theory*. Cambridge, Mass.: MIT Press, 1981.

Lucas, Robert E., Jr. and Thomas J. Sargent, "After Keynesian Economics." In Lucas and Sargent, eds., *Rational Expectations and Economic Practice*. Minneapolis: University of Minnesota Press, 1981, pp. 295–319.

Stiglitz, Joseph E., and Weiss, Andrew, "Credit Rationing and Its Implications for Macro-Economics," unpublished manuscript, 1988.

U.S. Government, Office of Management and Budget, *Special Analyses*, *Budget of the United States Government*, *Fiscal Year 1989*, Washington: Government Printing Office, 1988.

THE POLITICAL ECONOMY OF GOVERNMENT DEBT
H.A.A. Verbon and F.A.A.M. van Winden (editors)

Chapter 12

SELF-CORRECTING REAL DEFICITS: A NEW LESSON IN FUNCTIONAL FINANCE

Robert Eisner and Sang-In Hwang*

Department of Economics, Northwestern University, Evanston, Illinois 60208, USA

1. Introduction

A number of previous works[1] have pointed to the significance of the 'real budget deficit'. By this is meant a measure of the change in the real net debt of the US Federal government. This corresponds in large part - except for debt held by state and local government and by the rest of the world - to an important segment of financial assets of the private sector.

Measures of the structural or high-employment real budget deficit have been found, in US data for 1955 to 1988, to relate positively to subsequent increases in real GNP, consumption, and gross private domestic investment, and negatively to unemployment and net exports. Perhaps as a consequence of the last, following from a positive relation between deficits and increases in imports, US deficits were found to be related positively to growth in GDP in Canada, France, Italy, Japan, the United Kingdom and West Germany.

In this paper we present a multi-equation, structural model of the economy which is consistent with these findings and with the further hypothesis that increases in nominal budget deficits, far from creating a doomsday scenario of domestic and foreign debt, may generate new equilibria with higher rates of output and inflation. Real budget and current account deficits and debt burdens, domestic and international, may increase or decrease, dependent upon monetary policy.

* Respectively, William R. Kenan Professor of Economics and Research Assistant, Northwestern University. We are most grateful to WEFA Associates and to Alphametrics Corporation for furnishing the Modler software employed in our simulations and in particular to Charles Renfro for guidance and assistance in its use and the to WEFA again for the AREMOS software used in later simulations. Paul J. Pieper was of invaluable help in getting us started on simulations of simple models antecedent to those presented here. Stacey M. Tevlin has contributed mightily to our various computer manipulations, along with Craig Safir, Marc Sokol, Oliver Haberstroh, and John Applegate. Our work has enjoyed the financial support of National Science Foundation grant SES-8707979.

1 Eisner (1986, 1989, 1991), Eisner and Pieper (1984, 1986, 1987, 1988).

2. Theory and Hypotheses

Theoretical underpinnings for these relations are to be found in the neoclassical formulations of Haberler, Pigou and Patinkin, as well as in Keynes, and in later-day consumption functions of Modigliani and Friedman and modern formulations of the investment function. Simply enough, real deficits add to the permanent income and/or real wealth perceived by private agents in the form of public debt or the monetary and nonmonetary assets the debt may back. This increase in perceived wealth increases current and planned future consumption. These increases in turn raise the demand for physical capital and hence increase investment. (Portfolio effects of increases in financial assets on the demand for real assets may also contribute to a rise in investment.) Unless exchange rate adjustment can and does compensate, the increases in consumption and investment demand are effected in foreign goods as well as domestic goods, thus generating the observed increase in imports and decrease in net exports.

This formulation diverges from the currently dominant version of the neoclassical model, which essentially presumes market-clearing full-employment and, at least in the short run, fixed output. Here budget deficits increase consumption only at the expense of investment, either domestic or foreign or both.

A market-clearing, neoclassical model would appear to require neutrality with respect to equi-proportionate increases of government interest-bearing and non-interest-bearing debt, the latter corresponding to what may be called outside money. These would generate no real effects in a comparative statics formulation. They would result only in proportionate increases in prices, with no change in the total real debt of the government and hence no change in aggregate demand or any of its components.

Without the assumption of market clearing, or admitting the possibility of underemployment, increases in the nominal net debt of the government need not bring proportionate increases in prices. If they do not and hence if the real debt increases, they may be expected to increase aggregate demand and output. If they prove sufficient to bring the economy to full employment, we are back in a situation where greater nominal aggregate demand can only bring higher prices. Hence there is no further increase in the real net debt. All this suggests that fears that government budget deficits or public dissaving must absorb private saving and crowd out private investment are misguided. Over recent US history we have had substantial underemployment. Hence, as observed, real budget deficits have been associated with increases in consumption and investment. We have had crowding in, not crowding out. If nominal and real deficits persist to the point of bringing the economy to full employment, inflation will rise to a rate sufficient to reduce the real deficit to a level consistent with real full-employment growth. At this point, real domestic investment will be reduced only if monetary policy is such as to prevent the hypothesized equi-proportionate increases of money and interest-bearing debt held by private agents. In this case, real interest rates would rise and investment would be reduced. The cause though would not be the budget deficits themselves but the clash between fiscal expansion and monetary contraction.

Monetary policy may also impact total gross investment through its effect on exchange rates and real net foreign investment. Real budget deficits, by increasing aggregate demand, as noted, will increase the demand for foreign goods as well as domestic goods. This in itself implies negative foreign investment; the other side of the coin of a current account deficit is a capital account surplus, that is, foreign accumulation of claims to domestic assets, for the US, foreign holdings of dollars.

Unless foreigners are given some reason to hold the increased quantity of dollars, they will try to reduce their holdings[2]. In the aggregate, however, they will succeed only by bringing about a depreciation of the dollar and hence a reduction in the *real* value of their claims in terms of their own currencies. This depreciation will go on until the current account deficit is eliminated and/or is brought in line with the rate at which they may be willing to increase their real holdings of dollar assets. Nominal budget deficits need not therefore permanently reduce real net foreign investment (as by driving it negative from an initial 'balance' of zero) unless monetary intervention or stringency keeps the dollar from declining.

Expectations are implicitly rational in the sense that agents' behavior is consistent with implications of the model and they make use, with appropriate lags because of adjustment costs and the time necessary to distinguish permanent from transitory or stochastic changes, of all available information. We have endeavored to specify a set of equations to give structure to this model of the economy. One critical assumption is that the rate of inflation, not the acceleration of the rate of inflation, is a positive function of the rate of output. Higher output, with greater pressure on capacity, will generate a higher rate of inflation. But with any constant rate of output, the rate of inflation will also be constant. We have no razor's edge or NAIRU (non-accelerating inflation rate of unemployment), departures from which would bring ever-increasing inflation or deflation. Attempts to bring output beyond the limits set by resources would, however, if carried far enough, eventually bring prohibitive rates of inflation.

We have experimented with a related assumption - that nominal interest rates do not adjust fully to expected rates of inflation. However much this denial of the Fisher effect may be inconsistent with some perfect-market models - although it may follow from the Tobin-Mundell effect of a lower rate of return on money spilling into real assets - it does seem to square with economic history, at least for the relatively mild inflation known in the United States. Thus higher rates of inflation, in one variation of our models, would be associated with lower real rates of interest. In our major simulations herein discussed, however, we have allowed the Fisher effect to hold in the long run to avoid coloring the results with what may seem, to some, excessively positive effects on investment, via inflation, from budget deficits.

The supply side of the model is built around a constant-returns, CES production function and an exogenous labor force. It is assumed that the rate of inflation is a distributed lag function of the pressure of output on capacity and changes in the price of imported goods. In the growth version, the labor force and labor productivity, and hence the effective labor supply, are assumed to grow at constant percentage rates. Employment is determined by output, subject to the production function and existing capital. Investment then proceeds, also subject to the production function, in response to the need to replace depreciating capital and add (or subtract) capital as a consequence of changes in output.

Essential control parameters are an exogenous component of taxes and in some simulations government expenditures for goods and services, the elasticity of the money supply with respect to nominal GNP and, in a few simulations, an exogenous component or exogenous growth of the money supply. All other parameters are assumed but are generally in line with conventional macroeconomic theory and the structures of macroeconometric models. We hope

2 We assume that foreigners always hold 20 per cent of US government debt. Adjustments to their investment position are effected only in other portions of their portfolios.

ultimately to substitute estimated parameters for at least a number of those here specified a priori.

3. Description of Equations

The building blocks of the model are of course the individual behavioral equations and identities. These are here described briefly, generally for the main 'S'-version of the model, with numbers corresponding to the equations specified in Appendix 1.

1. Consumption demand is a distributed lag function of the components of real disposable income and, except in the 'T'-model, of net private financial wealth. (Tangible wealth is ignored.)
2. Real disposable income is defined as output minus taxes but plus government interest payments minus price and interest effects (explained below) on the real market value of domestically held government debt.
3. Net private financial wealth equals the market value of net debt of the government minus net foreign financial claims on domestic assets. The government debt includes both the non-interest-bearing monetary base and interest-bearing government bonds of five-year maturities.
4. Depreciation or capital consumption is a constant proportion of capital.
5. Replacement investment is a function of capital consumption, the rental cost of capital and capital demanded.
6. Accelerator investment demand is a distributed lag function of changes in output and the rental cost of capital.
7. Accelerator investment equals accelerator investment demand except that it has a lower bound of −1.1 times the rate of depreciation (taken to be the maximum feasible postponable replacement and liquidation of inventories).
8. Gross private domestic investment is then the sum of replacement investment and accelerator investment, both subject to a CES production function and an elasticity of the capital-output ratio with respect to the rental cost of capital of −0.5, and embodying a putty-clay model.
9. The rental-cost-of-capital index is based on the real rate of interest and depreciation. For a real rate of interest of0 .03, the index has a value of unity.
10. The real rate of interest is equal to the nominal rate of interest minus the expected rate of inflation.
11. The expected rate of inflation is the mean, with declining weights, of the rates of actual inflation over the twenty previous quarters.
12. The real rate of government expenditures for goods and services is exogenous (in the growth model, growing at a rate of 3 per cent per year).
13. Taxes are a function of gross income, that is, output and government interest payments. Taxes adjust fully to changes in interest payments, so that the change in the budget deficit is always equal to the change in the primary deficit, that is, the deficit exclusive of government interest payments.
14. Real imports of goods and services, other than the capital services measured by payments to foreigners on their net financial claims on US assets, valued in units of domestic output, are a distributed lag function of domestic output demanded and exchange rates. The elasticity of import demand with respect to output is unity. The long-run elasticity

is 0.25 with respect to real exchange rates (the amount of foreign currency, multiplied by the relative prices of US and foreign goods, that can be purchased for a dollar). A 'J-curve' reaction to exchange rate changes is built in, however, as the cost of imported goods changes with a shorter set of lags than the quantity of imports demanded.

15. Real imports of financial or capital services equal the real rate of interest times the amount of outstanding net financial claims of foreigners, exclusive of their holdings of government debt. (Government interest payments to foreigners enter into net foreign investment but are not considered imports of services in the national income and product accounts.)
16. Total imports are the sum of imports of capital services and of all other goods and services.
17. The foreign demand for US exports is a distributed lag function of an exogenous component, relating to world economic conditions (in the growth model, growing at 3 per cent per year), and of exchange rates.
18. The real exchange rate, defined as an index, initially set at unity, of the value of the dollar in terms of foreign currencies, multiplied by the relative price of US and foreign goods, is a function of real interest rates, the adjusted measure of real net foreign investment, which includes the price and interest effects on government debt held by foreigners,[3] and the value in foreign currencies of foreign claims to domestic assets.
19. US financial claims on foreigners denominated in foreign currencies are taken as exogenous, initially equal to $800 billion and growing at the rate g.
20. US financial claims on foreigners denominated in dollars are also taken as exogenous, initially equal to $800 billion and growing at the rate g.
21. The dollar value of US financial claims on foreigners equals the claims denominated in foreign currencies, divided by the exchange rate index, plus the value of claims denominated in dollars.
22. The change in foreign financial claims on the US equals the current flow increase of US claims on foreigners minus US adjusted real net foreign investment. Foreign claims are assumed equal initially to $2,120 billion.
23. Net foreign financial claims on the US (the negative of the net international investment position of the US) equal the value of financial claims of foreigners on the US minus the dollar value of total financial claims of the US on foreigners. This is thus initially equal to $520 billion. Net foreign financial claims are decreased by the sum of (US) net foreign investment and gains, due to falls in the exchange rate, in the dollar value of US claims denominated in foreign currencies.
24. Aggregate demand is the sum of consumption demand, investment demand, government expenditures for goods and services and foreign demand for US exports, minus imports.

[3] In simulations of effects of a tax cut of $300 billion, the high rates of inflation that were generated produced an explosive cycle of price and interest effects and adjusted net foreign investment, interacting with exchange rate and import fluctuations. Output and/or disposable income eventually turned negative and the simulations halted. To correct this breakdown and achieve stability we reduced the coefficient of net foreign investment in the exchange rate equation from 10 to 5 in the $300 billion tax-cut simulations reported in Table 4 below. (It also proved possible to correct the breakdown by substituting conventional net foreign investment, NFIC, in the exchange rate equation, thus eliminating the interaction with price and interest effects.)

25. The maximum possible or ceiling rate of output is a CES function of the labor force and the stock of capital. In the growth model the labor force is assumed to grow at 2 per cent per year and the productivity of labor at 100[(1.03/1.02) - 1] per cent per year so that the effective supply of labor grows at 3 per cent annually.
26. The 'zero-extra-inflation' rate of output is the output corresponding to a ratio of employment to the labor force equal to z, assumed to have a value of 0.92, thus corresponding to 8 per cent unemployment.
27. The labor force is initially assumed equal to 120 (million); in the growth model it increases at an annual rate of 2 per cent.
28. Actual output is a function of aggregate demand and the proximity of demand to capacity so that as demand exceeds 97 per cent of capacity actual output falls increasingly short of demand and, with increasing demand, can only asymptotically approach (and never exceed) capacity.
29. The ratio to be applied in keeping consumption, investment and exports below consumption demand, investment demand and export demand when aggregate demand exceeds output is formed by dividing output plus imports minus government expenditures for goods and services by aggregate demand plus imports minus government expenditures.
30. Consumption is consumption demand multiplied by the ratio defined in 29.
31. Investment is investment demand multiplied by the ratio defined in 29.
32. Exports are export demand multiplied by the ratio defined in 29.
33. Net exports equals exports minus imports.
34. Conventional net foreign investment equals net exports minus government interest payments to foreigners.
35. Unemployment equals the labor force minus employment, initially 9.6 million, which equals 120 million minus 110.4 million.
36. Output, which is determined by aggregate demand 24 and the supply constraints of 28, is consistent with the production function.
37. The change in capital stock equals gross investment minus capital consumption.
38. Capital stock demanded, which is determined by equating marginal product and marginal factor cost, is a function of output and the rental cost of capital.
39. Employment is determined by the requirements of the production function, with the existing capital stock.
40. The rate of inflation is a function of the previous rate of inflation, the proximity of output to capacity, the ratio of output demanded and output, and increases in the cost of imports brought on by decreases in the exchange rate. (It does not entail accelerating inflation.) The initial equilibrium rate of inflation for an output of $4,000 billion is taken to be 5 per cent.
41. The rate of change of the price level equals the rate of inflation.
42. The supply of (high-powered) money or the monetary base, which is an asset of the private sector, is a function of output. It is set initially at $160 billion, or 4 per cent of GNP. Departures of the money supply from its initial value or, in the growth case from baseline, are then defined by an elasticity parameter (EM), variously assumed to be - 1, 0, 1 and 2.
43. The supply of money is increased by $25 billion above its baseline.

44. The rate of growth of the nominal quantity of money, initially equal to the rate of growth of nominal GNP, is increased by two percentage points.
45. The nominal interest rate is a function of the nominal value of output, the nominal quantity of money and expected inflation. Expected inflation is fully reflected in interest rates in the main ('S') versions of our models (and in the 'T'-version). In the 'Q' version only 90 per cent of expected inflation is reflected in the nominal interest rate.
46. The nominal par value of net government debt increases by the amount of the conventional budget deficit.
47. The nominal market value of the debt equals the sum of the monetary base and the present value of outstanding interest-bearing issues.
48. The present value of outstanding interest-bearing issues is a function of their face values, the interest rates when they were issued, their remaining times to maturity, and the current interest rate.
49. The price effect equals the loss in value of the debt due to inflation.
50. The interest effect equals the difference between the change in the market value of the debt and the change in its par value.
51. The conventional budget surplus equals taxes minus government expenditures for goods and services and interest payments.
52. The nominal value of interest payments is defined by the volume of new bond issues and the nominal interest rates on those issues, over the previous five years.
53. New bond issues are equal to the sum of the refinancing of old issues (those of 20 quarters earlier) and what is necessary to finance the current deficit over and beyond monetization or increases in the monetary base.
54. The real budget surplus in current dollars equals the conventional budget surplus plus the 'price effect', or reduction in the real value of outstanding government debt due to inflation (what might be called an 'inflation tax'), and the 'interest effect', the reduction in the market value of outstanding debt due to increases in the market rate of interest (which is assumed equal to the rate on *new* issues). The real budget surplus in constant dollars, like all other variables, is its current dollar value divided by the price index.
55. Real interest payments received by domestic agents are 80 per cent of total interest payments, as domestic agents are assumed to hold 80 per cent of government debt.
56. Real interest payments received by foreigners are 20 per cent of total interest payments.
57. The price effect on domestically held debt equals 80 per cent of the total price effect.
58. The interest effect on domestically held debt equals 80 per cent of the total interest effect.
59. The domestically held debt equals 80 per cent of the total debt.
60. The debt held by foreigners equals 20 per cent of the total debt.
61. Net foreign financial claims other than net debt equal net foreign financial claims minus the debt held by foreigners.
62. Net national product equals gross national product minus depreciation.
63. Private saving equals disposable income minus consumption.
64. Gross saving equals disposable income minus consumption plus the real budget surplus; gross saving equals gross investment.
65. Real or adjusted net foreign investment equals conventional net foreign investment plus price and interest effects on foreign held debt.
66. Gross investment equals gross private domestic investment plus net foreign investment; gross investment equals gross saving.
67. Net private domestic investment equals gross private domestic investment minus depreciation.

68. Net investment, what is conventionally known as 'national saving', equals gross investment minus depreciation.

4. Characteristics of the Models

The models are set up with the economy in initial equilibrium in the first quarter of 1990. Baseline values of variables correspond roughly to current real figures for the United States. Output is set at $4,000 billion (pretty much its 1988 figure in 1982 dollars) and government expenditures for goods and services at $800 billion. The initial government debt at $1,600 billion is 40 per cent of output, the monetary base at $160 billion is 4 per cent, and net foreign claims on US assets, at $520 billion, are 13 per cent. The nominal interest rate is 8 per cent, inflation is at 5 per cent and the real rate of interest is therefore 3 per cent.

4.1. The Stationary Model

In the stationary model, net private domestic investment is set initially at zero and consumption above and gross domestic investment below their real figures. The conventional measure of the budget deficit stands initially at $77.59 billion or 1.9397 per cent of output but the real budget deficit, adjusted for the inflation tax (price effect) is zero, as seen, for example, in Table 1 (see at the end of the paper). Net exports are positive in the amount of real government interest payments to foreigners but the conventional measure of net foreign investment, NFIC, is negative, reflecting nominal interest payments to foreigners. These are matched, however, by net exports and the inflation tax on the foreign holdings of US government debt, so that real net foreign investment by our adjusted measure, NFI, is initially zero.

A permanent tax cut of $100 billion results initially in an increase in the real budget deficit by that amount. This causes increases in equilibrium output, consumption, gross investment, and inflation and the public debt, as may be noted in Table 1.[4] The equilibrium nominal interest rate rises with increased inflation. How much the nominal rate rises and what happens to the real interest rate and the rental cost of capital, however, depend on monetary policy. With exact accommodation to the increases in output (EM=1), the real interest rate and the rental cost of capital remain unchanged. Restraining monetary postures (EM=0 or the countercyclical EM= − 1) causes them to rise, while leaving the increase in the nominal rate of interest, with lesser rates of inflation, virtually unaffected. Expansionary monetary policy (EM=2) reduces the real rate of interest and the rental cost of capital. It also lessens the increase in the debt.

The increase in output initially generates an increase in real imports of goods and non-financial services (IMQ) as shown in Table 2. What happens subsequently, though, is affected by the course of real exchange rates (what the dollar is worth in foreign currencies, adjusted for the relative prices of US and foreign goods), and this depends very considerably on monetary policy. If it is restraining, and drives up real interest rates, the exchange rate rises and real net exports and conventional net foreign investment decline significantly. This begins to push the dollar down and exports rise.

[4] 'Equilibrium' results are not necessarily analytically precise but are those obtained in the simulations after 344 quarters. Tables 2 and 5 through 8 indicate initial values of variables, values when the exogenous change is imposed, and values after 1, 2, 10, 20, 40 and 86 years. Charts in Figures 1 through 4 graph the paths of key variables in the $100 billion tax cut simulations.

The negative net foreign investment of course raises net foreign claims - the US 'debt' to the rest of the world - and all the more with tight money and consequent higher exchange rates. The sharply negative foreign investment and increasing claims, relative to what foreigners may consider prudent, generate increasing pressure on the dollar, which stabilizes at less than its initial rate. Net foreign investment thus returns to zero. With accommodative monetary policy (EM=2), the initial fall in net foreign investment is curbed and then for a while substantially reversed so that net foreign claims actually decline and settle down below where they started, as shown in Figures 1 and 2.

At the new equilibrium the initial increase in the *real* budget deficit is eliminated. Real budget balance is effected by increases in explicit tax receipts from higher output and increases in the inflation tax, due to both the higher rate of inflation and the greater value of outstanding debt, which act to counterbalance the initial cut in taxes. The less accommodative is monetary policy the less the increase in output, but parameters are such that even an overtly countercyclical regime - one with an income elasticity of the money supply of −1.0 - is not sufficient to damp completely the increase in real GNP. Fiscal posture is kept exogenous with respect to monetary policy by adjusting tax payments to offset changes of Treasury interest payments due to changing interest rates.[5] More restrictive monetary policy then has the unambiguous consequence of holding down the increases in output and inflation resulting from the tax reduction.[6] It raises the cost of capital and thus reduces the capital-output ratio; even with EM = −1, though, the actual capital stock and gross investment are higher since the decrease in that ratio remains somewhat less than the relative increase in output.

The lag structure is such that permanent exogenous tax cuts generate oscillations and overshooting. We have extended our simulations over 86 years - 344 quarters - to confirm that the system eventually appears to converge. Restrictive monetary policy tends to damp the oscillations, as shown in charts (Figures 1 through 4) graphing transition paths, and the bulk of the movement to a new equilibrium is attained in five and ten years, as shown in Table 2.

Disturbance of an initial equilibrium output of $4,000 billion by an exogenous tax cut of $100 billion then leads eventually to a new equilibrium in which output, employment and consumption *and* gross investment and the capital stock, the public debt, inflation and nominal interest rates are all higher. Unemployment and exchange rates are lower. The budget and adjusted or real net foreign investment (the current account adjusted for price and interest effects on foreign holdings of US government debt) both return to real balance.

The real budget balance is effected by a combination of the higher tax revenues generated by higher output and increases in price effects - the 'inflation tax' on holders of public debt - that finally counterbalance the initial tax cut. Real net foreign investment, after initially moving negative with the conventional current account deficit from higher income-induced imports, returns to zero as a consequence of the fall in the value of the dollar generated by the negative foreign investment reinforced by the foreign resistance to accumulating holdings of US assets.

[5] The initial tax cut itself results in increased Treasury interest payments as it generates increased Treasury borrowing and debt. This added fiscal stimulus is neutralized by compensating increases in taxes. The change in the nominal structural deficit is thus kept constant at the amount of the original tax reduction.

[6] If increased interest payments were allowed to swell the deficit and disposable income, we could have the result that tigher money and higher interest rates would actually engender automatically an expansionist fiscal policy that would be sufficient to dominate the monetary contraction.

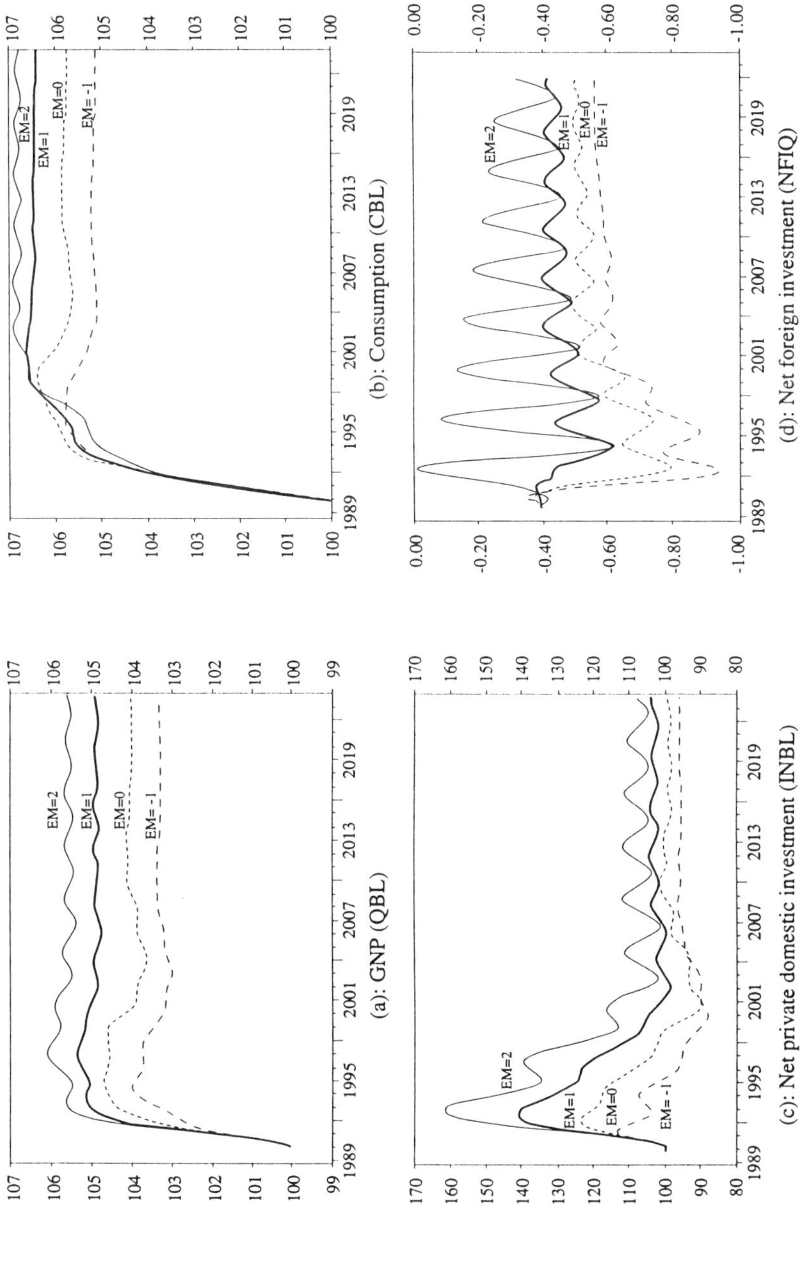

Figure 1. Effects of $100 billion tax cut, growth model (g = 0.03), income elasticities of money supply (EM) = 1, -1, 0 and 2: GNP (QBL), consumption (CBL), net private domestic investment (INBL), and net foreign investment (NFIQ) as percents of baseline

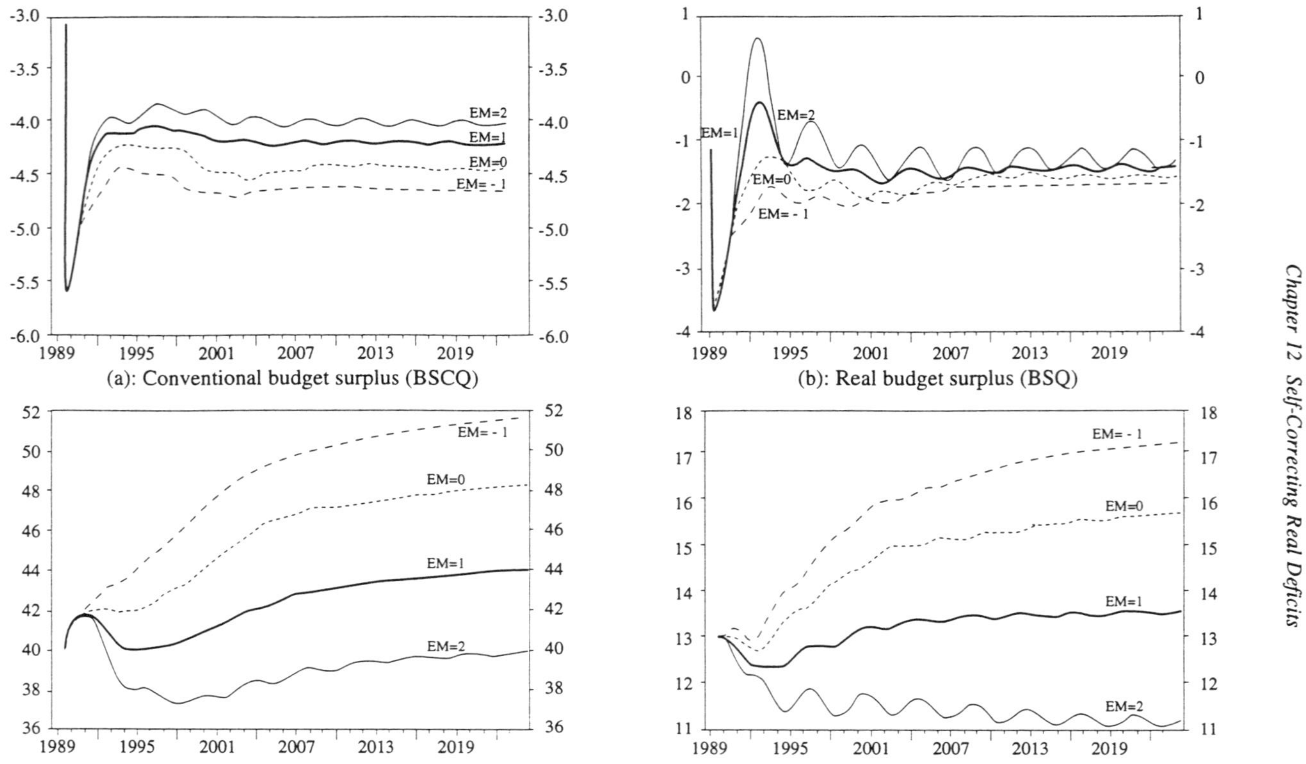

(a): Conventional budget surplus (BSCQ)

(b): Real budget surplus (BSQ)

(c): Market value of net debt (NDMQ)

(d): Net foreign financial claims (FCFNQ)

Figure 2. Effects of $100 billion tax cut, growth model (g = 0.03), income elasticities of money supply (EM) = 1, -1, 0 and 2: conventional budget surplus (BSCQ), real budget surplus (BSQ), market value of net debt (NDMQ) and net foreign financial claims (FCFNQ), as percents of GNP

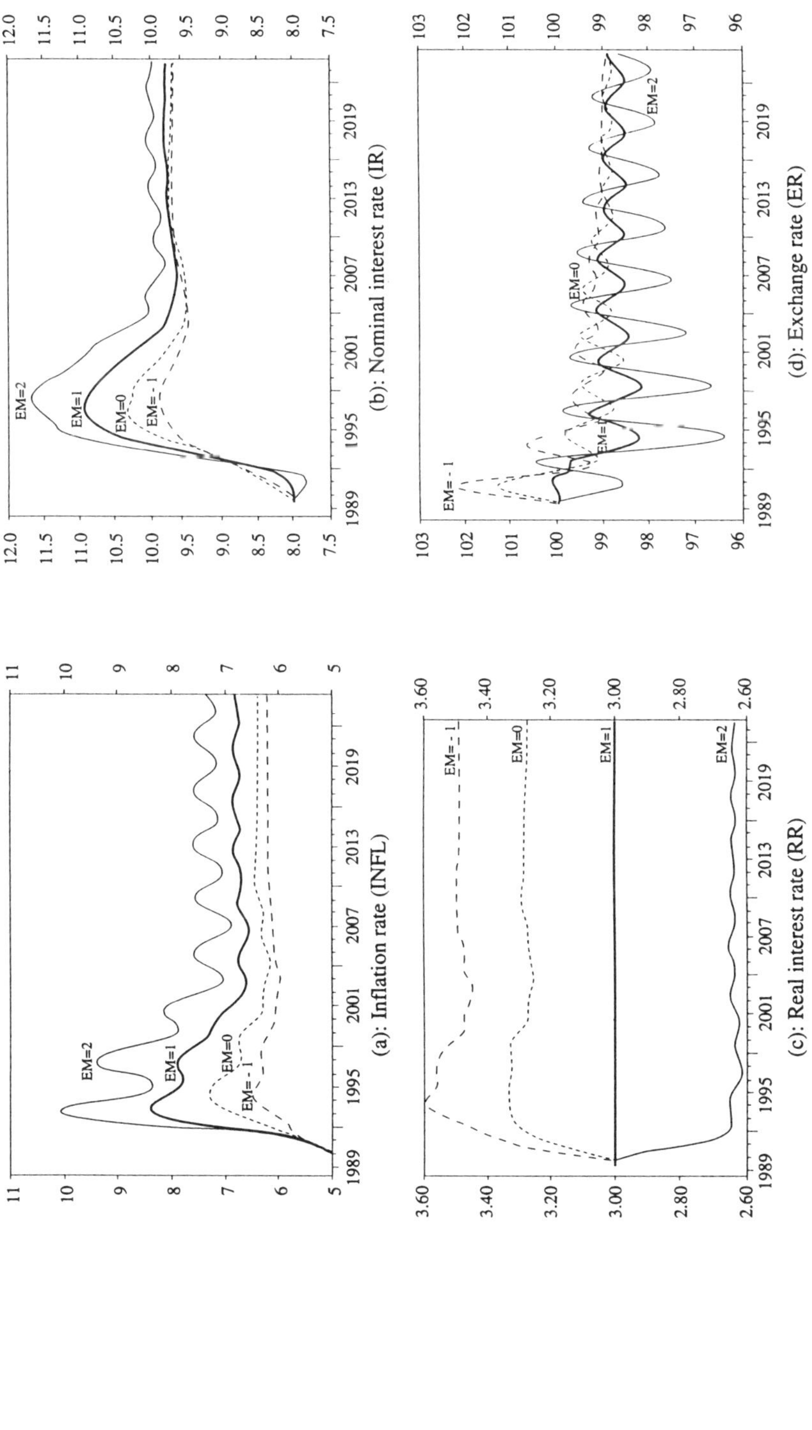

Figure 3. Effects of $100 billion tax cut, growth model (g = 0.03), income elasticities of money supply (EM) = 1, -1, 0 and 2: inflation rate (INFL), nominal interest rate (IR), real interest rate (RR) and exchange rate (ER), as percents

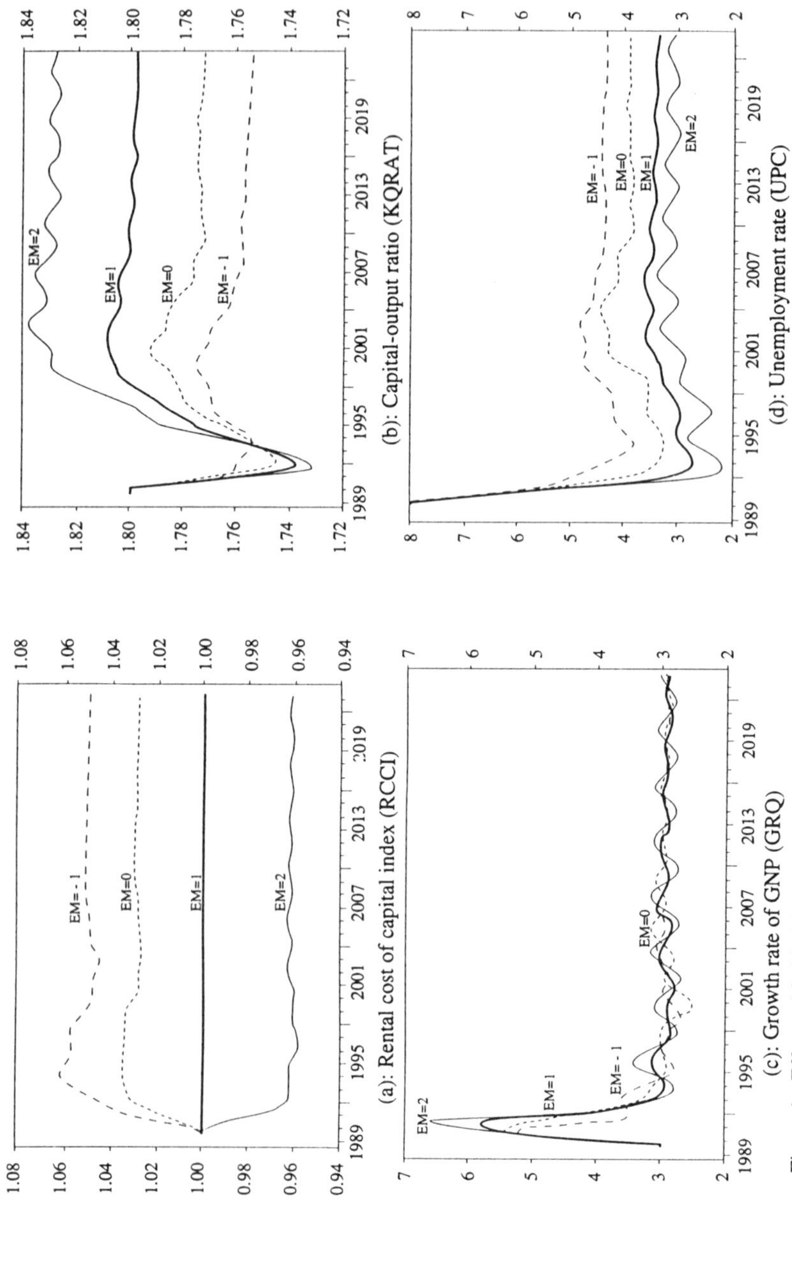

Figure 4. Effects of $100 billion tax cut, growth model (g = 0.03), income elasticities of money supply (EM) =1, -1, 0 and 2: rental cost of capital index (RCCI) and capital-output ratio (KQRAT), and growth rate of GNP (GRQ) and unemployment rate (UPC) as percents

4.2. The Growth Model

In the more realistic growth model the baseline growth rate is 3 per cent. This is generated by allowing exogenous components of government expenditures, taxes, exports and the real (high-powered) money supply to rise at that rate. It is instructive to consider the growth case in some detail. Here a tax cut in the first quarter of 1990 leaves GNP (Q) after 85 years up 4.06 per cent above the baseline 3 per cent growth path, for non-accommodative EM=0, and up 5.59 per cent for stimulative EM=2. For what we would regard as the essentially neutral monetary regime of EM=1, the rise, as shown in the lines for QBLPC in Tables 3 and 4, is 4.87 per cent. The easier the monetary policy the greater is the final capital-output ratio but then the less is the increase in net national product relative to the increase in gross product. Thus, for EM=2, where KQRAT rises from 1.8 to 1.829, the increase over baseline for net product is 0.23 per cent less than the increase of gross product. For the non-accommodating, restrictive policy of EM=0, net product increases above baseline by 0.21 per cent *more* than does gross product.

The rate of unemployment, it may be noted, is down from 8 per cent to 3.5 per cent in the EM=1 case. It is down less, but still substantially, when money is tight (EM=0), or very tight (EM=−1), as even the more modest increases in output require substantial increases in employment as a consequence of the decline in the capital-output ratio.

On that perennial issue of alleged 'crowding-out', Figure 1 and the line for IBLPC in Table 3 indicate that even with our most restrictive monetary policy, gross private domestic investment ends above baseline. That squares with US experience of the 1980s where, despite prophets of doom, gross private domestic investment held up well. What did happen in this past decade, and shows up in Figure 1, is an at least intermediate-run decline in total *net* investment (INBLPC). This reflects increasingly negative net exports and real net foreign investment and a consequent fall in accelerator-induced investment as GNP growth slows and the capital-output ratio falls, when money is tight and exchange rates rise. Temporary reduction of investment is a consequence then not of the exogenous budget deficit but essentially of the tight money policy that may be - but need not be - associated with it. Eventually, in our model, the pressure of accumulating foreign claims lowers the exchange rate and restores balance in real net foreign investment (in the sense of a constant ratio of net foreign claims to GNP), regardless of the monetary regime.

The real budget, as well as the conventional measure, initially shows a deficit in the growth model. Indeed, although this arithmetic relation is so often ignored, there must be a deficit in a growing economy if we are to have balance in the sense of real government debt growing at the same percentage rate as output. There is thus initially a real budget deficit equal to 1.178 per cent of output, as shown in Table 3. That is just sufficient for the real value of the net debt, which is 40 per cent of output, to grow at the baseline 3 per cent annual rate.

The tax cut of course brings on an immediate increase in both the real and conventional budget deficits. As output increases, both deficits, as ratios of GNP, decline. This relates partly to the increase in GNP itself but chiefly to the consequent increase in tax revenues. Higher inflation and the increase in public debt associated with increased deficits then generate a greater 'inflation tax' or price effect that reduces the real deficit further.

With the supplementary monetary stimulus of EM=2, the effect of lower real interest rates is such that the ratio of the real public debt to GNP, NDMQPC, is ultimately reduced to almost exactly what it was before the tax cut, as shown in Table 3 and Figure 2. Thus the ratio of the budget deficit to GNP also returns to approximately what it was before the tax cut.

With the neutral money policy of EM=1 or the tighter policies of EM=0 or -1, however, the debt ratio rises, as seen again in Figure 2 and in Table 3. And indeed it would rise all the more if our simulations did not have taxes altered to cover changes in Treasury interest payments, so that the original change in the structural deficit is kept intact. Thus, in our simulations, the tighter is the monetary regime the higher is TQPC, the ratio of taxes to GNP, but in no case does it rise to its pre-tax-cut proportion of output.

While in the growing economy the public debt, like everything else, grows without bound, the *ratio* of the public debt to output, NDMQPC, is bounded. As the ratio of the real deficit to output, -BSQPC, settles to its equilibrium value so does the debt ratio.[7]

Similarly, conventional net foreign investment (the official current account deficit) is initially negative, in the growth model, at -0.768 per cent of GNP. This implies that adjusted or real net foreign investment is -0.383 per cent of output, so that net foreign financial claims, initially 13 per cent of GNP, can remain at a constant ratio as long as the economy is on its 3 per cent baseline growth path. As seen in Figures 1 and 2 and Table 3, both of these variables, NFIQPC and FCFNQPC, move in what are generally considered adverse directions, down and up respectively, unless monetary policy is stimulative. With EM=1, however, NFIQPC moves briefly, if trivially, above its starting point, as the exchange rate goes down, and FCFNQPC moves down as the dollar value of US foreign-currency-denominated investment rises, as seen in Table 4. With sufficiently easy monetary policy, EM=2, real net foreign investment oscillates well above its initial value, reflecting inclusion of the price effects or inflation taxes on foreign holdings of US debt, not included in the conventional measure of net foreign investment. Net foreign financial claims actually end well below their baseline path; the easier money, despite the initially increased budget deficit, permits the US to become less of a 'debtor nation'!

4.3. Other Simulations

We have also undertaken simulations of the effects of increases in the structural deficit as a consequence of a $100 billion increase in government expenditures for goods and services. Results, shown in Table 5, are essentially similar to those for the tax cut case. In line with traditional theory, the government expenditures multiplier - actually the initial multiplicand of increased demand - is slightly larger.

To test the bounds built into our model, we also simulated an enormous cut of $300 billion in taxes, 7.5 per cent of GNP. If monetary policy is accommodative (EM=1), GNP rises to

[7] In a continuous time model that ratio, as has been pointed out on a number of occasions [see Eisner, (1989, p. 90, fn. 17), for example], is defined as b=d/g, where d is the ratio of the deficit to ouptut (-BSQPC in our nomenclature) and g is the relative rate of growth of output. For discrete time periods, with the debt measured at the end of the period, this becomes b=d(1+g)/g. Finally, with quarterly time series but the deficit and the rate of growth taken at annual rates, we have

$$b = d[0.25(1+g)^{.25}/\{(1+g)^{.25}-1\}].$$

For g=0.03, as assumed in our simulations, the value of the expression in square brackets is 33.955896. Hence, the equilibrium or long-run debt to GNP percentage turns out to be

$$\text{NDMQPC} = -33.955896 * \text{BSQPC}.$$

This may be verified in Table 3, for example, where at the original equilibrium in 198904 we have 40=39.955896*1.178 and, after the tax cut, for EM=1, 44.55 = 39.955896*1.312. The latter figure does differ slightly from the value of 44.341 shown for 207504, reflecting the fact that even after 86 years, oscillations have not ceased and variables have not fully settled down at their long run equilibria.

more than 6 per cent above baseline, but is sharply restrained by lack of capacity. The rate of capacity utilization, QUTPC (the ratio of output, Q, to capacity output QC), reaches 98.34 per cent, and in the growth model (Table 5), 98.357 per cent. Aggregate demand, QD, defined as the sum of consumer demand, export demand, government expenditures for goods and services, so exceeds the output limited by supply constraints that the ratio of output to aggregate demand, QQDPC, is down to 98.43 per cent.

Since government expenditures for goods and services are kept on their exogenous paths, there is some curtailment of domestic investment, along with consumption and exports, and the capital-output ratio is depressed. Net national saving and investment (INBLPC), nevertheless, rise to 1.66 per cent above their baseline. This comes only to 4.75 per cent of output, though, slightly (if trivially) below their 4.96 per cent starting point.

The effects of changes of monetary policy, aside from exogenous fiscal moves, may be seen in Table 6. In the first set of changes we introduce an increase of $25 billion, or 15.625 per cent, in the monetary base. This lump sum increase is then maintained indefinitely in *real* terms, with no accommodation to changes in output (EM=0). The result is a substantial increase in output; GNP after 85 years is 3.31 per cent above baseline, with unemployment down to 5.95 per cent. The real rate of interest is driven to 2.24 per cent, the rental cost of capital index from 1.0 to 0.919, and the exchange rate to 0.994. As a consequence, the capital-output ratio rises from 1.8 to 1.877 (and capacity output rises apace). Real net foreign investment turns positive and eventually settles at a negative ratio of GNP of −0.228 per cent, only 60 per cent of its initial negative figure. Total net national saving and investment rise 11.13 per cent above baseline. Net foreign financial claims fall to 7.61 per cent of output, not much more than half of their initial ratio of 13 per cent. The rate of inflation rises from 5 per cent to 5.6 per cent.

In another experiment, we examine the effect of switching from a regime in which the nominal monetary base grows at 8.15 per cent, accommodating the baseline increase in nominal GNP (5 per cent inflation plus 3 per cent real), to one in which the nominal monetary base grows two percentage points faster, that is, at an annual rate of 10.15 per cent. We stick here, however, to this fixed rule of constant growth in the nominal money supply and allow no responses to changes in real output or the rate of inflation. The permanent two percentage point increase in the rate of growth of the nominal money supply has the very real effect of lowering real interest rates, while raising the rate of inflation and slightly increasing nominal interest rates. The rental cost of capital and exchange rates fall and the capital-output ratio, all components of investment, and output rise. Both nominal and real budget deficits, the real debt and unemployment fall.

We can indicate the results of some other simulations which give an indication of the robustness of our model and its sensitivity to various critical parameter specifications. In the 'Q' variation, shown in Table 7, the Fisher effect is denied and a 'Tobin-Mundell effect' is included: nominal interest rates varied with 90 per cent rather than all of expected inflation. Thus, increases in real output, raising the rate of inflation, raise nominal interest rates but, with accommodative monetary policy (EM=1), lower real rates. In a 'T'-variation of the model, shown in Table 8, we modify the consumption function to make consumption demand dependent only on disposable income (although still including the implicit taxes or gains and losses of price and interest effects in that measure), excluding the financial wealth term.

In the 'Q' variation of the model, the lower real interest rates and costs of capital generate greater gross private domestic investment and lower exchange rates. We thus have higher paths for output, consumption and, initially, net exports. We end with a lesser budget deficit, a lesser debt-GNP ratio (almost precisely where we started) and net foreign claims somewhat below their starting point. In the 'T'-variation, the stimulus and output, investment and consumption are all generally less than in the other variations. The budget deficit, net debt and net foreign claims correspondingly end somewhat higher than in the basic 'S'-model. But even without the wealth effect on consumption the qualitative results of the basic model are confirmed.

5. Conclusions

Crucial assumptions in our basic ('S') model are: (a) deficits contribute to the permanent income or wealth perceived by private agents and hence contribute to consumption; the Barro-Ricardian equivalence effect is thus, at least in part, denied; (b) higher rates of output generate greater inflation but not a continuing acceleration of inflation. Not crucial, but important for some of the results in at least the basic, preferred model are: (c) increases in inflation are fully reflected in nominal interest rates, so that higher inflation thus does not lower real interest rates; (d) increases in foreign claims on domestic assets - that is, the accumulation of negative real net foreign investment - generate downward pressure on the value of the dollar. An upper bound is thus set for net foreign financial claims and, hence, a higher lower bound for real net foreign investment.

Major conclusions, given these assumptions, are:

1. Real budget deficits in a free economy are self-adjusting. A tax cut increasing the nominal deficit and, initially, the real deficit, generates a rise in the rate of inflation. This raises the price effect (inflation tax) on a larger real government debt. In a stationary economy that is eventually sufficient to restore the real budget to balance. In a growing economy, where a real budget deficit is a necessary condition for balanced growth, the ratio of the real deficit to output is dependent on the ratio of government debt to GNP. This, in turn, is dependent on monetary policy. Tighter money - supply inelastic or even varying negatively with respect to real GNP - raises the debt and deficit ratios above their initial values. Easier money lowers them. In all cases, however, the ratios of deficit and of debt to GNP are bounded, settling down to new equilibrium values.
2. The current account deficit and real net foreign investment are also self-adjusting in response to an initial increase in the budget deficit, as the exchange rate responds to the current account deficit, higher interest rates and the accumulation of net foreign claims. Net foreign investment stabilizes at lower or higher values or ratios, and this foreign 'debt' stabilizes at higher or lower levels or ratios than their starting points, depending on whether monetary policy is tight or easy.
3. In both the stationary and growth cases, output and employment are increased and unemployment decreased by budget deficits in all the monetary regimes simulated and in all variations of the models with non-restraining monetary policy. Gross private domestic investment was always crowded in, not crowded out, by increases in the budget deficit. Total net investment, or what has been called national saving, also increased in simulations of the basic model except where monetary policy was extremely constraining. In this case, with exchange rates initially rising, total net investment in the intermediate run did decline.
4. Monetary stimulus, itself, raises output and investment and reduces budget deficits or brings intermediate-run surpluses and reduces net foreign claims.
5. Additional work is in order in a number of directions. In particular, all parameters, while seemingly reasonable, have been assumed. The sensitivity of results to the particular parametric assumptions may be explored further and estimated parameters, as far as feasible, may be substituted for the 'reasonable' ones that we have assumed.

Table 1
Effect of $100 billion tax cut on long run equilibrium: income elasticity of money supply (EM) equals -1, 0, 1 and 2, stationary model (g=0)

Variable	198904	199001	207504			
			EM=-1	EM=0	EM=1	EM=2
Q	4000.000	4000.000	4148.995	4176.243	4198.830	4222.556
QBLPC	100.000	100.000	103.725	104.406	104.971	105.564
QN	3532.000	3532.000	3677.148	3695.554	3708.233	3720.292
QNBLPC	100.000	100.000	104.110	104.631	104.990	105.331
QUTPC	93.368	93.368	96.701	97.011	97.182	97.331
QQDPC	100.000	100.000	100.000	99.993	99.874	99.756
QC	4284.123	4284.123	4290.528	4304.935	4320.571	4338.326
QZ	4000.000	4000.000	4005.583	4018.137	4031.756	4047.213
DY	3193.410	3293.410	3336.984	3366.419	3390.893	3419.396
C	2725.410	2725.410	2865.188	2885.783	2900.423	2916.703
CBLPC	100.000	100.000	105.129	105.884	106.442	107.019
I	468.000	468.000	471.808	480.657	490.722	501.712
IBLPC	100.000	100.000	100.814	102.704	104.855	107.203
IAC	0.000	0.000	-0.000	0.003	0.132	-0.439
IRE	468.000	468.000	471.808	480.689	491.270	503.503
IG	468.000	468.000	471.691	480.594	491.085	500.463
IN	0.000	-0.000	-0.156	-0.095	0.487	-1.801
INQPC	0.000	-0.000	-0.004	-0.002	0.012	-0.043
IT	0.000	0.000	-0.038	-0.032	0.125	-0.552
ITQNPC	0.000	0.000	-0.001	0.001	0.003	-0.015
D	468.000	468.000	471.846	480.689	490.597	502.264
NFIC	-15.518	-15.518	-28.164	-26.760	-25.337	-25.193
NFI	0.000	-0.000	-0.117	-0.063	0.362	-1.249
NFIQPC	0.000	-0.000	-0.003	-0.002	0.009	-0.030
NE	6.590	6.590	11.999	9.803	7.685	4.141
X	400.000	400.000	426.359	423.373	419.651	416.187
IM	393.410	393.410	414.360	413.569	411.966	412.046
IMQ	0.000	387.410	400.066	402.888	405.574	409.535
INTF	22.108	22.108	40.163	36.564	33.022	29.334
G	800.000	800.000	800.000	800.000	800.000	800.000
INT	110.540	110.540	200.817	182.819	165.110	146.672
T	832.950	732.950	860.476	849.290	837.227	824.721
BSC	-77.590	-177.590	-140.341	-133.529	-127.883	-121.951
NEW	80.646	105.646	122.561	112.387	101.990	90.906
PE	77.590	77.590	140.235	133.471	128.248	120.511
IE	0.000	0.000	0.000	0.017	0.249	-0.789
SP	468.000	568.000	471.797	480.636	490.470	502.693
BS	0.000	-100.000	-0.106	-0.042	0.615	-2.229
NDP	1600.000	1625.000	2276.676	2097.580	1914.018	1718.660
NDM	1600.000	1625.000	2276.676	2097.580	1913.977	1718.706

Table 1 *(continued)*

FCF	2120.000	2120.000	2471.596	2345.250	2206.051	2050.403
FCUS	1600.000	1600.000	1614.319	1612.665	1610.287	1611.465
FCFN	520.000	520.000	857.276	741.585	595.764	438.938
FCOND	200.000	195.000	401.942	322.076	212.968	95.197
FW	1080.000	1105.000	1419.395	1355.958	1318.213	1279.768
M	160.000	160.000	154.040	160.000	167.954	177.803
IRPC	8.000	8.000	9.961	9.939	9.970	10.048
INFLPC	5.000	5.000	6.404	6.625	6.990	7.333
RRPC	3.000	3.000	3.557	3.316	3.000	2.644
RCCI	1.000	1.000	1.059	1.033	1.000	0.963
ER	1.000	1.000	0.982	0.984	0.987	0.986
K	7200.000	7200.000	7259.171	7395.211	7547.651	7727.141
KQRAT	1.800	1.800	1.750	1.771	1.798	1.830
N	110.400	110.400	115.196	115.658	115.920	116.150
U	9.600	9.600	4.804	4.342	4.080	3.850
UPC	8.000	8.000	4.003	3.618	3.400	3.208

Table 2
Effect of $100 billion tax cut, income elasticity of money supply (EM) equals 1, path in selected quarters, stationary model (g=0)

Variable	198904	199001	199101	199501	200001	201001	203001	207504
Q	4000.000	4000.000	4087.797	4207.989	4210.613	4198.250	4197.947	4198.830
QBLPC	100.000	100.000	102.195	105.200	105.200	104.956	104.949	104.971
QN	3532.000	3532.000	3619.342	3722.344	3722.344	3706.027	3706.858	3708.233
QNBLPC	100.000	100.000	102.473	105.389	105.389	104.927	104.951	104.990
QUTPC	93.368	93.368	95.400	97.569	97.569	97.112	97.145	97.182
QQDPC	100.000	100.000	100.000	99.533	99.790	99.926	99.902	99.874
QC	4284.123	4284.123	4284.885	4312.821	4327.834	4323.086	4321.333	4320.571
QZ	4000.000	4000.000	4000.664	4025.006	4038.080	4033.946	4032.419	4031.756
DY	3193.410	3293.410	3348.942	3408.572	3411.103	3400.015	3393.782	3390.893
C	2725.410	2725.410	2780.871	2877.212	2907.279	2904.538	2901.882	2900.423
CBLPC	100.000	100.000	102.035	105.570	106.673	106.573	106.475	106.422
I	468.000	468.000	500.981	539.304	496.876	490.160	490.192	490.722
IBLPC	100.000	100.000	107.047	115.236	106.170	104.735	104.742	104.855
IAC	0.000	0.000	22.923	49.824	5.381	-0.622	-0.423	0.132
IRE	468.000	468.000	478.058	492.264	492.645	491.182	491.143	491.270
IG	468.000	468.000	501.241	529.190	494.565	487.020	488.503	491.085
IN	0.000	-0.000	32.786	43.546	-0.750	-5.203	-2.586	0.487
INQPC	0.000	-0.000	0.802	1.035	-0.018	-0.124	-0.062	0.012
IT	0.000	0.000	32.526	53.659	1.561	-2.064	-0.897	0.125
ITQNPC	0.000	0.000	0.899	1.442	0.042	-0.056	-0.024	0.003
D	468.000	468.000	468.455	485.644	495.316	492.223	491.089	490.597
NFIC	-15.518	-15.518	-17.502	-34.798	-25.446	-27.054	-26.630	-25.337
NFI	0.000	-0.000	0.260	-10.114	-2.311	-3.140	-1.689	0.362
NFIQPC	0.000	-0.000	0.006	-0.240	-0.055	-0.075	-0.040	0.009
NE	6.590	6.590	5.945	-8.527	6.458	3.552	5.873	7.685
X	400.000	400.000	399.996	408.274	421.451	415.799	418.306	419.651
IM	393.410	393.410	394.051	416.801	414.993	412.246	412.433	411.966
IMQ	0.000	387.410	388.594	411.299	408.664	405.939	406.112	405.574
INTF	22.108	22.108	23.447	26.271	31.904	30.606	32.503	33.022
G	800.000	800.000	800.000	800.000	800.000	800.000	800.000	800.000
INT	110.540	110.540	117.234	131.357	159.522	153.030	162.516	165.110
T	832.950	732.950	761.593	805.764	834.585	825.003	834.413	837.227
BSC	-77.590	-177.590	-155.641	-125.593	-124.937	-128.027	-128.103	-127.883
NEW	80.646	105.646	98.829	102.861	98.688	100.902	101.816	101.990
PE	77.590	77.590	86.994	129.302	119.715	119.058	125.207	128.248
IE	0.000	0.000	1.817	-5.879	-4.037	0.513	-0.501	0.249
SP	468.000	568.000	568.071	531.360	503.823	495.477	491.900	490.470
BS	0.000	-100.000	-66.830	-2.170	-9.258	-8.457	-3.398	0.615
NDP	1600.000	1625.000	1707.856	1717.024	1697.125	1812.328	1889.126	1914.018
NDM	1600.000	1625.000	1707.259	1677.563	1704.945	1810.856	1888.830	1913.977

Table 2 *(continued)*

FCF	2120.000	2120.000	2119.897	2136.883	2163.410	2183.024	2200.397	2206.051
FCUS	1600.000	1600.000	1599.775	1615.722	1609.474	1611.395	1612.145	1610.287
FCFN	520.000	520.000	520.123	521.161	553.937	571.629	588.252	595.764
FCOND	200.000	195.000	178.671	185.648	212.948	209.457	210.486	212.968
FW	1080.000	1105.000	1187.136	1156.402	1151.008	1239.227	1300.578	1318.213
M	160.000	160.000	163.510	168.315	168.428	167.934	167.919	167.954
IRPC	8.000	8.000	8.019	10.780	10.795	9.853	9.966	9.970
INFLPC	5.000	5.000	5.316	8.097	7.351	6.862	6.916	6.990
RRPC	3.000	3.000	3.000	3.000	3.000	3.000	3.000	3.000
RCCI	1.000	1.000	1.000	1.000	1.000	1.000	1.000	1.000
ER	1.000	1.000	1.000	0.981	0.988	0.986	0.985	0.987
K	7200.000	7200.000	7207.000	7471.453	7620.239	7572.664	7555.216	7547.651
KQRAT	1.800	1.800	1.763	1.776	1.810	1.804	1.800	1.798
N	110.400	110.400	113.313	116.471	116.084	115.822	115.867	115.920
U	9.600	9.600	6.687	3.529	3.916	4.178	4.133	4.080
UPC	8.000	8.000	5.572	2.940	3.264	3.482	3.444	3.400

Table 3
Effect of $100 billion tax cut on long run equilibrium: income elasticity of money supply (EM) equals -1, 0, 1 and 2, growth model (g=0.03)

Variable	198904	199001	207504			
			EM= -1	EM = 0	EM = 1	EM = 2
Q	3970.550	4000.000	52131.602	52495.043	52906.594	53269.027
QBLPC	100.000	100.000	103.336	104.056	104.872	105.590
QNBLPC	100.000	100.000	103.680	104.262	104.881	105.362
QUTPC	93.368	93.368	96.353	96.721	97.095	97.358
QQDPC	100.000	100.000	100.000	100.000	99.936	99.733
QCBLPC	107.103	107.103	107.247	107.584	108.009	108.456
QZBLPC	100.000	100.000	100.126	100.419	100.789	101.179
DYBLPC	100.000	103.086	104.478	105.304	106.237	107.015
CBLPC	100.000	100.000	105.152	105.812	106.474	106.865
CQPC	63.179	63.179	64.290	64.245	64.144	63.942
IBLPC	100.000	100.000	100.740	102.500	104.790	107.345
IQPC	17.040	17.040	16.612	16.785	17.027	17.323
IACQPC	5.340	5.340	5.206	5.260	5.339	5.448
IREQPC	11.700	11.700	11.406	11.525	11.700	11.926
IGBLPC	100.000	100.000	99.808	101.886	104.593	107.797
IGQPC	16.657	16.657	16.089	16.310	16.615	17.006
INBLPC	100.000	100.000	97.607	100.437	104.105	108.947
INQPC	4.957	4.957	4.683	4.785	4.921	5.115
ITQPC	5.340	5.340	5.206	5.260	5.335	5.433
ITQNPC	6.048	6.048	5.876	5.946	6.041	6.166
DQPC	11.700	11.700	11.406	11.525	11.692	11.891
NFICQPC	-0.768	-0.768	-1.140	-1.071	-0.988	-0.882
NFIQPC	-0.383	-0.383	-0.523	-0.475	-0.414	-0.318
NEQPC	-0.219	-0.219	-0.256	-0.251	-0.242	-0.206
XQPC	10.000	10.000	10.038	9.995	9.951	9.932
IMQPC	10.219	10.219	10.294	10.246	10.193	10.138
IMQQPC	10.070	10.070	10.045	10.043	10.049	10.056
INTFQPC	0.549	0.549	0.884	0.820	0.746	0.676
GQPC	20.000	20.000	19.354	19.220	19.071	18.941
INTQPC	2.743	2.743	4.420	4.101	3.729	3.380
TQPC	19.640	17.140	19.159	18.911	18.618	18.338
BSCQPC	-3.103	-5.603	-4.616	-4.411	-4.182	-3.983
NEWQPC	2.154	2.779	2.962	2.759	2.507	2.254
PEQPC	1.925	1.925	3.084	2.979	2.872	2.817
IEQPC	0.000	0.000	0.000	-0.000	-0.002	0.006
SPBLPC	100.000	114.017	102.092	103.507	105.399	107.546
SPQPC	17.835	20.335	17.621	17.741	17.925	18.166
BSQPC	-1.178	-3.678	-1.532	-1.431	-1.312	-1.160
NDPQPC	40.000	40.625	52.013	48.594	44.340	40.097
NDMQPC	40.000	40.625	52.013	48.594	44.341	40.100

Table 3 *(continued)*

FCFQPC	53.000	53.000	56.476	54.576	52.076	49.269
FCUSQPC	40.000	40.000	38.903	38.648	38.376	38.121
FCFNBLPC	100.000	100.000	139.681	127.486	110.519	90.553
FCFNQPC	13.000	13.000	17.572	15.927	13.700	11.149
FWBLPC	100.000	102.315	131.815	125.895	119.012	113.223
FWQPC	27.000	27.625	34.441	32.667	30.641	28.952
MQPC	4.000	4.000	3.742	3.844	4.000	4.212
IRPC	8.000	8.000	9.698	9.713	9.808	10.010
INFLPC	5.000	5.000	6.202	6.423	6.800	7.399
RRPC	3.000	3.000	3.496	3.291	3.000	2.643
RCCI	1.000	1.000	1.052	1.031	1.000	0.962
ER	1.000	1.000	0.990	0.989	0.988	0.988
GRQPC	3.000	3.000	3.000	2.999	3.001	3.009
GRFCFNPC	3.000	3.000	3.001	2.999	3.023	3.037
GRMPC	3.000	3.000	3.000	3.000	3.001	3.017
GRM$PC	8.150	8.150	9.388	9.615	10.006	10.640
KQRAT	1.800	1.800	1.755	1.773	1.799	1.829
NLPC	92.000	92.000	95.577	96.032	96.496	96.823
UPC	8.000	8.000	4.423	3.968	3.504	3.177

Table 4
Effect of $100 billion tax cut, income elasticity of money supply (EM) equals 1, path in selected quarters, growth model (g=0.03)

Variable	198904	199001	199101	199501	200001	201001	203001	207504
Q	3970.550	4000.000	4206.667	4874.172	5651.037	7574.384	13683.789	52906.594
QBLPC	100.000	100.000	102.104	105.113	105.123	104.844	104.872	104.872
QNBLPC	100.000	100.000	102.369	105.296	105.067	104.831	104.877	104.881
QUTPC	93.368	93.368	95.315	97.495	97.207	97.046	97.091	97.095
QQDPC	100.000	100.000	100.000	99.608	99.856	99.970	99.940	99.936
QCBLPC	107.103	107.103	107.122	107.813	108.143	108.035	108.014	108.009
QZBLPC	100.000	100.000	100.017	100.619	100.906	100.812	100.794	100.789
DYBLPC	100.000	103.086	104.725	106.597	106.638	106.370	106.267	106.237
CBLPC	100.000	100.000	102.026	105.635	106.625	106.533	106.483	106.474
CQPC	63.179	63.179	63.131	63.493	64.082	64.197	64.150	64.144
IBLPC	100.000	100.000	104.933	111.197	105.587	104.740	104.773	104.790
IQPC	17.040	17.040	17.512	18.027	17.116	17.023	17.024	17.027
IACQPC	5.340	5.340	5.818	6.406	5.442	5.330	5.336	5.339
IREQPC	11.700	11.700	11.695	11.699	11.700	11.699	11.700	11.700
IGBLPC	100.000	100.000	105.069	110.040	105.334	104.252	104.547	104.593
IGQPC	16.657	16.657	17.141	17.438	16.691	16.563	16.606	16.613
INBLPC	100.000	100.000	116.805	124.929	104.842	102.622	103.884	104.105
INQPC	4.957	4.957	5.671	5.892	4.944	4.852	4.911	4.921
ITQPC	5.340	5.340	6.042	6.480	5.369	5.312	5.329	5.335
ITQNPC	6.048	6.048	6.825	7.326	6.083	6.017	6.035	6.041
DQPC	11.700	11.700	11.470	11.546	11.747	11.711	11.695	11.692
NFICQP	-0.768	-0.768	-0.801	-1.166	-0.965	-1.011	-0.987	-0.988
NFIQPC	-0.383	-0.383	-0.371	-0.588	-0.425	-0.460	-0.418	-0.414
NEQPC	-0.219	-0.219	-0.232	-0.547	-0.223	-0.296	-0.245	-0.242
XQPC	10.000	10.000	9.793	9.728	9.996	9.908	9.954	9.951
IMQPC	10.219	10.219	10.025	10.274	10.219	10.204	10.198	10.193
IMQQPC	10.070	10.070	9.892	10.143	10.071	10.060	10.055	10.049
INTFQPC	0.549	0.549	0.570	0.619	0.742	0.715	0.743	0.746
GQPC	20.000	22.000	19.588	19.027	19.025	19.076	19.071	19.071
INTQPC	2.743	2.743	2.848	3.096	3.710	3.576	3.713	3.729
TQPC	19.640	17.140	17.463	18.008	18.623	18.462	18.602	18.618
BSCQPC	-3.103	-5.603	-4.973	-4.115	-4.112	-4.190	-4.182	-4.182
MEWQPC	2.154	2.779	2.562	2.551	2.456	2.505	2.508	2.507
PEQPC	1.925	1.925	2.108	2.984	2.778	2.754	2.853	2.872
IEQPC	0.000	0.000	0.043	-0.097	-0.075	0.001	-0.008	-0.002
SPBLPC	100.000	114.017	114.287	110.007	106.682	105.796	105.504	105.399
SPQPC	17.835	20.335	19.964	18.666	18.100	17.997	17.943	17.925
BSQPC	-1.178	-3.678	-2.822	-1.228	-1.409	-1.434	-1.337	-1.312
NDPQPC	40.000	40.625	41.792	40.908	40.687	43.218	44.198	44.340
NDMQPC	40.000	40.625	41.778	40.048	40.866	43.194	44.202	44.341

Table 4 *(continued)*

FCFQPC	53.000	53.000	51.907	50.855	51.405	51.878	52.055	52.076
FCUSQPC	40.000	40.000	39.164	38.387	38.243	34.417	38.384	38.376
FCFN*	100.000	100.000	100.082	100.809	106.435	108.562	110.278	110.519
FCFQPC	13.000	13.000	12.743	12.468	13.162	13.461	13.670	13.700
FWBLPC	100.000	102.315	109.800	107.372	107.863	115.454	118.588	119.012
FWQPC	27.000	27.625	29.035	27.580	27.704	29.732	30.531	30.641
MQPC	4.000	4.000	4.000	4.000	4.000	4.000	4.000	4.000
IRPC	8.000	8.000	8.018	10.545	10.522	9.706	9.797	9.808
INFLPC	5.000	5.000	5.301	7.874	7.161	6.697	6.776	6.800
RRPC	3.000	3.000	3.000	3.000	3.000	3.000	3.000	3.000
RCCI	1.000	1.000	1.000	1.000	1.000	1.000	1.000	1.000
ER	1.000	1.000	1.001	0.983	0.990	0.986	0.987	0.988
GRQPC	3.000	3.000	5.731	3.058	2.923	2.995	3.023	3.001
GRFC**	3.000	3.000	3.183	4.815	4.226	3.135	3.271	3.023
GRMPC	3.000	3.000	5.731	3.058	2.923	2.995	3.023	3.001
GRM$PC	8.150	8.150	11.336	11.173	10.294	9.892	10.004	10.006
KQRAT	1.800	1.800	1.765	1.776	1.807	1.802	1.799	1.799
NLPC	92.000	92.000	94.325	96.970	96.633	96.438	96.490	96.496
UPC	8.000	8.000	5.675	3.030	3.367	3.562	3.510	3.504

* FCFN is abbreviation of FCFNBLPC

** GRFC is abbreviation of GRFCFNPC

Table 5
Effect of $100 billion tax cut, $100 billion government expenditure increase and $300 billion tax cut on long run equilibrium: income elasticity of money supply (EM) equals 1, growth model (g=0.03)

Variable	198904	199001	207504		
		ΔT = - 100[c]	ΔT = - 100[c]	ΔG = - 100[c]	ΔT = - 300[c]
Q	3970.550	4000.000	52854.168	53036.730	53538.559
QBLPC	100.000	100.000	104.768	105.130	106.125
QNBLPC	100.000	100.000	104.768	105.167	106.365
QUTPC	93.368	93.368	97.005	97.327	98.337
QQDPC	100.000	100.000	99.996	99.760	98.430
QCBLPC	107.103	107.103	108.003	108.017	107.919
QZBLPC	100.000	100.000	100.784	100.797	100.711
DYBLPC	100.000	103.086	106.134	103.386	108.496
CBLPC	100.000	100.000	106.385	103.039	108.618
CQPC	63.179	63.179	64.154	61.922	64.664
IBLPC	100.000	100.000	104.764	104.845	104.305
IQPC	17.040	17.040	17.040	16.994	16.748
IACQPC	5.340	5.340	5.340	5.340	5.340
IREQPC	11.700	11.700	11.700	11.700	11.700
IGBLPC	100.000	100.000	104.264	104.294	103.519
IGQPC	16.657	16.657	16.577	16.525	16.248
INBLPC	100.000	100.000	103.085	102.993	101.662
INQPC	4.957	4.957	4.878	4.857	4.749
ITQPC	5.340	5.340	5.340	5.326	5.249
ITQNPC	6.048	6.048	6.048	6.029	5.931
DQPC	11.700	11.700	11.700	11.668	11.500
NFICQPC	-0.768	-0.768	-1.036	-1.047	-1.827
NFIQPC	-0.383	-0.383	-0.462	-0.469	-0.500
NEQPC	-0.219	-0.219	-0.283	-0.319	-0.258
XQPC	10.000	10.000	9.949	9.962	10.023
IMQPC	10.219	10.219	10.232	10.280	10.280
IMQQPC	10.070	10.070	10.042	10.061	10.174
INTFQPC	0.549	0.549	0.753	0.728	1.569
GQPC	20.000	20.000	19.090	21.402	18.846
INTQPC	2.743	2.743	3.765	3.639	7.846
TQPC	19.640	17.140	18.644	20.931	18.143
BSCQPC	-3.103	-5.603	-4.211	-4.110	-8.549
NEWQPC	2.154	2.779	2.568	2.356	4.111
PEQPC	1.925	1.925	2.871	2.887	6.636
IEQPC	0.000	0.000	0.000	-0.000	0.000

Table 5 *(continued)*

SPBLPC	100.000	114.017	105.248	104.614	108.065
SPQPC	17.835	20.335	17.917	17.748	18.162
BSQPC	-1.178	-3.678	-1.340	-1.223	-1.913
NDPQPC	40.000	40.625	45.489	41.520	64.954
NDMQPC	40.000	40.625	45.489	41.520	64.954
FCFQPC	53.000	53.000	53.875	53.977	54.658
FCUSQPC	40.000	39.624	38.398	38.306	38.114
FCFNBLPC	100.000	102.890	124.730	126.732	135.055
FCFNQPC	13.000	13.376	15.477	15.671	16.544
FWBLPC	100.000	100.923	116.454	100.648	190.277
FWQPC	27.000	27.249	30.012	25.849	48.410
MQPC	4.000	4.000	4.000	4.000	4.000
IRPC	8.000	8.000	9.619	10.323	13.990
INFLPC	5.000	5.000	6.619	7.323	10.990
RRPC	3.000	3.000	3.000	3.000	3.000
RCCI	1.000	1.000	1.000	1.000	1.000
ER	1.000	1.019	0.989	0.987	0.978
GRQPC	3.000	3.000	3.000	3.000	3.000
GRFCFNPC	3.000	15.432	3.000	3.000	3.000
GRMPC	3.000	3.000	3.000	3.000	3.000
GRM$PC	8.150	8.150	9.818	10.543	14.319
KQRAT	1.800	1.800	1.800	1.795	1.769
NLPC	92.000	92.000	96.387	96.773	97.987
UPC	8.000	8.000	3.613	3.227	2.013

[c] The coefficient of NFI used in ER equation is 5 instead of 10. See footnote 3 above.

Table 6
Effect of monetary stimulus, income elasticity of money supply (EM) equals 0, path in selected quarters, growth model (g=0.03)

A: Increase of $25 billion, or 15.625 percent, in real monetary base

Variable	198904	199001	199101	199501	200001	201001	203001	207504
QBLPC	100.000	100.045	104.333	105.550	103.563	103.688	103.176	103.091
QNBLPC	100.000	100.051	104.846	105.458	102.913	103.249	102.589	102.506
IGBLPC	100.000	96.849	124.933	122.162	108.181	112.389	108.660	108.587
INBLPC	100.000	89.413	182.704	159.737	107.492	125.092	111.149	111.129
NFIQPC	-0.383	-0.907	0.498	0.293	-0.168	-0.076	-0.243	-0.228
TQPC	19.640	19.642	19.732	19.466	19.189	18.905	18.845	18.833
BSCQPC	-3.103	-3.091	-1.936	-1.626	-2.137	-2.104	-2.238	-2.261
SPBLPC	100.000	113.012	111.596	110.755	104.709	107.797	105.999	106.037
SPQPC	17.835	20.147	19.077	18.715	18.033	18.542	18.323	18.345
BSQPC	-1.178	-4.022	0.869	0.564	-0.633	-0.487	-0.781	-0.800
NDMQPC	40.000	40.693	38.069	30.672	27.682	28.017	27.161	27.196
FCFNBLPC	100.000	86.090	101.362	89.895	78.202	67.419	61.176	60.324
FCFNQPC	13.000	11.187	12.630	11.072	9.817	8.453	7.708	7.607
FWBLPC	100.000	109.332	98.300	76.622	68.525	75.132	74.334	74.794
FWQPC	27.000	29.506	25.439	19.600	17.865	19.564	19.452	19.589
MQPC	4.000	4.623	4.433	4.382	4.466	4.460	4.483	4.486
IRPC	8.000	7.051	7.246	9.395	8.642	7.836	7.897	7.835
INFLPC	5.000	5.000	5.986	7.599	5.919	5.852	5.633	5.601
RRPC	3.000	2.051	2.309	2.383	2.263	2.271	2.240	2.235
RCCI	1.000	0.900	0.927	0.935	0.922	0.923	0.920	0.919
ER	1.000	0.912	1.026	1.012	0.990	1.002	0.992	0.994
GRQPC	3.000	3.186	8.617	3.435	1.407	3.393	2.910	3.001
GRFCFNPC	3.000	-43.421	34.268	4.318	-6.700	2.720	2.622	3.008
GRMPC	3.000	84.096	3.000	3.000	3.000	3.000	3.000	3.000
GRM$PC	8.150	93.301	9.166	10.827	9.096	9.028	8.802	8.769
KQRAT	1.800	1.799	1.733	1.812	1.885	1.858	1.877	1.877
UPC	8.000	7.950	3.244	3.024	5.603	5.213	5.877	5.954

B: Two percentage points increase in rate of growth of nominal monetary base

Variable	198904	199001	199101	199501	200001	201001	203001	207504
QBLPC	100.000	100.000	100.162	102.933	104.112	105.268	106.374	106.933
QNBLPC	100.000	100.000	100.183	103.064	103.909	104.727	105.308	105.573
IGBLPC	100.000	100.000	100.783	111.457	112.991	116.708	118.308	119.598
INBLPC	100.000	100.000	102.611	133.921	130.323	134.073	127.481	125.256
NFIQPC	-0.383	-0.383	-0.364	-0.229	-0.145	-0.037	-0.034	-0.074
TQPC	19.640	19.640	19.640	19.595	19.425	18.932	18.380	18.084
BSCQPC	-3.103	-3.103	-3.058	-2.303	-1.993	-1.697	-1.419	-1.281
SPBLPC	100.000	100.000	100.923	105.153	106.378	109.653	112.261	113.977
SPQPC	17.835	17.835	17.971	18.220	18.223	18.578	18.578	19.010
BSQPC	-1.178	-1.178	-1.210	-0.183	-0.145	-0.111	-0.111	-0.380

Table 6 *(continued)*

NDMQPC	40.000	40.000	40.013	36.723	31.695	25.477	17.567	13.584
FCFNBLPC	100.000	100.000	98.662	94.584	88.676	69.094	41.118	21.813
FCFNQPC	13.000	13.000	12.805	11.946	11.073	8.533	5.025	2.652
FWBLPC	100.000	100.000	100.932	94.461	79.519	66.062	49.412	43.298
FWQPC	27.000	27.000	27.207	24.778	20.622	16.944	12.542	10.932
MQPC	4.000	4.000	4.071	4.206	4.334	4.653	4.994	5.215
IRPC	8.000	8.000	7.868	8.073	8.607	8.269	8.297	8.346
INFLPC	5.000	5.000	4.970	5.798	6.196	6.419	6.692	6.971
RRPC	3.000	3.000	2.876	2.652	2.454	2.013	1.608	1.378
RCCI	1.000	1.000	0.987	0.963	0.943	0.896	0.854	0.829
ER	1.000	1.000	0.991	0.990	0.989	0.984	0.984	0.984
GRQPC	3.000	3.000	3.419	3.675	2.981	3.235	3.022	3.003
GRFCFNPC	3.000	3.000	2.351	2.520	1.211	0.715	0.484	2.479
GRMPC	3.000	3.000	4.992	4.170	3.780	3.562	3.298	3.028
GRM$PC	8.150	8.150	10.210	10.210	10.210	10.210	10.210	10.210
KQRAT	1.800	1.800	1.797	1.783	1.827	1.870	1.936	1.973
UPC	8.000	8.000	7.821	5.111	4.503	3.893	3.535	3.368

Table 7
Effect of $100 billion tax cut on long run equilibrium, 'Q' variation nominal interest rate varies with 90 percent of expected inflation, growth model (g=0.03), income elasticity of money supply (EM) equals 1

Variable	198904	199001	199101	199501	200001	201001	203001	207504
Q	3970.550	4000.000	4206.676	4892.422	5688.818	7599.383	13740.017	53121.137
QBLPC	100.000	100.000	102.104	105.506	105.825	105.190	105.303	105.297
QNBLPC	100.000	100.000	102.370	105.705	105.642	105.008	105.165	105.164
QUTPC	93.368	93.368	95.315	97.814	97.590	97.106	97.245	97.247
QQDPC	100.000	100.000	100.000	99.255	99.512	99.929	99.826	99.824
QCBLPC	107.103	107.103	107.122	107.864	108.439	108.325	108.286	108.278
QZBLPC	100.000	100.000	100.017	100.663	101.164	101.065	101.030	101.023
DYBLPC	100.000	103.086	104.730	106.576	107.144	106.837	106.726	106.705
CBLPC	100.000	100.000	102.026	105.300	106.480	106.869	106.724	106.716
CQPC	63.179	63.179	63.131	63.055	63.570	64.188	64.032	64.030
IBLPC	100.000	100.000	104.934	114.013	109.642	105.304	106.228	106.297
IQPC	17.040	17.040	17.513	18.414	17.655	17.059	17.200	17.202
IACQPC	5.340	5.340	5.818	6.592	5.675	5.319	5.398	5.401
IREQPC	11.700	11.700	11.695	11.973	12.074	11.754	11.835	11.834
IGBLPC	100.000	100.000	105.065	114.234	110.442	105.171	106.428	106.433
IGQPC	16.657	16.657	17.141	18.035	17.384	16.654	16.836	16.837
INBLPC	100.000	100.000	116.791	138.372	118.066	101.881	106.636	106.752
INQPC	4.957	4.957	5.671	6.502	5.531	4.801	5.020	5.026
ITQPC	5.340	5.340	6.043	6.881	5.802	5.206	5.384	5.391
ITQNPC	6.048	6.048	6.825	7.778	6.582	5.906	6.106	6.113
DQPC	11.700	11.700	11.470	11.534	11.853	11.853	11.815	11.811
NFICQPC	-0.768	-0.768	-0.801	-1.031	-0.841	-0.935	-0.928	-0.932
NFIQPC	-0.383	-0.383	-0.372	-0.379	-0.271	-0.404	-0.364	-0.365
NEQPC	-0.219	-0.219	-0.232	-0.426	-0.124	-0.260	-0.224	-0.226
XQPC	10.000	10.000	9.793	9.816	10.066	9.908	9.938	9.934
IMQPC	10.219	10.219	10.025	10.242	10.190	10.168	10.162	10.161
IMQQPC	10.070	10.070	9.892	10.129	10.080	10.059	10.057	10.056
INTFQPC	0.549	0.549	0.570	0.605	0.717	0.675	0.704	0.706
GQPC	20.000	20.000	19.588	18.956	18.899	19.013	18.993	18.994
INTQPC	2.743	2.743	2.848	3.026	3.583	3.376	3.519	3.528
TQPC	19.640	17.140	17.463	17.976	18.564	18.296	18.449	18.458
BSCQPC	-3.103	-5.603	-4.973	-4.006	-3.919	-4.094	-4.062	-4.064
NEWQPC	2.154	2.779	2.562	2.494	2.288	2.353	2.361	2.362
PEQPC	1.925	1.925	2.108	3.244	2.965	2.630	2.821	2.834
IEQPC	0.000	0.000	0.039	0.018	-0.115	0.023	-0.001	-0.000
SPBLPC	100.000	114.017	114.308	111.095	109.494	106.723	106.735	106.666
SPQPC	17.835	20.335	19.967	18.780	18.454	18.095	18.078	18.067
BSQPC	-1.178	-3.678	-2.827	-0.745	-1.070	-1.441	-1.242	-1.230
NDPQPC	40.000	40.625	41.792	40.290	38.092	40.541	41.605	41.762
NDMQPC	40.000	40.625	41.779	39.399	38.147	40.605	41.613	41.762

Table 7 *(continued)*

FCFQPC	53.000	53.000	51.907	50.396	49.933	50.300	50.371	50.380
FCUSQPC	40.000	40.000	39.167	38.309	38.079	38.274	38.233	38.235
FCFN*	100.000	100.000	100.056	98.092	96.497	97.309	98.322	98.376
FCFNQPC	13.000	13.000	12.739	12.068	11.854	12.026	12.138	12.146
FWBLPC	100.000	102.315	109.818	106.726	103.054	111.343	114.955	115.502
FWQPC	27.000	27.625	29.040	27.312	26.293	28.579	29.475	29.617
MQPC	4.000	4.000	4.000	4.000	4.000	4.000	4.000	4.000
IRPC	8.000	8.000	8.016	10.532	11.256	9.663	9.927	9.925
INFLPC	5.000	5.000	5.301	8.718	8.225	6.810	7.132	7.138
RRPC	3.000	3.000	2.998	2.719	2.638	2.815	2.786	2.786
RCCI	1.000	1.000	1.000	0.970	0.962	0.981	0.977	0.977
ER	1.000	1.000	1.000	0.980	0.985	0.987	0.987	0.987
GRQPC	3.000	3.000	5.732	3.189	2.921	3.002	3.005	3.000
GRFC**	3.000	3.000	3.102	3.400	2.871	3.381	3.091	3.004
GRMPC	3.000	3.000	5.732	3.189	2.921	3.002	3.005	3.000
GRM$PC	8.150	8.150	11.336	12.185	11.386	10.016	10.350	10.353
KQRAT	1.800	1.800	1.765	1.774	1.824	1.824	1.818	1.817
NLPC	92.000	92.000	94.326	97.355	97.100	96.518	96.684	96.686
UPC	8.000	8.000	5.674	2.645	2.900	3.482	3.316	3.314

* FCFN is abbreviation of FCFNBLPC

** GRFC is abbreviation of GRFCFNPC

Table 8
Effect of $100 billion tax cut on long run equilibrium, growth model (g=0.03), income elasticity of money supply (EM) equals 1, model T

Variable	198904	199001	199101	199501	200001	201001	203001	7207504
Q	3970.550	4000.000	4203.329	4870.593	5645.003	7521.369	13568.416	52376.547
QBLPC	100.000	100.000	102.023	105.035	105.010	104.110	103.987	103.821
QNBLPC	100.000	100.000	102.278	105.217	104.947	104.096	103.989	103.821
QUTPC	93.368	93.368	95.240	97.434	97.112	96.485	96.411	96.282
QQDPC	100.000	100.000	100.000	99.665	99.925	100.000	100.000	100.000
QCBLPC	107.103	107.103	107.122	107.801	108.133	107.902	107.858	107.830
QZBLPC	100.000	100.000	100.016	100.608	100.897	100.696	100.658	100.633
DYBLPC	100.000	103.086	104.655	106.534	106.582	105.701	105.373	105.114
CBLPC	100.000	100.000	101.940	105.491	106.458	105.583	105.246	104.991
CQPC	63.179	63.179	63.128	63.453	64.050	64.073	63.944	63.891
IBLPC	100.000	100.000	104.772	111.142	105.539	103.653	103.905	103.805
IQPC	17.040	17.040	17.499	18.031	17.126	16.966	17.027	17.038
IACQPC	5.340	5.340	5.804	6.399	5.440	5.266	5.327	5.338
IREQPC	11.700	11.700	11.696	11.699	11.700	11.699	11.700	11.700
IGBLPC	100.000	100.000	104.903	110.106	105.254	103.342	103.775	103.678
IGQPC	16.657	16.657	17.128	17.462	16.696	16.534	16.623	16.634
INBLPC	100.000	100.000	116.253	125.306	104.705	101.280	103.303	103.341
INQPC	4.957	4.957	5.649	5.914	4.943	4.823	4.925	4.935
ITQPC	5.340	5.340	6.021	6.484	5.373	5.254	5.328	5.338
ITQNPC	6.048	6.048	6.801	7.330	6.089	5.951	6.034	6.045
DQPC	11.700	11.700	11.479	11.547	11.753	11.712	11.699	11.700
NFICQPC	-0.768	-0.768	-0.801	-1.146	-0.962	-0.981	-0.984	-0.999
NFIQPC	-0.383	-0.383	-0.372	-0.569	-0.430	-0.431	-0.403	-0.403
NEQPC	-0.219	-0.219	-0.231	-0.525	-0.221	-0.249	-0.204	-0.192
XQPC	10.000	10.000	9.801	9.729	9.989	9.934	9.960	9.958
IMQPC	10.219	10.219	10.032	10.254	10.211	10.183	10.164	10.150
IMQQPC	10.070	10.070	9.899	10.125	10.068	10.053	10.049	10.048
INTFQPC	0.549	0.549	0.570	0.620	0.741	0.732	0.780	0.807
GQPC	20.000	20.000	19.604	19.041	19.046	19.210	19.233	19.264
INTQPC	2.743	2.743	2.851	3.101	3.704	3.662	3.902	4.033
TQPC	19.640	17.140	17.458	18.006	18.607	18.477	18.705	18.820
BSCQPC	-3.103	-5.603	-4.997	-4.136	-4.143	-4.395	-4.430	-4.477
NEWQPC	2.154	2.779	2.570	2.573	2.493	2.652	2.763	2.851
PEQPC	1.925	1.925	2.106	2.951	2.745	2.732	2.901	2.979
IEQPC	0.000	0.000	0.042	-0.071	-0.083	0.019	0.002	-0.000
SPBLPC	100.000	114.017	114.272	110.227	107.023	106.119	105.825	105.553
SPQPC	17.835	20.335	19.977	18.717	18.177	18.180	18.151	18.133
BSQPC	-1.178	-3.678	-2.849	-1.256	-1.481	-1.645	-1.527	-1.499
NDPQPC	40.000	40.625	41.836	41.309	41.325	45.626	48.643	50.465
NDMQPC	40.000	40.625	41.822	40.506	41.498	45.648	48.646	50.466

Table 8 *(continued)*

FCFQPC	53.000	53.000	51.948	50.867	51.420	52.118	52.230	52.237
FCUSQPC	40.000	40.000	39.195	38.385	38.283	38.636	38.654	38.704
FCFN*	100.000	100.000	100.079	100.856	106.114	107.974	108.596	108.080
FCFNQPC	13.000	13.000	12.752	12.483	13.137	13.482	13.576	13.533
FWBLPC	100.000	102.315	109.843	109.016	110.305	124.029	135.067	142.015
FWQPC	27.000	27.625	29.070	28.023	28.361	32.166	35.070	36.933
MQPC	4.000	4.000	4.000	4.000	4.000	4.000	4.000	4.000
IRPC	8.000	8.000	8.018	10.322	10.332	9.266	9.242	9.176
INFLPC	5.000	5.000	5.291	7.693	6.961	6.273	6.243	6.174
RRPC	3.000	3.000	3.000	3.000	3.000	3.000	3.000	3.000
RCCI	1.000	1.000	1.000	1.000	1.000	1.000	1.000	1.000
ER	1.000	1.000	1.001	0.984	0.990	0.989	0.990	0.991
GRQPC	3.000	3.000	5.586	3.061	2.908	3.017	3.016	2.999
GRFC**	3.000	3.000	3.178	4.606	4.105	3.071	3.074	2.999
GRMPC	3.000	3.000	5.586	3.061	2.908	3.017	3.016	2.999
GRM$PC	8.150	8.150	11.172	10.989	10.071	9.480	9.447	9.358
KQRAT	1.800	1.800	1.766	1.777	1.808	1.802	1.800	1.800
NLPC	92.000	92.000	94.235	96.897	96.520	96.761	95.671	95.516
PC	8.000	8.000	5.765	3.103	3.480	4.239	4.239	4.484

* FCFN is abbreviation of FCFNBLPC

** GRFC is abbreviation of GRFCFNPC

Appendix 1

List of equations of the 'S'-model (unless otherwise indicated)

$$CD_t = (2/39)\sum_{j=1}^{12}(13-j)\{a[DY_{t-j} + IED_{t-j} - (.125\sum_{i=0}^{7} IED_{t-i})_{t-j}] + b(1+g)^{.25}FW_{t-j}\} \quad (1)$$

where

a = .208351728 in stationary model (g=0); a = .196781865 in growth model(g=.03), and

b = 16/1080 = 0.148148148 [in 'T'-variation of models, $FW_0(1+g)^{(t-j)/4}$ is substituted for FW_{t-j}; FW_0=1080.]

$$DY_t = Q_t + INTD_t - T_t - PED_t - IED_t \quad (2)$$

$$FW_t = NDM_t - FCFN_t \quad (3)$$

$$D_t = \delta K_t; \quad \delta = .065 \quad (4)$$

$$IRE_t = D_t[(\sum_{j=1}^{56} RCCI_{t-j}/56)/(.25\sum_{j=1}^{4} RCCI_{t-j})]^{.5} * KD_t/K_t \quad (5)$$

$$IACD_t=(2v/111)\sum_{i=1}^{36}(37-j)(Q_{t-j}-Q_{t-j-1})(.25\sum_{j=1}^{4} RCCI_{t-j})^{-.5}$$

where v = 0.6 for g = 0; v = 0.662439579 for g = 0.03 (6)

$$IAC_t=IACD_t \text{ when } IACD_t > -1.1D_t; \quad IAC_t=-1.1D_t \text{ when } IACD_t \leq -1.1D_t \quad (7)$$

$$ID_t = IRE_t+IAC_t \quad (8)$$

$$RCCI_t = (RR_t+\delta)/(RR_0+\delta), \quad RR_0 = .03 \quad (9)$$

$$RR_t = IRE_t - INFLEXP_t \quad (10)$$

$$INFLEXP_t = (1/210)\sum_{j=1}^{20}(21-j)INFL_{t-j} \quad (11)$$

$$G_t = \bar{G}(1+g)^{t/4}$$

where $\bar{G}$=800 and g=0 in stationary model; g=0.03 growth model (12)

$$T_t = \bar{T}(1+g)^{t/4} + .25(Q_t+INT_t) + r[INT_t-INT_0(1+g)^{1/4}] \quad (13)$$

where

r = 0.75, so that taxes adjust to cover changes in interest payments, and

$\bar{T}$ = −194.68485 where g=0; $\bar{T}$ = −241.84375 where g=0.03.

$$IMQ_t = [(5m/136)\sum_{j=1}^{16}(16-j)QD_{t-j}ER_{t-j-1}]/(.25\sum_{j=1}^{4} ER_{t-j})^{-/75} \quad (14)$$

where m=0.019370498 where g=0; m=0.0210453563 where g=0.03

$$IMFC_t = RR_tFCOND_{t-1} \quad (15)$$

$$IM_t = IMQ_t + IMFC_t \quad (16)$$

$$XD_t = (5x/136)\sum_{j=1}^{16}(16-j)[80-300(ER_{t-j-1}-1)](1+g)^{(t-j)/4} \tag{17}$$

where x=1 where g=0; x=1.04491013 where g=0.03

$$ER_t = [(1+RR)/1.03]^{10} + 10NFI_{t-1}/Q_{t-1}$$
$$- 0.5\{FCF_{t-1}/FCF_0ER_0(1+g)^{(t-1)/4}] - 1\} + y \tag{18}$$

where y=0 where g=0; y=0.038284 where g=0.03, and 5 NFI_{t-1}, instead of 10 NFI_{t-1}, was used in the $\Delta T = -300$ simulations

$$FCUSF_t = FCUSF_0(1+g)^{t/4};\ \text{with } FCUSF_0 = 800 \tag{19}$$
$$FCUSD_t = FCUSD_0(1+g)^{t/4};\ \text{with } FCUSD_0 = 800 \tag{20}$$
$$FCUS = FCUSF/ER + FCUSD \tag{21}$$
$$FCF_t = FCF_{t-1} - .25NFI_t + FCUSD_t - FCUSD_{t-1} + FCUSF_t - FCUSF_{t-1}; \tag{22}$$

where FCF_0 = 2,120

$$FCFN_t = FCF_t - FCUS_t;\ \Delta FCFN_t = -(.25NFI_t + \Delta\{FCUSF/ER\}_t - \Delta FCUSF_t) \tag{23}$$
$$QD_t \equiv CD_t + ID_t + G_t + (XD_t - IM_t) \tag{24}$$

The maximum possible or ceiling rate of output is

$$QC_t = c\{d[((1+g)/(1+n))^{t/4}L_t]^{-1} + (1-d)K_t^{-1}\}^{-1} \tag{25}$$

and the zero-extra-inflation output is

$$QZ_t = c\{d[((1+g)/(1+n)^{t/4}zL_t]^{-1} + (1-d)K_t^{-1}\}^{-1}, \tag{26}$$

where c=3.2486214, d=0.000074329757 and n=0 where g=0; n=0.02 where g=0.03 and z=0.92, the proportion of the labor force employed corresponding to that zero-extra inflation

$$L_t = (1+n)^{t/4}L_0;\quad L_0 = 120 \tag{27}$$
$$Q_t = QD_t + X1\{0.97QC_t - QD_t + .03QC[1 - (0.97QC_t/QD_t)^{20}]\}, \tag{28}$$

where X1 = 0 if $QD_t < 0.97QC_t$; X1 = 1 if $QD_t \geq 0.97QC_t$

$$QRAT_t = (Q_t - G_t + IM_t)/(QD_t - G_t + IM_t) \tag{29}$$
$$C_t = CD_t\ QRAT_t \tag{30}$$
$$I_t = ID_t\ QRAT_t \tag{31}$$
$$X_t = XD_t\ QRAT_t \tag{32}$$
$$NE_t = X_t - IM_t \tag{33}$$
$$NFIC_t = NE_t - INTF_t \tag{34}$$
$$U_t = L_t - N_t;\quad N_0 = 110.4;\quad U_0 = 9.6 \tag{35}$$
$$Q_t = c\{d[((1+g)/(1+n)^{t/4}N_t]^{-1} + (1-d)K_t^{-1}\}^{-1} \tag{36}$$

But since Q_t is determined by (24) and (28) and

$$K_t = K_{t-1} + .25(I_{t-1} - D_{t-1}) \quad (37)$$

$$KD_t = 1.8 * (Q^2_{t-1}/Q_{t-2})/(.25\sum_{j=1}^{4} RCCI_{t-j})^{.5} \quad (38)$$

$$N_t = d/\{[(1+g)(1+n)]^{t/4}[c/Q-(1-d)/K_t]\} \quad (39)$$

$$\begin{aligned} INFL_t = {} & .5INFL_{t-1} + \{[QC_{t-1} - QZ_{t-1}/(QC_{t-1} - Q_{t-1}]^f - 1\} \\ & - (IM_{t-1}\Delta ER_{t-1})/(Q_{t-1}ER_{t-2} + [(QD_{t-1}/Q_{t-1}) - 1] + 0.25 \end{aligned} \quad (40)$$

where f = 0.01

$$P_t = P_{t-1}(1 + INFL_t)^{.25} \quad (41)$$

where $P_0 = 1.0$

$$MS\$_t/P_t = \alpha Q_t + \beta(1+g)^{t/4}$$

For EM = −1: $(\alpha,\beta) = (-.04,320)$
For EM = 0: $(\alpha,\beta) = (0,160)$
For EM = 1: $(\alpha,\beta) = (.04,0)$
For EM = 2: $(\alpha,\beta) = (.08,-160)$ (42)

where EM is elasticity of money supply with respect to departures of Q from baseline.

$$\begin{aligned} MS\$/P_t &= 160(1+g)^{t/4}, & t \le -1 \\ MS\$/P_t &= (160+25)(1+g)^{t/4}, & t \ge 0 \end{aligned} \quad (43)$$

$$\begin{aligned} MS\$_t &= 160[1.05(1+g)]^{t/4}, & t \le -1 \\ MS\$_t &= 160[1.07(1+g)]^{t/4}, & t \ge 0 \end{aligned} \quad (44)$$

$$IR_t = (P_tQ_t/M\$_t)^{1.2}/800 + rINFLEXP_t + k \quad (45)$$

where k = −0.02948918558, r=1, while in ‘Q’ variation of models, k = −0.02448918558, r=0.9.

$$NDP\$_t = NDP\$_{t-1} - .25BSC\$_t \quad (46)$$

$$NDM\$_t = M\$_t + \sum_{j=0}^{19} PV_{t,j} \quad (47)$$

where

$$PV_{t,j} = \sum_{i=1}^{20-j} [IRQ_{t-j}NEW\$_{t-j}/(1+IRQ)^i] + NEW\$_{t-j}/(1+IRQ)^{20-j} \quad (48)$$

$$PE\$_t = 4[(P_t/P_{t-1})-1]NDM\$_{t-1} \quad (49)$$

$$IE\$_t = -4[(NDP\$_t-NDP\$_{t-1}) - (NDM\$_t-NDM\$_{t-1}] \quad (50)$$

$$BSC\$_t = T\$_t - G\$_t - INT\$_t \quad (51)$$

$$INT\$_t = 4(\sum_{i=1}^{20} IRQ_{t-i}NEW\$_{t-i}) \quad (52)$$

$$NEW\$_t = NEW\$_{t-20} - .25BSC\$_t - \Delta M\$_t \quad (53)$$

$$BS\$_t = BSC\$_t + PE\$_t + IE\$_t \tag{54}$$

where, for all variables V, $V_t = V\$_t/P_t$

$$INTD_t = .8INT_t \tag{55}$$
$$INTF_t = .2INT_t \tag{56}$$
$$PED_t = .8PE_t; \quad PEF_t = .2PE_t \tag{57}$$
$$IED_t = .8IE_t; \quad IEF_t = .2IE_t \tag{58}$$
$$NDMD_t = .8NDM_t \tag{59}$$
$$NDMF_t = .2NDM_t \tag{60}$$
$$FCOND_t = FCFN - NDMF_t \tag{61}$$
$$QN_t = Q_t - D_t \tag{62}$$
$$SP_t = DY_t - C_t \tag{63}$$
$$SG_t = DY_t - C_t + BS_t = IG_t \tag{64}$$
$$NFI_t = NFIC_t + PEF_t + IEF_t \tag{65}$$
$$IG_t = I_t + NFI_t = SG_t \tag{66}$$
$$IT_t = I_t - D_t \tag{67}$$
$$IN_t = IG_t - D_t = SN_t \tag{68}$$

Appendix 2

List of Variables

BS	Real budget surplus
BSC	Conventional budget surplus
BSCQPC	BSC as a percent of output
BSQPC	BS as percent of output
C	Consumption (personal consumption expenditures)
CBLPC	C as a percent of baseline C
CQPC	C as percent of output
D	Depreciation
DQPC	D as percent of output
DY	Disposable income
DYBLPC	DY as a percent of baseline DY
EM	Elasticity of M with respect to Q
ER	Exchange rate (real value of $ in foreign currency)
FCF	Foreign net worth in US
FCFN	Net foreign financial claims
FCFNBLPC	FCFN as a percent of baseline FCFN
FCFNQPC	FCFN as a percent of output
FCFQPC	FCF as a percent of output
FCOND	Net foreign financial claims other than net debt
FCUS	US net worth abroad, total dollar value
FCUSD	US net worth abroad, portion denominated in dollars
FCUSF	US net worth abroad, portion denominated in foreign currencies
FCUSQPC	FCUS as a percent of output
FW	Net private financial wealth
FWBLPC	FW as a percent of baseline FW

FWQPC	FW as a percent of output
G	Government expenditures for goods and services
GBAR	Base component of government expenditures
GQPC	G as a percent of output
GRFCFNPC	Growth rate, in percent, of FCFN
GRQPC	Growth rate, in percent, of output
GR[V]PC	Growth rate of variable [V] in percent
I	Investment (gross private domestic)
IAC	Accelerator investment
IACD	Accelerator investment demand
IACQPC	IAC as a percent of output
IBLPC	I as a percent of baseline I
IE	Interest effect
IED	Interest effect, domestic
IEF	Interest effect, foreign
IEQPC	IE as a percent of output
IG	Gross investment
IGBLPC	IG as a percent of baseline IG
IGQPC	IG as a percent of output
IM	Imports
IMFC	Imports of financial services
IMQ	Import of other goods and services
IMQPC	IM as a percent of output
IMQQPC	IMQ as a percent of output
IN	Net investment
INBLPC	IN as a percent of baseline IN
INQPC	IN as a percent of output
INFL	Inflation rate
INFLEXP	Expected inflation rate
INFLPC	INFL as a percent
INT	Interest payments by government
INTD	Interest payments by government, domestic
INTF	Interest payments by government to foreigners
INTFQPC	INTF as a percent of output
INTQPC	INT as a percent of output
IQPC	I as a percent of output
IR	Nominal interest rate
IRE	Replacement investment
IREQPC	IRE as a percent of output
IRPC	IR as a percent
IRQ	IR, quarterly rate, $=(1+IR)^{.25}-1$
IT	Net private domestic investment
ITBLPC	IT as a percent of baseline IT
ITQNPC	IT as a percent of QN
ITQPC	IT as a percent of output
K	Capital stock (beginning of quarter)
KD	Capital stock demanded
KQRAT	Capital output ratio
L	Labor force
M	Real monetary base (high-powered money)
MD$	Nominal money demand (for monetary base)
MS$	Nominal money supply (of monetary base)
MQPC	M as a percent of output

N	Employment
NDM	Market value of net debt
NDMD	Market value of net debt, domestic
NDMQPC	NDM as a percent of output
NDP	Par value of net debt
NDPQPC	NDP as a percent of output
NE	Net exports
NEQPC	NE as a percent of output
NEW	Newly issued bonds
NEWQPC	NEW as a percent of output
NFI	Real net foreign investment
NFIC	Conventional net foreign investment
NFIQPC	NFI as a percent of output
NFICQPC	NFIC as a percent of output
NLPC	Employment as a percent of labor force
P	Price level
PE	Price effect
PED	Price effect, domestic
PEF	Price effect, foreign
PEQPC	PE as a percent of output
$PV_{t,j}$	Present value of bonds issued j quarters ago
Q	Output (GNP)
QBLPC	Q as a percent of baseline output
QC	Maximum possible or ceiling rate of output
QCBLQPC	QC as a percent of baseline Q
QD	Output demanded
QN	NNP
QNBLPC	QN as a percent of baseline QN
QQDPC	Q as a percent of QD
QUTPC	Utilization of capacity, as a percent of output
QZ	Zero-extra-inflation rate of output
QZBLPC	QZ as a percent of baseline QZ
RCCI	Rental cost of capital index
RR	Real interest rate
RRPC	RR as a percent
SG	Gross saving
SGQPC	SG as a percent of Q
SN	Net saving or 'national saving'
SP	Private saving
SPBLPC	SP as a percent of baseline SP
SPQPC	SP as a percent of Q
T	Taxes
TBAR	Tax equation component
TQPC	T as a percent of output
U	Unemployment
UPC	Unemployment as a percent of labor force
X	Exports
XQPC	X as a percent of output
z	Proportion of labor employed corresponding to QZ
$	Denotes nominal value of variable

References

Eisner, R., 1986, *How Real is the Federal Deficit?*, The Free Press, New York.

Eisner, R., 1989, Budget deficits: Rhetoric and reality, *Journal of Economic Perspectives*, 3, 2, 73-93.

Eisner, R., 1991, Deficits and us and our grandchildren, in: J. Rock, ed., *The Debt and the Twin Deficits Debate*, Bristlecone Books/Mayfield, Mountain View, California, pp. 81-131.

Eisner, R. and S.-I. Hwang, 1990, Real deficits, inflation and output in a demand-side model, to be published in *Prévision et Analyse Economique*.

Eisner, R. and P.J. Pieper, 1984, A new view of the federal debt and budget deficits, *American Economic Review*, 74, 1, 11-29.

Eisner, R. and P.J. Pieper, 1986, 1987, Measurement and effects of government debt and deficits, in: *Economic Policy and National Accounting in Inflationary Conditions, Studies in Banking and Finance*, North-Holland, Amsterdam, 115-144. Updated and revised as: Dette et déficit gouvernementaux: mesures et effêts, in: *Annales d'Economie et de Statistique*, 1986, 3, 27-52.

Eisner, R. and P.J. Pieper, 1988, Deficits, monetary policy and real economic activity, in: K.J. Arrow and M. Boskin, eds., *Economics of Public Debt*, MacMillan, London, 3-40.

PART III

BUDGET DEFICITS AND SAVING

[22]

NATIONAL SAVING AND THE TWIN DEFICITS: MYTH AND REALITY

Robert Eisner and Paul J. Pieper
Northwestern University and University of Illinois at Chicago

Reality: National saving in the United States went down in the last decade, at least during the 1982–83 recession, budget deficits went up, and the trade and current accounts moved to deficit.

Myth: Eliminating or reducing budget deficits will both eliminate or reduce the current account deficit *and* increase national saving.

That our budget and trade deficits have reduced national saving has been argued widely. But much discussion of saving and deficits is careless of definitions and irrelevant to the economic variables that should concern us. Net foreign investment, the other side of the coin of the trade deficit—or more properly, the current account deficit—is not what it appears to be. And the budget deficit may actually contribute to more national saving, rather than less.

1. The Measurement of Saving

The conventional or official measure of gross saving in the United States is produced by the Bureau of Economic Analysis (BEA) of the Department of Commerce as part of the National Income and Product Accounts (NIPA). As shown in table 3–1, NIPA is equal to the sum of personal saving—personal income minus personal taxes and personal outlays for consumption expenditures, interest, and transfer payments—corporate

Table 3–1. Net Saving and Investment Account, 1990* (billions of dollars)

Gross private domestic investment	745.0	Personal income	4,645.6
		Less: Personal tax and nontax payments	699.8
Less: Capital consumption allowances with capital consumption adjustment	575.7	Less: Personal outlays	3,766.8
		Personal consumption expenditures	3,658.1
Net private domestic investment	169.3	Interest paid by consumers to business	107.8
Net foreign investment	−90.1	Personal transfer payments to foreigners	0.9
		Personal saving	179.1
		Undistributed corporate profits with inventory valuation and capital consumption adjustment	29.1
		Government surplus or deficit (−), national income and product accounts	−126.0
		Federal	−161.3
		State and local	35.4
		Net saving	82.2
		Statistical discrepancy	−3.1
Net Investment	79.2	*Net Saving and Statistical Discrepancy*	79.2

* Adapted from *Survey of Current Business*, January 1991, tables 1.1, 1.9, 2.1 and 5.1, pp. 6, 8, 10 and 13.

saving (undistributed profits), and what is sometimes called "government saving." This last measure comprises the sum of the federal, state, and local government surpluses. Gross saving is equal, except for a statistical discrepancy, to gross investment, the sum of gross private domestic investment and net foreign investment. Net national saving plus the statistical discrepancy is then equal to net private domestic investment—gross private domestic investment minus capital consumption allowances—and net foreign investment. Because gross private domestic investment includes only the acquisition of reproducible tangible capital by business, fixed capital by nonprofit institutions, and residential housing by households, national saving is thus restricted to a part of private investment in tangible assets and the acquisition of assets in the rest of the world, net of foreign acquisitions in the United States.

This NIPA measure of saving and investment is quite narrow. From an economic perspective, investment may be defined simply as any type of activity that will yield future benefits. The BEA is now committed to some broadening by moving our accounts into conformity with the UN-recommended System of National Accounts, which explicitly includes public investment along with private investment and which may also advise taking into account investment in R&D and other intellectual property. The current NIPA measure of investment, however, excludes (1) all investment by government, at all levels; (2) all investment by government enterprises; (3) all investment by households except that in new housing; (4) all investment in the intangible capital of education and

Table 3–2. Federal Government Investment by Type, 1989

Investment	*Expenditure (billions of dollars)*	*Percent of Federal Expenditures*
Tangible capital	124.4	10.5
Direct	99.6	8.4
Structures	13.4	1.1
Equipment	86.2	7.3
Grants-in-aid	24.8	2.1
Education and training	25.8	2.2
Direct	3.7	0.3
Grants-in-aid	13.8	1.2
Transfer payments	8.3	0.7
Research and development	61.7	5.2
Total	211.9	17.8
Addendum:		
Health expenditures	164.9	13.9
Direct	23.3	2.0
Grants-in-aid	40.2	3.4
Transfer payments	101.4	8.5

Sources: *National Income and Product Accounts of the United States*, tables 3.7 and 3.15; and *Special Analyses: Budget of the United States Government*, Table D-8.

training, research, and health; (5) most increases in the real value of existing assets, including assets held in the rest of the world; and (6) most investment in land and natural resources. Clearly, from the extent of these exclusions, this most widely used or conventional measure of national saving relates to only a small part of the capital that we provide for the future, in the order of some 15 to 20 percent (see Eisner, 1989, 1991*a*). An account of just the federal government component of these exclusions is shown in table 3–2. Whatever the effect of these exclusions on the narrow, conventional measure of national saving, reduction of budget deficits would seem almost certainly to reduce the full, relevant measure by curtailing household or consumer investment and government tangible and intangible investment.

2. Deficits and the Saving–Investment Identity

We take as the starting point for our analysis, ignoring the statistical discrepancy, the following national income accounting identity:

$$S^P - D^F + S^{S\&L} = I + \text{NFI}, \qquad (3\text{–}1)$$

where S^P is private saving, D^F is the federal deficit, $S^{S\&L}$ is the composite state and local government surplus, I is gross private domestic investment, and NFI is net foreign investment. The left-hand side of the equation is of course equal to gross saving.

The saving–investment identity is a useful foundation for economic analysis. It is not a substitute for it. Because national saving is the sum of public saving and private saving, many assert, with little argumentation, that increasing public saving or reducing public dissaving in the form of federal budget deficits will increase national saving. But this is assuredly true only if other public saving (state and local government surpluses) and private saving are not reduced or, looking at the other side of the coin, if the sum of net private domestic investment and net foreign investment is increased. This is unlikely to be the case, however, for three major reasons.

First, as another look at table 3–1 will show, one frequently ignored first effect of reducing the federal budget deficit may be to reduce the composite state and local surplus. This reduction would occur quite directly if the federal government reduced its deficit by cutting grants-in-aid to states and localities, currently running over $130 billion per year, more than 17 percent of total state and local government expenditures. Empirical confirmation that this may be so is found in the following

AR(1) regression between federal grants-in-aid to state and local governments, GIA, and the price-adjusted high-employment deficit, PAHED, both expressed as a percent of GNP:

$$\Delta GIA_t = \underset{(0.052)}{0.138X1} - \underset{(0.049)}{0.059X2} + \underset{(0.027)}{0.086\Delta PAHED_t}, \quad t = 1956-1989, \quad (3-2)$$

$R^2 = .397$, $D - W = 2.21$, $\rho = 0.298$. Equation (3–2) was estimated with a first-order correction for serial correlation. $X1$ is a constant term for the 1956–1972 period, and $X2$ is a constant for the 1973–1989 period. The estimates indicate that each dollar more of the inflation-and-cyclically-adjusted federal surplus was accompanied by 8.6 cents less in federal grants-in-aid to state and local governments.

The federal deficit can also affect state and local government saving indirectly by increasing the burden on state and local services or by encroaching on state and local sources of revenue. A proposal floated in Washington in the summer of 1990 to limit federal tax deductibility of state and local taxes offers another example of a measure to reduce the federal deficit at the expense of state and local budgets. These latter budgets would be plagued by great resistance to the taxes necessary to maintain *their* surpluses or lower *their* deficits.

Second, identity (3–1) has in practice been applied to conventional measures of the deficit and saving. However, the conventional deficit measure includes many types of investment expenditures, such as expenditures on infrastructure, education, and R&D.[1] Even if the deficit did reduce private investment dollar for dollar, its effect on total investment would be less if the deficit were partly a result of increased expenditures on government investment. As may be seen in table 3–2, about 18 percent of federal government spending is in the form of investment in tangible capital, education and training, and research and development. Another 14 percent of federal spending is devoted to health care, some portion of which represents investment in human capital. In addition, because some items of federal spending such as interest payments on the debt are relatively fixed, government investment is likely to be more than proportionally affected by cuts in the budget deficit.

Third, looking to the behavior of private agents, we must recognize first that any change in the federal deficit is likely to change personal income and/or personal tax and nontax payments, thus affecting disposable personal income (DPI). If the deficit is reduced—either by cutting spending or raising income taxes—DPI will be reduced. Since personal saving is the difference between DPI and personal outlays, unless the latter change dollar for dollar with DPI, personal saving will decline.

Increases in excise or sales taxes will generally raise the cost or value of personal consumption expenditures, thus also reducing personal saving. Increases in corporate taxes (or reductions in government payments to corporations) will similarly reduce undistributed corporate profits, a component of national saving.

Simply enough then, we cannot tell, in terms of the saving identity itself, whether increases in the budget deficit will reduce national saving or whether reductions will raise it. We can, of course, state that a reduction in the federal deficit will increase national saving *if* all other components of saving remain the same, but this result is hardly to be expected and is indeed almost impossible, given the further identities between federal net payments to other sectors and their receipts from the federal government.

The effect of the federal deficit on saving may be better understood by examining its effect on the other side of the saving–investment identity: private domestic investment and net foreign investment. What will a reduction in the federal deficit do to either measure?

Some conventional wisdom suggests that a reduction of the federal deficit will increase private domestic investment by freeing funds and resources otherwise used for lending to the government or for financing consumption expenditures. But the reduction in the flow of private funds to finance the deficit is, in the first instance, exactly matched by a reduction in the funds available because the Treasury has either reduced what it is paying out or increased what it is taking in taxes. And if consumption is reduced, can we be sure that business will find it more profitable to invest? If consumers do not buy that new U.S. car, will that make GM or Chrysler more likely to invest? Or less?

We may go all the way back to Lange (1938) for the classic argument that there is a rate of consumption that will maximize investment, given the dual effects of increased consumption in raising the demand for capital to facilitate greater output and its effect in reducing the demand for capital by raising interest rates. If consumption is initially at or below this maximization point, reductions in consumption are likely to lower investment, not increase it. In fact, throughout the last several decades, changes in consumption have been positively correlated with changes in domestic investment. And, as we have reported in other work, budget deficits themselves have been positively related to increases in gross private domestic investment (Eisner 1986; Eisner and Pieper, 1988).

But what about net foreign investment? Here we may anticipate a different scenario. Net foreign investment is equal to exports, plus the usually zero or trivial item of net capital grants received by the United

States, minus imports, transfer payments to foreigners from persons and government, and interest paid by government to foreigners, as shown in Table 3–3. But then, just as an increase in taxes or a reduction of income receipts from the federal government may lead us not to buy a Ford or a Chrysler, it may lead some of us not to buy a Toyota or a Mazda. Any reduction in imports, other things equal, must reduce foreign accumulation of dollars. It thus reduces foreign investment in the United States and hence U.S. net foreign investment. And in this case, a number of the other items in the net foreign investment identity are likely to move in the direction of reinforcing the negative correlation between deficits and net foreign investment.

This scenario is clear, for example, if a reduction in the deficit entails reductions of government transfer payments to foreigners or, with the decline in DPI, if personal transfer payments to foreigners are reduced. And in the long run, reduction of the deficit, to the extent that it holds down the federal debt, may lower interest paid by government to foreigners. (More to the point, if budget deficits do contribute to negative U.S. foreign investment, they add to foreign claims on the United States. Higher claims result in higher business interest, dividend, and profit payments to foreigners, thus raising imports, and to higher government interest payments to foreigners to the extent the claims are on government debt.)

Thus we have what should be an obvious way by which a reduction in the federal deficit can reduce the current account deficit and raise foreign investment: by bringing on a recession. Lower income and output will certainly reduce imports. Unless the exchange rates can and are allowed to adjust sufficiently and/or unless the rest of the world moves as deeply into recession as the United States, exports will not fall as much as

Table 3–3. Net Foreign Investment, 1990* (billions of dollars)

Exports of goods and services	672.8
Plus: Capital grants received by the United States (net)	0
Less: Imports of goods and services	704.0
Transfer payments to foreigners (net)	15.5
From persons (net)	0.9
From government (net)	14.6
Interest paid by government to foreigners	38.8
Net foreign investment	−85.5

* Adapted from *Survey of Current Business*, April 1991, Account 4.1, p. 14.

imports, if at all. It is rarely put this way, but it is precisely by causing a recession that reducing the budget deficit will reduce the trade deficit. And it is precisely because budget deficits have stimulated the U.S. economy, and some of the relative prosperity has spilled into greater purchases of foreign goods, that budget deficits have contributed to the trade deficit.

Whether reductions in the structural or cyclically adjusted deficit will do more to increase net foreign investment than they do to reduce net private domestic investment, however, is extremely doubtful. If they do not, they obviously will not increase national saving.

We shall undertake a look at the historical record and then a more rigorous analysis of the empirical relation between budget deficits and current account deficits or its negative; net foreign investment, and between budget deficits and gross private domestic investment, the other component of the conventional measure of gross and net national saving. This will entail exploration as well of the role of the monetary regime and exchange rates. We shall devote attention, as we proceed, to appropriate measures of budget deficits, net foreign investment, and national saving and note the relations involving these broader and generally economically more relevant variables.

3. U.S. Investment in the Eighties—A Historical Perspective

Conventional wisdom holds that the rate of U.S. saving, and investment with it, fell during the decade of the eighties. Because the eighties were also a period of large government budget deficits, this condition has, in turn, fostered a belief that government deficits have reduced investment and that the way to increase investment is to reduce the deficit.

The conclusion that U.S. investment fell during the eighties is usually based on the NIPA measure of gross investment, which is included in table 3–4. The major component of gross private domestic investment has in fact fallen only slightly from its level in the seventies and is actually higher than its level in the fifties and sixties. Net foreign investment, though, has swung sharply negative. As a result, NIPA gross investment in the eighties has fallen by about 2 percent of GNP compared to the sixties and seventies. Even worse, this measure did not rebound during the latter part of the decade, when the economy rebounded, but instead fell further, with a precipitous decline in net foreign investment.

As we have pointed out, however, the NIPA measure of investment is quite narrow. The more comprehensive measures of investment in table

Table 3–4. Measures of Real Gross Investment, Mean Percentage of GNP

Investment Measure	*(1) 1953–1959*	*(2) 1960–1969*	*(3) 1970–1979*	*(4) 1980–1989*	*(5) 1984–1989*
Gross private domestic	15.86	16.50	17.15	16.87	17.73
Net foreign	0.21	0.62	0.24	−1.64	−2.70
Gross (BEA)	16.07	17.12	17.40	15.23	15.03
Consumer durables	5.92	6.24	7.85	9.23	10.04
Federal tangible	4.83	2.92	1.56	2.44	2.61
S&L tangible	2.84	3.30	2.54	1.92	1.95
Total tangible (including net foreign)	29.66	29.57	29.35	28.83	29.64
R&D	1.91	2.76	2.27	2.55	2.62
Education & training	4.24	5.41	6.37	5.91	5.81
Intangible[1]	6.15	8.17	8.64	8.44	8.43
Total tangible and intangible	35.81	37.74	37.99	37.27	38.06

See appendix for data sources.
[1] R&D plus education and training.

3–4 show that investment in consumer durables has increased throughout the postwar period, with a particularly large increase occurring during the eighties. Government tangible investment was largely unchanged from the seventies to the eighties, with a decline in state and local investment offset by an increase in federal investment. However, government tangible investment as a percent of GNP has fallen significantly from its level in the fifties and sixties.

The portion of GNP devoted to total tangible investment was only 0.5 percent to 0.8 percent less than the portion invested during the previous three decades. The large drop in net foreign investment has been offset to a large extent by increased investment in consumer durables. Further, all of the drop in investment in the eighties occurred during the first part of the decade. Expressed as a fraction of GNP, tangible investment in the 1984–1989 period was as large or larger than its value in the previous three decades.

Table 3–4 also offers measures of intangible investment. We define intangible investment narrowly to include only expenditures on research and development, education, and government-financed training. Intangible investment as a fraction of GNP has been roughly constant over the past three decades. During the eighties, the fraction of GNP spent on education fell, but this decrease was largely offset by an increase in R&D expenditures.

Looking at the comprehensive investment measures in table 3–4, it may be seen that the BEA NIPA investment is only about 40 percent of the total of tangible, including net foreign, and intangible investment. Our total investment measure, which includes all types of tangible investment and some types of intangible investment, tells a story different from that suggested by the NIPA measure. Total investment in the eighties was about the same as the U.S. postwar average and only slightly below the level of the sixties and seventies. Declines in net foreign investment have been offset largely by increases in investment in consumer durables.

To the extent this occurred is not to be dismissed glibly as a "consumption binge." Households buying automobiles are, after all, providing for their future transportation services just as are Avis and Hertz or as private companies might be doing in buying new busses. Most of the small decline in total investment that did occur took place in the deep recession in the first part of the decade. Gross investment in the latter part of the decade, when concern about deficits was greatest, was actually a higher proportion of GNP than average.

We can therefore dismiss the simple argument that large deficits in the eighties caused a reduction in investment.[2] This argument is based on the false premise that investment fell during the eighties. Further, the measures of investment presented so far have been expressed as a percentage of GNP. This practice will understate the effect of deficits on investment if deficits have a stimulatory effect on GNP. Deficits may very well increase total investment even if the fraction of GNP that is invested remains the same.

All this is not to argue that total saving and investment are necessarily adequate or well focused to provide optimally for our future. But this may relate more to the distribution between public and private and tangible and intangible investment. A third of a generation growing up functionally illiterate and millions of our more advantaged youth woefully behind their foreign counterparts in math and science may reflect our most important, real deficits.

4. The Effect of Deficits on Investment— An Empirical Analysis

The effect of deficits on saving may be better understood by examining the investment side of the saving–investment identity. Obviously, deficits cannot reduce saving unless they reduce one or more components of investment.

We hypothesize first the following relationship between investment and the deficit:

$$I_{j,t}/\text{GNP6}_t = b_{0j} + b_{1j}\text{PAHES6}_{t-1} + u_{j,t}, \qquad t = 1957 \text{ to } 1990, \quad (3-3)$$

where I_j is real investment of type j, GNP6 is an estimate of the GNP associated with a 6 percent unemployment rate, and PAHES6 is the price-adjusted 6 percent high-employment surplus as a percent of actual GNP, taken from the BEA for the years 1970 to 1990 and extrapolated backward on the basis of the BEA middle expansion trend deficit for the earlier years.

Equation (3–3) differs in three respects from the usual formulation of the deficit–investment relationship. First, we express investment as a fraction of potential GNP rather than actual GNP. Using actual GNP in the denominator would result in an understatement of the effect of deficits on investment if deficits have an expansionary effect on output.

Second, our deficit measure is cyclically adjusted to remove the reverse causation of the economy on the deficit. In addition, our deficit measure is "price-adjusted," which means it in effect includes only *real* interest among federal outlays, or counts as an "inflation tax" the loss in the value of government debt due to inflation. This correction is approximately equal to the rate of inflation times the net federal government debt (financial liabilities less financial assets). A reduction in the real value of government debt would be expected to reduce the private sector's wealth, thereby decreasing consumption and increasing or decreasing investment, depending on whether the output effect is greater or less than the substitution effect of possible lower real interest rates. And finally, the deficit variable is lagged, to permit its hypothesized stimulatory effects to operate on investment in accordance with widely shared views of the investment function. To control for serial correlation, equation (3–3) was estimated by AR(1) (Cochrane-Orcutt) regressions.

Table 3–5. Adjusted Deficit and Private Tangible Investment ($I_{j,t} = b_0 + b_1 PAHED6_{t-1}$)

	Regression Coefficients[1]					
		$PAHED6_{t-1}$				
I_j	b_0	b_1	R^2	$D-W$	ρ	n
Gross private domestic	16.488 (0.527)	0.769 (0.297)	0.315	1.63	0.513 (0.181)	34
Net foreign	−0.250 (0.749)	−0.407 (0.086)	0.882	2.05	0.891 (0.088)	34
Gross	16.072 (1.134)	0.473 (0.309)	0.443	1.73	0.762 (0.129)	34
Consumer durables	16.052 (45.080)	0.299 (0.072)	0.931	1.57	0.989 (0.059)	34
Private domestic tangible	24.030 (0.618)	1.335 (0.317)	0.613	1.54	0.539 (0.159)	34
Private tangible	24.064 (0.784)	0.785 (0.355)	0.393	1.60	0.616 (0.159)	34

[1] Ordinary least squares with a first-order correction for serial correlation. Standard errors are shown in parentheses. Sample period is 1957–1990.

Variable definitions:

PAHED6 = price-adjusted 6 percent high-employment deficit, as estimated by the BEA for the years 1970–1990 and extrapolated backward by the Holloway method on the basis of the BEA middle expansion trend deficit for the earlier years, as percent of GNP.

I_j = real investment of type j—GPDI, NFI, gross, and consumer durables from the BEA—taken as a percentage of GNP. Private domestic tangible is the sum of gross private domestic investment and consumer durables. Private tangible is the sum of gross investment and consumer durables.

Estimates for private investment are shown in table 3–5. We may note first that the lagged price-adjusted high employment deficit, PAHED6, clearly is related *positively* to gross private domestic investment. Each percentage point of deficit was associated with 0.769 percentage point *more* of subsequent investment as a ratio of potential GNP.

However, the lagged deficit showed a significant negative relation with subsequent net foreign investment, reflecting the stimulatory effect of deficits on imports. On balance, the positive effect on domestic investment appeared larger than the negative effect on foreign investment so that the total effect on the BEA measure of gross investment was positive, although not significantly so in this regression.[3]

As we have pointed out though, private investment properly includes all acquisitions of assets that contribute future returns. An automobile purchased by a household contributes to transportation services as does an automobile the household rents from Hertz. Our lagged deficit variable shows a highly significant positive relationship with investment in consumer durables, which is excluded from the official measures of investment. Each additional dollar of deficit was associated with an additional 30 cents of consumer durables expenditures in the following year.

The relation between our deficit variable and private tangible investment (excluding investment in land and household investment in semidurables and inventories, however) is substantially and significantly positive, with a coefficient of +1.335 for the lagged deficit variable in the regression of domestic capital tangible investment. Although the adjusted structural budget deficit does appear to relate negatively to net foreign investment, there is certainly no evidence that it reduces even the narrow BEA total of gross private investment, domestic and foreign, let alone a broader total that would include household investment in consumer durables. Here, the coefficient for the deficit variable is a highly significant +.785.

Of course, the price-adjusted high employment deficit does not fully, or perhaps even accurately, define the exogenous fiscal parameters affecting investment, let alone all of the parameters, including specifically those relating to monetary policy. As in previous work, therefore, we have introduced as a regressor the real change in the monetary base—defined here as the mean monetary base in the month of December as reported by the Federal Reserve Board of Governors, deflated by the fourth-quarter GNP implicit price deflator. This variable was taken as a percentage of GNP, but a consistent series was available only from 1960 on, thus reducing our sample period, because of the lags introduced, to one beginning in 1962.

The results of regressions including this monetary variable, shown in table 3–6, point to a strong and significant positive role for increases in the monetary base in affecting domestic investment and a negative role in net foreign investment, as might have been expected. Easier money, as it stimulates the economy, will again encourage imports. If it also brings about a lowering of the exchange rate, moreover, it will have a further effect of encouraging exports and discouraging imports.[4] The signs of coefficients of the deficit variable remain as before, but the magnitude and significance of the coefficients in the case of gross private investment and the BEA's gross investment are reduced. Apparently, some of the presumed impact of inflation in reducing the real deficit was captured by its effect in reducing the real increase in the monetary base. Nevertheless, its coefficient in the gross investment equation, though not manifesting a high level of statistical significance, suggested that the lagged, appropriately adjusted deficit increased, rather than decreased, the conventional measure of investment and saving.

We still see, however, a significant, positive role for the deficit variable with regard to investment in consumer durables and private domestic tangible investment as a whole. Each percentage point of the deficit–GNP ratio was associated with 1.2 percentage points *more* of the latter and .682 percentage point more even of total private tangible investment, including the negative component of net foreign investment.

Getting further away from the narrow BEA, NIPA measure of private investment, however, to include tangible public investment sharpens the picture considerably. Whatever its effect on private investment, one should expect an immediate impact of reductions in budget deficits on government expenditures, whereas increase in deficits should be associated with greater expenditures. One should further expect that at least some of this impact on government expenditures should be felt in public investment. That effect is precisely what is shown in table 3–7.

The impact of the federal deficit on federal investment is, not surprisingly, the clearest and most substantial. Most of the impact is in the same year; the regression coefficient indicates that each additional dollar of deficit was associated with an additional 12.1 cents of federal tangible investment expenditures in that year and another 4.6 cents the following year, a total then of 16.7 cents over the two years. The impact on state and local government investment, perhaps directly or indirectly through grants-in-aid or contributions to jointly financed programs, was considerably less, but still positive, coming to 6.3 cents over the two years.

Introducing the monetary variable, as shown in table 3–8, sharpens the relation considerably. We now see that the sum of the coefficients of

Table 3–6. Adjusted Deficit, Change in Monetary Base, Real Exchange Rate, and Private Tangible Investment ($I_{j,t} = b_0 + b_1 PAHED6_{t-1} + b_2 DMB_{t-1}\ ERR_{t-2}$)

	Regression Coefficients[1]						
I_j	b_0	$PAHED6_{t-1}$ b_1	DMB_{t-1} b_2	ERR_{t-2} b_3	R^2	$D-W$	ρ
Gross private domestic	20.846 (3.738)	0.507 (0.373)	5.578 (2.270)	−0.045 (0.039)	0.364	1.83	0.489 (0.213)
Net foreign	2.028 (2.044)	−0.267 (0.111)	−0.322 (0.642)	−0.032 (0.013)	0.897	2.26	0.931 (0.089)
Gross	22.730 (3.941)	0.485 (0.341)	5.132 (1.935)	−0.074 (0.038)	0.603	2.02	0.847 (0.129)
Consumer durables	13.026 (11.129)	0.282 (0.085)	1.157 (0.496)	−0.009 (0.001)	0.936	1.51	0.971 (0.061)
Private domestic tangible	30.320 (4.326)	1.119 (0.389)	5.759 (2.592)	−0.062 (0.045)	0.603	1.67	0.535 (0.190)
Private tangible	32.665 (4.229)	0.682 (0.395)	6.321 (2.350)	−0.087 (0.044)	0.460	1.76	0.646 (0.183)

[1] Ordinary least squares with a first-order correction for serial correlation. Standard errors are shown in parentheses. Sample period is 1962–1990; there are 29 observations.

Variable definitions:

PAHED6 = price-adjusted 6 percent high-employment dificit as percent of GNP.

DMB = change in the real monetary base as a percent of GNP (December figures divided by 4th quarter GNP implicit price deflator).

ERR = trade weighted real exchange rate (1972–100).

I_j = real investment of type j—GPDI, NFI, gross, and consumer durables, from the BEA, taken as a percent of potential GNP. Private domestic tangible is the sum of gross private domestic investment and consumer durables. Private tangible is the sum of gross investment and consumer durables

Table 3–7. Adjusted Deficit and Public Investment ($I_{k,t} = b_0 + b_1\text{PAHED6}_t + b_2\text{PAHED6}_{t-1}$)

	Regression Coefficients[1]							
I_k	b_0	$PAHED6_t$ b_1	$PAHED6_{t-1}$ b_2	$\Sigma PAHED6$ $b_1 + b_2$	R^2	$D-W$	ρ	n
Federal tangible	1.829 (0.372)	0.121 (0.037)	0.046 (0.036)	0.167 (0.051)	0.938	1.14	0.891 (0.031)	34
S&L tangible	0.148 (3.609)	0.025 (0.030)	0.038 (0.030)	0.063 (0.042)	0.904	1.14	0.981 (0.040)	34
Total government tangible	3.591 (1.256)	0.140 (0.058)	0.080 (0.057)	0.220 (0.081)	0.943	1.12	0.938 (0.038)	34
Education & training[2]	0.036 (0.057)	0.041 (0.014)	−0.003 (0.014)	0.038 (0.022)	0.516	1.93	0.729 (0.129)	32
Government R&D[2]	−0.016 (0.025)	0.001 (0.009)	0.013 (0.009)	0.014 (0.015)	0.464	2.19	0.592 (0.122)	32
Total government	8.258 (6.335)	0.183 (0.066)	0.102 (0.065)	0.285 (0.093)	0.934	1.08	0.977 (0.043)	33

[1] Ordinary least squares with a first-order correction for serial correlation. Standard errors are shown in parentheses. Sample period is 1957–1990 for federal tangible, S&L tangible, and total government tangible. Sample period is 1957–1989 for education and training, government R&D, and total government.

[2] Estimated as first differences.

Variable definitions:

PAHED6 = price-adjusted 6 percent high-employment dificit as percent of GNP.

I_k = real investment of type k – federal tangible, S & L tangible, education & training, government R&D, and total government – generally from the BEA, taken as percentage of potential GNP.

Table 3–8. Adjusted Deficit, Change in Monetary Base, and Public Investment ($I_{k,t} = b_0 + b_1\text{PAHED6}_t + b_2\text{PAHED6}_{t-1} + b_3\text{DMB} + b_4\text{DMB}_{t-1}$

	Regression Coefficients[1]										
I_k	b_0	$PAHED6_t$ b_1	$PAHED6_{t-1}$ b_2	DMB_t b_3	DMB_{t-1} b_4	$\Sigma PAHED6$ $b_1 + b_2$	ΣDMB $b_3 + b_4$	R^2	$D-W$	ρ	n
Federal tangible	1.836 (0.333)	0.121 (0.049)	0.079 (0.054)	−0.346 (0.333)	−0.119 (0.329)	0.200 (0.080)	−0.465 (0.572)	0.845	1.42	0.873 (0.059)	29
S&L tangible	0.857 (3.279)	0.036 (0.038)	0.099 (0.043)	−0.436 (0.263)	−0.418 (0.260)	0.135 (0.064)	−0.854 (0.452)	0.948	1.20	0.974 (0.040)	29
Total government tangible	3.581 (1.136)	0.152 (0.074)	0.173 (0.083)	−0.780 (0.512)	−0.541 (0.505)	0.325 (0.124)	−1.321 (0.879)	0.929	1.25	0.928 (0.046)	29
Education & training[2]	0.008 (0.082)	0.033 (0.016)	−0.004 (0.017)	0.007 (0.110)	0.027 (0.105)	0.029 (0.029)	0.034 (0.197)	0.596	1.63	0.810 (0.127)	27
Government R&D[2]	−0.018 (0.032)	−0.001 (0.011)	0.002 (0.012)	0.112 (0.076)	0.093 (0.073)	0.001 (0.020)	0.205 (0.136)	0.557	2.04	0.680 (0.162)	27
Total government	7.931 (5.084)	0.204 (0.088)	0.190 (0.097)	−0.906 (0.629)	−0.388 (0.587)	0.394 (0.148)	−1.294 (1.041)	0.936	1.16	0.968 (0.045)	28

[1] Ordinary least squares with a first-order correction for serial correlation. Standard errors are shown in parentheses. Sample period is 1962–1990 for federal tangible, S&L tangible, and total government. Sample period is 1962–1989 for education and training and government R&D.

[2] Estimated as first differences.

Variable definitions:

PAHED6 = price-adjusted 6 percent high-employment dificit as percent of GNP.

DMB = change in the real monetary base as a percent of GNP. (December figures divided by 4th quarter GNP implicit price deflator)

I_k = real investment of type k taken as percentage of potential GNP. See appendix for data sources.

the current and lagged deficit variable is +.200 for federal tangible investment and +.135 for state and local tangible investment. For government as a whole, therefore, the coefficients suggest that each additional dollar of deficit was associated with an *additional* 32.5 cents of tangible investment. If we include government intangible investment in education and training and in R&D, the total impact of each additional dollar of deficit would appear to be an additional 39.4 cents in investment.

We are led finally to table 3–9, in which we present regression results for all domestic tangible investment and for total tangible investment, including net foreign investment, both as measured and adjusted. First, the simple regression of total domestic tangible investment on the lagged, price-adjusted 6 percent unemployment budget deficit yields a highly significant positive coefficient of 1.325 over the years 1957 to 1990. Introducing the lagged change in the monetary base brings a significant positive coefficient for that variable as well, while still leaving a highly significant, though reduced, positive coefficient of .971 for the deficit.

Considering the role of the current deficit blurs matters some, however. Although a larger adjusted deficit is associated with more current public investment, it is also associated with less private investment. Notice, however, that the coefficient of the current deficit will be biased downward if policy makers follow a countercyclical fiscal policy. The sign of the current change in the monetary base is also negative, suggesting that a coefficient bias due to stabilization policy exists. The sum of coefficients of the current and lagged deficit variables is still a substantially positive .748 but has a large standard error of .546.

Turning to total tangible investment, despite the negative relation with the net foreign investment component included in the total, the coefficient of the lagged deficit variable remains significantly positive when standing alone in the regression. Introducing the monetary base variable, however, again reduces the coefficient of the deficit variable. With both current and lagged deficits in the regression, we find the sum of the coefficients further reduced, but still positive, although not significantly so.

One last adjustment may be undertaken, to correct net foreign investment for the official measure's exclusion of much of the changes in dollar market value of international assets, particularly direct investment (see Eisner and Pieper, 1990). We now see a significant positive coefficient of 1.211 for the lagged deficit variable and still a substantial positive coefficient of .935 in a regression including both the lagged change in the monetary base and the real exchange rate lagged two years.

We have also regressed measures of net national saving, working from changes in stocks of durable goods – in business, households, and government – thus in effect subtracting out capital consumption allowances. We

Table 3–9. Adjusted Deficit, Change in Monetary Base, Real Exchange Rate, and Domestic and Total Tangible Investment ($I_{k,t} = b_0 + b_1 PAHED6_t + b_2 PAHED6_{t-1} + b_3 DMB_t + b_4 DMB_{t-1} + b_5 ERR_{t-2}$)

	Regression Coefficients[1]											
I_k	b_0	$PAHED6_t$ b_1	$PAHED6_{t-1}$ b_2	DMB_t b_3	DMB_{t-1} b_4	ERR_{t-2} b_5	$\Sigma PAHED6$ b_1+b_2	ΣDMB b_3+b_4	R^2	$D-W$	ρ	n
Total domestic tangible	29.092 (0.639)		1.325 (0.321)						.584	1.55	0.562 (0.153)	34
Total domestic tangible	29.031 (0.756)		0.971 (0.388)		5.261 (2.459)				.627	1.58	0.605 (0.187)	29
Total domestic tangible	29.519 (0.736)	−0.481 (0.364)	1.229 (0.395)	−1.803 (2.613)	4.493 (2.571)		0.748 (0.546)	2.690 (4.355)	.656	1.51	0.581 (0.184)	29
Total tangible	28.934 (1.012)		0.871 (0.344)						.468	1.62	0.706 (0.131)	34
Total tangible	28.881 (1.321)		0.601 (0.387)		5.135 (2.283)				.572	1.61	0.783 (0.139)	29
Total tangible	29.580 (1.141)	−0.525 (0.364)	0.795 (0.394)	−2.078 (2.476)	4.244 (2.432)		0.270 (0.562)	2.167 (3.855)	.624	1.54	0.758 (0.150)	29
Total adjusted tangible	27.999 (1.582)		1.211 (0.602)						.508	1.51	0.676 (0.214)	18
Total adjusted tangible	34.865 (6.030)		0.935 (0.639)		9.511 (4.003)	−0.077 (0.061)			.605	1.77	0.718 (0.201)	18

[1] Ordinary least squares with a first-order correction for serial correlation. Standard errors are shown in parentheses. Sample period is 1957–1990 for total tangible. Sample period is 1957–1989 for private tangible plus total government.

[2] Estimated as first differences.

Variable definitions:

PAHED6 = price-adjusted 6 percent high-employment dificit, as estimated by the BEA for the years 1970–1990 and extrapolated backward by the Holloway method on the basis of the BEA middle expansion trend deficit for the earlier years, as percent of GNP.

DMB = change in the real monetary base as a percent of GNP (December figures divided by 4th quarter GNP implicit price deflator).

ERR = Trade weighted real exchange rate (value of the dollar, March 1973 = 100).

I_k = real investment of type k, taken as percent of potential GNP.

have some reason to question the appropriateness of measures of capital consumption and net capital stocks and do not report these results. They do not, however, differ significantly (see Eisner, 1991*b*) from those for the gross investment series that we have reported.

5. Conclusion

The ultimate concern of many, appropriately, is the total of national saving. A major, probably *the* major, argument against budget deficits is that they have depressed national saving, by crowding out private domestic investment and by turning net foreign investment negative, thus increasing our debt to the rest of the world. They have thus, it is argued, put an undue burden on the future. A full response to that contention would take us beyond the scope of this chapter to the critical issues of investment in human and intangible capital.[5] What may most be jeopardizing the lives of those living in the future, as we have suggested, are the developing inadequacies of millions of a generation growing up semiliterate, the inferior education of millions more of our more advantaged students compared to their counterparts in other advanced and advancing nations, our slippage in basic research and investment in advanced technology, and our inability to eliminate the scourges of crime and drugs.

None of our empirical results should be taken as definitive. Estimation of this kind is treacherous. Unrecognized spurious correlations or transient peculiarities of data may well mislead. But our results should give pause to those who see in recent budget deficits, certainly as they are usually measured, harbingers of doom, as the national saving that they view as inadequate is all the more depressed. Our results should give all the more pause because they are particularly consistent with the body of macroeconomic theory that recognizes our economy as it is, one subject to recurrent if not persistent departures from full employment and potential output. In such an economy, real structural budget deficits may be expected to have precisely the outcomes indicated in this chapter.

By increasing aggregate demand, these deficits raise employment and output. With or without the further impact of increases in exchange rates, they thus contribute to greater imports and a trade deficit and hence less foreign investment, thus depressing national saving. With room for increases in national income and output (or, conversely, the reality of declines where real, structural deficits are reduced), budget deficits may, and apparently do, contribute more to national saving by stimulating domestic private investment. They do so all the more if we go beyond the narrow BEA measure of private investment and include household investment in consumer durables. And the effect is magnified still more when we add public investment, as federal deficits seem clearly related to contemporaneous federal tangible investment.

For those concerned with the rate of national saving the lesson would seem to be: Either work to *in*crease real, structural deficits, particularly for worthwhile public investment, or look elsewhere for solutions to our saving problems.

Acknowledgments

Maurice Ewing, Oliver Haberstroh, Satish Reddy, Craig Safir, and Marc Sokol have been of invaluable research assistance. The authors are indebted to the National Science Foundation (grants SES-8707979 and SES-8913660) for financial support.

Notes

1. See Aschauer (1989) and various of the works of Edwin Mansfield, Gary Becker, and many others for arguments and findings that the productivity of tangible public infrastructure, R&D, and human capital in general are at least as high if not considerably higher than that of conventionally measured gross private domestic investment.

2. Measures of net saving have declined from their levels of the fifties and sixties. The measures of the decline and their interpretation are likely, however, to be misleading for several reasons. First, the BEA's measure of depreciation is uncertain. The BEA measures depreciation essentially as a weighted average of past investment, using weights assumed to be constant over time. Our knowledge is limited regarding actual depreciation rates for different types of capital and how these rates may change with changing economic and technological conditions and changing productivity of new investment. The last should be taken into account in any measure of net saving and investment. Second, the conventional measure of net foreign investment ignores revaluations of existing assets on the U.S. net international investment position. These revaluations are often sizable and in recent years have generally been in favor of the United States (see Eisner and Pieper, 1990). Third, net saving measures reflect the rate of growth of capital, which in turn reflects the rate of growth of output, rather than saving propensities per se. A decline in GNP growth, such as that which occurred with the post-1973 productivity slowdown, will result in an increase in the ratio of depreciation allowances to GNP and a reduction in net saving (see Pieper 1989).

3. It is arguable that the social return to domestic investment is greater than the return to foreign investment, so that even if the deficit caused an offsetting change in these two items, the net return might still be positive. In addition to providing a return to the owners of capital, greater domestic investment will raise the level of productivity and real wages of the labor force by increasing the capital–labor ratio. The comparable externality for net foreign investment will accrue to foreign labor forces. The real rate of return to foreign

investors in the United States has appeared to be quite low; we estimated it in the neighborhood of 4 percent in 1989.

4. The real exchange rate merits inclusion as an independent variable both because its value is clearly not determined entirely by the fiscal and monetary variables and because it may be expected to have its effects with some considerable lag. Unfortunately, data on its value prior to 1973 are not available. The exchange rate variable was assumed, in the regressions that included such observations, to have a value of 100 for those earlier years. The base for the underlying trade-weighted index was March 1973 = 100.

5. Measures of investment in intangible capital for the years 1946 to 1981 may be found in Eisner (1988, 1989). Their contributions to national saving are discussed further in Eisner (1991), and their relation to budget deficits is considered in Eisner (1992).

Appendix: Data Sources

1. High-Employment Surplus and High-Employment GNP

The high-employment surplus is defined for a 6.0 percent rate of unemployment. The sources for both series for the years beginning with 1970 are the issues of the *Survey of Current Business* of December 1983, May 1985, August 1989, and August 1990. For the years from 1955 to 1969, the high-employment surplus is estimated by taking the Department of Commerce "mid-expansion trend" cyclically adjusted series and using Holloway's (1989) estimation procedure to convert it to a 6 percent basis. The Holloway procedure is in fact now used by the Commerce Department to estimate the 6 percent unemployment surplus.

High-employment GNP for the years from 1970 on is taken from the already mentioned *Survey of Current Business*. For the years prior to 1970, high-employment GNP is estimated as $GNP6 = GNPME^*[1 + .02(UME - 6)]$, where GNPME is the Commerce Department of "mid-expansion trend GNP" and UME is the percentage point unemployment rate associated with mid-expansion trend GNP. (The BEA estimates that in the post-1970 period each percentage point of unemployment is associated with 1.9 percent less of cyclically adjusted output. With productivity probably greater prior to 1970, it has seemed reasonable to round the 1.9 percent up to .02 in our formulation.) The mid-expansion trend GNP, unemployment rate, and cyclically adjusted deficit are published in the December 1983 *Survey of Current Business*.

2. Price-Adjusted Surplus (and Deficit)

The price-adjusted surplus is equal to the 6 percent high-employment surplus already defined plus price effects on the federal net debt. Price effects on the federal debt are in turn estimated as

$$PE_t = [(A - 1)\ D_{t-1} + (B - 1)\ (D_t - D_{t-1})]/B,$$

where

PE = price effects
D = net federal debt at market value
$A = P^e{}_t / P^e{}_{t-1}$
$B = P^e{}_t / P_t$
P^e = end-of-year GNP deflator (taken as the mean of the fourth quarter deflator and the deflator for the first quarter of the subsequent year) and
P = annual GNP deflator.

The deficit is of course simply the negative of the surplus.

3. *Monetary Base*

The nominal monetary base is taken from the *Economic Report of the President*. The figures are averages for the month of December. The monetary variable used in the regression is defined as the change in end-of-period real stocks divided by real GNP. Algebraically, this may be written as

$$\text{MBCH}_t = 100\ [(\text{MB82}_t - \text{MB82}_{t-1})/\text{GNP82}_{t-1}],$$

where MB82 is the real monetary base and GNP82 is real GNP. The fourth quarter implicit GNP deflator is used to deflate the monetary base.

4. *Real Exchange Rate*

The real exchange rate is a trade-weighted index of ten major trading partners of the United States. The series is constructed by the Federal Reserve Board and published in the *Economic Report of the President*. The index is available for 1973 onward. The index is assumed to be constant prior to 1973.

5. *Investment Measures*

NIPA refers to the *National Income and Product Accounts of the United States*. The number of following the NIPA designation refers to the table and line number.

Consumer Durables	NIPA 1.2.3
Gross Private Domestic	NIPA 1.2.6
Net Foreign Investment	NIPA 4.1.22 deflated by GNP implicit price deflator
Net Foreign, Adjusted	Net foreign investment (NIPA 4.1.22) plus difference between changes in adjusted international investment position of the United States at market value and changes in official international investment position, from Eisner and Pieper (1990), columns 7 and 2 of table 3–8, deflated by the GNP implicit price deflator
Federal Tangible	NIPA 3.8.4 + 3.8.11 + 3.8.13 + 3.8.30
State & Local Tangible	NIPA 3.8.22 + 3.8.27.
Research & Development	NSF'(1987), appendix table B.5, and for later years, *U.S. Statistical Abstract*, deflated by GNP implicit price deflator.
Education	
Federal	NIPA 3.15.20 + 3.15.48 + 3.15.78, deflated by deflator for nondefense government purchases constructed by dividing nominal by constant dollar purchases reported in NIPA 3.7 and 3.8
State and Local	NIPA 3.16.9 + 3.16.40 − 5.5.47, deflated as for federal
Private	NIPA 2.5.85

References

Aschauer, David. "Is Public Expenditure Productive?" *Journal of Monetary Economics* (March 1989): 177–200.

Eisner, Robert. *How Real Is the Federal Deficit?* New York: The Free Press, 1986.

———. "Extended Measures of National Income and Product." *Journal of Economic Literature* (December 1988) 26: 1611–1684.

———. *The Total Incomes System of Accounts*. Chicago: University of Chicago Press, 1989.

———. "The Real Rate of U.S. National Saving." *Review of Income and Wealth*, Series 37, no. 1 (March 1991): 13–32.

———. "U.S. National Saving and Budget Deficits." For *The Political Economy of Investment, Saving and Finance: A Global Perspective*, Gerald Epstein and

Herbert Gintis, eds., A Project of the World Institute for Development and Economic Research (WIDER), The United Nations University, Helsinki, Finland, manuscript copy, 6/20/92.

Eisner, Robert and Pieper, Paul J. "A New View of the Federal Debt and Budget Deficits." *American Economic Review* 74 (March 1984): 11–29.

———. "Deficits, Monetary Policy and Real Economic Activity." In Kenneth J. Arrow and Michael J. Boskin, eds., *The Economics of Public Debt*.Macmillan Press in association with the International Economic Association, 1988, London, pp. 3–40.

———. "'The World's Greatest Debtor Nation'?" *The Review of Economics and Finance* 1 (1) (1990): pp. 9–32.

Holloway, Thomas M. "Measuring the Cyclical Sensitivity of Federal Receipts and Expenditures: Simplified Estimation Procedures." *International Journal of Forecasting* 5 (1989): 347–360.

Lange, Oscar. "The Rate of Interest and the Optimal Propensity to Consume." *Economica* (New Series) 5 (February 1938): 12–32. Reprinted in American Economic Association, *Readings in Business Cycle Theory*. Philadelphia: Blakiston, 1944, pp. 169–192.

Pieper, Paul. "Why Net Investment Has Fallen." Paper presented at Western Economic Association meeting, June 1989.

[23]

US national saving and budget deficits

Robert Eisner

It has been widely argued that the decline of "national saving" in the United States in the 1980s was brought on by large federal budget deficits.[1] This is frequently taken as a matter of a simple accounting identity. Gross saving is the sum of private saving and public saving, the latter defined as the government budget surplus. The greater the federal deficit, it is then assumed, the greater is public dis-saving and hence the less is the arithmetic sum of private and public saving. Since national saving is merely gross saving minus capital consumption allowances, it too must then be less.

To take this accounting identity as evidence that reducing the federal deficit must raise national saving should be recognized, on even the slightest reflection, as patently absurd. It is startlingly akin to the assumption, more than half a century ago, that saving and investment would be increased if we all undertook to save more by consuming less. Perhaps! But that is exactly the proposition to be proved, or supported by empirical evidence, not assumed.[2]

The difficulty, going back to the national income accounts, is that while the saving–investment identity must hold by definition, it does not follow that changing one component of saving must change major components of investment or the total of saving–investment by the same amount or even in the same direction, as Gordon has pointed out in the preceding chapter of this volume, unless we short circuit the entire argument by assuming all other things constant. Thus, gross saving is the sum of undistributed corporate profits, capital consumption allowances, personal saving, and the total government – federal, state, and local – surplus. These (plus the statistical discrepancy) are in turn equal to the sum of gross private domestic investment and net foreign investment. Can we properly assume that raising one component of public saving by reducing the federal deficit, by raising taxes or cutting expenditures, will leave these other components unchanged? Will it increase total investment? If it does not, of course, it cannot raise total saving. The issue is complementary to that raised by Gordon in the preceding chapter regarding the relations between personal and private saving and investment.

At the most obvious level, will not reducing federal grants in aid to states and localities, currently running at some $150 billion per year, in the first instance cause an equal decrease in state and local surpluses?[3] Will not increasing taxes in the first instance reduce both undistributed profits and disposable income, in the latter case, further reducing personal saving? And if, as most prevalent theory and empirical evidence suggest, consumption is reduced, may not the resultant sluggishness of demand and sales bring about reductions in business investment as well as residential housing construction, thus further reducing income and saving?

It is of course possible that slack capacity may reduce supply prices of investment goods and that a lower demand for money for transactions purposes, perhaps along with policy-induced increases in money supply, may combine to reduce the cost of capital enough to bring about an increase in investment. In principle, this would be more likely to occur if the economy were at or near full employment and full utilization of capacity, with enough pent-up demand to prevent fiscal tightening from bringing on a general slowdown. But again such results do not necessarily come automatically – except for those dogmatically committed to faith in perpetually and instantaneously clearing markets – and are not to be assumed.

We shall here examine relations involving national saving, federal budget deficits, and changes in the money supply in the United States, along with real exchange rates, to see what has actually occurred. While we shall not ignore the traditional or conventional, "official" measure of national saving, we shall consider, as well, broader measures of saving, encompassing government and household investment in all forms of tangible capital and investment in intangible capital, and measures of net foreign investment adjusted for changes in the market values of US and foreign assets.[4]

1 Issues and concepts

Is the United States rate of national saving too low? Do US budget deficits reduce national saving and hence, like termites, eat away at the foundations of future well being? The answers are, you cannot tell unless you measure right. And if saving is too low, you cannot tell what to do about it unless you know what you are talking about.

The conventional measure of "gross saving," as reported by the United States Bureau of Economic Analysis, is identically equal to the sum of gross private domestic investment and net foreign investment, minus the statistical discrepancy. On the saving side of the account, as we have indicated, it is the sum of personal saving, corporate saving (undistributed corporate profits), private capital consumption allowances, and the government budget surplus (Federal and state and local, combined).[5] The "national saving" of common parlance is then *net* saving, calculated by subtracting capital consumption allowances, as shown in table 4.1. This measure is deficient or misleading on several major counts.

First, personal saving is defined as personal income minus personal taxes (and non-tax payments), personal consumption expenditures, interest paid by consumers to business, and personal transfer payments to foreigners. The problem here is that "personal consumption expenditures" include vast amounts for consumer durables and semi-durables, which in meaningful terms would properly be counted as investment, and hence as saving.

Second, unlike in the United Nations System of National Accounts followed in much of the world, none of US government expenditures for goods and services is included in investment, which, as designated, comprises only *private* investment. Correspondingly, all government expenditures for goods and services are subtracted from government revenues in arriving at the budget surplus, which is the conventional definition of government saving.

Third, the net foreign investment figure, highly negative in recent years, reflects changes in the US net international investment position where a major component, direct investment, is measured at original cost rather than current value. Appropriate corrections, indicated by Eisner and Pieper (1990), Dewald and Ulan (1989), and now, for the US Bureau of Economic Analysis, Landefeld and Lawson (1991), very substantially reduce or eliminate the negative US position. These corrections imply a considerable increase, in recent years, in appropriate measures of net foreign investment and hence of national saving.

Fourth, while the net foreign investment measure is a particularly significant example, in general, measures of both income and saving and investment exclude the value of real capital gains and losses, so that net saving will correspond only by chance to economically relevant changes in wealth. Further, increased realization of capital gains will increase taxable income but not the conventional income of the national income accounts. By increasing income taxes, greater realized capital gains will, by conventional measures, reduce private saving while increasing public saving. Increased capital gains in themselves, aside from tax consequences, are likely to reduce the conventional measure of national saving if they raise consumption more than they raise measured income. If

Table 4.1. *Net saving and investment account, 1992* (billions of dollars)*

Gross private domestic investment	770.9	Personal income	5,056.8
		Less: Personal tax and nontax payments	627.2
Less: Consumption of fixed capital	653.5	Less: Personal outlays	4,216.1
		Personal consumption expenditures	4,093.9
Net private domestic investment	117.3	Interest paid by consumers to business	112.0
Net foreign investment	– 47.1		
		Personal transfer payments to foreigners	10.2
		Personal saving	213.5
		Undistributed corporate profits with inventory valuation and capital consumption adjustment	107.2
		Government surplus or deficit (–), national income and product accounts	– 281.0
		Federal	– 295.3
		State and local	14.2
		Net saving	39.7
		Statistical discrepancy	30.5
Net investment	70.2	Net saving and statistical discrepancy	70.2

Source: * Adapted from *Survey of Current Business*, April 1993, tables 1.1, 1.9, 2.1, and 5.1, pp. 8, 10, 12, and 15.

they are accompanied by more measured investment included in national income, national saving will rise.

Fifth, and of overwhelming importance for critical questions of growth for which saving matters, conventional measures exclude all saving and investment in intangible and human capital. Such saving and investment far exceed in magnitude, and very likely in importance, the private saving in tangible capital that gets so much attention.

And sixth, a major factor in the presumed decline of the widely regarded measure of *net* national saving has been the very large relative, as well as absolute, increase in depreciation or capital consumption allowances. As shown by Pieper (1989), however, this may as well be viewed as a consequence rather than a cause of declining real growth. As growth of output approaches zero, unless the capital–output ratio increases, the net saving and investment rates must also approach zero. At any point in time, the ratio of depreciation to fixed investment, and hence of net saving to gross investment and saving, may depend much more on the rate of past investment than the propensity to save.

The differences between real net national saving and the conventional measure of national saving, about which there has been so much hand wringing, are large. These differences have substantial import for international and intertemporal comparisons. With proper focus on a full, relevant measure we may still find reason for concern. The causes, however, will prove different. And so will reasonable remedies.

Take investment in transportation, as one salient example. In an earlier century in the United States, this involved in considerable part private investment in railroads. Through much of this century it has entailed huge amounts of government investment in roads and airports and private investment in automobiles. The former is financed by taxes and the latter is counted as consumption. Neither shows up as part of "saving." Is it proper then to judge our saving reduced to the extent the reduction is due to this shift from business to non-business investment?

Similar issues arise in international comparisons. France and more recently Germany have undertaken and are undertaking large amounts of investment in high-speed trains. This swells OECD figures for their total saving and capital formation. But US figures include all government investment as "government consumption." US investment in new airports and runways (however inadequate) is generally a government project and not counted in "investment." With comparable inclusion of all public and private investment, the widely commented on excess of Japanese over US saving[6] would be reduced. But then, if capital formation in education took into account hours spent in school and study and were, properly, to include the opportunity cost of students' time, Japanese

Table 4.2. *Saving measures and components, mean percents of GNP, 1971–81 and 1982–90*

Series	1971–81	1982–90	Difference
(Current dollars)			
GSD	16.82	13.29	– 3.53
CCAD	9.94	11.01	+ 1.07
NS0D	6.87	2.28	– 4.59
GPDID	16.58	15.26	– 1.32
NPDID	6.64	4.25	– 2.39
INVRAD	9.11	7.60	– 1.51
NFIDMISD	0.24	– 1.97	– 2.21
NS1D	9.35	5.62	– 3.73
INVLAND	4.11	0.35	– 3.76
NS7D	13.46	5.97	– 7.49
NFICORD	– 0.01	0.71*	+ 0.72
NS3D	13.45	7.30*	– 6.15
INVINTAD	17.02		
INVSDID	0.25		
NRD	6.57		
NRMLND	3.01		
(1982 dollars)			
GS	17.38	14.92	– 2.46
CCA	10.39	12.02	+ 1.63
NS0	6.98	2.90	– 4.08
GPDI	17.14	16.89	– 0.25
NPDI	6.75	4.87	– 1.88
INVRA	8.93	7.81	– 1.12
NFIMS82	0.24	– 1.97	– 2.21
NS1	9.17	5.84	– 3.33
INVLAN	4.11	0.35	– 3.76
NS7	13.28	6.19	– 7.09
NFICOR	– 0.01	0.71*	+ 0.72
NS3	13.27	7.50*	– 5.77
INVINTA	16.72		
INVSDI	0.27		
NR82	6.39		
NRMLN82	2.94		

Note: * 1982–89.

investment in this vital form of human capital might be seen to dwarf that of the United States.

2 Measures

The decline in conventional US national saving over the last two decades may be viewed in the movements of its components. In table 4.2, I present comparisons, for the years from 1971 to 1981 and 1982 to 1990, in current and 1982 dollars, of the major elements of conventional US "national saving" (NS0 and NS0D) and of suggested alternate measures (see definitions below), all as percents of GNP.[7,8]

We may note first that the conventional measure of national saving fell from 6.87 percent in the period 1971–81 to 2.28 percent in years 1982–90, a drop of 4.59 percentage points. This represented a drop of 3.53 percentage points in the *gross* saving rate, which was coupled with a rise of 1.07 percentage points in the rate of capital consumption. Gross saving, it may be remembered though, is identically equal to gross private domestic investment plus net foreign investment minus the statistical discrepancy. The total of these last two (NFIDMISD) fell by 2.21 percentage points, which means that gross saving available to the US to finance gross private domestic investment (GSD − NFIDMISD = GPDID) declined by only 1.32 percentage points. Gross private domestic investment in 1982 dollars as a percent of GNP, GPDI, it should be noted, was virtually unchanged, declining by only 0.25 percentage points. Real net private domestic investment as a percent of GNP, NPDI, declined by 1.88 percentage points, however, the decline reflecting almost entirely the increase in capital consumption allowances.

Net foreign investment, we have pointed out though, should correspond to changes in the market values of assets, net of liabilities, of the home country in the rest of the world and of assets, net of liabilities, of the rest of the world in the home country. Applying a net foreign investment correction (NFICORD), to make net foreign investment consistent with such changes in market values, does not make a substantial difference in the conventional measures, NFI or NS0, over the entire periods of comparison. There was, however, a substantial swing in that correction from 1981–4 to 1985–9, of 2.38 percentage points, from − 1.13 percent of GNP to + 1.25 percent, as shown in table 4.3. This suggests corresponding corrections over those years in the private, business, and government components of gross saving, the proportions depending on which sector held the assets whose market values moved differently from evaluations used in the official accounts.

A move to a comprehensive measure of saving entails relating it to a

Table 4.3. *Net foreign investment corrections*

	Percents of GNP		
	1981–4	1985–9	Change, 1981–4 to 1985–9
Net foreign investment (NFID)	− 0.77	− 2.76	− 1.99
Net foreign investment correction (NFICORD)	− 1.13	+ 1.25	2.38
Adjusted net foreign investment (NFIADJD)	− 1.90	− 1.51	0.39

comprehensive measure of investment. This is effected by taking the change in the BEA's "constant-cost net stock of fixed reproducible tangible wealth,"[9] which includes government and household fixed capital as well as that of business and non-profit institutions, multiplying it by a price deflator calculated as the ratio of current cost to constant cost net stocks, and adding the change in business inventories. The totals as percents of GNP, denoted INVRAD for investment in reproducible assets in current dollars, and the corresponding constant dollar series, INVRA, are shown in table 4.2. We then add NFIDMISD, net foreign investment minus the statistical discrepancy (NFIMSD82 in the constant dollar series) to obtain measures of national saving which include government and household net investment. These, however, are still exclusive of government and household investment in semi-durables and inventories and of all investment in land.

Substantial growth in stocks of consumer durables kept down the decline in investment in reproducible assets. From 1971–81 to 1982–90, the fall in the mean value of INVRAD was only 1.51 percentage points as compared to 2.39 percentage points for NPDID (the current United States Bureau of Economic Analysis measure of net private domestic investment, as a percent of GNP), from 9.11 percent of GNP to 7.60 percent, and only 1.12 percentage points for INVRA, in 1982 dollars. The drop in the corresponding measure of national saving, NS1D, with the inclusion of net foreign investment, was again considerable however, coming to 3.73 percentage points; the drop was 3.33 percentage points for NS1, in 1982 dollars.

We may secure a still further expanded measure of saving, NS7D or NS7 in 1982 dollars, by adding increases in the real value of land. These are calculated from the "Balance Sheets for the US Economy" prepared by the Federal Reserve's Flow of Funds division. We take the year-end values of land at market prices and deflate by year-end GNP price deflators (the average of fourth-quarter and subsequent first-quarter figures) and consider the differences in these deflated values as real saving in land. We then multiply these differences by the corresponding annual GNP implicit price deflators to get the current dollar values of saving in the form of increases in the value of land, INVLAND (INVLAN in the constant dollar series), over and above that accountable to general inflation.[10]

The saving measure, NS3D (NS3 in the constant dollar series) adds the net foreign investment correction, NFICORD (or NFICOR in constant dollars). NS3D (and NS3) are thus equal to NS7D (and NS7), including investment in land, plus the net foreign investment correction.

Our measure of investment in land (INVLAND), which may suffer from infirmities in the underlying data, indicate a sharp fall, from 4.11 percent of GNP in 1971–81 to 0.35 percent in 1982–90. This in turn brings down the current dollar measures, NS7D and NS3D, by 7.49 and 6.15 percentage points, from 13.46 percent to 5.97 percent and from 13.45 percent to 7.30 percent, respectively.

By far greatest in amount and possibly, we may suggest, in current significance at the margin, is investment in intangible capital. We fall back here on my TISA ("Total Incomes System of Accounts") estimates.[11] These were built up in some detail in current and 1972 dollars for various components of investment in education and training, research and health.[12] Constant dollar totals used in this chapter were crudely converted to 1982 dollars by dividing by the GNP 1982 dollar implicit price deflator for 1972.

The ratio of net investment in intangible capital to GNP in current dolars (INVINTAD) averaged 17.02 percent over the years 1971 to 1981. (TISA estimates, beginning in 1945 and 1946, extend only to 1981.) This may be compared to the conventional saving ratio, NS0D, of 6.87 percent for that period, the ratio of 9.35 percent for NS1D, which includes investment in all reproducible fixed capital, and the ratio of 13.45 percent for NS3D, which also includes investment in land.

We add net investment in intangible capital and the relatively small amounts of net investment by government and households in inventories and semi-durables to NS1D to get a measure of saving, NS14D, including all investment in tangible reproducible capital and in intangible capital. We add investment in land to obtain the measure, NS15D. And now the ratios of saving to GNP, as seen in table 4.4, turn really large: 26.36 percent for NS14D over the 1971–81 period and 30.47 percent for NS15D, the measure including investment in land.

Table 4.4. *Comparison of mean saving ratios, 1971–81*

Current dollars		Constant dollars	
Measure	Mean (% of GNPD)	Measure	Mean (% of GNP)
NS0D	6.87	NS0	6.98
NS1D	9.35	NS1	9.17
NS7D	13.46	NS7	13.28
NS3D	13.45	NS3	13.27
NS14D	26.36	NS14	25.88
NS15D	30.47	NS15	29.98
NS16D	32.93	NS16	32.27
NS17D	33.48	NS17	32.92
NS0D/NS14D	26.06	NS0/NS14	26.97
NS0D/NS15D	22.55	NS0/NS15	23.28
NS0D/NS16D	20.86	NS0/NS16	21.63
NS0D/NS17D	20.52	NS0/NS17	21.20

Finally, we can add saving in the form of net revaluations of tangible assets, that is, capital gains over and above those accountable to inflation. These give us ratios of national saving to GNP of 32.93 percent for NS16D and 33.48 percent for NS17D, the measure including investment in land.

We may note how far we have gone by observing that the mean for the current dollar ratios for the years 1971 to 1981 of conventional national saving, NS0D, divided by the mean for our comprehensive measure including all investment in tangible and intangible capital other than net revaluations, NS15D, is only 22.55 percent. The corresponding proportion involving the measure including net revaluations, NS17D, is 20.52 percent.

Some of the findings from these old and new measures merit highlighting. First, despite all the complaint about the fall in conventional national saving in the 1980s decade of high budget deficits, that most critical component for domestic growth, the share of real gross private domestic investment in GNP, fell hardly at all. The drop in conventional national saving stemmed first rather from the rise in the capital consumption allowance ratio, which may be somewhat suspect itself and in any event would seem to be more the effect than the cause of a decline in growth. And it stemmed second from the decline in net foreign investment, also suspect at least in its failure to include changes in the market value of US direct foreign investment. With appropriate correction, net foreign investment, thanks in part to the decline in the value of the US dollar, in fact turned up in the latter part of the 1980s. In any event, the declines in net foreign investment that did occur would not appear to have the negative effects on domestic productivity associated with declines in real domestic investment, and hence would be of lesser consequence for economic growth.

We may also note again that the decline in real net private domestic investment, as reported by the BEA, is partially compensated by a rise in investment in consumer durables, so that the total decline in the ratio to GNP of net investment in reproducible assets, including household and government investment, is less. This, along with the very large amounts of investment in intangible capital that are in considerable part financed by government, should give pause to those who would think to curb or reverse presumed declines in national saving by either of the usual prescriptions for reducing budget deficits – raising taxes or cutting government expenditures.

Designations and definitions of elements of adjusted measures of national saving

First designations, ending in "D," denote current dollars; second designations refer to 1982 dollars.

GSD, GS	Gross saving from national income and product accounts
CCAD, CCA	Capital consumption allowances with adjustment, from national income and product accounts
GPDID, GPDI	Gross private domestic investment
INVRAD, INVRA	Net investment in reproducible assets, excluding investment in consumer semi-durables and government and household inventories
NFIDMISD, NFIMSD82	Net foreign investment minus statistical discrepancy, national income and product accounts
INVLAND, INVLAN	Net investment in land
NFICORD, NFICOR	Net foreign investment correction
INVINTAD, INVINTA	Net investment in intangible capital
INVSDID, INVSDI82	Net investment in consumer and government semi-durables
NRD, NR82	Net revaluations
NRMLND, NRMLN82	Net revaluations excluding land

Definitions and derivations of saving rates and other variables

NS0	Conventional net national saving = gross saving − capital consumption allowances with adjustment, from national income and product accounts as of March 1991
NS1	Change in total fixed reproducible capital, from "Summary Fixed Reproducible Tangible Wealth Series, 1925–89," *Survey of Current Business*, October 1990, pp. 31–2, updated to 1990 with unpublished data furnished by John Musgrave of the Bureau of Economic Analysis, plus net foreign investment minus statistical discrepancy from national income and product accounts
NS7	Change in total fixed reproducible capital plus net foreign investment minus statistical discrepancy (NS1), plus change in real value of land from Board of Governors of the Federal Reserve System, Flow of Funds Division, *Balance Sheets for the US Economy 1945–90*, March 1991, end-of-year land values deflated by average of fourth quarter and subsequent first quarter GNP implicit price deflators
NS3	Change in total fixed reproducible capital plus adjusted net foreign investment, calculated from changes in the net international investment position of the United States adjusted to market value (Eisner and Pieper, 1990), minus statistical discrepancy, plus change in real value of land
NS14	Change in total fixed reproducible capital plus adjusted net foreign investment minus statistical discrepancy plus investment in intangible capital and in government and household inventories and semi-durables from Total Incomes System of Accounts (TISA, Eisner, 1989c)
NS15	Change in total fixed reproducible capital plus adjusted net foreign investment minus statistical discrepancy plus change in real value of land (NS3), plus investment in intangible capital and in government and household inventories and semi-durables
NS16	Change in total fixed reproducible capital plus adjusted net foreign investment minus statistical discrepancy plus investment in intangible capital and in government and household inventories and semi-durables (NS14), plus total net revaluations from TISA
NS17	Change in total fixed reproducible capital plus adjusted net foreign investment minus statistical discrepancy plus change in real value of land plus investment in intangible capital and in government and household inventories and semi-durables (NS15), plus net revaluations exclusive of net revaluations on land
DMB	Change in monetary base as percent of GNP in 1982 dollars, from *Economic Report of the President*, February 1991, December averages of monetary base deflated by GNP fourth quarter implicit price deflator
ERR	Real exchange rate index, multilateral trade-weighted value of the US dollar (March 1973 = 100), adjusted by changes in consumer prices, from *Economic Report of the President*, February 1991, p. 410

PAHED6 Price-adjusted high-employment deficit as percent of GNP, the negative of PAHES6, the price-adjusted high-employment surplus as percent of GNP, on a 6 percent unemployment basis, taken from Bureau of Economic Analysis series published in *Survey of Current Business* for the years from 1970 to 1990 and adjusted for "price effects" (changes in real value of net Federal debt due to inflation), as reported in Eisner and Pieper (1984) and Eisner (1986). The high-unemployment surplus for years prior to 1970 was calculated as indicated in the Data sources appendix below.

3 Deficits and conventional national saving

In searching for the influence of federal deficits on saving it is important to distinguish it from the common effect of cyclical movements on public and private saving. Lower GNP of course means lower national income and almost certainly lower private saving. The associated reduction of tax revenues and increase in transfer payments for unemployment increase the federal deficit and thus lower public saving. A minimum necessity in the analysis therefore is use of a cyclically adjusted measure of the deficit.

Further, conventional measures of the deficit fail to take properly into account the role of inflation. They include nominal rather than real interest expenditures and correspondingly do not count as a "tax" the reduction in the real value of government debt due to inflation. I have presented both of these corrections in earlier works[13] and offer here an extended measure of a federal "price-adjusted high-employment deficit," PAHED6.

I have noted previously that higher values of a price or inflation-adjusted, high-employment deficit, or lesser surpluses, were associated with *greater* subsequent growth in real GNP, personal consumption expenditures, and gross private domestic investment, but with lesser growth, or decline of net exports over the period 1955 to 1984.[14] These relations proved robust to the introduction of monetary variables, particularly real changes in the monetary base, which were themselves positively related to the growth of GNP, consumption, and domestic investment. The theoretical rationale for the relations, and the results, it was explained, fit well the life-cycle theory of consumption and neoclassical and accelerator theories of investment, reinforced perhaps by portfolio choice considerations. Real budget deficits imply increases in wealth as perceived by private agents in the form of government debt and thus generate increases in consumption demand, for both domestic and foreign goods. To the extent that some private agents are liquidity constrained, the flow of after-tax income corresponding to budget deficits, even apart from the wealth effect, further contributes to the private demand for goods. The initial increases in output, or even rational anticipations of increases in output, and the greater financial wealth in turn induce an increase in demand for physical capital. It may be useful to present these relations more formally.[15]

First, real consumption may be viewed as a function of real income, real capital, real financial wealth of the private sector consisting of the domestically held, interest-bearing and non-interest-bearing government debt ("outside money") and the real rate of interest.

$$C/P = C(Y/P, K, GD/P, M_x/P, r);$$
$$0 < C_1 < 1;\ C_2,\ C_3,\ C_4 > 0;\ C_5 \gtreqless 0. \quad (1)$$

Then, real investment is a function of current output, the expected path of future output, the existing stock of capital and its marginal rental cost, the last a function of the real rate of interest, and the net stock of financial capital held by the private sector.

$$I/P = I(Y(t)/P(t),\ K, c, \{GD + M_x\}/P);\ I_1, I_4 > 0;\ I_2, I_3 < 0 \quad (2)$$

where $Y(t)/P(t)$ represents some appropriately weighted average of the series of expected real future outputs, itself a function of current and past real output.

Exports, given foreign income and wealth, are a function of real exchange rates, appropriately lagged, and imports are a function of real exchange rates (measured as a trade-weighted index of the amount of foreign currencies that can be bought for a dollar) and real income and output. Thus net exports may be written

$$NE = X/P - M/P = E(ERR_{-2}, Y/P);\ E_1, E_2 < 0. \quad (3)$$

We then have the identity

$$Y/P = C/P + I/P + NE + G \quad (4)$$

where G denotes real government expenditures for goods and services.

The real interest rate and hence the rental cost of capital are determined by the condition of equality of money supply and money demand

$$M_s = M_d = P^*L(Y/P, i, \dot{P}^e);\ L_1 > 0;\ L_2, L_3 < 0 \quad (5)$$

where $\dot{P}^e$ is the expected rate of inflation (so that r, above, $= i - \dot{P}^e$).

Real net foreign investment is net exports minus net government interest payments and transfers to foreigners. The real exchange rate is then a function of the real interest rate, real net foreign investment, and the value in foreign currencies of foreign claims on US assets. This last stock is affected by both the accumulation of negative flows of net foreign investment and the changes in values of those accumulations as a result of revaluations in own currencies and changing exchange rates themselves. Briefly

$$ERR = R(r, NFI, FC); \;\; R_r, R_{NFI} > 0; \;\; R_{FC} < 0. \qquad (6)$$

On the supply side there are production functions dependent on capital and labor. These indicate marginal rates of substitution and the elasticity of investment with respect to the rental cost of capital and the effects of increasing demand on prices and inflation. Rates of inflation are more responsive to real demand as output approaches the capacity determined by factor supply and the production function. Expected inflation and nominal interest rates may adjust more or less completely, with some lag, to actual inflation.

This model is spelled out in much greater detail, with suggested plausible parameters, in Eisner and Hwang (1993). Simulations, with these parameters, suggest that greater real structural deficits increase consumption and also increase domestic investment, where output effects generally dominate substitution effects relating to the rental cost of capital. However, they decrease net foreign investment as, depending on the monetary regime, they tend to raise real interest rates and real income. Real exchange rates ultimately adjust to keep net foreign claims from growing relative to GNP. The real deficit and the real domestically held debt also stabilize as ratios of GNP. The net effect of real structural deficits on saving – the sum of gross private domestic investment and net foreign investment – is positive.

The issue at hand, however, is not what our model generates – however plausible I find it and its parameters. It is rather what the data, applied to structural or reduced-form equations that may be drawn from the model, actually show. Government budget deficits, we must acknowledge, may bring about increases in gross private domestic investment such as those we have observed and still lower the national saving rate. Net foreign investment was in fact reduced, as imports soared, with larger budget deficits and more rapidly growing GNP. Higher real exchange rates would be expected, with some lag, further to lower net exports and net foreign investment. With the ratio of capital consumption allowances presumably little if at all affected, greater deficits could then generate gross private domestic investment and still reduce the national saving rate.

In fact, as may be seen in figure 4.1, the conventional national saving rate, which we have designated NS0, along with various expanded measures of saving, moved generally downward from early in the 1970s, and was distinctly lower in the 1980s, when budget deficits were relatively high. Figure 4.2, graphing conventional national saving and the prior year's adjusted high-employment deficit, PAHED6(– 1), would seem to

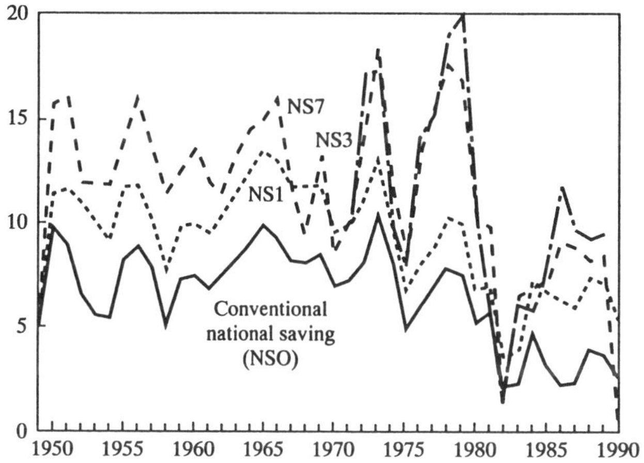

Figure 4.1 Measures of national saving (0, 1, 3, 7) as percents of GNP

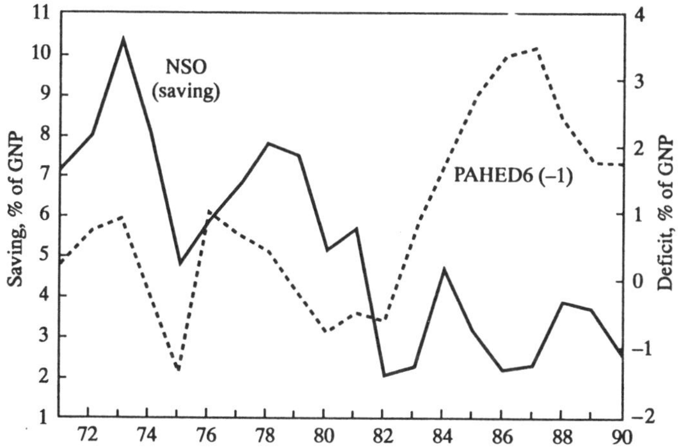

Figure 4.2 Conventional measure of national saving and lagged adjusted deficit

confirm, at least for the high-deficit 1980s, that the greater inflation-adjusted high-employment deficits were associated with less national saving. It is important, however, to look further.

Deficits add to the total debt, interest bearing and non-interest bearing, of the Federal government and consequently to the assets of the private sector (and of state and local government). As indicated above this may be expected to lead directly to more consumption and income and saving and, with accelerator and possibly portfolio effects, possibly to a higher

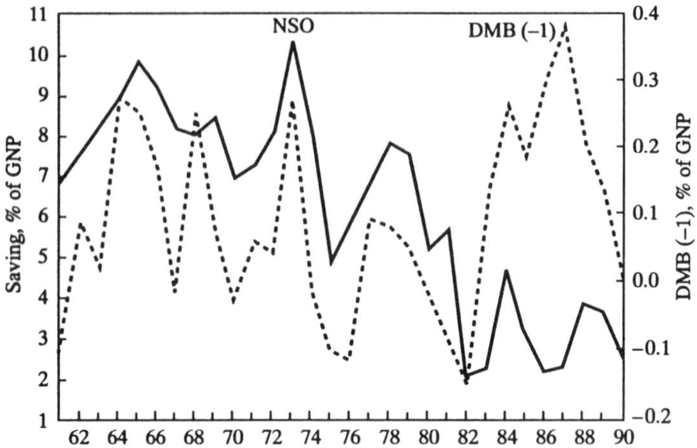

Figure 4.3 Conventional national saving, and lagged change in monetary base, DMB(− 1), as percents of GNP

proportion of income saved. To the extent the Federal Reserve buys government securities, however, part of that debt is monetized and shows up in the monetary base. It is appropriate to recognize the possible special role of monetary factors and include real changes in the monetary base, along with the deficit, in relations explaining saving. Figure 4.3 indeed offers suggestive evidence of a positive relation between real changes in the monetary base and subsequent saving. And finally, very large swings in real exchange rates over the last two decades may be expected to have substantial effects on net foreign investment and hence on national saving. They should be included in relations to be estimated.

Saving rates and deficits are both highly autocorrelated. Table 4.6 presents the results of AR(1) regressions in levels and first-difference regressions of alternative measures of national saving on the lagged inflation or price-adjusted high-employment deficit, PAHED6(− 1), real changes in the monetary base, lagged one and two years, DMB(− 1) and DMB(− 2), all expressed as percents of gross national product, and an index of the twice-lagged, trade-weighted real exchange rate, ERR(− 2), over the years 1972 to 1990. Beginning with the conventional national saving rate, NS0, we note a statistically significant coefficient of 0.887 for PAHED6(− 1). With an AR(1) coefficient (rho) of 0.984, estimates are essentially of a first-difference relation, where the coefficient of PAHED6(− 1) is 0.905; in the considerable number of other cases where the AR(1) coefficient was in the neighborhood of unity, we have reported only the first-difference regressions. Each percentage point increase in the

Table 4.6. *Adjusted budget deficits, changes in monetary base and alternate measures of real national saving, NS0, NS1, NS7, 1972–90, and NS3, 1972–89* ($NSk_t = b_0 + b_1 \text{PAHED6}_{t-1} + b_2 \text{DMB}_{t-1} + b_3 \text{DMB}_{t-2} + b_4 \text{ERR}_{t-2}$), $k = 0, 1, 7, 3$)

	Regression coefficients and standard errors						
Variable	AR(1)	First differences					
or parameter	NS0	NS0	NS1	NS7	NS7	NS3	NS3
C	− 9.501	− 0.381	− 0.395	− 0.737	− 0.699	− 0.321	− 0.321
	(135.709)	(0.253)	(0.272)	(0.756)	(0.741)	(0.942)	(0.902)
PAHED6(− 1)	0.887	0.905	1.124	2.606	2.584	2.351	2.351
	(0.368)	(0.366)	(0.393)	(1.093)	(1.074)	(1.328)	(1.279)
DMB(− 1)	8.237	8.429	9.139	16.022	15.301	9.298	9.288
	(2.178)	(2.191)	(2.354)	(6.551)	(6.356)	(8.235)	(7.778)
DMB(− 2)	5.835	6.116	7.072	3.845	—	0.039	—
	(1.849)	(1.852)	(1.989)	(5.536)		(6.818)	
ΣDMB	14.072	14.545	16.211	19.867	—	9.337	—
	(3.046)	(3.085)	(3.314)	(9.222)		(11.687)	
ERR(− 2)	− 0.135	− 0.149	− 0.146	− 0.171	− 0.152	− 0.079	− 0.078
	(0.037)	(0.041)	(0.044)	(0.122)	(0.117)	(0.148)	(0.139)
AR(1)	0.984	—	—	—	—	—	—
	(0.081)						
$\hat{R}^2$	0.808	0.618	0.657	0.446	0.465	0.195	0.253
D–W	2.728	2.826	2.837	2.226	2.044	1.625	1.624
n	19	19	19	19	19	18	18

Table 4.6 *(continued)*

Notes: * Significant at 0.05 probability level.

C	Constant term.
AR(1)	First-order autoregressive coefficient.
$\hat{R}^2$	Adjusted coefficient of determination.
D–W	Durbin–Watson coefficient.
n	Number of observations.
PAHED6(– 1)	Lagged price-adjusted, BEA 6 percent high-employment budget deficit as percent of GNP.
DMB(– 1)	Lagged real change in monetary base as percent of GNP (December figures divided by fourth quarter GNP implicit price deflator).
DMB(– 2)	Two-year lagged real change in monetary base as percent of GNP (December figures divided by fourth quarter GNP implicit price deflator).
ERR(– 2)	Trade weighted, real exchange rate, lagged two years (March 1973 = 100).
NS0	Conventional net national saving = gross saving – capital consumption allowances with adjustment.
NS1	Change in total fixed reproducible capital plus net foreign investment minus statistical discrepancy.
NS7	Change in total fixed reproducible capital plus net foreign investment minus statistical discrepancy (NS1) plus change in real value of land.
NS3	Change in total fixed reproducible capital plus adjusted net foreign investment minus statistical discrepancy plus change in real value of land.

deficit (as a ratio of GNP) was thus associated with almost a percentage point *in*crease in conventional national saving. We may also note the significant positive coefficients for increases in the real monetary base and the expected negative coefficient for the real exchange rate. It might be inferred from these estimated parameters that an easier monetary policy would increase national saving both directly and by bringing down exchange rates. But reducing the budget deficit in itself, if these regressions for data of the last two decades can be considered relevant, would appear not to increase national saving, as has been widely argued, but rather to reduce it.

Questions may be raised about the endogeneity of variables in our least squares regressions. I can also present the results of VARs (vector autoregressions), however, that would appear to confirm the individual equation least squares results. Working with two lags of PAHED6, DMB, ERR and NS0, included in that order, we may note, from impulse response functions shown in table 4.10 and figure 4.4, that a percentage point increase in the ratio to GNP of the structural, inflation-adjusted deficit, PAHED6, was associated with a small contemporaneous decline in the national saving ratio, NS0 (of which the deficit is itself, of course, a negative component), but subsequent increases of a percentage point or more in saving over each of the next three years. The national saving rate indeed remained higher for nine more years, gradually dwindling as the initial increase in the deficit was reversed.

Over the period of our observations, innovations in the deficit – or positive shocks – were associated, with a two-year lag, with roughly equal subsequent negative movements in the deficit. If policymakers, counterfactually, had actually kept the deficit higher, the gains in saving might perhaps have been even greater and further repeated.

The VARs indicated that similar, if shorter-lived, increases in subsequent saving were associated with initial increases in the real monetary base. Increases in the real exchange rate, however, brought decreases in national saving.

4 Extended measures of national saving

As I have argued on a number of occasions,[16] our interest in national saving, as it relates to provision for the future, must certainly call for focus on much more than the conventional measure of saving. Investment in new automobiles provides future transportation sevices whether it consists of gross private domestic investment by Hertz or Avis, government purchases by a municipal police department, or private "consumption" expenditures for durable goods by households. Business, government, and

129

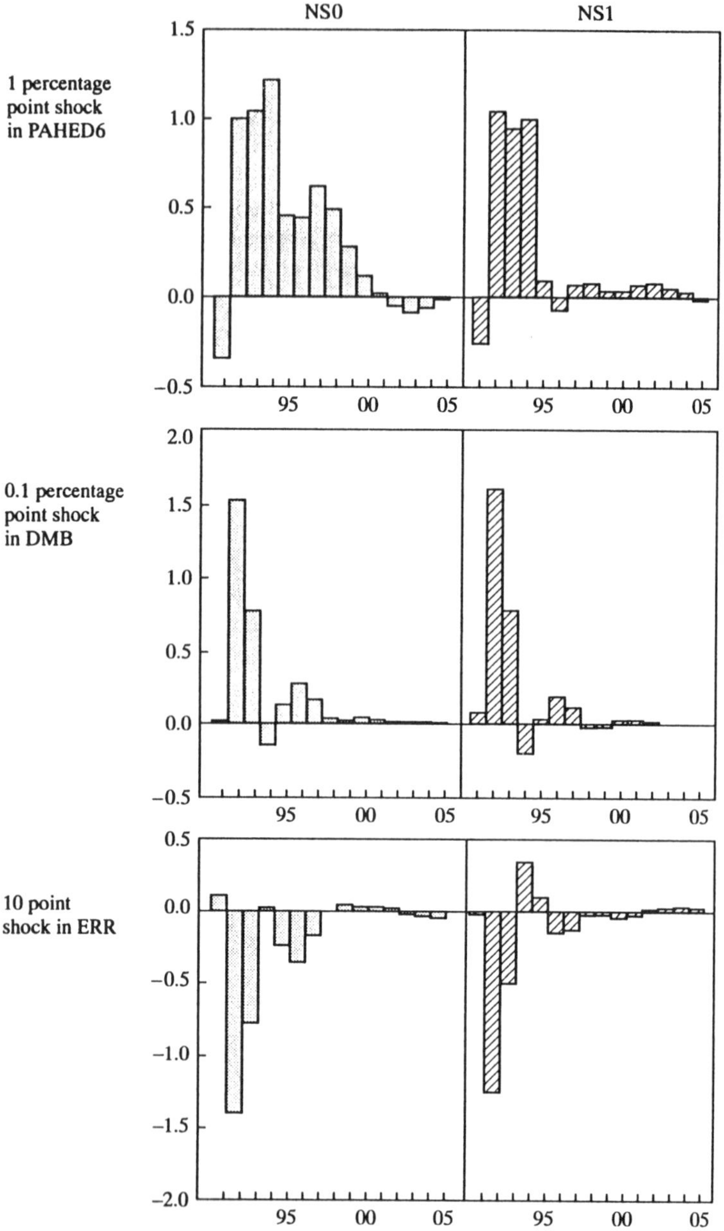

Figure 4.4 VARs with two lags, 1972–90 observations. Impulse response functions for national saving, as percent of GNP (conventional, NS0, and expanded, NS1), to 1991 shocks: one percentage point shock in price-adjusted high-employment deficit as percent of GNP (PAHED6): 0.1 percentage point shock in change in real monetary base as percent of GNP (DMB); 10 point shock in trade-weighted real exchange rate index (ERR)
Note: * Ordering is shocked variable first and saving variable last in each case.

university expenditures for research may prove a more important investment than much business spending for plant and equipment. Households and businesses may save by investing in land and its resources as well as in the buildings constructed above them. A good half of the decline in conventional US national saving rate in the 1980s is to be found in the reported fall in net foreign investment. But the net foreign investment figures must surely be adjusted for changes in the market value of US and foreign claims. This would be essential to get any meaningful measure of increases in our "debt" to the rest of the world that are alleged to pose an increasing burden on our future.[17] Only an adjusted measure of net foreign investment, taking this into account, should go into our measure of national saving.

Broader measures of national saving may not alter the trend to lower rates, we have observed in the conventional measure. In fact, they generally do not. In figure 4.1, for example, we can see that saving that includes all government and household investment in fixed reproducible capital, NS1, while higher than the conventional NS0 was also distinctly lower in the 1980s than previously.[18] Similarly, NS7, the measure including the saving constituted by increases in the real value of land, is higher yet, but still lower in the 1980s than previously.

The critical question, though, is what effect on saving we can expect from lower budget deficits. Would an increase in personal income taxes that effects a reduction in consumer expenditures for new automobiles and other durable goods raise national saving? The regressions of NS0 suggest it would not. But then it would almost certainly not raise national saving if this is taken, as it should be, to include the consumer investment in durable goods as a form of saving. If the reduction in the budget deficit is accomplished, as well it might, by a reduction in government expenditures for roads, bridges, and airports, we may also expect that it would also *lower* and not raise the expanded measure of national saving.

And this is indeed precisely what we observe. In table 4.7 we relate the lagged price-adjusted high-employment deficit, PAHED6(− 1) to private tangible investment, which we take to include, in addition to gross private domestic investment (GDPI) and net foreign investment (NFI, not all of the latter of which, to be sure, is "tangible"), investment in consumer durables (CD). In AR(1) regressions over the period 1957–90, we note highly significant positive coefficients for both the GPDI and CD components, along with the highly significant negative coefficient for NFI. The coefficient for all of private tangible investment is a significantly positive 0.785, suggesting that each additional percentage point of inflation-adjusted structural deficit, as a ratio of GNP, was associated with almost 0.8 of a percentage point *more* of private saving and investment. If

Table 4.7. *Adjusted deficit and private tangible investment* ($I_{j,t} = b_0 + b_1 \text{PAHED6}_{t-1}$)

I_j	Regression coefficients*					
	b_0	PAHED6_{t-1} b_1	$\hat{R}^2$	D–W	rho	n
Gross private domestic	16.488	0.769	0.315	1.63	0.513	34
	(0.527)	(0.297)			(0.181)	
Net foreign	− 0.250	− 0.407	0.882	2.05	0.891	34
	(0.749)	(0.086)			(0.088)	
Gross	16.072	0.473	0.443	1.73	0.762	34
	(1.134)	(0.309)			(0.129)	
Consumer durables	16.052	0.299	0.931	1.57	0.989	34
	(45.080)	(0.072)			(0.059)	
Private domestic tangible	24.030	1.335	0.613	1.54	0.539	34
	(0.618)	(0.317)			(0.159)	
Private tangible	24.064	0.785	0.393	1.600	0.616	34
	(0.784)	(0.355)			(0.159)	

Notes: * Ordinary least squares with a first-order correction for serial correlation. Standard errors are shown in parentheses. Sample period is 1957–90.

Variable definitions:
PAHED6 = price-adjusted 6 percent high-employment deficit, as estimated by the BEA for the years 1970–90 and extrapolated backward by the Holloway method on the basis of the BEA middle expansion trend deficit for the earlier years, as percent of GNP.
I_j = real investment of type j – GPDI, NFI, gross, and consumer durables from the BEA – taken as a percent of GNP. Private domestic tangible is the sum of gross private domestic investment and consumer durables. Private tangible is the sum of gross investment and consumer durables.

Table 4.8. *Adjusted deficit, change in monetary base, real exchange rate and private tangible investment (first differences)* ($\Delta I_{j,t} = b_0 + b_1 \Delta PAHED6_{t-1} + b_2 \Delta DMB_{t-1} + b_3 \Delta DMB_{t-2} + b_4 \Delta ERR_{t-2}$)

	Regression coefficients*							
ΔI_j	b_0	$\Delta PAHED6_{t-1}$ b_1	ΔDMB_{t-1} b_2	ΔDMB_{t-2} b_3	$\Sigma \Delta DMB$ $b_2 + b_3$	ΔERR_{t-2} b_4	$\hat{R}^2$	D–W
Gross private domestic	− 0.097	0.734	6.716	6.207	12.923	− 0.071	0.610	2.15
	(0.209)	(0.271)	(1.694)	(1.444)	(2.526)	(0.036)		
Net foreign	− 0.059	− 0.241	0.016	− 0.900	− 0.884	− 0.032	0.470	2.19
	(0.081)	(0.105)	(0.658)	(0.561)	(0.918)	(0.014)		
Gross	− 0.156	0.493	6.732	5.307	12.039	− 0.103	0.528	2.40
	(0.204)	(0.264)	(1.652)	(1.408)	(2.462)	(0.035)		
Consumer durables	0.135	0.257	1.477	0.801	2.278	− 0.009	0.525	1.70
	(0.063)	(0.082)	(0.513)	(0.437)	(0.765)	(0.011)		
Private domestic tangible	0.039	0.991	8.194	7.007	15.201	− 0.080	0.639	1.97
	(0.246)	(0.318)	(1.989)	(1.695)	(2.965)	(0.042)		
Private tangible	− 0.020	0.750	8.209	6.108	14.317	− 0.113	0.571	2.21
	(0.240)	(0.310)	(1.941)	(1.654)	(2.893)	(0.041)		

Notes: * Ordinary least squares. Standard errors are shown in parentheses. Sample period is 1962–90; there are twenty-nine observations.

Variable definitions:
PAHED6 = price-adjusted 6 percent high-employment deficit as percent of GNP
DMB = change in the real monetary base as a percent of GNP (December figures divided by 4th quarter GNP implicit price deflator)
ERR = trade weighted real exchange rate (March 1973 = 100)
I_j = real investment of type j – GPDI, NFI, gross, and consumer durables, from the BEA, taken as a percent of potential GNP. Private domestic tangible is the sum of gross private domestic investment and consumer durables. Private tangible is the sum of gross investment and consumer durables.

we eliminate NFI, we find the coefficient for private *domestic* tangible investment is a considerably higher 1.335, suggesting that each percentage point more of deficit was associated with four-thirds of a percentage point more of subsequent investment.

In table 4.8, in first-difference regressions (the results of AR(1) regressions in the levels, with values of the autoregression coefficient close to unity, were similar), we add the change in the lagged change in monetary base variables, ΔDMB(– 1) and ΔDMB(– 2), and the change in a two-year lagged real exchange rate variable, ΔERR(– 2). Lack of consistent monetary data forces us to restrict our sample to years beginning in 1962. Further, with the available real exchange series beginning only in 1973, we arbitrarily set the values of ERR at 100 for all years prior to 1973 (March 1973 = 100). Despite these limitations, results were essentially consistent with those already reported. The coefficient of ΔPAHED6(– 2) for gross private domestic investment was a still significant, positive, if reduced, 0.734; the coefficient for all private domestic tangible investment, including consumer durables, was 0.991; and the coefficient for all of private tangible investment was a still positive, and significant, 0.750. The real exchange rate variable, ΔERR(– 2) had the expected negative signs. The coefficients of ΔDMB(– 1) and ΔDMB(– 2) are generally positive and significantly so, consistent with the theory that their stimulative effects along with lower real interest rates will, with appropriate lags, increase domestic investment, but may, by generating more imports, reduce net foreign investment.[19] The deficit coefficient for NFI is again negative, as expected.

We also report in table 4.6 the results of regressions, in first difference form, of *net* saving, NS1, NS7, and NS3, which incorporate successively government and consumer fixed investment, investment in land, and the net foreign investment correction. The size of the positive coefficients of PAHED6(– 1) are now distinctly larger, 1.124, 2.606, and 2.351 (this last only for the eighteen observations from 1972 to 1989), respectively. Coefficients of the monetary variables, DMB(– 1) and DMB(– 2), are again positive and significantly so for NS1, but less clear, particularly for DMB(– 2), for NS7 and NS3. Coefficients of the exchange rate are negative, but significantly so only for NS1.[20]

In table 4.9, we can report the results of regressions of our broadest measures of national saving, incorporating from my total incomes system of accounts (TISA)[21] investment in intangible capital, government and household inventories and semi-durables, and net revaluations or real capital gains. Since the TISA accounts have not been extended beyond 1981, I had only ten useable observations for these regressions. Further, with the real exchange rate index only available from 1973, there would

Table 4.9. *Adjusted budget deficits, changes in monetary base and alternate measures of real national saving, NS14, NS15, NS16, and NS17, 1972–81* ($NSk_t = b_0 + b_1 PAHED6_{t-1} + b_2 DMB_{t-1} + b_3 DMB_{t-2}$, k = 14, 15, 16, 17)

Variable or parameter	Regression coefficients* and standard errors			
	NS14	NS15	NS16	NS17
C	25.689	30.126	31.154	32.268
	(1.109)	(1.324)	(2.851)	(2.109)
PAHED6(− 1)	2.180	3.424	9.179	8.591
	(1.805)	(2.049)	(2.524)	(1.983)
DMB(− 1)	16.055	20.283	23.385	21.086
	(11.412)	(14.401)	(17.412)	(13.325)
DMB(− 2)	12.866	7.801	32.724	28.398
	(10.555)	(13.384)	(17.659)	(13.051)
ΣDMB	28.921	28.084	56.109	49.484
	(12.555)	(15.481)	(24.506)	(18.428)
AR(1)	− 0.014	− 0.010	0.350	0.336
	(0.679)	(0.509)	(0.544)	(0.389)
$\hat{R}^2$	0.416	0.468	0.713	0.780
D–W	1.610	1.519	1.068	1.967
n	10	10	10	10

Notes: * Significant at 0.05 probability level.

C	Constant term.
AR(1)	First-order autoregressive coefficient.
$\hat{R}^2$	Adjusted coefficient of determination.
D–W	Durbin–Watson coefficient.
n	Number of observations.
PAHED6(− 1)	Lagged price-adjusted, high-employment budget surplus as percent of GNP.
DMB(− 1)	Lagged real change in monetary base as percent of GNP (December figures divided by fourth quarter GNP implicit price deflator).
DMB(− 2)	Two-year lagged real change in monetary base as percent of GNP (December figures divided by fourth quarter GNP implicit price deflator).
NS14	Change in total fixed reproducible capital plus adjusted net foreign investment minus statistical discrepancy plus investment in intangible capital and in government and household inventories and semi-durables.

have only been six meaningful observations in AR(1) relations and not very meaningful results if the ERR(− 2) variable had been included. Nevertheless, in all cases, it may be noted, the coefficient of the PAHED6 variable was substantially positive. In the regressions of NS16 and NS17, these positive coefficients were again statistically significant at the 0.05 level or below.[22] The DMB coefficients were uniformly positive.

We may also report the results of vector autoregressions involving the extended saving ratio, NS1. As with those for NS0, discussed above, key results of these VARs, also shown in table 4.10 and figure 4.4, are remarkably consistent with those of the ordinary least squares and AR(1) regressions we have been discussing. Positive shocks of one percentage point to PAHED6 were associated, again after slight contemporaneous declines, with positive impulse responses in NS1 of about a percentage point of GNP in each of the next three years.

As in the case of the conventional saving rate, NS0, real increases in the monetary base were also associated with increases in the expanded saving measure, NS1. Increases in the real exchange rate were similarly associated with declines in the expanded saving measure.

5 Conclusion

We purport to nothing definitive about this analysis. National saving has certainly many determinants, the impact of which may vary with the state of the economy, policy regimes, and the complicated and perhaps changing relations among current variables and the probability distributions of expectations of their future values. Results in full-scale, multi-equation, macroeconomic models may prove more persuasive to some – although not to others – than the essentially reduced forms considered in this chapter.

Table 4.9 (*cont.*)

NS15	Change in total fixed reproducible capital plus adjusted net foreign investment minus statistical discrepancy plus change in real value of land (NS3) plus investment in intangible capital and in government and household inventories and semi-durables.
NS16	Change in total fixed reproducible capital plus adjusted net foreign investment minus statistical discrepancy plus investment in intangible capital and in government and household inventories and semi-durables (NS14) plus total net revaluations.
NS17	Change in total fixed reproducible capital plus adjusted net foreign investment minus statistical discrepancy plus change in real value of land plus investment in intangible capital and in government and household inventories and semi-durables (NS15) plus net revaluations exclusive of net revaluations on land.

Table 4.10. *VARs with 2 lags, orderings PAHED6, DMB, ERR, and NS0 or NS1, impulse response functions to one percentage point shock in price-adjusted high-employment deficit (PAHED6), from VARs and from 100-observation samples*

From VARs

Year	NS0	PAHED6	DMB	ERR
1	−0.33	1.00	0.017	0.6
2	0.99	0.10	0.084	−2.3
3	1.04	−0.29	−0.017	−10.3
4	1.22	−0.86	−0.106	−9.8
5	0.45	−0.84	−0.093	−8.6
6	0.44	−0.72	−0.068	−5.4
7	0.61	−0.58	−0.048	0.5
8	0.48	−0.30	−0.021	5.1
9	0.27	0.01	0.010	6.9

Year	NS1	PAHED6	DMB	ERR
1	−0.26	1.00	0.020	1.2
2	1.03	0.28	0.086	−0.1
3	0.93	−0.01	0.009	−7.7
4	0.99	−0.55	−0.074	−7.8
5	0.08	−0.59	−0.069	−7.5
6	−0.09	−0.55	−0.054	−5.8
7	0.06	−0.50	−0.043	−1.5
8	0.07	−0.32	−0.026	2.7
9	0.03	−0.07	−0.001	5.0

From samples

NS0			NS1		
Year	Mean	Stan. err.	Year	Mean	Stan. err.
1	−0.26	0.66	1	−0.28	0.72
2	1.21	1.10	2	1.14	1.14
3	1.27	1.35	3	1.07	1.25
4	1.56	1.46	4	1.29	1.33
5	0.61	1.75	5	0.10	1.38
6	0.94	1.95	6	0.19	1.37
7	1.24	2.39	7	0.12	1.57
8	1.24	2.77	8	0.42	2.02
9	1.21	2.99	9	−0.14	2.86

Cumulative	Mean	Stan. err.	Cumulative	Mean	Stan. err.
1	−0.26	0.66	1	−0.28	0.72
2	0.95	1.57	2	0.87	1.66
3	2.21	2.58	3	1.94	2.51
4	3.77	3.62	4	3.22	3.36
5	4.38	4.85	5	3.33	4.13
6	5.32	6.45	6	3.52	4.73
7	6.56	8.48	7	3.64	5.27
8	7.80	10.81	8	4.06	5.77
9	9.01	13.37	9	3.92	6.58

One may ask how our estimates compare with others that might justify the apparent conventional wisdom that budget deficits reduce national saving. To my knowledge – although that knowledge may well be imperfect – no appropriate, data-based estimates have been presented. Where support for the assertion has been offered it has consisted of naive comparisons of contemporaneous, conventional, actual – not prior, structural, or cyclically adjusted or inflation adjusted or investment adjusted deficits – and conventional measures of saving. In many cases the "analysis" has entailed nothing more than looking at the saving–investment identity and the naive assumption that if one component of (conventional) saving – federal government "saving" – goes up, all the other components will remain the same and therefore the total will go up.

The evidence presented here, however inconclusive all such evidence must be, does offer support to the hypothesis that, as relevant theory suggests may well be the case, real budget deficits have increased rather than decreased national saving, even by its narrow, conventional measure. With the broader, more comprehensive measures of national saving with which we should be most concerned, the effects may be greater. The solution to imagined or real problems of an insufficiency of saving[23] would not appear, on the findings from data of the last two decades, to be found in reducing or eliminating "the budget deficit." This conclusion complements that of Gordon, in the preceding chapter, that encouraging personal or private saving does not appear to increase investment.

A constructive approach would point rather to an easier monetary policy, that would raise domestic and foreign investment and, most important, to shifts of priorities in the direction of more public and private household investment[24] in both tangible and intangible capital.

Appendix Data sources

1 High-employment surplus and high-employment GNP

The high-employment surplus is defined for a 6.0 percent rate of unemployment. The source for both series for the years beginning with 1970 is the issues of the *Survey of Current Business* of December 1983, May 1985, August 1989, and August 1990. For the years from 1955 to 1969, the high-employment surplus is estimated by taking the Department of Commerce "mid-expansion trend" cyclically adjusted series, and using Holloway's (1989) estimation procedure to convert it to a 6 percent basis. The Holloway procedure is in fact now used by the Commerce Department to estimate the 6 percent unemployment surplus.

High-employment GNP for the years from 1970 on is taken from the *Survey of Current Business* issues listed above. For the years prior to 1970, high-employment GNP is estimated as GNP6 = GNPME × [1 + 0.02(UME − 6)], where GNPME is the Commerce Department of "mid-expansion trend GNP" and UME is the percentage point unemployment rate associated with mid-expansion trend GNP. (The BEA estimates that in the post-1970 period each percentage point of unemployment is associated with 1.9 percent less of cyclically adjusted output. With productivity probably greater prior to 1970 it has seemed reasonable to round the 1.9 percent up to 0.02 in our formulation.) The mid-expansion trend GNP, unemployment rate and cyclically adjusted deficit are published in the December 1983, *Survey of Current Business.*

2 *Price-adjusted surplus (and deficit)*

The price-adjusted surplus is equal to the 6 percent high-employment surplus defined above plus price effects on the federal net debt. Price effects on the federal debt are in turn estimated as

$$PE_t = [(A - 1)D_{t-1} + (B - 1)(D_t - D_{t-1})]/B, \quad \text{where}$$

PE = price effects,
D = net federal debt at market value,
$A = P^e_t / P^e_{t-1}$,
$B = P^e_t / P_t$
P^e = end-of-year GNP deflator (taken as the mean of the fourth-quarter deflator and the deflator for the first quarter of the subsequent year) and
P = annual GNP deflator.

The deficit is of course simply the negative of the surplus.

3 *Monetary base*

The nominal monetary base is taken from the *Economic Report of the President.* The figures are averages for the month of December. The monetary variable used in the regression is defined as the change in end of period real stocks divided by real GNP. Algebraically, this may be written as

$$\text{DMB}_t = 100[(\text{MB82}_t - \text{MB82}_{t-1})/(\text{GNP82}_{t-1}],$$

where MB82 is the real monetary base and GNP82 is real GNP. The fourth-quarter implicit GNP deflator is used to deflate the monetary base.

4 Real exchange rate

The real exchange rate is a trade-weighted index of ten major trading partners of the US. The series is constructed by the Federal Reserve Board and published in the *Economic Report of the President*. The index is available for 1973 onwards. The index is assumed to be constant prior to 1973.

5 Investment measures

The abbreviation NIPA refers to the *National Income and Product Accounts of the United States*. The number following the NIPA designation refers to the table and line number.

Consumer durables	NIPA 1.2.3
Gross private domestic	NIPA 1.2.6
Net foreign investment	NIPA 4.1.22 deflated by GNP implicit price deflator
Net foreign, adjusted	Net foreign investment (NIPA 4.1.22) plus the difference between changes in the adjusted international investment position of the US at market value and changes in the official international investment position, from Eisner and Pieper (1990), table 8, columns 7 and 2, deflated by the GNP implicit price deflator
Federal tangible	NIPA 3.8.4 + 3.8.11 + 3.8.13 + 3.8.30
State and local tangible	NIPA 3.8.22 + 3.8.27
Research and development	NSF (1987), appendix table B.5, and for later years, *US Statistical Abstract*, deflated by GNP implicit price deflator
Education	
Federal	NIPA 3.15.20 + 3.15.48 + 3.15.78, deflated by deflator for non-defense government purchases constructed by dividing nominal by constant dollar purchases reported in NIPA 3.7 and 3.8
State and local	NIPA 3.16.9 + 3.16.50 − 5.5.47, deflated as above
Private	NIPA 2.5.85

Notes

William R. Kenan Professor of Economics, Northwestern University. Much of this chapter is based on or derived from joint work with Paul J. Pieper. I have borrowed most recently from Eisner and Pieper (1992). I have enjoyed the research assistance of John Applegate, Maurice Ewing, Oliver Haberstroh, Satish Reddy, Craig Safir, Marc Sokol, and Stacey M. Tevlin, and the continued financial support of the National Science Foundation, most recently through grant #SES-8909600, for the underlying research, but I alone am of course responsible for the contents of this chapter.

1 See Friedman (1983b and 1990), Summers and Carroll (1987), Gramlich (1989), Schultze (1990 and 1991), and Rivlin (1991), among many.

2 One might have thought that an appropriate theoretical formulation was given by Oskar Lange (1938) in his "Optimal Propensity to Consume . . ." article setting forth a model of Keynes' *General Theory*. There is a rate of consumption, private and public, that will maximize investment. On the one hand, increased consumption will raise the demand for capital to facilitate greater output. On the other, it will reduce investment by raising interest rates (or the supply price of capital goods, thus reducing the marginal efficiency of investment). If consumption is initially at or below this maximization point, reductions in consumption are likely to lower investment, not increase it.

3 Empirical confirmation that this may be so is found in the following AR(1) regression between federal grants in aid to state and local governments, GIA, and the price-adjusted high-employment deficit, PAHED6 (explained below), both expressed as a percent of GNP:

$$(2)\quad \Delta GIA_t = \underset{(0.053)}{0.142\,X1} - \underset{(0.048)}{0.046\,X2} + \underset{(0.027)}{0.083\,\Delta PAHED6_t},$$

$$t = 1957\text{–}90,\ \hat{R}^2 = 0.367,\ DW = 2.17,\ rho = 0.297.$$

This was estimated with a first-order correction for serial correlation, with rho the estimated autoregression coefficient. X1 is a constant term for the 1957–72 period while X2 is a constant for the 1973–90 period. The estimates indicate that each dollar more of the inflation and cyclically adjusted federal deficit was accompanied by 8.3 cents more in federal grants in aid to state and local governments.

4 These broader measures of national saving are presented in detail in Eisner (1991) which, with some updating, forms the basis of much of the first two sections of this chapter. A number of measures are taken or derived from the annual time series put together in my total incomes system of accounts (Eisner, 1989c). The net foreign investment adjustments are based on work in Eisner and Pieper (1990) and (1991).

5 We might suggest that here, as elsewhere, it is perfectly appropriate to include the total national income accounts surplus (or deficit) without distinguishing among surpluses in social security trust funds and deficits in the rest of the budget. The fact that politicians or others may choose to designate some revenues for one subaccount does not alter the relevant totality. They all go into the same pot. It may be added that what accountants designate as "in" the social security trust funds has nothing to do, in any economic sense, with what may be available to pay retirees or other beneficiaries in the future. That will depend upon the productivity of the people producing in the future, in turn related to the real wealth that has been accumulated. And this will relate to the real saving discussed in this chapter.

6 See Hayashi (1986) for an illuminating analysis of this.

7 This section, updated to 1990 where possible, draws heavily upon Eisner (1991), in which are to be found detailed series for all of the years from 1946 to 1989 for which they are

available. The underlying figures, in billions of current and constant (1982) dollars, are available on request to the author.

8 National saving in 1982 dollars is calculated, using the saving–investment identity, as NS0 = GPDI − CCA + (NFID − SD)/GNPDEF, where GPDI and CCA are gross private domestic investment and capital consumption allowances with adjustment, both in 1982 dollars, NFID and SD are net foreign investment and the statistical discrepancy, in current dollars, and GNPDEF is the implicit price deflator for gross national product.

9 From "Summary Fixed Reproducible Tangible Wealth Series, 1925–89," *Survey of Current Business*, October 1990, pp. 31–2, updated from tables furnished by John Musgrave, of the US Bureau of Economic Analysis.

10 Changes in the Federal Reserve's value of land at market prices in principle reflect: (1) general increases in land prices in excess of increases in all prices – what we refer to as net revaluations; (2) changes in the general level of all prices or gains corresponding to inflation; and (3) increases in the value of land as a consequence of investment expenses or development. With the available data, our measure of investment in land in fact cannot distinguish between (1) and (3) and hence includes both. In the measures of saving presented below including both investment in land and net revaluations, NS17D and NS17, we therefore include from TISA, as indicated below, total net revaluations *exclusive* of land.

11 See Eisner (1988 and 1989c). Kendrick (1976) laid foundations for much of the TISA accounts. Note also the work of Ruggles and Ruggles (1982), particularly with regard to revaluations and integration of stocks and flows.

12 A full description of sources and methods of TISA series is to be found in Eisner (1989c).

13 Eisner and Pieper (1984) and Eisner (1986), among others.

14 See Eisner (1986 and 1989b) and Eisner and Pieper (1988).

15 A brief, generally specified presentation of a relevant model of an economy with budget deficits is to be found in Eisner (1986), pp. 182–4. A full set of equations, of which some of the relations estimated in this chapter may be seen as reduced forms, is spelled out in Eisner and Hwang (1991).

The model underlying these equations is to be distinguished from that underlying Barro–Ricardian equivalence. According to the equivalence theorem, private agents would generally be indifferent to the financing of government expenditures by taxes or deficits, on the understanding that the present value of the taxes they would have to pay over their relevant horizons, including the lifetimes of successive generations, would be unaffected. The equivalence theorem would suggest that a larger deficit – reduced public saving – would induce greater private saving to pay anticipated larger future taxes. National saving would hence be unaffected. The model behind our equations – and the evidence presented in our estimates of parameters – suggest, however, that national saving may be increased by government deficits, particularly under conditions of less than full employment and excess capacity. Reductions of deficits, if they drive the economy away from full employment, may then reduce national saving.

16 See Eisner (1988a, 1989a, 1989c, and 1991), for example.

17 See Eisner and Pieper (1990) and (1991) for an explanation and presentation of necessary adjustments.

18 Summary descriptions of the various measures of national saving discussed here are presented in the "Definitions and Derivations of Saving Rates and Other Variables," above. Numerical designations correspond to those assigned in Eisner (1991), which offers complete series, in current and constant dollars and as percentages of GNP, of the measures of saving and their components, and an explanation of the sources and methods by which they were derived.

19 One should not be misled by the absolute size of the DMB coefficients. The standard deviation of the DMB variable – the change in the monetary base as a percent of GNP – is relatively small, some 11 percent of that of PAHED6. Large coefficients do not necessarily then imply correspondingly large effects of DMB on the various dependent investment variables.

20 Impulse response functions from VARs involving NS1, but otherwise similar to those with NS0 mentioned above, are again consistent with our ordinary regression results.

21 Eisner (1989c).

22 The absolute values of some of the coefficients, it should be noted, are awkwardly large. It is hard to see why each dollar of deficit should be associated with as much as eight or nine dollars of additional national saving, as some of the coefficients in table 4.8 would seem to suggest. There may be temporary accelerator effects and non-repeatable capital gains involved, indicating that not all of the estimated relationship can be taken as depicting states of long-run equilibrium. And there may, of course, be other, non-permanent and spurious effects that have been picked up in at least some of the estimates.

23 Some portion of the decline of conventionally measured national saving is indeed more imagined than real. Major portions, as we have indicated above and as further discussed in Eisner and Pieper (1991) and Goldstein (1990), relate to the measures of capital consumption allowances and net foreign investment, both of which are suspect.

24 See Aschauer (1989) for evidence that *non-military*, public tangible investment has proved a major contributor to private productivity. This suggests that reductions in military spending – including investment in weapons system and weapons research – associated with the end of the Cold War, might well be devoted to non-military public investment, rather than to deficit reduction.

References

Aschauer, David Alan, 1989. "Is Public Expenditure Productive?," *Journal of Monetary Economics*, 23(2) (March): 177–200.

Dewald, William G. and Michael Ulan, 1989. "The US Net International Investment Position: Misstated and Misunderstood," in James A. Dorn and William A. Niskanen (eds.), *Dollars, Deficits, and Trade*, Norwall, MA: Kluwer Academic Publishers for the Cato Institute.

Eisner, Robert, 1986. *How Real is the Federal Deficit*?, New York: The Free Press.

1988. "Extended Measures of National Income and Product," *Journal of Economic Literature*, 26 (December): 1611–84.

1989a. "Divergences of Measurement and Theory and Some Implications for Economic Policy" (1988 Presidential Address to the American Economic Association), *The American Economic Review*, 79 (March): 1–13.

1989b. "Budget Deficits: Rhetoric and Reality," *Journal of Economic Perspectives*, 3 (Spring): 73–93.

1989c. *The Total Incomes System of Accounts*, Chicago: University of Chicago Press.

1991. "The Real Rate of US National Saving," *The Review of Income and Wealth*, 37(1) (February): 15–32.

Eisner, Robert and Sang-In Hwang, 1993. "Self-Correcting Real Deficits: A New Lesson in Functional Finance," manuscript copy, 3/16/91, for F. van Winden and H.A.A. Verbon (eds.), *The Political Economy of Government Debt*, Amsterdam: Elsevier, pp. 255–94.

Eisner, Robert and Paul J. Pieper, 1984. "A New View of the Federal Debt and Budget Deficits," *American Economic Review*, 74 (March): 11–29.

1990. "'The World's Greatest Debtor Nation'?" *The North American Review of Economics and Finance*, 1 (Spring): 9–32.

1991. "Real Foreign Investment in Perspective," *Annals, American Academy of Political and Social Science*, 516 (July): 22–35.

Friedman, Benjamin, 1983b. "Implications of the Government Deficit for U.S. Capital Formation," in Federal Reserve Bank of Boston, *The Economics of Large Government Deficits*, Proceedings of a Conference Held in October.

1990. "Views on the Likelihood of Financial Crisis," National Bureau of Economic Research, Working Paper No. 3407.

Goldstein, Henry N., 1990. "Should We Fret About Our Low Net National Saving Rate?," *The Cato Journal*, 9 (Winter): 441–62.

Gordon, David M., 1995. "Putting the Horse (Back) Before the Cart: Disentangling the Macro Relationship between Investment and Saving," in Gerald A. Epstein and Herbert M. Gintis (eds.), *Macroeconomic Policy after the Conservative Era*, Cambridge: Cambridge University Press.

Gramlich, Edward M., 1989. "Budget Deficits and National Saving: Are Politicians Exogenous?," *The Journal of Economic Perspectives*, 3 (Spring): 23–35.

Hayashi, Fumio, 1986. "Why is Japan's Saving Rate So Apparently High?," in Stanley Fischer (ed.), *NBER Macroeconomics Annual 1986*, Cambridge, MA: MIT Press, pp. 145–210.

Holloway, Thomas M., 1989. "Measuring the Cyclical Sensitivity of Federal Receipts and Expenditures: Simplified Estimation Procedures," *International Journal of Forecasting*, 5: 347–60.
Kendrick, John W., 1976. *The Formation and Stocks of Total Capital*, New York: National Bureau of Economic Research.
Landefeld, J. Steven and Ann M. Lawson, 1991. "Valuation of the US Net International Investment Position," Survey of Current Business, 71 (May): 40–9.
Lange, Oskar, 1938. "The Rate of Interest and the Optimal Propensity to Consume," *Economica* (February), New Series, 5: 12–32. Reprinted in American Economic Association, *Readings in Business Cycle Theory*, Philadelphia: Blakiston, 1944, 169–92.
Pieper, Paul J., 1989. "Why Net investment Has Fallen," paper presented to Western Economic Association Meetings (June 20).
Rivlin, Alice M., 1991. Statement Before the Committee on Ways and Means, US House of Representatives (December 17).
Ruggles, Richard and Nancy D. Ruggles, 1982. "Integrated Economic Accounts for the United States, 1947–1980," *Survey of Current Business*, 62 (May): 1–53.
Schultze, Charles L., 1990. "Cut Defense to Increase Saving," *Challenge*, 33 (March/April): 11–17.
1991. Statement Before the Committee on Ways and Means, US House of Representatives (December 17).
Summers, Lawrence, and Chris Carroll, 1987. "Why Is US National Saving So Low?," *Brookings Papers on Economic Activity*, 2: 607–35.

ELSEVIER

Journal of Economic Behavior and Organization
23 (1994) 111-126

JOURNAL OF
Economic Behavior
& Organization

Real government saving and the future

Robert Eisner*

Department of Economics, Northwestern University, 2003 Sheridan Road, Evanston, IL 60208-2400, USA

Received January 1993, final version received August 1993

Abstract

Government saving should properly include government-financed investment. Changes in public tangible investment and investment in education are found to be *positively* related to changes in inflation-adjusted, structural deficits. Changes in these deficits have also been associated with changes in the same direction in gross private domestic investment and even changes in narrow measures of national saving. Hence, changes in real deficits have been associated a fortiori with changes in the same direction in a broader measure of national saving, including government and household investment in tangible capital. Our data also suggest that the pay-off to more public *tangible* investment, at least, is distinctly positive and very possibly larger than that to more private investment.

Key words: Saving; Investment; Government; Deficit

JEL classification: E62; H62; H60

1. Introduction

Conventional accounts measure government saving as the sum of Federal and state and local budget surpluses. Large reported deficits in the last decade have hence been viewed as major depressants of 'national saving', the sum of private and government saving. Consequently lower national saving, it is then argued, leaves a greater burden to the future. The appropriate

* William R. Kenan Professor of Economics, Northwestern University. I am greatly indebted to a number of research assistants who have helped in processing and statistical analysis of the data and, most important in recent work, Satish Reddy. Underlying series, frequently unpublished, have been generously made available by Gerald Donahoe, Bruce Grimm and John Musgrave of the Bureau of Economic Analysis.

SSDI 0167-2681(93)E0041-W

corrective is reduction of government dis-saving, that is, the reduction of budget deficits.

There is in fact evidence that cyclically-adjusted, inflation-adjusted or 'real' federal deficits have been associated with more not less subsequent national saving, even as conventionally mismeasured. This results, apparently, from the stimulatory effect of these deficits on real GNP and its components of gross private domestic investment as well as consumption. The increases in domestic investment have exceeded the declines in net foreign investment so that, after abstracting from the role of monetary variables and exchange rates, total investment and saving have increased.

Real government saving, in any economically meaningful and relevant sense, however, is a far cry from the conventional measure of budget surpluses or deficits. The failure to have separate capital accounts even for the tangible reproducible fixed capital of structures and equipment, let alone expenditures for the intangible capital of R&D and education, makes the traditional measures a very poor, even perverse guide to provision for the future.

In this paper we will present a comprehensive measure of government saving, drawing on capital accounts being put together by the Bureau of Economic Analysis for R&D and similar accounts for education. We shall then offer estimates of parameters of relations determining these expanded measures of government saving. Finally, we shall endeavor to estimate a production function including private and public tangible capital stocks among its arguments, to suggest the productivity of at least some of government investment, and hence its contribution to future output.

2. Correcting the accounts

We can have no meaningful picture of public saving, conventionally viewed in the United States as the excess of tax revenues over government outlays, without making the government accounts at least consistent with private business accounting practice. That means setting up current accounts that exclude capital outlays but include depreciation or capital consumption allowances as charges against revenues. Such accounts would then recognize net government capital expenditures as a component of public saving.

Further adjustments, beyond merely bringing government accounts into conformity with private accounting practice, are important to have a measure of economically relevant saving and provision for the future. These include recognizing household tangible investment in what are referred to as 'consumer durables'. In current, conventional accounts government purchase of an automobile is lumped into 'government expenditures for goods and services', counted neither as consumption nor investment. Household purchases of automobiles are counted as consumption. But if Hertz were to buy the same vehicles and rent them to government or households they would be counted as investment. An economically relevant measure, consistent with the fact that all motor vehicles are expected to provide services over a substantial future, would classify all acquisitions of new cars as investment, regardless of the sector of legal ownership.

But probably most important is intangible investment, particularly in education and in research. Much, perhaps most, of these expenditures should be recognized as saving.[1]

In Table 1 we offer total government current and capital accounts for 1991. They add, to the national income and product accounts, Bureau of Economic Analysis measures of government investment in fixed capital and education along with National Science Foundation figures on government-financed R&D expenditures.

This investment spending is put into a separate capital account, with depreciation included as capital consumption allowances in the current account. The \$193 billion government deficit on conventional national income and product account, presumably offsetting private saving and thus reducing 'national saving' by that amount, is now reduced to a deficit of only \$24 billion on current account. Government capital expenditures, nowhere explicitly recognized in the conventional accounts, come to \$530 billion, of which \$184 billion are tangible investment (both military and civilian). Intangible investment amounted to a considerably greater \$346 billion, of which \$279 billion are in education and \$67 billion in R&D. With total capital consumption allowances of \$361 billion, net capital expenditures – the deficit on capital account, to be financed by borrowing (or printing money) – are \$169 billion.

These revised government accounts are then reflected in the revised gross saving and investment account of Table 2. We add to the conventional gross private domestic investment figure of \$721 billion the \$530 billion of 'gross public domestic investment' and we add, on the other side of the account, the \$361 billion of public capital consumption allowances. Net national saving, about the low level of which so much concern has been expressed, is thus increased by the \$169 billion of net public investment, from \$82 billion (\$275 billion minus the conventional consolidated deficit of \$193 billion) to \$251 billion. Perhaps more important, the revised accounts make clear that efforts to reduce government deficits, if they reduce public investment, are perverse in their effects on an economically relevant measure of national saving. Similarly, increases in public sector deficits, if used to finance public investment, *increase* national saving.

[1] See Eisner (1988, 1989, 1991a) for detailed presentation of concepts and measures of extended accounts for output, capital accumulation and saving.

Table 1
Government receipts and expenditures accounts, 1991 (billions of dollars).

Current account			
Credits: Revenues			1,747
Charges: Current expenditures			1,771
Goods and services		560	
Net interest, transfer payments and other		850	
Capital consumption allowances		361	
Surplus or deficit (−)			−24
Capital account			
Credits: Capital consumption allowances			361
Charges: Gross capital expenditures			530
Tangible		184	
Intangible		346	
Education	279		
R&D	67		
Surplus or deficit: Net capital expenditures (−)			−169
Consolidated account			
Revenues			1,747
Expenditures			1,940
Total surplus or deficit (−)			−193

Sources: National Income and Product Accounts, *Survey of Current Business*, September 1992, pp. 29–30; 'Federal Government Expenditures by Type and Function' and 'State and Local Government Expenditures by Type and Function' Tables 3.16 and 3.17; *Survey of Current Business*, July 1992, Table 3.1, p. 66, 3.7B p. 69; Bureau of Economic Analysis, 'Fixed Government Capital (including residential) historical-cost valuation, gross investment, depreciation and net investment', total; National Science Foundation, *Science and Technology (1991)*, Appendix A, Table 4-2, p. 306; U.S. Department of Commerce, *Government Finances*, December 1991, Tables 4 and 5, pp. 4, 6. Intangible capital consumption allowances assumed equal to two-thirds of gross intangible capital expenditures.

3. Determinants of public and private investment and saving

In fact, increases in inflation-adjusted Federal structural deficits have been associated over the past 30 years with increases in Federal tangible investment, as should be apparent in Fig. 1 and is confirmed by the statistically significant regression coefficient of 0.102 in the first row of Table 3. There was little obvious association between the Federal structural deficit and contemporaneous state and local government tangible investment, but changes in total government tangible investment,apparently reflecting their

Table 2
Gross saving and investment account, 1991 (billions of dollars).

Gross private domestic investment	721	Net private saving		275
		Personal saving	200	
Gross public domestic investment	530	Business saving	76	
Net foreign investment	9	Net public saving		−24
		Capital consumption allowance		987
		Private	626	
		Public	361	
		Statistical discrepancy		22
Gross investment	1,260	Gross saving and statistical discrepancy		1,260

Sources: Table 1, above, and National Income and Product Accounts, Table 5.1. Gross Saving and Investment, *Survey of Current Business*, July 1992, p. 76.

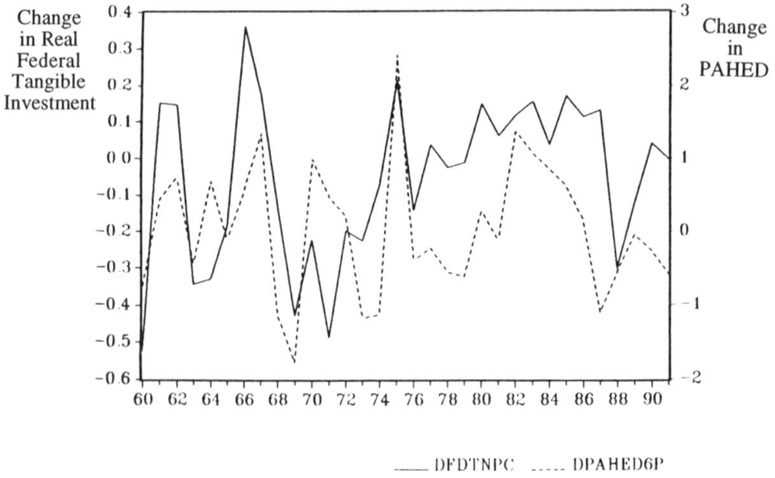

Fig. 1. Changes in price-adjusted high employment deficit and real federal tangible investment as percent of GNP.

Federal component, were also positively related to Federal structural deficits, as may be seen in Fig. 2 and in the statistically significant regression reported on the third row of Table 3.

Changes in total government expenditures for education and training were even more positively associated with changes in the inflation-adjusted, Federal structural deficit, as shown in Fig. 3 and the regression results on the

Table 3
Adjusted deficit and public investment; $\Delta I_k = b_0 + b_1 \Delta \text{PAHED6}$.[1]

ΔI_k	b_0	b_1	$\hat{R}^2$	$D\text{–}W$	rho	n
Federal tangible	−0.035	0.102	0.250	1.52	0.336	31
	(0.049)	(0.035)			(0.166)	
S&L tangible	−0.018	0.006	0.274	1.86	0.566	31
	(0.040)	(0.017)			(0.157)	
Total government tangible	−0.048	0.110	0.302	1.37	0.473	31
	(0.079)	(0.042)			(0.160)	
Education & training	0.052	0.135	0.347	1.73	0.510	31
	(0.070)	(0.035)			(0.158)	
Government R&D	−0.021	0.011	0.291	2.08	0.525	30
	(0.019)	(0.009)			(0.163)	
Total government	−0.056	0.228	0.354	1.70	0.390	30
	(0.093)	(0.059)			(0.176)	

[1]Ordinary least squares with a first-order correction for serial correlation. Standard errors are shown in parentheses. Estimated as first differences. Sample period is 1961–1991 for federal tangible, S&L tangible, and total government tangible, and education and training and 1962–1991 for government R&D and total government.
Variable definitions:
ΔPAHED6 = price-adjusted 6 percent high-employment deficit as percent of GNP, first difference.
ΔI_k = real investment of type k – federal tangible, S&L tangible, education & training, government R&D and total government – generally from the BEA, taken as percent of potential GNP, first differences.

fourth row of Table 3. And all this is reflected clearly in Fig. 4, relating the Federal deficit to total government investment expenditures, tangible and intangible, and in the corresponding regression results reported in the bottom row of Table 3. Each one percentage point change in the ratio of the inflation-adjusted 6-percent-unemployment deficit to GNP was associated on average with a 0.228 percentage point change in public investment in the *same* direction.

Granted that Federal structural deficits have been associated then with more public investment and hence real government saving, is it not still possible that these deficits have absorbed so much private saving and crowded out so much *private* investment that they actually reduced total or national saving? This would indeed be inevitable, except possibly for foreign financing of our investment, if national income and product were fixed. For then more output going to public expenditures would have to mean less output going to private expenditures or to foreigners. With the presumption

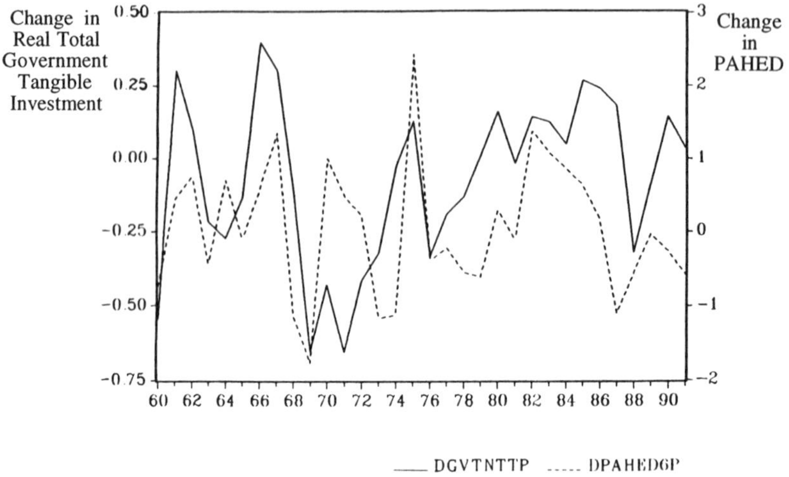

Fig. 2. Changes in price-adjusted high employment deficit and real total government tangible investment as percent of GNP.

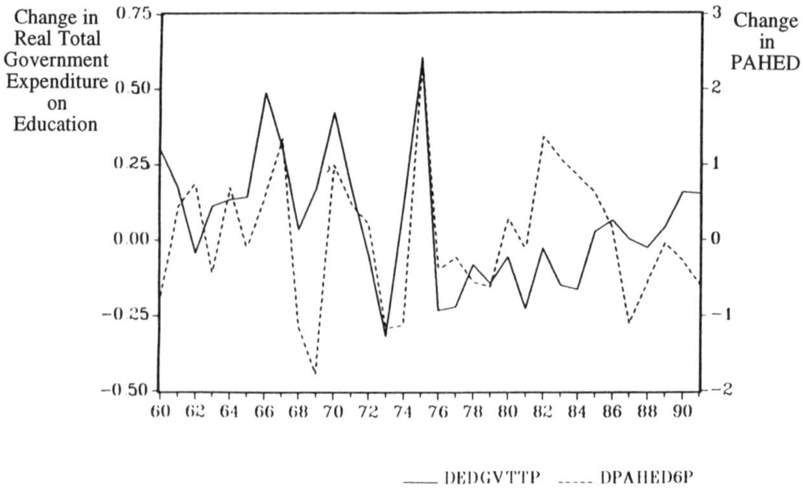

Fig. 3. Changes in price-adjusted high employment deficit and real total government expenditures on education as percent of GNP.

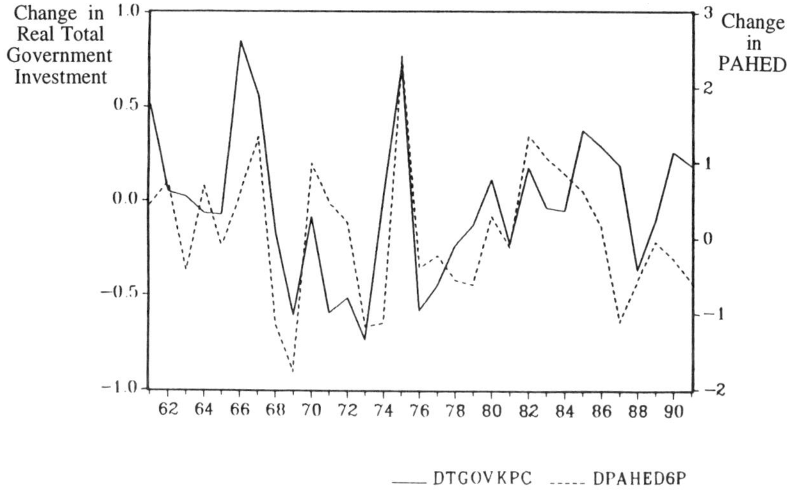

Fig. 4. Changes in price-adjusted high employment deficit and real total government investment as a percent of GNP.

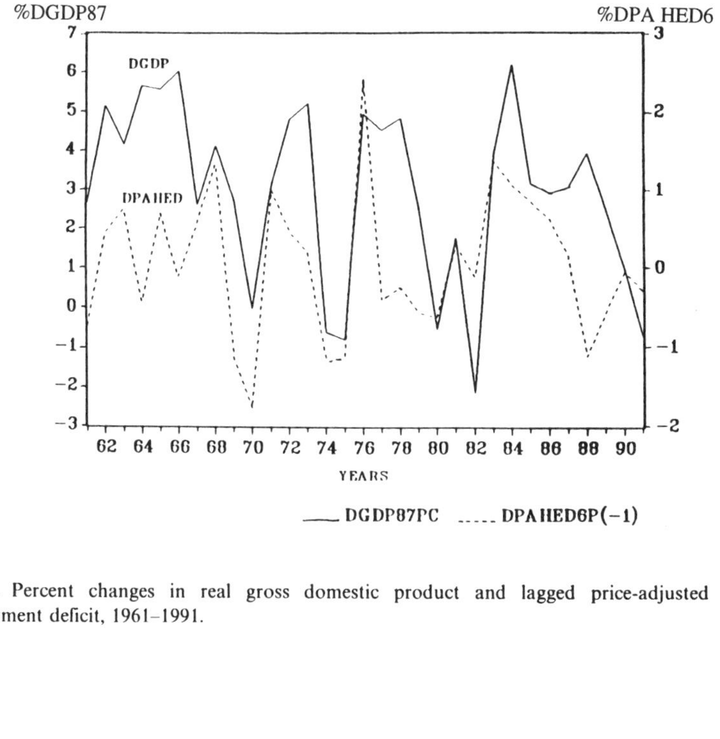

Fig. 5. Percent changes in real gross domestic product and lagged price-adjusted high-employment deficit, 1961–1991.

of any reasonably substantial marginal propensity to consume domestic goods, deficit-financed public expenditures which would raise after-tax income would generate sufficient additional consumption to lower private investment more than any increase in public investment.

But that crucial assumption, that national income and product – and with them, unemployment and employment – are fixed, is a source of major error. In fact, they are not fixed. The United States economy, whatever its myriad virtues, like most other market economies, suffers much more often than not from less-than-full employment and a consequent capacity for variation in income and output. If a bigger structural deficit, for whatever purpose, increases employment, income and output, it is quite possible that we can have more public investment and more private investment too. Indeed, we can have more consumption, public or private, and more private investment. More consumption may actually bring about more investment. There may be 'crowding in' rather than crowding out of private investment, a possibility that was elegantly laid forth by Oscar Lange (1938) over half a century ago. It is an empirical question whether on balance our economy has tended to have sufficient slack for us to be below 'the optimum propensity to consume', that is to have so little consumption or government expenditures that increasing them would bring an increase in private investment.[2]

Fig. 5 makes clear that this possibility is open. Changes in the inflation-adjusted (or 'price-adjusted'), structural (or 'high-employment') deficit have been positively associated with subseqent changes in real gross domestic product. Fig. 6 manifests a corresponding relation with unemployment; increases in the budget surplus, or decreases in the deficit, have been associated with increases in unemployment. And these relations are confirmed by the regression results reported in Table 4. Those regressions are better fits with the inclusion of changes in the real monetary base as an independent variable but they are robust, as well, in the simple relations with only the deficit variable.

More directly to the point at issue, however, are the relations reported in Table 5. Here we note that the deficit and monetary base variables are positively related to gross private domestic investment. There *has* been crowding in.

Has that been entirely at the expense of net foreign investment, though? My results, as well as those of others, indicate that deficits have encouraged imports and reduced net exports.[3] Thus, the conventional measure of

---

[2] See Eisner (1986) for an early, comprehensive treatment of some of these issues and, for more up-to-date treatments, focussing more considerably on national saving, Eisner (1992a and 1992b).

[3] See, for example, Eisner and Pieper (1992).

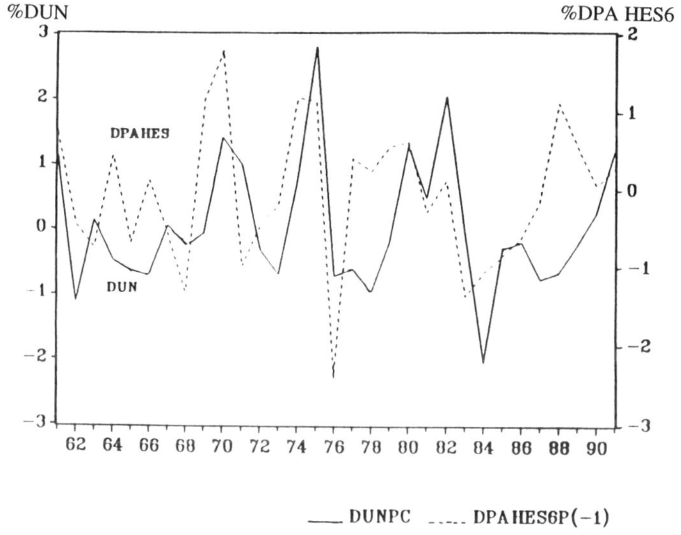

Fig. 6. Percent changes in unemployment and lagged price-adjusted high-employment surplus, 1961-1991.

national saving – the sum of gross private domestic investment and net foreign investment – might still be negatively related to these deficits.

That, however, is not the case. As shown in the second column of Table 5, reporting the regression of NS0, after taking into account the effects of real changes in exchange rates, we find that each percentage point of structural deficit, expressed as a ratio of GNP, was associated with almost exactly one percentage point *more* of subsequent national saving over the period from 1973 to 1991.[4]

But finally, what about a broader measure of national saving, one that at least includes government and household investment in tangible capital. Fig. 7, graphing changes in the real structural deficit against changes in NS1, this expanded measure of national saving, both taken as percentages of GDP, tells a striking story. It is clear to the naked eye that changes in the deficit have been positively associated with subsequent changes in national saving over the years from 1961 to 1991. And this relation is confirmed in the regression, for the years 1973 to 1991, where the monetary base and

[4] Earlier years were excluded because of the absence of earlier measures of trade-weighted, real exchange rates.

Table 4
Changes in adjusted budget deficits, monetary base, real GDP and unemployment, 1962–1991; $\Delta Y_t = b_0 + b_1 \Delta \text{PAHED6}_{t-1} + b_2 \text{DMB}_{t-1}$.

Variable or parameter	ΔY_t GDP	ΔY_t Unemployment
C	1.922	0.462
	(0.570)	(0.170)
ΔPAHED6$_{t-1}$	1.227	−0.486
	(0.317)	(0.162)
DMB$_{t-1}$	8.510	−4.414
	(2.493)	(1.052)
AR(1)	0.378	−0.010
	(0.208)	(0.235)
$\hat{R}^2$	0.481	0.444
D–W	1.713	1.771
n	30	30

C	Constant term
$AR(1)$	First-order autoregressive coefficient
$\hat{R}^2$	Adjusted coefficient of determination
D–W	Durbin–Watson coefficient
n	Number of observations
ΔPAHED6$_{t-1}$	Lagged price-adjusted, BEA 6% high-employment budget deficit as percent of GNP
DMB$_{t-1}$	Lagged real change in monetary base as percent of GNP (December figures divided by 4th quarter GNP implicit price deflator).

exchange rate variables are also included. With deficits to some extent financing household and government investment, the relation is even stronger than that for the narrower measure of national saving. We now note that each percentage point change in the deficit was associated with an average move in the same direction of 1.193 percentage points of national saving as a ratio of GNP. The deficits have apparently contributed to more government saving and investment and to more total, national saving and investment as well.

Table 5

Adjusted budget deficits, changes in monetary base, and real exchange rates and gross private domestic investment and alternate measures of real national saving, NS0 and NS1, first differences, 1973–1991; $\Delta Y_t = b_0 + b_1 \Delta \text{PAHED6}_{t-1} + b_2 \Delta \text{DMB}_{t-1} + b_3 \Delta \text{DMB}_{t-2} + b_4 \Delta \text{ERR}_{t-2}$.

Variable or parameter	ΔY_t		
	GDPI	NS0	NS1
C	−0.295	−0.376	−0.430
	(0.190)	(0.241)	(0.169)
$\Delta \text{PAHED}_{t-1}$	1.258	1.004	1.193
	(0.274)	(0.241)	(0.263)
ΔDMB_{t-1}	5.646	6.925	7.605
	(1.440)	(1.211)	(1.318)
ΔDMB_{t-2}	4.142	5.953	6.223
	(1.284)	(1.149)	(1.180)
$\Sigma \Delta \text{DMB}$	9.788	12.877	13.828
	(2.001)	(1.806)	(1.834)
ΔERR_{t-2}	−0.092	−0.122	−0.124
	(0.030)	(0.026)	(0.027)
AR(1)	−0.049	0.282	−0.062
	(0.327)	(0.297)	(0.322)
$\hat{R}^2$	0.696	0.746	0.796
D–W	1.866	2.135	1.822
n	19	19	19

C	Constant term
AR(1)	First-order autoregressive coefficient
$\hat{R}^2$	Adjusted coefficient of determination
D–W	Durbin–Watson coefficient
n	Number of observations
PAHED_{t-1}	Lagged price-adjusted, BEA 6% high-employment budget deficit as percent of GNP
DMB_{t-1}	Lagged real change in monetary base as percent of GNP (December figures divided by 4th quarter GNP implicit price deflator)
DMB_{t-2}	Two-year lagged real change in monetary base as percent of GNP (December figures divided by 4th quarter GNP implicit price deflator)
ERR_{t-2}	Trade weighted, real exchange rate, lagged two years (March 1973 = 100)
GPDI	Gross private domestic investment as percent of GNP
NS0	Conventional net national saving = gross saving − capital consumption allowances with adjustment, as percent of GNP
NS1	Change in total fixed reproducible capital plus net foreign investment, as percent of GNP

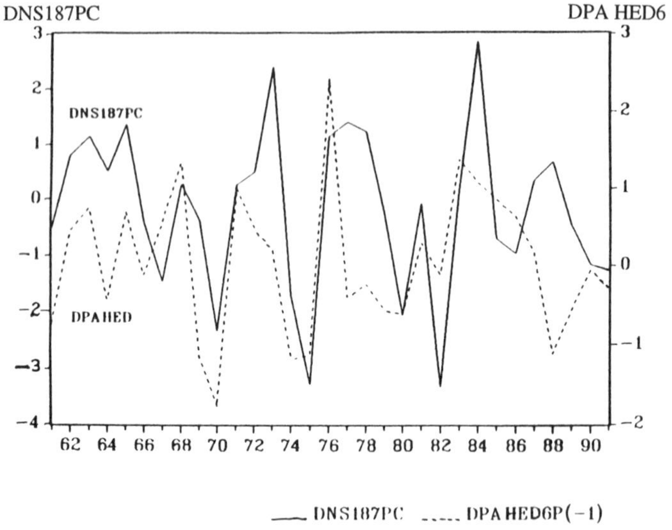

Fig. 7. Percent changes in ratios to GDP of total, real, tangible, national saving and lagged price-adjusted high-emp. deficit.

4. Tangible public investment and productivity

Finally, we may bring some of our data to bear on the critical question of the productivity of public tangible investment, of which infrastructure investment is of course a significant part, a part that we may expect will rise with the decline of military spending and the policy commitments of the new Clinton Administration. We have estimated a log-linear production function from data on total labor hours worked and the end-of-previous-year stocks of private and public tangible capital.[5] Parameter estimates indicate the expected major role of labor and suggest the usually observed increasing returns to scale. Most interesting for our purposes, however, are the significantly positive coefficients to *both* private and public tangible capital. We may indeed note that, while the differences are hardly statistically significant, the coefficient of public capital is larger than that of private capital. One percent more of private capital was associated with 0.19 percent more of GDP, while one percent more of public capital was associated with

[5] We lack useful series on stocks of government-financed capital stocks of education and R&D. We are further inhibited from entering even crude approximations into our production function by the unreasonableness of expecting changes in such stocks from having any effect on output other than with long and variable lags.

Table 6
Production function: gross domestic product and labor hours and private and public tangible capital; $\text{LGD87}_t = b_0 + b_1\text{LLBRHRS}_t + b_2\text{LKPRVTTAN}_{t-1} + b_3\text{LKPUBTAN}_{t-1}$.

Variable or parameter	Regression coefficients and standard errors
C	−0.462
	(0.212)
LLBRHRS_t	0.973
	(0.081)
LKPRVTTAN_{t-1}	0.190
	(0.054)
LKPUBTAN_{t-1}	0.270
	(0.068)
AR(1)	0.007
$\hat{R}^2$	0.998
D–W	1.167
n	31

C	Constant term
AR(1)	First-order autoregressive coefficient
$\hat{R}^2$	Adjusted coefficient of determination
D–W	Durbin–Watson coefficient
n	Number of observations
LGDP87_t	Logarithm of gross domestic product in 1987 dollars
LLBRHRS_t	Logarithm of labor hours
LKPRVTTAN_{t-1}	Logarithm of private tangible capital stock in 1987 dollars at end of previous year
LKPUBTAN_{t-1}	Logarithm of public tangible capital stock in 1987 dollars at end of previous year
t	1961 to 1991

0.27 percent more of GDP. Inasmuch as the measured public capital stock was much less than the measured private capital stock, this suggests a much greater marginal productivity of public capital. If we could take the numbers seriously – I would caution that they be viewed as just one more bit of evidence in a very difficult, tricky and controversial set of estimation efforts[6] – they would imply a gross marginal product of public capital investment 4.5 times that of private capital investment.[7]

5. Summary and conclusion

Government saving should properly include government-financed investment. Accounts that do so show national saving to be much more than that shown in conventional measures and the negative accounting contribution of government budget deficits to national saving to be much less. This, of course, does not imply incorrectness of the widespread view that national saving in the United States is in some sense 'too low'. It does, however, put new light on proposals to increase it.

First, changes in public tangible investment and investment in education are found to be *positively* related to changes in price-adjusted, high-employment deficits (inflation-adjusted, structural deficits). This suggests that direct efforts to reduce Federal deficits, particularly subject to the public constraint of aversion to tax increases, are likely to reduce public investment. Increases in the deficit, if past history is to be a guide, may conversely be associated with increases in public investment and government saving.

Second, changes in these deficits have also been associated with changes in the same direction in gross private domestic investment and even changes in narrow measures of national saving, excluding government and household investment in tangible capital. Hence changes in real deficits have been associated a fortiori with changes in the same direction in a broader measure of national saving, including government and household investment in tangible capital.

Finally, our findings suggest, as have those of some others, that the pay-off to public tangible investment, at least, is distinctly positive and very possibly larger at the current margin, than that to private investment.

---

[6] See, for a not entirely representative sample, Aschauer (1989), Munnell (1990) and Eisner (1991b).

[7] The mean of the observations of LKPRVTTAN, the natural logarithm of private tangible capital stock, is 8.8850, corresponding to 7,222.7 billions of 1987 dollars. The mean of observations of LKPUBTAN, the natural logarithm of private capital stock, is 7.7377, corresponding to $2,293.1 billion. The ratio of (geometric) means is thus 3.15. The mean of the observations of LGDP87, the natural logarithm of gross domestic product is 8.0852, corresponding to 3,245.9 billion in 1987 dollars. The implied gross marginal product of private tangible capital is thus 0.0855358. The implied gross marginal product of public tangible capital is 0.3817155, or 4.46264 times the marginal product of private capital.

References

Aschauer, D., 1989, Is public expenditure productive?, Journal of Monetary Economics, March, 177–200.

Eisner, R., 1986, How real is the federal deficit? (The Free Press, New York).

Eisner, R., 1988, Extended measures of national income and product, Journal of Economic Literature 26, December, 1611–1684.

Eisner, R., 1989, The total incomes system of accounts (University of Chicago Press, Chicago).

Eisner, R., 1991a, The real rate of U.S. national saving, Review of Income and Wealth 37, no. 1, March, 13–32.

Eisner, R., 1991, Infrastructure and regional economic performance: Comment, New England Economic Review, September/October, 47–58.

Eisner, R., 1992a, Deficits: Which, how much and so what?, American Economic Review 82, no. 2, May, 295–298.

Eisner, R., 1992b, U.S. national saving and budget deficits, For The political economy of investment, saving and finance: A global perspective, Gerald Epstein and Herbert Gintis, eds., A project of the World Institute for Development and Economic Research (WIDNER), The United Nations University, Helsinki, Finland, manuscript copy, 6/20/92.

Eisner, R. and P.J. Pieper, 1992, National saving and the twin deficits: myth and reality, in: The Economics of Saving, James H. Gapinski, ed. (Kluwer Academic Publishers).

Lange, O., 1938, The rate of interest and the optimal propensity to consume, Economica 5, February, 12–32. Reprinted in American Economic Association, Readings in Business Cycle Theory (Blakiston, Philadelphia) 169–192.

Munnell, A.H., 1990, How does public infrastructure affect regional economic performance?, New England Economic Review, September/October, 11–32.

[25]

Sense and nonsense about budget deficits

Almost everybody talks about federal budget deficits. Almost everybody is against them in principle. And almost no one knows what he or she is talking about.

Maybe it goes back to something deep in our Calvinist heritage, that we must suffer rather than borrow. 'No gain without pain', goes the modern version. We must raise taxes or cut useful government spending now to pay for a better future.

Or perhaps it has more recent political roots. Franklin D. Roosevelt pledged but never managed to 'balance the budget', and Republicans attacked Democrats over budget deficits for the next 50 years. Then, with the huge Reagan-era deficits, Democrats thought they had their chance and turned the tables on the issue. In charting his independent course, Ross Perot has made the deficit his principal issue and has advanced a number of extreme 'solutions' to the problem, including a balanced-budget amendment to the Constitution. President Clinton, in his initial State of the Union address on the economy, was constrained to present a comprehensive deficit reduction package.

The public has always agreed in wide proportions that the deficit should be eliminated. But it is far from clear that any candidate - Republican, Democrat, or Independent - has ever won an election with this position. In fact, many have lost by opposing popular deficit-increasing measures or by supporting tax increases to reduce it. With all the hoopla about deficit reduction, a Gallup poll reported at the time of Clinton's first State of the [99] Union address is significant. Asked, 'Which is more important, creating jobs or reducing the deficit?', 65 per cent of respondents chose 'creating jobs' and only 28 per cent 'reducing the deficit'.

The public may well not understand the choice, but, as we shall confirm, deficits can indeed create jobs. Deficits can be good for us, as well as bad. And deficits can be too small as well as too large. To know which, you at least have to measure them right.

What is the deficit and how is it measured?

Few people have any notion how the federal budget deficit is measured. Many, including the major TV news anchors, editorialists in leading newspapers such as *The New York Times*, and countless politicians, do not even seem to know the difference between deficit and debt. The deficit is the amount by which expenditures exceed tax revenues in a given period or, in the more comprehensive official jargon, 'outlays' exceed 'receipts', and hence the amount that must be borrowed or added to the debt over that period. The debt is the amount owed at any point in time - what has been borrowed and not paid back.

President Clinton himself, in his Inaugural Address, succumbed to the public looseness of phrase, if not general confusion, in saying that we must 'cut our massive debt'. If he meant the federal debt, that in fact is quite beyond reasonable possibility in the foreseeable future. Clinton has more realistically talked of cutting the *deficit* by $140 billion as against forecasts of what it will be in 1997. But that would still leave a deficit of some $206 billion and the debt hence *growing* by that amount annually. Only a budget *surplus* would reduce the debt.

Yet we still hear the President and others talking about reducing the debt. Witness the pious Mobil advertisement that argues, 'Clearly, one of President Clinton's and the 103rd Congress's primary tasks must be to reduce the federal debt to the extent practical as soon as possible', adding inexplicably the internally redundant clause, 'and to balance the budget to prevent further deficits'.

Many do not understand the measures of the debt about which they speak so much. The most frequently cited figure, something over $4 trillion now, is a gross 'total', which includes over $1 trillion of 'debt' held within the government, largely by trust funds such as those for Social Security for old age and retirement. But a more meaningful figure, relevant to household spending, financial markets, and business decisions, and excluding accounting transactions between one arm of government and another, is for what is called the 'gross federal debt held by the public'. This came, at the end of the 1992 fiscal year, to almost exactly $3 trillion.

We have a vast number of measures of the federal deficit, most of which would horrify any private or public accountants worth their salt. Aside from differences between the Bureau of Economic Analysis national income accounts and the Office of Management and Budget and Congressional budgets, budgets with and without 'deposit insurance' outlays (chiefly for the Savings and Loan bailout), our federal accounting violates a basic principle of accounting for private business, most state and local governments in the United States, and national governments across the globe: it does not distinguish between current or operating outlays and capital expenditures.

If there were no separate capital accounts, almost every large corporation in the United States would be reporting 'deficits' or losses. Of course, this is not so. Private businesses exclude capital outlays from their current accounts and charge only depreciation when presenting their income (or profit) and loss statements. In a growing company, current investment is virtually always greater than depreciation, which is an average of past investment. Including depreciation rather than current investment thus permits profitable companies to keep their bottom line in the black. And many state and local governments in the United States, required by their constitutions to balance their current or operating budgets, finance capital outlays (like roads and bridges and new water systems or school buildings) separately, by borrowing.

Even this, however, would not now do much for the federal government deficit. Assume, counter-factually, that federal accounting conformed to private business practice and included in the budget only the depreciation on past tangible investment, not current tangible capital investment. The resulting US federal budget deficit would be [100] virtually the same as the overall deficits generally reported. This is a manifestation of something of which we should be much more aware – virtually zero net public investment in physical infrastructure. Our public physical plant is wearing out at least as fast as it is being replaced. A more comprehensive measure of investment, though, would include the Office of Management and Budget (OMB)'s estimates of 'Major Federal Capital Outlays' for research and development and education and training as well as physical capital. If we used this measure, net investment, reflecting (however inadequately) the needs of our growing population, would be positive. Its exclusion would reduce the measure of the deficit by perhaps $80 billion of the $290 billion reported for our last fiscal year.

Given some $175 billion per year of federal grants to state and local governments, it might make some sense to present a consolidated account for all of government, as the US Bureau of Economic Analysis does in its national income and product accounts. If we do that and then separate out all capital expenditures, for both tangible and intangible investment, we find that while the total consolidated 1991 budget retains a deficit of $193 billion, the current account portion of that deficit is only $24 billion.

A large part of the deficit is accountable directly to our slow economy and high unemployment. The US Congressional Budget Office indeed estimates that each percentage point of unemployment adds, in the short term, $50 billion to the deficit, with the amount growing over time as additional deficit adds more to debt and subsequent interest payments.

If national unemployment in 1993 were merely back at its 5.3 per cent average of the years 1988 to 1990 – instead of hovering at nearly 7 per cent – the deficit would be $100 billion less; by 1996, as a consequence of interest payment savings on a lesser accumulated debt, it would be some $130 billion less. Virtually all of the Clinton–Gore Administration's commitment to deficit reduction could be realized by that minimal reduction in unemployment. Achieving a 4 per cent unemployment rate, which has long been a target, or a 3 per cent rate such as during the Vietnam War, could bring about an even greater reduction in the deficit.

The Office of Management and Budget, in its final document released by President Bush, offered 'baseline' deficit estimates grounded on the relatively pessimistic economic outlook of 51 private 'blue chip' forecasters. They foresaw real GDP growth of only 3 per cent in 1993, 2.9 per cent in 1994, and [101] then down to 2.5 per cent from 1995 to 1998; unemployment was still projected at 5.7 per cent for 1998.

The OMB also presented deficit estimates on the basis of 'high-growth' projections, which had the GDP increasing in successive years at 3.5 per cent, 4.0 per cent, 3.7 per cent, 3.4 per cent, 3.2 per cent, and 3.0 per cent, with unemployment down to 5.0 per cent in 1998, its level in March 1989 at the beginning of the Bush Administration. I have added estimates of what the deficit would have been in any year over which unemployment had averaged 5 per cent. These were calculated on the assumption, consistent with Congressional Budget Office calculations, that each percentage point reduction in unemployment is associated in the short run, without including eventual interest savings with a reduction in the deficit equal to 0.8 per cent of the GDP.

I have compared deficit projections under the different assumptions as to growth and employment, and the results are striking. With no additional spending cuts or tax increases, the deficit would have fallen, in the high-growth scenario from 4.9 per cent of the GDP in 1992 to 2.1 per cent in 1998, more than meeting the Clinton

Administration's goals. If unemployment had been down to 5 per cent throughout the period, instead of just in any given year, there would have been growing interest savings on a lower debt, and the deficit would have shrunk even more than shown in my short-run 5 per cent unemployment curves.

The deficit in a growing economy

In an expanding economy with an increasing population, almost everything grows: births and deaths, marriages and divorces, borrowing and repayment, income and wealth, and assets and debt. The criterion for increasing debt - how much borrowing there should be - is directly related to income. This is true for the government as well as for prudent private borrowers, banks, and businesses. Governments, as well as people, should not indefinitely allow their debt to grow faster than their income.

One may well argue that a responsible deficit target, similar to responsible targets for private business and households, is that debt over the long run grow no faster than income or, for the nation, Gross Domestic Product (GDP). At the end of the 1939 fiscal year, as the New Deal was giving way to World War II, the gross federal debt held by the public came to $41 billion, 47 per cent of GDP. In 1946, after World War II, it reached $242 billion, or 114 per cent of GDP. By 1980, with federal budget deficits in all of the years from 1961 on, the debt had grown to $709 billion, but had fallen, relatively, to 27 per cent of GDP. At the end of the 1992 fiscal year, the debt held by the public was $2999 billion, up to 51 per cent of GDP, but still only a little more than it was in 1939 and less than half of its proportion just after World War II. We may note both the short-period changes and the secular swings of the debt-GDP

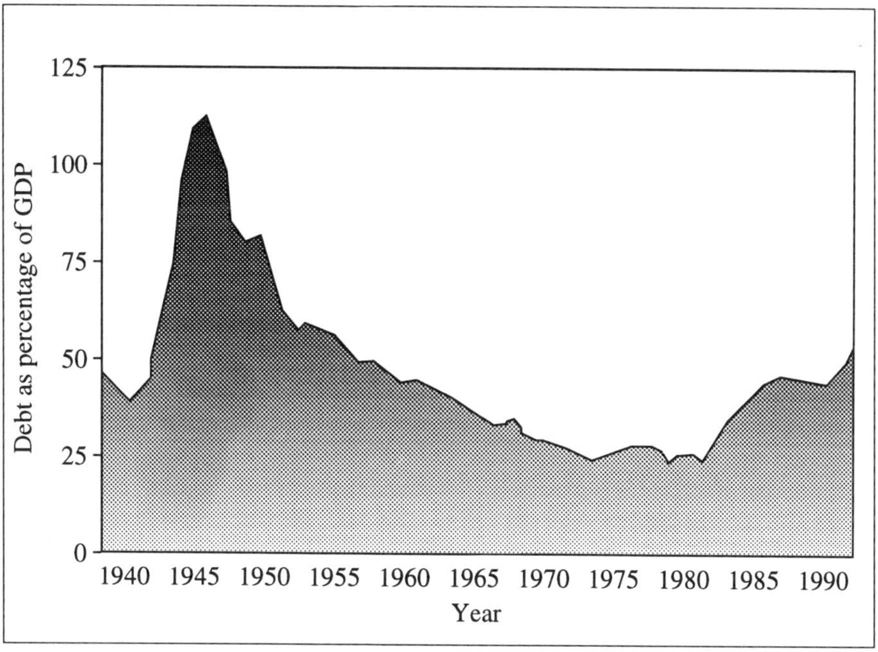

Figure 1 Debt as percentage of GDP 1940-90

ratio in the graph in Figure 1.

There is nothing sacrosanct about any particular debt–GDP ratio. In periods of recession we may expect deficits to rise and the debt to grow more rapidly than GDP, which will itself be growing much less rapidly, if at all. If there is need for major investment, debt may again grow faster than GDP.

But suppose we were to keep the debt–GDP ratio constant. It is instructive to note what this 'equilibrium' target would imply for our current situation. If we maintained the approximate 1992 debt–GDP ratio of 0.5 and assumed an estimated 7 per cent growth then the projected 1993 deficit would be $210 billion. Compare this with the final Bush OMB projected 1993 deficit of $327 billion as well as with the $227 billion that deficit would be if unemployment were two percentage points less.

The Bush OMB's final deficit projections are based on the 'blue chip' private forecasters' anticipation of an unemployment rate averaging 7.2 per cent for all of calendar 1993! Greeted with much expression of concern, the OMB had its mismeasured deficit declining from $327 billion in 1993 to $270 billion in 1994 and $230 billion in 1995 before beginning to rise again to $266 billion in 1996, $305 billion in 1997, and $320 billion in 1998. They assumed unemployment above 6 per cent through 1995 and at 5.7 per cent in 1998. The OMB [102] also assumed interest rates on 91-day Treasury bills would rise, unaccountably, from their current rate of less than 3 per cent to over 5 per cent, thus adding perhaps another $50 billion to the annual deficit.

Those projections, though, even if correct, would still have the deficit-to-GDP ratio below 3.9 per cent, with the debt–GDP ratio virtually stable, at 57 per cent, by 1998. The debt would then be growing at a 6.67 per cent per annum rate with a projected nominal GDP growth of 5.93 per cent. If the rate of growth of GDP were over 6.67 per cent, the debt–GDP ratio would be declining. If unemployment were down only to its 5.2 per cent rate of 1989 and Treasury bill rates were still around 3 per cent, the resulting 1997 deficit would be not $305 billion but of the order of $200 billion, or 2.5 per cent of GDP. With a slightly more ambitious 7 per cent rate of growth of GDP, the debt–GDP ratio would then be headed for an equilibrium ratio of 36 per cent, well below its current figure of about 51 per cent. In a meaningful, relative sense, President Clinton would have reduced 'our massive debt'.

How do deficits hurt? Or do they?

Much of what is written and said about the damage done by federal budget deficits is sheer nonsense, no matter how often repeated. First, of course, the notion that the federal government will go bankrupt because it is unable to pay off or service its debt is absurd. A sovereign government need never overtly repudiate a debt in its own currency. It can always tax those subject to its laws, including bondholders, to get the necessary proceeds. Or it can simply print the money needed – in the case of the United States, have the Federal Reserve buy Treasury securities. That may have other consequences, which we will consider. But in any event, there is no issue of bankruptcy for debt in dollars. (Debt denominated in a foreign currency, which is not the case for the United States, is quite another matter.) The debt may be repaid in cheaper dollars, but there is no reason why it cannot be repaid.

Ross Perot warned repeatedly that we are 'spending our children's money'. But our children's money has not yet been printed and will of course be printed or supplied when our children need it, in whatever quantities the interaction of the monetary authorities and our banking and financial system then determine. Alan Greenspan's successors in the Federal Reserve will always be able to supply money for our children. What they cannot supply and, we shall see, what may be lacking are the real resources of capital - public and private, tangible and intangible, human and nonhuman - with which we are failing now to endow our children.

We are also told that our continuing deficits mean we are passing ever greater debt on to our children. This is literally true. Our children will be the *owners* of all those Treasury bills, notes and bonds that constitute the debt. That will give them a nice cushion of accumulated savings. Is that necessarily so bad?

We are further told that the interest burden of the debt, currently about $185 billion per year, is a heavy drag on the economy. In fact it comes to only about 3 per cent of GDP. But, more fundamentally, the interest payments of the Treasury are, after all, income to their recipients. Any taxes that may be levied to finance the payments are then matched by added income.

There are those who call this a regressive redistribution of income, on the assumption that the rich receive interest income financed by taxes paid by the poor. A moment's reflection casts major doubt on that assumption. The ultimate beneficiaries of the interest receipts - via pension funds, insurance, and banking services, as well as savings bonds - must for the most part be in the large middle class. And relatively little is paid in taxes by the very poor. The social cost of debt and deficits will have to be found elsewhere.

On a more sophisticated level, some might argue that if marginal tax rates are three percentage points higher to finance interest payments, work-effort may be discouraged. People receiving large proportions of their income in the form of interest would not wish to work to earn more with Uncle Sam taking still another three cents out of every additional dollar. But with interest income only 3 per cent of GDP (a bit higher as a percentage of national income), we are a long way from having to worry about that.

It is also said that large deficits will cause inflation. The first answer to this is that we have had some large deficits in the last decade, and inflation has declined sharply. It is running currently at no more than 3 per cent by official measure and is [103] probably less, perhaps zero with full adjustment for product improvement. Indeed, the times series relation between deficits and inflation in the United States has generally been negative; bigger deficits have come with less inflation and smaller deficits with more inflation. To be fair, however, this reflects primarily the effect of the economy on the deficit, rather than the deficit on the economy. In recessions, inflation tends to be less, and, with lesser tax revenues and greater outlays for unemployment benefits, deficits are larger. In booms, inflation may be more while tax revenues are greater and unemployment benefits less, so that deficits are less.

An appropriate test of the effect of deficits on inflation, or on any other economic variables, would have then to abstract from the reverse effect of those variables on the deficit. One way to get at this is to work with a measure of the deficit that is not affected by the fluctuations of the economy. For this purpose we may use what has variously been called the structural, the cyclically-adjusted, or the 'high-employment' budget. This indicates what tax revenues, outlays, and the deficit *would* be if the economy were on some fixed path as, say, a 6 per cent unemployment path for a measure that has been published periodically by the Bureau of Economic Analysis. The size of the high-employment deficit may then be a measure of fiscal stimulus. But larger high-employment deficits have also not been associated with more inflation.

The reason for this negative finding brings us closer to the fundamental relation of government [104] deficits and government debt to the economy. That depends very considerably on the state of the economy, whether it is zooming along at top speed or is in a sluggish, slack-resources, unemployment mode. Recognizing this will lead us to the conclusion, however shocking to some, that *deficits can be good for us*. This is not to say that they are always beneficial, but they will be good if they generate otherwise lacking purchasing power for the products of American business. In general, deficits can be too small as well as too large. And for most of the past half-century, including right now, contrary to the conventional wisdom, we will find that deficits have been too small. Far from struggling to reduce the deficit, as President Clinton has constrained himself, or offering demagogic appeals for zero deficits (or even surpluses to 'pay off' the debt), as has Mr Perot, we should be looking for the most productive ways to increase it.

Are deficits relevant?

There is a school of thought, led by Harvard's Robert Barro, which argues that deficits essentially do not matter. This is not my argument. What Barro and his many followers (still a minority among economists) claim is that financing government expenditures by borrowing and by taxes (at least non-distortionary 'lump-sum' ones) are equivalent in their effects on the economy. This proposition is called 'Ricardian equivalence', [105] after the great classical economist, David Ricardo, who first suggested the possibility before later rejecting it. It reasons that if taxpayers have greater after-tax incomes because government expenditures are financed by borrowing instead of by taxes, they will not spend their extra income. Instead, they will save it to pay the future taxes necessary to service the resulting debt, or else leave the money to their children, who will pay those taxes.

The arguments against Ricardian equivalence are myriad: the difference between borrowing and lending costs of government and private agents who frequently have liquidity constraints; the lack of certainty or even knowledge by any of us that taxes will in fact be higher in the foreseeable future or that others, including the parents of our children's spouses or the other grandparents of our grandchildren, will not pay those taxes; and finally the case where we have no children or else consider them worthless and not worth providing for. But I leave that debate to the economics journals, which have filled many pages with it.

How deficits do matter

We return then to the mainstream argument that deficits do matter; the question is how. Simply enough, deficits, as opposed to government outlays financed by taxes, matter because they add to the purchasing power and aggregate demand of the private sector. A person or business is likely to spend more when holding a government security than a receipt for payment of taxes. The former, after all, is part of the person's or business's wealth. All of our economic theory and empirical evidence indicate that people with more wealth, other things being equal, will spend more.

The argument that increases in the real value of the government debt to the private sector increase consumption and aggregate demand is old neoclassical economics, a line of reasoning to be found in the works of Gottfried Haberler and A.C. Pigou. The Keynesian argument is parallel, that real deficits increase consumption by adding to current real disposable income. Keynes also included changes in the value of wealth as an argument of his consumption function, warning that ignoring them would be perilous in times in which they changed.

Failure to take into account the huge increase in debt held by the public during World War II - the debt–GDP ratio was well over 100 per cent in 1946 - was a major factor in the alarmist, erroneous predictions that the end of the war would bring on a major recession. And that failure was part of the background and motivation for the path-breaking work of Nobel Laureates Milton Friedman and Franco Modigliani in developing our modern theory of the consumption function. Wealth, or the permanent income to be expected from that wealth, are critical determinants of consumption expenditures.

If we doubt that theory, we can try a quick mental experiment. Suppose I could arrange with Lloyd Bentsen, our new Secretary of the Treasury, for each reader of this article to be given $100 000 in new Treasury bills. How many would feel poorer? How many would spend none of their new holdings? And how many might just buy a new car or take a more expensive vacation trip? If even some fall into that last category, the result is higher consumption expenditures and more business to those producing the additional goods or services purchased. But this additional holding of Treasury bills - or other Treasury securities, or cash to the extent that the Federal Reserve buys some of the additional debt - is exactly what happens when the government runs a deficit.

There is one important qualification, however, too often overlooked: inflation. If prices today are 3 per cent higher than a year ago, then today's $100 000 are the equivalent, roughly, of $97 000 in last year's purchasing power. We may be expected to feel richer and spend more only to the extent that the deficit raised our wealth in government securities by more than enough to keep up with inflation. A deficit is a *real* deficit only to the extent that it adds to the real value, that is the value in constant dollars, of our holdings of government debt. We may view the loss in real value of outstanding debt due to inflation as an 'inflation tax' levied by the government on debt holders, thus reducing that real deficit. Another way of looking at this is to see that of the $185 billion of interest payments swelling the nominal deficit, some $90 billion represents the amount the government finds it necessary to pay, because of higher nominal interest rates, to compensate bondholders for their inflation losses.

The short run: consumption, output, and employment

While the greater wealth the public holds in government debt as a result of deficits will induce more consumption, greater deficits are actually [106] often accompanied by less consumption. This is because recessions and associated unemployment reduce consumption and also, as we have noted, increase deficits. As warned before, we have to avoid confusing cause and effect, the effect of deficits on the economy and the effect of the economy on deficits.

To ascertain the effect of an independent increase in the deficit, one not brought on by the decline of the economy, we need again to consider the high-employment budget, which indicates what the deficit *would be*, aside from fluctuations of the economy, if unemployment were fixed. And further, since we can expect that it is only real increases in the wealth in the form of government debt held by the public that can be expected to affect consumption, we should also adjust the deficit for the loss in the real value of the debt due to changes in the price level.

The impact of deficits on the economy should then be found in the relation between an inflation-adjusted and cyclically adjusted deficit and the economic variables with which we are concerned. I have accordingly constructed (along with Paul J. Pieper of the University of Illinois at Chicago, my collaborator in many of these investigations), time series of what I call the price-adjusted, high-employment deficit. And I have worked these into simple charts and tables and more rigorous least-squares regressions as well as, more recently, VARs (vector autoregressions). These latter put together past and current values of the presumably underlying variables and try to estimate their relations and interrelations without preconditions or confining specifications as to lags or what determines what. The results have confirmed, over and over as I have tested the relations for robustness over time as well as for variations in formulations, that deficits, over the past three decades at least, have been good for us.

Specifically, we have found that higher values of the price-adjusted, high-employment deficit, taken as a percent of GNP or GDP, have been associated with more rapid subsequent growth in real product, as may be seen in the graph in Figure 2, sparing readers of this article more sophisticated statistical presentation. (This may be found in my 1986 book, *How Real is the Federal Deficit?*, and in numerous periodical articles.) And since more rapid growth in real product is associated with alleviated unemployment, it comes as no surprise that we have also found that larger deficits have been associated with less subsequent unemployment.

There is one condition that must have been necessary for this result. There must have been slack resources for most of the last 30 years over which I have estimated these relations. Unemployment could not have been reduced by bigger deficits if it were already at its rock-bottom, full-employment level. And output could not have increased faster if there were no additional workers and no additional capacity for increased production. Sadly, this slack-resource condition was met.

It must be recognized that, except for wartime – unemployment reached the 3 per cent level during the Vietnam War – we have rarely if ever had truly full employment. Herein is a vital caution to President Clinton and the Congress as they put into place [107] a program for economic recovery and sustained, high-investment growth. We entered 1993 with unemployment still over 7 per cent and most forecasts, including those used by the OMB, the Congressional Budget Office, and the Clinton Administration itself, indicating that this unemployment rate would subside only very slowly.

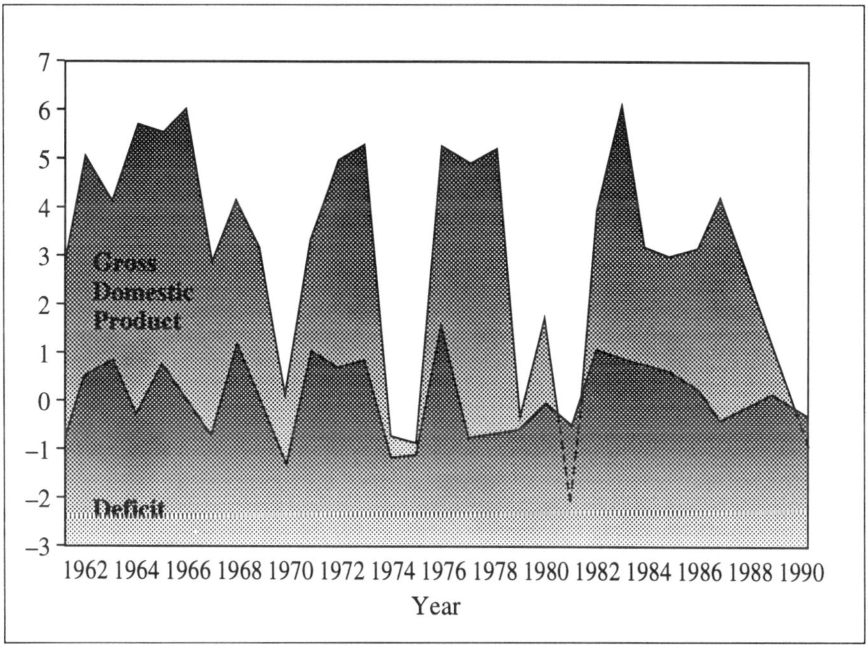

Figure 2 Changes in price-adjusted high-employment deficit and real GDP as percentages of GDP, 1961-91

Yet the economic program the President presented in his February 17 address to Congress included a reduction of the structural deficit by $55 billion from 1993 to 1994. Is this a time for the restraint of deficit reduction or for the stimulus of *more* government spending - preferably for public investment - and *lower* taxes?

This fundamental fact of excess unemployment may be challenged by devotees of the pernicious 'natural rate' of unemployment or 'non-accelerating-inflation-rate of unemployment (NAIRU)'. They may find 6 per cent or 6.5 per cent or even the 7+ per cent of the past year to be natural. They may think that in our perfect market economy whatever *is* must be optimal and natural. I recall the joke about the graduate student who in January 1983 wrote on the board the flash, depth-of-recession news from the Bureau of Labor Statistics: 'The natural rate of unemployment has just reached 10.7 per cent'.

But I will maintain that involuntary unemployment due to a lack of aggregate demand or purchasing power is a fundamental fact of our economy, as confirmed by these effects of deficits. And this fundamental fact makes all the difference, making a mockery of most arguments for reducing the deficit at this time, and exposes the error of the conventional wisdom of too many, although not all, macroeconomic theorists.

The long run: national saving

The fact that increases in the real, structural deficit have usually ushered in growth or greater growth in output and reductions in unemployment becomes central to the one legitimate possible argument that deficits may be too large. It relates to the future, not to their current effect. As long as there is some slack in the economy, fiscal stimulus in the form of bigger deficits will in the short term raise output and employment. But, some insist, these deficits reduce 'national saving'. In so doing they reduce the capital we will have in the future and hence reduce future product. That is - or would be, if it were true - the real burden that deficits place on our children and grandchildren and indeed, except for those near the end of their lives, on all of us.

Is it true, though? Do our deficits reduce national saving and investment or capital accumulation? There is one argument that gives the false impression that this is inevitable. Conventional gross national saving, GS, is defined as the sum of private saving - personal saving, PS, and business saving, BS - and public saving, or the consolidated federal, state, and local budget surpluses, FS plus SLS. And the total of gross national saving (except for a statistical discrepancy) is identically equal to the total of gross investment, GI:

$$GS \equiv PS + BS + FS + SLS \equiv GI$$

Deficits are then seen as negative surpluses, or negative public saving that offsets positive private saving. Bigger federal deficits constitute a still greater negative value to FS and hence mean less total or national saving, GS, and less gross investment [108], GI, or less accumulation of capital for the future. Reducing the deficit would raise national saving and investment. All this may seem apparent from the identity above.

This argument is alas just too simplistic. It entails the elementary fallacy of assuming *ceteris paribus*: other things being the same. But imagine more realistically, for example, that the federal deficit is reduced - FS is made less negative - by cutting grants to state and local governments, which have been running about $175 billion per year. Would this not immediately reduce state and local government surpluses, SLS, and thus offset the reduction in the federal deficit or algebraically higher value of FS?

Or suppose the federal deficit is reduced by raising income taxes. This would reduce disposable personal income and surely reduce personal saving, PS, the difference between disposable personal income and consumption, even if, as is likely, consumption were also reduced. So here we would have another offset to the increase in public saving or reduction in public spending. Similarly, an increase in corporate profits taxes would reduce undistributed corporate profits and thus reduce business saving, BS. And a like consequence, it should be noted, would flow from a reduction in government expenditures, either in transfer payments like Social Security benefits or in government outlays for goods and services. In both events, disposable income and private saving would be reduced. A decline in business saving and private saving would at least partly offset the algebraic increase in the negative federal surplus.

Looking at investment

A nation invests either by accumulating real assets on its own soil or by acquiring claims to assets in the rest of the world. Gross investment is the sum of gross private domestic investment and net foreign investment.

$$GI \equiv GPDI + NFI$$

And gross national saving, GS, we have noted, is identically equal to gross investment. We can thus better consider how reduced federal deficits would affect national saving by finding its effects on the components of gross investment.

By far the larger element here is gross private domestic investment, the sum of business and non-profit institution expenditures on new equipment and structures, construction of new housing, and increases in business inventories. Would the cuts in consumption and government expenditures for goods and services result in more or less private domestic investment? If we cut our purchases of new cars, is that going to lead the automobile industry to spend more or less on new facilities? If our disposable income is cut, will we buy more or fewer new houses?

I may seem to be loading the questions, but the answer is not that obvious. Classical economists and the conventional wisdom would argue that if the government is borrowing less, interest rates will be lower, and this will stimulate more business investment and purchases of new houses. But will this positive effect outweigh the negative effect of lower sales to ultimate consumers and of lower incomes?

A half-century ago Oscar Lange examined this issue in a seminal review of Keynes's *General Theory*. He pointed out that there was an 'optimal propensity to consume' that would maximize investment. This would be reached when the stimulative effect on investment of more consumption was eventually just balanced by the increasing negative effects of higher interest rates. [109]

What happens is that as consumption increases from low levels the developing pressure on capacity stimulates investment, and there is little rise in recession interest rates and little negative effect on investment. As full employment is approached, more consumption begins to crowd out investment simply because there is no more capacity to increase both consumption and investment. In a free market, interest rates rise as business struggles to get the funds to finance additional capital to increase capacity. But these higher interest rates increasingly choke off investment. Thus, whether more consumption or more government expenditures crowd out domestic private investment may again depend on how close the economy is to full employment. If we are at full employment – or some people's 'natural rate' – so that output cannot be increased, then it is clear that, aside from getting goods from the rest of the world, more output going to consumption or government must mean less output to private investment. If we are not at full employment, then the outcome of changes in budget deficits and changing consumption and/or government spending is not clear. We can get a pretty good idea, however, by looking at the historical facts.

Here again, my charts, tables, and regressions provide clear results. As shown in Figure 3, larger inflation-adjusted, structural deficits have been associated with *more* subsequent gross private domestic investment, and smaller deficits have been associated with less investment. My multiple regression results add the information

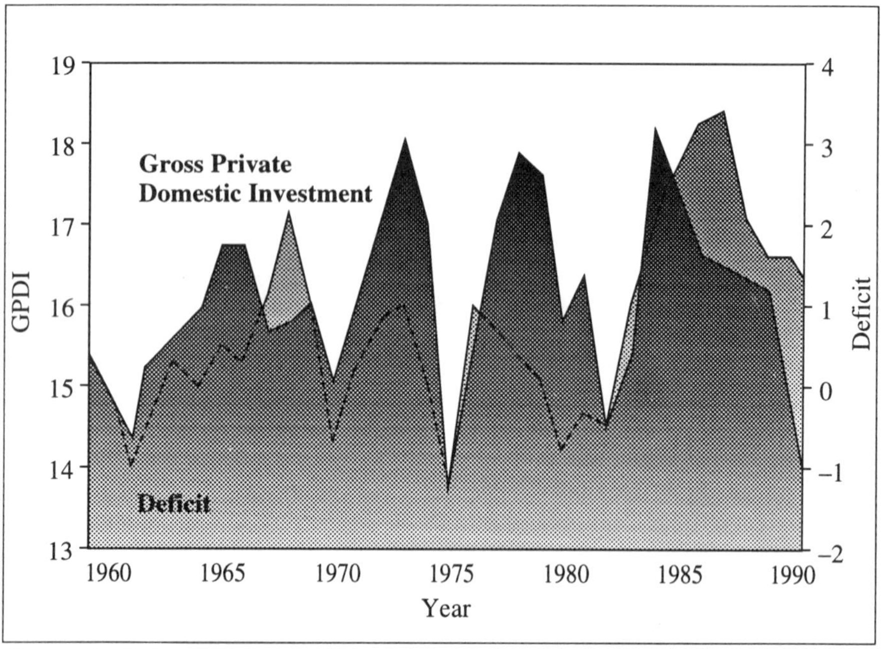

Figure 3 Price-adjusted high-employment deficit and GPD as percentages of GDP, 1959-91

that easier money, as measured by increases in the real monetary base, has also been associated with increases in real output *and* domestic investment. The remedy to any increases in interest rates would thus appear to be supportive, stimulatory monetary policy by the Federal Reserve.

This, however, still does not tell the whole story. Gross investment, which is equal to gross saving, is the sum of gross private domestic investment and net foreign investment. And net foreign investment is largely net exports or, a bit more generally, the current account surplus in our balance of international payments. If we export more than we import, to the extent that we do not give foreigners' payments back to them, we acquire foreign assets. We thus have net foreign investment. But if we import more than we export, we pay for this excess by giving foreigners net additional claims, in debt or equity, on us. We have negative net foreign investment, reducing total gross investment.

Will not increased deficits stimulate the demand for all goods, foreign as well as domestic, and thus increase imports and reduce net foreign investment? Indeed they will. And reductions in the deficit would reduce imports - perhaps by causing a recession - and raise net foreign investment! Whether the cutting of deficits raises or reduces national saving then depends on the balance of the two effects, the increase in net foreign investment and the reduction in gross private domestic investment.

Once more, we can turn to the data. The results of statistical analysis, while not as sharp as in the case of domestic investment alone, take the ground out from the argument that reducing deficits is likely to raise national saving. The historical [110] record has shown the opposite. Larger, real structural deficits have been associated with more saving and smaller deficits with less saving.

Deficits and total national saving

The statistical relation involving the conventional, narrow measure of national saving, it must be acknowledged, is not that strong. It is strengthened in a major way, however, when we recognize that what is relevant for our future, and that of our children and grandchildren, is not merely the accumulation of capital in the form of gross private domestic investment and net investment in the rest of the world. Of vital significance is public investment in all of the tangible infrastructure on which private industry depends, as well as all investment, public and private, in education and training and research and the basic services of public security on which social living depends.

Increased federal deficits may well go toward financing increased public investment. They have apparently done so already, if insufficiently. Inflation-adjusted, strategic deficits have been positively related to total government *tangible* investment. As shown in Figure 4, they have also been positively related to total government expenditures on education.

As a start to measuring this broader effect of deficits, I have related our real, structural deficits to expanded measures of national saving, and once again I find a sharp positive relation, as seen in the graph in Figure 5. Larger price-adjusted, high-

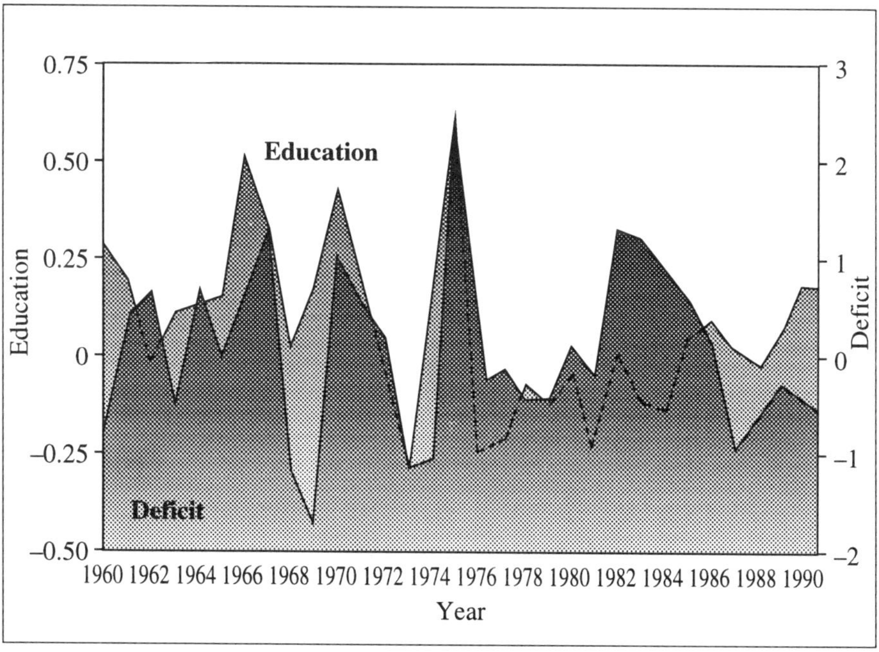

Figure 4 Changes in price-adjusted high-employment deficit and real total government expenditures on education as percentages of GNP, 1960–91

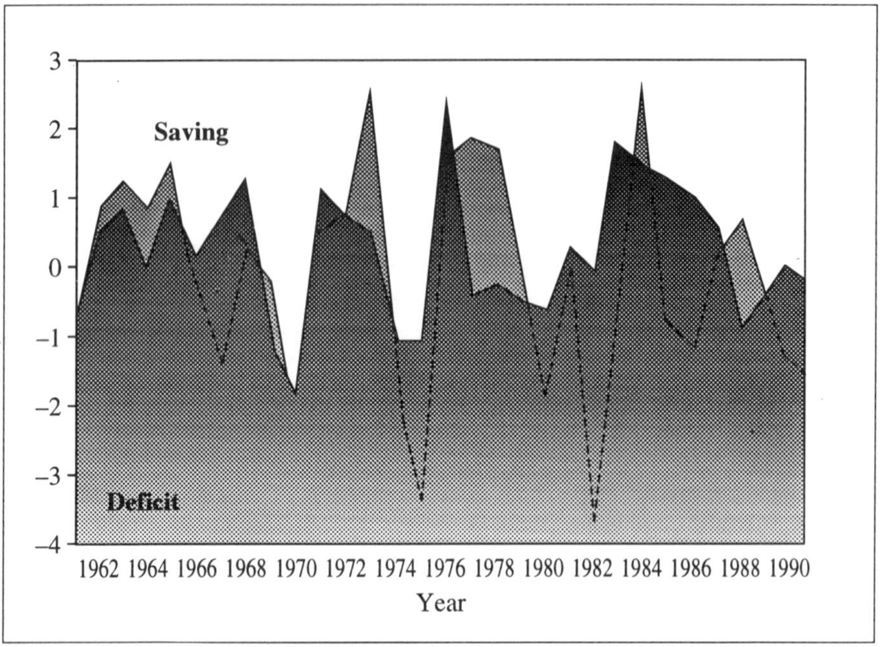

Figure 5 Changes in price-adjusted high-employment deficit and real total tangible national saving as percentages of GNP, 1961–91

employment deficits have historically been associated with more, not less, national saving.

Providing for the future

Given the state of our economy, present deficits are not too large. They will naturally come down as we reduce unemployment, speed economic growth, and achieve a prosperous economy.

Real, structural deficits have helped and not hurt current output, employment, consumption, and well-being. They also encourage more, not less, investment in our future.

President Clinton, in advancing a broad-based program for investment and economic growth, has stated explicitly, 'Deficit reduction is not an end in itself'. The purpose of deficit reduction is rather to help provide for our future and our children's future by increasing national saving and investment. But we must then be clearly aware of the danger that deficit-cutting measures will curtail or reduce conventionally measured gross private domestic or business investment, household investment, and the public investment in physical capital and in people that he sees, correctly I believe, as vital to that future. [111]

[26]

NATIONAL SAVING AND BUDGET DEFICITS

Robert Eisner*

Abstract—It has been widely argued that government budget deficits reduce national saving. Estimated relations indicate otherwise, both for the traditional or conventional, "official" measure of national saving and a broader, more relevant measure, encompassing government and household as well as private business investment in tangible capital. Greater price-adjusted, high-employment deficits, increases in the real monetary base, and declines in real exchange rates have all been associated with more subsequent national saving. These relations, manifest in AR(1) regressions over the 1972–91 period, were confirmed in VARs.

It has been widely argued that the decline of "national saving" in the United States in the 1980s was brought on by large federal budget deficits. In this paper I shall examine relations involving national saving, federal budget deficits and changes in the money supply in the United States, along with real exchange rates, to see what has actually occurred. I shall consider both the traditional or conventional, "official" measure of national saving, which (plus the statistical discrepancy) equals the sum of gross private domestic investment and net foreign investment, and a broader, more relevant measure, encompassing government and household as well as private business investment in tangible capital.[1]

In searching for the influence of federal deficits on saving it is important to distinguish it from the common effect of cyclical movements on public and private saving. Lower GNP of course means lower national income and almost certainly lower private saving. The associated reduction of tax revenues and increase in transfer payments for unemployment increase the federal deficit and thus lower public saving. A minimum necessity in the analysis therefore is use of a cyclically adjusted measure of the deficit.

Further, conventional measures of the deficit fail to take properly into account the role of inflation. They include nominal rather than real interest expenditures and correspondingly do not count as a "tax" the reduction in the real value of government debt due to inflation. I have presented both of these corrections in

Received for publication August 28, 1990. Revision accepted for publication April 30, 1993.

* Northwestern University.

I have enjoyed the research assistance of John Applegate, Maurice Ewing, Oliver Haberstroh, Satish Reddy, Craig Safir, and Marc Sokol and Stacey M. Tevlin, financial support of the National Science Foundation, through Grant #SES-8909600, for the underlying research, and helpful comments of two anonymous referees and Martin Eichenbaum and Mark Watson, but I alone am of course responsible for the contents of this paper.

[1] Still broader measures of national saving are presented in detail in Eisner (1991a). They include measures of investment in intangible capital drawing on annual time series put together in my total incomes system of accounts (Eisner, 1989c) and measures of net foreign investment based on adjustments of assets to market value found in Eisner and Pieper (1990). Consideration of the relations between budget deficits and these broader measures of saving is to be found in Eisner (1993).

earlier works[2] and offer here an extended measure of the federal "price-adjusted high-employment deficit," *PAHED*.

In previous work it was noted that higher values of this price- or inflation-adjusted, high-employment deficit, or lesser surpluses, were associated with *greater* subsequent growth in real GNP, personal consumption expenditures, and gross private domestic investment, but with lesser growth, or decline of net exports over the period 1955 to 1984.[3] These relations proved robust to the introduction of monetary variables, particularly real changes in the monetary base, which were themselves positively related to the subsequent growth of GNP, consumption and domestic investment. The theoretical rationale for the relations, and the results, it was explained, fit well the life cycle theory of consumption and neoclassical and accelerator theories of investment, reinforced perhaps by portfolio choice considerations. Real budget deficits imply increases in wealth as perceived by private agents in the form of government debt and thus generate increases in consumption demand, for both domestic and foreign goods. To the extent that some private agents are liquidity constrained, the flow of after-tax income corresponding to budget deficits, even apart from the wealth effect, further contributes to the private demand for goods. The initial increases in output, or even rational anticipations of increases in output, and the greater financial wealth in turn induce an increase in demand for physical capital.[4]

The issue at hand offers a harder test, however. Government budget deficits may bring about increases in gross private domestic investment such as those we have observed and, if net foreign investment declines sufficiently, still lower the national saving rate. In fact, imports have soared and net foreign investment turned negative with larger budget deficits and more rapidly growing GNP.

Deficits add to the total debt, interest-bearing and non-interest bearing, of the Federal government and consequently to the assets of the private sector (and of state and local government). As indicated above this may be expected to lead directly to more consumption and income and saving and, with accelerator and possibly portfolio effects, possibly to a higher proportion of income saved. To the extent the Federal Reserve buys government securities, however, part of that debt is monetized and shows up in the monetary base. It is appropriate to recognize the possible special role of monetary factors and include real changes in the monetary base, along with the deficit, in relations explaining saving. And finally, very large swings in real exchange rates over the last two decades may be expected to have substantial effects on net foreign investment and hence on national saving, which is identically equal to the sum of net foreign investment and gross domestic investment. They should be included in relations to be estimated.

Table 1 presents the results of AR(1) regressions of alternative measures of national saving on the lagged inflation-adjusted or "price-adjusted" high-employment deficit, *PAHED*(-1), and real change in the monetary base, all expressed as percentages of gross national product, and an index of the trade-weighted real exchange rate, over the years 1972 to 1991.[5] Beginning with the conventional national saving rate, *NS*0, we note a statistically significant coefficient of 0.757 for *PAHED*(-1). Each dollar of deficit was thus associated with roughly 75 cents *more* of conventional national saving.[6] We may also note the significant positive coefficients for increases in the real monetary base and the expected negative coefficient for the real exchange rate. It might be inferred from these estimated parameters that an easier monetary policy, with some lags, would increase national saving both directly and by bringing down exchange rates.[7] But reducing the

[2] Eisner and Pieper (1984) and Eisner (1986), among others.

[3] See Eisner (1986 and 1989b) and Eisner and Pieper (1988).

[4] A full set of equations, of which some of the relations estimated in this paper may be seen as reduced forms, is to be found in Eisner and Hwang (1993).

The model underlying the equations estimated in this paper is to be distinguished from that underlying Barro-Ricardian equivalence. According to the equivalence theorem, private agents would generally be indifferent to the financing of government expenditures by taxes or deficits, on the understanding that the present value of the taxes they would have to pay over their relevant horizons, including the lifetimes of successive generations, would be unaffected. The equivalence theorem would suggest that a larger deficit—reduced public saving—would induce greater private saving to pay anticipated larger future taxes. National saving, the sum of public and private saving, would hence be unaffected. The model behind this paper suggests, however, that national saving may be increased by government deficits, particularly under conditions of less-than-full-employment and excess capacity. Reductions of deficits, if they drive the economy away from full employment, may then reduce national saving.

[5] Saving rates and deficits are both highly autocorrelated and the autoregressive coefficients shown in table 1 are close to unity. Equations estimated in first differences thus gave virtually identical coefficients.

[6] Our positive coefficient of 0.757 for the deficit variable may be viewed as a Keynesian result to be contrasted with the value of zero that would be predicted by Ricardian equivalence and with the value of minus unity that would follow from complete "crowding out" in a neoclassical model.

[7] While the monetary base is contaminated by large and possibly varied holdings of currency in an underground economy and abroad, it would appear in principle still to be the best available measure of the exogenous intervention of the monetary authority. It is in effect the non-interest-bearing component of Federal liabilities which constitute non-Federal financial assets, similar in dimension to the interest-bearing debt. The change in the monetary base is thus the portion of the deficit which is monetized.

One alternative measure of monetary policy that may be suggested is M2. This, however, may be expected to be much less exogenous and less a policy instrument than the monetary base. Changes in M2 may rather reflect changes in the

TABLE 1.—ADJUSTED BUDGET DEFICITS, CHANGES IN MONETARY BASE, REAL EXCHANGE RATE AND ALTERNATE MEASURES OF NATIONAL SAVING, 1972–91

Variable or Parameter	Regression and Coefficients and Standard Errors	
	*NS*0	*NS*1
C	50.478	60.456
	(312.737)	(380.945)
PAHED(−1)	0.757	1.089
	(0.334)	(0.365)
DMB(−1)	5.999	6.858
	(1.935)	(2.109)
DMB(−2)	6.584	7.360
	(1.692)	(1.846)
ERR(−2)	−0.107	−0.099
	(0.035)	(0.038)
AR(1)	1.009	1.010
	(0.082)	(0.083)
$\hat{R}^2$	0.798	0.782
D.W.	2.583	2.630
n	20	20

Note: *C* = Constant term
AR(1) = First-order autoregressive coefficient
$\hat{R}^2$ = Adjusted coefficient of determination
D-W = Durbin-Watson coefficient
n = Number of observations
PAHED(−1) = Lagged price-adjusted, BEA 6% high-employment budget deficit as percentage of GNP
DMB(−1), *DMB*(−2) = Lagged real changes in monetary base as percentage of GNP
ERR(−2) = Real exchange rate index, March 1973 = 100, lagged two years
*NS*0 = Conventional net national saving = gross saving − capital consumption allowances with adjustment, as percentage of GNP
*NS*1 = Change in total fixed reproducible capital plus change in business inventories and net foreign investment minus statistical discrepancy, as percentage of GNP.

budget deficit in itself, if these regressions for data of the last two decades can be considered relevant, would appear not to increase national saving, as has been widely argued, but rather to reduce it.

As I have argued on a number of occasions,[8] our interest in national saving, as it relates to provision for the future, must certainly call for focus on much more than the conventional measure of saving. Investment in new automobiles provides future transportation services whether it consists of gross private domestic investment by Hertz or Avis, government purchases by a municipal police department, or private "consumption" expenditures for durable goods by households. Business, government and university expenditures for research and education and training may prove more important investments than much business spending for plant and equipment. Households and business may save by investing in land and its resources as well as in the buildings constructed above them.

Broader measures of national saving may not alter the trend to lower rates found in the conventional measure. In fact, they generally do not. Saving that includes all government and household investment in fixed reproducible capital, *NS*1, while higher than the conventional *NS*0, was also distinctly lower in the 1980s than previously.

The critical question, though, is what effect on saving can we expect from lower budget deficits? Would an increase in personal income taxes that effects a reduction in consumer spending raise national saving? The regressions of *NS*0 suggest it would not. But then it would almost certainly not raise national saving if this is taken, as it should be, to include consumer investment in durable goods as a form of saving. If the reduction in the budget deficit is accomplished, as well it might, by a reduction in government expenditures for roads, bridges and airports, we may also expect that it would *lower* and not raise the expanded measure of national saving.

And this is indeed precisely what we observe in table 1 in the report of the regression of *NS*1, which incorporates government and consumer fixed investment. The coefficient of *PAHED*(−1) is now indeed somewhat larger, 1.089, than in the regression of the narrower measure of saving, *NS*0. Coefficients of the monetary variables, *DMB*(−1) and *DMB*(−2), are again positive and the coefficient of the exchange rate negative.

Impulse response functions from vector autoregressions (VARs) of *PAHED*, *DMB*, *ERR* and either *NS*0 or *NS*1 appear to confirm these results. As shown in table 2 and figure 1, responses with the equation for the shocked variable first and the saving rate last[9] suggest that positive shocks to the cyclically- and inflation-adjusted deficits contribute, after some modest contemporaneous decline, to substantially higher saving rates.[10] Positive shocks to changes in the real

demand for money. They may even prove a perverse measure of exogenous forces, positive and larger when the FED is endeavoring to slow the economy by reducing bank reserves. In response to resultant higher interest rates, depository institutions may then solicit more in the way of liabilities which are a part of M2, increasing this broader measure of the money supply at the expense of M1.

I have experimented with changes in M2 as a monetary variable and find that while it does substantially lower the statistical significance of the deficit and monetary variables and reduce the value of the coefficient of *PAHED*; it leaves the coefficients of the latter positive and substantial, 0.441 in the *NS*0 regression and 0.864 in the regression of *NS*1. Our findings with regard to the effects of the deficit on saving would thus appear reasonably robust in the face of even the introduction of this questionable monetary parameter.

[8] See Eisner (1988, 1989a, 1989c, 1989d, and 1992), for example.

[9] This is the least supportive ordering, permitting the structural deficit to impact the unlagged saving ratio of which it is a negative component.

[10] Unlike for the single equation estimated parameters shown in table 1, however, standard errors of the VAR shock-responses, as estimated from Monte Carlo simulations generated by RATS, are relatively high.

TABLE 2.—VARS WITH 2 LAGS, *NS0* OR *NS1*, *PAHED*, *DMB*, *ERR*, IMPULSE RESPONSE FUNCTIONS TO ONE PERCENTAGE POINT SHOCK IN PRICE-ADJUSTED HIGH-EMPLOYMENT DEFICIT (*PAHED*), FROM VARS AND FROM 100-OBSERVATION SAMPLES

		From VARs		
Year	*NS0*	*PAHED*	*DMB*	*ERR*
1	−0.32	1.00	0.020	−0.1
2	0.64	−0.03	0.048	−3.8
3	−0.17	−0.35	0.023	−12.0
4	0.56	−0.71	−0.119	−9.5
5	0.24	−0.64	−0.075	−3.1
6	−0.27	−0.33	0.009	−1.2
7	0.27	−0.14	−0.013	3.6
8	0.59	0.07	−0.019	9.0
9	0.16	0.34	0.034	7.4
Year	*NS1*	*PAHED*	*DMB*	*ERR*
1	−0.19	1.00	0.029	0.3
2	1.16	0.12	0.060	−1.6
3	0.37	−0.25	0.032	−9.0
4	0.60	−0.57	−0.106	−7.9
5	−0.11	−0.57	−0.070	−4.0
6	−0.75	−0.35	0.010	−3.8
7	−0.09	−0.29	−0.022	0.5
8	0.38	−0.12	−0.039	6.9
9	0.17	0.23	0.019	7.3

From Samples					
NS0			*NS1*		
Year	Mean	Standard Error	Year	Mean	Standard Error
1	−0.29	0.68	1	−0.14	0.81
2	0.87	1.21	2	1.39	1.25
3	−0.13	1.31	3	0.49	1.53
4	1.01	1.25	4	0.75	1.25
5	0.34	1.32	5	−0.06	1.34
6	−0.07	1.32	6	−0.65	1.24
7	0.38	1.48	7	−0.06	1.34
8	0.66	1.33	8	0.58	1.66
9	−0.08	1.75	9	0.25	1.38
Cumulative	Mean	Standard Error	Cumulative	Mean	Standard Error
1	−0.29	0.68	1	−0.14	0.81
2	0.59	1.64	2	1.25	1.83
3	0.46	2.70	3	1.74	3.07
4	1.47	3.57	4	2.49	4.03
5	1.81	4.36	5	2.43	4.68
6	1.74	5.19	6	1.78	5.19
7	2.12	6.08	7	1.71	5.86
8	2.78	6.79	8	2.29	6.75
9	2.71	7.68	9	2.55	7.23

Note: Ordering is *PAHED*, *DMB*, *ERR*, and *NS0* or *NS1*.

monetary base are also related to subsequently higher saving. Positive shocks to the real exchange rate, by contrast, are associated with less subsequent national saving.

We pretend to nothing definitive about this analysis. National saving has certainly many determinants, the impact of which may vary with the state of the economy, policy regimes and the complicated and perhaps changing relations among current variables and the probability distributions of expectations of their future values. Results in full-scale, multi-equation macroeconomic models may prove more persuasive to some than the essentially reduced forms considered in this paper.

The evidence presented here, though, does offer support to the hypothesis that, as relevant theory suggests may well be the case, real budget deficits have

FIGURE 1.—VARS WITH 2 LAGS, 1972–91 OBSERVATIONS. IMPULSE RESPONSE FUNCTIONS FOR NATIONAL SAVING, AS PERCENTAGE OF GNP, *NS0* AND *NS1*, TO 1992 SHOCKS: ONE PERCENTAGE POINT SHOCK IN PRICE-ADJUSTED HIGH-EMPLOYMENT DEFICIT AS PERCENTAGE OF GNP (*PAHED*); 0.1 PERCENTAGE POINT SHOCK IN CHANGE IN REAL MONETARY BASE AS PERCENTAGE OF GNP (*DMB*); 10 POINT SHOCK IN TRADE-WEIGHTED REAL EXCHANGE RATE INDEX (*ERR*)

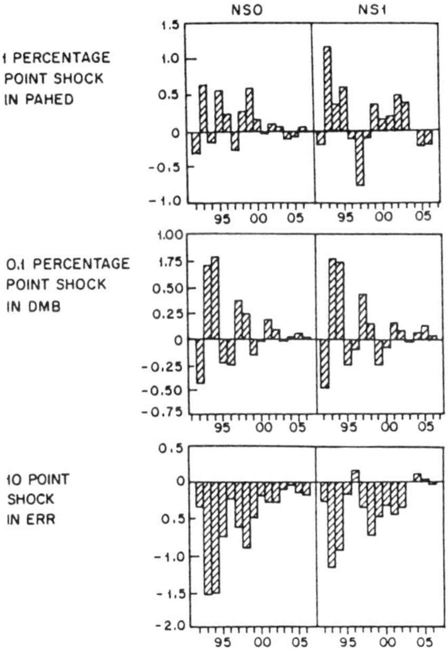

Note: Ordering is shocked variable first and saving variable last in each case.

increased rather than decreased national saving, even by its narrow, conventional measure. With the broader, more comprehensive measures of national saving with which we should be most concerned, the effects may be greater. The solution to imagined or real problems of an insufficiency of saving[11] would not appear, on the findings from data of the last two decades, to be found in reducing or eliminating "the budget deficit."

A constructive approach would point rather to an easier monetary policy, that would raise domestic and foreign investment and, most important, to shifts of priorities in the direction of more public and private household investment.[12]

APPENDIX

Definitions and Derivations of Saving Rates and Other Variables

NS0 = Conventional net national saving = gross saving minus capital consumption allowances with adjustment, from national income and product accounts as reported in *Economic Report of the President* (Feb. 1992), table B-26, p. 328, and *Survey of Current Business* (Mar. 1992), table 5.1.

NS1 = Change in total fixed reproducible capital, from "Summary Fixed Reproducible Tangible Wealth Series, 1925–90," *Survey of Current Business* (Jan. 1992), updated to 1991 with unpublished data furnished by John Musgrave of the Bureau of Economic Analysis, plus change in business inventories and net foreign investment minus statistical discrepancy from national income and product accounts.

DMB = Change in monetary base as percentage of GNP in 1987 dollars, from *Economic Report of the President* (Feb. 1992), December averages of monetary base deflated by GNP fourth-quarter implicit price deflator.

ERR = Real exchange rate index, multilateral trade-weighted value of the U.S. dollar adjusted by changes in consumer prices (Mar. 1973 = 100; 1970 to 1972 unavailable and assumed equal to 100), from *Economic Report of the President* (Feb. 1992), p. 420.

PAHED = Price-adjusted high-employment deficit as percentage of GNP, the negative of *PAHES*, the price-adjusted high-employment surplus as percentage of GNP. High employment surplus estimates, supplied by Michael Webb of the Government Division of the Bureau of Economic Analysis, were calculated on the basis of 6% unemployment through the first two quarters of 1991 (used as the 1991 annual figure) and adjusted for "price effects" (changes in real value of net Federal debt due to inflation) with the GNP implicit price deflator, as reported in Eisner and Pieper (1984) and Eisner (1986).

REFERENCES

Aschauer, David, "Is Public Expenditure Productive?," *Journal of Monetary Economics* (Mar. 1989), 177–200.

Eisner, Robert, *How Real Is the Federal Deficit?* (New York: The Free Press, a Division of Macmillan, 1986).

______, "Extended Measures of National Income and Product," *Journal of Economic Literature* 26 (Dec. 1988), 1611–1684.

______, "Divergences of Measurement and Theory and Some

[11] Some part of the decline of conventionally measured national saving is indeed more imagined than real. Major portions relate to the measures of capital consumption allowances and net foreign investment, both of which are suspect, as pointed out by Eisner (1991) and Goldstein (1990).

[12] See Aschauer (1989) for evidence that *non-military*, public tangible investment has proved a major contributor to private productivity. This suggests that reductions in military spending—including investment in weapons system and weapons research—associated with the end of the Cold War, might well be devoted to non-military public investment, rather than to deficit reduction.

Implications for Economic Policy" (1988 Presidential Address to the American Economic Association), *The American Economic Review* 79 (Mar. 1989a), 1–13.

______, "Budget Deficits: Rhetoric and Reality," *Journal of Economic Perspectives* 3 (Spring 1989b), 73–93.

______, *The Total Incomes System of Accounts* (Chicago: University of Chicago Press, 1989c).

______, "The Real Rate of National Saving," *The Review of Income and Wealth* 37 (Feb. 1991), 15–32.

______, "Deficits: Which, How Much and So What?" *The American Economic Review* 82 (May 1992), 295–298.

______, "U.S. National Saving and Budget Deficits," for Gerald Epstein and Herbert Gintis (eds.), *The Political Economy of Investment, Saving and Finance: A Global Perspective*, A Project of the World Institute for Development and Economic Research (WIDER), The United Nations University, Helsinki, Finland (1993).

Eisner, Robert, and Sang-In Hwang, "Self-Correcting Real Deficits: A New Lesson in Functional Finance," in F. van Winden and H. A. A. Verbon (eds.), *The Political Economy of Government Debt* (Amsterdam: Elsevier, 1993), 255–294.

Eisner, Robert, and Paul J. Pieper, "A New View of the Federal Debt and Budget Deficits," *American Economic Review* 74 (Mar. 1984), 11–29.

______, "Deficits, Monetary Policy and Real Economic Activity," in Kenneth J. Arrow and Michael J. Boskin (eds.), *The Economics of Public Debt* (London: Macmillan Press in association with the International Economic Association, 1988), 3–40.

______, "'The World's Greatest Debtor Nation'?" *The North American Review of Economics and Finance* 1 (Spring 1990), 9–32.

Goldstein, Henry N., "Should We Fret About Our Low Net National Saving Rate?," *The Cato Journal* 9 (Winter 1990), 441–462.

[27]

The balanced budget crusade

ROBERT EISNER

A "BALANCED budget," no matter that few know what it means, particularly by archaic federal accounting rules, seems to be an American icon. Republicans and President Clinton now both proclaim it as a goal, differing only on timing and the means of achieving it.

The politics of all this seem overwhelming. Republicans think they have an issue to gain the support of most of the 20 million 1992 Perot voters who seem obsessed over the deficit and the debt it creates. Democrats, apparently scared witless that the Republicans are right on the politics, are reduced largely to saying, "Me too, but not your way!"

It has not always been so. In his 1864 annual message to Congress, Abraham Lincoln said:

> The public debt on the first day of July last, as appears by the books of the treasury, amounted to $1,740,690,489.49. Probably, should the war continue for another year, that amount may be increased by not far from five hundred million dollars. Held as it is for the most part, by our own people, it has become a substan-

> tial branch of national, though private, property. For obvious reasons, the more nearly this property can be distributed among all the people the better.... The great advantage of citizens being creditors as well as debtors, with relation to the public debt, is obvious. Men can readily perceive that they cannot be much oppressed by a debt which they owe themselves.

In 1962, President John F. Kennedy declared, "Obviously deficits are sometimes dangerous—and so are surpluses.... What we need is not labels and cliches but more basic discussion of the sophisticated and technical questions involved in keeping a great economic machine moving ahead." And, in 1981, Congressman Jack Kemp stated, "The Republican party no longer worships at the altar of a balanced budget."

Everybody tells the pollster that a balanced budget is good, until it is learned how it might be balanced and whom it will hurt. That many would be hurt is clear. Senate Republicans, in the fall of 1995, put forth proposals that take large bites out of prospective outlays for Medicare, Medicaid, education, research, and countless other programs. House Republicans were generally ready to go their Senate colleagues one better by adding more massive tax cuts, thus necessitating still more draconian cuts in spending.

But it is not just the "special interests" of those directly affected that may be hurt by budget cuts. Slashing productive public investment—in human capital and in physical infrastructure—can have damaging effects on the private economy and our present and future welfare. And, if the loss of purchasing power, whether due to the government giving the public less as it reduces outlays or taking from it more as it raises taxes, depresses the economy or brings us into a recession, the damage will be enormous.

False alarm

By conventional measures, the deficit has, in fact, dramatically decreased, from $290 billion or 4.9 percent of Gross Domestic Product (GDP) in 1992 to $203 billion or 3.1 percent of GDP in 1994 and to $164 billion or 2.3 percent of GDP in 1995. The debt, which increases each year by the amount of the deficit, is no longer growing faster than the nation's income.

If we look at budgets of other leading nations, we find that almost all of them have larger deficits—in proportion to the size of their economies—than we do. Indeed, the Maastricht agreement for the European Economic Union sets a limit on deficits of no more than 3 percent of GDP, a figure that we will be well below this year and, even by conservative (or alarmist?) Congressional Budget Office projections, below this entire century.

If we account for capital outlays the way the federal budget does, we would find that most cities and states frequently, if not chronically, run deficits. And composite balance sheets of American households and businesses would show that both add hugely to their debt every year, which means, by federal accounting rules, that they are running massive deficits, generally greater than that of the federal government. Why then should the federal government balance its budget, particularly if to do so will entail massive sacrifice by such "special interests" as the elderly, the ill, the young, the poor, businessmen, farmers, veterans—indeed, the great bulk of the population?

Most of the simplistic arguments for a balanced budget are without merit. First, we will not go "bankrupt." The deficit contributes not to a national debt owed to other countries but to a federal government debt overwhelmingly owed to its own people in our own currency. A sovereign government can always get or create the money necessary to roll over such a debt or to pay it off.

Second, the deficit and debt are not adding to the burdens of our children. As President Lincoln knew—and it was hardly original with him—for every debtor there is a creditor, and our children will eventually be just as much creditors as debtors. Every savings bond and Treasury bill, note, and bond constituting the debt, except for the minor portion owned by foreigners, will be an asset of our posterity. If we are putting an extra burden on our children, it is not in those pieces of paper, which will in fact be their inheritance of wealth.

Third, our deficits are not causing others to lose confidence in us and, hence, driving down the value of the dollar. We remain the greatest and strongest economy in the world. If a balanced budget "strengthens" the dollar, it will only do so because it slows the economy so that we import less and, hence, supply fewer dollars to the rest of the world.

Fourth, our deficits are not driving up inflation or interest rates. The historical relation between deficits and interest rates is murky indeed. Federal Reserve policy, the state of the economy, and expected inflation are what really matter.

How a balanced budget hurts

What then do analytical economists see as the role of the deficit and its possible effect on the current economy and our future? Conservative economist Robert Barro of Harvard University and his many followers argue for "Ricardian Equivalence," which holds that, as a first approximation, it does not matter whether government expenditures are financed by current taxes or by current borrowing—a deficit. The reasoning is that, if taxes are cut, thus creating a deficit, taxpayers' behavior will not be affected. They will say to themselves that the resulting debt will have to be serviced and/or paid off in the future. Hence, their lower taxes now will be matched by higher taxes later. They will not therefore spend the money they are no longer paying in taxes. They will either set it aside to pay their higher taxes in the future themselves or they will leave the money to their children to pay the taxes.

Most professional economists, however, believe that Ricardian Equivalence is of limited applicability and reject the argument that deficits do not matter. Contradicting Barro's views, most of us apparently feel richer when, other things being equal, we own our share of $3.5 trillion dollars of Treasury obligations than when we don't. And we feel still richer if deficits increase our real holdings of those assets. Hence, we generally spend more on consumption.

If we are already buying everything our economy is capable of producing—we are operating at full employment and full capacity—production of more goods to satisfy our consumption demand can only come at the expense of production of investment goods. We may then put a burden on our children by leaving them less productive because we leave them fewer capital goods. But suppose, as in most of our history except during wartime, we are not producing at full capacity. Then, more spending induced by deficits can, and is likely to, increase consumption and, concomitantly, to increase business investment and production, thus providing for the increased consumption. Far from burdening our children, we are actually aiding them even as we help ourselves.

Further, increased holdings of government debt will induce us to spend more of our incomes only if our holdings have risen in real terms adjusted for inflation and, more fundamentally, have *risen relative to our incomes*. Since the debt held by the public averaged about $3,500 billion in fiscal year 1995, inflation, at the roughly 3 percent of the past year, would mean that holders of that debt suffered a loss in its purchasing power or real value equal to (approximately) 3 percent of $3,500 billion, or some $100 billion. Thus the real increase in the debt, and therefore the real deficit, is only the nominal deficit of $164 billion minus $100 billion, or $64 billion. And, with national income growing at 6 percent per year, the debt would have to grow at more than 6 percent of that $3.5 trillion—a nominal deficit of more than $210 billion or some $50 billion *more* than last year's $164 billion—to cause us to spend a larger proportion of our incomes.

A "balanced budget" would hardly be balanced in a growing economy. It would imply a debt-to-income ratio declining by about 6 percent per year, thus reducing our spending and bringing the risk of recession.

If our concern is that we provide properly for the future, it is absurd to try to balance a budget that makes no distinction between government expenditures for current consumption and government expenditures of an investment nature—for physical infrastructure, basic research and the development of new technology, the education of our children, and the health of our people. We might well wish to balance a current operating budget and restrict our borrowing to net investment, borrowing and investing enough, as a rule of thumb, to have a total deficit that keeps the ratio of debt to national income or GDP constant. But balancing the budget at the expense of our public investment in the future is one way that we really borrow from our children—and never pay them back.

Will a balanced budget drive down interest rates, perhaps abetted by the Federal Reserve, so that we have more private investment? That is a dicey proposition. Lower interest rates tend to encourage investment, particularly in housing, although they also lower the interest income of millions of households. But the loss of $200 billion of purchasing power *each year* is likely to slow the economy so much that private investment, despite the best efforts of the Fed, will be less, not more.

Some deficit hawks

What are the arguments in favor of balancing the budget, even as it is currently measured? Perhaps the most important one does not really relate to budget balancing at all but to reducing the role of government. Nobel Laureates Milton Friedman of the Hoover Institution and James Buchanan of George Mason University see the discipline of a balanced budget as preventing excessive government spending. Friedman and Buchanan, and many others, believe that in a representative form of government such as ours there are major incentives for our legislators to enact programs that may not even be in the long-term interests of the groups that promote them, much less society as a whole. The public is, however, notoriously reluctant to support higher taxes. If the programs had to be paid for by tax increases, the legislators would not dare to enact them. Economists arguing for a balanced budget on the grounds that it is necessary to reduce the role of government are not therefore arguing for a balanced budget per se. They generally disapprove of raising taxes to balance budgets more than they do of deficits.

"Supply-side economists" would reduce taxes, particularly marginal tax rates, regardless of their effect on the deficit (although some have claimed that the lower rates will increase taxable income so much that tax revenues would rise and, hence, reduce the deficit). The application of their views, along with the military buildup and the recession of 1982-1983, contributed to the large, much decried Reagan deficits. It may well be argued that those deficits, by pumping purchasing power into the economy, were a major factor in the recovery from that recession.

Many economists, including such prominent figures as Charles Schultze of the Brookings Institution, chairman of the Council of Economic Advisers under President Carter, Nobel Laureate Franco Modigliani of MIT, and Benjamin Friedman, chairman of Harvard's Economics Department, argue that deficits crowd out private investment. They claim that deficits reduce the nation's productivity and place a burden on future generations. When it is pointed out that, despite (or because of?) our recent deficits, gross private domestic investment has soared to record heights, both in absolute real terms and as a percentage of GDP, the reply is that this investment has been financed by foreigners. And this, we are told, has its cost: The interest and dividends on this investment will be paid to foreigners over the years ahead.

Budget deficits, by my estimates, do indeed contribute to trade or current account deficits with other nations. Essentially, they do so by raising our GDP and national income, thereby increasing our imports. If balancing the domestic budget were to eliminate those international deficits, they would do so by slowing our own economy. We would buy fewer Toyotas (the variety made in Japan, not Kentucky) but fewer Chryslers and Fords as well. And, further, it must be pointed out, even current account deficits averaging \$100 billion a year for the next five years would add only \$500 billion to net foreign claims on the United States. At a 4 percent real rate of return, that would cost us \$20 billion per year, less than 0.3 percent of our GDP, hardly a burden worth risking a recession over. In the long run, we should expect a lower exchange rate to balance our current accounts, at least to a point where foreign claims become a constant proportion of our GDP.

On the larger question of deficits crowding out the total of all investment, domestic and foreign, the critical issue is how much slack there is in the economy. What Schultze, Modigliani, and Benjamin Friedman apparently have in mind is an economy that, over the long run, is essentially at full employment or, at least, at a level of employment—some call it the "natural rate"—that deficits and aggregate demand cannot generally affect. Increased government demand or consumption demand has no free resources to draw upon. The consequence will be increased inflation. It is not clear why this alone would reduce private investment. But, if the response of the Federal Reserve to the inflation is to increase nominal *and* real interest rates, the result may be expected to be a reduction in real investment and an increased burden on the future.

If, however, the economy is at less than full employment,

the increased effective demand resulting from a structural deficit will increase total output, carrying increased investment to meet the increased demand for consumer goods. My own research has indicated that this is exactly what is happening. Correctly measured, real structural deficits have been followed by lower unemployment, greater output, and more consumption *and* private investment. They have also been accompanied by more *public* investment. Far from contributing to an increased burden on our future, they have provided for greater well-being for our children and our grandchildren.

Dissident voices

Many economists agree that deficit reduction is desirable in the appropriate circumstances. But they view the current crusade for a balanced budget under current federal accounting rules that do not separate out capital expenditures—let alone a constitutional amendment that would put the economy into a fiscal straight jacket—as misguided and ill-informed. The list of dissidents includes Nobel Laureates (and past presidents of the American Economic Association) Kenneth Arrow of Stanford University, Gérard Debreu of the University of California, Berkeley, Lawrence Klein of the University of Pennsylvania, Franco Modigliani and Robert M. Solow of MIT, and James Tobin of Yale University. Also included are Moses Abramovitz of Stanford, William Baumol of New York University, Charles P. Kindleberger of MIT, John Kenneth Galbraith of Harvard University, William Vickrey of Columbia University, all past presidents of the American Economic Association, and Hyman Minsky of the Levy Economic Institute, Robert Heilbroner of the New School for Social Research, Peter Bernstein, formerly with Shearson-Lehman, Paul Davidson of the University of Tennessee, and many others. Many have spoken out, but their voices have not broken through.

Some economists think that, while changing the level and composition of government expenditures may matter, a balanced budget will do no good or harm to the economy as a whole. Others think it can do serious harm. Whichever group is right, the sacrifice to attain that "balance" will be as useful as the ancient sacrifices to propitiate pagan gods—or those Western religious crusades of yesteryear.

[28]

Capital budgeting for government

Private business accounts separate capital from current expenditures. State and local governments generally do. The Federal government budget and our national income and product accounts do not, and therein hangs a tale.

There is much talk of budget deficits and there have been major efforts to reduce what are purported to be our deficits. Deficits do matter. But the failure to distinguish capital from current expenditures contributes to misleading measures of our deficits and what might be done about them. It obscures from the public information vital to allocation of the nation's resources. Most important, it contributes to faulty public policy regarding our provision for the future.

Take the Federal budget, which is the major culprit. We were told to anticipate a deficit of $400 billion in fiscal year 1992. But it turned out that this included some $80 billion of outlays for 'deposit insurance', which were essentially financing of a liability already incurred in Government guarantees of Savings and Loan Bank deposits. If we kept a balance sheet of government assets and liabilities, this would properly show up in a shuffling of the portfolio, no current change in net worth and no entry at all in the current account. This is indeed recognized implicitly in the Administration's budget by separate measures of the 'deficit' without deposit insurance, and by the Bureau of Economic Analysis in excluding purely financial transactions outright. If the Federal government eliminated these purely financial capital transactions from its measure of the deficit, it would prevent these confusing variations in reported deficits as varying amounts of them enter the budget or the actual amounts vary from what is budgeted. We do not in our personal finances report a 'deficit' when we borrow to buy into the stock market. [16] And we do not report a surplus when we sell the stock and pay off the debt. The Federal government should view and account for these transactions similarly.

Financial capital transactions, however, are only the tip of the capital investment iceberg left out of Federal government accounts. Any acquisition of assets, financial or real, is included in the budget as an outlay and thus adds to the 'deficit'. And sales of assets are treated as subtractions from outlays which reduce the deficit. This leads to the anomaly that one could eliminate the deficit for a number of years by selling off title to government assets and then leasing them back. We could start with the White House and Capitol, go on to the interstate highway system and Federal lands and perhaps conclude by selling all of our military hardware back to our defense contractors. The Federal government currently owns more than $1.6 trillion in fixed reproducible capital - equipment and structures - alone. If we sold-leased-back this equipment and structures to the amount of several hundred billion dollars a year, we could show a 'balanced budget' for a number of years, until we ran out of assets!

The Federal government ought to have a capital budget. Businesses' income

Table 1 Federal government investment in fixed capital, 1987, 1990, 1991, 1992 (billions of dollars)

	1987	1990	1991	1992
Gross investment	76.3	73.6	72.6	71.2
Depreciation	46.3	53.4	56.4	59.3
Net investment	30.0	20.2	16.1	11.9

Source Bureau of Economic Analysis, 'Fixed Government Capital (including residential) historical-cost valuation, gross investment, depreciation and net investment', Federal.

statements include only current expenditures and capital depreciation, not the outlays for new machinery or the building of factories. State and local governments are generally required to balance current operating budgets but keep separate capital accounts.

A separate capital budget for the Federal government would generally, although not necessarily always, leave a remaining current account in less deficit than the composite account now presented. The magnitude of the adjustment would depend on the level of net investment - that is, the amount by which gross investment exceeds the level of depreciation in the existing capital stock. If the capital budget were to include only investment in equipment and structures, [17] the 1992 deficit as calculated in the national income and product accounts would have been lowered by only a small amount because net investment was so low (see Table 1). In prior years, the change would have been more substantial. The great virtue of a capital budget is that it would have alerted us to trends that might warrant attention - such as the very large decrease in the level of Federal net investment in fixed capital from $30 billion in 1987 to $12 billion in 1992.

A capital budget might reasonably include other items where expenditures are made today with an expectation of benefits in the future. Taking OMB budget figures in fiscal 1991, these would comprise a more inclusive $103.5 billion for direct Federal invesment in physical capital, grants to state and local governments for physical capital of $26.5 billion, research and development expenditures of $66.0 billion, and education and training expense of $35.8 billion. If we put all of this investment into a capital budget but, appropriately, put depreciation on Federally-financed capital, reasonably about two-thirds of gross investment, back into the current budget, we would reduce the OMB measure of 'the deficit' by a substantial $77.9 billion.

Focusing on the composite account for all levels of government, a meaningful capital account would include investment in human and intangible capital as well as fixed capital. In Tables 2 and 3, I have projected some very rough and summary figures for 1990 and for 1992 respectively to show what such an account might look like. We find that the composite Federal, state and local *current* budget in 1990 was $25 billion in surplus. Total expenditures exceed total receipts by $140 billion, the amount of the deficit reported in the official national income and product accounts, but this related to and was equal to the excess of net capital expenditures over the current account surplus. In effect, there was a deficit of $165 billion on capital account. [18]

Table 2 Government receipts and expenditures account, 1990 (billions of dollars)

	Current account			
Credits: Revenues				1697
Charges: Current expenditures				1672
Goods and services			549	
Net interest, transfer payments and other			794	
Consumption of capital			329	
Surplus or deficit (−)				25
	Capital account			
Credits: Consumption of capital				329
Charges: Gross capital expenditures				494
Tangible		187		
Intangible		307		
Education	245			
R&D	62			
Net capital expenditures				165
Surplus or deficit (−)				−165
	Consolidated account			
Revenues				1697
Expenditures				1837
Total surplus or deficit (−)				−140

Sources National Income and Product Accounts, *Survey of Current Business*, January 1992, p. 42; 'Government Expenditures by Function', Table 3.15, *Survey of Current Business*, January 1992, p. 48; Bureau of Economic Analysis, 'Fixed Government Capital (including residential) historical-cost valuation, gross investment, depreciation and net investment', total. National Science Foundation, *Federal funds for research and development; fiscal years 1989, 1990 and 1991*, volume XXXIX, Table C-1, p. 35; US Department of Commerce, *Government Finances*, December 1991, Tables 4 and 5, pp. 4, 6. Intangible capital consumption allowances assumed equal to two-thirds of gross intangible capital expenditures.

In 1992 the total deficit was a considerably greater $269 billion but Table 3 indicates that all of this increase could be accounted for by a move in the current account from that $25 billion surplus to a deficit of $97 billion - a $122 billion swing, a great portion due to the deterioration of the economy. It clearly was not related to investment in our future.

What is particularly important is how this translates into total saving and investment accounts, shown in Tables 4 and 5. Here we can compare the conventional, official saving and investment account with an extended measure that includes 'gross public domestic investment' along with gross private domestic

Table 3. Government receipts and expenditures account, 1992 (billions of dollars)

Current account				
Credits: Revenues				1849.4
Charges: Current expenditures				1946.1
Goods and services			601.8	
Total		1131.8		
Minus cap. exp.		530.0		
Net interest, transfer payments and other			986.7	
Consumption of capital			357.6	
Surplus or deficit (−)				−96.7
Capital account				
Credits: Consumption of capital				357.6
Tangible		135.4		
Intangible		222.2		
Charges: Gross capital expenditures				530.0
Tangible		196.7		
Intangible		333.3		
Education	261.7			
R&D	71.6			
Net capital expenditures				172.4
Surplus or deficit (−)				−172.4
Consolidated account				
Revenues				1849.4
Expenditures				2118.5
Total surplus or deficit (−)				−269.1

Sources National Income and Product Accounts, *Survey of Current Business*, September 1993, p. 12, Tables 3.2 and 3.3, Federal and State and Local Government Receipts and Expenditures, respectively; pp. 30, 32, 34, Tables 3.15, 3.16 and 3.17, 'Government Expenditures by Function', 'Federal Government Expenditures by Type and Function', and 'State and Local Government Expenditures by Type and Function'; Bureau of Economic Analysis, from John Musgrave, 'Fixed Government Capital (including residential) historical-cost valuation, gross investment, depreciation and net investment', total; National Science Foundation/SRS, *National Patterns of R&D Resources; 1992*, pp. 47, 48, Tables B-2 and B-3, and data and estimates from Carol Evans of Bureau of Economic Analysis; consumption of intangible capital assumed equal to two-thirds of gross intangible capital expenditures.

investment. The extended measures of Tables 4 and 5 are still narrow measures of saving in that they exclude non-government investment in R&D and education and training as well as household investment in durable goods. But they include gross public investment on the investment side of the account and the saving that

Table 4 Extended gross saving and investment account, 1990 (billions of dollars)

Gross private domestic investment	803	Net private saving		257
		Personal saving	207	
		Business saving	50	
Gross public domestic investment	494	Net public saving		25
Net foreign investment	−83	Capital consumption allowance		924
		Private	595	
		Public	329	
		Statistical discrepancy		8
Gross investment	1214	Gross saving and statistical discrepancy		1214

Sources Table 2, above, and National Income and Product Accounts, Table 5.1. - Gross Saving and Investment, *Survey of Current Business*, January 1992, p. 58.

corresponds to it on the other. This makes clear the following:

1. Increasing current expenditures reduces net public saving (the 1990 current surplus of Table 2) or increases net public *dis*-saving (the 1992 current account deficit of Table 3). Unless private saving is increased, possibly as a result of increases in income, total or national saving must decline.

Table 5 Extended gross saving and investment account, 1992 (billions of dollars)

Gross private domestic investment	796.5	Net private saving		329.0
		Personal saving	238.7	
		Business saving	90.3	
Gross public domestic investment	530.0	Net public saving		−96.7
Net foreign investment	−55.1	Consumption of capital		1015.5
		Private (fixed)	657.9	
		Public	357.6	
		Statistical discrepancy		23.6
Gross investment	1271.4	Gross saving and statistical discrepancy		1271.4

Sources Table 3, above, and *Survey of Current Business*, August 1993, p. 55, Table A. - Summary National Income and Product Accounts, 1992, Account 5 - Gross Saving and Investment Account.

2. Increases in government capital expenditures, on the other hand, must increase national saving unless they implausibly bring about equal or greater decreases in the sum of private domestic and net foreign investment.

Introduction of a capital budget to the government account puts a quite different light on the much misunderstood issue of government deficits and their effect on national saving. The Bureau of Economic Analysis of the Department of Commerce is indeed now working on the presentation of accounts that separate government current expenditures from government capital expenditures. This would be in line with the United Nations System of National Accounts followed by most other nations. But currently the government deficit in the national income and [19] product accounts is treated as a direct offset to private saving. The assertion is routinely made that the greater the deficit, the less is total saving and along with it, total investment. This is in fact a dubious proposition, as actions to reduce the deficit, either by raising taxes or cutting expenditures, are likely to depress the economy and hence reduce private investment and saving.

A capital budget for the government sector, with associated revisions of the saving and investment account, would highlight the impact of public investment on gross investment. Reduction of the conventional 'deficit' by reducing government investment spending is virtually certain to reduce total investment and hence, contrary to much conventional wisdom, reduce national saving and increase the burden we pass to the future. [20]

PART IV

NATURAL RATE OF UNEMPLOYMENT AND NAIRU

OUR NAIRU LIMIT

THE GOVERNING MYTH OF ECONOMIC POLICY

BY ROBERT EISNER

We mustn't have it too good. Too much growth—too little unemployment—is a bad thing. These are not the idle thoughts of economic nail-biters; they are the economic policy of the United States. After real growth of gross domestic product (GDP) hit 4.5 percent in the last quarter of 1994 and unemployment dipped to 5.4 percent in December, the Federal Reserve moved on February 1 to raise interest rates for the seventh time in less than a year. Why? To slow our too rapid rate of growth and stop or reverse the fall in unemployment. Why do that? To fight inflation.

Ordinary people may wonder. Overall inflation, as measured by the GDP implicit price deflator, was down to 2.1 percent, its lowest in three decades. The Consumer Price Index rose only 2.7 percent in 1994 and knowledgeable analysts, including the Fed's chairman, Alan Greenspan, recognize that this measure overstates the rise in consumer costs, perhaps by as much as two percentage points.

Hard-nosed economic analysts and business leaders are also raising questions. They point to technological advances and downsizing in U.S. industry and suggest that productivity and output potential may well be rising more rapidly than the 2.5 percent long-term growth rate that Greenspan and others think marks the outer limit for the economy. Furthermore, as people lose old, high-paying jobs and look desperately even for lower-paying employment, there is slack in the labor force. Perhaps most important, increasing globalization and world competition may limit the ability of American firms to raise prices and workers to push for higher wages.

These heretical observations have so far failed to dent the dominant dogma haunting economic policy. The central tenet of that dogma is a concept familiarly known among economists as the NAIRU—the "nonaccelerating-inflation-rate of unemployment." While unknown to the general public, the NAIRU has become one of the most powerful influences on economic policy this century. My recent work, however, shows that even on the basis of a conventional model used to estimate the NAIRU, there is no basis for the conclusion that low unemployment rates threaten permanently accelerating inflation. And, according to an alternative model more consistent with the data, inflation might actually be lower at lower unemployment levels than we are experiencing today.

THE NAIRU FRAMEWORK

The basic proposition of the NAIRU is simple: Policymakers cannot use deficit spending or an increase in the money

UNEMPLOYMENT RATES

Unemployment and NAIRU: Actual unemployment has bounced all around its supposed natural rate in the last half century.

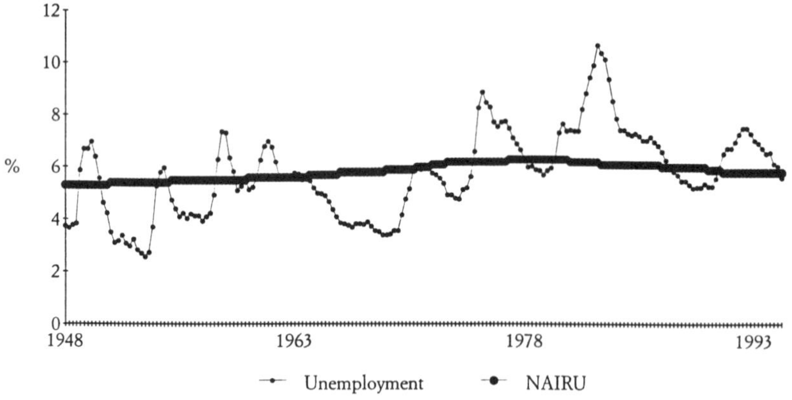

supply to reduce unemployment below some "equilibrium" rate, except at the cost of accelerating inflation. This is a sharp departure from the Keynesian view that inflation poses a danger only when increased spending or demand presses against full or near-full employment.

The concept of the NAIRU, derived from Milton Friedman's notion of a "natural rate of unemployment," rejects the assumed trade-off between unemployment and inflation described by the Phillips Curve, named after A.W. Phillips, an innovative economist from New Zealand. The Phillips Curve suggests that maintaining lower unemployment does produce higher inflation, but the inflation is constant. In the NAIRU view, the Phillips Curve is only a short-run relation. Trying to reduce unemployment by increasing spending or aggregate demand may work for a while, but then the higher inflation will cancel out the effects of the stimulus. Increased actual inflation will raise expectations of future inflation; only the excess of actual inflation over what workers, employers, borrowers, and lenders expect will stimulate the economy. At each round, higher spending and inflation will be necessary to maintain the original reduction in unemployment.

Thus, according to the NAIRU, fiscal or monetary policies aimed at reducing unemployment would leave us like a dog chasing its tail. If policy were aimed at keeping total spending sufficiently high to keep unemployment below its "natural rate," inflation would rise more and more rapidly. Ultimately, policymakers would give up in the face of runaway prices. Unemployment would then be back at its natural rate and inflation would stop accelerating, but it would stay at its new, higher level until unemployment rose above the natural rate and the process was painfully reversed.

In this view, the only way to reduce unemployment, except possibly in the short run, is to change conditions affecting the supply of labor—for example, by cutting the minimum wage, reducing or eliminating unemployment benefits, or upgrading the skills of workers. If the NAIRU is taken seriously, supply-side measures are the only ways to get unemployment down and keep it down. And if unemployment is at or close to the NAIRU, the monetary authority must take prompt anti-inflationary action to prevent the economy from "overheating." Otherwise, inflation will not only be higher but will be launched on its accelerating course, from which it can be diverted only by the medicine of excess unemployment—that is, unemployment above the NAIRU.

This is the view that underlies the otherwise inexplicable policy of the Federal Reserve. Most of our central bankers believe that we are at the natural rate of unemployment or below it, and we need more unemployment before it is too late. The main difference among macroeconomists today is that conservatives tend to put the NAIRU higher, at say 6-plus or 7 percent, while liberals put it at 6 or perhaps 5-plus percent. A few brave souls suggest that since our estimates of the NAIRU are imprecise, we should cautiously try to bring down unemployment until we have signs of inflation. But others say by then it will be too late.

Few economists have challenged the basic concept of the NAIRU. Keynes observed six decades ago that economists could stubbornly stick to their assumptions in the face of crushing reality, as when they argued in the depths of the Great Depression that there could be no involuntary unemployment. Another such episode of professional obstinacy may well be unfolding. Business leaders report, and national statistics confirm, that despite unemployment falling below the conventional NAIRU, accelerating inflation is nowhere in sight. But many economists are unmoved by mere evidence.

The available data do not, in fact, show that the NAIRU has much to do with historical levels of unemployment. In the United States, as shown in the figure on page 59, actual unemployment has bounced all around a NAIRU that was altered only slightly to keep up with it. Why, for example, did unemployment dip well below the NAIRU through most of the 1960s? The theory does not tell us why it was possible then but impossible now.

The conventional model could simply be ignoring many factors affecting inflation or the interaction of unemployment and inflation. These factors may also have a different impact when unemployment is high and when it is low. When unemployment is high, workers may indeed hesitate to press for higher wages because they are worried about losing their jobs. Still higher unemployment and falling demand may lead to more competition for limited markets, which may further check inflation.

But when unemployment is low, inflation may also be held in check. Low unemployment is usually associated with more efficient use of all resources. Persistent low unemployment rates that might lead to higher wages may encourage the substitution of capital for labor and raise anticipated future productivity, which would curb inflation. And with profits high and overhead costs spread broadly, firms may keep down prices to discourage others from entering their markets. Firms that are flush with profits may consider moving into new areas. Firms already there may well hesitate to raise prices and thus offer greater invitation to would-be interlopers.

> The premises of the Fed's anti-inflation policy are now in doubt.

This is, of course, just a sketch of why low unemployment and the high profits usually associated with it may inhibit inflation. Thus, the relationship may be different from what is usually assumed. It may be true that high unemployment reduces inflation, while it is false that low unemployment raises inflation.

The Conventional Formulation

Two crucial assumptions are necessary to arrive at the usual concept of the NAIRU. The first is that, left to itself, any given rate of inflation is self-perpetuating; the second, that unemployment is a key factor in changing inflation rates—specifically, that higher unemployment lowers inflation, and lower unemployment raises inflation.

There has been something of a cottage industry in estimating the NAIRU over the years. An exemplary case is the formulation by the Congressional Budget Office (CBO) in its August 1994 *Economic and Budget Outlook: An Update*, which is similar to influential work a decade earlier by Robert Gordon. The general idea is that inflation is a function of a number of variables such as presumably independent food and energy price movements, changes in productivity, the imposition and removal of price controls, and, most important, past inflation and current and past unemployment. The idea that inflation is self-perpetuating is embodied in the assumption that past inflation enters the equations

UNEMPLOYMENT AND INFLATION

High levels of unemployment do cut inflation...

...but low levels do *not* bring rising inflation; they actually appear to reduce inflation.

with a coefficient of one. The formulation then has an estimated constant term—which is positive, pushing inflation up—and negative coefficients of unemployment to hold inflation down. The size of those negative coefficients determines how much unemployment will be necessary to keep inflation from increasing. The rate of unemployment just sufficient to do this is the NAIRU.

I have replicated the CBO estimates and have confirmed the agency's results using its own model. The sum of the past inflation coefficients is at or above that crucial value of unity necessary for inflation to be self-perpetuating unless stopped. The constant terms are positive and the sums of the unemployment coefficients negative. My estimates yield a NAIRU at just about CBO's figure of 5.8 percent. (The measure of unemployment used by the CBO is the unemployment rate for married men, which it then adjusts to estimate the general rate of unemployment.)

> We have no basis for deliberately raising unemployment.

However, even this model does not support some of the implications usually drawn for policymaking. Many economists argue that we must never let the genie of inflation out of the bag because even a brief, inflation-accelerating experience of low unemployment will be disastrous and difficult to correct. Testing that proposition, I found that a one percentage point reduction in the married-male unemployment rate to 2.55 percent (one percentage point below the CBO estimate of the married-male NAIRU) generates a sharp increase and fluctuation in CPI inflation for several quarters, which subsides quickly if unemployment goes back up to the NAIRU. Even permanent unemployment of 2.55 percent does not, after five years, get inflation past 7 percent.

These results are based on the conventional formulation, but that is only the beginning of the story. The conventional model constrains the unemployment and inflation parameters in ways that are in fundamental conflict with the data. Freeing the model from those constraints leads to dramatically different conclusions; this calls into question the use of the NAIRU as a justification for blocking fiscal and monetary policies that might bring "full employment," or distinctly lower unemployment than what is now widely viewed as acceptable.

An Alternative Model

My reformulation of the conventional model suggests that the effect of unemployment on inflation is different when unemployment is low compared to when it is high. The key question, then, is what happens to the estimated values of the unemployment coefficients when unemployment is low. Do they differ consistently from the coefficients when unemployment is high?

First, estimates of separate relations for high and low unemployment show that differences between the unemployment coefficients are clearly statistically significant.

Second, the unemployment coefficients in the low-unemployment regressions are generally positive, though usually modest in size. This suggests that, whatever the effect on inflation of unemployment below the NAIRU, once below the NAIRU, lowering unemployment further may reduce inflation.

Third, under low unemployment, the sums of inflation coefficients were below unity, contradicting a critical assumption underlying the NAIRU. Inflation left to itself would not be self-perpetuating, and low unemployment would not cause accelerating inflation. Even if unemployment below the NAIRU did raise inflation, it would raise it by a finite amount—the old Phillips-Curve relation, not permanently accelerating inflation.

Simulations and Forecasts

One way to reveal the effects of the various interacting coefficients is to simulate or forecast ahead. I show results based on a single equation for inflation in the consumer price index. The high-unemployment inflation paths in the figure on page 61 fit the conventional view. Unemployment above the NAIRU drives inflation down, although the implicit NAIRU is closer to 6.8 percent in my simulations based only on high-unemployment observations. It takes still higher unemployment to break the back of inflation. But high enough unemployment does eventually turn inflation negative; that is, it drives prices down.

The low-unemployment paths shown, however, offer quite a different picture. At 5.8 percent unemployment, contrary to Alan Greenspan's fears, there is no accelerating inflation. By the end of the century, inflation settles at about 4.4 percent. Strikingly, at lower unemployment rates, inflation is no higher. At 4.8 percent unemployment, the simulation shows inflation coming down to 3.6 percent. At 3.8 percent unemployment, inflation comes down to 2.9 percent. At 2.8 percent unemployment, inflation at the end of 1999 is down to 2.1 percent.

NAIRU Escape?

I would not bet the family farm or the nation's economy on any set of econometric estimates, even my own. But promoters, defenders, and practitioners of the conventional NAIRU have done exactly that, with increasingly dogmatic assertion. They have paralyzed macroeconomic policy that should be aimed at the "high" and "full" employment targets set by the Employment Act of 1946 and the Humphrey-Hawkins Full Employment and Balanced Growth Act of 1978.

If accelerating inflation is not our fate, some might think a few extra percentage points of constant inflation might offer a pretty good bargain. Lower unemployment would generate large increases in output. According to the robust Okun's Law, named after Arthur Okun, the late Yale economist, each percentage point of unemployment costs at least two percentage points of output. That would amount to more than $130 billion of GDP this year.

Those committed to the concept of a NAIRU cannot easily dismiss the evidence of asymmetry that I have presented. I am not proposing a new dogma that lowering unemployment will reduce inflation. Even if my formulation is right, my standard errors are often too high—as, I should add, are those of practitioners of the conventional model— to permit any precise conclusions. There may be no stable, universal relation among unemployment and all the various factors contributing to inflation.

But the results reported here should clearly show the lack of empirical support for the NAIRU and the policies based upon it. They suggest that we have no sound basis for deliberately raising unemployment. On the contrary, we ought to be trying to reduce it, not only by supply-side measures, but by ensuring that the economy is not starved for adequate aggregate demand or productivity-increasing public investment. These measures should aim at reducing both underlying structural unemployment and the unemployment caused by misguided anti-inflation policy. The fight against inflation can then be focused where it should be—on promoting the greatest measure of domestic and international competition. ❑

[30]

The retreat from full employment

Robert Eisner

Six decades ago, in the work that so much influenced Paul Davidson and me and at least two generations of economists, John Maynard Keynes found in long continuing unemployment a critical failing in our economic system. His work also exposed a critical failing in classical economics.

FULL EMPLOYMENT, EFFECTIVE DEMAND AND INVOLUNTARY UNEMPLOYMENT

In the three-dimensional world that included involuntary unemployment and consequent departures from full employment, along with the supply and demand for labour, parallel lines did actually cross. One could no longer argue that encouraging saving would necessarily increase saving and investment. One could no longer argue that cutting wages would necessarily increase employment. One could no longer argue that increasing the money supply would necessarily increase prices proportionately – if at all. And one could no longer argue that public spending or government budget deficits would necessarily crowd out private investment.

Full employment meant everyone working who wanted to work at a wage equal to but not necessarily more than his or her marginal product. It meant workers on their supply curves, that is, supplying labour to the point where the declining utility of the real wage equalled the rising marginal disutility of labour. The existence of persons voluntarily not working, not supplying their labour, because the disutility of work exceeded the utility of the product (equal to the real wage) that they could produce, was not viewed as inconsistent with full employment.

But there were also millions of *in*voluntarily unemployed, those without jobs not because they were not supplying their labour but rather because nobody was demanding it. And this lack of demand for labour was due to the inability of business to sell the products that labour could produce. There was a shortage of aggregate effective demand.

This shortage could exist because there was no automatic mechanism to equate the demand for goods to their potential or full-employment supply. Contrary to Say's Law, supply did not create its own demand. Those supplying goods or labour were not necessarily ready to spend all the proceeds. Households, very rationally looking to the future, might be expected to consume currently less than their income, which was in the aggregate equal to their output. Whether business would want to purchase the output that households did not, would depend upon whether their expectations of gross profits from investment exceeded the costs of investment, as might be measured simplistically by the rate of interest or, in modern, more sophisticated fashion, by the rental price of capital.

The problem could then be reduced to the issue of whether expectations of gross profits from investment, because of gloomy foreboding or real lacks of profitable opportunities, would exceed a rate of interest – or rental price of capital – which could not be expected necessarily to get sufficiently low to compensate for insufficiently buoyant expectations of profits. There was thus this basic, real potential failing of insufficient effective demand.

A shortage of money in real terms could contribute to the problem by keeping interest rates above their potential minimum. In principle, a remedy could be found then in lower prices and lower wages, which would increase the real quantity of money. The path to this was treacherous if not impassable, however, as the dynamic downwards movement of wages and prices would only create expectations of further price declines that would further reduce current demand. It would also bring on extreme hardship and bankruptcy to those with fixed obligations and lesser nominal proceeds.

Some remedy might be found in a monetary authority that would increase the real quantity of money by increasing its nominal amount, rather than waiting for prices to fall. Such a remedy was indeed to be sought, but it was likely to be of limited efficacy because of the limitations on how low interest rates could be brought by these means. In the last analysis short-term interest rates could not be brought below zero and, because of varied and uncertain expectations of the future, relevant long-term rates would have to be higher.

Haberler (1941) and Pigou (1943) pointed to another solution. Lower prices would imply a greater real value of private wealth in the form of existing government money or more generally, as explained by Patinkin (1948), all government obligations, interest-bearing as well as non-interest-bearing. Unemployment would then be dissipated as lower wages and prices that increased private wealth would increase consumption.

This solution would not suffer from an upper bound such as that due to the interest rate floor. But it would suffer the same negative effects of falling prices and, aside from the existence of huge government debt, could not be expected to be more than modest in magnitude. And that debt, in the minds of believers in Ricardian equivalence, would in any event have little or no effect. Finally, benefits would at best be long delayed as prices could hardly be expected to fall considerably in a short time.

Keynesian theory – contrary to the Marxian model with its reserve army of the unemployed, necessary to hold down wages and keep up profits – did not imply that there always had to be involuntary unemployment. Households might want to consume a lot. Businesses might want to invest a lot. But this could not be guaranteed. Full employment, far from being a universal condition, might not exist for long periods, with few if any automatic forces to generate it. The dark decade of the 1930s seemed to confirm the notion that substantial unemployment, if not an equilibrium condition, was more the norm than the exception.

FISCAL AND MONETARY POLICY FOR FULL EMPLOYMENT

The policy implications of all this seemed clear. Efforts to drive down wages and/or prices would be of little avail and, more likely, counterproductive. The monetary authority should be asked to increase the quantity of money and ease credit to lower interest rates as far as possible, not neglecting the long end of the bond market. A corollary not often noted is that, in the interest of developing and confirming expectations of low long-run interest rates, the central bank should avoid as far as possible, if not entirely, increases in short-term rates to lop off booms or to combat imagined inflation.

But the limitations in the effectiveness of monetary policy in the face of severe shortages of effective demand suggested major resort to fiscal policy. This would include increased government spending for goods and services, particularly for public investment – moves to the socialization of investment. In the words of Keynes, 'I expect to the State, which is in a position to calculate the marginal efficiency of capital-goods on long views and on the basis of the general social advantage, taking an ever greater responsibility for directly organizing investment…' (1936, p. 164).

It would also include reductions in net taxes, by increasing transfer payments as well as reducing tax obligations. Disposable income and household consumption would thus be increased. And this would encourage investment to provide the capacity to produce the increased quantities of consumer goods.

It may be noted that this does not necessarily imply, as many claim today, that it is permissible to brook public budget deficits in periods of recession and high unemployment but then necessary to run surpluses or at least balance when recessions are over. If unemployment is long-standing or even chronic, it may be best to run deficits, of varying size, all the time. In economies in which nominal income and output are growing – which includes virtually all economies – this is eminently feasible without continuously raising the critical debt to income ratio. If excess unemployment is or has become the norm, rather than the exception, as seemed clear in the 1930s, chronic deficits are indicated to eliminate the unemployment or at least reduce it.

And, recognizing that economies are not closed, currencies should not be maintained at higher than equilibrium values. Unemployment should certainly not be created in order to defend an overvalued pound, a strong franc or an expensive dollar.

The Second World War brought the inadvertent application of Keynesian demand stimulus with a vengeance, and the elimination of mass unemployment throughout the Western world. The end of the war brought a huge explosion of pent-up consumer demand in the United States and demand for new investment to rebuild after the vast destruction in other warring nations. The United States offered financial aid to other nations to support that demand and the huge holding of government bonds by the public – the public debt to GDP ratio was over 110 per cent at the end of the war in comparison with about 50 per cent now – supported the American consumption and investment binge. Contrary to forecasts of gloom and doom, there was no major postwar recession.

The 20 to 25 per cent unemployment rates of the 1930s in the United States had given way to 1.2 per cent in 1944 but remained under 6 per cent for over a decade thereafter, until the recession of 1958, and indeed averaged 4.5 per cent over the period from 1946 to 1957. We operated under the Employment Act of 1946, committing us to maximum employment, and the figure of 4 per cent was widely accepted as attainable full employment.

With unemployment averaging 6.8 per cent in 1958, Arthur Burns, President Eisenhower's hardly Keynesian chairman of the Council of Economic Advisors, saw to it that adequate fiscal stimulus, largely in the form of acceleration of implementation of government military contracts, was brought to bear. Unemployment fell to 5.5 per cent in 1959. After rising briefly to 6.7 per cent in 1961, it began to drift down again, helped by the tax cut of 1964 and then the Vietnam War, which saw unemployment below 4 per cent for each of the years 1966 to 1969.

While some of us thought we could do better, particularly in training and finding jobs for those on the fringes of the labour force, we seemed to many to have finally reached our goal of full employment. We had at least eliminated most of the unemployment directly traceable to inadequate aggregate demand.

ABANDONMENT OF FULL EMPLOYMENT

That achievement had significant effects on the body politic and interests of the economics profession. At the political level, except in periods of recession, more concern was expressed about inflation than unemployment. With unemployment hitting disproportionately the poor and minorities least likely to vote, the political economic dynamic shifted.

And the generation that came to the economics profession dedicated to doing good and saving the system by curing its Achilles' heel of unemployment found itself increasingly outnumbered by younger cohorts more fond of exploring the properties of assumed equilibria – which usually entailed clearing of all markets, including the labour market – and solving essentially technical problems. As unemployment drifted up following the end of the Vietnam War stimulus, explanations other than those relating to demand came to the fore.

At first there were purely mechanical arguments. Various segments of the labour force – women, blacks, youths, veterans – were doomed to fixed rates of presumably structural unemployment, unrelated to aggregate demand. As the proportions of high-unemployment segments in the labour force grow, so must aggregate unemployment. Left unexplained was why, over US history, new groups came to replace old in the high-unemployment segments, without affecting aggregate unemployment. First it was the Irish, then newer immigrants from Eastern and Southern Europe. The Second World War saw the elimination of unemployment in all groups but then it rose among blacks and youths and women. Now women's unemployment is no higher than that of men and Hispanic unemployment is adding to that of blacks. Currently, numerous white-collar workers and even some upper-class executives are losing their jobs!

I would suggest that there is nothing immutable about rates of unemployment among different strata of the population. Labour is certainly heterogeneous, a fact ignored in some theoretical discussions. But changes in aggregate demand are likely to impact most on marginal workers, whoever they are. Their grim complaint that they are 'the last to be hired and the first to be fired' reflects largely that fact. High aggregate demand, if it does not raise all boats fully, actually raises employment most among those considered hard to employ.

And high aggregate demand does reduce the structural and frictional unemployment supposed by some to be impervious to demand increases. As firms strive to produce more, job openings increase and job seekers more quickly find the positions that meet their skills.

THE 'NATURAL RATE OF UNEMPLOYMENT' AND THE NAIRU

With the end of the 1960s came the really sophisticated rationalizations of significant unemployment in the notions of a 'natural rate of unemployment' and its counterpart the non-accelerating inflation rate of unemployment or 'NAIRU'. According to the old Phillips curve (Phillips, 1958), which drew inflation of wages (or prices, which differed only by the rate of growth of labour productivity), on the vertical axis, as a function of unemployment, on the horizontal axis, we could reduce unemployment by increasing aggregate demand if we were willing to brook the costs of higher inflation. This trade-off became more and more costly in terms of higher inflation as unemployment was driven lower and lower and the Phillips curve became steeper and steeper. It presumably approached the vertical as it approached full employment.

But according to the newer doctrine, associated initially with the names of Milton Friedman (1968) and E.S. Phelps (1968), such trade-off was at best temporary. Increases in demand that lowered unemployment below its natural rate or NAIRU would move us up a short-run Phillips curve defined by a given expected rate of inflation equal to its initial current rate. The resulting higher actual inflation would, in due course, raise expected inflation and thus raise the short-run Phillips curve.

The only way to maintain the lower rate of unemployment was then to stimulate demand further, thus raising inflation further and in turn raising the short-run Phillips curve still further. If finally the monetary authority gave up in this game – somehow it was always the monetary authority; fiscal policy was ignored – we would be left with the higher rate of inflation but unemployment would rise back to its original 'natural' rate.

The long-run Phillips curve was thus vertical. Increasing demand could only raise inflation. Trying to maintain unemployment below its natural rate would only bring accelerating inflation. Reduction of inflation would require painful excess unemployment, above its natural rate.

We had moved a long way. Economics was back at being its most dismal. The pain and waste of the system – in this case involuntary unemployment – were again an inevitable part of the natural order of things. Efforts to eliminate it would be unsuccessful, and only add to the pain. Indeed, by the accepted explanation the unemployment was not really involuntary. Except for the usual frictional unemployment, somehow viewed as constant, those without jobs did not want them because they did not find the current real wage sufficient and/or preferred to be idle now and work later when the real wage would be higher.

This view of the world suggests that sharp increases in unemployment should be seen, in the words of Modigliani (1977), as 'epidemics of contagious laziness' (p. 6). How else explain the increases in unemployment from 3.5 per cent in 1969 to 5.9 per cent in 1971, from 4.9 per cent in 1973 to 8.5 per cent in 1975, from 5.8 per cent in 1979 to 9.7 per cent in 1982 (10.7 per cent in December 1982) and, most recently, from 5.0 per cent in March of 1989 to 7.7 per cent in June of 1992, falling again to 5.4 per cent in December of 1994? And how can we explain the huge increases in unemployment in Western Europe over the past two decades, from rates in the 2 and 3 per cent range to double digits such as France's current 12 per cent? Can that be 'natural', while Japan's 3 per cent is also natural? Nature or God must treat different countries very differently!

How can we explain all this if we rule out fluctuations and differences in aggregate demand, either endogenous or the consequence of the exogenous forces of government or the rest of the world? If we recognize them, we find powerful effects on employment and output and saving and investment stemming from inflation-adjusted structural budget deficits, monetary conditions as measured by changes in the real monetary base, and impacts from outside as measured by changes in real exchange rates, as I have reported in a number of works.[1]

But macroeconomic policy makers shield themselves from this evidence behind the wall of dogma of their NAIRU. In the United States today neither conservatives nor liberals generally challenge this dogma. Martin Feldstein puts the NAIRU at 6.5 to 7 per cent while Alan Blinder, President Clinton's appointee as vice-chairman of the Fed, puts it at 5.5 to 6 per cent, and the Congressional Budget Office estimates it currently (1995) at 6.0 per cent. Going below that, or even anticipating going below that, apparently triggers grave concerns in Alan Greenspan, Federal Reserve Board Chairman, and most of his colleagues; interest rates were raised six times in 1994 in an effort to slow the economy.

The policy had its reward. The 1994, fourth-quarter real growth in GDP of 5.1 per cent came down to 2.7 per cent in the first quarter of 1995. Unemployment rose from that 5.4 per cent rate of December 1994 to 5.8 per cent in April. While it declined slightly to 5.7 per cent in May and 5.6 per cent in June, the Federal Reserve in early July, then seeing greater risks of recession than inflation, changed policy and moved to cut the federal funds rate.

WHAT IS WRONG WITH THE NAIRU

What is the power of the NAIRU, other than its ideological appeal to those who believe that significant unemployment is valuable in a flexible, dynamic economy or those who, in an anti-government crusade, would abdicate government responsibilities for macroeconomic policy altogether? In the face of its glaring failures of prediction in Europe, where its implications of accelerating deflation in the face of persistent unemployment far higher than any plausible 'natural' rates have been so sharply falsified, competing theories of hysteresis have come to the fore. There have been efforts to explain a varying NAIRU, varying even with the rate of government spending! But I have found that the general formulation of the NAIRU does not stand up, in US data, to plausible alternative formulations.

There are two crucial assumptions necessary to arrive at the usual concept of the NAIRU. One is that, left to itself, any given rate of inflation is somehow self-perpetuating. The mechanism would appear to involve the equality of expected future inflation to some weighted average of past inflation, although it is not at all clear why rational agents should always form their expectations in this way. Then, given these expectations, they act in such a manner that somehow expected future inflation is realized in actual future inflation, unless again some other variables intervene to affect the result. The second crucial assumption is that unemployment lowers inflation and that lower unemployment raises the rate of inflation. The combination of these two assumptions generates the result that increases in demand that may lower unemployment can do so only in the short run. And rational agents recognizing the truth of these assumptions make the short run very short indeed – soon becoming infinitesimal in length.

The dynamic process that supposedly effectuates all this has been elaborated in various fashions. Most frequently involved are more or less ignorant workers who initially mistake increases in nominal wages associated with inflation as increases in real wages and hence increase their supply of labour. In fact, the argument goes, prices have initially risen more than wages so that employers, faced with an actual decline in the real wage, move down their marginal labour productivity curves and hire more workers. But when workers sooner or later note that prices have gone up at least as much as wages, they withdraw their 'excess' labour and employers are left hiring the same number of workers as before, at the initial real wage.[2]

I have long been puzzled by why many economists should take this contrived scenario, or others, involving island parables and the like, seriously. There is little evidence that fluctuations in real wages or changes in labour supply account for much if any of the fluctuations in unemployment observed in the United States. And much of the evidence, on resignations, for example, indicates that lower unemployment is associated with reductions in labour supply, as more workers voluntarily give up their jobs. Higher unemployment is correspondingly associated with fewer resignations, as workers are fearful that they will not easily find other jobs if they give up the ones they have.

There is at best an important ellipsis in the argument, not easily papered over. The NAIRU after all relates not to changes in prices and wages, but to changes in inflation. Agents are somehow assumed to adjust current labour supply and demand, in terms of levels of prices and wages, to perceived changes in rates of change of those variables. And when we come to changes in inflation, we somehow assume that expectations are single-valued and held, accurately or not, with certainty. As all of us know, we are faced with at best rather uncertain probability distributions of expected future inflation, and we do not even have a good idea of the parameters of those probability distributions. Why, under these circumstances, should agents be concerned only with their first moment? Is it only the single-valued mean that should affect their actions? Or is it also the variance of the distribution or higher moments yet? Might those other moments not be expected to influence behaviour under conditions of risk aversion and costs of planning and decision making for an uncertain future? And what other variables might affect all these moments and affect them differently under different circumstances? How clear and how stable then is the path from past inflation to future inflation?

THE CONVENTIONAL FORMULATION OF THE NAIRU AND AN ALTERNATIVE

The general mathematical formulation leading to the NAIRU might be written:

$$IN = b_1 \, IN_{-1} + b_2 \, (U - \text{NAIRU}) + \Sigma b_g Z_g, \qquad (1)$$

where IN = inflation, IN_{-1} is lagged inflation or an average of past inflation rates, U = unemployment, and the Z_g represent other factors that might affect the rate of inflation. The value of b_2 is expected to be negative; U less than the NAIRU will raise inflation. If the value of b_1 is less than 1 we are faced with the proposition that inflation is not self-sustaining. Left to itself, any given rate of inflation would then decay, a devastating blow to the NAIRU and the vertical long-run Phillips curve. The model is thus frequently put in its strong form, with b_1 assumed equal to one, or the sum of regression coefficients in estimates relating to a series of lagged values of inflation constrained to equal unity. If we further ignore any other factors (not necessarily independent of rates of inflation) which may affect inflation, we are left with the formulation:

$$\Delta IN = b_2 \, (U - \text{NAIRU}), \qquad b_2 < 0. \qquad (2)$$

Inflation will remain constant, that is, $\Delta IN = 0$ if, and only if, $U - \text{NAIRU} = 0$, that is, if unemployment is at the NAIRU. Higher unemployment will reduce inflation, but unemployment below the NAIRU will increase inflation, and keep increasing it; we will have that accelerating inflation.

I have taken this conventional formulation and data used by the US Congressional Budget Office to estimate values of the NAIRU just as the CBO does (CBO, 1994, 1995), including 20 lagged values of inflation, current and four or five lagged values of unemployment, a measure of inflation in food and energy prices, defined as the difference between the rates of change of the fixed weight price index for personal consumption expenditures and the index less food and energy, the difference between the rates of change of labour productivity in the non-farm business sector and segmented trends of labour productivity and dummy variables for the imposition and removal of the Nixon price controls in the 1970s. I confirmed CBO estimates of the NAIRU at about 5.8 per cent and 6.0 per cent. And I found the sum of the inflation coefficients close to unity and the unemployment coefficients negative.

But is that formulation the only reasonable one, or even the correct one? May there not be others and, in particular, may not the relation be asymmetrical? May unemployment not have a different impact when it is low and when unemployment is high? When unemployment is high, more unemployment may lead to more competition for limited markets, which may check inflation. But when unemployment is low, reducing unemployment further may have little impact on inflation. Let me suggest several hypotheses pointing to a theoretical formulation in which low unemployment tends to hold inflation in check.

First, low measured unemployment is usually associated with greater, more efficient utilization of all resources as fixed factors of labour, management and capital are put to fuller use. This may entail increases in productivity and decreases in average costs (not necessarily captured fully by the productivity variable) which militate against price increases.[3] Second, persistent low unemployment may set up forces of capital–labour substitution and further increases in anticipated future productivity (also not necessarily captured in the PRD variable) which curb inflation. Third, some game-theoretical considerations suggest that in a collective bargaining situation real wages may tend to move countercyclically, so that in periods of low unemployment upward wage pressure may be less.[4] And fourth, with profits high and overhead costs spread broadly, various oligopolistic considerations – such as a desire to discourage new entry – may become more important. Firms that are flush with profits are threats to move into new areas. Firms already there may well hesitate to offer greater invitation to would-be interlopers with moves for additional price increases.

This is of course just a sketch of a theory as to why low unemployment and the high profits usually associated with it may militate against inflation.

Table 7.1 Inflation and total unemployment, separate high- and low-unemployment regressions

Variable or statistic	Regression coefficients and standard errors					
	INC (CPI-U)			INF (GDP implicit price deflator)		
	All *U*	*U*≥NAIRU	*U*<NAIRU	All *U*	*U*≥NAIRU	*U*<NAIRU
Constant	3.683	−1.890	0.914	3.489	−1.526	0.930
	(0.881)	(0.359)	(0.230)	(0.787)	(0.383)	(0.251)
ΣINF coef.	1.189	1.234	0.926	1.108	1.143	0.885
	(0.082)	(0.050)	(0.031)	(0.087)	(0.049)	(0.032)
ΣU coef.	−0.722	−0.814	0.234	−0.670	−0.881	0.050
	(0.181)	(0.225)	(0.267)	(0.173)	(0.247)	(0.275)
U_t	−0.683	−1.219	−0.699	−1.652	−0.632	−0.444
	(0.482)	(0.287)	(0.474)	(0.470)	(0.314)	(0.494)
U_{t-1}	−0.294	0.544	0.963	1.130	−0.333	0.224
	(0.925)	(0.312)	(0.621)	(0.885)	(0.329)	(0.648)
U_{t-2}	0.788	−0.128	−0.457	0.567	0.285	0.189
	(0.915)	(0.318)	(0.619)	(0.861)	(0.330)	(0.643)
U_{t-3}	−0.553	0.173	0.115	−0.297	−0.129	−0.228
	(0.853)	(0.317)	(0.624)	(0.807)	(0.333)	(0.640)
U_{t-4}	0.020	−0.185	0.312	−0.417	−0.072	0.309
	(0.473)	(0.252)	(0.472)	(0.452)	(0.274)	(0.485)
ΣFAE coef.	0.101	−0.425	−0.020	0.925	0.584	0.895
	(0.378)	(0.342)	(0.406)	(0.256)	(0.264)	(0.279)

Table 7.1 (continued)

Variable or statistic	Regression coefficients and standard errors					
	INC (CPI-U)			INF (GDP implicit price deflator)		
	All *U*	*U*≥NAIRU	*U*<NAIRU	All *U*	*U*≥NAIRU	*U*<NAIRU
PRD_t	−0.028	−0.017	−0.058	−0.059	−0.019	−0.035
	(0.048)	(0.043)	(0.044)	(0.049)	(0.045)	(0.045)
$NIXON_t$	−1.713	−2.409	−1.980	−1.195	−1.915	−1.211
	(0.821)	(0.829)	(0.898)	(0.817)	(0.894)	(0.955)
$NIXOFF_t$	1.158	1.009	0.690	2.140	1.975	1.631
	(0.776)	(0.757)	(0.796)	(0.744)	(0.790)	(0.810)
$\hat{R}^2$	0.783	0.793	0.769	0.753	0.727	0.710
n	152	152	152	152	152	152
D–W	1.969	1.966	1.959	2.083	1.992	1.938
NAIRU	5.883	5.837	1.942	5.691	6.051	−6.800
ΣUVH-ΣUVL coefficients		1.048			0.931	
Standard error		0.349			0.370	
t-statistic		3.003			2.518	

Notes: Independent estimates of 20 inflation lags, sums not constrained to equal unity, four lags of food and energy inflation, asymmetric relation (U≥NAIRU = UVH and U<NAIRU = UVL), *U* > or < CBO varying NAIRU time series, 1956.I to 1993.IV.

Possible causes of asymmetry in the relation between inflation and unemployment are myriad. But what do the econometric estimates show?

We have estimated independent regressions for high and low unemployment, relative to the CBO estimates of a varying NAIRU. Results of the conventional relation and separate high and low unemployment regressions for inflation as measured by the consumer price index and the GDP implicit price deflator are presented in Table 7.1. They reveal great disparities in the relations involving high and low unemployment. I estimate the standard error of the sums of differences of coefficients of high and low unemployment on the assumption of zero covariance, that is that the variance of the difference in sums is equal to the sum of the variances of the sums, an assumption which, judging from the variances of differences in the single regressions, rather *over*states the variance of the differences. Still we find *t*-statistics of 2.5 and 3. The differences between the sums of high and low unemployment coefficients are clearly statistically significant.

Second, the unemployment coefficients in the low-unemployment regressions are generally positive, though usually modest in size. This suggests that, whatever the effect on inflation of unemployment below the NAIRU, once below the NAIRU, lowering unemployment further may reduce inflation.

Third, the sums of inflation coefficients, which had tended to be slightly above unity in the conventional regressions, were even higher in the separate, high-employment regressions, thus offering support to the accelerationist hypothesis for high unemployment. *But they were below unity in the low-employment regressions!* This would indicate that, even if unemployment below the NAIRU did raise inflation it would effect an old Phillips curve relation, and not accelerating inflation.

In the separate regressions the sums of the inflation coefficients are about the same in the high-unemployment regressions, 1.234 and 1.143, as in the single regression. The results are quite different in the low-unemployment regressions. The sums of the inflation coefficients are now, respectively, 0.926 and 0.885. And the sums of the low-unemployment coefficients are both positive, 0.234 for INC and a small 0.050 for INF.

It should be noted finally that there are substantial, positive constant terms in the low-unemployment regressions. The combination of all these coefficients would lead us to think that unemployment below the NAIRU might raise inflation initially but that it would not be accelerating, and lowering unemployment, at least in the case of INC, would again lower inflation.

The estimation of separate constant terms, both in single regressions and, of course, with separate regressions, effects certain anomalies of discontinuity at the NAIRU in the simulations and projections discussed below. I have hence regressed inflation (INC, measured by the consumer price index) on

Table 7.2 Inflation in consumer price index (CPI-U) and total unemployment, single regression, single constant term, high- and low-unemployment variables

Variable or statistic	Regression coefficients and standard errors	
	$U \geq$NAIRU	$U <$NAIRU
Constant	0.325	0.325
	(0.341)	(0.341)
ΣINF coef.	0.940	0.940
	(0.076)	(0.076)
ΣU coef.	–0.243	0.141
	(0.310)	(0.348)
U_t	–0.470	0.278
	(0.384)	(0.670)
U_{t-1}	0.431	–0.030
	(0.565)	(1.034)
U_{t-2}	0.020	–0.613
	(0.584)	(1.050)
U_{t-3}	0.124	–0.133
	(0.574)	(1.032)
U_{t-4}	–0.458	0.723
	(0.549)	(1.019)
U_{t-5}	0.110	–0.084
	(0.373)	(0.661)
ΣFAE coef.	–0.038	–0.038
	(0.479)	(0.479)
PRD_t	–0.075	–0.075
	(0.049)	(0.049)
$NIXON_t$	–1.155	–1.155
	(0.964)	(0.964)
$NIXOFF_t$	0.484	0.484
	(0.866)	(0.866)
$\hat{R}^2$	0.735	0.735
n	152	152
D–W	1.932	1.932
NAIRU	7.896	3.862
(Assuming 3% inflation)		

Notes: Independent estimates of 20 inflation lags, sums not constrained to equal unity, current and five lagged high-unemployment coefficients (UVH) and low-unemployment coefficients (UVL), and four lagged coefficients of food and energy inflation, asymmetric relation ($U \geq$NAIRU = UVH and $U <$NAIRU = UVL), $U \geq$ or < CBO varying NAIRU time series, 1956.I to 1993.IV.

high- and low-unemployment variables with a single constant term, estimating all lagged coefficients independently.[5] As shown in Table 7.2, the sums of the unemployment coefficients are a modestly negative –0.243 for unemployment greater than or equal to the variable NAIRU but a positive 0.141 for unemployment below the NAIRU. The constant term is a positive but small 0.325 and the sum of the inflation coefficients is 0.940, thus less than the value of unity critical to permanent acceleration. In no case, however, are the coefficients statistically significantly different from zero (or in the case of the inflation coefficients, from unity).

SIMULATIONS AND PROJECTIONS

One way to reveal the effects of the various, interacting coefficients is to simulate or forecast ahead. Since our equations were estimated with observations ending in the last quarter of 1993 and we now have observations for the first three quarters of 1994, we have chosen to forecast ahead the 21-quarter period from 1994.IV to 1999.IV. For these quarters we have first assumed total unemployment to remain constant at the 5.8 per cent rate of October 1994, which was the current, old series CBO estimate of the NAIRU.[6] We have then assumed unemployment to be constant at any of eight other levels, at one percentage point intervals. We thus have quarter-by-quarter projections of inflation for constant unemployment rates of 5.8 per cent, 6.8 per cent, 7.8 per cent and 8.8 per cent, and also for 4.8 per cent, 3.8 per cent, 2.8 per cent, 1.8 per cent and the admittedly unrealistic 0.8 per cent. We have used the regressions of Tables 7.1 and 7.2 for these forecasts.

Results again are striking, as shown in Tables 7.3 to 7.5 and Figures 7.1 to 7.4. Figure 7.1, based on the standard model with no distinction among unemployment rates, UN, offers at least modest confirmation of the usual accelerationist result. Inflation in the consumer price index, INC, remains constant if UN is kept at 5.8 per cent (not rising, as the Fed appears to fear). But for lower unemployment INC is greater and keeps rising over the five-year period, particularly for unemployment at 3.8 per cent and below. Still, it may be noted in Table 7.3, from which Figure 7.1 is derived, that even after five years of unemployment at 4.8 per cent, a full percentage point below the NAIRU, inflation would be up to only 8.7 per cent. In view of the enormous gains of output likely with one percentage point less of unemployment, some might think the trade-off worthwhile, particularly if other measures to improve competition and labour markets might be introduced to lower that inflation.

Examining the effects on inflation of unemployment above the NAIRU, as projected in the standard model, we note quite sharp deflationary results, as

Table 7.3 Projections of INC, inflation in consumer price index (CPI-U), for unemployment rates above and below varying CBO NAIRU, conventional model (From Table 7.1)

	Unemployment (%)								
Period	0.8	1.8	2.8	3.8	4.8	5.8	6.8	7.8	8.8
	Inflation (%)								
1994.I	2.1	2.1	2.1	2.1	2.1	2.1	2.1	2.1	2.1
1994.II	1.6	1.6	1.6	1.6	1.6	1.6	1.6	1.6	1.6
1994.III	4.7	4.7	4.7	4.7	4.7	4.7	4.7	4.7	4.7
1994.IV	7.2	6.5	5.9	5.2	4.5	3.8	3.1	2.4	1.8
1995.I	9.8	8.5	7.3	6.0	4.7	3.4	2.1	0.9	–0.4
1995.II	6.4	5.8	5.3	4.7	4.1	3.6	3.0	2.4	1.9
1995.III	8.4	7.6	6.7	5.9	5.0	4.2	3.3	2.5	1.6
1995.IV	11.9	10.3	8.7	7.1	5.5	3.9	2.2	0.6	–1.0
1996.I	12.7	10.9	9.0	7.2	5.4	3.6	1.7	–0.1	–1.9
1996.II	11.8	10.2	8.7	7.1	5.5	4.0	2.4	0.8	–0.8
1996.III	13.3	11.4	9.5	7.7	5.8	3.9	2.1	0.2	–1.7
1996.IV	15.0	12.7	10.3	8.0	5.6	3.3	1.0	–1.4	–3.7
1997.I	14.8	12.5	10.2	7.9	5.6	3.3	1.0	–1.3	–3.6
1997.II	15.4	13.1	10.9	8.6	6.3	4.1	1.8	–0.5	–2.8
1997.III	17.2	14.4	11.7	9.0	6.3	3.6	0.9	–1.8	–4.6
1997.IV	19.1	16.1	13.0	10.0	7.0	3.9	0.9	–2.2	–5.2
1998.I	18.7	15.7	12.7	9.7	6.7	3.8	0.8	–2.2	–5.2
1998.II	20.0	16.8	13.6	10.3	7.1	3.9	0.7	–2.5	–5.8
1998.III	21.6	18.1	14.6	11.0	7.5	4.0	0.4	–3.1	–6.7
1998.IV	22.4	18.7	14.9	11.2	7.4	3.6	–0.1	–3.9	–7.7
1999.I	23.4	19.5	15.6	11.8	7.9	4.0	0.1	–3.7	–7.6
1999.II	24.7	20.6	16.5	12.4	8.2	4.1	0.0	–4.1	–8.2
1999.III	27.0	22.4	17.9	13.3	8.7	4.2	–0.4	–5.0	–9.5
1999.IV	27.7	23.0	18.2	13.5	8.7	4.0	–0.8	–5.5	–10.3

Summary statistics, projection period 1994.IV to 1999.IV

	Unemployment (%)								
Stat.	0.8	1.8	2.8	3.8	4.8	5.8	6.8	7.8	8.8
	Inflation (%)								
Mean	16.60	14.04	11.48	8.92	6.37	3.81	1.25	–1.31	–3.87
σ	6.36	5.11	3.86	2.61	1.37	0.27	1.19	2.43	3.68
Max	27.74	22.99	18.24	13.48	8.73	4.16	3.31	2.46	1.89
Min	6.38	5.82	5.26	4.69	4.13	3.31	–0.78	–5.53	–10.29

Table 7.4 *Projections of INC, inflation in consumer price index (CPI-U), for unemployment rates above and below varying CBO NAIRU, asymmetric model, with separate high unemployment and low unemployment equations (from INC equations in Table 7.1)*

	Unemployment (%)								
	Low-unemployment eqn						High-unemployment eqn		
Period	0.8	1.8	2.8	3.8	4.8	5.8	5.8	6.8	7.8
	Inflation (%)								
1994.I	2.1	2.1	2.1	2.1	2.1	2.1	2.1	2.1	2.1
1994.II	1.6	1.6	1.6	1.6	1.6	1.6	1.6	1.6	1.6
1994.III	4.7	4.7	4.7	4.7	4.7	4.7	4.7	4.7	4.7
1994.IV	7.1	6.4	5.7	5.0	4.3	3.6	3.5	2.3	1.1
1995.I	4.4	4.3	4.2	4.1	4.0	3.9	2.7	1.4	0.1
1995.II	4.3	4.3	4.2	4.2	4.2	4.1	2.9	1.8	0.6
1995.III	6.2	5.9	5.6	5.3	4.9	4.6	3.6	2.2	0.8
1995.IV	6.0	5.7	5.5	5.3	5.1	4.8	3.3	1.1	−1.0
1996.I	4.2	4.4	4.6	4.8	5.0	5.3	2.7	0.2	−2.3
1996.II	4.5	4.7	5.0	5.2	5.5	5.8	3.1	0.6	−1.9
1996.III	5.5	5.5	5.6	5.6	5.7	5.8	3.1	0.2	−2.7
1996.IV	3.9	4.2	4.5	4.8	5.1	5.5	2.4	−1.1	−4.6
1997.I	2.7	3.3	3.9	4.6	5.2	5.8	2.2	−1.4	−5.0
1997.II	3.7	4.2	4.8	5.4	6.0	6.6	2.9	−0.9	−4.7
1997.III	3.9	4.3	4.8	5.2	5.6	6.0	2.4	−2.0	−6.4
1997.IV	2.9	3.7	4.4	5.2	5.9	6.7	2.6	−2.3	−7.1
1998.I	2.7	3.5	4.3	5.1	5.8	6.6	2.2	−2.9	−8.1
1998.II	3.4	4.1	4.8	5.5	6.2	6.9	2.4	−3.1	−8.6
1998.III	3.2	4.0	4.8	5.5	6.3	7.0	2.4	−3.7	−9.7
1998.IV	2.3	3.3	4.2	5.1	6.0	6.9	1.8	−4.8	−11.4
1999.I	2.3	3.3	4.4	5.4	6.4	7.5	2.1	−4.8	−11.7
1999.II	3.2	4.1	4.9	5.8	6.6	7.5	2.2	−5.4	−12.9
1999.III	2.8	3.7	4.7	5.7	6.6	7.6	2.0	−6.2	−14.3
1999.IV	2.1	3.2	4.3	5.4	6.5	7.7	1.7	−7.1	−15.9

Summary Statistics, Projection Period 1994.IV to 1999.IV

	Unemployment (%)								
Stat.	0.8	1.8	2.8	3.8	4.8	5.8	5.8	6.8	7.8
	Inflation (%)								
Mean	3.87	4.30	4.72	5.15	5.58	6.01	2.58	−1.70	−5.99
σ	1.38	0.91	0.52	0.44	0.79	1.25	0.53	2.86	5.24
Max	7.12	6.42	5.72	5.77	6.64	7.65	3.55	2.32	1.11
Min	2.07	3.19	3.94	4.10	3.99	3.62	1.66	−7.12	−15.91

Table 7.5 *Projections of INC, inflation in consumer price index (CPI-U), for unemployment rates above and below varying CBO NAIRU, asymmetric model, with single equation and single constant term (from equation in Table 7.2)*

	Unemployment (%)										
	Low-unemployment variables				High-unemployment variables						
Period	2.8	3.8	4.8	5.8	4.8	5.8	6.8	7.8	8.8	9.8	10.8
	Inflation (%)										
1994.I	2.1	2.1	2.1	2.1	2.1	2.1	2.1	2.1	2.1	2.1	2.1
1994.II	1.6	1.6	1.6	1.6	1.6	1.6	1.6	1.6	1.6	1.6	1.6
1994.III	4.7	4.7	4.7	4.7	4.7	4.7	4.7	4.7	4.7	4.7	4.7
1994.IV	2.8	3.1	3.4	3.6	4.6	4.1	3.6	3.2	2.7	2.2	1.7
1995.I	2.4	2.8	3.2	3.7	4.1	3.8	3.4	3.1	2.8	2.4	2.1
1995.II	4.5	4.3	4.1	4.0	4.4	4.3	4.2	4.1	4.0	3.9	3.8
1995.III	6.1	5.5	4.9	4.3	5.0	4.9	4.8	4.8	4.7	4.7	4.6
1995.IV	3.7	3.9	4.0	4.1	5.6	4.9	4.3	3.7	3.1	2.4	1.8
1996.I	3.0	3.4	3.8	4.3	5.7	5.0	4.2	3.5	2.8	2.1	1.4
1996.II	4.4	4.5	4.5	4.6	5.9	5.4	4.8	4.3	3.7	3.2	2.6
1996.III	4.6	4.6	4.5	4.5	6.2	5.5	4.8	4.2	3.5	2.9	2.2
1996.IV	2.9	3.3	3.6	3.9	5.9	5.0	4.1	3.2	2.2	1.3	0.4
1997.I	2.8	3.2	3.6	4.0	6.0	5.0	4.1	3.2	2.2	1.3	0.4
1997.II	3.8	4.0	4.3	4.5	6.5	5.6	4.7	3.9	3.0	2.1	1.2
1997.III	2.8	3.2	3.6	4.1	6.5	5.4	4.2	3.1	2.0	0.9	–0.2
1997.IV	2.5	3.2	3.9	4.6	7.0	5.8	4.6	3.3	2.1	0.9	–0.4
1998.I	2.4	3.0	3.7	4.3	6.8	5.6	4.3	3.1	1.9	0.6	–0.6
1998.II	3.0	3.5	3.9	4.4	6.9	5.7	4.6	3.4	2.2	1.0	–0.2
1998.III	2.7	3.3	3.9	4.5	7.2	5.9	4.6	3.3	2.0	0.7	–0.7
1998.IV	2.0	2.8	3.5	4.2	7.1	5.7	4.2	2.8	1.4	0.0	–1.4
1999.I	2.4	3.1	3.8	4.5	7.4	6.0	4.6	3.2	1.8	0.4	–1.0
1999.II	2.5	3.2	3.9	4.6	7.6	6.1	4.7	3.2	1.7	0.3	–1.2
1999.III	2.2	3.0	3.8	4.6	7.7	6.2	4.6	3.1	1.5	0.0	–1.6
1999.IV	1.8	2.7	3.6	4.5	7.7	6.1	4.5	2.8	1.2	–0.4	–2.0

Summary Statistics Projection Period, 1994.IV to 1999.IV

	Unemployment (%)										
Stat.	2.8	3.8	4.8	5.8	4.8	5.8	6.8	7.8	8.8	9.8	10.8
	Inflation (%)										
Mean	3.12	3.50	3.88	4.26	6.27	5.33	4.39	3.44	2.50	1.56	0.62
σ	1.05	0.71	0.41	0.30	1.10	0.67	0.37	0.51	0.91	1.35	1.81
Max	6.10	5.49	4.88	4.58	7.71	6.16	4.85	4.79	4.73	4.67	4.62
Min	1.81	2.69	3.23	3.64	4.11	3.77	3.44	2.82	1.23	–0.38	–2.00

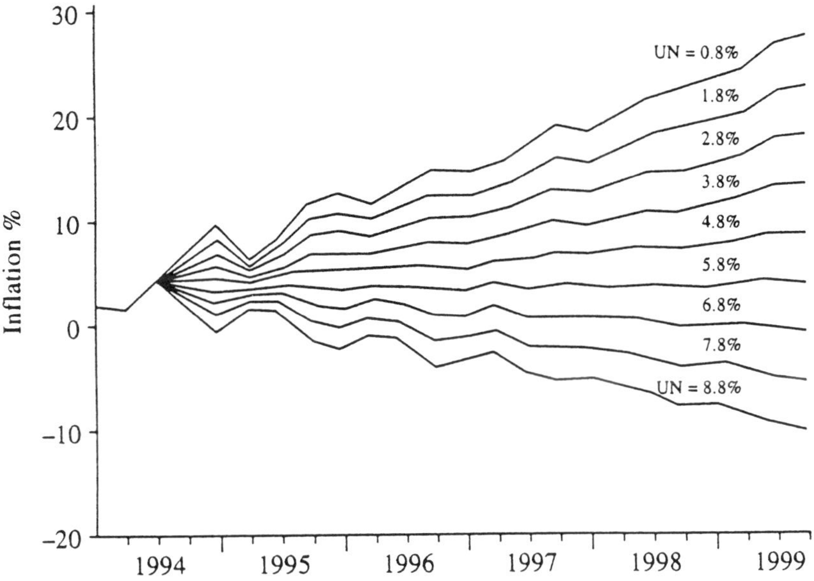

Figure 7.1 Conventional model, unemployment (UN) above and below 5.8% and CPI-U inflation, projections from Tables 7.1 and 7.3

shown in Figure 7.1, revealing the symmetrical results of the standard formulation: low unemployment brings accelerating inflation and high unemployment brings accelerating deflation. The projections with high-unemployment regressions, shown in Table 7.4, are even more extreme in their predictions of deflation as unemployment gets above and stays above the NAIRU. It is the projections of inflation for unemployment below the NAIRU, *derived from the separate low-unemployment regressions*, however, that are most striking. Table 7.4, depicted in Figure 7.2, indicates a forecast of INC with a constant unemployment rate at the NAIRU of 5.8 per cent, taken at preliminary estimates of 4.7 per cent inflation in 1994.III, rising to 7.7 per cent inflation by 1999.IV (as opposed to stabilizing at about 4 per cent according to projections on the conventional regression). But for 4.8 per cent unemployment the 1999.IV projection is 6.5 per cent inflation and for 3.8 per cent unemployment it is 5.4 per cent inflation. And so it goes! For further percentage point drops in unemployment INC by 1999.IV falls successively to 4.3 per cent and 3.2 per cent (and for the admittedly unrealistic 0.8 per cent unemployment to 2.1 per cent). It is true that lower unemployment leads, in the forecasts, to an immediate surge in inflation and the surge is greater the lower the unemployment. This is perhaps the kind of evidence that leads analysts to conclude precipitously that lower unemployment must be inflationary. But, particularly

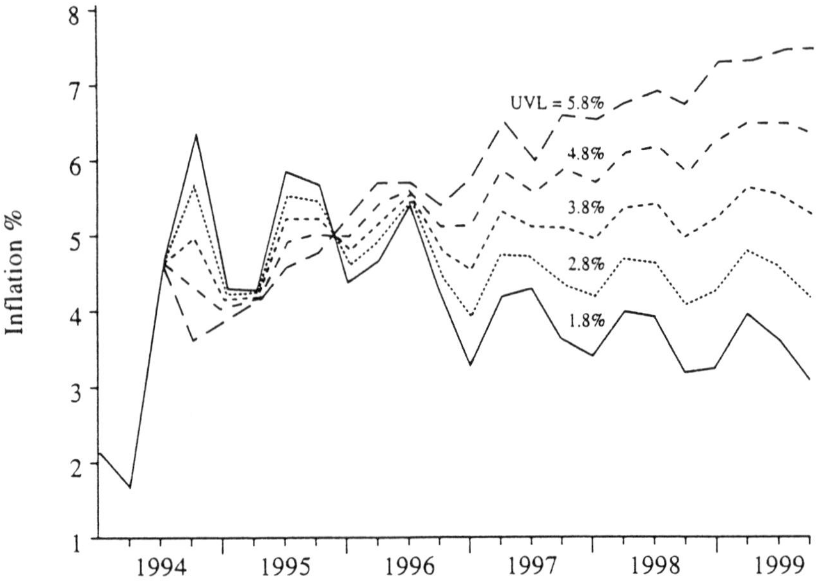

Figure 7.2 Asymmetric model 'low unemployment' (UVL) of 5.8%, 4.8%, 3.8%, 2.8%, and 1.8%, and CPI-U inflation, projections from Tables 7.1 and 7.4

in the lower-unemployment scenarios, inflation turns down as low unemployment persists, even falling below its starting point.

We may look finally at the projections of inflation in the consumer price index (INC) based upon a single equation with a single constant term shown in Table 7.5 (based on the regression shown in Table 7.2) and Figures 7.3 and 7.4. If unemployment remains constant at 5.8 per cent, the 1994 CBO NAIRU,[7] with inflation at 4.7 per cent in 1994.III, the low-unemployment coefficients generate inflation of 4.5 per cent in 1999.IV. With unemployment at 4.8 per cent, inflation in 1999.IV is down to 3.6 per cent. With unemployment at 3.8 per cent, inflation comes down to 2.7 per cent and with unemployment at 2.8 per cent, inflation would end the simulation period at only 1.8 per cent. One would be hard-pressed to see any evidence of accelerating inflation here or that lower unemployment adds to inflation. It is only projections based on the high-employment coefficients that show accelerating inflation at low unemployment – and sharp deceleration as unemployment gets high.

Summarizing briefly from Eisner (1995), from which this section is taken, I find, as shown in Tables 7.1 and 7.2, that the critical sum of current and past unemployment coefficients is generally negative, as in the conventional model, when unemployment is above the NAIRU. This indicates that high unem-

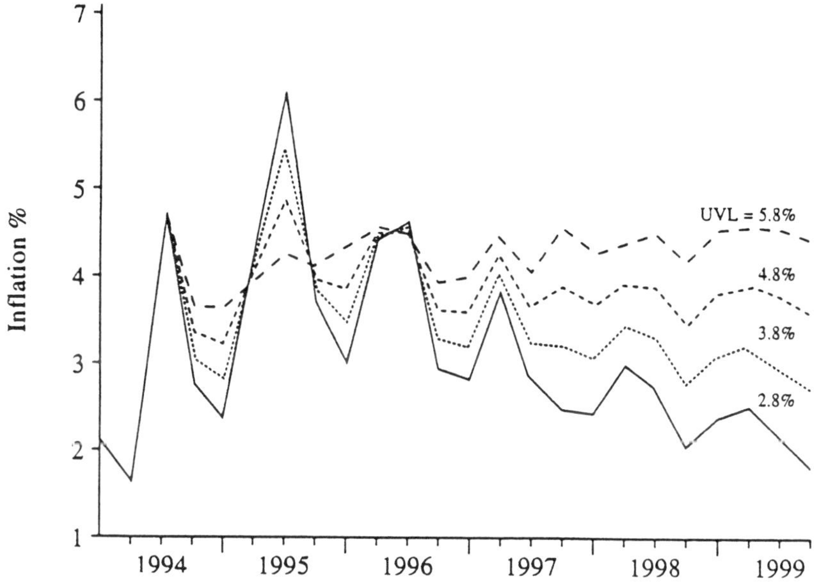

Figure 7.3 Asymmetric relation: projections from single equation with single constant term, 'low unemployment' (UVL, below variable NAIRU) and CPI-U inflation, from Tables 7.2 and 7.5

ployment will lower inflation and still higher unemployment will then lower it further. But the sums of low-employment coefficients are far less than those of the high-employment coefficients and indeed are not infrequently positive, indicating that driving unemployment below the NAIRU may actually *reduce* inflation. In addition, that critical sum of past inflation coefficients, which does meet the crucial assumption of unity in the conventional formulation, turns out to be less than unity in separate regressions of low-unemployment variables or in regressions with separate low- unemployment and high-unemployment variables but a common constant term and a common set of those inflation variables.

Thus, a stimulus to demand that would reduce unemployment may well reduce inflation. In any event, with sums of lagged inflation coefficients below unity, they may not cause permanently accelerating inflation. They would then, at worst, raise the steady rate of inflation – the old 'short-run' Phillips curve becomes long-run again. Increases in aggregate demand that might reduce unemployment would do so only at a cost of a higher, but still steady rate of inflation, or at no cost of higher inflation at all.

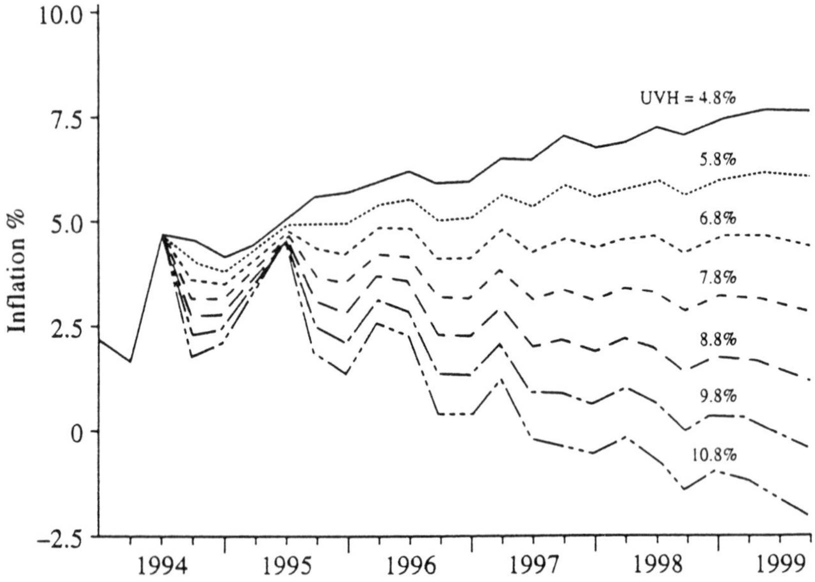

Figure 7.4 *Asymmetric relation: projections from single equation with single constant term, 'high unemployment' (UVH, above variable NAIRU) and CPI-U inflation, from Tables 7.2 and 7.5*

CONCLUSION

Unemployment due to inadequate aggregate demand remains, despite changing political and economic winds, a major source of inefficiency and loss in market economies. The old arguments that this is not possible are as inadequate as they always were. The current dogma, that the economy is doomed to a 'natural' rate of unemployment which is not necessarily – and not likely – full, is neither theoretically nor empirically robust. The NAIRU, proclaiming that efforts to reduce unemployment by stimulating demand will, in the long run at least, cause nothing but accelerating inflation, turns out to be a very thin reed – or weed – on which to base so much painful if not disastrous policy.

Even with the conventional NAIRU model, low unemployment has a long lagged effect in raising inflation. Simulations indicate further that a cut in unemployment for a quarter or even a year, with a subsequent return to the NAIRU, brings only a temporary increase in inflation. Inflation then comes back to its original rate without the necessity of excess unemployment, thus contradicting the presumed implications of the model.

And even with the conventional model, standard errors are substantial. Who can be sure that the estimated NAIRU is stable, or is not 5.5 per cent or even 5 per cent instead of 6 per cent? Dooming the economy to an extra per cent of unemployment loses some 2 per cent of output by a conservative application of Okun's Law, or $150 billion of output in today's American economy – a hefty price to pay on the basis of anybody's uncertain econometrics.

I would not bet the family farm or the nation's economy on any set of econometric estimates, even my own. But promoters, defenders and practitioners of the conventional NAIRU have done exactly that, with increasingly dogmatic assertion, in recent years. They have paralysed macroeconomic policy making that should be aimed at the 'high' and 'full' employment targets mandated in the United States, respectively, in the Employment Act of 1946 and the Full Employment and Balanced Growth (Humphrey-Hawkins) Act of 1978. Without allowing a real-world test of the proposition that lower unemployment would cause significantly more inflation, let alone continuously accelerating inflation, they have generally stymied programmes of fiscal stimulus and monetary easing.

There may indeed be no stable, universal relation among unemployment and all the various factors that may contribute to inflation, let alone accelerating inflation. My own results should make clear the lack of empirical support for the conclusion that approach to the presumed NAIRU should lead us to slow the economy and turn off a path to fuller employment. They suggest rather that we should pursue aggressively all reasonable measures to reduce unemployment, by removing supply-side impediments and adding supply-side incentives – *and* by seeing to it that the economy is not starved of adequate aggregate demand.

NOTES

1. Among them, Eisner (1986, 1988, 1989, 1994a, 1994b).
2. The old notion of involuntary unemployment due to shortage of demand for the products that could be produced by a full-employment economy is thus discarded. The onus is now put on workers who are *voluntarily* unemployed because they do not like the real wage that they are currently offered.
3. Chirinko (1995), seeking to explain procyclical movements in productivity, finds evidence that marginal cost is below average cost and falls relative to average cost in expansions. Rotemberg and Summers (1990) have presented evidence of countercyclical movement in mark-ups. Chirinko and Fazzari (1994), while not supporting a general finding of countercyclical mark-ups, do find substantial evidence of increasing returns. Decreasing marginal costs, increasing returns and countercyclical or even acyclical mark-ups would all be consistent with a finding that upward pressure on prices is less under conditions of low unemployment.
4. See Eberwein and Kollintzas (1994) and the works cited therein.

5. I have also estimated the coefficients with PDL estimators. Results are about the same.
6. The CBO raised its 1993 estimate of 5.8 per cent to 6.0 per cent for 1994 on the basis of predictions that new US Bureau of Labor Statistics measures of unemployment would raise the series by 0.2 percentage points. It is not clear, *ex post*, as the CBO has noted, that they have raised it that much.
7. Currently (1996) put at 5.83 per cent on the basis of the new, adjusted measures of unemployment.

REFERENCES

Chirinko, R.S. (1995), 'Non-Convexities, Labor Hoarding, Technology Shocks, and Procyclical Productivity: A Structural Econometric Approach', *Journal of Econometrics*, **66**(1), 61–99.

Chirinko, R.S. and S.M. Fazzari (1994), 'Economic Fluctuations, Market Power, and Returns to Scale: Evidence from Firm-Level Data', *Journal of Applied Econometrics*, **9**(1), 47–69.

Congressional Budget Office (CBO) (1994), *The Economic and Budget Outlook: An Update*, Washington, DC: Congressional Budget Office, August.

Congressional Budget Office (CBO) (1995), *The Economic and Budget Outlook: Fiscal Years 1996–2000*, Washington, DC: Congressional Budget Office, January.

Eberwien, C.J. and T. Kollintzas (1994), 'A Dynamic Model of Bargaining in a Unionized Firm With Irreversible Investment', manuscript, Northwestern University.

Eisner, R. (1986), *How Real Is the Federal Deficit?*, New York: The Free Press.

Eisner, R. (1988), 'Deficits, Monetary Policy and Real Economic Activity' in K.J. Arrow and M.J. Boskin (eds), *The Economics of Public Debt*, London: Macmillan in association with the International Economic Association.

Eisner, R. (1989), 'Budget Deficits: Rhetoric and Reality', *Journal of Economic Perspectives*, **3**(2), 73–93.

Eisner, R. (1994a), 'National Saving and Budget Deficits', *The Review of Economics and Statistics*, **76**(1), 181–6.

Eisner, R. (1994b), *The Misunderstood Economy: What Counts and How to Count It*, Boston, Mass.: Harvard Business School Press.

Eisner, R. (1995), 'A New View of the NAIRU', manuscript, Northwestern University, 24 July, paper presented at the World Econometric Congress, Tokyo, 25 August 1995.

Friedman, M. (1968), 'The Role of Monetary Policy', *American Economic Review*, **58**(1), 1–17.

Haberler, G. (1941), *Prosperity and Depression*, third edition, Geneva: League of Nations.

Keynes, J.M. (1936), *The General Theory of Employment, Interest, and Money*, London: Harcourt Brace Jovanovich (1953 reprint).

Modigliani, F. (1977), 'The Monetary Controversy or, Should We Forsake Stabilization Policies?', *American Economic Review*, **67**(1), 1–19.

Patinkin, D. (1948), 'Price Flexibility and Unemployment', *American Economic Review*, **38**(7), 543–64.

Phelps, E.S. (1968), 'Money-Wage Dynamics and Labor-Market Equilibrium', *Journal of Political Economy*, **76**(4), Part 2, 678–711.

Phillips, A.W. (1958), 'The Relation Between Unemployment and the Rate of Change of Money Wage Rates in the United Kingdom, 1861–1957', *Economica*, **25**(10), 283–99.

Pigou, A.C. (1943), 'The Classical Stationary State', *Economic Journal*, **53**(10), 343–51.

Rotemberg, J.J. and L.H. Summers (1990), 'Inflexible Prices and Procyclical Activity', *The Quarterly Journal of Economics*, **105**(4), 851–74.

[31]

DEFICITS AND UNEMPLOYMENT

Dogmas Blocking Economic Policy

by Robert Eisner

MUCH OF THE ECONOMICS PROFESSION AND BODY POLITIC HAVE BEEN infected by a virus spreading the belief, if not the reality, of policy impotence. Monetary policy—changing the quantity of money or its rate of growth—will generally, except possibly for brief "surprises," have no real effect. Monetary expansion will only raise prices or the rate of inflation, in the latter case raising nominal rates of interest but leaving real rates ultimately unchanged. Fiscal expansion by means of deficits will not be stimulatory because the public will understand that lower taxes now will have to be paid for in higher taxes later; people will hence save for that grim future rather than spend more now.

Further, we are doomed, we are told, to a "natural" rate of unemployment with which we cannot tamper without wreaking economic havoc. According to this dogma, permitting unemployment to get "too low," let alone actively trying to reduce it, will set off not just higher inflation but inflation getting higher and higher and higher. Simply returning to the natural level of unemployment will still leave inflation at the higher rates it reached in our period of delinquency. Reasonable price stability can only be restored then by excess unemployment.

As if all this is not enough, those who might see some merit in using fiscal policy for good see the "huge" deficits left from the Reagan years as making impossible any "costly" new initiatives. We cannot, we are told, interfere with deficit reduction and add even more to the debt. And raising taxes is a political no-no, and perhaps particularly bad for the economy as well.

Robert Eisner is the William R. Kenan professor emeritus of economics at Northwestern University and a past president of the American Economic Association.

It is time to reject these counsels of doom and do-nothing. Government and its fiscal policy can help the economy and improve our lives. To open the path we must expose the humbug of the current discussion of the public debt and deficits. And we must dispel the notion that we are bound by a natural rate of unemployment short of full employment.

Debt and Deficits Can Be Good for You

A first step is to eliminate the deficit paranoia that infects political discourse. *There is nothing wrong with prudent, responsible deficits.* By the methods of federal accounting we all run them—households, businesses, and state and local governments. Families borrow to buy homes, automobiles, and other durable goods and to send their children to college. Corporations borrow to finance the capital investment so widely viewed as a key to growth. And state and local governments borrow, unconstrained by "balanced budget" requirements in their constitutions, to finance their capital outlays. All such spending financed by borrowing, considered prudent financial planning when anyone else initiates it, constitutes what we call a deficit in the federal budget.

What is important for government, as for individuals and business, is not that there be no deficit but that the deficit be such that the resulting debt does not get out of line with income. Current and prospective federal deficits for the rest of this century meet that test. With a debt held by the public of $3.5 trillion and a growth of national income of 6%—and a greater growth is quite possible—an increase in the debt of $210 billion would leave the ratio of debt to income unchanged. The 1994 deficit was $203 billion, the 1995 deficit is projected at $160 billion, and for the year 2000 the Office of Management and Budget forecast a deficit of $208 billion.[1] That would constitute a growth in the debt significantly *less* than the growth in income.

There is in fact nothing sacrosanct about the current ratio of debt to income. That ratio, in terms of gross domestic product, was 51.7% at the end of the 1994 fiscal year.[2] The ratio was only 26.1% in 1981 before the big Reagan-era deficits, but it was as high as 114% in 1946, a year that ushered in a quarter century of unparalleled growth and prosperity. But even maintaining the current ratio over the long run would permit large increases in deficits to combat recessions or to undertake major public investment. These would be balanced by the decreases in deficits in booms or when the investment paid off in higher incomes.

The one meaningful argument against deficits is that they absorb private saving that would otherwise go to private investment. And by thus permitting excessive consumption, they are presumed to sacrifice the future for the benefit of the present.

The argument seems unassailable to many as they repeat the mistake of economists of more than six decades ago. Simply enough, the argument assumes full employment or full utilization of our resources. In the words of John Maynard Keynes, they apply the rules of plane geometry to a world of more than two dimensions, particularly to a world where the level of employment is an additional dimension whose variability cannot be ignored.

Of course, if employment is full and income and output are therefore fixed at what can be produced at full employment, more output going to consumption must mean less going to investment. If a deficit finances increased consumption there must be less investment. And since reducing the deficit, whether by cutting government spending or raising taxes, must reduce after-tax income, it must reduce consumption. Again, with given output, less consumption must mean more investment.

But in the real United States economy of this century we have rarely had full employment, except in times of war.[3] Higher employment has coincided with greater output—and more saving and investment. And lower employment has coincided with lesser output—and less saving and investment. What can be said of the role of deficits in such a world?

To accurately assess the effect of the deficit on the economy we must make two adjustments to the deficit as it is ordinarily measured. First, we must adjust for the impact of the business cycle. Even if there are no changes whatsoever in tax and spending policy, the deficit will fluctuate as the economy goes through the high and low points of the business cycle. At the low point, large numbers of workers are unemployed and incomes are low. The deficit then becomes larger mostly for two reasons: there are more unemployed or underemployed workers collecting unemployment, food stamps, or other government benefits, and there is less money collected in taxes, since people are earning less. The opposite effect occurs at the high point of the business cycle: government spending on benefits falls because fewer people are out of work, and tax collections increase because incomes are high.

Removing the effect on the deficit of these cyclical fluctuations allows us to construct a structural or cyclically adjusted measure of the deficit.[4] This is a measure of what the deficit would be year by year holding the level of unemployment constant, at, say, 6%.[5] Changes in this measure of the deficit are entirely attributable to changes in tax or spending policy, not fluctuations in the economy.

Second, we must adjust the deficit by the extent to which inflation reduces the real value of the government's debt. A large amount of government spending each year (currently about $200 billion) goes to pay interest on the government debt. A portion of this interest is not real interest but is actually an inflation premium that compensates for the loss of purchasing power due to inflation.

This point can be illustrated with a simple example. Suppose the government's debt is $3 trillion and that it must pay 7% interest on the debt this year, or $210 billion. Let's also assume that inflation over the course of the year is 3%. What this means is that the $3 trillion in debt that the government owes bondholders will be worth 3%, or $90 billion, less at the end of the year because of the impact of inflation. The bondholders receive $210 billion in interest payments, but the first $90 billion just compensates them for their losses due to inflation. After adjusting for the loss of purchasing power of their bonds, the amount of real interest they received was just $120 billion.

This inflation premium rises whenever inflation goes up, meaning that the actual deficit rises even though the amount of real interest paid out remains the same. By removing this effect of the inflation premium, we get a better idea of the real value of the deficit.

I have constructed a measure of the deficit, which I call the price-adjusted, high-employment[6] deficit (PAHED), that adjusts for these two factors. It removes the effects of both the business cycle and inflation on the deficit. In widely reported work over a number of years,[7] I have found that PAHED has exactly the sort of effects that would be expected if the economy were operating below its full employment levels of output. Specifically, larger deficits in one year are associated with higher real GDP growth and decreases in unemployment the next. They are also associated with higher levels of investment and national saving, even though the effect on the trade deficit and foreign investment flows is somewhat negative.

Monetary policy and real exchange rates also play a role. Easier money, as measured by the rate of increase in the money supply, has also been associated with higher GDP and saving and investment and lower unemployment a year later. Similarly, but after a lag of two or three years, lower real exchange rates have proved stimulatory. Neither of these factors, however, obscures the clear role of real, inflation-adjusted budget deficits, in themselves, as stimulants to the economy and contributors to real economic growth.

If these results of analysis of data over a period of almost 40 years are to be accepted—and I have seen no persuasive rejection of the fundamental findings—some clear conclusions must follow for policy makers. Fiscal policy, as measured by budget deficits, has had a significant impact on the economy. Larger structural deficits should be accepted and indeed pursued when the economy is sluggish. They have proved potent—whether consciously applied or stumbled into without acknowledgment, as was the case with the supposedly "supply side" tax cuts and increases in military expenditures of the 1980s. And rather than blindly striving to reduce the deficit regardless of the shape of the economy, let alone reduce it to zero with a "balanced budget," we should aim at a deficit sufficiently large to provide the effective demand for all of the goods and services our economy can produce.

There is more to the issue, though, than merely the size of the deficit. What the government and the private sector do with the money is also important. Just as the amount of private investment matters for the future, so does the amount of public investment or private investment financed by the government. One of the ironies of the deficit reduction rhetoric that says we must reduce the burden on our children and grandchildren is that deficit reduction is likely to take a heavy toll on public investment of all kinds—crucial infrastructure of roads, bridges, harbors, and airports; protection of the environment; support of basic research; food for children and pregnant women and their infants; and the basic education at all levels that is most vital to our future.

These needs suggest a policy rule of thumb: we should aim, on the average, at a high-employment deficit such that the debt-to-GDP ratio remains constant. What this would mean now, with a ratio of about 50%

and a rate of growth of GDP of (at least) 6%, is a deficit that would grow year by year but that would generally remain at 3% of GDP. (As indicated above, that would mean a current deficit of about $210 billion, significantly more than we have.) This deficit, however, should be used to finance net public investment, broadly defined to include human and intangible capital of education and research as well as the tangible capital of public infrastructure. The growth and improved supply of labor that such investment would bring would help the economy attain and maintain the high employment that would correspond to the employment rate for which the deficit was set. And high employment would also be brought about by a monetary policy aimed at low interest rates, which would promote private investment, and the lower real exchange rates that they would bring.

THE BUGABOO OF THE "NATURAL" LEVEL OF UNEMPLOYMENT[8]

A major force blocking the path to sane macroeconomic policy is the continuing hold, in the face of increasing contrary evidence, of the doctrine of a natural or "non-accelerating inflation rate of unemployment," or NAIRU. The argument, going back to Milton Friedman and Edmund S. Phelps,[9] is that basic structural forces in the economy dictate an equilibrium rate of unemployment; this rate may involve considerably more unemployment than just the modest proportions of "frictionally" jobless traditionally associated with full employment.[10] In Europe, double-digit rates have been accepted by many now for some years as "natural." I have quipped with considerable accuracy that the difference between conservative and liberal economists in the United States may be characterized by the views of those, like Martin Feldstein, who see the natural rate at 6½% to 7%, and of those, like Alan Blinder, who suggest it is between 5½% and 6%. A few brave souls are willing, given our uncertainties and the standard errors of our estimates, to allow unemployment to edge down into the danger range. But certainly too few reject the notion as a dismal dogma, never unambiguously supported by the facts.

According to the NAIRU dogma, increased demand due to fiscal or monetary policy may only temporarily increase the rate of employment.

The theory rejects the old Phillips Curve notion of a tradeoff between inflation and unemployment, whereby increased demand may reduce unemployment but only at the cost of higher inflation. The NAIRU idea is that any such reduction in unemployment occurs only because inflation is temporarily higher than had been expected. This higher inflation leads workers, apparently voluntarily and not involuntarily unemployed, to make themselves available for work because they note the increase in wages before they become aware of the increase in prices. They hence respond to what appears to them to be higher real wages by supplying themselves for jobs. Employers, on the other hand, recognize that the prices they can get for their products are higher and are going up faster than wages. Real wages to them are lower and hence they eagerly hire the additional workers.

This happy situation, however, cannot last. As workers come to realize that prices have in fact risen more than wages, they demand still higher wages or quit their jobs if they don't get them. Employers, faced with wages catching up to prices, no longer see any profit in the additional workers and let them go. We are thus back where we started, at the natural rate of unemployment.

But then the cycle repeats itself. Unemployment can only be kept below its natural rate by constantly raising inflation above what has been expected, thus producing the "accelerating" inflation that gives the concept its name. If the natural rate is, say, the 5.8% that the Congressional Budget Office has recently calculated,[11] allowing it to stay at the 5.7% of July 1995 (or the 5.4% of several months earlier!) would have the annual rate of price increase rising from its current 2% or 3% to 4%, 6%, 10%, 20%, and on into an endless hyperinflation.

If we give up this effort to keep unemployment "too low," or the Federal Reserve is successful, after inflation has reached, say, 10%, in getting unemployment back up to the natural rate of 5.8%, this will not end the inflation. It will stop accelerating, but it will remain stuck at that rate of 10%. To lower inflation we will then have to go through the painful experience of high unemployment, that is, unemployment in excess of the natural rate. The clear policy implication, to Alan Greenspan and others, is that we must not allow unemployment to get too low in the first place. And that also means that we cannot permit the economy to grow too fast. Since 2.5% growth in real GDP is associated with a fairly constant rate of unemployment, any signs that the economy is growing or will be growing faster than that must be combatted by tighter fiscal policy (cutting government expenditures and deficits) and/or tighter monetary policy (holding down bank reserves and raising interest rates).

Is there any solid justification for all this? To answer that question, I have put the NAIRU idea through two series of tests. First, assembling the data used by the Congressional Budget Office, I used CBO's model to re-estimate the NAIRU. Second, I made a slight change to the model to better reflect a different, though plausible, scenario for the effect of low unemployment.

In testing CBO's model, I found, as did CBO, that, other things equal, inflation experienced in the recent past gets passed on into the present. I too found that high rates of unemployment lead to decelerating inflation and vice versa. Most importantly, I got their precise results for the estimate of the NAIRU, a number that varied closely around CBO's then estimate of 5.8%, depending on the measure of inflation that was used.

When I made projections for the future using this standard model, I found, as expected, that unemployment below the NAIRU led to accelerating inflation. But interestingly, even with the standard model, low unemployment did not lead to sharply accelerating inflation.[12] Most striking, however, are the results of the second test, in which I made a change to the standard model.

Suppose we accept that high unemployment lowers inflation, as it apparently does. A relation estimated with observations of both high and low unemployment may well show unemployment and inflation moving in opposite directions solely because of those high unemployment observations. But suppose high and low unemployment aren't mirror images, one causing inflation to rise by a point and the other causing it to fall the same amount. Suppose low unemployment does not raise inflation and maybe even lowers it.

There are many reasons why such an asymmetrical relationship is plausible. When unemployment is low, productivity tends to be high, since firms will be trying to make full use of previously idle labor. This will tend to lower average costs, and possibly even marginal costs.[13] Also, during periods of low unemployment workers will be putting in more overtime and more hours in general. This means that they will have higher weekly pay even at the same basic wage rate, so they may feel less need to insist on hourly pay increases. Both of these factors under competitive conditions will tend to hold down prices. It is also possible that at a time when high demand will be already producing high profits, firms with current control of the market will be reluctant to raise prices out of fear of encouraging new competition, which would lower profits in the long run.

Whatever the theoretical formulation, what are the facts? I have re-estimated the NAIRU equations by separating the data into two pools, one for periods when unemployment was above the conventionally measured estimate of the NAIRU, and one for periods when it was below. The results are dramatically different. During the first period, high unemployment had an even larger effect than previously estimated on reducing inflation. However, in the period of low unemployment, there was no evidence whatsoever that low unemployment leads to accelerating inflation.

I find in fact that, on the basis of the low-unemployment observations, 5.8% unemployment yields forecasts over the rest of the century of fairly constant and modest inflation. Lower unemployment, as shown in **Figure A**, actually traces a path of *lower* inflation.

FIGURE A
Low Unemployment and Inflation Simulation,1995-99

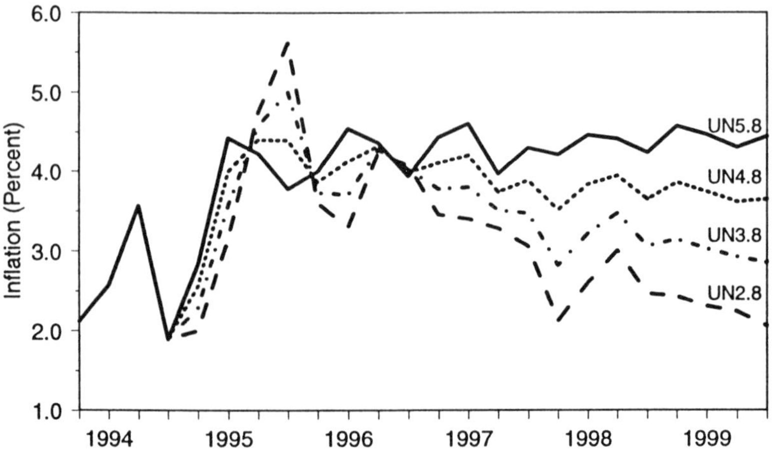

Source: Author's analysis of CBO data.

I am fond of stating that I would not bet my life—or the economy—on anyone's econometric estimates, including my own. I do not mean to substitute for the old dogma that low unemployment causes permanently accelerating inflation a new dogma that low unemployment can be relied upon to lower inflation. But I think these results[14] should give pause to those who have for some years been contributing to keeping economic policy in a nasty straight-jacket.

Perhaps we should proceed after all to implement the policies aimed at maximum and full employment that are mandated in the laws of the land.[15]

NOTES

1. Congressional Budget Office (1995), p. 28.

2. Of that, 5.4% was held by the Federal Reserve, leaving only 46.4% held by the rest of the "public." See Office of Management and Budget (1995c), Table 7.1, p. 89.

3. And forecasts by the Organization for Economic Cooperation and Development (OECD) now warn of the likelihood of double-digit unemployment rates in Europe on into the next century.

4. I believe the concept was first developed by Herbert Stein, later chairman of President Nixon's Council of Economic Advisers, when he was with the business-supported Committee for Economic Development. It was later presented more widely by Walter Heller and Arthur Okun, chairmen of the CEA under Presidents Kennedy and Johnson.

5. There is nothing significant in the particular percentage chosen. It could be a full-employment figure, such as 4% unemployment. It could be a low employment figure, say 8% unemployment. The important point is that, by not varying with cyclical fluctuations, it sets aside those cyclical effects of the economy on the deficit.

6. Generally calculated at the 6% rate used for some time by the Bureau of Economic Analysis or at the fairly similar "standardized employment" rates provided by the Congressional Budget Office.

7. See Eisner (1986, 1989, 1991, 1992, 1994a, and 1994b), and Eisner and Pieper (1984, 1988, and 1992), for example.

8. This section is based on findings reported in considerable detail in Eisner (1995a). A brief popular presentation of some of the arguments is to be found in Eisner (1995b).

9. See Friedman (1968) and Phelps (1968).

10. People who quit their jobs or leave school to start work generally don't get a job immediately. This portion of the workforce (perhaps 2-3%) is referred to as the "frictionally" jobless.

11. Congressional Budget Office (1994), p. 62 for 1993; raised to 6.0%, based on new calculations of the unemployment rate, for 1994.

12. Thus, simulations over the period 1994 (fourth quarter) to 1999 (fourth quarter) of a major one percentage point reduction below its NAIRU in the married-male unemployment rate, used by the CBO in estimating its equations, had inflation rising about 3 percentage points after five years. This is not clearly an inadmissible tradeoff. One percentage point of married-male unemployment might well correspond to 1½ percentage points of total unemployment. By Okun's law this would correspond to some 3 percentage points of GDP, or about $200 billion of output. Would 3 percentage points of steady inflation be too much to accept for that much more output?

13. See Chirinko (1995).

14. Shown in considerable detail in Eisner (1995a).

15. The Employment Act of 1946 and the Balanced Growth and Full Employment Act (Humphrey-Hawkins) of 1978.

References

Chirinko, Robert S. 1995. "Non-Convexities, Labor Hoarding, Technology Shocks, and Procyclical Productivity: A Structural Econometric Approach," *Journal of Econometrics*.

Congressional Budget Office. 1994, 1995. *The Economic and Budget Outlook: An Update*. Washington, D.C.: Congressional Budget Office.

Eisner, Robert. 1986. *How Real Is the Federal Deficit?* New York: Free Press.

Eisner, Robert. 1989. "Budget Deficits: Rhetoric and Reality." *Journal of Economic Perspectives*, Vol. 3, Spring, pp. 73-93.

Eisner, Robert. 1991. "Our Real Deficits." *Journal of the American Planning Association*, Vol. 57, Spring, pp. 131-135.

Eisner, Robert. 1992. "U.S. National Saving and Budget Deficits." In G. Epstein and H. Gintis, eds., *The Political Economy of Investment, Saving and Finance: A Global Perspective*. Project of the World Institute for Development and Economic Research (WIDER), United Nations University. Helsinki, Finland. Manuscript copy.

Eisner, Robert. 1994a. "National Saving and Budget Deficits." *The Review of Economics and Statistics*, February, pp. 181-186.

Eisner, Robert. 1994b. *The Misunderstood Economy: What Counts and How to Count It.* Boston: Harvard Business School Press.

Eisner, Robert. 1995a. "A New View of the NAIRU." Northwestern University, presented to the 7th World Congress of the Econometrics Society, Tokyo, August 1995.

Eisner, Robert. 1995b. "Our NAIRU Limit: The Governing Myth of Economic Policy." *American Prospect*, Spring 1995.

Eisner, Robert and Paul J. Pieper. 1984. "A New View of the Federal Debt and Budget Deficits." *American Economic Review*, Vol. 74, March, pp. 11-29.

Eisner, Robert and Paul J. Pieper. 1988. "Deficits, Monetary Policy and Real Economic Activity." In K.J. Arrow and M.J. Boskin, eds., *The Economics of Public Debt.* Macmillan Press in association with the International Economic Association, London.

Eisner, Robert and Paul J. Pieper. 1992. "National Saving and the Twin Deficits: Myth and Reality." In J. H. Gapinski, ed. *The Economics of Saving.* Boston: Kluwer Academic Publishers.

Friedman, Milton. 1968. "The Role of Monetary Policy." *American Economic Review*, Vol. 58, March, pp. 1-17.

Office of Management and Budget. 1995a. *Budget of the United States Government, Fiscal Year 1996.* Washington, D.C.: U.S. Government Printing Office.

Office of Management and Budget. 1995b. *Budget of the United States Government, Fiscal Year 1996, Analytical Perspectives.* Washington, D.C.: U.S. Government Printing Office.

Office of Management and Budget. 1995c. *Budget of the United States Government, Fiscal Year 1996, Historical Tables.* Washington, D.C.: U.S. Government Printing Office.

Phelps, Edmund S. 1968. "Money-Wage Dynamics and Labor-Market Equilibrium." *Journal of Political Economy*, Vol. 76, August, Part 2, pp. 678-711.

[32]

The decline and fall of the NAIRU*

The persistence of double-digit unemployment in much of Western Europe has made it increasingly difficult to defend the concept of a stable, meaningful 'NAIRU' – the supposed 'natural' or 'Non-Accelerating-Inflation Rate of Unemployment'. Unemployment in the United States has been below its presumed NAIRU for three years. The doctrine – or dogma – of the NAIRU, which has had a major role in macroeconomic theory and policy making for several decades, indicates that this should have caused accelerating inflation. But inflation by all measures has, if anything, declined[1] and shows no signs of increasing. In this chapter I shall challenge the robustness of the conventional model of the NAIRU, its econometric estimates, and its implications for macroeconomic policy.

Introduction

Tied to the notion of a 'natural rate of unemployment', introduced by Milton Friedman (1968) and almost simultaneously propounded by Phelps (1968), the NAIRU variously indicates that increasing aggregate demand cannot reduce unemployment permanently below some minimum, usually short of previous targets of 'full employment', or that this could be done only at the cost of accelerating inflation.

This concept was thus a sharp departure not only from the old Keynesian argument that there would be little to fear from inflation unless increases in demand pressed against a supply that, under conditions of full or close-to-full unemployment, could not be augmented with additional workers. It also rejected the old 'Phillips curve', which indicated a trade-off, becoming more and more expensive as full unemployment was approached, so that increased demand could reduce and maintain lower unemployment but only at the cost of higher, *but constant* inflation.

The new argument was that this old Phillips curve was a 'short-run' relation that shifted with changes in expectations of future inflation. Reductions in unemployment, which raised actual inflation as they moved us up the short-run Phillips curve, would then raise expectations of future inflation and thus raise the curve so that the rate of inflation corresponding to any given rate of unemployment would be higher. If fiscal or monetary policy aimed at keeping aggregate demand sufficiently high to maintain any rate of unemployment below the natural rate, the short-run curve would keep rising and with it actual inflation. As agents came to perceive such a policy regime, they would adjust their expectations more and more quickly. Inflation would rise more and more rapidly and ultimately the higher nominal aggregate demand would translate into no change in real demand or the policy makers would give up in the face of the runaway inflation.

Unemployment would then be back at its natural rate and inflation would stop accelerating, but would stay at its new, higher rate until unemployment was raised above the natural rate and the process was, painfully, reversed. The long-run Phillips curve was thus in effect vertical at the natural rate of unemployment or NAIRU. Unemployment less than the NAIRU would set up not merely higher inflation, but continuously increasing inflation. Unemployment above the NAIRU would bring constantly decreasing inflation, presumably leading eventually to sharp *de*flation.

The only way to reduce unemployment, except possibly in the very short run, was then to improve supply and thus reduce the NAIRU. This might be done by eliminating or softening minimum wage restrictions and taxes on labour and restrictions on firing and discriminatory or other impediments to hiring, by reducing or eliminating unemployment benefits, by increasing wage flexibility, by improving labour markets, by upgrading education and training of workers and perhaps by offering subsidies to new hiring. Many of these measures have considerable merit in their own right, others are more dubious or bring serious welfare costs. But in any event, if the NAIRU is taken seriously, these supply-side measures are the *only* ways that long-run or average unemployment can be reduced. Fiscal stimulus packages or easier money and lower nominal interest rates will not work. And if unemployment is deemed already at or close to the NAIRU, the monetary authority must take prompt anti-inflationary action to prevent the economy from 'overheating'. Otherwise, inflation will not only be higher but will be launched on its accelerating course, from which it can be diverted only by the medicine of excess unemployment, that is, unemployment above the NAIRU.

The results of this view have been reflected in policy decisions of the Federal Reserve in the United States. The Federal Reserve tightened the reins and raised interest rates six times in 1994. It was seen by many as likely to raise rates again – until GDP growth slowed substantially in the first quarter of 1995 – even though inflation had been generally running at a constant or slowing rate of under 3 per cent. But unemployment was falling and by September 1994 had fallen below 6 per cent. To most of our central bankers, that was the natural rate, or already below it. Hence more unemployment had to be booked before it was too late.[2]

There have been growing theoretical and statistical criticisms of the NAIRU.[3] The main differences among policy-oriented macroeconomists, however, most of whom seem to accept the concept, is that conservatives tend to put the NAIRU higher, at say 6.5 or 7 per cent, while liberals put it lower, at 6 or perhaps 5.5 per cent. A few brave souls suggest that, since our estimates do have standard errors[4] and we are not quite sure exactly where the NAIRU is, we should cautiously try to drive unemployment lower until demand pressures have clearly resulted in at least the beginnings of that much-feared accelerating inflation. But still fewer have risen to challenge the basic concept.

In this chapter, I shall do just that, arguing that the NAIRU has never had any sound base in theory and has not found support in the historical data. I shall debate the issues on the home grounds of supporters of the NAIRU, using their usual basic specifications of the model. I shall show that their estimates of the impact of low unemployment depend critically on their inclusion of high unemployment observations in their regressions. And I shall show that what meaningful relation may exist is apparently asymmetric. Estimates of a variant of the conventional model that permits such a distinction suggest that while unemployment above the

NAIRU may have lowered inflation in the United States, unemployment *below* the NAIRU has had little or no lasting effect in increasing inflation.

The usual formulation of the NAIRU

There are two crucial assumptions necessary to arrive at the usual concept of the NAIRU. One is that, left to itself, any given rate of inflation is somehow self-perpetuating. The mechanism would appear to involve the equality of expected future inflation to some weighted average of past inflation, although it is not at all clear why rational agents should always form their expectations in this way. Then, given these expectations, they act in such a manner that somehow expected future inflation is realized in actual future inflation, unless again some other variables intervene to affect the result. The second crucial assumption is that unemployment lowers inflation and that lower unemployment raises the rate of inflation. The combination of these two assumptions generates the result that increases in demand that may lower unemployment can do so only in the short run. And rational agents recognizing the truth of these assumptions make the short run very short indeed – soon becoming infinitesimal in length.

The dynamic process that supposedly effectuates all this has been elaborated in various fashions. Most frequently involved are more or less ignorant workers who initially mistake increases in nominal wages associated with inflation as increases in real wages and hence increase their supply of labour. In fact, the argument goes, prices have initially risen more than wages so that employers, faced with an actual decline in the real wage, move down their marginal labour productivity curves and hire more workers. But when workers sooner or later note that prices have gone up at least as much as wages, they withdraw their 'excess' labour and employers are left hiring the same number of workers as before, at the initial real wage. Workers are always on their supply curves, so that what unemployment exists is voluntary. No ugly shortages of effective demand prevent markets from clearing.

I have long been puzzled why many economists should take this contrived scenario or others – involving island parables or what have you – seriously. There is little evidence that fluctuations in real wages or changes in labour supply account for much, if any, of the fluctuations in unemployment observed in the United States. And much of the evidence, on quits for example, indicates that lower unemployment is associated with reductions in labour supply, as more workers voluntarily give up their jobs. Higher unemployment is correspondingly associated with fewer quits, as workers are fearful that they will not easily find other jobs if they give up the ones they have.

There is at best an important ellipsis in the argument, not easily papered over. The NAIRU after all relates not to changes in prices and wages, but to changes in inflation.[5] Agents are somehow assumed to adjust current labour supply and demand, in terms of levels of prices and wages, to perceived changes in rates of change of those variables. And when we come to changes in inflation, we somehow assume that expectations are single-valued and held, accurately or not, with certainty. As all of us know, we are faced with at best rather uncertain probability distributions of expected future inflation, and we do not even have a good idea of the parameters of those probability distributions. Why, under these circumstances should agents be concerned only with their first moment? Is it only the single-valued mean that should affect their actions? Or is it also the variance of the distribution or higher moments yet? Might those other moments not be expected to influence behaviour under conditions of risk-aversion and costs of planning and decision making for an uncertain future? And what other variables might affect all of these moments and affect them differently under different circumstances? How clear and how stable then is the path from past inflation to future inflation?

The general mathematical formulation leading to the NAIRU might be written:

$$IN = b_1\, IN_{-1} + b_2\,(U - \text{NAIRU}) + \Sigma\, b_g\, Z_g, \qquad (1)$$

where IN = inflation, IN_{-1} is lagged inflation or an average of past inflation rates, U = unemployment, and the Z_g represent other factors that might affect the rate of inflation. The value of b_2 is expected to be negative; U less than the NAIRU will raise inflation. If the value of b_1 is less than 1 we are faced with the proposition that inflation is not self-sustaining. Left to itself, any given rate of inflation would then decay, a devastating blow to the NAIRU and the vertical long-run Phillips curve. The model is thus frequently put in its strong form, with b_1 assumed equal to one, or the sum of regression coefficients in estimates relating to a series of lagged values of inflation constrained to equal unity. If we further ignore any other factors (not necessarily independent of rates of inflation) which may affect inflation, we are left with the formulation:

$$\Delta\, IN = b_2\,(U - \text{NAIRU}),\ b_2 < 0. \qquad (2)$$

Inflation will remain constant, that is, $\Delta\, IN = 0$ if, and only if, $U - \text{NAIRU} = 0$, that is, if unemployment is at the NAIRU. Higher unemployment will reduce inflation, but unemployment below the NAIRU will increase inflation, and keep increasing it; we will have that accelerating inflation.

Estimates of the conventional model

There has been something of a cottage industry of estimates of the NAIRU over the years. I shall take as exemplary a recent formulation by the Congressional Budget Office (CBO) (1994), similar to the early influential work of Gordon (1982).[6] Coefficients are estimated from what are called 'Phillips Curve Regressions' of quarterly time series of the form:

$$IN_t = C + \Sigma\, b_i\, IN_{t-i} + \Sigma\, b_j\, U_{t-j} + b_f\, FAE_{t-l} + b_p\, PRD_t + b_c\, NIXON_t + b_o\, NIXOFF_t. \qquad (3)$$

The lagged inflation variables, IN, run variously from $t-1$ to $t-12$, $t-18$ and $t-20$. The lagged unemployment variables, U, are taken from t to $t-4$ (not $t-1$ to $t-4$, as erroneously indicated in CBO, 1994). FAE is a measure of inflation in food and energy prices, defined as the difference between the rates of change of the fixed-weight price index for personal consumption expenditures (PCE) and the fixed-weight index for PCE less food and energy.[7] PRD is the difference between the rates of change of labour productivity in the non-farm business sector and segmented trends of labour productivity. *NIXON* is a dummy variable for the quarters of Nixon price controls, 0.8 for the five quarters between 1971.3 and 1972.3, and zero otherwise. *NIXOFF* is a dummy variable for the termination of wage and price controls in 1974, 0.4 in 1974.2 and 1975.1, and 1.6 in 1974.3 and 1974.4, and zero otherwise.

CBO estimates its basic regressions with unemployment for married males with the sum of the inflation coefficients constrained to come to one. It then attempts to convert its estimate of the NAIRU for married males to a NAIRU for total unemployment on the basis of the demographic composition of the labour force.

The NAIRU is estimated simply enough, by the CBO, by assuming that $\Sigma\, b_i = 1$, so that for constant *IN*, or $IN_t = IN_{t-i}$ for all i, $IN_t - \Sigma\, b_i\, IN_{t-i} = 0$, and that the means of FAE_{-l} and *PRD* are their expected values of zero. Ignoring the quarters where *NIXON* and *NIXOFF* are non-zero, we then have for constant or non-accelerating inflation:

$$\Delta\, IN_t = 0 = C + \Sigma\, b_j U_{t-j} \tag{4}$$

The constant rate of *U* which satisfies this equation is the estimated value of the NAIRU. Hence, we have:

$$\text{NAIRU} = -\ C\,/\,\Sigma\, b_j\,. \tag{5}$$

The CBO's 'preferred equation', that for the benchmark-years-weighted GDP price index, gave a NAIRU for married males (NAIRU-MM) of 3.55 per cent. This was reported to translate into an overall NAIRU of about 5.8 per cent in 1993.[8]

I have replicated the CBO estimates, as reported in Eisner (1995a, 1996b, 1997a and 1997b) without constraining the sum of the inflation coefficients to equal unity. Equation (4) is then replaced by

$$0 = C - IN_t + \Sigma\, b_i IN_{t-i} + \Sigma\, b_j\, U_{t-j}\,. \tag{6}$$

This would reduce to (4) if the constant, non-accelerating rate of inflation were zero. I have rather taken it to equal 3 per cent. Where the sum of the estimated inflation coefficients is not necessarily unity, we hence have:

$$\text{NAIRU} = -\ (C + 3 * \{\Sigma\, b_i - 1\})\,/\,\Sigma\, b_j\,. \tag{7}$$

Despite my not imposing the constraint that the sum of the inflation coefficients equal unity, my results were virtually identical with those of the CBO.[9]

I then re-estimated the conventional, CBO model working directly with total unemployment instead of unemployment of married males. The results, shown in Table 1, were fully consistent with those of the CBO.[10] The sums of the inflation coefficients were again not less than unity, in fact, about 1.16 for both the CPI-U and the GDP implicit price deflator, and slightly higher for estimates for 'core inflation', excluding the food and energy component from the measure of inflation and from the regressors. The sums of the unemployment coefficients were all in the

Table 1 Inflation and unemployment: conventional model

Variable or statistic	Regression coefficients and standard errors*		
	CPI-U	GDP implicit price deflator	Core inflation
	(INC)	(INF)	(INR)
Constant	3.871 (0.880)	3.777 (0.589)	3.255 (0.743)
ΣIN_{t-i} Coef. ($1 \leq i \leq 20$)	1.162 (0.083)	1.154 (0.069)	1.256 (0.085)
ΣU_{t-j} Coef. ($0 \leq j \leq 4$)	−0.737 (0.179)	−0.747 (0.131)	−0.739 (0.163)
FAE_{t-f} ($1 \leq f \leq 4$)	0.389 (0.279)	0.531 (0.150)	
PRD_t	−0.030 (0.039)	−0.076 (0.027)	−0.019 (0.040)
$NIXON_t$	−1.581 (0.819)	−1.113 (0.595)	−1.623 (0.808)
$NIXOFF_t$	0.443 (0.815)	2.668 (0.603)	3.469 (0.748)
$\hat{R}^2$	0.768	0.849	0.806
$D-W$	1.988	2.091	1.960
NAIRU	5.914	5.673	5.442

Note *Based on 163 quarterly observations from 1956.1 to 1996.3 for CPI-U and GDP implicit price deflator and 138 observations from 1962.2 to 1996.3 for core inflation.

neighborhood of −0.74. The direct estimates of the total-unemployment NAIRU were about 5.9 per cent for the CPI-U, 5.7 per cent for the GDPIPD and close to 5.4 per cent for core inflation.

While my parameter estimates, using the conventional model then, correspond predictably to the CBO (and presumably other similar) estimates, some of the implications usually drawn for policy purposes are not supported. In particular, it is often argued that we must not let the genie of inflation out of the bottle; even a brief, inflation-accelerating experience of low unemployment will be disastrous because it will be so difficult to correct. I have tested that proposition initially by simulating dynamic projections using the Table 1 equations for INC, inflation in the consumer price index, and INF, inflation in the GDP implicit price deflator (see Table 2). Assuming no effects of food and energy price inflation, FAE, or PRD, deviation of

Table 2 Projections of inflation in CPI-U and GDPIPD for one percentage point reduction in unemployment rates beginning in 1996.4, for one quarter, four quarters, eight quarters and permanently, conventional model (from equations in Table 1)

	Total unemployment									
	Consumer price index					GDP implicit price deflator				
Unemployment	5.70%	4.70% 96.4	4.70% 96.4–97.3	4.70% 96.4–98.3	4.70%	5.70%	4.70% 96.4	4.70% 96.4–97.3	4.70% 96.4–98.3	4.70%
Period	Inflation per cent									
1996.4	2.72	3.51	3.51	3.51	3.51	2.10	3.37	3.37	3.37	3.37
1996.4–1997.3	3.03	3.23	3.92	3.92	3.92	2.31	2.36	3.02	3.02	3.02
1997.4–1998.3	3.23	3.48	3.96	4.86	4.86	2.06	2.34	2.49	3.20	3.20
1998.4–1999.3	3.28	3.42	3.80	4.54	5.44	2.03	2.14	2.54	2.97	3.67
2003.4	4.01	4.25	4.98	5.93	10.09	1.45	1.70	2.03	2.77	5.78

productivity from trend, I have experimented with projections of the quarters from 1996.4 to 2003.4 on the basis of varying assumptions:

1. Unemployment is constant at a NAIRU of 5.7 per cent.
2. Unemployment falls to 4.7 per cent for one quarter and then returns to the NAIRU.
3. Unemployment falls to 4.7 per cent for one year and then returns to the NAIRU.
4. Unemployment falls to 4.7 per cent for two years and then returns to the NAIRU.
5. Unemployment falls to 4.7 per cent and stays there.

Since the lower unemployment would be expected to generate huge increases in output, some might think a few extra percentage points of inflation, even if there were not large standard errors to the forecasts so that we could predict them accurately, and even if they could not be counteracted by means other than by slowing the economy, would offer a pretty good bargain, or tradeoff, as it used to be called. (By 'Okun's Law', each percentage point of *total* unemployment translates into at least 2 percentage points of output – more than $150 billion of GDP this year.) Simulations with this conventional model, and others to be presented later, also indicate that a mere return to the NAIRU, let alone a slight increase of unemployment above it, would quickly eliminate most of the increase in inflation that had occurred.

The simulations suggest that lowering unemployment by one percentage point does increase inflation, but slowly. The initial 5.7 per cent baseline inflation of 2.1 per cent in the GDPIPD is 0.6 percentage points lower in 2003.4 and 0.4 percentage points lower even if unemployment is reduced a percentage point for one quarter. Inflation is virtually unchanged if unemployment is kept lower for a full year. It is only 0.7 percentage points higher at the end of the seven-year period if unemployment is initially lower for two years. Inflation is 5.8 per cent by 2003.4, only 4.3 percentage points higher than the 5.7 per cent baseline solution, even if unemployment is kept permanently at 4.7 per cent. Estimates for the CPI-U indicate somewhat greater inflation from lower unemployment, but even there the worst inflation result, for unemployment kept permanently a percentage point lower, is an inflation difference after seven years of 6.1 percentage points.

But that is only the beginning of my story. The conventional model, it will be shown, constrains the unemployment and inflation parameters in ways that are in fundamental conflict with the data.

An alternative model with asymmetrical effects of departures from the NAIRU

As equation (1) indicates, there are certainly in principle other variables, there dubbed Z_g, which may affect inflation. The CBO, as do others, acknowledges this in adding variables for food and energy price inflation (*FAE*), presumably at least in part exogenous, deviations of productivity from trend (*PRD*), and the imposition and removal of price controls. May there not be others and may they not have different impacts when unemployment is low and when unemployment is high?

When unemployment is high, more unemployment may lead to more competition for limited markets, which may check inflation. But when unemployment is low, reducing unemployment further may have little impact on inflation. Let me suggest several hypotheses pointing to a theoretical formulation in which low unemployment tends to hold inflation in check.

First, low measured unemployment is usually associated with greater, more efficient utilization of all resources as fixed factors of labour, management and capital are put to fuller use. This may entail increases in productivity and decreases in average costs (not necessarily captured fully by the PRD variable) which militate against price increases.[11]

Second, persistent low unemployment may set up forces of capital–labour substitution and further increases in anticipated future productivity (also not necessarily captured in the *PRD* variable) which curb inflation. Third, some game-theoretical considerations suggest that, in a collective bargaining situation, real wages may tend to move counter-cyclically, so that in periods of low unemployment upward wage pressure may be less.[12] And fourth, with profits high and overhead costs spread broadly, various oligopolistic considerations – such as a desire to discourage new entry – may become more important. Firms that are flush with profits are threats to move into new areas. Firms already there may well hesitate to offer greater invitation, with moves for additional price increases, to would-be interlopers.

This is of course just a sketch of a theory as to why low unemployment and the high profits usually associated with it may militate against inflation. Possible causes of asymmetry in the relation between inflation and unemployment are myriad. Yet, the issue has not to my knowledge, except summarily in Eisner (1994), been explored. We shall in this section indicate a formulation to examine it, and offer some dramatic results of our empirical analysis.

To do so, initially we replace equation (3) by

$$IN_t = CH + CL + \Sigma\, b_i\, IN_{t-i} + \Sigma\, b_{jH}\, UH_{t-j+1} + \Sigma\, b_{jL}\, UL_{t-j+1} + \Sigma\, b_f\, FAE_{t-f} + b_p\, PRD_t + b_c\, NIXON_t + b_o\, NIXOFF_t\,, \qquad (8)$$

$i = 1$ to 20, $j = 1$ to 5, $f = 1$ to 4, $UH = U$ when $\geq$ NAIRU and zero otherwise, $UL = U$ when $U <$ NAIRU and zero otherwise,[13] and *CH* and *CL* are the constant terms corresponding respectively to *UH* and *UL*. They are calculated as the regression coefficients of dummy variables defined as: $UHD = 1$ when $U \geq$ NAIRU and zero otherwise, and $ULD = 1$ when $U <$ NAIRU and zero otherwise. In an alternative formulation, we constrained the constant term to be the same for all observations. The NAIRU is the CBO series for total unemployment, derived from its 3.55 per cent married-male NAIRU, but varying on the basis of demographic changes between 5.5 and 6.3 per cent over the observation period.

Our reformulation of the conventional model will raise two critical questions. 1) Will the estimated values of $\Sigma\, b_{jL}$ in equation (8) differ consistently from $\Sigma\, b_{jH}$ and differ significantly from zero? 2) Will $\Sigma\, b_i$, the sum of the inflation coefficients, remain at or above unity?

Results for regressions with separate constant terms for high and low unemployment observations, as seen in Table 3a, show absolute values of the $\Sigma\, b_{jL}$

Table 3a Inflation and unemployment, unemployment above NAIRU (UH) and unemployment below NAIRU (UL): separate constants

Variable or statistic	Regression coefficients and standard errors		
	CPI-U	GDP implicit price deflator	Core inflation
	(INC)	(INF)	(INR)
UH constant	−1.633 (0.486)	−1.521 (0.441)	−2.076 (0.580)
UL constant	0.275 (0.306)	0.020 (0.264)	−0.216 (0.353)
ΣIN_{t-i} Coef. ($1 \le i \le 20$)	1.173 (0.083)	1.149 (0.075)	1.239 (0.090)
ΣUH_{t-j} Coef. ($0 \le j \le 4$)	−0.777 (0.272)	−0.905 (0.230)	−0.913 (0.295)
ΣUL_{t-j} Coef. ($0 \le j \le 4$)	−0.096 (0.262)	−0.308 (0.211)	−0.356 (0.273)
$\Sigma UL_{t-j} - \Sigma UH_{t-j}$ Coef.	0.682 (0.304)	0.597 (0.255)	0.577 (0.300)
FAE_{t-f} ($1 \le f \le 4$)	0.056 (0.299)	0.378 (0.169)	
PRD_t	−0.012 (0.036)	−0.041 (0.029)	−0.555 (0.039)
$NIXON_t$	−2.043 (0.851)	−1.661 (0.682)	−1.838 (0.865)
$NIXOFF_t$	0.827 (0.835)	3.096 (0.670)	3.191 (0.752)
$\hat{R}^2$	0.778	0.837	0.813
$D-W$	2.016	1.920	2.089

sharply less than those of the $\Sigma\, b_{jH}$. The differences were reasonably statistically significant, with *t*-statistics of 2.24 and 2.34 for the CPI-U and GDPIPD regressions, respectively, although only 1.92 for core inflation. Unemployment above the NAIRU did appear to reduce inflation. The sums of the negative coefficients differed very significantly from zero. But for unemployment below the NAIRU, the $\Sigma\, b_L$ were much lower, in the case of the CPI-U, close to zero, and were never significantly negative.

Let us spell out that critical asymmetry. Turning to inflation in the GDP implicit price deflator in Table 3a, we find that the sum of the coefficients for unemployment above the CBO NAIRU was a highly significant −0.905. This suggests an even greater anti-inflationary impact of high unemployment than the coefficient sum of −0.747 estimated in the conventional relation, shown in Table 1. But the coefficients for the low-unemployment variable, summed to only −0.308. Results for core inflation were consistent with those for the GDPIPD, while those for CPI-U inflation were, if anything, even more striking. The high-unemployment coefficients in this case summed to −0.777 while the low-unemployment coefficients summed to only −0.096. The sums of the inflation coefficients, however, were greater than unity in all regressions, indicating that a considerable amount of unemployment would be necessary to keep inflation from getting out of hand.

When we do not allow separate constant terms for high and low unemployment observations, results are somewhat different, as shown in Table 3b, but again damaging to the conventional NAIRU model. Now the sums of the inflation coefficients are less than unity, suggesting that inflation, left to itself, would decay to some equilibrium value, depending on the level of unemployment. At 5.7 per cent unemployment these would be about 5.7 per cent inflation for the CPI-U, 2.2 per cent for the GDPIPD, and 6.0 per cent for core inflation on the basis of the low-unemployment coefficients.[14]

The sums of the high-unemployment coefficients are considerably less in absolute value than in the regressions with separate constant terms, ranging from −0.261 to −0.386 for the various measures of inflation. They indicate a lesser anti-inflationary impact of high unemployment. The sums of the low-unemployment coefficients are again less in absolute value and, for the CPI-U, actually positive. Hence, the low-unemployment CPI-U coefficients indicate that unemployment below the NAIRU will not raise the 5.7 per cent equilibrium rate and would, if we could believe the point estimate for the sums of both the inflation and unemployment coefficients, *reduce* it about 1 percentage point for each percentage point less of unemployment. Each percentage point reduction in unemployment would raise that equilibrium GDPIPD inflation by about 1.8 percentage points. An unemployment rate of 4 per cent would generate equilibrium rates of inflation of about 4.0 per cent in the CPI-U, 5.2 per cent in the GDPIPD and 4.9 per cent in core inflation.[15]

So far we have been constraining parameters other than those of the unemployment variables to be the same. Of most importance, what will happen to our estimates of the sum of the inflation coefficients when those constraints are removed? We have therefore estimated completely separate, independent, high-unemployment and low-unemployment regressions.

Turning to the regressions shown in Table 4a, we find that the sums of the unemployment coefficients in the low-unemployment regressions are close to zero, and less in absolute value, but not significantly less than the high-unemployment coefficients, which are considerably less than in the composite regressions. The sum of the unemployment coefficients in the CPI-U regression is in fact again slightly positive (but not significantly so), and larger in a regression with a shift dummy for the quarters from 1990.1 to 1996.3.

The GDPIPD regressions suggest that each one percentage point increase in high

Table 3b Inflation and unemployment, unemployment above NAIRU (UH) and unemployment below NAIRU (UL): single constants

Variable or statistic	Regression coefficients and standard errors		
	CPI-U	GDP implicit price deflator	Core inflation
	(INC)	(INF)	(INR)
Constant	0.368 (0.337)	0.352 (0.282)	0.345 (0.374)
ΣIN_{t-i} Coef. ($1 \leq i \leq 20$)	0.926 (0.075)	0.900 (0.063)	0.937 (0.075)
ΣUH_{t-j} Coef. ($0 \leq j \leq 4$)	−0.261 (0.280)	−0.323 (0.221)	−0.386 (0.308)
ΣUL_{t-j} Coef. ($0 \leq j \leq 4$)	0.072 (0.287)	−0.177 (0.231)	0.040 (0.292)
$\Sigma UL_{t-j} - \Sigma UH_{t-j}$ Coef.	0.333 (0.328)	0.146 (0.264)	0.426 (0.333)
FAE_{t-f} ($1 \leq f \leq 4$)	0.213 (0.328)	0.606 (0.180)	
PRD_t	−0.038 (0.039)	−0.077 (0.029)	−0.096 (0.042)
$NIXON_t$	−0.906 (0.908)	−0.558 (0.713)	−0.495 (0.918)
$NIXOFF_t$	−0.018 (0.904)	1.890 (0.692)	1.873 (0.788)
$\hat{R}^2$	0.730	0.803	0.767
$D-W$	1.978	1.909	2.011

unemployment would lower inflation by 2.2 percentage points. But each reduction of unemployment by one percentage point below the NAIRU would raise inflation by only 0.75 percentage points ($0.116 \div \{1-0.846\}$). At 4 per cent unemployment the steady rate of inflation would settle at 4.5 per cent. On the basis of the 1990–96 observations, it would settle at 2.7 per cent. The corresponding equilibrium inflation rate in the CPI-U at 4 per cent unemployment would be all of 1.6 per cent, with each percentage point further reduction in unemployment lowering equilibrium inflation another percentage point!

Table 4a Inflation and unemployment, unemployment above NAIRU (UH) and unemployment below NAIRU (UL): separate regressions

	Regression coefficients and standard errors					
	CPI-U			GDPIPD		
Variable or statistic	High unemployment regression UH	Low unemployment regression UL	UL	High unemployment regression UH	Low unemployment regression UL	UL
Constant	0.426 (0.314)	0.539 (0.285)	0.625 (0.299)	0.424 (0.262)	0.580 (0.232)	0.691 (0.254)
C9096	–	–	−0.313	–	–	−0.280
	–	–	(0.331)	–	–	(0.265)
ΣIN_{t-i} Coef. $(1 \leq i \leq 20)$	0.914 (0.070)	0.886 (0.061)	0.879 (0.062)	0.884 (0.059)	0.846 (0.050)	0.832 (0.052)
ΣUH_{t-j} Coef. $(0 \leq j \leq 4)$	−0.202 (0.254)	0.065 (0.263)	0.126 (0.271)	−0.258 (0.206)	−0.116 (0.216)	−0.050 (0.225)
ΣFAE_{t-f} Coef. $(1 \leq f \leq 4)$	0.323 (0.297)	0.281 (0.321)	0.267 (0.322)	0.561 (0.174)	0.631 (0.179)	0.620 (0.179)
PRD_t	−0.040 (0.037)	−0.051 (0.037)	−0.052 (0.037)	−0.072 (0.028)	−0.077 (0.028)	−0.077 (0.028)
$NIXON_t$	−1.093 (0.874)	−0.996 (0.904)	−1.127 (0.915)	−0.671 (0.687)	−0.397 (0.719)	−0.520 (0.728)
$NIXOFF_t$	−0.350 (0.864)	−0.217 (0.891)	−0.221 (0.892)	1.772 (0.681)	1.673 (0.689)	1.696 (0.689)
$\hat{R}^2$	0.733	0.729	0.729	0.799	0.795	0.796
$D-W$	1.975	1.977	1.984	1.943	1.945	1.949

The core-inflation regressions are generally in line with those for the other measures of inflation. As reported in Table 4b, the sums of the high-unemployment coefficients are −0.362, the sums of the low-unemployment coefficients are virtually zero and the sums of the inflation coefficients are below unity. The low-unemployment regression calculated with the jump variable for the 1990–96 observations indicates for 4 per cent unemployment an equilibrium inflation rate of 2.3 per cent, with each percentage point further reduction in unemployment generating a further reduction of 0.2 percentage points in inflation.

Table 4b Inflation and unemployment, unemployment above NAIRU (UH) and unemployment below NAIRU (UL), separate regressions: core inflation

Variable or statistic	Regression coefficients and standard errors		
	High unemployment regression	Low unemployment regression	
	UH	UL	UL
Constant	0.409 (0.339)	0.521 (0.327)	0.688 (0.360)
C9096	- -	- -	−0.383 (0.345)
ΣIN_{t-i} Coef. $(1 \leq i \leq 20)$	0.925 (0.066)	0.894 (0.061)	0.876 (0.063)
ΣU_{t-j} Coef. $(0 \leq j \leq 4)$	−0.362 (0.277)	−0.047 (0.275)	0.026 (0.283)
PRD_t	−0.092 (0.041)	−0.104 (0.043)	−0.105 (0.043)
$NIXON_t$	−1.124 (0.895)	−0.473 (0.933)	−0.666 (0.948)
$NIXOFF_t$	2.164 (0.782)	1.187 (0.791)	1.805 (0.790)
$\hat{R}^2$	0.758	0.743	0.743
$D-W$	1.880	1.973	1.982

A declining NAIRU

Robert Gordon, whose estimates of the conventional model have been prominent and influential, has long put the NAIRU at 6 per cent. Recently, however, he has developed a 'time-varying' NAIRU (Gordon, 1997), which adjusts quarter-by-quarter, on the basis of a disturbance parameter that he sets, to the errors generated by previous estimates. The 'TV-NAIRU' based on his preferred value for the parameter turns out to have fallen over the period 1990.1 to 1996.2 from 6.3 per cent to 5.5 per cent when related to the CPI and to 5.6 per cent when related to the GDPIPD.

This would seem to vitiate at least some of the presumed usefulness of the NAIRU in setting policy. If unemployment is pushed or allowed to drift below the previous NAIRU it may perhaps do so without bringing on that accelerating inflation after all; the NAIRU may drift down along with actual unemployment and inflation!

Perhaps Gordon's TV-NAIRU does not, nevertheless, adjust enough. As shown in

Table 5a Inflation and unemployment, unemployment above time-varying NAIRU (UHTV) and below time-varying NAIRU (ULTV): separate constants

Variable or statistic	Regression coefficients and standard errors		
	CPI-U	GDP implicit price deflator	Core inflation
	(INC)	(INF)	(INR)
UHTV constant	−1.491 (0.483)	−1.401 (0.443)	−2.030 (0.575)
ULTV constant	0.401 (0.300)	0.230 (0.287)	−0.029 (0.360)
ΣIN_{t-i} Coef. ($1 \leq i \leq 20$)	1.131 (0.080)	1.115 (0.078)	1.202 (0.088)
$\Sigma UHTV_{t-j}$ Coef. ($0 \leq j \leq 4$)	−0.600 (0.255)	−0.723 (0.225)	−0.712 (0.262)
$\Sigma ULTV_{t-j}$ Coef. ($0 \leq j \leq 4$)	−0.032 (0.241)	−0.173 (0.213)	−0.213 (0.254)
$\Sigma ULTV_{t-j} - \Sigma UHTV_{t-j}$	0.568 (0.283)	0.550 (0.246)	0.499 (0.276)
FAE_{t-f} ($1 \leq f \leq 4$)	0.121 (0.284)	0.381 (0.169)	
PRD_t	−0.023 (0.033)	−0.045 (0.026)	−0.045 (0.037)
$NIXON_t$	−2.137 (0.861)	−1.859 (0.709)	−2.087 (0.860)
$NIXOFF_t$	0.606 (0.812)	2.986 (0.664)	3.179 (0.726)
$\hat{R}^2$	0.784	0.838	0.818
$D-W$	2.047	1.950	2.071

Table 5a, in regressions involving separate constant terms, the sums of high-unemployment coefficients were again sharply and significantly negative but the sums of the low-unemployment coefficients were close to zero and generally significantly more (less in absolute value) than the high-employment coefficients, except in the case of core inflation where the difference of 0.5 with a standard error 0.276 implied a probability level of only 0.07.

Table 5b Inflation and unemployment, unemployment above time-varying NAIRU (UHTV) and below time-varying NAIRU (ULTV): single constants

Variable or statistic	Regression coefficients and standard errors		
	CPI-U	GDP implicit price deflator	Core inflation
	(INC)	(INF)	(INR)
Constant	0.489 (0.329)	0.524 (0.315)	0.511 (0.393)
ΣIN_{t-i} Coef. ($1 \leq i \leq 20$)	0.897 (0.073)	0.860 (0.070)	0.897 (0.077)
ΣUH_{t-j} Coef. ($0 \leq j \leq 4$)	−0.106 (0.261)	−0.112 (0.221)	−0.176 (0.276)
ΣUL_{t-j} Coef. ($0 \leq j \leq 4$)	0.168 (0.262)	−0.033 (0.236)	0.173 (0.277)
$\Sigma UL_{t-j} - \Sigma UH_{t-j}$ Coef.	0.274 (0.305)	0.079 (0.258)	0.348 (0.312)
ΣFAE_{t-f} ($1 \leq f \leq 4$)	0.240 (0.312)	0.623 (0.183)	
PRD_t	−0.047 (0.036)	−0.078 (0.028)	−0.082 (0.041)
$NIXON_t$	−0.784 (0.904)	−0.479 (0.742)	−0.431 (0.914)
$NIXOFF_t$	−0.241 (0.875)	1.701 (0.696)	1.740 (0.768)
$\hat{R}^2$	0.739	0.798	0.766
$D-W$	1.995	1.944	1.982

The TV-NAIRU regressions with a single constant also indicated results similar to those with the CBO NAIRU, as shown in Table 5b. The sums of the high-unemployment coefficients were even smaller in absolute value, running close to −0.1 for the CPI-U and GDPIPD, and −0.176 for core inflation. The sums of the low-unemployment coefficients were virtually zero for the GDPIPD and a *positive* 0.17 for both the CPI-U and core-inflation regressions. Sums of the inflation coefficients in all cases were 0.9 or less, pointing again to a (weak) old-style Phillips curve even in the long run rather than a NAIRU.

Finally, the separate regressions for unemployment above and below the TV-

Table 6a Inflation and unemployment, unemployment above time-varying NAIRU (UHTV) and unemployment below time-varying NAIRU (ULTV), separate regressions: CPI-U and GDPIPD inflation

	Regression coefficients and standard errors					
	CPI-U			GDPIPD		
Variable or statistic	High unemployment regression UHTV	Low unemployment regression ULTV	ULTV	High unemployment regression UHTV	Low unemployment regression ULTV	ULTV
Constant	0.496 (0.314)	0.540 (0.280)	0.625 (0.292)	0.548 (0.275)	0.593 (0.237)	0.725 (0.262)
C9096	– –	– –	−0.318 (0.317)	– –	– –	−0.313 (0.268)
ΣIN_{t-i} Coef. $(1 \leq i \leq 20)$	0.897 (0.069)	0.883 (0.060)	0.877 (0.061)	0.855 (0.062)	0.844 (0.052)	0.826 (0.054)
ΣU_{t-j} Coef. $(0 \leq j \leq 4)$	−0.091 (0.248)	0.171 (0.243)	0.209 (0.246)	−0.089 (0.198)	−0.033 (0.217)	−0.047 (0.228)
ΣFAE_{t-f} Coef. $(1 \leq f \leq 4)$	0.347 (0.298)	0.235 (0.306)	0.229 (0.306)	0.614 (0.174)	0.603 (0.179)	0.589 (0.179)
PRD_t	−0.047 (0.036)	−0.047 (0.036)	−0.048 (0.036)	−0.078 (0.028)	−0.075 (0.028)	−0.076 (0.028)
$NIXON_t$	−1.053 (0.871)	−0.846 (0.891)	−0.967 (0.899)	−0.536 (0.673)	−0.456 (0.742)	−0.621 (0.754)
$NIXOFF_t$	−0.370 (0.865)	−0.180 (0.860)	−0.184 (0.860)	1.638 (0.673)	1.676 (0.689)	1.710 (0.689)
$\hat{R}^2$	0.730	0.743	0.743	0.802	0.794	0.794
$D-W$	1.974	2.003	2.014	1.946	1.938	1.944

NAIRU, reported in Tables 6a and 6b, are also fairly consistent with those for the CBO NAIRU. The sums of the low-unemployment coefficients for CPI-U and core inflation are all positive. The low-unemployment GDPIPD coefficients sums are negative but close to zero. So indeed are all of the sums of high-unemployment coefficients, except for that for core inflation, which is a modest −0.177. The sums of the inflation coefficients range from 0.908 to 0.826, hardly any comfort to those who would insist that there is a vertical long-run Phillips curve.

The TV-NAIRU series would thus first seem to confirm that in recent years the

Table 6b Inflation and unemployment, unemployment above time-varying NAIRU (UHTV) and unemployment below time-varying NAIRU (ULTV): separate regressions: core inflation

Variable or statistic	Regression coefficients and standard errors		
	High unemployment regression UHTV	Low unemployment regression ULTV	ULTV
Constant	0.457 (0.361)	0.603 (0.332)	0.787 (0.362)
C9096	– –	– –	−0.424 (0.336)
ΣIN_{t-i} Coef. $(1 \leq i \leq 20)$	0.908 (0.070)	0.876 (0.062)	0.856 (0.064)
ΣU_{t-j} Coef. $(0 \leq j \leq 4)$	−0.177 (0.267)	0.099 (0.264)	0.158 (0.267)
PRD_t	−0.090 (0.043)	−0.081 (0.042)	−0.081 (0.042)
$NIXON_t$	−0.917 (0.908)	−0.599 (0.936)	−0.801 (0.947)
$NIXOFF_t$	2.163 (0.804)	1.949 (0.775)	1.942 (0.772)
$\hat{R}^2$	0.737	0.748	0.750
$D-W$	1.910	1.941	1.952

presumed NAIRU has been declining. They also support our more fundamental argument that the entire concept is not robust against the separation of high-unemployment and low-unemployment observations.

Simulations and forecasts

One way to reveal the effects of the various, interacting coefficients is to simulate or forecast ahead, as we did for the conventional model with results shown above in Table 2, with different assumed values of unemployment. With equations estimated with observations ending in 1996.3 we have forecast ahead the 29-quarter period from 1996.4 to 2003.4. For these quarters we have again first assumed total unemployment to remain constant at the 5.7 per cent that we have taken to be the NAIRU on the basis of our estimates of the conventional model; this is close to the 5.83 per cent CBO estimate of the current NAIRU noted above.

Table 7 Projections of inflation in CPI-U and GDPIPD for one percentage point reduction in total unemployment rates beginning in 1996.4, for one quarter, four quarters, eight quarters and permanently, based on separate high and low unemployment regressions (from equations in Table 6a)

	High unemployment regression									
	Consumer price index					GDP implicit price deflator				
	5.70%	4.70% 96.4	4.70% 96.4–97.3	4.70% 96.4–98.3	4.70%	5.70%	4.70% 96.4	4.70% 96.4–97.3	4.70% 96.4–98.3	4.70%
Period	Inflation per cent									
1996.4	3.62	4.12	4.12	4.12	4.12	3.11	3.46	3.46	3.46	3.11
1996.4–1997.3	3.64	3.69	3.91	3.91	3.91	3.09	3.20	3.43	3.43	3.43
1997.4–1998.3	4.34	4.44	4.59	4.86	4.86	3.47	3.52	3.70	4.03	4.03
1998.4–1999.3	3.88	3.84	3.79	3.76	3.88	3.95	3.99	4.14	4.37	4.71
2003.4	6.18	6.20	6.28	6.41	7.51	5.34	5.36	5.44	5.58	6.76

Table 7 (continued)

	Low unemployment regression									
	Consumer price index					GDP implicit price deflator				
	5.70%	4.70% 96.4	4.70% 96.4–97.3	4.70% 96.4–98.3	4.70%	5.70%	4.70% 96.4	4.70% 96.4–97.3	4.70% 96.4–98.3	4.70%
Period	Inflation per cent									
1996.4	2.85	2.96	2.96	2.96	2.96	2.48	2.73	2.73	2.73	2.73
1996.4–1997.3	3.32	3.42	3.37	3.37	3.37	2.60	2.64	2.78	2.78	2.78
1997.4–1998.3	3.78	3.68	3.70	3.75	3.75	2.56	2.59	2.66	2.84	2.84
1998.4–1999.3	3.88	3.84	3.79	3.71	3.76	2.71	2.73	2.77	2.87	3.05
2003.4	4.50	4.49	4.47	4.44	4.15	2.92	2.93	2.96	2.90	3.47

We present in Table 7 results for the separate high-unemployment and low-unemployment regressions (of Table 4a), analogous to those from the conventional model shown in Table 2 (on the basis of the equations in Table 1). We note now that the high-unemployment regressions indicate that, even at the NAIRU, inflation would rise some over seven years, but that lowering unemployment a percentage point would make little difference. At the worst, with a permanent reduction in unemployment of one percentage point, inflation would have increased only 1.3 percentage points more in the CPI-U and 1.4 percentage points in the GDPIPD. In the case of the low-unemployment regressions, as would be predicted by the positive sum of unemployment coefficients, a permanent one percentage point reduction in unemployment actually left CPI-U inflation lower in 2003.4, by 0.35 percentage points, than it would have been with continuation at the 5.7 per cent NAIRU baseline. It raised GDP inflation by about 0.6 percentage points.

In Table 8 we compare projections over the 1996.4–2003.4 period for unemployment rates at, above, and below the 5.7 per cent NAIRU. The conventional model offers the expected stability of inflation at the NAIRU, increasing inflation at lower unemployment and deceleration, turning to price declines, at higher unemployment. Simulations with the separate high-unemployment regressions also indicate faster, and increasing inflation with lower unemployment, although each percentage point of lesser unemployment, as anticipated above, is associated, even at the end of seven years, with only 1.3 percentage points more of inflation in the CPI-U and only 1.4 percentage points more in the GDPIPD.

The low-unemployment simulations indicate only 0.5 percentage points more of GDP inflation by 2003.4 for each percentage point reduction in unemployment. Even 2.7 per cent unemployment would raise average annual inflation from 3.0 per cent in 1996.4 to 4.6 per cent in 2003.4, as compared to an increase from 2.5 per cent to 2.9 per cent if unemployment were left at 5.7 per cent. On the basis of the 1990–96 observations, inflation would remain virtually constant regardless of the unemployment rate, averaging about 2.3 per cent for each of the years from 1996 to 2003 with 5.7 per cent unemployment, and about 2.9 per cent with 2.7 per cent unemployment.

The CPI-U, low-unemployment simulations suggest again that lower unemployment actually *reduces* inflation. With 5.7 per cent unemployment, inflation would have risen from 2.9 per cent in 1996.4 to 4.5 per cent in 2003.4. With 2.7 per cent unemployment it would have gone only from 3.2 per cent to 3.4 per cent. On the basis of the 1990–96 observations, with 2.7 per cent unemployment inflation would have *fallen* from 2.9 per cent in 1996.4 to 1.1 per cent in 2003.4.

Some of the contrasting results of the low-employment regressions and the conventional, all-employment regressions are illustrated in Figure 1. Complete lack of support for the NAIRU is shown clearly in Figure 2, based on low-employment regressions reflecting the shift in the 1990–96 observations.

In all cases, it should be acknowledged, standard errors of forecasts are considerable, running over 2 percentage points. Confidence levels, even at the 5 per cent probability level, would run 4 or five percentage points above and below the projections.

What these simulations may reflect is a set of observations generating a short-run

Table 8 Projections of inflation in CPI-U and GDPIPD for unemployment rates above and below NAIRU, based on conventional model regression and on separate high unemployment and low unemployment regressions (from equations in Tables 1 and 4a)

	Conventional model regression							
	Consumer price index				GDP implicit price deflator			
	Unemployment							
	4.7%	5.7%	6.7%	7.7%	4.7%	5.7%	6.7%	7.7%
Period	Inflation per cent							
1996.4	3.5	2.7	1.9	1.1	3.4	2.1	0.8	−0.4
96.4–97.3	3.9	3.0	2.1	1.2	3.0	2.3	1.6	0.9
97.4–98.3	4.9	3.2	0.0	1.6	3.2	2.1	0.9	−0.2
98.4–99.3	5.4	3.3	1.1	−1.0	3.7	2.0	0.4	−1.3
2003.4	10.1	4.0	−2.1	−8.2	5.8	1.4	−2.9	−7.2

	High unemployment regression							
	Consumer price index				GDP implicit price deflator			
	Unemployment							
	4.7%	5.7%	6.7%	7.7%	4.7%	5.7%	6.7%	7.7%
Period	Inflation per cent							
1996.4	4.1	3.6	3.1	2.6	3.5	3.1	2.8	2.4
96.4–97.3	3.9	3.6	3.4	3.1	3.4	3.1	2.8	2.4
97.4–98.3	4.9	4.3	3.8	3.3	4.0	3.5	2.9	2.3
98.4–99.3	5.4	4.7	4.0	3.3	4.7	4.0	3.2	2.4
2003.4	7.5	6.2	4.9	3.5	6.8	5.3	3.9	2.5

Table 8 (continued)

	Low unemployment regression							
	Consumer price index				GDP implicit price deflator			
	Unemployment							
	2.7%	3.7%	4.7%	5.7%	2.7%	3.7%	4.7%	5.7%
Period				Inflation per cent				
1996.4	3.2	3.1	3.0	2.9	3.2	3.0	2.7	2.5
96.4–97.3	3.5	3.4	3.4	3.3	3.1	3.0	2.8	2.6
97.4–98.3	3.7	3.7	3.8	3.8	3.4	3.1	2.8	2.6
98.4–99.3	3.5	3.6	3.8	3.9	3.7	3.4	3.1	2.7
2003.4	3.4	3.8	4.1	4.5	4.6	4.0	3.5	2.9

	Low unemployment regression based on 1990–96 observations							
	Consumer price index				GDP implicit price deflator			
	Unemployment							
	2.7%	3.7%	4.7%	5.7%	2.7%	3.7%	4.7%	5.7%
Period				Inflation per cent				
1996.4	2.9	2.8	2.7	2.6	3.0	2.8	2.5	2.3
96.4–97.3	3.0	3.0	3.0	3.0	2.8	2.6	2.5	2.4
97.4–98.3	2.6	2.8	2.9	3.1	2.7	2.4	2.5	2.2
98.4–99.3	2.0	2.4	2.7	3.1	2.8	2.6	2.4	2.3
2003.4	1.1	1.8	2.5	3.2	2.9	2.7	2.4	2.2

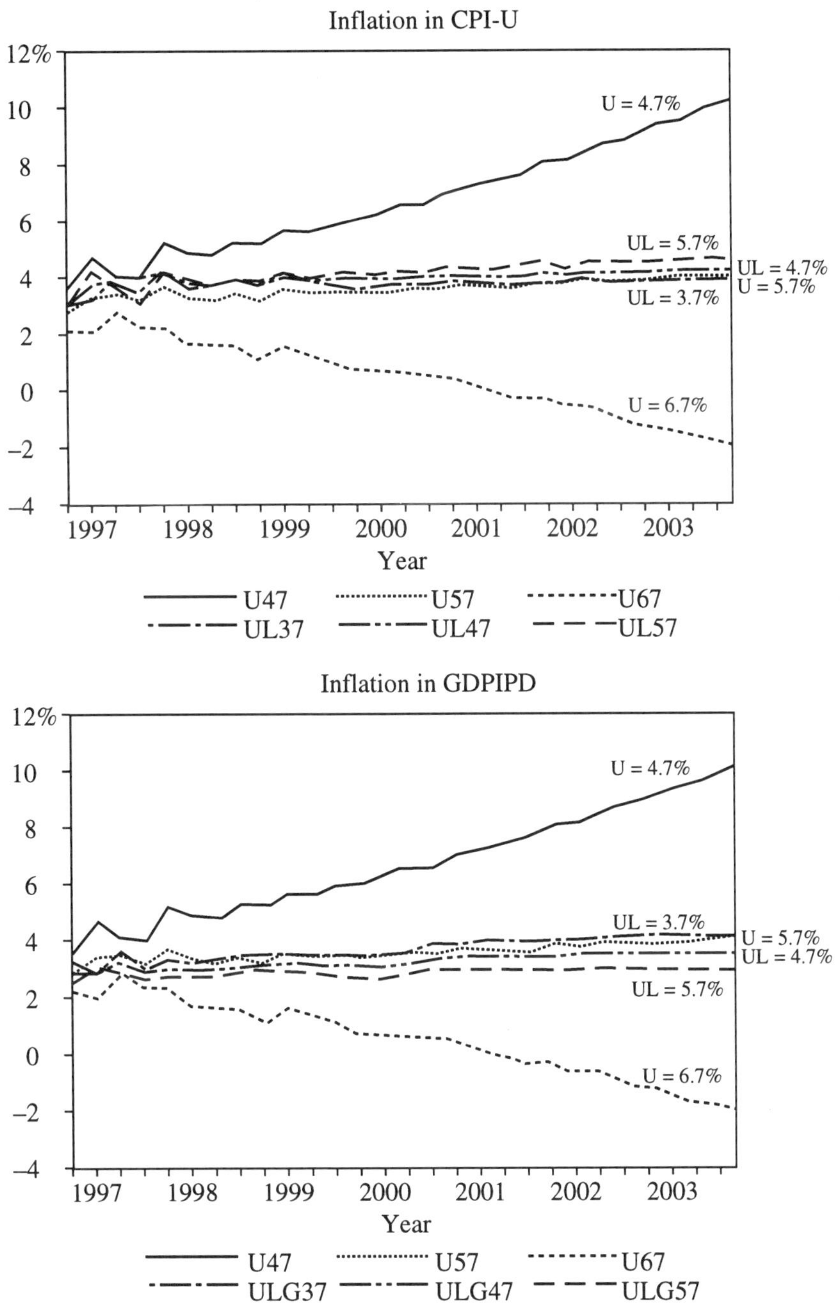

Figure 1 *Conventional model: all-unemployment, U, and low-unemployment, UL, Regression forecasts of inflation, 1996.4–2003.4. U = 6.7%, 5.7% (NAIRU) and 4.7%; UL = 5.7%, 4.7%, and 3.7%*

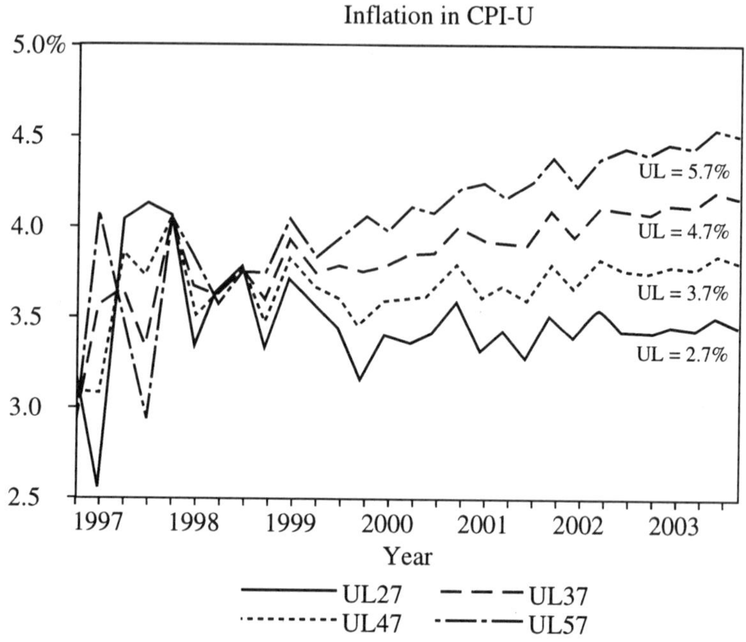

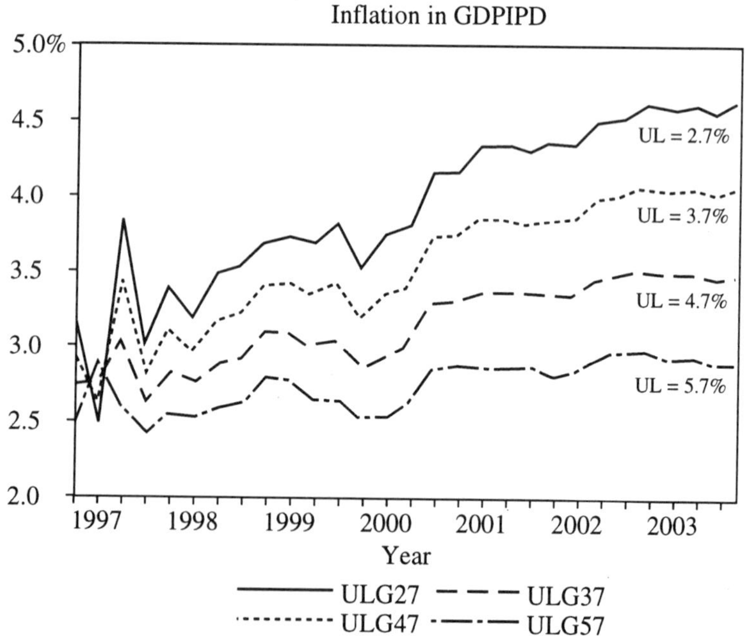

Figure 2 Low-unemployment regression forecasts of inflation, 1996.4–2003.4, reflecting shift in 1990–1996 observations. UL (low unemployment) = 5.7%, 4.7%, 3.7% and 2.7%

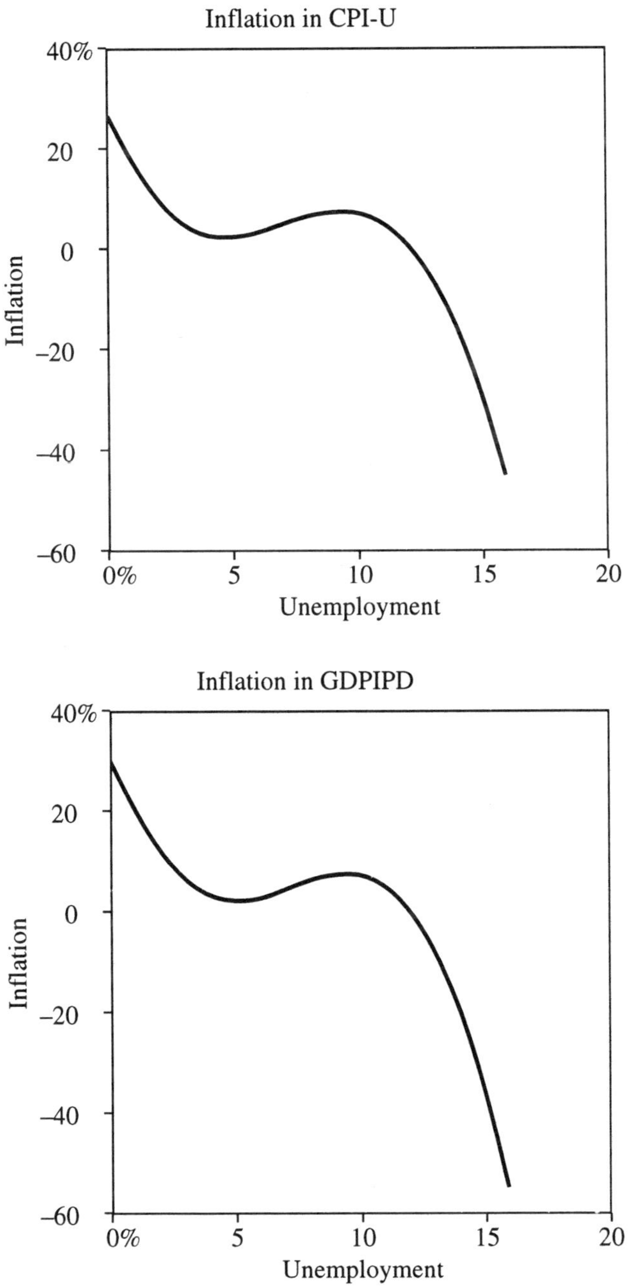

Figure 3 *Phillips curves from third degree regressions, based on 163 observations from 1956.1 to 1996.3*

Phillips curve quite different from its original hyperbolic shape. Phillips curves calculated and plotted from cubic equations relating inflation to current and four lagged values of unemployment over our 1956–96 estimation period, shown in Figure 3, appear rather to confirm the original suggestion by Tobin (1955) that they are S-shaped. *Very* low unemployment is indeed associated with considerably more rapid inflation, but the curves turn upward, as we reduce unemployment, after inflation reaches minima at 4.8 per cent and 5.0 per cent unemployment, as shown in Table 9. Higher unemployment is associated with *higher* inflation until it reaches maxima, at 9.4 per cent unemployment for the CPI-U and 9.3 per cent unemployment for the GDPIPD.

Looking at the CPI-U, lower unemployment is associated with higher inflation, but only when unemployment is above 9.4 per cent or below 4.8 per cent. At the old target of 4 per cent unemployment, inflation is 3.3 per cent, little above its minimum of 2.9 per cent. Much higher unemployment would be associated with the end of inflation, but these data suggest unemployment would have to be in the neighbourhood of 12 per cent before prices actually began to come down.

Table 9 Phillips curve from third degree regression, inflation in CPI-U and GDPIPD, based on observations over 163 quarters from 1956.1 to 1996.3

Unemployment	Inflation in CPI-U	Inflation in GDPIPD
	Percentage	
0.0	26.74	33.46
1.0	16.53	20.75
2.0	9.59	11.97
3.0	5.37	6.48
4.0	3.33	3.65
4.8	2.91 (min)	2.88
5.0	2.95	2.84 (min)
6.0	3.69	3.42
7.0	5.01	4.74
8.0	6.38	6.17
9.0	7.26	7.08
9.3	7.35	7.16 (max)
9.4	7.36 (max)	7.16
10.0	7.13	6.83
11.0	5.44	4.78
12.0	1.67	0.30
13.0	−4.72	−7.25
14.0	−14.27	−18.50

Conclusion

I would not bet the family farm or the nation's economy on any set of econometric estimates, even my own, and these have substantial standard errors, as just pointed out. I welcome further tests and estimates of the relations that I have presented. However, those committed to the concept of a NAIRU - which I find poorly based to begin with - may not easily dismiss unexplained estimates of its substantial, recent decline and its breakdown when we distinguish between responses to high and low unemployment.

I do not claim a robust basis for a new dogma that says that lowering unemployment will reduce inflation. There may indeed be no stable, universal relation among unemployment and all the various factors that may contribute to inflation, let alone accelerating inflation. But there is no robust empirical support for holding down economic growth to avoid unemployment less than a presumed NAIRU.

Notes

* I am indebted to the Congressional Budget Office and to Robert Arnold, in particular, for the series that they used in preparing their estimates of the NAIRU. I am indebted to Robert J. Gordon for his estimates of a 'time-varying' NAIRU series. I have also benefited from the fine research assistance of Suken Shah, James Gill, Jay Hoffman, and Daniel A. Pasini. I am grateful to participants in the Northwestern macroeconomics seminar, and particularly to Gordon, for helpful comments and for corrections to a draft of an earlier presentation of some of this work. And I am also grateful to participants in seminars at the Congressional Budget Office, the Federal Reserve Bank of Chicago, and the University of Wisconsin, and to Robert S. Chirinko, Martin Eichenbaum, Allen Sinai, Robert M. Solow, Daniel Sullivan, Mark W. Watson, and Kenneth D. West for further helpful comments. A lengthy version of the earlier work was presented at the 7th World Congress of the Econometric Society in Tokyo (Eisner, 1995a) and a revised version of that is to be published in Eisner (1997a) with a French translation in Eisner (1997b). Some of the conclusions from the earlier paper have been published in Eisner (1995b and 1996a). Portions of the earlier version have also been published in Eisner (1996b).

1. Unemployment fell below a presumed NAIRU of 6 per cent - many put it higher - in the third quarter of 1994, with inflation by the GDP implicit price deflator running at 2.2 per cent; it ran at 1.6 per cent in the third quarter of 1996, with unemployment by then averaging 5.2 per cent. In the second quarter of 1997, the GDP implicit price deflator rose 2.2 per cent, with unemployment averaging 4.9 per cent. Inflation as measured by the CPI-U fell from 3.75 per cent in the third quarter of 1994 to 1.0 per cent, at annual rates, for the three months ending June 1997.
2. Stock and bond markets crashed in the United States the day it was reported that the February 1996 unemployment rate had fallen to 5.5 per cent. Investors concluded that the Fed. would now certainly not move to lower interest rates as it had been expected to do in response to previous evidence of a slowing economy. The markets plummeted again in early May 1996 after reports that first quarter real GDP growth was at 2.8 per cent, deemed too high to leave unemployment constant, and that the April unemployment rate was back down 0.3 percentage points to 5.4 per cent. The Fed's refusal to raise interest rates in the fall of 1996, despite widespread expectation that it would do so, may, however, reflect a shift in a more pragmatic direction. This shift seems to have been concerned both by remarks by Chairman Alan Greenspan and by Open Market Committee decisions to leave rates unchanged as late as their meeting in August 1997, despite a July unemployment rate of 4.8 per cent.
3. See, for example, Blanchard (1990), Blanchard and Katz (1997), Galbraith (1997), Rogerson (1997), Tobin (1967, 1972, 1993 and 1995), Solow (1987), Setterfield, Gordon and Osberg (1992), Setterfield (1996), and Hahn (1995), Cross (1995b) and other chapters in Cross (1995a).
4. See Staiger, Stock and Watson (1996 and 1997).
5. Ray Fair (1996), working with data for 29 other countries and the United States, has argued that the NAIRU is 'two derivatives' off. He found unemployment to be associated with higher prices but not rising prices, let alone rising inflation.
6. Other recent similar work has been done by Weiner (1993).
7. I have responded to a suggestion (by Dean Baker of the Economic Policy Institute) that general levels of prices might react to changes in food and energy prices over some period of time. I have hence introduced the *FAE* variable with four distributed lags and have found their explanatory

power to be superior to that of the single-lagged *FAE* variable used by the CBO.

8. In later estimates (CBO, 1995, Table E-1, p. 91, footnote b), it was judged 0.2 percentage points higher to correspond to new estimates of actual unemployment, so that the NAIRU for 1994 was put at 6.0 per cent. The earlier increases suggested by the new estimates were subsequently thought to be exaggerated and the CBO's estimates for 1996 are at 5.83 per cent.
9. The unconstrained estimates of that sum in fact come out close to unity: 1.038 for the CPI-U deflator and 1.037 for the GDP implicit price deflator (GDPIPD). The estimate was 0.994 for the old benchmark-weighted GDP deflator for observations from 1955.1 to 1993.4 used in the original CBO estimates. And the critical sums of unemployment coefficients were a comparable −0.742 in my replication. My NAIRU estimates were 3.611 per cent for the CPI-U deflator, as against the CBO's 3.72 per cent, and 3.566 per cent for the GDPIPD, calculated from current-dollar and chained 1992-dollar measures of GDP, as against 3.55 per cent for the CBO estimate for a benchmark-weighted GDP deflator. I have calculated inflation in the GDPIPD from the series in current dollars and the new real gross domestic product in chained 1992 dollars, for the quarters beginning in 1959.1, for which these are presently available. I have used the old series in 1992 benchmarked dollars for the quarters before 1959.1.
10. All of the results reported in this chapter are based on regressions of 163 quarterly observations from 1956.1 to 1996.3 relating to inflation in the CPI-U and the GDP implicit price deflator and on regressions of 138 observations from 1962.2 to 1996.3 for core inflation.
11. Chirinko (1995), seeking to explain pro-cyclical movements in productivity, finds evidence that marginal cost is below average cost and falls relative to average cost in expansions. Robert Hall (1988 and 1991) has contended that price is frequently well above marginal costs and capacity constraints not binding, which might suggest that there is little reason to raise prices as employment increases. Rotemberg and Summers (1990) have presented evidence of counter-cyclical movement in markups. Chirinko and Fazzari (1994), while not supporting a general finding of counter-cyclical markups, do find substantial evidence of increasing returns. Decreasing marginal costs, increasing returns and counter-cyclical or even acyclical markups would all be consistent with a finding that upward pressure on prices is less under conditions of low unemployment.
12. See Eberwein and Kollintzas (1994) and the works cited therein.
13. To prevent any bias from the differences between the differences of the means of the high and low unemployment variables and these assigned values of zero, I normalized these variables around zero. Thus, for each sample, the means of *UNH* and *UNL* were subtracted from each valid observation.
14. In general, the equilibrium inflation rate may be written:

$$IN_{EQ} = (C + \Sigma\, b_j\, U_j)/(1 - \Sigma\, b_i),$$

where again C is the constant term, U is unemployment, and the b_j and the b_i are, respectively, the coefficients of unemployment and inflation. Our constant terms reflect the fact that the unemployment variables have been normalized about their mean, so that unemployment of 5.7 per cent in the low unemployment regressions is measured as 5.7 −4.951. Calculation of the equilibrium inflation rate for the GDP implicit price deflator on the basis of the low unemployment regression is, for example: (0.352 − 0.177 {5.7 − 4.951} ÷ (1 − 0.9) = 2.194.

15. Assuming exogenous factors not operative (that is, in our formulation, $FAE = PRD = 0$), the change in the steady rate of inflation, *IN*, resulting from a permanent change in the rate of unemployment, *U*, is calculated as

$$\Delta IN = \Delta U * \Sigma\, b_j \div (1 - \Sigma\, b_i)$$

where $\Sigma\, b_j$ is the sum of the unemployment coefficients and $\Sigma\, b_i$ is the sum of the inflation coefficients. Designating the constant term as C, the equilibrium rate of inflation for the mean values of unemployment, which was normalized to zero for the high and low unemployment variables, *UH* and *UL*, is

$$IN_{EQ} = C \div (1 - \Sigma\, b_i).$$

Since $UH = 0$ corresponds to an unemployment rate of 7.272 per cent and $UL = 0$ corresponds to an unemployment rate of 4.951 per cent, the equilibrium rate of inflation as a function of the rate of unemployment may be written:

$INH_{EQ} = (C + \Sigma\, b_{jH} * \{U - 7.272\}) \div (1 - \Sigma\, b_i)$, for the high unemployment relations, and
$INL_{EQ} = (C + \Sigma\, b_{jL} * \{U - 4.951\}) \div (1 - \Sigma\, b_i)$, for the low unemployment relations.

References

Blanchard, O.J. (1990), 'Unemployment: getting the questions right and some of the answers', in J.H. Drèze and C.R. Bean (eds), *Europe's Unemployment Problem*, Cambridge, MA: MIT Press.

Blanchard, O.J. and Lawrence F. Katz (1997), 'What we know and do not know about the natural rate of unemployment', *The Journal of Economic Perspectives* **11**(1), 51-72.

Chirinko, Robert S. (1995), 'Non-convexities, labour hoarding, technology shocks, and procyclical productivity: a structural econometric approach', *Journal of Econometrics*.

Chirinko, R.S. and S.M. Fazzari (1994), 'Economic fluctuations, market power, and returns to scale: evidence from firm-level data', *Journal of Applied Econometrics*, **9**, 47-69.

Congressional Budget Office (1994), *The Economic and Budget Outlook: An Update*, Washington, DC: Congressional Budget Office, August.

Congressional Budget Office (1995), *The Economic and Budget Outlook: Fiscal Years 1996-2000*, Washington, DC: Congressional Budget Office, January.

Cross, Rod (ed.) (1995a), *The Natural Rate of Unemployment; Reflections on 25 Years of the Hypothesis*, Cambridge University Press.

Cross, Rod (1995b), 'Is the natural rate hypothesis consistent with hysteresis?', in Cross (1995a).

Eberwein, Curtis J. and Tryphon Kollintzas (1994), 'A dynamic model of bargaining in a unionized firm with irreversible investment', Northwestern University.

Eisner, Robert (1994), *The Misunderstood Economy: What Counts and How to Count It*, Boston: Harvard Business School Press.

Eisner, Robert (1995a), (1997a), (1997b), 'A new view of the NAIRU', Northwestern University, presented to the 7th World Econometric Congress in Tokyo, August 1995 (1995a), a later version to appear in P. Davidson and J. Kregel (eds), *Improving the Global Economy: Keynesianism and the Growth in Output and Employment*, Edward Elgar, Cheltenham, UK, and Brookfield, US, October 1997 (1997a), pp. 106-30, and in French translation, 'Une autre interprétation du NAIRU', in *Cahiers de l'Espace Europe*, March 1997, pp. 9-38 (1997b).

Eisner, Robert (1995b), 'Our NAIRU limit, the governing myth of economic policy', *The American Prospect*, Spring 1995, pp. 58-63. Reprinted in *Macroeconomics*, 1996/1997 Annual Edition, Dushkin Publishing Group, pp. 134-9.

Eisner, Robert (1996a), 'Deficits and unemployment', in *Reclaiming Prosperity: A Blueprint for Progressive Economic Reform*, Economic Policy Institute, pp. 27-38.

Eisner, Robert (1996b), 'The retreat from full employment', in Philip Arestis (ed.), *Employment, Economic Growth and the Tyranny of the Market*, Edward Elgar, Cheltenham, UK, and Brookfield, US, pp. 106-30.

Fair, Ray C. (1996), 'Testing the standard view of the long-run unemployment-inflation relationship', Cowles Foundation, Yale University, March.

Friedman, Milton (1968), 'The role of monetary policy', *American Economic Review*, **58**, 1-17.

Galbraith, James K. (1997), 'Time to ditch the NAIRU', *The Journal of Economic Perspectives*, **11**(1), 93-108.

Gordon, Robert J. (1982), 'Inflation, flexible exchange rates, and the natural rate of unemployment', in M.N. Baily (ed.), *Workers, Jobs and Inflation*, Washington, DC: Brookings Institution.

Gordon, Robert J. (1997), 'The time-varying NAIRU and its implications for economic policy', NBER Working Paper 5735 and *Journal of Economic Perspectives*, **11**(1), 11-32.

Hahn, Frank (1995), 'Theoretical reflections on the "natural rate of unemployment"', in Cross (1995a).

Hall, Robert E. (1988), 'The relation between price and marginal cost in US industry', *Journal of Political Economy*, **96**, 921-47.

Hall, Robert E. (1991), 'Labor demand, labor supply, and unemployment volatility', in Olivier Jean Blanchard and Stanley Fischer (eds), *NBER Macroeconomics Annual* 1991.

Phelps, Edmund S. (1968), 'Money-wage dynamics and labor-market equilibrium', *Journal of Political Economy*, vol. **76**, Part 2, 678-711.

Rogerson, Richard (1997), 'Theory ahead of language in the economics of unemployment', *The Journal of Economic Perspectives*, **11**(1), 73-92.

Rotemberg, J.J. and L.H. Summers (1990), 'Inflexible prices and procyclical activity', *The Quarterly Journal of Economics*, **105**, 851-74.

Setterfield, M.A. (1996), 'Using the NAIRU as a basis for macroeconomic policy: an evaluation', in B. Maclean and L. Osberg, *The Unemployment Crisis: All for Nought?*, McGill-Queen's.

Setterfield, M.A., D.V. Gordon and L. Osberg (1992), 'Searching for a will o' the wisp: an empirical study of the NAIRU in Canada', *European Economic Review*, **36**, 119-36.

Solow, Robert M. (1987), 'Unemployment: getting the questions right', *Economica*, **53**, S23-34.

Staiger, Douglas, James Stock and Mark Watson (1996), 'How precise are estimates of the natural rate of unemployment?', National Bureau of Economic Research Working Paper 5477, March.

Staiger, Douglas, James Stock and Mark Watson (1997), 'The NAIRU, unemployment and monetary policy', *The Journal of Economic Perspectives*, **11**(1), 33-49.
Tobin, James (1955) 'A dynamic aggregative model', *Journal of Political Economy*, **63**(1), 103-15.
Tobin, James (1967), 'Unemployment and inflation: the cruel dilemma', in A. Phillips (ed.), *Price Issues in Theory, Practice and Policy*, Philadelphia: University of Pennsylvania Press.
Tobin, James (1972), 'Inflation and unemployment', *American Economic Review*, **62**(1), 1-18.
Tobin, James (1993), 'Price flexibility and output stability: an old Keynesian view', *Journal of Economic Perspectives*, **7**, 45-65.
Tobin, James (1995), 'The natural rate as new classical economics', in Cross (1995a).
Weiner, Stuart E. (1993), 'New estimates of the natural rate of unemployment', *Economic Review*, Federal Reserve Bank of Kansas City, pp. 53-69.

Appendix: Results of VARS

Results of vector autoregressions with eight lagged values of unemployment and inflation, along with the exogenous variables *PRD*, *FAE*(−1), *NIXON* and *NIXOFF*, as shown in Tables A.1 and A.2 and Figure A.1, would appear consistent with those of the ordinary least-squares regression presented in the text.

Noting first the VARs involving the CPI-U, we find that a one percentage point (positive) shock to the regression of UN, the series for all unemployment, is associated with an immediate decline in inflation. The reduction reaches a maximum of 2.67 per cent in quarter 6 and is persistent throughout the 28 periods of forecast. The one percentage point shock in the high-employment VAR reduces inflation by a maximum of only 0.55 percentage points, in quarter 5, and subsequent quarters indicate a considerable easing of that effect.

The low-unemployment VAR results are quite different. A one percentage point shock here is associated with a 0.24 per cent reduction in inflation in quarter 1, followed immediately by a cancelling increase. From quarter 6 on we see *in*creases in inflation. A *re*duction in unemployment below the NAIRU would seem to reduce inflation.

Results of the VARs relating to the GDP implicit price deflator are similar in that again the shock in the all-unemployment regression is associated with a substantial though lesser reduction in inflation and the shock in the high-employment regression is associated with only a very modest reduction in inflation. The low-unemployment shock here is not followed by generally higher inflation but again it is not associated with markedly lower inflation.

Table A.1 VAR percentage point responses of inflation in CPI-U (INC) to one percentage point increases in all unemployment (UN), high unemployment (UH), and low unemployment (UL): eight quarter lags of inflation and unemployment variables with PRD, FAE*(-1)*, FAE*(-2)*, FAE*(-3)*, FAE*(-4)*, NIXON, *and* NIXOFF *exogenous, based on observations from 1956.1 to 1996.3*

Percentage response of INC (inflation in CPI-U) to one percentage point shock of UN, UH, and UL

	All unemployment		High unemployment		Low unemployment	
Quarter	UN	INC	UH	INC	UL	INC
1	1.00	−0.50	1.00	−0.43	1.00	−0.24
2	1.58	−1.91	0.66	−0.10	0.93	0.28
3	1.81	−1.82	0.37	−0.14	0.91	−0.04
4	1.71	−1.32	0.31	−0.18	0.79	−0.20
5	1.40	−2.59	0.34	−0.55	0.76	−0.32
6	1.07	−2.67	0.25	−0.11	0.71	0.12
7	0.82	−2.61	0.00	0.14	0.66	0.21
8	0.60	−2.13	−0.03	−0.01	0.50	0.60
9	0.38	−2.32	−0.04	−0.42	0.36	0.52
10	0.15	−2.22	−0.08	−0.34	0.25	0.50
11	−0.05	−1.93	−0.13	−0.02	0.16	0.63
12	−0.22	−1.93	−0.12	−0.18	0.09	0.86
13	−0.37	−1.88	−0.12	−0.38	0.02	0.93
14	−0.49	−1.68	−0.12	−0.33	−0.04	0.84
15	−0.57	−1.43	−0.09	−0.17	−0.09	0.84
16	−0.63	−1.42	−0.06	−0.26	−0.10	0.85
17	−0.68	−1.38	−0.06	−0.33	−0.11	0.83
18	−0.71	−1.19	−0.07	−0.22	−0.11	0.77
19	−0.73	−1.08	−0.04	−0.18	−0.10	0.73
20	−0.74	−1.05	−0.02	−0.24	−0.09	0.66
21	−0.75	−0.98	−0.03	−0.22	−0.07	0.57
22	−0.74	−0.86	−0.04	−0.11	−0.05	0.51
23	−0.72	−0.80	−0.02	−0.13	−0.02	0.47
24	−0.71	−0.78	−0.01	−0.18	−0.01	0.41
25	−0.69	−0.70	−0.03	−0.12	0.01	0.34
26	−0.66	−0.62	−0.03	−0.06	0.02	0.30
27	−0.64	−0.59	−0.02	−0.10	0.04	0.26
28	−0.61	−0.56	−0.02	−0.12	0.05	0.23

Table A.2 VAR percentage point responses of inflation in GDPIPD (INF) to one percentage point increases in all unemployment (UN), high unemployment (UH), and low unemployment (UL): eight quarter lags of inflation and unemployment variables with PRD, FAE(*-1*), FAE(*-2*), FAE(*-3*), FAE(*-4*), NIXON, *and* NIXOFF *exogenous, based on observations from 1956.1 to 1996.3*

Percentage response of INF (inflation in GDPIPD) to one percentage point shock of UN, UVH, and UYL

	All unemployment		High unemployment		Low unemployment	
Quarter	UN	INF	UVH	INF	UVL	INF
1	1.00	−1.12	1.00	−0.41	1.00	−0.31
2	1.58	−1.54	0.67	−0.16	0.93	0.27
3	1.84	−1.51	0.35	−0.17	0.93	−0.59
4	1.79	−0.57	0.27	−0.27	0.77	−0.19
5	1.50	−1.28	0.34	−0.41	0.78	−0.20
6	1.20	−0.87	0.26	−0.21	0.73	0.22
7	1.00	−1.33	0.02	0.03	0.68	0.02
8	0.78	−1.10	−0.04	−0.19	0.53	0.01
9	0.56	−1.17	−0.04	−0.15	0.41	−0.16
10	0.33	−0.98	−0.06	−0.04	0.31	−0.17
11	0.12	−0.79	−0.11	0.04	0.23	−0.27
12	−0.01	−0.62	−0.13	−0.06	0.16	−0.28
13	−0.09	−0.69	−0.09	−0.09	0.09	−0.29
14	−0.14	−0.64	−0.07	0.00	0.02	−0.29
15	−0.19	−0.61	−0.06	0.01	−0.03	−0.30
16	−0.24	−0.56	−0.06	−0.04	−0.06	−0.29
17	−0.27	−0.55	−0.03	−0.06	−0.08	−0.29
18	−0.30	−0.53	−0.01	−0.02	−0.10	−0.29
19	−0.30	−0.47	0.00	−0.02	−0.11	−0.29
20	−0.30	−0.44	0.00	−0.05	−0.11	−0.28
21	−0.30	−0.42	0.00	−0.05	−0.11	−0.26
22	−0.30	−0.40	0.01	−0.04	−0.10	−0.24
23	−0.31	−0.36	0.01	−0.03	−0.09	−0.23
24	−0.31	−0.35	0.00	−0.04	−0.08	−0.21
25	−0.30	−0.34	0.00	−0.04	−0.07	−0.19
26	−0.30	−0.32	0.00	−0.03	−0.05	−0.17
27	−0.29	−0.29	0.00	−0.03	−0.04	−0.16
28	−0.29	−0.28	−0.01	−0.03	−0.03	−0.15

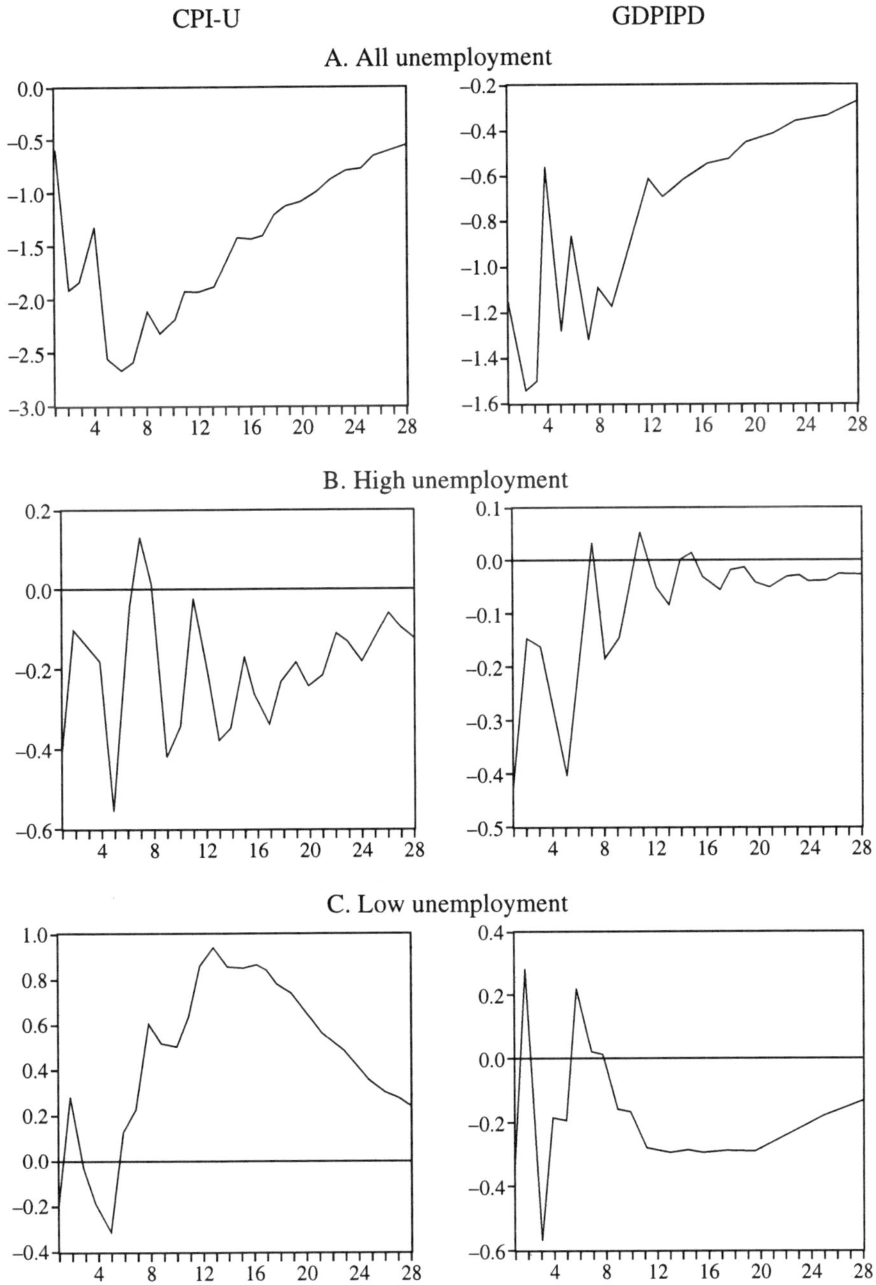

Figure A.1 *VAR percentage point responses, over 28 quarters, of inflation in CPI-U (INC) and inflation in GDPIPD (INF), to one percentage point increases in all unemployment (UN), high unemployment (UH), and low unemployment (UL): eight quarter lags of INC and unemployment variables, with* PRD, FAE(*-1*), FAE(*-2*), FAE(*-3*), FAE(*-4*), NIXON, *and* NIXOFF *exogenous, based on VARS from observations from 1956.1 to 1996.3*

Appendix: complete list of publications

A. Books and monographs

1. *Determinants of Capital Expenditures; An Interview Study*, University of Illinois, 1956.
2. 'Determinants of business investment' (with Robert H. Strotz) Research Study Two in *Impacts of Monetary Policy*, prepared for the Commission on Money and Credit, Prentice-Hall, Englewood Cliffs, NJ, 1963, pp. 60-337. Parts reprinted in Arnold Zellner (ed.), *Readings in Economic Statistics and Econometrics*, Little Brown, Boston, 1968, pp. 463-516, and Norman F. Keiser (ed.), *Readings in Macroeconomics, Theory, Evidence and Policy*, Prentice-Hall, Englewood Cliffs, NJ, 1970, pp. 133-40.
3. *Some Factors in Growth Reconsidered*, Center of Planning and Economic Research, Athens, 1966. (Two Lectures: 'On unemployment and growth' and 'Investment durability and growth'.)
4. *Factors in Business Investment*, Ballinger Press, Cambridge, Mass., for National Bureau of Economic Research, 1978.
5. *How Real is the Federal Deficit?*, The Free Press, a Division of Macmillan, New York, 1986.
6. *The Total Incomes System of Accounts*, University of Chicago Press, Chicago, 1989.
7. *The Misunderstood Economy: What Counts and How to Count It*, Boston: Harvard Business School Press, 1994; paperback, 1995; Japanese translation, 1995; Korean translation, 1996; Chinese translation, 1997; Portuguese, Russian, and Indonesian translations forthcoming.
8. *The Great Deficit Scares: The Federal Budget, Trade and Social Security*, The Twentieth Century Fund Press, New York, 1997. Swedish translation: Ordfront, 1997.
9. *Social Security: More, Not Less*, A 20th Century Foundation Report, New York, The Century Foundation Press, 1998.
10. *The Keynesian Revolution, Then and Now: The Selected Essays of Robert Eisner*, Volume 1, Edward Elgar, Cheltenham, UK and Northampton, USA, 1998.
11. *Investment, National Income and Economics Policy: The Selected Essays of Robert Eisner*, Volume 2, Edward Elgar, Cheltenham, UK and Northampton, USA, 1998.

B. Articles

1. 'The Investment Multiplier', *Review of Economic Studies*, 1949-50, **XVII**(3), no. 44, pp. 198-202.
2. 'Underemployment equilibrium rates of growth', *American Economic*

Review, March 1952, pp. 43–58. (Reprinted in E3 below, pp. 812–27.)

3. 'Accelerated amortization, growth and net profits', *Quarterly Journal of Economics*, November 1952, pp. 533–44.
4. 'Depreciation allowances, replacement requirements and growth', *American Economic Review*, December 1952, pp. 820–31. French translation as 'Provisions pour dépréciation, necessité de remplacement, expansion', in *Rayonne et Fibres Synthétiques*, January 1954, pp. 1–8.
5. 'Guaranteed growth of income', *Econometrica*, January 1953, pp. 169–71.
6. 'Conventional depreciation allowances vs. replacement cost', *The Controller*, May 1954, pp. 134–8. Reprinted in Sydney Davidson *et al.* (eds), *An Income Approach to Accounting Theory*, Prentice-Hall, Englewood Cliffs, NJ, 1964, pp. 266–72.
7. 'Depreciation under the new tax law', *Harvard Business Review*, January–February 1955, pp. 66–74 (plus duplicated mathematical appendix). Reprinted in *Congressional Record*, March 11, 1955, pp. 2264–7.
8. 'Accelerated depreciation: some further thoughts', *Quarterly Journal of Economics*, May 1955, pp. 285–96.
9. 'Interview and other survey techniques and the study of investment', in *Problems of Capital Formation*, Studies in Income and Wealth, volume 19, Princeton University Press for the National Bureau of Economic Research, 1957, pp. 513–84, 596–601.
10. 'Technological change, obsolescence and aggregate demand', *American Economic Review*, March 1956, pp. 92–105.
11. 'Expectations, plans and capital expenditures: a synthesis of *ex post* and *ex ante* data', in Mary Jean Bowman (ed.), *Expectations, Uncertainty and Business Behavior*, S.S.R.C., New York, 1958, pp. 165–88. (Summary of earlier draft in *Journal of the American Statistical Association*, June 1954, p. 356.)
12. 'An appraisal of proposals for tax differentials affecting investment', in *Income Tax Differentials*, Symposium, Tax Institute, Princeton, 1958, pp. 154–71; also discussion, pp. 172 ff., passim.
13. 'On growth models and the neo-classical resurgence', *Economic Journal*, December 1958, pp. 707–21. (Reprinted in E3, below pp. 829–44.)
14. 'The permanent income hypothesis: comment', *American Economic Review*, XLVIII, December 1958, pp. 972–90.
15. 'A distributed lag investment function', *Econometrica*, January 1960, pp. 1–29. (Summary of earlier version presented at Econometric Society meetings, December 1958, appears in *Econometrica*, April 1959, pp. 307–8.)
16. 'Flight insurance and the theory of choice' (with Robert H. Strotz), *Journal of Political Economy*, August 1961, pp. 355–68.
17. 'Investment plans and realizations', *American Economic Review*, May 1962, pp. 190–203.
18. 'Investment: fact and fancy', *American Economic Review*, May 1963, pp. 237–46.
19. 'Another look at liquidity preference', *Econometrica*, July 1963, pp. 531–8, and 'Reply', p. 550.

20. 'Capital expenditures, profits and the acceleration principle', in *Models of Income Determination*, Studies in Income and Wealth, vol. 28, Princeton, 1964, pp. 137–65, 172–6.
21. 'Bestimmungsgründe von Abweichungen zwischen antizipierten und tätsachlichen Investitionen: Ein Beitrag zum Vierteljahrlichen ökonometrischen Modell für die USA', *Ifo Studien* 9, 1963, No. 1/2, pp. 1–37. (German translation of 'Realization of investment anticipations in a quarterly econometric model of the United States economy', presented to CIRET Conference in Vienna, April 1963.)
22. 'Forecasting investment spending', in *The Economic Outlook for 1964*, University of Michigan, Ann Arbor, 1963, pp. 71–95.
23. 'Income distribution, investment and growth', *Indian Economic Journal*, April–June 1964, pp. 400–412; French translation, as 'Répartition des revenus, investissement et croissance', *Économie Appliquée*, No.3, 1963, pp. 343–60.
24. 'Capacity, investment and profits', presented to National Industrial Conference Board meetings in May 1964, in *Quarterly Journal of Economics and Business*, Sept. 1964, pp. 7–12. Reprinted slightly abridged in *Business Scope*, Nov. 28, 1964, **8**(19), pp. 2–7. Also in D.R. Starleaf (ed.), *Economics, Readings in Analysis and Policy*, Scott Foresman, Glenview, Illinois, 1969, pp. 243–7.
25. 'An overall view of the model', *1963 Proceedings of the Business and Economic Statistics Section, American Statistical Association*, pp. 260–63.
26. 'Realization of investment anticipations', in Lawrence R. Klein *et al.*, *The Brookings Quarterly Econometric Model of the United States*, Rand McNally and North-Holland, 1965, pp. 95–128.
27. 'Fiscal and monetary policies for growth', in M.R. Ross (ed.), *The Future of Economic Policy*, Ann Arbor, Michigan, 1967, pp. 14–27.
28. 'A permanent income theory for investment: some empirical explorations', *American Economic Review*, June 1967, pp. 364–90.
29. 'Capital and labor in production: some direct estimates', in Murray Brown (ed.), *The Theory and Empirical Analysis of Production*, Studies in Income and Wealth, vol. 31, New York, 1967, pp. 431–62, 472–5.
30. 'The aggregate investment function', *International Encyclopedia of Social Sciences*, Macmillan, 1968, vol. 8, pp. 185–94.
31. 'War and taxes: the role of the economist in politics', *Bulletin of Atomic Scientists*, June 1968, pp. 13–18.
32. 'Investment behavior and neo-classical theory' (with M.I. Nadiri), *Review of Economics and Statistics*, August 1968, pp. 369–82. Also in *Aggregate Investment: Selected Readings*, edited by J.F. Helliwell, Penguin Books Ltd., Middlesex, England, 1976, pp. 109–32.
33. 'Factors affecting the level of interest rates: Part II' (Originally 'The liquidity trap and the liquidity leak') in *Conference on Savings and Residential Financing, 1968 Proceedings*, United States Savings and Loan League, Chicago, 1968, pp. 28–40. Also in *High Interest Rates*, Senate Committee Hearings, 1969, pp. 102–13; *Monetary Economics: Readings on Current*

Issues, William E. Gibson and George G. Kaufman (eds), McGraw-Hill, 1971, pp. 303–10.
34. 'Investment and the frustrations of econometricians', *American Economic Review*, May 1969, pp. 50-64.
35. 'Fiscal and monetary policy reconsidered', *American Economic Review*, Dec. 1969, pp. 897-905. (Also in E11 below, pp.159 ff.)
36. 'Economics, freedom, and the draft', *Public Policy*, Fall 1970, pp. 733–41.
37. 'The war and the economy', Sam Brown and Len Ackland (eds), *Why Are We Still in Vietnam*, Random House, 1970, pp. 108–23. (Also in E12 below, pp. 665–78.)
38. 'What went wrong?', *Journal of Political Economy*, May/June 1971, pp. 629–41.
39. 'The 1971 report of the President's council of economic advisers: inflation and recession', *American Economic Review*, September 1971, pp. 522–6.
40. 'What went wrong: further thoughts on fiscal and monetary policy', in *Issues in Fiscal and Monetary Policy: The Eclectic Economist Views the Controversy*, edited by James J. Diamond, DePaul University, 1971, pp. 75-91.
41. 'Non-linear estimates of the liquidity trap', *Econometrica*, September, 1971, pp. 861-64.
42. 'Components of capital expenditures: replacement and modernization versus expansion', *Review of Economics and Statistics*, August 1972, pp. 297-305. Also condensed and translated in *Mercurio* (Italy).
43. 'Tax incentives for investment', *National Tax Journal*, September 1973, pp. 397-401.
44. 'Bonanzas for business investment', *Challenge*, Nov./Dec., 1973, pp. 38–44.
45. 'Econometric studies of investment behavior: a comment', *Economic Inquiry* - The Journal of the Western Economic Association, March 1974, pp. 91–104. (Also in Panayotis G. Korlinas and Richard S. Thorn, *Modern Macroeconomics, Major Contributions to Contemporary Thought*, 1979, Harper and Row, pp. 77–86.)
46. 'Business Investment Preferences', *George Washington Law Review*, March 1974, pp. 486-500.
47. 'Tax policy and investment: an analysis of survey responses', (with Patrick Lawler), *American Economic Review*, March 1975, pp. 206–12.
48. 'The Keynesian revolution reconsidered', *American Economic Review*, May 1975, pp. 189-94.
49. 'Government and inflation, or what is wrong with the old-time religion', in *Economic Outlook for 1975*, University of Michigan, Ann Arbor, 1975, pp. 58–66.
50. 'Money and other illusions in economic policy', prepared for the David Horowitz Lectures in Tel Aviv and Jerusalem, May 1976, translated into Hebrew, *Quarterly Banking Review*, **XV**(60), July 1976, pp. 33–44, and **XVI**(62), Jan. 1977, pp. 17–28. Later versions published in part and in whole in English in *Sozialwissenschaftliche Annalen*, 1979, and in *Economic Forum*, 1980.

51. 'The corporate role in financing future investment needs', in Joint Economic Committee, *US Economic Growth from 1976-1986: Prospects, Problems and Patterns*, vol. **3**, *Capital*, Nov. 15, 1976 (USGPO, 78-611, 1976), pp. 16–32.
52. 'Capital shortage: myth and reality', *American Economic Review*, February 1977, pp. 110–15.
53. 'The outlook for business investment', in Eli Shapiro and William White (eds), *Capital for Productivity and Jobs*, New York, Prentice-Hall, 1977, pp. 50–72 and further comment 'Outlook for business investment and profits', December 2, 1977.
54. 'Inflation', in John Carr (ed.), *Full Employment and Economic Justice*, Huntington, Indiana: Our Sunday Visitor, Inc. Press, April 1977, pp. 61–75.
55. 'Government policy, investment and the return on capital', Jacques de Bandt (ed.), *Le Capital dans la Function de Production*, Paris, 1978, pp. 239-52. (Originally presented at the *Colloque International*, Paris X, Nanterre, November 18–20, 1976).
56. 'Government policy and investment', in *Financing Economic Growth: The Problem of Capital Formation*, Center for the Study of American Business, Washington University, St. Louis, and Federal Reserve Bank of St. Louis, Working Paper 19, June 1977, pp. 7-37.
57. 'Government and inflation', in Bergstrom, Catt, Peston and Silverstone (eds), *Stability and Inflation*, New York: John Wiley and Sons, 1977, pp. 103–11.
58. 'Total incomes in the United States, 1959 and 1969', in *Review of Income and Wealth*, Series 24, no. 1, May 1978, pp. 41–69. (Originally presented at International Association for Research in Income and Wealth, 14th General Conference, York, England, August 1977.)
59. 'Machlup on academic freedom', in Jacob S. Dreyer (ed.), *Breadth and Depth in Economics: Fritz Machlup - The Man and His Ideas*, Boston: Lexington Books of D.C. Heath and Co., 1978, pp. 3–12.
60. 'More on capital anticipations', Werner H. Strigel (ed), *Problems and Instruments of Business Cycle Analysis*, New York: Springer-Verlag, 1978, pp.329–90. (Originally presented at 13th CIRET Conference, Munich, Sept., 1977.)
61. 'Cross section and time series estimates of investment functions', *Annales de l'INSEE*, no. 30/31/1978 (April–Sept., 1978), pp. 99–129.
62. 'Employment taxes and subsidies', in *Work Time and Employment*, National Commission for Manpower Policy, Washington, DC, 1978, pp. 275–310. (Originally presented at Conference on Work Time and Employment, Washington, DC, October 6–7, 1978.)
63. 'Incitation à l'emploi plutôt qu'à l'investissement', *Revue Économique*, **31**(1), January 1980, 5–15.
64. 'Total income, total investment and growth', *American Economic Review*, May 1980, pp. 225–31.
65. 'Capital gains and income: real changes in the value of capital in the United States, 1946–1975', in Dan Usher (ed.), *The Measurement of Capital*, University of Chicago Press for National Bureau of Economic Research,

1980, pp. 175-342. (Originally presented at Conference on Research in Income and Wealth, Toronto, October 1976; revised and updated version August 1979.)

66. 'Limitations and potentials of countercyclical fiscal and monetary policies', in *The Business Cycle and Public Policy 1929-1980, A Compendium of Papers*, Joint Economic Committee, Congress of the United States, Washington, DC: USGPO, 1980, pp. 147-71.

67. 'Expectations in economics', in Joint Economic Committee of the US, *Expectations and the Economy*, Washington, DC, USGPO, 85 830 0, 1981, pp. 54-65.

68. 'An extended measure of government product: preliminary results for the United States, 1946-1976' (with David H. Nebhut), *Review of Income and Wealth*, May 1981, pp. 33-64.

69. 'The effects of tax parameters in the investment equations in macroeconomic econometric models' (with Robert S. Chirinko, from OTA Paper 47), in Marshall Blume, Jean Crockett, and Paul Taubman (eds), *Economic Activity and Finance*, Cambridge, Mass., Ballinger, 1982, pp. 25-84.

70. 'Tax policy for investment: implications for innovation', in National Science Foundation, *Tax Policy and Investment in Innovation*, Washington, DC, 1982.

71. 'The state of fiscal policy - and some alternatives', in Conference Board Public Policy Forum, *Colloquium on Alternatives for Economic Policy*, 1982, pp. 28-35.

72. 'Money, taxes and budgets: demand or supply-side economics?', *Economic Papers* (published by the Economic Society of Australia), **1**(1), April 1982, pp. 38-48.

73. 'Differential impacts of tax incentives for investment' (with Steven Bender), *Journal of Policy Modeling*, **4**(2): June 1982, 143-59.

74. 'Total incomes in the United States, 1946 to 1976: a summary report' (with Emily Simons, Paul J. Pieper and Steven Bender), *Review of Income and Wealth*, June 1982, pp. 133-74.

75. 'Business investment in new plant and equipment', 'Capital formation', 'Investment function', and 'Profits in economic theory', in Douglas Greenwald (ed.), *Encyclopedia of Economics*, New York, McGraw-Hill, 1982, pp. 105-7, 113-16, 553-7, and 773-5.

76. 'Tax policy and investment', in *Public Finance and Economic Growth*, Proceedings of the 37th Congress of the International Institute of Public Finance, Tokyo 1981; Wayne State University Press, 1983, pp. 167-80.

77. 'Social security, saving, and macroeconomics', in *Journal of Macroeconomics*, **5**(1), 1983, pp. 1-19.

78. 'Government policy, saving and investment', in *Journal of Economic Education*, Spring 1983, pp. 38-49.

79. 'The economics of an effective jobs tax credit', in American Institute of CPAs, *Tax Equity Conference Volume*, 1983, pp. 33-42.

80. 'Tax policy and investment in major US macroeconomic econometric models' (with Robert S. Chirinko, from OTA Paper 46), *Journal of Public*

Economics, **20**(2), 1983, pp. 139–66.

81. 'Which way for France?' *Challenge*, July/August 1983, pp. 34–41.
82. 'Transfers in a total incomes system of accounts', in *Economic Transfers in the United States*, Marilyn Moon (ed.) (NBER, Studies in Income and Wealth, vol. **49**), University of Chicago Press, 1984, pp. 9–35.
83. 'A new view of the federal debt and budget deficits' (with Paul J. Pieper), *American Economic Review*, March 1984, **74**(1), pp. 11–29. Reprinted in United States Information Agency, *Portfolio: International Economic Perspectives*. A Spanish translation, 'Una nueva perspectiva de la deuda publica Y los déficits presupuestarios', published in *Hacienda Publica Español*, 1985.
84. 'Which budget deficit? Some issues of measurement and their implications', *American Economic Review*, May 1984, **74**(2), pp. 138–43.
85. 'Inflation, unemployment, and the budget', in Albert T. Sommers (ed.), *Reconstructing the Federal Budget*, New York, Praeger, 1984, pp. 150–63. (Earlier version published in Conference Board, *Toward a Reconstruction of Federal Budgeting*, 1983, pp. 59–64.)
86. 'The new incremental tax credit for R&D: incentive or disincentive?' (with Steven H. Albert and Martin A. Sullivan), *National Tax Journal*, June 1984, pp. 171–83.
87. 'Tax incentives and R&D expenditures' (with Steven H. Albert and Martin A. Sullivan), *Proceedings of the Conference on Quantitative Studies of Research and Development in Industry*, École Nationale de la Statistique et de l'Administration Economique, Paris, 1985. A shorter version was published in *Leading Indicators and Business Cycle Surveys*, Karl A. Oppenländer and Günter Poser (eds), Aldershot, England, Gower Publishing Company, Ltd., 1984, pp. 385–419.
88. 'On Keynesian underemployment, prices, and wealth effects of government debt', in *Money Credit and Prices in Keynesian Perspective*, Alain Barrère (ed.), Macmillan, 1988, pp. 162–9. French version is: 'Chìmage Kéynésian, prix et effets de richesse de la dette publique', in A. Barrère (ed.), *Keynes aujourd'hui: Théories et Politiques*, Paris, 1985, pp. 413–18.
89. 'The total incomes system of accounts', *Survey of Current Business*, January 1985, pp. 24–48.
90. 'How to make sense of the deficit' (with Paul J. Pieper), *The Public Interest*, Winter 1985, pp. 101–18. Reprinted in *Dealing with the Deficits Theory and Policy*, University Publications of America. Italian translation, 'Che significato dare al deficit di bilancio', published in *Problemi Di Amministrazione Publica*, No. 4, 1985, pp.175–204. Reprinted in *A Nation in Debt: Economists Debate the Federal Budget Deficit*, Richard H. Fink and Jack High (eds), University Publications of America, Inc., Frederick, MD., 1987, pp. 87–101.
91. 'The R&D tax credit: a flawed tool', *Issues in Science and Technology*, **1**(4), Summer 1985.
92. 'Measurement and effects of government debt and deficits' (with Paul J. Pieper), in *Economic Policy and National Accounting in Inflationary*

Conditions, Proceedings of an international conference in Dorga/Bergamo, Italy in January 1984, J. Mortensen (ed.), in *Studies in Banking and Finance*, Bertrand Jacquillat, Arnold W. Sametz, Marshall Sarnat, Giorgio P. Szego (eds), vol. **2**, 1985, pp. 115-44. An updated and revised version is published in French as 'Dette et déficit gouvernementaux: mesures et effets' in *Annales d'Économie et de Statistique*, 3, July/September 1986, pp. 27-52.

93. 'Fact and fancy on debt and deficits', in *Confronting the Federal Deficit*, Hugh W. Long (ed.), Dover, Mass., Auburn House Publishing Company, 1986, pp. 1-15.
94. 'The real federal deficit', in Congress of the United States, Joint Economic Committee, *The American Economy in Transition: from the Second World War to the 21st Century*, A symposium on the Fortieth Anniversary of the Joint Economic Committee, Washington, USGPO, forthcoming (presented January 16, 1986). Also published as 'The federal budget crisis' in *The Changing American Economy*, David Obey and Paul Sarbanes (eds), Oxford and New York, Basil Blackwood, 1986, pp. 73-107.
95. 'Will the real federal deficit stand up?', *Challenge*, May/June 1986, pp. 13-21. (An abbreviated version of B93, above.)
96. 'The real deficit', in *Quarterly Model Outlook*, Wharton Econometric Forecasting Associates, May 1986, **5**(5), 99-108.
97. 'The real federal deficit: what it is, how it matters and what it should be', in *The Quarterly Review of Economics and Business*, Winter 1986, pp. 6-21, (presented as the C. Woody Thompson Lecture for the Midwest Economic Association, March 20, 1986).
98. 'The revolution restored: Keynesian unemployment, inflation and budget deficits', *Eastern Economic Journal*, July-September, 1986, pp. 217-21. Presented at the Twelfth Annual Convention of Eastern Economic Association, Plenary Session II: The *General Theory* after 50 Years, Philadelphia, April 10, 1986.
99. 'The burden of the public debt', in *The New Palgrave: A Dictionary of Economics*, John Eatwell, Murray Milgate, Peter Newman (eds), vol. 1, London: Macmillan, pp. 294-6.
100. 'Investment' (with Robert M. Coen), in *The New Palgrave: A Dictionary of Economics*, John Eatwell, Murray Milgate and Peter Newman (eds), vol. 2, London, Macmillan Press, 1987, pp. 980-85.
101. 'The federal deficit: how does it matter?', *Science*, September 25, 1987, pp. 1577-82.
102. 'Deficits, monetary policy and real economic activity' (with Paul J. Pieper), presented at the International Economic Association Conference on Economics of Public Debt, Stanford University, June 24-26, 1986. Published in *The Economics of Public Debt*, Kenneth J. Arrow and Michael J. Boskin (eds), Macmillan Press in association with the International Economic Association, 1988, London, pp. 3-40.
103. 'Taxes, budget deficits and capital formation', Proceedings of Conference of International Institute of Public Finance, Paris. (Presented at I.I.P.F. 43rd Congress of Public Finance and the Performance of Enterprises, August

24-28, Paris, 1987.) Hungarian translation in *Penzugyi Szemle*, XXXII, February 1988, pp. 147-57. Also published in *Public Finance and Performance of Enterprises*, Wayne State University Press, Detroit, Michigan, 1989, pp. 15-29.

104. 'Extended accounts for national income and product', *Journal of Economic Literature*, **XXVI**, December 1988, pp. 1611-84.
105. 'Employer approaches to reducing unemployment', presented at Conference on 'Rethinking employment policy', at Urban Institute, Washington, September 5-6, 1985. Published in conference volume *Rethinking Employment Policy*, D. Lee Bawden & Felicity Skidmore (eds), Washington, DC, Urban Institute Press, 1989, pp. 135-59.
106. 'Debt and deficit and other illusions' in *The Economics of Imperfect Competition and Employment*, George R. Feiwel (ed.), London, Macmillan, 1989, pp. 709-20.
107. 'Budget deficits: rhetoric and reality', *Journal of Economic Perspectives*, **3**(2), Spring 1989, 73-93. French version, 'Les déficits budgétaires: de la Rhétorique à la réalité', in *Économie Appliquée*, **XLII**, 1989, Nos. 1-2, pp. 135-59.
108. 'Fiscal policy' (with Nancy S. Barrett), in *America's Transition: Blueprints for the 1990s*, Mark Green and Mark Pinsky (eds), New York, Democracy Project, 1989, pp. 8-27.
109. 'Divergences of measurement and theory and some implications or economic policy', presidential address to the American Economic Association, Dec. 29, 1988, *American Economic Review*, **79**(1), March 1989, 1-13. French version 'Divergences entre empirisme et théorie, implications pour la politique économique', *Revue française d'économie*, **79**(1), Winter 1989, pp. 39-64.
110. 'Inflation-adjusted government budget deficits and real economic activity: rejoinder' with Paul J. Pieper, *Annales d'Économie et de Statistique*, 1989, January-March, 1989, pp. 139-147.
111. 'Learning about economics and the economy', chapter in *The Principles of Economics Course: A Handbook for Instructors*, Philip Saunders and William Walstad (eds), New York, McGraw-Hill, 1990, pp. 10-18.
112. 'Social security, saving and the future', presented at the Public Trustees' Policy Symposium on Social Security Trust Fund Build-Up, Washington, DC, Sept. 16, 1988, published in the *Conference Proceedings, Social Security Trust Funds: Issues for the 1990s and Beyond*, Public Policy Institute, American Association of Retired Persons, 1990, pp. 25-30.
113. 'Public policy and manufacturing: back to basics', presented at conference on American Manufacturing in the 1990s, Nov. 9-10, 1988, at the Center for the Study of American Business at Washington University in St. Louis. Published in *American Manufacturers in A Global Market*, Kenneth W. Chilton, Melinda E. Warren, Murray L. Weidenbaum (eds), Boston, Kluwer Academic Publishers, 1990, pp. 9-16.
114. 'Debunking the conventional wisdom in economic policy', *Challenge*, May-June, 1990, pp. 4-11.

115. 'The world's greatest debtor nation?', (with Paul J. Pieper), *The North American Review of Economics and Finance*, **1**(1), 1990, pp. 9-32. (Tables updated and revised in 1991.)
116. 'Deficits and us and our grandchildren', in James M. Rock (ed.), *The Debt and the Twin Deficits Debate*, Mountain View, CA, Bristletone Books/Mayfield, 1991, pp. 81-107.
117. 'Self-correcting real deficits: a new lesson in functional finance' (with Sang-In Hwang), *The Political Economy of Government Debt*, Harrie A.A. Verban, Frans A.A.M. Van Winden (eds), North Holland, Amsterdam, 1993, pp. 255-94.
118. 'The real rate of US national saving', *The Review of Income and Wealth*, Series 37, number 1, March 1991, pp. 1-18.
119. 'The Gramm-Rudman-Hollings balanced budget act', in *The New Palgrave Dictionary of Money and Finance*, Vol. 2, Peter Newman, Murray Milgate, John Eatwell (eds), Macmillan Press Limited, London, 1992, pp. 275-9.
120. 'Budget deficits: problems of measurement', in *The New Palgrave Dictionary of Money and Finance*, Vol. 1, Peter Newman, Murray Milgate, John Eatwell (eds), Macmillan Press Limited, London, 1992, pp. 245-7.
121. 'The total incomes system of accounts', in *The New Palgrave Dictionary of Money and Finance*, Vol. 3, Peter Newman, Murray Milgate, John Eatwell (eds), Macmillan Press Limited, London, 1992, pp. 670-73.
122. 'Real foreign investment in perspective' (with Paul J. Pieper), *The Annals of the American Academy of Political and Social Science*, July 1991, pp. 22-35.
123. 'Macroeconomic consequences of disarmament', presented at ECAAR-IPPS Conference on Economic Issues of Disarmament, Institute for International Peace Studies, University of Notre Dame, November 23-24, 1990, published in *Challenge*, January-February 1991, pp. 47-50. Also to be published in *Economic Issues of Disarmament*, Jurgen Brauer and Manas Chatterji (eds), London: Macmillan, 1993, pp. 33-41.
124. 'Our real deficits', *Journal of the American Planning Association*, **57**(2), Spring 1991, pp. 131-5.
125. 'No new taxes for S&L bailout', *Challenge*, March/April 1991, pp. 34-8.
126. 'National saving and the twin deficits: myth and reality' (with Paul J. Pieper), *The Economics of Saving*, James H. Gapinski (ed.), Kluwer Academic Publishers, pp. 109-33.
127. 'US national saving and budget deficits', in *Macroeconomic Policy after the Conservative Era*, Gerald A. Epstein and Herbert Gintis (eds), Cambridge University Press, Cambridge, England, 1995, pp. 109-142.
128. 'Infrastructure and regional economic performance: comment', *New England Economic Review*, September/October 1991, pp. 47-58.
129. 'Debt and deficits', in *The McGraw-Hill Encyclopedia of Economics*, Douglas Greenwald (ed.), New York: McGraw-Hill, 1994, pp. 248-52.
130. 'Federal debt', in *The Fortune Encyclopedia of Economics*, David R. Henderson (ed.), New York, Warner Books, 1993, pp. 248-53.
131. 'Real deficits and real growth: a further view' (with Paul J. Pieper), *Journal*

of Post-Keynesian Economics, Fall 1992, pp. 43-9.

132. 'Deficits, which, how much and so what', presented at Round Table Discussion at the American Economic Association, New Orleans, January 4, 1992, in *The American Economic Review Papers and Proceedings*, May 1992, pp. 295-8.
133. 'Some measurement and policy issues of national saving and investment', in *Personal Saving, Consumption, & Tax Policy*, Marvin H. Kosters (ed.), AEI Press, 1992, pp. 119-24.
134. 'Fiscal and monetary policy reconsidered, again: basic lessons', *Journal of Economic Education*, Summer 1993, pp. 245-59.
135. 'The twin deficits', in *Profits, Deficits, and Instability*, Dimitri B. Papadimitriou (ed.), Macmillan Academic and Professional, Ltd, pp. 255-67.
136. 'Real government saving and the future', *Journal of Economic Behavior and Organization*, January 1994, pp. 1-15.
137. 'Measure, theory, fact and fancy: the case of the budget deficit', *Bulletin of the American Academy of Arts and Sciences*, April 1993, pp. 27-43.
138. 'Clinton, deficits, and the US economy', *Challenge*, May/June 1993, pp. 47-51. (Also published in Japanese in *Weekly Economist.*)
139. 'Déficits, Épargne, et Politique Economique', *Economies et Sociétés*, January/February 1994, pp. 231-72. (Unpublished English version presented as 'Debt and deficits: myth and reality', at Statistics Canada Seminar, April 1993.)
140. 'Deficits, saving and economic policy', John R. Commons Lecture at Allied Social Science Association Meetings, January 4, 1994, published in *American Economist*, Spring 1994, pp. 1-9.
141. 'Quelques considérations macroéconomiques sur le désarmement', in *Les cahiers de l'espace europe*, March 1994, No. 4, pp. 53-71. (Slightly abridged version has been published in Japanese, English title: 'Some macroeconomics of disarmament'.)
142. 'Sense and nonsense about budget deficits', *Harvard Business Review*, May/June 1993, pp. 99-111.
143. 'National saving and budget deficits', *The Review of Economics and Statistics*, February 1994, pp. 181-6.
144. 'Expansion of boundaries and satellite accounts', *Socio-Economic Accounts: Developments, Issues, Prospects*, John W. Kendrick (ed.), Norwell, Kluwer Academic Publishers, 1995, pp. 91-113.
145. 'Disarmament and unemployment', in Manas Chatterji, Jacques Fontanel, and Akira Hattori (eds), *Arms Spending, Development and Security*, New Delhi, APH Publishing, 1996, pp. 70-86.
146. 'Keynes is not dead, just drugged and dormant', *Journal of Post Keynesian Economics*, Winter 1994-5, pp. 211-29.
147. 'Our NAIRU limit, the governing myth of economic policy', *The American Prospect*, Spring 1995, pp. 58-63. Reprinted in *Macroeconomics*, 1996/1997 Annual Edition, Dushkin Publishing Group, pp. 134-9. Reprinted in *Economics*, 1996/1997 Annual Edition, Dushkin Publishing Group, pp.

126–131.
148. 'Saving, economic growth, and the arrow of causality', *Challenge*, May–June, 1995, pp. 10–14. Reprinted in *Macroeconomics*, 1996/1997 Annual Edition, Dushkin Publishing Group, pp. 65–9.
149. 'How about a really fair flat tax?', *Durell Journal of Money and Banking*, Spring, 1995, pp.8–14.
150. 'The retreat from full employment', *Volume 2: Employment, Economic Growth and the Tyranny of the Market: Essays in Honour of Paul Davidson*, 1996, pp.106–30.
151. 'Gross domestic product: its greatness and its limitations', *New Economy*, 1996, pp. 2–5.
152. 'Désarmement et chômage aux Etats-Unis', *Reconversion des Industries d'Armement*, Paris, 1995, pp. 47–62.
153. 'Deficits and unemployment', in *Reclaiming Prosperity: A Blueprint for Progressive Economic Reform*, Economic Policy Institute, 1996, pp. 27–38.
154. 'Tax reform', in *Reclaiming Prosperity: A Blueprint for Progressive Economic Reform*, Economic Policy Institute, 1996, pp. 79–90.
155. 'Fiscal policy', in *Encyclopedia of Business Cycles, Panics, Crises, and Depressions*, David Glasner (ed.), Garland, 1996, pp. 233–7.
156. 'The proposed sales and wage tax: fair, flat or foolish', in American Enterprise Institute, *Fairness and Efficiency in the Flat Tax*, Washington, AEI Press, 1996, pp. 42–95.
157. 'The balanced budget crusade', *The Public Interest*, Number 122, Winter 1996, pp. 85–92.
158. 'The marginal efficiency of capital and investment', in G.C. Harcourt and Peter Riach (eds), The Second Edition of *The General Theory*, Routledge, 1996, pp. 175–87.
159. 'State of the union: black holes in the statistics', *Challenge*, **40**(1), January–February 1997, 6–15. Published in *Accuracy, Timeliness and Relevance of Economic Statistics*, 1997.
160. 'A new view of the NAIRU', in P. Davidson and J. Kregel (eds), *Improving the Global Economy: Keynesianism and the Growth in Output and Employment*, Edward Elgar, Cheltenham, UK, and Northampton, USA, 1997, pp. 196–230.
161. 'Une autre interprétation du NAIRU' (French translation of 'A new view of the NAIRU'), in *Cahiers de l'Espace Europe*, March 1997, pp. 9–37.
162. 'Don't sock the elderly, help them: old age is hard enough', in *The Elder Law Journal*, University of Illinois Law School, Spring 1997, **5** (1), pp. 181–93.
163. 'Damn the NAIRU - and full speed ahead', in Jerry J. Jasinowski (ed.), *The Rising Tide*, New York, Wiley, 1998, pp. 61–9.
164. 'Budgets and taxes', in Ray Marshall (ed.), *Restoring Broadly Shared Prosperity: A Collection of Essays*, Washington, DC, The Economic Policy Institute, pp. 13–29.
165. 'Education in a system of national accounts', *International Journal of Educational Research*, 1998, pp. 527–31.
166. 'Budget deficits, unemployment and economic growth: a cross-section time-

series analysis', *Annales d'Economie*, forthcoming.

167. 'The decline and fall of the NAIRU', in *The Keynesian Revolution, Then and Now: The Selected Essays of Robert Eisner*, volume 1, Edward Elgar, Cheltenham, UK and Northampton, USA, 1998.
168. 'Save social security from its saviours', *Jobs and Capital*, 1998, and *Journal of Post-Keynesian Economics*, **21**, Fall, 1998.

C. Notes and briefer comments

1. Rejoinder to comment on 'Underemployment equilibrium rates of growth', *American Economic Review*, June 1953, pp. 385–93.
2. Rejoinder to comment on 'Depreciation allowances, replacement requirements and growth', *American Economic Review*, September 1953, pp. 614–21.
3. 'Depreciation allowances and replacement restated', *The Controller*, May 1954, pp. 228–48.
4. Comment in *Short-Term Economic Forecasting*, Studies in Income and Wealth, vol. 17, Princeton, 1955, pp. 484–88.
5. Technological change,. obsolescence, and aggregate demand: a reformulation', *American Economic Review*, September 1956, pp. 666–9.
6. Comment on 'Implications of depreciation policy' in *Problems of Capital Formation*, Studies in Income and Wealth, vol. 19, Princeton, 1957, pp. 210–12.
7. Comment in Irwin Friend and Robert Jones (eds), *Consumption and Savings*, vol. 1, University of Pennsylvania, 1960, pp. 159–64.
8. Comments in National Bureau of Economic Research volume on *The Quality and Economic Significance of Anticipations Data*, Princeton, 1960, pp. 82–6, 139–42, 237–8, 366–8, 458–9.
9. Comment in *Output, Input and Productivity Measurement*, Studies in Income and Wealth, vol. 25, Princeton, 1961, pp. 76–7.
10. Comment on papers on permanent income hypothesis at 1960 European meetings of Econometric Society, *Econometrica*, pp. 196–7.
11. Comments in *Bulletin de L'Institut International de Statistique*, report of the 32nd session, Tokyo, 1961, pp. 72, 114.
12. 'Determinants of business investment' (with Robert H. Strotz), report by Robert Eisner published in American Statistical Association, *1961 Proceedings of the Business and Economic Statistics Section*, pp. 5–7.
13. 'Comment' on Robert M. Solow, 'Capital, labor and income in manufacturing', in *The Behavior of Income Shares*, Studies in Income and Wealth, vol. 27, Princeton, 1963, pp. 128–37.
14. 'Comment' for Robert Ferber (ed.), *Determinants of Investment Behavior*, New York, 1967, pp. 589–96.
15. 'Comment' for Universities – National Bureau Conference on the Economics of Defense, New York, 1967.
16. 'The proposed income tax increase', *Illinois Business Review*, University of Illinois, November 1967, pp. 6–8.
17. 'Tax policy and investment behavior: comment', *American Economic*

Review, June 1969, pp. 379–88.
18. 'Neo-classical theory of investment behavior: a comment' (with M.I. Nadiri), *Review of Economics and Statistics*, May 1970, pp. 216–22.
19. 'Tax policy and investment behavior: further comment', *American Economic Review*, Sept. 1970, pp. 746–52.
20. 'Non-income: a foreword' (with Arthur B. Treadway), American Statistical Association, *1970 Proceedings of the Business and Economic Statistics Section*, p. 131.
21. 'Socioeconomic accounting: comment', American Statistical Association, *1970 Proceedings of the Business and Economic Statistics Section*, pp. 224–5.
22. The 1972 Federal Budget, *Illinois Business Review*, February 1971, pp. 6–8.
23. 'The asset depreciation range system', Statement of April 12, 1971, for Treasury Department Hearings, in *Congressional Record*, pp. S5301–4.
24. 'Asset depreciation reform', in *Proceedings, National Conference on Depreciation Reform and Capital Recovery*, NAM, April 1971, pp. 27–30.
25. 'Fiscal and monetary policy reconsidered: reply', *American Economic Review*, June 1971, pp. 458–61.
26. 'New twists to income and product', *Survey of Current Business*, July 1971, Part II, pp. 67–8.
27. 'Investment, obsolescence and foreign competition', *Conference Board Record*, preprinted in *Vital Speeches*, February 15, 1972, pp. 285–8.
28. 'Fiscal and monetary policy reconsidered: further reply', *American Economic Review*, December 1972, p. 957.
29. 'Man and machine and taxes', *Social Policy*, Sept./Oct., 1973, pp. 44–5.
30. Comment on Christensen and Jorgenson, 'Measuring economic performance in the private sector', in Milton Moss (ed.), *The Measurement of Economic and Social Performance*, Studies in Income and Wealth, no. 38, NBER, New York, 1974, pp. 343–9.
31. Comment on Juster, 'A framework for the measurement of economic and social performance', and on Comment by Jaszi, *ibid.*, pp. 99–102.
32. 'Issues in econometric studies of investment behavior: a comment', *Journal of Economic Literature*, March 1974, pp. 49–50.
33. 'Discussion' of papers by Nichols, Tobin and Litvack, Malkiel and Quandt on concepts and measurement of income from endowments, *American Economic Review*, May 1974, pp. 438–42.
34. 'A hard look at corporate taxes', *Business Week*, Dec. 14, 1974, pp. 18–19.
35. 'Econometrics', *The World Book Encyclopedia*, Edition 75A, p. E38b.
36. 'Maximizing welfare', from Symposium at the University of Chicago, *Society*, March/April, 1977, pp. 92–4.
37. 'Corporate taxes and economic growth', *National Journal Conference Proceedings*, edited transcript of Conference Proceedings of Nov. 14–15, 1977, Washington: The Government Research Corporation, 1978, pp. 31–2.
38. 'The administration's investment credit proposals', *Tax Notes*, April 3, 1978, pp. 347–9.
39. 'A direct attack on unemployment', March 1977. Revised copy 'A direct

attack on unemployment and inflation', *Challenge*, July/August 1978, pp. 49-51. Also published in David C. Colander (ed.), *Solutions to Unemployment*, Harcourt Brace Jovanovich, NY, 1981, pp. 177-80.

40. 'No tax relief on capital gains', *Challenge*, January/February 1979, pp. 62–4.
41. Comment on 'Increasing job opportunities in private sector' in Conference Report No. 29, National Commission for Manpower Policy, Washington, DC, November 1978.
42. 'Stopping inflation, reducing unemployment and solving the oil problem', *Journal of Post-Keynesian Economics*, Spring 1980, pp. 432-5.
43. Contribution to Round Table Discussion, in Charles R. Hulten (ed.), *Depreciation, Inflation and the Taxation of Income from Capital*, the Urban Institute, Washington, DC, 1981, pp. 282–7, 296–7, 298, 300.
44. 'Asset depreciation', *Harvard Business Review*, Jan./Feb. 1981, pp. 184, 186, 188.
45. Comment on 'Effects on firm behavior', in Robert H. Haveman and John L. Palmer (eds.), *Jobs for Disadvantaged Workers*, Brookings Institution, Washington, DC, 1982, pp. 252–6.
46. Comment on 'Policy initiatives to stimulate productivity', Urban Institute Conference on Depreciation, *Conference Proceedings*, 1981.
47. 'Discussion', in Federal Reserve Bank of Boston, *Saving and Government Policy* (Conference in October 1982), pp. 104–9.
48. Comment on 'Individual saving behavior and capital formation', by George M. Furstenberg in *Saving for Retirement*, American Council of Life Insurance and Columbia Graduate School of Business, 1982, pp. 187–94.
49. 'Inflation, unemployment and the federal budget', in the Conference Board, *Toward a Reconstruction of Federal Budgeting*, 1983, pp. 59–64.
50. 'Comments' on discussion papers at the Dorga Conference on 'Economic policy and national accounting in inflationary conditions', in *Studies in Banking and Finance*, North Holland, Vol. **2**, 1985, pp. 67–8.
51. 'Reply' on R&D Tax Credits, *Issues in Science and Technology*, **I**(5), Fall 1985, p.9.
52. 'Discussion', of Kopcke paper on 'Tax reform and capital formation', in Federal Reserve Bank of Boston, *Economic Consequences of Tax Simplification*, Proceedings of a conference in October 1985, pp. 149–52.
53. 'Discussion', *National Tax Policy: The Impact on R&D*, Proceedings of National Science Foundation, Association of American Universities, The Conference Board, Oct. 23, 1985, pp. 18–20.
54. 'Comment' on 'The changing cyclical variability of economic activity in the United States', by Bradford DeLong and Lawrence H. Summers for *The American Business Cycle: Continuity and Change*, Robert J. Gordon (ed.), University of Chicago Press for the NBER, 1986, pp. 719–27.
55. 'Debt and deficits: curse, or blessing in disguise', Northwestern University *Arts & Sciences*, Spring 1986, pp. 16–19.
56. 'Government accounting and the budget deficit', *Fiscal Policy Forum*, Tax Foundation, **4**(2), Spring/Summer 1986, pp. 3, 6–9.
57. 'What's in a deficit?', *American Politics*, **1**(8), Sept. 1986, pp. 14, 28.

58. 'A new view of the federal debt and budget deficits: reply' (with Paul J. Pieper), *American Economic Review*, December 1986, **76**(5), pp. 1156–7.
59. 'Comment', in *Macro-Dynamique et Déséquilibres*, Jean-Paul Fitousi and Pierre-Alain Muet (eds), Paris, Economica, 1987, pp. 243–4.
60. 'Rejoinder' (with Paul J. Pieper, to comment on budget deficits), *Journal of Post-Keynesian Economics*, Fall 1988, **11**(1), pp. 161–8.
61. 'The federal budget deficit and what to do about it', in *National Economic Commission*, Staff Papers and Major Testimony, March 1989, pp. 81–4.
62. 'Comment', on 'Government saving, capital formation, and wealth in the US 1947–85', by Boskin *et al.* in *The Measurement of Saving, Investment and Wealth*, Lipsey and Tice (eds), University of Chicago Press, 1989, pp. 353–6.
63. 'Challenges of macro policy in the open US economy', *Contemporary Policy*, January 1989, **VII**(1), 1–12.
64. 'Inflation-adjusted government budget deficits and real economic activity: Rejoinder' (with Paul J. Pieper), *Annales d'Économie et de Statistique*, January–March, 1989, pp. 139–47.
65. 'Reply' to comment by Maurice Scott on 'Extended accounts for national income and product', *Journal of Economic Literature*, **XXVIII**, September 1990, pp. 1180–3.
66. 'Reply to Robert Solo', *Journal of Economic Issues*, March 1991.
67. 'The new world order', published in Japanese in *Weekly Economist*, October 22, 1991, pp. 33ff.
68. 'The federal budget deficit', *Jobs and Capital*, **I**(2), Summer 1992.
69. Comment on William A. Niskanen 'Fiscal effects on US economic growth', and Norman B. Ture, 'Capital formation, economic growth and jobs: a heretical tax strategy for economic growth', *Economic Policy, Financial Markets, and Economic Growth*, Benjamin Zycher and Lewis C. Solomon (eds), Westview Press, 1993, pp. 267–9 (Niskanen), pp. 269–73 (Ture).
70. 'National saving and our real deficits', *Durell Journal of Money and Banking*, **IV**(4), December 1992, pp. 6–16.
71. 'Clinton, deficits, and the US economy', January 23, 1993, published in Japanese in *Weekly Economist.*
72. 'The three trillion dollar asset', *Siemens Review*, February, 1994, pp. 32–5.
73. 'The economic aspects of President Clinton's budgetary politics', *Public Budgeting and Finance*, Fall 1994, pp. 19–23.
74. 'The index of sustainable economic welfare: comment', in *The Green National Product: A Proposed Index of Sustainable Economic Welfare*, Clifford W. Cobb and John B. Cobb, Jr. (eds), Lanham, Maryland, University Press of America, 1994, pp. 97–110.
75. 'The great deficit debate', interview debate in *The American Legion*, January, 1995, pp. 40–42, 84, 86, 88.
76. 'Borrow now to invest in the future', in *Five Hundred Ways to Make America Better*, George Magazine and Random House, 1998.

D. Newspaper and popular magazine articles

1. 'Nixon's old economic policy', *The Progressive*, October 1971, pp. 21–3.

2. 'A hard look at corporate taxes', *Business Week*, Dec. 14, 1974, pp. 18–19.
3. 'Corporate income taxes', for *Los Angeles Times Syndicate*, Jan. 24, 1975.
4. 'A way to create jobs: cut payroll taxes', *New York Times*, August 17, 1975.
5. Thrice-yearly articles on economics for the *Chicago Tribune*, 1975, 1976, 1977, 1978.
6. 'On unemployment', *The New Leader*, March 28, 1977, p. 24.
7. 'Tackling inflation, unemployment and the oil problem', *USA Today*, March 1980, pp. 21–2.
8. 'Tight money policy could choke recovery', in *USA TODAY*, August 12, 1983.
9. 'Will the real deficit please stand up?', in *The New York Times*, September 25, 1983.
10. Articles for the Scripps-Howard News Service, every fourth week, 1984, 1985.
11. 'Are things really better after 4 years?', *The New York Times*, July 8, 1984.
12. 'What do rising rates portend?', *Chicago Tribune*, Perspective, July 19, 1984.
13. 'The great mirage - deficits and interest rates', *The Wall Street Journal*, August 3, 1994.
14. 'Social security: a program at risk', *The New York Times*, November 11, 1984.
15. 'Reconsidering the deficit', *Chicago Tribune*, May 13, 1985.
16. 'Starving the states to feed business', *The New York Times*, June 16, 1985.
17. 'Auctioning off the nation's wealth: cut deficits, but not by selling assets', *The New York Times*, January 19, 1986.
18. 'Deficit? The true danger may be a budget surplus', *The Washington Post*, February 2, 1986.
19. 'Piercing the myths of the budget deficit', *The New York Times*, May 4, 1986.
20. 'The real federal budget deficit', *Chicago Tribune*, May 22, 1986.
21. 'Sense and nonsense on the budget deficit', Standard and Poor's *CreditWeek*, December 15, 1986, pp. 1 and 47.
22. 'Not what they seem', *Financial Planning*, April 1987, pp. 152–5.
23. 'No, inflation isn't the Fed's top priority', *The New York Times*, June 15, 1987.
24. 'How big a budget deficit?', *Wall Street Journal*, Sept. 9, 1987.
25. 'The federal deficit: how does it matter?', *Science*, September 25, 1987.
26. 'Don't blame the deficit for the crash', *The New York Times*, October 25, 1987.
27. 'Commentary', in *Cortlandt Forum*, February 1988, p. 9.
28. 'Not so good, but not so bad', *The World & I*, a publication of The Washington Times Corp., July 1988, pp. 20–26.
29. 'To raise the saving rate, try spending', *The New York Times*, August 29, 1988. (French translation, 'Les États-Unis doivent dépenser pour sortir de la crise de l'épargne', appeared in *Libération*, September 1988.
30. 'La demande crée l'offre', *Le Monde*, France, September 27, 1988.
31. 'Don't privatize social security', *The New York Times*, October 1, 1988.
32. 'The dollar: rhetoric and reality', *WorldLink*, published by CITICORP/Global Payment Products, November 1988.

33. 'About that deficit: hold on a minute', *Business Month*, December 1988.
34. 'Real deficit is in human capital', *Los Angeles Times*, December 26, 1988.
35. 'The budget deficit? Which deficit?', *Chicago Tribune*, January 3, 1989.
36. 'The great deficit debate: liberal Keynesian', *National Review*, January 27, 1989, p. 47.
37. 'More on pussycats and termites', *The Brookings Review*, Fall 1989, p. 43.
38. 'The deficit: an exchange', *The New York Review*, September 28, 1989.
39. 'Commentary', *Northwestern Perspective*, Fall 1989, p. 48.
40. 'Dollars and deficits walk the high wire together', *The New York Times*, November 2, 1989.
41. 'Interview with Robert Eisner', *Research*, February, 1990 (Publication of NLI Research Institute, Tokyo), pp. 2–17.
42. 'Low US savings rate: a myth', *The New York Times*, March 1, 1990.
43. 'The (non)problem, the budget deficit', *The Wall Street Journal*, June 19, 1990.
44. 'The S&L bailout has nothing to do with taxes', *Chicago Tribune*, September 7, 1990.
45. 'Baker is right about "Jobs"...', *The New York Times*, November 26, 1990.
46. 'Tax cuts will not solve this slump', *Newsday*, November 1991.
47. 'No new taxes for S&L bailout', *Challenge*, March/April 1991, pp. 34–8.
48. 'Should we aid the Soviet Union?', *The New York Times*, *OP-ED*, August 27, 1991.
49. 'Should the Feds adopt a capital budget? Yes: "It would highlight the impact of public investment"', *Governing*, October 1992, pp. 57–8.
50. 'Will gift horse or workhorse give us a pull?', *Newsday*, Sunday, March 6, 1992.
51. 'Clinton's plan passes the test', *Chicago Tribune*, July 24, 1992.
52. 'Perot plan is an Rx for disaster', *Newsday*, October 2, 1992.
53. 'Deficit-reduction plans: a lot of pain that may add up to no gain', *Los Angeles Times*, January 30, 1994.
54. 'Balancing Act - Budget amendment creates, not solves, problems', *Chicago Tribune*, February 18, 1994.
55. 'Off balance', *The New York Times*, Saturday, March 19, 1994.
56. 'Concept of a "Natural rate of unemployment" is grossly inflated', *Los Angeles Times*, April 3, 1994.
57. 'Putting government back in the equation', *Chicago Tribune*, May 15, 1994.
58. 'Fed treats the economy when it isn't ill', *Newsday*, May 19, 1994.
59. 'In Fed's inflation ambush, recovery may get shot in the foot', *Los Angeles Times*, May 29, 1994.
60. 'Putting together the pieces of the economic puzzle', *Chicago Tribune*, July 1, 1994.
61. 'The great mirage - deficits and interest rates', *The Wall Street Journal*, August 3, 1994.
62. 'What's so terrible about employers helping with health care?' *Los Angeles Times*, August 7, 1994.
63. 'GOP "contract" soaked in snake oil', *Newsday*, October 5, 1994.

64. 'Is this a contract or a GOP con job?', *Chicago Tribune*, October 9, 1994.
65. 'Address other issues and trade deficit will take care of itself', *Los Angeles Times*, October 9, 1994.
66. 'A choice and an echo', *The New York Times*, October 26, 1994.
67. 'The grandkids can relax', *The Wall Street Journal*, November 9, 1994.
68. 'Balanced-budget amendment would spell disaster for economy', *Los Angeles Times*, December 11, 1994.
69. 'We don't need balanced budgets', *The Wall Street Journal*, January 11, 1995.
70. 'What better to invest in than education?', *Los Angeles Times*, January 17, 1995.
71. 'US investment in education should increase, not decrease', *Dallas Morning News*, January 22, 1995.
72. 'There's good in the "Middle-class bill of rights"', *Chicago Tribune*, February 2, 1995.
73. 'For a real shocker, read proposed balanced budget amendment', *Los Angeles Times*, February 5, 1995.
74. 'Make taxes fair, not flat', *The Wall Street Journal*, April 11, 1995.
75. 'Despite critics, hiking minimum wage may make good sense', *Los Angeles Times*, April 23, 1995.
76. 'Kerry-Simpson package would destroy social security benefits', *Los Angeles Times*, July 9, 1995.
77. 'Social Security – the real issues', *Newsday*, July 28, 1995.
78. 'Should government be made smaller – or just made better?', *Los Angeles Times*, September 17, 1995.
79. 'Social security's not in a fix', *Chicago Tribune*, September 20, 1995.
80. 'Opening up the growth debate', *The Wall Street Journal*, September 25, 1995.
81. 'Republican counter-revolution will be a net loss and a lost net', *Los Angeles Times*, November 5, 1995.
82. 'The deficit is budget battle's red herring', *The Wall Street Journal*, November 28, 1995.
83. 'Balancing the federal budget with some common sense', *Chicago Tribune*, November 30, 1995.
84. 'Balancing our deficit thinking', *The Nation*, December 11, 1995.
85. 'These figures spell good times, not bad', *The New York Times*, Sunday Business Section, December 24, 1995.
86. 'China may yet make good on its promise of increased prosperity', *Los Angeles Times*, January 14, 1996.
87. 'No need to sacrifice seniors or children', *The Wall Street Journal*, February 2, 1996.
88. 'Talk of a flat-tax plan overlooks burdens placed on consumers', *Los Angeles Times*, February 4, 1996.
89. 'Who's afraid of jobs and growth?', *The New York Times*, March 31, 1996.
90. 'Flat tax would hit the poor and middle class', *The Miami Herald*, April 3, 1996.
91. 'Make taxes fair, not flat', *The Wall Street Journal*, April 11, 1996.

92. 'Beware of tax fads?', *The Wall Street Journal*, April 23, 1996.
93. 'We can begin to tackle income disparity', *Los Angeles Times*, April 28, 1996.
94. 'A reduction in the capital gains tax would benefit relatively few', *Los Angeles Times*, June 30, 1996.
95. 'Nothing to fear but fear of good news', *The Wall Street Journal*, July 9, 1996.
96. 'Dole's tax package not friendly to most families', *Chicago Tribune*, August 7, 1996.
97. 'Dole's tax plan: deficit would increase', *The Miami Herald*, August 7, 1996 (plus correction, August 8).
98. 'Bad math makes bad economics', *Los Angeles Times*, August 14, 1996.
99. 'What US Social Security crisis?', *The Wall Street Journal*, August 30, 1996.
100. 'The Fed should keep its head', *The New York Times*, September 19, 1996.
101. 'What counts and how to count it', *The Wall Street Journal*, November 12, 1996.
102. 'There's no need to pick on the elderly', *Los Angeles Times*, November 24, 1996.
103. 'Keep social security out of private hands', *Newsday*, December 20, 1996.
104. 'Painless cures for Medicare, Social Security', *The Miami Herald*, January 6, 1997.
105. 'Balanced budget: bad economics', *The Wall Street Journal*, January 22, 1997.
106. 'The BBA: a spent idea', *The Nation*, February 24, 1997.
107. 'Is Greenspan sure investors are irrational?', *Los Angeles Times*, March 23, 1997.
108. 'Untie the balanced-budget knot', *Newsday*, May 6, 1997 and, somewhat abbreviated, as 'Politicians perform a bad balancing act with nation's budget', *Chicago Tribune*, May 7, 1997.
109. 'In doing nothing, Fed did a world of good', *Los Angeles Times*, May 25, 1997.
110. 'A French lesson', *The Wall Street Journal*, June 4, 1997.
111. 'Budget nearly balanced - but tax plans aren't', *Los Angeles Times*, July 20, 1997.
112. 'Whatever you call it, a tax goes to the treasury', *Wall Street Journal*, July 29, 1997.
113. 'Time to rest our tired economic Dogmas', *Los Angeles Times*, September 21, 1997.
114. 'When bad economic theory threatens good times', *The New York Times*, October 11, 1997.
115. 'A free trade primer', *The Wall Street Journal*, October 13, 1997.
116. 'What Social Security needs is a "publicization"', *Los Angeles Times*, November 30, 1997.
117. 'Cut Social Security? No, expand it', *Wall Street Journal*, December 10, 1997.
118. 'Budget surpluses and Social Security nonsense', *Wall Street Journal*, February 17, 1998.
119. 'Social Security is worth saving. Here's how to do it', *Wall Street Journal*,

March 26, 1998.

120. 'The great surplus debate: understand it', *The American Prospect*, May–June, 1998, pp. 86–7.

121. 'Must we save for our grandchildren?', *Wall Street Journal*, June 3, 1998.

E. Statements before congressional committees, commissions

1. 'Changes in methods of depreciation and their effects', in *Federal Tax Policy for Economic Growth and Stability* (USGPO, 68595, Washington, 1955), pp. 515–27. (See also transcript of oral testimony in *Hearings before the Subcommittee on Tax Policy of the Joint Economic Committee on the Economic Report* (USGPO, 70325, 1956), pp. 413–56, including testimony of Eisner and others on panel.)

2. 'Factors affecting economic growth', in *Hearings before the Joint Economic Committee*, Congress of the US (USGPO, 36379, 1959), pp. 257–8 and passim.

3. 'The income–expenditure approach to the theory of money relations', and 'A note on *Money and Prices', in Employment, Growth and Price Levels*, Hearings before Joint Economic Committee of the Congress of the US, Part IV (USGPO, 38563, 1959), pp. 792-910, also discussion with Committee, pp. 767–92.

4. 'Effects of depreciation allowances for tax purposes', in *Tax Revision Compendium*, vol. 2, on Committee on Ways and Means of the House of Representatives, 86th Congress, 1st session (USGPO, 47060, 1959), pp. 793–9.

5. 'Capital expenditures and expectations', for Joint Economic Committee, Congress of the US, in *Variability of Private Investment in Plant and Equipment, Part II, Some Elements Shaping Investment Decisions* (USGPO, 75924, 1962), pp. 31-6. Reprinted in Walter L. Johnson and David R. Kamerschen (eds), *Macroeconomics, Selected Readings*, Houghton Mifflin Co., Boston, 1970, pp. 129–33.

6. 'Investment tax credits', for Senate Finance Committee, April 1962, in *Revenue Act of 1962*, Hearings before the Committee on Finance, US Senate, 87th Congress, second session, on HR 10650, April 24 and 25, 1962, part 6 (USGPO, 82190 0, 1962), pp. 2476–80.

7. 'Provision regarding "Treatment of investment credit by federal regulatory agencies"', for Senate Finance Committee, in *Revenue Act of 1963*, Hearings before the Committee on Finance, US Senate, 88th Congress, first session, on HR 8363, Nov. 12–15 and Nov. 21–2, 1963, Part 2 (USGPO, 1963), pp. 1871–9.

8. 'A fiscal policy for peace, prosperity and progress', for the Subcommittee on Fiscal Policy of the Joint Economic Committee of the Congress of the US, in *Fiscal Policy Issues of the Coming Decade*, Statements by Individual Economists and Representatives of Interested Organizations, 89th Congress, First Session (USGPO, 1965), pp. 42–5.

9. 'Monetary policy and inflation', for Senate Committee on banking and currency hearings on 'High interest rates', *Congressional Record*, April 1,

1969, pp. 97–101.
10. 'Proposals to extend 10% tax surcharge and certain excise tax rates and to repeal 5% investment tax credit', for House Ways and Means Committee, *Congressional Record*, May 28, 1969, pp. E4418–9.
11. 'Effects of tight money', in *Emergency Home Financing*, Hearings before the Committee on Banking and Currency, House of Representatives, February 5, 1970 (USGPO, 1970), pp. 159–64.
12. 'The war and the economy', in *Changing National Priorities*, Hearings before the Subcommittee on Economy in Government of the Joint Economic Committee, Part II, June 15, 16, 17 and 18, 1970 (USGPO, 1970), pp. 665–78, 686–7, 702–20, passim.
13. '*1971 Economic Report of the President*', Hearings of the Joint Economic Committee, February 24, 1971 (USGPO, Part II), pp. 500–34.
14. Statement for House Banking and Currency Committee, Congress of the US, October 14, 1971.
15. 'Investment credit and accelerated depreciation and amortization', Committee on Ways and Means, *General Tax Reform*, Part 3 of 11, February 7, 1973, pp. 370–91.
16. 'Employment, taxes, and small business', for Joint Hearings before the Select Committee on small business and the Subcommittee on financial markets of the Committee on Finance, US Senate, 94th Congress, first session on *Study of the Business Tax Structure as it Affects Small Business*, June 17, 18, and 19, 1975 (USGPO, 54-3970, 1975), pp.122–31.
17. Proposal for a 'Job development credit: a tax credit for investment in human capital', Supplement to Statement of June 17, 1975, *ibid.*, pp. 121–30.
18. 'Current economic policy', before the Joint Economic Committee of the Congress of the US, *Midyear Review of the Economic Situation and Outlook*, First Session, July 23, 24, 25, 29, 30 and 31, 1975 (USGPO, 65-201, 1976), pp. 266–78.
19. 'Capital formation tax policy questions', before the Task Force on Tax Policy and Tax Expenditures and the Task Force on Capital Needs and Monetary Policy of the Committee on the Budget, US Senate, 94th Congress, 1st session, *Encouraging Capital Formation Through the Tax Code*, September 18–19, 1975 (USGPO, 59-987 0, 1975), pp. 3–11.
20. 'Current economic policy', before the Joint Economic Committee of the Congress of the US, Regional Hearings in Chicago, *Jobs and Prices in Chicago*, 94th Congress, 1st session, October 20, 1975 (USGPO, 65-222, 1976), pp. 42–6.
21. 'Capital formation and the tax structure', for Committee on the Budget, House of Representatives, 94th Congress, *Fiscal Year 1977 Budget and the Economy*, second session, January 29, 1976, Washington (USGPO, 67-103, Jan., Feb., March, 1976), pp. 125–30.
22. 'Full Employment and Balanced Growth Act of 1976' (Humphrey-Hawkins Bill), for Subcommittee on Manpower, Compensation and Health and Safety, Committee on Education and Labor, Congress of the US, April 2, 1976, Washington (USGPO, 72-531 0, 1976), pp. 117–22.

23. 'Issues regarding capital formation', prepared for the Joint Economic Committee of the Congress of the US, June 1976, Washington (USGPO, 83-402 0, 1977), pp. 84–5.
24. 'Administration stimulus proposals and employment tax credit', for Ways and Means Committee, Feb. 8, 1977, Washington (USGPO, 83-959 0, 1977), serial 95-1), pp. 497–505.
25. Statement and 'Supplementary Statement' on Employment Tax Credit, printed for the use of the Select Committee on Small Business, Feb. 22, 1977, Washington (USGPO, 92-525 0, 1977), pp. 93–104.
26. Statement for Joint Economic Committee, Subcommittee on Economic Growth and Stabilization, *The Role of Federal Tax Policy in Stimulating Capital Formation and Economic Growth*, July 12–14, 1977, Washington (USGPO, 22-686, 1978), pp. 129–35.
27. 'Full Employment and Balanced Growth Act of 1977', Senate Human Resources Committee, Subcommittee on Employment, Poverty and Migratory Labor, Feb. 3, 1978, Washington (USGPO, 32-931, 1978), pp. 3–13.
28. 'Employment and unemployment statistics', National Commission, Joint Economic Committee, Congress of the US, Chicago, June 13, 1978, Washington (USGPO, 40-394 0, 1978), pp. 260–63.
29. 'Tax credits to increase employment and reduce inflation', prepared for the Senate Finance Committee, Subcommittee on Administration of Internal Revenue Code, Senate Committee on Small Business, July 20, 1978, Washington (USGPO, 34-840-0, 1978), pp. 54–66.
30. 'Proposals to reduce taxation of capital gains', for Hearings before the Senate Committee on Finance, August 23, 1978, Washington (USGPO, 052-070-0, 1978), pp. 704–16.
31. 'Employment opportunities', Subcommittee of Committee on Education and Labor, House of Representatives, Congress of the US, Feb. 13, 1979, Washington (USGPO, 1979), pp. 35–49.
32. 'Investment tax credit', Subcommittee on Oversight Committee on Ways and Means, House of Representatives, Congress of the US, March 27, 1979, Washington (USGPO, 50-104-0, 1979), pp. 342–7.
33. 'Impact of inflation on business investment', for the Task Force on Inflation of the Committee on the Budget, June 19, 1979, Washington (USGPO, 49-145-0, 1979), vol. 2, pp. 391–5.
34. 'Unreported income and the underground economy: estimates and implications', in *Underground Economy*. Hearings before the Subcommittee on Oversight of the Committee on Ways and Means, House of Representatives, 96th Congress, Sept. 10, 1979, Serial 96-70, (USGPO, 56-5380, 1980), pp. 136–48.
35. 'Tax policy for 1980', Committee on the Budget, US House of Representatives, January 30, 1980, Washington.
36. Statement in *Savings and Economic Growth*, Hearing of Joint Economic Committee of Congress of the US, July 30, 1980, Washington (USGPO, 73-460-0, 1981), pp. 12–18.

37. 'Economic issues for fiscal year 1981', for Committee on the Budget, US House of Representatives, December 30, 1980, Washington (USGPO, 74-360, Jan. 30, 1981), pp. 146–230.
38. 'Statement before Committee on Banking & Urban Affairs, Subcommittee on Economic Stabilization in *Revitalization and the US Economy*, Congress of the US, serial no. 97-11, Feb. 25, 1981, Washington (USGPO, 76-240-0), pp. 9–23.
39. Statement before House Committee on Education and Labor, April 2, 1981, Washington.
40. 'Proposed administration tax cuts', before House Committee on Small Business, Subcommittee on Tax, Access to Equity Capital and Business Opportunities, April 2, 1981, Washington (USGPO, 78-250-0), pp. 366–78.
41. Statement before House Committee on Education and Labor and on Small Business, Subcommittees on Labor Standards and on SBA and SBIC Authority, Minority Enterprise and General Small Business Problems, April 29, 1981, Washington.
42. 'Total income, total investment and growth', before Subcommittee on Oversight and Investigations of the Committee on Energy and Commerce, Congress of the US, June 24, 1981, Washington (USGPO, 15-870-0), pp. 388–407.
43. Statement for Joint Economic Committee of the Congress of the US on *The Unemployment Crisis and Policies for Economic Recovery*, October 15, 1982, Washington (USGPO, 17-871-0, 1983), pp. 4–20.
44. 'Monetary and fiscal policy and beyond', prepared for Joint Economic Committee, Hearings on Industrial Policy, Economic Growth, and the Competitiveness of US Industry, June 29, 1983, Washington (USGPO, Y4, EC7: IN2/14/Part I), pp. 211–26.
45. 'Policies for full employment and price stability', before the Joint Economic Committee Hearings on The State of the Economy and Economic Policy, Washington, February 21, 1984 (USGPO, Y4EC7:21), pp.1–60.
46. 'Research and experimentation tax credits', before the Subcommittee on Oversight, Committee on Ways and Means, US House of Representatives, August 1, 1984, Committee on Ways and Means, *Research and Experimentation Tax Credit*, August 2 and 3, 1984 (Serial 98-102), pp. 71–141.
47. 'The administration's proposed 1986 Budget and Economic Policy', before the Committee on Education and Labor, US House of Representatives, February 21, 1985 (USGPO 44.ED8/1199-13), pp. 4–34.
48. 'The US Catholic bishops on employment', before the Subcommittee on Economic Stabilization, House Committee on Banking, Finance and Urban Affairs, March 19, 1985 (USGPO Y4B 22/1 99-5), pp. 49–88.
49. 'Effects of tax reform legislation', for Joint Economic Committee, US House of Representatives, September 15, 1986.
50. 'The fiscal 1988 budget and the economy', for the Committee on the Budget, US House of Representatives, February 4, 1987 (USGPO Y4B 85/3 100-1 Part I), pp. 509–37.

51. 'Overview of the President's budget for fiscal year 1988', Hearings before the Committee on Ways and Means, House of Representatives, February 11, 1987 (Serial 100-13, USGPO), pp. 176–82.
52. 'Monetary policy, the deficit and the economy', Committee on Banking, Subcommittee on Domestic Monetary Policy, US House of Representatives, February 25, 1987 (USGPO H241-29.1).
53. 'Proposals to increase and extend the research and experimentation tax credit', Senate Committee on Finance, Subcommittee on Taxation and Debt Management', April 3, 1987 (USGPO Y4F49:S.HRG.100-156), pp. 99–148.
54. 'Economic Bill of Rights', Committee on Education and Labor, Subcommittee on Employment Opportunities, US House of Representatives, November 23–24, 1987.
55. 'Economic outlook and appropriate economic policy for 1988', The Joint Economic Committee, US Senate, January 22, 1988.
56. 'The Federal budget deficit and what to do about it', National Economic Commission, July 25, 1988.
57. 'Tax credits and other measures to support research and technology', US House of Representatives, Committee on Science, Space and Technology, Subcommittee on Science, Research and Technology, May 18, 1989.
58. 'Proposed balanced budget amendment to constitution', US House of Representatives, Committee on the Judiciary, Subcommittee on Economic and Commercial Law, July 11, 1990.
59. Statement before Committee on Labor and Human Resources, United States Senate, Hearings on the Recession and the Changing Structure of the Workplace, January 7, 1991.
60. 'AEI Conference on personal savings, consumption, and tax policy', Comment on Personal Tax Incentives, Fiscal Policy, and National Savings, Washington, DC, August 16, 1991.
61. Statement on 'US economy, and proposals to provide middle-income tax relief, tax equity and fairness, economic stimulus and growth', for Committee on Ways and Means, US House of Representatives Hearings on the US Economy, December 17, 1991, USGPO, Serial 102-100, pp. 731–5.
62. 'Statement before Committee on Public Works and Transportation, US House of Representatives, Hearings on 'The anti-recession infrastructure jobs act of 1992', March 12, 1992 (USGPO, H.R. 4175) pp. 100–102.
63. Statement before Conseil Economique et Social, République Française, Paris, France, March 24, 1992.
64. Hearings on 'A balanced budget constitutional amendment: economic issues', for Congressional Research Service Seminar, Library of Congress, May 28, 1992.
65. Statement for Committee on Banking, Housing and Urban Affairs, US House of Representatives, Hearings on the US Economy, July 22, 1992.
66. Testified before Economic Development Sub-Committee of House Public Works Committee, Hearings on 'Investment in America's infrastructure: short and long-term strategies', January 15, 1993.
67. 'Capital budgeting for government', Statement before US House of

Representatives, Committee on Government Operations - Legislation and National Security Subcommittee, November 9, 1993, pp. 15–25.

68. 'Saving and economic growth', in *Importance of Savings In Our Economy*, Hearing Before the Committee on Finance, United States Senate, January 31, 1995, US Government Printing Office, Washington, 1995, pp. 41–50.
69. Statement for Joint Economic Committee, Congress of the United States, Hearings on The Humphrey-Hawkins Act and the Role of the Federal Reserve, March 16, 1995, US Government Printing Office, Washington, 1996, pp. 89–102 (oral testimony, pp. 8–12).
70. 'Investment and the capital stock: overview', Statement at 'National Conference on the economic accounts', US Chamber of Commerce, Economics and Statistics Administration, and Bureau of Economic Analysis, March 21, 1995.
71. 'Full employment and inflation: where we stand and where we can go', Statement for Committee on Banking and Financial Services, US House of Representatives, Hearing of July 23, 1997.
72. 'A capital budget for truth in packaging', prepared for the President's Commission to Study Capital Budgeting, Public Hearing, Washington, DC, April 24, 1998.

F. Reviews

1. Paul M. Sweezy (ed.), Bohm-Bawerk, *Karl Marx and the Close of His System* and Hilferding, *Bohm-Bawerk's Criticism of Marx*, *American Economic Review*, June 1950, pp. 431–2.
2. Harrod, *Economic Essays*, *American Economic Review*, March 1954, pp. 134-8.
3. Weintraub, *An Approach to the Theory of Income Distribution*, *American Economic Review*, December 1958, pp. 1004–6.
4. Chakravarty, *The Logic of Investment Planning*, *American Economic Review*, June 1960, pp. 449–52.
5. Matthews, *The Business Cycle*, *Journal of Political Economy*, October 1960, pp. 526–7.
6. Meij (ed.), *Depreciation and Replacement Policy*, *Journal of Political Economy*, February 1963, pp. 92–3.
7. Johnson, H.G., *Money, Trade and Economic Growth*, *American Economic Review*, March 1963, pp. 151–4.
8. Jaskari, *Depreciation Allowances and the Real Capital*, *Econometrica*, July 1963, pp. 619–20.
9. Saulnier, *The Strategy of Economic Policy*, *Journal of Political Economy*, February 1964, pp. 93–5.
10. Meyer and Glauber, *Investment Decisions, Economic Forecasting and Public Policy*, *Journal of Finance*, Dec. 1964, pp. 718–21.
11. Stigler, *Capital and Rates of Return in Manufacturing Industries*, *Econometrica*, January 1965, pp. 249–50.
12. Gordon and Klein (ed.), *American Economic Association Readings in Business Cycles*, *American Economic Review*, Sept. 1966, pp. 925–9.

13. Galbraith, *The New Industrial State*, in *Bulletin of the Atomic Scientists*, October 1967, pp. 30–2; also in *Quarterly Journal of Economics and Business*, Fall 1967, pp. 83–7.
14. Blum, *Drafted or Deferred: Practices Past and Present*, and Miller (ed.), *Why the Draft: The Case for a Volunteer Army*, *American Economic Review*, September 1968, pp. 951–5.
15. Reich, *The Greening of America*, *Saturday Review*, Dec. 5, 1970, pp. 23–6.
16. Owen, *The Price of Leisure*, *Journal of Economic Literature*, June 1971, pp. 463–4.
17. Galbraith, *The New Industrial State* (2nd edn, revised), *Saturday Review*, October 2, 1971, pp. 40–42.
18. Weisskopf, *Alienation and Economics*, *Saturday Review*, Dec. 25, 1971, p. 38.
19. McCarry, *Citizen Nader*, *Saturday Review*, April 1, 1972, pp. 73–4.
20. Phelps, *Inflation Policy and Unemployment Theory*, *Journal of Economic Literature*, June 1973, pp. 562–4.
21. Galbraith, *Money*, *Chicago Daily News*, September 3, 1975.
22. Minsky, *John Maynard Keynes*, 'On Keynes and Keynesians and revolution', Review article for *Nebraska Journal of Economics and Business*, Spring 1977, pp. 3–9.
23. Galbraith, *The Age of Uncertainty*, *Chicago Daily News*, April 2, 1977.
24. Leijonhufvud, *Information and Coordination in Macroeconomic Theory*, review essay for *Journal of Money and Banking*, August 1982, pp. 413–9.
25. Buiter *et al.*, *The Economics of Large Government Deficits*, Conference Series No. 27, Federal Reserve Bank of Boston, *Journal of Economic Literature*, June 1985.
26. McLeod, *The Principles of Financial Intermediation*, *Journal of Economic Literature*, **XXIII**, June 1985, pp. 637–40.
27. Robert Heilbroner, *21st Century Capitalism*, in *New York Times Book Review*, September 19, 1993, p. 18.
28. Daniel Shaviro, *Do Deficits Matter?*, in *Journal of Economic Literature*, 1997.

G. Unpublished manuscripts

1. *The Gallup Poll and Opinion on Conscription, A Study in Public Opinion and Polling Technique*, Columbia University, 1942 (MA thesis).
2. *Growth, Investment and Business Cycles: A Critique and Development of Some Recent Theories*, Johns Hopkins University Library, 1951 (doctoral dissertation).
3. Discussion of Federal Reserve Board Committee Reports on Inventory Statistics, Investment Expectations and General Business Expectations at Meetings of American Statistical Association and American Economic Association in New York, December 30, 1955, duplicated.
4. 'Potential for expansion of government programs', for Stanford Research Institute, 1960.
5. 'Capital expenditures in 1967: some guidelines for projections', presented at

National Industrial Conference Board Conference on Business in 1967, New York, October 6, 1966.
6. 'Investment, capacity and the current situation', presented at Board of Governors of the Federal Reserve System, February 17, 1967.
7. 'Capital goods: inventories, backlogs and price pressures', presented at National Industrial Conference Board Conference on Business in 1969, New York, Sept. 19, 1968.
8. 'War and peace: a new view of the game', 1968.
9. 'Investment anticipations and realizations: cross sections and time series of data of the McGraw-Hill surveys, 1955–66', presented at CIRET Conference in Madrid, September 1969.
10. 'Longer term capital expenditure anticipations and sales expectations: a micro-economic analysis', presented at Conference in Brussels, September, 1972.
11. 'Sales expectations and realizations in the McGraw-Hill surveys', presented at CIRET Conference in London, September 1973.
12. 'TISA: The Total Incomes System of Accounts', presented at Fourteenth General Conference of International Association for Research in Income and Wealth, Aulanko, Finland, August 1975.
13. 'The liberal agenda: private sector', prepared for Union for Democratic Action of Americans for Democratic Action, 1977.
14. 'The effects of tax policies on investment in macroeconometric models: full model simulations' (with Robert S. Chirinko), OTA Paper 46, US Department of the Treasury, Office of Tax Analysis, January 1981; revised and reduced version entitled 'Tax policy and investment in major US macroeconomic econometric models', published as B79.
15. 'The effects of tax parameters in the investment equations of macroeconomic econometric models' (with Robert S. Chirinko), OTA Paper 47, US Department of the Treasury, Office of Tax Analysis, January 1981. (Almost identical to an earlier version presented to the World Econometric Congress at Aix-en-Provence, France in August 1980, entitled 'The effects of tax policies on investment in large scale econometric models'.) Published in revised form as B69.
16. 'The ninth plan: a review and evaluation of the preparatory phase', prepared for the Commissariat General du Plan, Paris, 1983, also available in French.
17. 'Determinants of investment', presented at Conference on US–Mexico Investment Relations, Stanford University, January 24–26, 1985.
18. 'Real deficits, inflation and output in a demand-side macro-economic model', with Sang-In Hwang, January 5, 1990. (Version entitled 'Real budget deficits' presented at LINK Conference in Paris, August 1989.)
19. 'Deficits and capital markets – and banking', March 1990, forthcoming in a volume to be published by the Cambridge University Press.
20. 'Capital formation', presented at Conference on Research in Income and Wealth Workshop on the Revision of the United Nations System of National Accounts, Washington, DC, November 9, 1990.
21. 'Expanded measures of output and investment for now and the future',

presented at International Forum, 'Economics in transition: statistical measures now and in the future', Sochi, USSR, October 15–17, 1990. To be published in volume for International Institute for Applied Systems Analysis, Laxenburg, Austria.

22. 'Taxes, politics, and the economy', November 1991.
23. 'Underpinnings for economic revival', presented at Allied Social Science Associations, New Orleans, Joint Session of AEA and URPE, January 3, 1992.
24. 'A quick fix for the long run', March 1992.
25. 'A program to get out of recession and stagnation and promote long-run growth', prepared for Offit Bank, September 28, 1992.
26. 'Transcript of remarks at little rock economic conference', December 15, 1992.
27. 'Public and private saving and domestic and foreign investment: myths and realities', presented for the Federal Reserve Bank of Dallas Conference on 'The role of saving in economic growth', March 18–19, 1994.
28. 'The misunderstood world economy', for *International Seminar of Korean Institute for International Economic Policy*, 'The embarkment of WTO and Korea's economy', April 17, 1995.
29. 'A new view of the NAIRU', presented to the 7th World Congress of the Econometric Society, Tokyo, August 1995. (Later version published: B160 and B161, above.)
30. 'Korea and the US in the New World Order', presented to the First Korea US Forum of the Korea-America Friendship Society, Seoul, June 14, 1996, translated into Korean for publication.
31. 'The decline and fall of the NAIRU', presented to the American Economic Association Meetings, New Orleans, January 19, 1997.
32. 'Employment act and employment policies: an appraisal', presented to the Allied Social Science Associations Meetings, New Orleans, January 19, 1997.
33. 'Economic reform and macroeconomic policy: lessons from the United States and Korea', prepared for Yuido Institute conference on 'The effect of recent economic reforms in Korea (1993–1996)' on February 24, 1997 in Seoul. To be translated and published in Korean.

Name index

Economists of the Twentieth Century

Monetarism and Macroeconomic Policy
Thomas Mayer

Studies in Fiscal Federalism
Wallace E. Oates

The World Economy in Perspective
Essays in International Trade and European Integration
Herbert Giersch

Towards a New Economics
Critical Essays on Ecology, Distribution and Other Themes
Kenneth E. Boulding

Studies in Positive and Normative Economics
Martin J. Bailey

The Collected Essays of Richard E. Quandt (2 volumes)
Richard E. Quandt

International Trade Theory and Policy
Selected Essays of W. Max Corden
W. Max Corden

Organization and Technology in Capitalist Development
William Lazonick

Studies in Human Capital
Collected Essays of Jacob Mincer, Volume 1
Jacob Mincer

Studies in Labor Supply
Collected Essays of Jacob Mincer, Volume 2
Jacob Mincer

Macroeconomics and Economic Policy
The Selected Essays of Assar Lindbeck
Volume I
Assar Lindbeck

The Welfare State
The Selected Essays of Assar Lindbeck
Volume II
Assar Lindbeck

Classical Economics, Public Expenditure and Growth
Walter Eltis

Money, Interest Rates and Inflation
Frederic S. Mishkin

The Public Choice Approach to Politics
Dennis C. Mueller

The Liberal Economic Order
Volume I Essays on International Economics
Volume II Money, Cycles and Related Themes
Gottfried Haberler
Edited by Anthony Y.C. Koo

Economic Growth and Business Cycles
Prices and the Process of Cyclical Development
Paolo Sylos Labini

International Adjustment, Money and Trade
Theory and Measurement for Economic Policy
Volume I
Herbert G. Grubel

International Capital and Service Flows
Theory and Measurement for Economic Policy
Volume II
Herbert G. Grubel

Unintended Effects of Government Policies
Theory and Measurement for Economic Policy
Volume III
Herbert G. Grubel

The Economics of Competitive Enterprise
Selected Essays of P.W.S. Andrews
Edited by Frederic S. Lee
and Peter E. Earl

The Repressed Economy
Causes, Consequences, Reform
Deepak Lal

Economic Theory and Market Socialism
Selected Essays of Oskar Lange
Edited by Tadeusz Kowalik

Trade, Development and Political Economy
Selected Essays of Ronald Findlay
Ronald Findlay

General Equilibrium Theory
The Collected Essays of Takashi Negishi
Volume I
Takashi Negishi

The History of Economics
The Collected Essays of Takashi Negishi
Volume II
Takashi Negishi

Studies in Econometric Theory
The Collected Essays of Takeshi Amemiya
Takeshi Amemiya

Exchange Rates and the Monetary System
Selected Essays of Peter B. Kenen
Peter B. Kenen

Econometric Methods and Applications
(2 volumes)
G.S. Maddala

National Accounting and Economic Theory
The Collected Papers of Dan Usher, Volume I
Dan Usher

Welfare Economics and Public Finance
The Collected Papers of Dan Usher, Volume II
Dan Usher

Economic Theory and Capitalist Society
The Selected Essays of Shigeto Tsuru, Volume I
Shigeto Tsuru

Methodology, Money and the Firm
The Collected Essays of D.P. O'Brien
(2 volumes)
D.P. O'Brien

Economic Theory and Financial Policy
The Selected Essays of Jacques J. Polak
(2 volumes)
Jacques J. Polak

Sturdy Econometrics
Edward E. Leamer

The Emergence of Economic Ideas
Essays in the History of Economics
Nathan Rosenberg

Productivity Change, Public Goods and Transaction Costs
Essays at the Boundaries of Microeconomics
Yoram Barzel

Reflections on Economic Development
The Selected Essays of Michael P. Todaro
Michael P. Todaro

The Economic Development of Modern Japan
The Selected Essays of Shigeto Tsuru
Volume II
Shigeto Tsuru

Money, Credit and Policy
Allan H. Meltzer

Macroeconomics and Monetary Theory
The Selected Essays of Meghnad Desai
Volume I
Meghnad Desai

Poverty, Famine and Economic Development
The Selected Essays of Meghnad Desai
Volume II
Meghnad Desai

Explaining the Economic Performance of Nations
Essays in Time and Space
Angus Maddison

Economic Doctrine and Method
Selected Papers of R.W. Clower
Robert W. Clower

Economic Theory and Reality
Selected Essays on their Disparities and Reconciliation
Tibor Scitovsky

Doing Economic Research
Essays on the Applied Methodology of Economics
Thomas Mayer

Institutions and Development Strategies
The Selected Essays of Irma Adelman
Volume I
Irma Adelman

Dynamics and Income Distribution
The Selected Essays of Irma Adelman
Volume II
Irma Adelman

The Economics of Growth and Development
Selected Essays of A.P. Thirlwall
A.P. Thirlwall

Theoretical and Applied Econometrics
The Selected Papers of Phoebus J. Dhrymes
Phoebus J. Dhrymes

Innovation, Technology and the Economy
The Selected Essays of Edwin Mansfield
(2 volumes)
Edwin Mansfield

Economic Theory and Policy in Context
The Selected Essays of R.D. Collison Black
R.D. Collison Black

Location Economics
Theoretical Underpinnings and Applications
Melvin L. Greenhut

Spatial Microeconomics
Theoretical Underpinnings and Applications
Melvin L. Greenhut

Capitalism, Socialism and Post-Keynesianism
Selected Essays of G.C. Harcourt
G.C. Harcourt

Time Series Analysis and Macroeconometric Modelling
The Collected Papers of Kenneth F. Wallis
Kenneth F. Wallis

Foundations of Modern Econometrics
The Selected Essays of Ragnar Frisch
(2 volumes)
Edited by Olav Bjerkholt

Growth, the Environment and the Distribution of Incomes
Essays by a Sceptical Optimist
Wilfred Beckerman

The Economics of Environmental Regulation
Wallace E. Oates

Econometrics, Macroeconomics and Economic Policy
Selected Papers of Carl F. Christ
Carl F. Christ

Strategic Approaches to the International Economy
Selected Essays of Koichi Hamada
Koichi Hamada

Economic Analysis and Political Ideology
The Selected Essays of Karl Brunner
Volume One
Edited by Thomas Lys

Growth Theory and Technical Change
The Selected Essays of Ryuzo Sato
Volume One
Ryuzo Sato

Industrialization, Inequality and Economic Growth
Jeffrey G. Williamson

Economic Theory and Public Decisions
Selected Essays of Robert Dorfman
Robert Dorfman

The Logic of Action One
Method, Money, and the Austrian School
Murray N. Rothbard

The Logic of Action Two
Applications and Criticism from the Austrian School
Murray N. Rothbard

Bayesian Analysis in Econometrics and Statistics
The Zellner View and Papers
Arnold Zellner

On the Foundations of Monopolistic Competition and Economic Geography
The Selected Essays of B. Curtis Eaton and Richard G. Lipsey
B. Curtis Eaton and Richard G. Lipsey

Microeconomics, Growth and Political Economy
The Selected Essays of Richard G. Lipsey
Volume One
Richard G. Lipsey

Macroeconomic Theory and Policy
The Selected Essays of Richard G. Lipsey
Volume Two
Richard G. Lipsey

Employment, Labor Unions and Wages
The Collected Essays of Orley Ashenfelter
Volume One
Edited by Kevin F. Hallock

Education, Training and Discrimination
The Collected Essays of Orley Ashenfelter
Volume Two
Edited by Kevin F. Hallock

Economic Institutions and the Demand and Supply of Labour
The Collected Essays of Orley Ashenfelter
Volume Three
Edited by Kevin F. Hallock

Monetary Theory and Monetary Policy
The Selected Essays of Karl Brunner
Volume Two
Edited by Thomas Lys

Macroeconomic Issues from a Keynesian Perspective
Selected Essays of A.P. Thirlwall
Volume Two
A.P. Thirlwall

Money and Macroeconomics
The Selected Essays of David Laidler
David Laidler

The Economics and Politics of Money
The Selected Essays of Alan Walters
Edited by Kent Matthews

Economics and Social Justice
Essays on Power, Labor and Institutional Change
David M. Gordon
Edited by Thomas E. Weisskopf and Samuel Bowles

Practicing Econometrics
Essays in Method and Application
Zvi Griliches

Economics Against the Grain
Volume One
Microeconomics, Industrial Organization and Related Themes
Julian L. Simon

Economics Against the Grain
Volume Two
Population Economics, Natural Resources and Related Themes
Julian L. Simon

Advances in Econometric Theory
The Selected Works of Halbert White
Halbert White

The Economics of Imperfect Knowledge
Collected Papers of G.B. Richardson
G.B. Richardson

Economic Performance and the Theory of the Firm
The Selected Papers of David J. Teece
Volume One
David J. Teece

Strategy, Technology and Public Policy
The Selected Papers of David J. Teece
Volume Two
David J. Teece

The Keynesian Revolution, Then and Now
The Selected Essays of Robert Eisner
Volume One
Robert Eisner

Investment, National Income and Economic Policy
The Selected Essays of Robert Eisner
Volume Two
Robert Eisner

International Trade Opening and the Formation of the Global Economy
Selected Essays of Peter J. Lloyd
Peter J. Lloyd

Production, Stability and Dynamic Symmetry
The Selected Essays of Ryuzo Sato
Volume Two
Ryuzo Sato